AA

KEYGUIDE

# PROVENCE AND THE CÔTE D'AZUR

76

# CONTENTS

**KEY TO SYMBOLS**

- Map reference
- Address
- Telephone number
- Opening times
- Admission prices
- Underground station
- Bus number
- Train station
- Ferry/boat
- Driving directions
- Tourist office
- Tours
- Guidebook
- Restaurant
- Café
- Bar
- Shop
- Number of rooms
- Air conditioning
- Swimming pool
- Gym
- Other useful information
- ▷ Cross reference
- ★ Walk/drive start point

210

121

88

145

# UNDERSTANDING PROVENCE AND THE CÔTE D'AZUR

Understanding Provence and the Côte d'Azur is an introduction to the country, its geography, economy, history and its people, giving a real insight into the region. Living Provence and the Côte d'Azur gets under the skin of Provence today, while The Story of Provence and the Côte d'Azur takes you through the region's past.

# UNDERSTANDING PROVENCE AND THE CÔTE D'AZUR

In theory Provence is in France, but in truth it has always been a land apart. You'll know when you've crossed the border because in Provence everything is different: the pale rocky terrain, the herb-rich food, the outdoor life, the dry air and brilliant sunlight. There are markets bursting with life, shaded squares filled with café tables, astounding art galleries and superb music festivals. The landscape ranges from mountains and lavender fields to coastline and wetlands. The Côte d'Azur is the glitzy side of Provence, with exclusive beaches and marinas packed with luxury yachts.

## GETTING YOUR BEARINGS

Provence has an enviable position in France's sunny southeastern corner, with the warm waters of the Mediterranean to the south and Italy to the east. The western reaches of the Alps stretch to the north of Provence—in early spring you can ski in the morning, then drive to the Côte d'Azur for a stroll by the sea in the afternoon. The Côte d'Azur, with its celebrity glamour, is the area of coastline running from the Italian border in the east to St-Tropez in the west. It is also known as the French Riviera, although officially this stretches farther west along the coast. The tiny principality of Monaco, an independent nation-state though it covers just 2sq km (less than 1sq mile), sits on the eastern edge of the coast, between Nice and Menton.

## TOURISM

Tourism encompasses the whole of Provence, and the Riviera coastal strip is one of the most popular holiday destinations in the world. The Côte d'Azur accounts for one per cent of the world market for overnight stays, with almost 70 million guest nights per year. Annual visitor spending reaches around €5 billion. There have been environmental costs, however, and quality of life in the busier areas has inevitably suffered. Nevertheless, both regional and national decision-makers are determined to ensure further tourism growth. Yet thanks to a diverse landscape, with rocky hill districts and dense wilderness areas that defy development, most of inland Provence (and even some coastal stretches) remains largely undeveloped and there are plenty of opportunities to escape the crowds.

## THE ECONOMY

Provence by no means depends on tourism. Unlike some popular holiday destinations, Provence—even the Riviera tourist heartland—has a huge diversity of other industry. High-tech development, telecommunications and scientific research are all major contributors to the region's economy. One of Europe's leading technology parks, Sophia-Antipolis, is a short distance from Cannes. Viniculture and horticulture remain an important part of the economy—grapes, melons, lemons, olives and cut flowers are among the local produce. Provence provides 70 per cent of the world's lavender oil and is home to around a tenth of France's vineyards.

## CLIMATE AND LANDSCAPE

There's something absolutely joyous about the climate of Provence, with its balmy temperatures, the freshness of the shade on a summer afternoon and the comfortable warmth of long evenings outdoors. That, of course, is what has attracted visitors, from the aristocratic seekers of winter sun in the 19th century to today's holidaymakers here for two weeks in summer. Tour companies' brochures describe it as perfection, yet the climate of Provence has its harsher edge. The long rainless summer, zero humidity, high temperatures and sheer blue sky may sound like a dream come true, but for centuries such weather impoverished the population and made life hard. Only when the capricious rivers, especially the Durance, were tamed and the waters channelled for irrigation did agriculture really begin to flourish. Storms can be spectacularly sudden and violent, menacing skies illuminated by endless lightning, with downpours that can flood towns and villages within hours and send dangerous torrents surging down river beds that are usually bone dry. Mont Ventoux, especially, towering above the Vaucluse in western Provence, draws stormy weather to itself.

**Opposite** *Les Arènes, in Nîmes, is around 2,000 years old*
**Below** *Harvest time in Châteauneuf-du-Pape*

Provence locals are aware of the shifting winds and the weather they bring. Wind from the east brings turbulence, from the south, rain. The prevailing wind is the *mistral*, dry air flowing from the Alps to the sea. In winter it can howl icily down the Rhône valley, fanning out along the coast as it approaches the sea. In summer, though, it's lighter, sometimes almost gentle, and keeps skies cloudless for weeks at a time.

Provence's landscape ranges from the watery plains of the Camargue to the Mediterranean beaches, from the low inland hills to the snowy peaks of the Alps. To some extent, each of these areas has its own climate. The diversity is at its most striking in February, when spring flowers are opening on the Riviera, while an hour's drive north snow-covered mountain resorts in the Provençal Alps offer perfect skiing conditions.

## LANGUAGE

It's easy enough to hear that the *accent du Midi*—the strong southern inflection, with its emphatic tones ringing like church bells—is different from French as spoken farther north. Here every word ending is vigorously sounded, often with a resounding nasal 'ang'. *Vin* (wine) becomes *vang*, *pain* (bread) becomes *pang*, *demain* (tomorrow) becomes *demang*, *beau temps* (good weather) is *beau tang*.

The Provençal accent is a last remnant of a completely separate language. The language of southern France—whether called Provençal, Langue d'Oc or Occitan—came directly from Latin (like Spanish or Italian). It was the everyday speech of both the educated and the ordinary people. Above all, it was the language of the troubadours, whose lyric poems and songs of gallantry were all told in the Provençal tongue. In those days, the language was called Romans or Lenga Romana. The later name, Langue d'Oc, contrasts the southern word for yes, *oc*, with the word northerners once used, *oïl*. While the word *oc* has vanished, the talk of rural southerners is still liberally peppered with local dialect words.

Though Provençal was officially suppressed from the 15th century onwards, it continued in everyday use until the Revolution. The poet Frédéric Mistral (1830–1914) then led a 19th-century revival with his Félibrige movement and won the Nobel Prize for Literature in 1904 for his novels and poetry written in Provençal. Mistral remains a local hero, but his movement failed, and French replaced the old tongue.

Yet Provençal will not go away. Under the name Occitan, it has resurfaced as a symbol of southern independence, part of a wave of pride in southern culture and traditions. While the authentic language survives only as a country patois, many towns and villages have put up street signs and other public information in Provençal. Schools offer a chance to learn the local language, while in the universities of the south, it is possible to study Provençal more seriously. Many names, especially of southern dishes, are pure Provençal, like *anchoïade, aïoli, pistou* and *ratatouille*. At the same time, several towns still have their own patois, sometimes mixing Provençal with French and Italian, like the popular Nissart speech of Nice.

## SOCIETY

Provence is distinctly more 'Latin' than the rest of France. Siestas shut some shops from noon until 3pm, bullfights and races remain a spectator sport (especially in Arles and Nîmes) and politics are sometimes as turbulent as in nearby Italy.

The lively village market remains an important occasion, giving the chance to buy seasonal produce and catch up on the local gossip. Festivals also play a key role in Provence life. Nice celebrates the early spring with its Carnival and Menton with the *Fête du Citron*. The partying continues in the summer, with around 300 towns and villages staging their own festival.

**Above** *The pretty village of La-Bollène-Vésubie, nestled in the hillside not far from the Parc National du Mercantour*

# PROVENCE AND THE CÔTE D'AZUR AT A GLANCE

The Provence-Alpes-Côte d'Azur region is broken down into six *départements*. You can tell which *département* a town or attraction is in by looking at the first two digits of the postal code (these are given in brackets below). Also within Provence's boundaries, although not part of France, is the luxury-loving principality of Monaco. In the *Regions* chapter of this book (▷ 58–256) we have included it in the Alpes-Maritimes section.

**Bouches-du-Rhône (13)** is on the Mediterranean coast, on the western side of Provence. Its capital is the ancient port city of Marseille and its landscape includes the wetland reserves of the Camargue and the beautiful Chaîne des Alpilles hills. There are Roman reminders at Arles.

**Var (83)**, farther east, has the Côte d'Azur beach resorts of Fréjus, Le Lavandou and Hyères, as well as the celebrity's choice, St-Tropez. The interior has tranquil sun-basking villages, wild hills like the Massif des Maures, thriving country towns such as Draguignan and Romanesque sites such as the Abbaye du Thoronet.

**Alpes-Maritimes (06)** includes the northeastern stretch of the Côte d'Azur. Its resorts extend along the scenic waterfront from Cannes and Antibes to Menton and the Italian border. The whole strip is dedicated to relaxation, style and the good life, plus generous helpings of superb history dating back to Roman times and beyond, and world-famous art museums like the Fondation Maeght. Nice is the *département's* ancient capital and Queen of the Riviera. Inland are *villages perchés* (perched villages) like Èze and the mountainous Mercantour region.

**Monaco**, a short way up the coast from Nice, is the tiny principality that thinks big. Monaco-Ville, on its rock, is the stately little ceremonial capital, while Monte-Carlo is the principality's big-money quarter, dominated by its casino.

**Alpes-de-Haute-Provence (04)**, north of Var, takes in the spectacular Grand Canyon du Verdon, as well as the appealing old hill towns of Castellane, Forcalquier and Sisteron, and the spa town of Digne-les-Bains.

**Hautes-Alpes (05)**, in northern Provence, is popular for skiing in winter and hiking in summer.

**Vaucluse (84)**, north of Bouches-du-Rhône, includes medieval Avignon, Roman Orange and the wine town of Châteauneuf-du-Pape. Southern Vaucluse has an array of impressive sights, man-made and natural, including the gushing Fontaine de Vaucluse spring, ochre-tinted Roussillon and Romanesque abbeys like Sénanque. Northern Vaucluse has mountain scenery but also remarkable Roman sights like Vaison-la-Romaine.

# THE BEST OF PROVENCE AND THE CÔTE D'AZUR

## BOUCHES-DU-RHÔNE

**Aix-en-Provence** (▷ 65–67) An elegant town that has art museums and fine Renaissance mansions and is hometown of the painter Paul Cézanne.

**The Camargue** (▷ 74–75) Great for long, wild walks, peace and quiet, horseback riding and birdwatching.

**Chocolaterie de Puyricard** (▷ 102) Sample some of the best chocolates in France, at this shop in Aix-en-Provence.

***Fête des Gardians*** (▷ 107) Be entertained by the cowboys of the Camargue during this celebration in Arles in May.

**Marseille** (▷ 78–85) Soak up the history in the Vieux Port and Le Panier districts of this ancient city, then sample the lively nightlife…or the delicious local fish stew, bouillabaisse.

**Nîmes** (▷ 86–89) Venture just outside the Bouches-du-Rhône *département* to see one of the best-preserved Roman amphitheatres in the world.

**Oustau de Baumanière** (▷ 109) Enjoy exquisite food in the restaurant of this 16th-century country-house hotel.

## VAR

**Îles d'Hyères** (▷ 122–123) Catch a ferry to these peaceful islands, which represent a different side of the Côte d'Azur.

**Massif des Maures** (▷ 126) Here's real wilderness, just minutes from the Riviera resorts.

**St-Tropez** (▷ 128–129) More film set than fishing village, it's still popular with celebs.

**La Tarte Tropézienne** (▷ 133) Visit this St-Tropez patisserie to try the famous *tarte Tropézienne* cream cake that gave the shop its name.

**Windsurf** (▷ 276) L'Almanarre, near Hyères, is a popular spot with enthusiasts.

## ALPES-MARITIMES AND MONACO

**Antibes** (▷ 141–142) Stroll through the attractive historic quarter, visit the Picasso Museum, then take a break on one of the sandy beaches on the Cap d'Antibes.

**Cannes** (▷ 144–146) Shop 'til you drop in Provence's most glamorous destination.

**Èze** (▷ 148) Of all the perched villages of the Riviera, this is one of the most accessible and most impressive.

***Fête du Citron*** (▷ 189) Visit Menton in late February to experience the lively Lemon Festival.

**Fragonard** (▷ 184) Treat yourself to a fragrance from this renowned perfumery, in Grasse.

**Hôtel Negresco** (▷ 194–195) If you're feeling wealthy, book yourself into this luxury hotel—if not, wander past to admire the landmark dome.

**Le Louis XV** (▷ 191) Spend your Monte-Carlo Casino winnings (and you may need them) at this luxurious restaurant, part of the Hôtel de Paris, in Monaco.

**Monaco-Ville** (▷ 156–157) The sedate old city poised on The Rock has quiet pageantry and wonderful sea views.

**Monte-Carlo's Casino quarter** (▷ 158) At its most impressive admired from outside, the ornate Casino symbolizes the lavish opulence of the principality.
**Monte-Carlo Grand Prix** (▷ 189) Monte-Carlo becomes a racetrack in May and welcomes the top names in Formula 1.
**Musée Océanographique** (▷ 157) Dug into the cliff face of The Rock, this is one of the best sea-life museums in Europe.
**Nice** (▷ 163–167) Stroll the Promenade des Anglais, see the city's great art galleries and experience the hectic nightlife.
**Nice Carnival** (▷ 189) Join in the party at the Nice Carnival, in February. If you're visiting in summer, catch the Nice Jazz Festival (▷ 189) in July.

## ALPES-DE-HAUTE-PROVENCE AND HAUTES-ALPES

**La Citadelle** (▷ 215) This restaurant in Sisteron offers wonderful alpine views and tasty local dishes.
**Digne-les-Bains** (▷ 201) Relax in the thermal baths at this famous spa town.
**Entrevaux** (▷ 202) Vauban's fortifications add to the impressive natural defences of this mountain gateway to Provence.
**Grand Canyon du Verdon** (▷ 204–205) The deepest, longest river gorge in Europe makes a spectacular drive.
**Sisteron** (▷ 208) Napoleon Bonaparte paused at this dramatically sited fortified mountain town on his march back to Paris in 1815.
**Ski** (▷ 199) Hit the slopes surrounding the Val d'Allos or the Serre Chevalier resorts.

## VAUCLUSE

**Avignon** (▷ 224–227) The main draws of this riverside walled city are the magnificent Palais des Papes (Palace of the Popes) and the huge drama and dance festival held in July.
**Châteauneuf-du-Pape** (▷ 229) Discover a world-famous wine village nestled among immaculate vineyards, and maybe bring home a bottle or two.
**Christian Étienne** (▷ 252) Dine in a 14th-century palace in Avignon and enjoy creations by a former sous-chef at Paris' Ritz Hotel.
**Théâtre Antique** (▷ 234–235) Experience the wonderful acoustics of Orange's Roman amphitheatre during the *Chorégies* festival in July.
**Vaison-la-Romaine** (▷ 240–241) Step back 2,000 years by visiting the impressive Roman sites of this pleasant market town.

**Opposite** *Looking towards the Massif des Maures, in Var*
**Below left** *The awesome cliffs of Sisteron tower over nearby houses*
**Below right** *Inside the Hôtel Negresco, Nice*

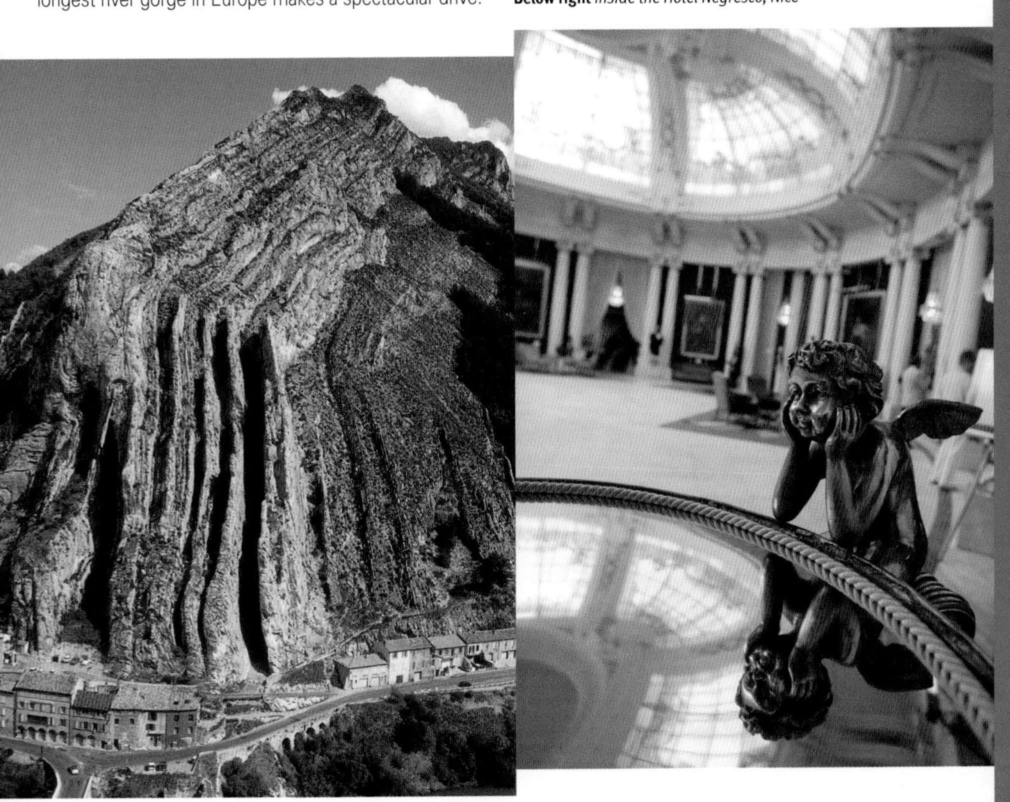

## TOP EXPERIENCES

**Buy Provençal** Check out vivid fabrics, local herbs, lavender toiletries and other evocative souvenirs of Provence.

**Dance the night away**—whether you're into clubbing or ballroom, Provence has it all.

**Drink** either a cooling Rosé de Provence wine or a rich Côte du Rhône red.

**Eat** bouillabaisse, ratatouille, *pan bagnat, salade niçoise* or one of the other delicious local dishes.

**Escape the crowds** and head for the mountains.

**Get festive** at one of the many *fêtes* on the Riviera or at an inland town.

**Go to a market** for a glimpse of the vivacity and richness that is Provence.

**Lie on a beach** There are plenty to choose from. The sandiest are from Cannes westward.

**Return to Rome** by visiting Provence's remarkable amphitheatres in Arles, Nîmes and Orange.

**See some art** at the Chagall in Nice, the Fondation Maeght near St-Paul-de-Vence or the Villa Ephrussi de Rothschild on Cap Ferrat.

**Ski** Yes, if you're here in spring, combine skiing at Isola with relaxing on the beach at Nice.

**Try luxury living** with a meal in a top hotel, like the Martinez in Cannes or the Negresco in Nice.

**Visit a monastery** and relax in the serene setting of a Romanesque abbey like Sénanque.

**Walk the ramparts** at fortified medieval towns and cities like Avignon and Aigues-Mortes.

**Watch the world go by** from an outdoor café table.

**Below** *An eye-catching sign at L'Espiguette beach, on the western Camargue coast*

# LIVING PROVENCE AND THE CÔTE D'AZUR

# PROVENCE LIFE

For a region with such rich and varied language, it is paradoxical that the greatest conveyor of emotion is in the shrug. The image of daily life in Provence is the most abiding of all pictures of regional France: pastel houses around dusty squares where old men while away the hours sipping pastis on a café *terrasse* and playing pétanque (bowls) under age-old plane trees. Taciturn they may be, but this very characteristic has inspired generations of writers. Their stories help perpetuate the timeless charm of the place, but it is the landscape—background to isolated villages perched above rolling fields of lavender and craggy olive groves—that really preserves Provence's character, with locals living life the old way. The Mediterranean climate helps keep any aggressive movement for change safely at bay, and the patois and dialects (whose imminent demise has been predicted for the past 400 years) have been regularly rescued by successive generations, from the 19th-century poet Frédéric Mistral to the second-generation immigrants in modern Marseille, keen to embrace the original language of the area. These immigrants are part of the secret of Provence's success. The clichéd images of village life may be as true as ever. But new blood—whether trans-Mediterranean communities in the ports or artists settling in picturesque hamlets—and a vibrant cultural life prove Provence is as much an ideal of today as a mirror to the past.

## THE DAY THE SHEEP CAME TO TOWN

Spring sees the *trans-humance*, when shepherds take their flocks from winter to summer grazing grounds. As the sheep are driven through the narrow streets of historic towns, it is a time for thanksgiving, music and wine. From little-known Vaucluse villages such as Jonquières to more established visitor destinations including St-Rémy-de-Provence and ski resorts in the Alps, thousands of sheep, dogs, donkeys and shepherds parade along the streets. Mass is said, tambourines are shaken and copious quantities of wine are quaffed until the animals are well on their way. Then, in autumn, the locals get ready for the return journey.

**Clockwise from above** *Shepherds guide their sheep to their summer grazing grounds during the* transhumance; *a float takes part in Nice's lively Mardi Gras celebrations; playing the accordion in the sunshine*

## GYPSIES AND COWBOYS BY THE SEA

Gypsies dance with the Camargue's cowboys during one of the most lively events of the Provençal calendar, the *Pèlerinage des Gitans*. The village of Saintes-Maries-de-la-Mer is where, legend has it, saints Marie-Jacobé, Marie-Salomé and Mary Magdalene arrived with their maid Sarah, patron saint of gypsies. Every year in late May, gypsies from all over Europe make their pilgrimage to the coast. Dressed in vibrant, traditional costumes, gypsies and *gardians* (local cowboys who look after wild black bulls) carry jewel-encrusted statues of St. Sarah and the Maries into the sea to be blessed. During the evening and into the night, the beach echoes to the sound of celebrations.

## PARTY TIME

Forget understated style—the Riviera has a gaudy party for a glorious two weeks, when the international visitors are looking the other way. Mardi Gras is the way to party out of winter and into spring. In Nice, massive papier-mâché heads join the marching bands and dancing crowds following floats parading daily through the streets and along the Promenade des Anglais to the sea. The giant papier-mâché King of the Carnival reigns supreme until he is set alight and put to sea, bringing the carnival to its dramatic close. Along the coast, the usually genteel folk of Menton provide a rival assault on the senses, when 145 tonnes of oranges and lemons are transformed into massive floats for the *Fête du Citron*.

## THE INVISIBLE MARKET

On Parisian menus, the black diamonds of Provence are known as *truffes* (truffles). In Vaucluse, the delicacy is better known as *rabasse*. Legends of countrymen wandering off before dawn with hounds snuffling out truffles in secret locations help fuel the mystique and high prices. These days, they're virtually farmed around the roots of the downy oak. Rows of trees are planted in *truffière* fields. Saturday markets in Carpentras, Valréas and Grillon see farmers and dealers trading openly. But the big money, say locals, changes hands in the invisible truffle markets. Word of mouth, not maps, and deep pockets instead of picturesque stalls are the backdrop to hard-core trade. To the uninitiated, these markets don't exist. But anonymous deals in village bars and cafés are serious business.

## WHEN ONE MOZART IS NOT ENOUGH

Some people can never have too much sun, nor too much Mozart. Thus Provence in summer reverberates to the sound of popular arias in historic settings. To add to Provence's lengthy list, a new festival arrived in 2002, when fashion designer Pierre Cardin launched his own opera festival in the ruins of the Château Lacoste, the *Festival d'Art Lyrique et de Théâtre de Lacoste* (www.festivaldelacoste.com). The opening star-studded production was Mozart's condemnation of loose morals, *Don Giovanni*. This was apt as the château was previously owned by the Marquis de Sade. Another great date on the musical calendar is the *Musique-Cordiale Festival* (www.musique-cordiale.com), when music is performed in churches and village squares in Seillans for ten days in August.

# CANNES, THE RICH AND THE FAMOUS

The Cannes Film Festival is the ultimate A-List event. The Mediterranean has more movie stars per square yacht than ever and 4,000 journalists from 75 countries compete for interviews with directors and photographs of starlets on the Croisette. More than a mere photo opportunity, the festival has been the scene of fights, booing and mass walkouts at screenings, with passion a lot closer to the surface than at other celebrity events. In the great spirit of 1968, when anarchy took to the streets of France, film-makers François Truffaut and Jean-Luc Godard stormed the stage at the festival, reflecting the volatile political climate. Cannes has always been political. Its founding in 1939 was in itself a reaction to Mussolini's fascist takeover of the Venice Film Festival—although World War II meant Cannes didn't properly take off until 1947. Idealism is only part of the story. Money matters at Cannes too. Half the world's movie deals take place here, from blockbusters to small art-house flicks. Not all today's celebrities on the Riviera come down to the Croisette to parade before the paparazzi. Tina Turner and George Michael are among the legends of the music industry finding solace and inspiration in private villas nearby.

**Clockwise from above** *You might find yourself parking next to a Ferrari in Monaco; Elton John has a villa near Nice; Brigitte Bardot relaxes in St-Tropez in 1962*

## THE BÉBÉ GROWS UP

Since Brigitte Bardot first stepped out in St-Tropez for Roger Vadim's classic film *Et Dieu Créa la Femme* in 1957, hers has been the face of the village resort, eclipsing previous high-profile residents such as the author Colette and artist Paul Signac. In her wake came the rock royalty of the 1960s, and the excesses of their front-page lifestyles, chic shopping and pricey wining and dining gave the resort the nickname *St-Trop* (too much!). The chances of seeing the famous Bardot pout in public these days are pretty slim, since the actress known to the French as *BB* (pronounced Bébé) famously gave up show business on her 40th birthday, establishing an animal sanctuary and leaving town in 1989, returning only to keep an eye on the animals.

## THERE'S SOMETHING ABOUT MARIANNE

Marianne, symbol of the French Republic, adorns civic buildings, coins and stamps. While the latest image (launched in 2003) features a stylized multi-ethnic figure, her image has been inspired by stars and models such as Brigitte Bardot, Cathérine Deneuve, Inès de la Fressange and Laetitia Casta. However, the Marianne in Menton's *Sale des Marriages*, where townsfolk register their weddings, is a little unusual. The room was decorated by the artist and film director Jean Cocteau and includes a Marianne that bears a striking resemblance to the legendary actor Jean Marais, star of *Beauty and the Beast, Orpheus* and *Les Misérables*.

## THEY CAN'T STAY AWAY FOR LONG

British author Peter Mayle was not the first big name to discover the enchanting delights of the Lubéron village of Ménerbes. Former French president François Mitterrand, actor John Malkovich, actress Jane Birkin and author Albert Camus had also been numbered among the VIP residents. But the publication of Mayle's bestseller *A Year In Provence* (1989) led to the Mayle Trail of tourists driving through the streets in search of locations from the book. The author finally left the village and moved to California. But such is the lure of the place, he returned to Provence within a decade—finding a house suitably off the beaten track.

## FLOWERS FOR ELTON

Since Elton John was granted honorary citizenship of Nice, he is often to be seen shopping for blooms at the world's oldest flower market. The cours Saleya, in the heart of the old town, is one of France's most picturesque markets, and fills the air with the scent of violets, mimosa and carnations for six days every week. Elton discovered the charms of the market back in the days when he was a regular guest at the Hôtel Negresco, and now hunts for exotic blooms for his luxury villa that stands high above the bay.

## ON THE BIG SCREEN

Provence is highly sought after for film locations, the landscape being wonderfully resistant to change. The link is not exclusively retro, though the perched village of Le Castellet had a starring role in *Jean de Florette* (1986), just as it had in the 1930s when Marcel Pagnol, on whose novel the movie is based, filmed *La Femme du Boulanger* here. Other films showing Provençal scenery include *Herbie Goes to Monte-Carlo* (1977), *To Catch a Thief* (1955), *French Kiss* (1995) with Meg Ryan and Ridley Scott's *A Good Year* (2006).

# PROVENCE INDUSTRIES

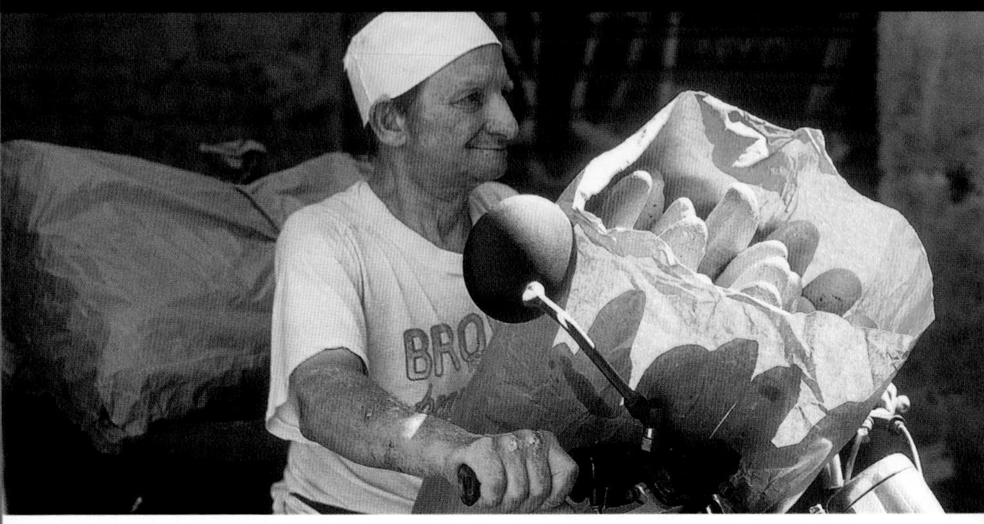


With a natural backdrop most regions could only envy, a slow pace of life and a near-perfect climate, it would be easy simply to declare that Provence's single industry is tourism. But that would be to miss the point of those rolling fields of lavender and centuries-old village workshops. The dazzling blooms earn their keep as a viable crop. Provence is, after all, the heart of France's perfume industry. Across the Var and Alpes-Maritimes, growing flowers is such serious business that mere prettiness is but a luxury. So important is the cultivation of ornamental plants and cut flowers that growers raise them in vast plastic tunnels, producing mimosa and carnations for flower markets and ornamental palm trees for offices and restaurants. Alongside the traditional crops of vines and olives, horticulture turns the great outdoors into the thriving heart of the region's economy. Provence's wealth comes not only from the land, but also the sea. Fishing fleets serve villages along the Med, but the days of the simple fishing boat putting out to sea are as numbered here as in the rest of the world. To meet demand, fish farming is developing, with sea bass (known as *loup*) and bream *(daurade)* being reared for the table as successfully as more traditional water crops such as mussels. Inland from the coast, France's first science park has created a silicon valley. The heart of trade has always been Marseille, whether the commodity was hemp, wine or grain. One Marseille product still manufactured in the region is the celebrated soap, *Savon de Marseille*.

**Clockwise from above** *Delivering the morning bread in Nice; delicate painting at the Atelier Soleil, in Moustiers-Sainte-Marie; lavender is grown in the region; Marseille soap makes a good souvenir*

**A NEW GENERATION**

Provence is famous for its crafts and rural professions. In many a rustic hamlet you'll find a *boulanger* up at the crack of dawn baking bread and a blacksmith hard at work beating horseshoes. Yet there is a place where the local skills are IT and cybernetics and you are more likely to encounter an astrophysicist than a basket weaver. On the Plateau de Valbonne, behind Antibes, is Sophia-Antipolis, dubbed France's silicon valley. New technology rules in the nation's first science park. Unlike nearby villages, where the past keeps the present alive, here 15,000 people with an eye firmly on the future work for more than 800 companies at the cutting edge of technology. Pharmaceuticals, chemicals and life sciences are the new Provençal trades. Maybe the next generation of visitors to Provence will come here to photograph the village robotics expert.

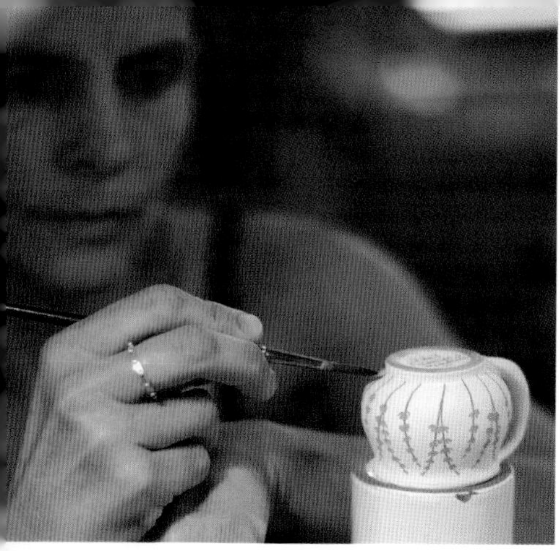

## THE ART OF THE BLACKSMITH

When demand for traditional village crafts dries up, what should a fellow do but upgrade from artisan to artist and move the client base from a remote farmstead to a metropolitan salon? Raymond Moralès (1926–2000) spent the bulk of his working life as a blacksmith, before deciding to transfer his skills to the world of the arts. His passion for creating huge and dramatic sculptures led him to open his own museum in 1982. Now hundreds of looming metal figures fill the open-air park and gallery on his estate between Fos and Martigues. The hulking exhibits have both a tribal and an erotic edge, and are not for the fainthearted!

## HOW RICE SAVED THE REGION'S GREENS

The fresh green vegetables sitting on the plates at fashionable Provençal restaurants may well owe their existence to the humble paddy fields of the Carmargue. Surprising as it may seem, the fact the fields of the area can now yield a wide variety of tasty greens is due to the planting of rice paddies in the 1950s. Until then, the pastures of the Camargue were too rich in salt to be used for anything other than grazing cattle, horses and sheep. In its heyday, the Camargue produced a third of the rice served in France. Now a fraction of the area covered 40 years ago, the rice fields have nonetheless revitalized arable production here by cleaning the soil of salt.

## LITTLE PEOPLE, BIG BUSINESS

For most of the country Christmas comes but once a year. In Provence, it's a 365-day industry. The production of nativity scene backdrops and figurines is a craft for which the region is justly famous. *Santons* (mini-saints) were wooden or wax dolls that were used in church displays. When the Revolution closed the churches, Marseille potter Jean-Louis Lagnel created the first mass production of the figures so each home could have its own crib, or *crèche*. Over the years the biblical cast was augmented with secular characters, such as doctors and farmers. In Aubagne, popular figures have included the actors Gérard Dépardieu and Yves Montand.

## A NOSE BY ANY OTHER NAME

The hillside town of Grasse is famous for its gloriously intoxicating fragrance industry. Each talented expert who creates the cocktail of aromas is known as 'The Nose'. Less well publicized is that Noses may well earn as much for coming up with new smells for disinfectants as they do for designer scents in expensive bottles. Grasse's best-known industry took on a deadly twist in the film *Perfume* (2006). The drama, starring Ben Whishaw, Dustin Hoffman and Alan Rickman, follows Whishaw's anti-hero on a murderous quest to create the world's finest perfume. Many scenes were shot in the lavender fields around Grasse.

# ART AND ARTISTS IN PROVENCE AND THE FRENCH RIVIERA

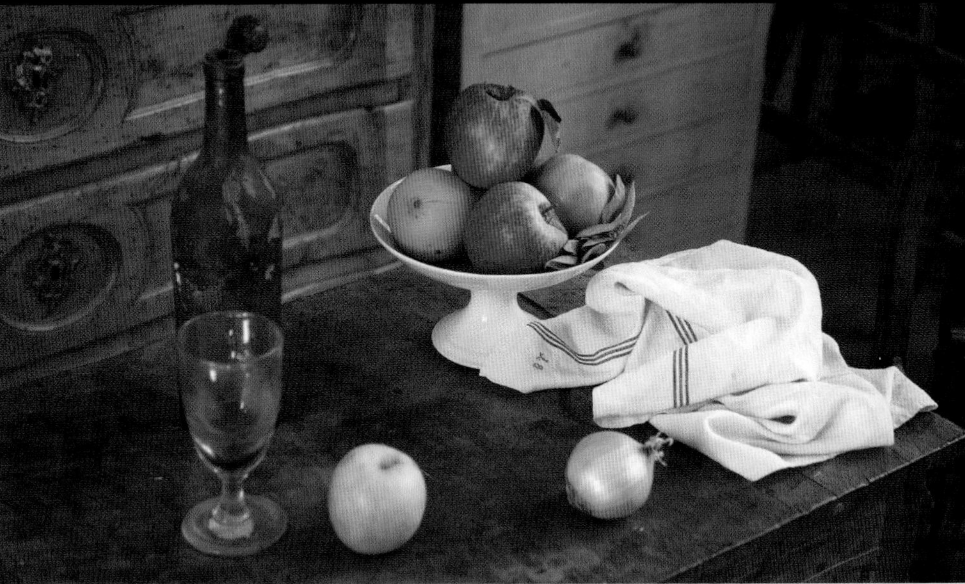

For more than a century, the world's most famous artists, from Pierre-Auguste Renoir to Pablo Picasso, have been drawn to the Côte d'Azur and Provence. Impressionist Claude Monet sparked the trend with a fleeting visit to Antibes during the 1880s, but it was really Vincent Van Gogh's arrival in Provence later that decade that paved the road southwards. Van Gogh splashed bold southern colours onto his canvasses while residing first in Arles, then later at the Monastère St-Paul-de-Mausole, just outside St-Rémy-de-Provence. Paul Cézanne, who spent most of his lifetime in and around Aix-en-Provence, devoted his career to painting interpretations of his hometown and its surrounding natural beauty. Henri Matisse first set foot in Nice in 1917. From his home at the eastern end of Nice's cours Saleya, Matisse's views took in floor-to-ceiling seascapes; from Villa le Rêve in Vence, he was within peeking distance of his late-life masterpiece, the Chapelle du Rosaire. The South of France had a similar, heart-capturing effect on Marc Chagall. He spent six decades—from 1925 until his death in 1985—returning time and again to the Riviera. Pablo Picasso, quite possibly the 20th century's most famous artist, also chose to make the Côte d'Azur his home.

### LA COLOMBE D'OR

Opening its doors for the first time in 1931, St-Paul-de-Vence's La Colombe d'Or began life as a simple village restaurant and pension. Artists, in particular, were welcomed; those who couldn't afford room and board paid with their canvasses instead. La Colombe d'Or's growing collection—artworks that started as the owner Roux family's sideline hobby—soon took centre stage. In 1960, 20 of these paintings were stolen. Although the pieces were recovered the following year, the Rouxs were forced to beef up their security. Today, only paying patrons are allowed indoors to admire La Colombe d'Or's priceless collection.

**Above** *Cézanne's studio, the Atelier Cézanne, has been preserved and is open to visitors*

#### FOLLOWING IN THEIR FOOTSTEPS

With a little preparation, it's easy for amateur artists to paint in the shadow of their favourite 20th-century masters. In Nice, pop into the tourist office and pick up the free pamphlet 'In the footsteps of Matisse'. These pages catalogue Matisse's artworks, places that inspired him and his various residences in the south of France. Of particular interest is the artist's former yellow mansion of a home at the eastern end of Nice's cours Saleya, where Matisse painted several local characters. Cézanne-lovers should head to Aix-en-Provence: the Aix tourist office hands out a similar booklet entitled 'In the steps of Cézanne'. Alternatively, simply keep an eye out for the chunky metal 'C's embedded in the city's pavements. These studs guide visitors to Cézanne's favourite spots around town.

#### HOUSES OF WORSHIP

Between 1947 and 1966, Matisse, Chagall and Picasso all devoted their artistic creativity to churches along the French Riviera. Inspired by his former nurse (later a Dominican nun), Matisse's Chapelle du Rosaire (▷ 171)—entirely designed and decorated by the artist—was completed in Vence in 1951. Picasso painted the massive panels for 'War and Peace', which adorn the small central chapel in nearby Vallauris (www.musee-picasso-vallauris.fr), in 1952 as an act of political defiance, highlighting his objection to the Korean War. Between 1954 and 1966 Chagall interpreted 17 stories from the Old Testament and the Hebrew book Song of Songs. These artworks, which are now housed in Nice's Chagall Museum (▷ 165), were originally intended for permanent display in Vence's cathedral.

#### ÉCOLE DE NICE

During the 1960s, a small group of avant-garde artists took the world by storm, transforming everyday objects and assembling mass-produced minutia into unique artworks. Known as 'l'École de Nice' (the 'Nice School'), the movement was led by Niçois local Yves Klein, renowned for his brilliant blue creations. Notable members of the school also included Arman, Ben, Niki de Saint-Phalle and César. A permanent section in Nice's Musée d'Art Moderne et d'Art Contemporain (MAMAC, ▷ 167) is devoted to works created by the artists from the Nice School.

#### CUTTING EDGE: PROVENÇAL ART TODAY

Visitors to Provence are frequently so focused on the south of France's late 19th- and 20th-century artistic heyday that the region's contemporary art is largely ignored. For current yet classic creations, visit the myriad galleries woven throughout St-Paul-de-Vence or Èze, or along Nice Old Town's rue Droite. For a more unconventional experience, head to Marseille: La Friche Belle de Mai (www.lafriche.org), located in a former tobacco factory, houses edgy exhibitions, as well as installations and performance art.

**Below left** *The entrance to the Musée Matisse*
**Below right** *The cloister at St-Paul-de-Mausole, where Van Gogh stayed in 1889*

# FOOD AND DRINK

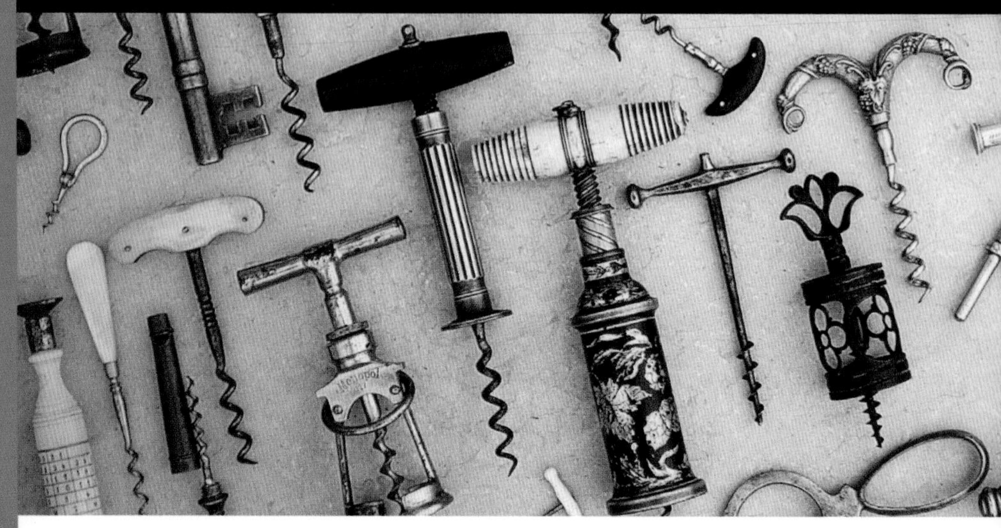

Olive oil, garlic, tomato, onions and herbs: The basic ingredients of Provençal cuisine came as something of a revelation to Northern Europe after the austerity of World War II. But before the recipe books from food writers such as Elizabeth David opened up the vista of French gastronomy to include something other than rich creamy sauces and complex combinations, the good folk of Provence had long cooked in the simple manner that has been credited with promoting longevity and good health. More recently, the cookbooks of Patricia Wells have repopularized Provençal cuisine to a worldwide audience. The very simplicity of the diet owes much to the climate. *Primeur* vegetables are available weeks before their regular season in the rest of the country. The long coastline means fish is plentiful. The traditional soup dish is, of course, bouillabaisse, practically a stew, filled with sea bass, mullet and shellfish cooked in a rich stock seasoned with saffron, fennel and other herbs. Originating in Marseille, this dish is prepared differently in every restaurant on the coast, the only constants being the accompanying dishes of *rouille* (spicy mayonnaise), croutons and grated cheese. No meal is complete unless served with a local wine. The heat of the summer sun encourages locals to sample a rosé at midday. The aperitif of choice is pastis. The waterfront dish of the Riviera is the wonderful *salade niçoise*—tomatoes, peppers, onions, olives, olive oil, anchovy, hard-boiled eggs, green beans, basil and crisp lettuce.

**Clockwise from above** *The Corkscrew Museum in Ménerbes; take some Provençal herbs home; or enjoy a bottle or two of the local wine*

**COOL CUISINE**

With a wealthy clientele and one eye on the daring restaurants of London and New York, Provence's culinary tradition has pulled away from classic French cuisine in recent years. Such centres of gastronomic tourism as Les Baux, Bormes-les-Mimosas and Mougins now attract patrons in search of experimental mixes of flavour—all topped with foam, emulsion or *jus*. The latter village has turned out many of Provence's cutting-edge chefs, including Roger Vergé, Alain Llorca and Sébastien Chambru, who all perfected their skills at the famed Moulin de Mougins restaurant (▷ 191–192). The town becomes an open-air eating festival in September, as Provence's top chefs perform for the public. Even more cutting-edge is Le Fooding (www.lefooding.com). This organization supports off-beat restaurants and arranges food events in Provence each summer.

## A TWIST IN THE TALE

How does a winemaker while away the months and years before his replanted vines bear fruit? The answer, in Ménerbes at least, is to make sure he has enough corkscrews to open the bottles once they are ready for drinking. Yves Rousset-Rouard collected corkscrews, in ivory, gold, silver and wood, until he had enough to open a museum in his Côte du Lubéron cellars. At his Musée du Tire-Bouchon, in Cavaillon, you can see more than 1,000, dating from the very first models of the 17th century to the latest high-tech boys'-toys gadgets. While his wines have garnered gold and silver medals for their quality, the vigneron has also won great reviews from the wine media for his collection of ornate tools.

## SOUP KITCHENS

Foodies from far afield pack their forks and prepare to tantalize the taste buds at the legendary Gastronomic Days festival in the Roman town of Vaison-la-Romaine in November. Master bakers, great chefs and award-winning winemakers descend on the town for five days of lip-smacking competition. Locals, though, prefer the earthier contest between some 14 nearby villages that takes place a week or so earlier. Which village housewife makes the best bowl of soup? To decide, all are invited to roll up their sleeves and dip their ladles in the pots, bowls and tureens of the makeshift soup bars in each village. Lots of music and dancing—and plenty of *potages, veloutés* and consommés—ward off the winter chill.

## A PROVENÇAL CHRISTMAS

If you dine out in Provence at the end of December you'll find that Christmas dinner is both a sweet and savoury occasion. The table is decked with symbolism and tradition in mind. The *Gros Souper* (Big Supper) on Christmas Eve is one of the south's most cherished rituals. With 13 desserts, the meal is known for its abundance of sweets and, paradoxically, for its so-called austerity. Dishes include modest marinated vegetables, *anchoaïde* (anchovy paste), salt cod and *escargots à l'aïoli* (snails in garlic), through to the finale of a spread of platters representing Christ and the apostles, with nougats, nuts and raisins, and plenty of fruit dishes, from delicious figs to sweet *confits* (candied fruits). The table is draped with three white cloths and set with bowls and candles symbolizing the Holy Trinity.

## A SPICIER CURE

With their traditional distrust for authority figures, the French have long preferred to seek advice from people who stand behind a counter rather than sit behind a desk. Thus it is the village pharmacist who dispenses wisdom on topics such as what ails the pet cat, which mushrooms in the basket are safe to eat and how to treat a bad back. In the south, locals are as likely to ask the herb seller in the market for tips on swollen feet and cramps as for seasoning a bouillabaisse. In 1970, British author Laurence Durrell was looking for a remedy for his eczema. He took the advice of Arles market trader Ludo Chardenon and brewed a pot of herbal tea. Chardenon then became a best-selling author in his own right. *In Praise of Wild Herbs* is still in print, with its suggested remedies for baldness, acne and cellulite.

# SPORT AND LEISURE

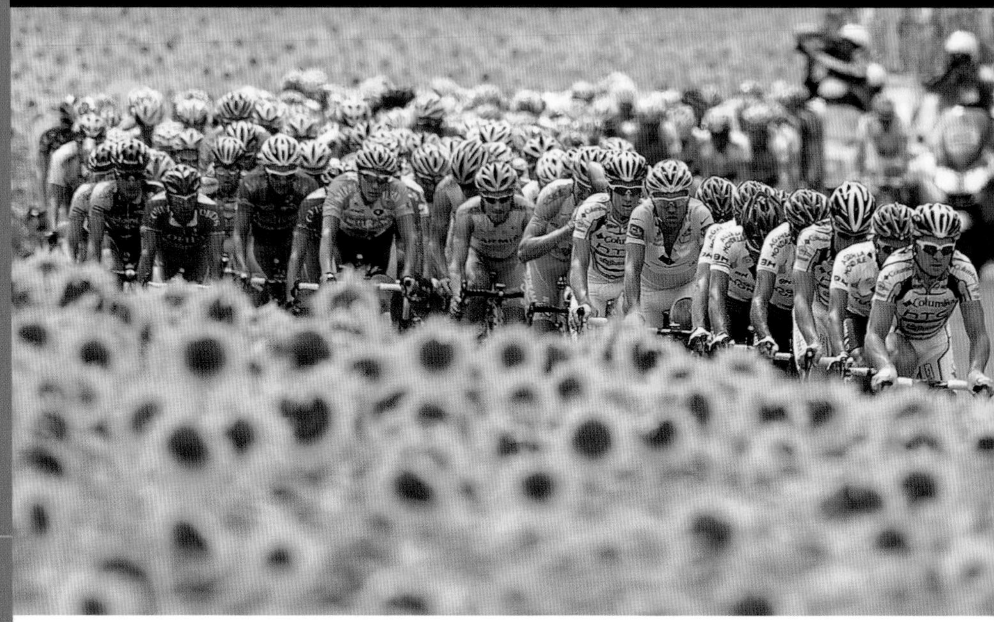

France is a nation of sports-lovers, even if, when it comes to participation, some may prefer to argue the latest scores and scandals over a drink at the local *bar des sports*. In Provence, those who like to take things easy choose the sedentary pleasures of pétanque, or bowls, in the town square. The game gets its name, depending on which story you prefer, from the patois version of the phrase *pieds tanques* (feet together) or the clanking sound of the balls clashing. Traditional boules is played over a long course of some 20m (66ft), whereas pétanque uses a smaller area. More energetic pursuits include white-water rafting, canoeing and other adventures on inland waterways. Water sports have grown up along the seaside resorts, with world-class windsurfing at Saintes-Maries-de-la-Mer. You can play golf at links along the coast or go horseback riding in the Camargue. Hikers can even travel with a donkey! Spectator sports range from rugby to bullfighting in the Roman arenas. The local *Courses Camarguaises* are less bloody than the traditional bullfight, with the bull being allowed to survive the contest. Compassionate visitors beware: At *ferias*, or festival days, the arenas of Arles and Nîmes stage Spanish-style corridas in which the bull is killed.

**Above** *The Tour de France cycles past a sunflower field*

**A STROLL WITH YOUR SNORKEL**

Ten per cent of France is protected parkland. However, should you fancy a ramble in the park of Port-Cros, don't forget your snorkel. This 687ha (1,700-acre) island, one of the Îles d'Hyères, is nestled in amazingly clear waters and was designated as a national park in 1963. The protected zone extends around the coast, some 600m (654 yards) out to sea. The nature trail here takes visitors under water more than 0.5km (0.3 miles) along the seabed. Signposted visitor trails continue from the island's paths down into the sparkling waters. To protect the wildlife, boats are not allowed to moor on the sandy beaches. Underwater guided tours from La Palud beach are free, but you should bring your own snorkel.

## SQUARE BALLS

Pétanque, the great bowling sport of the south of France, is an essential part of Provence life. No village is without its *boulodrome*, the grand name for a dusty square where locals roll boules in the late afternoon sun. But what of those steep perched villages on the hillside behind the Riviera, where streets are on such a slope that front and back doors may be on different floors? The answer, in Haut-de-Cagnes at least, is simple: Use square balls. In creating their cubed bowling balls, the villagers here have invented a whole new sport. *Boules Carrées* now has its own world championship, with around 300 players descending on Cagnes for the finals each summer.

## TURNING THE OTHER CHEEK

Everyone knows that Provence is the place to buy pétanque balls. However, less well known is Marseille's sideline industry selling reproduction buttocks to lovers of the sport. Traditionally players from the south of France have to pay a specific forfeit if they score no points at all in a match. The origins of the custom of kissing a sculpted or painted *derrière* after losing the game are lost in the mists of time. However, no self-respecting *boulodrome* is without a discreetly positioned pair of artificial buttocks. So do not be surprised when visiting the village potter to encounter a realistic-looking backside among the olive bowls, fruit platters and garlic graters.

## STUNT OF THE CENTURY

The Tour de France has been going for more than a century, which is not bad for a marketing stunt. Originally staged in 1903 to publicize *l'Auto* magazine, the first tour saw 60 riders covering 2,500km (1,550 miles) over 19 days. There were only six stages, so riders had to pedal their boneshakers through the night. In later years allegations of doping tarnished the reputation of the tour. But a recent series of close-run contests, not least in 2009 when 37-year-old Lance Armstrong chased Alberto Contador to the finish, have put the zest back into the race. The tour takes place in July and the cyclists follow a different route each year, often with a stretch outside France.

**Above** *There are plenty of opportunities for snorkelling off the coast of Provence*

**Below** *A game of boules in St-Tropez*

# URBAN VS. RURAL

The arrival of the TGV (*Train à Grande Vitesse*—super-fast train) cut journey times between Paris and Provence. But in the country your journey will still be measured in decades not hours. Away from the urban buzz, Provence's villages eschew the cult of internationalism, choosing to celebrate all things rural. People nod and bid each other a friendly *bonjour* when passing in the street. Of course, time does leave its mark, and those same fast trains that are making France smaller are nudging away at those differences. The Mediterranean is now only three hours from Paris, and city families are leaving behind the cosmopolitan life to move to the country. These families are buying rural houses not just for weekends but as their main homes. They believe their children will enjoy a better life in the country, so the breadwinner opts for a weekly commute to the city and staying in a studio pied-à-terre, while the rest of the family lives the country life.

**Above** *The pool area at the stylish Hi-hôtel, Nice*

### CABINS IN THE SUN

While New Yorkers have their summer houses in the Hamptons, the good people of Marseille have their *cabanons*. Most casual visitors pass through the coastal area south of Marseille unaware of its unique *cabanon* lifestyle. This is focused on weekend and holiday houses where families decamp to party and play boules or cards with their friends in huts, cabins, shacks and boathouses. The *Route des Cabanons* takes you through the enchanting yet little-known villages of Montredon, Madrague and Morgiou, as well as better-known fishing ports such as Vallon des Auffes. The tourist office in Marseille can suggest an early-evening driving itinerary through this hinterland of the south.

### DESIGNER HOTEL

The 21st century is the era of the designer hotel. Where once it was enough to have designer Philippe Starck come up with waiters' uniforms or a new chair, France's newest hotels vie for the most outrageous concepts. In Nice, the palatial elegance of the Negresco has a new rival in Matali Crasset's multi-concept Hi-hôtel, where you can choose the space that best suits your mood. Shower behind a plant screen in a room with an indoor terrace theme, relax on furniture created from computer monitors or sing along to the Sofablaster with its built-in music. Other places to try these latest hip hotel concepts, if only from the hotel bar, include the Hotel Windsor in Nice and Hotel 3.14 in Cannes.

# THE STORY OF PROVENCE AND THE CÔTE D'AZUR

# PREHISTORY, GREEKS AND ROMANS

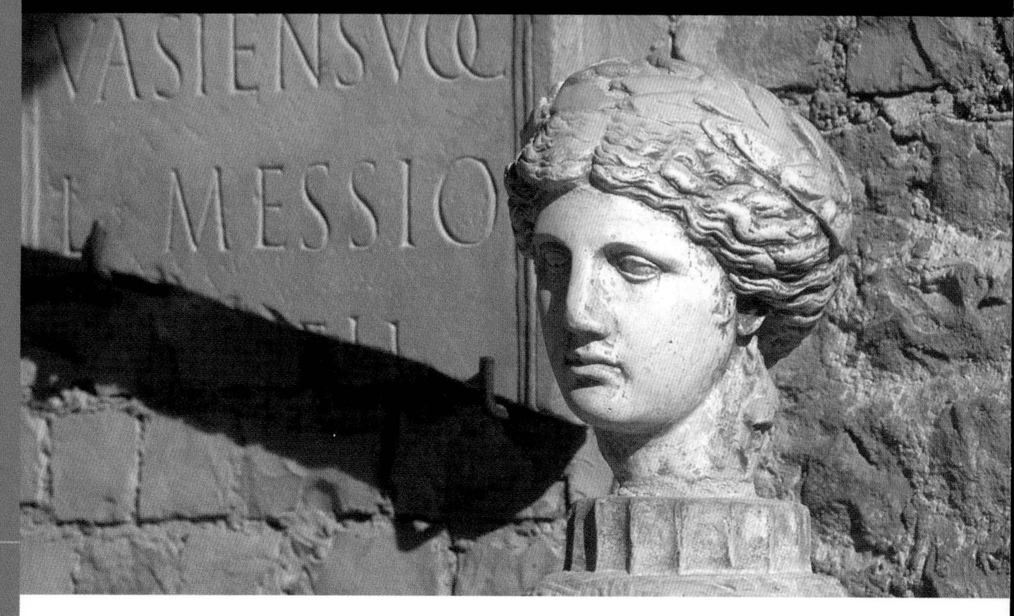


Provence took its name because it was indeed a province of Rome, while all of France farther north was a mere colony. The region boasts magnificent Roman constructions, ranging from arenas to the breathtaking Pont du Gard. However, beyond the grand edifices remain legacies of local communities dating back many thousands of years. The first known settlement is Terra Amata, behind the old port in Nice. Cro-Magnon hunters lived near freshwater springs by the beach. At Menton, Palaeolithic discoveries include a 30,000-year-old skull and burial sites with bodies draped in shell jewellery. Neolithic and Bronze Age Ligurians, who farmed the region 8,000 years ago, left their mark with rock engravings in the Vallée des Merveilles. The Ligurians began intermarrying with Celtic tribes, starting the trading migrations that changed the face of the Mediterranean. First arrivals were the Greek Phocaeans, who established the bridgehead of Massalia (Marseille). It was a relatively peaceful settlement until conflict with local Celts led the Greeks to appeal to Rome for back-up in 124BC. Canny Romans, who marched in under the command of Sextius Calvinius, saw the area's potential and made their first settlement at Aquae Sextiae (Aix-en-Provence). Founding a capital at Narbonne in 118BC, the Romans soon held a territory stretching from the Pyrenees in the west to the Alps in the east, and as far north as Lyon. Road building included the Via Agrippa, north from Arles and Avignon, the Via Aurelia, towards Italy, and the Via Domitia, to Spain.

**Above** *A Roman bust and a carved stone sign in Vaison-la-Romaine, a town with many Roman remains*

**THE UNLIKELY CAPITAL**

Proof, if any were needed, that political acumen is more than a match for natural resources is found in the speedy elevation of Arles to the capital of Roman Provence. The unlikely choice of Arles over the more obvious trading port of Marseille is due to the town's canny allegiances at the time of Julius Caesar's conflict with Pompey in the turmoil that followed Caesar's conquest of Gaul in 51BC. Marseille, or Massalia as it was then known, backed the wrong side, whereas Arles supported Caesar, even building a fleet of 12 boats for him. Thus Caesar sacked the port on the Med and elevated Arles to capital. Even when Marseille had re-established itself in later centuries, the legacy of Roman patronage guaranteed Arles' success through the Renaissance and beyond.

### THE GOOD LIFE

Leisure is not a modern concept. Provence was something of an arts and entertainment hub for the Roman Empire. The area's incredible legacy of theatres, arenas and bathhouses owes much to the reign of Augustus, who established a large number of settlements to be governed by military veterans. Towns such as Arles, Avignon and Vaison soon developed into cities and cultural hubs with grandiose architecture reflecting the artistic and relaxed lifestyle of a prosperous peace. Temples, sporting arenas, theatres, aqueducts and bridges made the cities more desirable outposts of the empire. The luxuries of life were funded by Provence's natural resources and the development of a skilled workforce. The region produced oil, grain and ships for the empire.

### CAVEMEN LEAVE THEIR MARK

While cave paintings in the Dordogne are visible proof of prehistoric life in France, Provence had long lacked this type of artistic legacy from its earliest inhabitants. Then, in 1991, Henri Cosquer went diving along the coast near Cassis, in the Bouches-du-Rhône *département*. The limestone cliffs are famous for their fjord-like *calanques* (inlets), and it was 37m (121ft) under the sea that Cosquer found an opening in one of them. Exploring further, he discovered a cave lined with hundreds of paintings of bison, deer, fish and horses—dating from around 25,000BC. The site became known as the underwater Lascaux and was listed as a historical monument in 1992. The caves are not on the visitor trail. They were walled up after other divers died trying to visit them.

### TO GREECE WITH LOVE

In surprising contrast to the warlike arrival of the Roman regime, the Greeks won Marseille in the most improbable manner: It was given as a wedding present. When a group of Greek traders dropped anchor at the Lacydon inlet on France's Mediterranean coast, they were fortunate enough to arrive just as the local king, Nann, was holding a banquet for his daughter to choose a husband. As luck would have it, the lass, Gyptis, was rather taken with Protis, the spokesman for the new arrivals. So she chose him as her fiancé. Better yet, King Nann gave Lacydon (the site of today's Vieux Port) to the couple. Thus, with no hint of aggression or unpleasantness, the Greeks were able to establish a colony at one of Europe's most strategic sites.

### ALL RHODES LEAD TO RHÔNE

Provence's greatest river pays tribute to an island across the Mediterranean, thanks to the trading routes into Gaul established by the Greeks. The river Rhône provided an unrivalled trade corridor between the Mediterranean and key settlements in Provence, with local tin, copper, gold and silver exchanged for Greek ceramics. The Greeks planted exotic fruits and vines along the river bank, tended with Hellenic know-how, and established a wine and olive oil trade. The river itself was named after the Greek island of Rhodes, with the adjective *Rhôdéenne* still used today to describe the plains along the river valley.

**Above left** *A rock engraving from the Vallée des Merveilles*
**Below** *Marseille's Vieux Port*

# CHRISTIANITY AND FEUDALISM

Christianity arrived in Provence towards the end of the Roman era. Preachers settled on the coast and St. Trophimus came to Arles quite early on, but it was after the open support of Emperor Constantine in the fourth century AD that Christianity established itself. The first Church Council took place in Arles in AD314 and the next century saw the construction of abbeys and monasteries around Marseille. As Rome's influence declined, so peace evaporated. The Visigoths made incursions into Arles and other invaders encroached on Provence. By AD536 the Franks were the leading power. Saracens from across the Pyrenees in Spain, seeing the destruction of a formerly unified province, began taking key towns in the eighth century AD. This resulted in a period of conflict between the Saracens and the Franks, led by General Charles Martel. The Franks forced the Saracens out of Provence throughout the 730s, but this was no lasting peace. For more than a century, Saracens continued to raid towns from their bases such as La Garde-Freinet, besieging Marseille in AD838 and Arles in AD842. Provence became a kingdom in its own right in AD855, but found itself subject to renewed attacks, from not only the Saracens but also the Normans. The Saracens were finally overwhelmed in 1032, when Guillaume le Libérateur banished them at the dawn of the era of the Counts of Provence. The feudal system saw local seigneurs governing their own fiefdoms. This coincided with a golden era of learning, thanks to the monasteries, and trade, developing after the Crusades.

**Clockwise from above** *Evocative castle ruins at Les Baux-de-Provence; sunlight strikes the trunk of a mature cork oak growing in the forests of the Massif des Maures; flower carvings on the cloister pillars of the Abbaye de Sénanque*

**REVENGE OF THE HAMMER**

Victor over the Saracens, Charles Martel (Charles the Hammer) famously began his own power-broking regimes towards the end of his life, arbitrarily announcing rulers and appointing leaders throughout the land. Charles did not put too much stock in the legal rules of succession, having suffered first hand from the vagaries of a step-grandmother who manipulated the fortunes of her own family, when Charles was in his 20s. To prevent Charles' objections to her policy, Plectrude, a lady with a will of iron, had arranged for the lad to be thrown into prison. He wrested power from Plectrude and, in a series of bloody battles, took on all Saracen uprisings, eventually defeating Saracen settlements in Avignon, Marseille and Aix-en-Provence, restoring Frankish Christian rule to the region.

## AN UNSUCCESSFUL HERMIT

While other offshore attractions lure hordes of visitors, the island of St-Honorat, one of the Îles de Lérins near Cannes, has managed to retain its monastic peace. A Christian community was accidentally established here in the fourth century AD by St. Honoratus, archbishop of Arles, a great teacher and one of history's least successful hermits. He chose the island as a place of solitary contemplation, yet, according to contemporary writers, he established an enormous monastery. The island soon earned an enviable reputation as a place of learning, despite not having any formal teaching structure. It produced many of the Church's best-known saints, among them Ireland's St. Patrick and Marseille's St. Cassian. The tranquil setting of today's Abbaye de Lérins belies a tumultuous history. The monks were slaughtered by Saracens in the seventh century AD.

## MIRACLE MADONNA

The oldest Black Madonna statue in France is in the Église Notre-Dame de Romigier, in Manosque (▷ 206). Said to have been found in a nearby forest in the sixth century AD, it mysteriously disappeared for generations before being rediscovered as the church was being built. The monks did not like the look of the statue (Black Madonnas were often the subject of fear and superstition) and decided to leave the Madonna outside the church door. Local legend has it that the Madonna then walked into the church and made her way to the altar. Despite this, the monks removed the icon and placed her outside once again. Whereupon, so the story goes, she returned to the church altar, where she has stayed ever since.

## SARACENS' LEGACY

Pillaging, laying siege to entire communities and a general warlike stance have given the invading Saracens some bad press over the years. However, just as the Greeks left their vines, and the Romans their infrastructure, the Saracens also gave Provence a pretty decent legacy. Flat tiled roofs can be traced back directly to their arrival in Provence, and (albeit less practical) the tambourine was their gift to music. The most profitable gift to the locals was the cork industry, which flourished for around 900 years after the Saracens left. In La Garde-Freinet, chestnut groves and eucalyptus trees surrounding the town are outnumbered by vast woods of cork oak trees. By the 19th century, La Garde-Freinet was France's principal producer of cork.

## FROM BATTLE TO BALLADS

Music hath charms to soothe the most savage beast. And so feuding barons of Les Baux-de-Provence, whose regimes were marked with bloodshed, were responsible for a mini-musical renaissance as well as for military aggression. From the 10th century the lords, who claimed kinship with the magi kings attending Christ's nativity, fought to assert their authority with regard to land. However, in wooing for love, they preferred a more gentle approach and would hire troubadours to pen ballads and sing serenades at the windows of potential wives. This led to Les Baux becoming a musical hot spot, with strolling players from far and wide descending on the citadel to sing in the streets in European song contests.

# CONFLICT AND CULTURE

The squabbles of the feudal lords were finally ended in the 13th century, when Count Raymond-Bérenger V of Barcelona took control of the region, establishing firm laws and an administrative structure based on his own Catalan regime. It was the marriage of his youngest daughter Beatrice that set Provence on the path to stability. In 1246 Beatrice married Charles of Anjou, brother to Louis IX, King of France, and part of a family with a strong track record of ruling. Britain's Plantagenet monarchs came from the same stock. Earlier in the century, in Languedoc, France waged war against the Cathars (followers of a Christian sect). Avignon made the mistake of allying itself with the losing side and was attacked by France and badly damaged in 1226. France seized control of the Comtat Venaissin, territories north of Avignon. This was in turn given to Rome in 1274, in a move that led to the Avignon papacy. This period brought an artistic and cultural boom to Provence. Under the patronage of the popes, a thriving university developed in Avignon and artists came from Siena to decorate the new palaces and chapels. Outside the charmed enclave, the rest of Provence found the 14th century less enjoyable. There was a great plague in 1348, and when Queen Jeanne died childless in 1382 it led to the inevitable warring over the succession. Louis II (died 1434) and the legendary Roi René (1409–80) brought stability back to Provence. Meanwhile Nice, no longer part of Provence, spent the coming centuries until the French Revolution warring with France and the Duchy of Savoy.

**THE POPES AT AVIGNON**

After years of violence at the hands of the citizens of Rome, the popes fled to the safety of Avignon in 1309, after an invitation from King Philip, who lusted after papal money and influence on French soil. The popes lived in a fortress-like palace, which the poet Petrarch called 'a sewer where all the filth of the universe had gathered', and by 1377 the court was so threatened by thieves and swindlers that Gregory XI returned to Rome. The sovereigns of Europe then sponsored their own candidates, and by 1414 there was the spectacle of three popes, each vying for pre-eminence. The prelates of the Sorbonne, among others, put a stop to this, and in 1418 a sole pope again sat in Rome.

## RENAISSANCE RENÉ

Roi René was a popular figure and credited with the golden age of Aix-en-Provence. Indeed, some historians pun his name, claiming the Renaissance as 'René essence'. Good King René of the House of Anjou boasted several dukedoms and was also King of Aragon, Hungary, Mallorca, Naples, Sardinia, Sicily, Valencia and even Jerusalem. He enjoyed something of a front-row seat at history, escorting Joan of Arc to visit the Dauphin in Orléans and giving Christopher Columbus his first naval commission. He was a true Renaissance man, speaking no less than six languages, writing a rule book for the sport of jousting, and excelling in the arts as a painter, poet and musician. When jailed by the Duke of Burgundy, he passed time by perfecting his skills at engraving on glass.

## HIDDEN DRAGON

June visitors to Tarascon are often surprised to see a dragon dance in the streets—an event that might seem more at home in a New Year's celebration in Hong Kong than a carnival in Provence. However, this is truly a Provençal tradition, even if the monster is not quite a dragon. The ritual was established in 1474 to commemorate the routing of the *Tarasque*, a legendary beast that supposedly emerged from the waters of the port and terrorized the town, eating children and cattle. The story goes that St. Martha tamed the beast by waving her crucifix at it. The monster allowed itself to be put on a lead and trotted off, leaving the townsfolk in peace. The dragon dance, with its attendant bonfires and fireworks, represents the taming of the beast—a symbol of Christianity's supremacy over paganism.

## BEGINNING OF THE END

When Louis XI inherited Provence after the death of King René in 1480, the French king set about bringing the region under closer royal control. As Louis began measures to dilute the powers of Provence's *États-Généraux* (States General), Aix's politicians voiced public opposition. Eventually, as Provence was a crucial buffer zone between the French and Italian provinces—what is now the Riviera had long been ceded to Savoyard and Genovese control—the Crown relented. In 1486, a treaty was signed granting Provence freedom to run its own legal institutions.

## WHEN IS A MONK NOT A MONK?

From the 12th century, Monaco belonged to Genoa, a city-state split between two factions, the papist Guelfs and the Ghibellines. When the Guelf Grimaldi family was chased out of Genoa in the 13th century, they seized their rivals' land along the Riviera. The prize of Monaco was won when François Grimaldi and an accomplice, disguised as monks, gained access to the fortress, then drew swords from under their habits to take control of Monaco. This is remembered today on the family crest—two sword-wielding monks.

**Clockwise from opposite** *The Grimaldi coat of arms on Monaco's Palais Princier; the procession of Roi René at Aix-en-Provence; the dragon parade in Tarascon*

# FINALLY FRENCH

Provence lost its language in 1539. With the Edict of Villers-Cotterêts, King François I delivered the death sentence on Provençal, one of several *langues d'Oc* (languages of the south). He made it illegal to use any language other than French in schools, churches and local administration. The 16th century brought fresh religious conflict to Provence, with the rise of Protestantism, as much a challenge to the monarchy as to the Catholic Church. Various sects around the country were regarded as hotbeds of insurgency, and the State took revenge with bloody massacres in the Petit Lubéron: Around 3,000 people were slaughtered over five April days in 1545. Protestants attacked Orange Cathedral and churches across Haute-Provence, bringing an inevitable backlash of State-sanctioned massacre. The return of plague and the coronation of the former Huguenot Henri IV at the end of the century calmed the situation, with the 1598 Edict of Nantes securing freedom of worship for Protestants. It was a short-lived peace, as after Henri's assassination in 1610, Louis XIII and Cardinal Richelieu flexed the monarchy's muscles against the regions. In 1685, Louis XIV revoked the Edict of Nantes, leading to a mass Protestant exodus. Decadence in Louis' court and corruption in successive reigns, coupled with a decline in Provence's fortune after blighted harvests, meant the region was ready to follow Paris' lead when it came to Revolution in 1789. Churches were looted and the guillotine was set up in Marseille.

**Above** *The French flag, flying from a building in Arles*

**MAN OF THE CENTURIES**

Michel de Nostre Dame was born in St-Rémy-de-Provence in 1503 into a family of recent converts from Judaism to Catholicism. A stargazer from his school days, Nostradamus studied medicine. He devoted his early years to finding a cure to the plague that ravaged 16th-century Provence, experimenting with herbalism and blending established medical practice with country lore. Gaining a reputation as a doctor, he moved to Salon-de-Provence in 1547, but within a decade he had become better known as the court astrologer, with his first book of predictions published in 1555. Nostradamus died in 1566, but his work lives on, his own immortality guaranteed by the *Siècles* (centuries), cryptic predictions re-appraised by each successive generation to reveal visions of tyrants and natural disasters. His home is now a museum of his life (▷ 95).

## THE GIRL IN THE VELVET MASK, PERHAPS?

Not all prisoners in 17th-century France were granted the respect paid to the most famous resident of the Fort Royal, on the island of Sainte-Marguerite (▷ 146). Contemporary accounts state the guards would take off their hats in his presence. For this was the Man in the Iron Mask. The writer Voltaire dropped hints as to his identity, suggesting he bore a resemblance to a famous Frenchman. A popular story is that the prisoner was the twin brother of Louis XIV. Another claims the man was in fact a woman, the female heir to the throne, and other conspiracy theorists say the prisoner had proof of the king's illegitimacy. It is not just the man who is the subject of conjecture. Experts dispute the nature of the mask. Some swear it was made of black velvet.

## HOW MARSEILLE GOT ITS SONG

The French national anthem, *La Marseillaise*, is probably the best-known link between the Republic and Marseille. So it is surprising to discover that it was written about an army that could not have been farther from Marseille, and by a loyal supporter of the monarchy. The Revolution was well under way when the aristocratic mayor of Strasbourg commissioned a marching song from Claude-Joseph Rouget de Lisle in 1792. The song of the Rhine army was then promoted as the song of the border armies. Then François Mireur came to Marseille to recruit volunteers to storm Louis XVI's Tuileries palace. The soldiers of the south sang the song so lustily when they marched into Paris that the Parisians renamed it *La Marseillaise*. It became a national anthem in 1795.

## ULTIMATE PEST CONTROL

When a village calls itself Contes (stories), it is no surprise that its history is made up of myths and legends. Among many *contes* in the village, in the Alpes-Maritimes, was the tale of an invasion of voracious caterpillars in 1508. The grubs took to the streets, devouring everything in sight and secreting a poison causing rashes and illness among the residents. As the creatures munched their way through pine needles and foliage, the citizens appealed to the Bishop of Nice, who came to the village in order to perform the exorcism that finally rid Contes of its most unwelcome invaders.

## THE PRICE OF FREEDOM

Marseille rose up against Louis XIV in 1659 and the king retaliated by building a fortress to keep an eye on the city's citizens. However, in the early 18th century, the king granted Marseille the status of Free Port, increasing its fortunes. Unfortunately, as the port grew, so did the risk of infection from dubious cargoes. In 1720 a ship brought the third and worst outbreak of plague to Marseille, killing half the population of the city and claiming 100,000 lives across Provence.

**Above** *The cover of a song sheet for* La Marseillaise

**Left** *Religious conflict in the Petit Lubéron*

# THE 19TH CENTURY

The 19th century was the hundred years that began to define modern France, politically and artistically. Napoleon Bonaparte seized power at the turn of the century, bringing an end to the Terror that had followed the French Revolution. Provence was less supportive of Napoleon's imperial wars and downright cross at losing a swathe of the Alpes-Maritimes to Sardinia on his defeat in the Russian campaign. After his abdication, the former emperor made one final march through the region after escaping from Elba before being defeated at Waterloo. The subsequent return to power of the royal family led to a revival of the old political skirmishing in Provence. After a lull at the coronation in 1830 of 'Citizen King' Louis-Philippe, Provençal tempers flared up again in support of his overthrow in the 1848 revolution and passions still simmered during the reign of Napoleon III from 1850. The second half of the century saw a flourishing of art and literary movements, with the poet Frédéric Mistral reclaiming local identity. Rail links brought tourism to the south of France and also moved artists from the dark skies of northern Europe to the vibrancy of the Riviera. Commercially, Provence changed during this period, with modern shipbuilding and the opening of the Suez Canal reforming industries and establishing global markets. Marseille became a base for sugar refining and exporting soap.

**Clockwise from above** *A plaque of artist Paul Cézanne; celebrity chef Auguste Escoffier; a poster advertises winter in Nice*

## LOCAL BOY PAINTS GOOD

Although the tortured artist most often associated with Provence is Vincent Van Gogh, his famous link with Arles and St-Rémy lasted just two years. The local boy with an intense passion for his art was in fact Paul Cézanne. Born in Aix-en-Provence on 10 January 1839, he moved to Paris in his twenties and joined the young Impressionists, but was disillusioned at the reception their work received and returned to his home town. Here he worked alone, developing his style in the Provence countryside and his attic studio in rue Boulegon. Like Van Gogh, Cézanne became extraordinarily prolific during his final years, creating more than 300 paintings after 1895. As he finally achieved recognition, he built a typical Provençal-style house, called Les Lauves, by Aix Cathedral. He died on 22 October 1906.

**LOOKS FAMILIAR**

The *tricolore* blue, white and red flag of the French Republic was a long time coming. At the start of the Revolution in 1789 a simple blue and red cockade was used as the national symbol. Blue, white and red were agreed as the republican colours in 1794. With the restoration of the monarchy, a combination of the *tricolore* with the national emblem of a cockerel proved an unsatisfactory compromise. By the revolution of 1848 the simple blue, white and red symbol came back into fashion, and the state adopted the *tricolore* we know today, taken from the original flag of the Provençal town of Martigues. The royalists never accepted the dismissal of their cockerel, but the blue, white and red was officially enshrined as a national symbol, with the blue stripe always flown closest to the flagpole.

**MISTRAL BLOWS AWAY THE COBWEBS**

The rediscovery of the once banned Provençal language can be traced to the region's most famous poet, Frédéric Mistral (1830–1914), a Nobel prize winner. After conventional schooling near his home in St-Rémy-de-Provence, Mistral studied in Avignon, where he found a fellow lover of the old tongue in Joseph Roumanille. On 21 May 1854, Roumanille, Mistral and five other writers founded the Félibrige movement for the revival of the traditional language of Provence. A year later, Mistral established the annual *Armanan Provençau*, the first publication to be written in Provençal since the 16th century. He went on to open a museum of traditional culture in Arles with his Nobel prize money. You'll find plaques featuring his poems across the area.

**RECIPE FOR FAME**

These days, television produces a never-ending stream of celebrity chefs, but in the 19th century, cooks remained anonymous. The first kitchen master to become a celebrity in his own right was Auguste Escoffier, who learned his trade in the family restaurant in Nice back in the 1880s. By the turn of the century he had launched the Ritz in Paris and Savoy in London. Escoffier was quick to see the advantages of fame, and he swiftly launched spin-off industries marketing his own brand of utensils and a stream of cookbooks. His birthplace, in the village of Villeneuve Loubet, is home to the Fondation Escoffier museum, where foodies may salivate at exhibitions of simple country cooking and haute cuisine.

**THE CÔTE D'AZUR**

British people of the upper class in the 19th century often went on the Grand Tour in Europe. In 1834, Lord Brougham, a member of the English aristocracy, was forced to spend the night in the village of Cannes and loved the place so much he built a villa there. His wealthy friends soon followed him and over the years British aristocrats opened up the rest of the coast, resulting in a rail line connecting London directly to Menton (via a ferry) by 1868. Royalty were not averse to the Riviera's charms—Queen Victoria spent winters at Nice in the 1890s, away from the chills and fogs of England. Even today there is a little bit of Nice that is forever England—the waterfront is named Promenade des Anglais.

# THE 20TH CENTURY

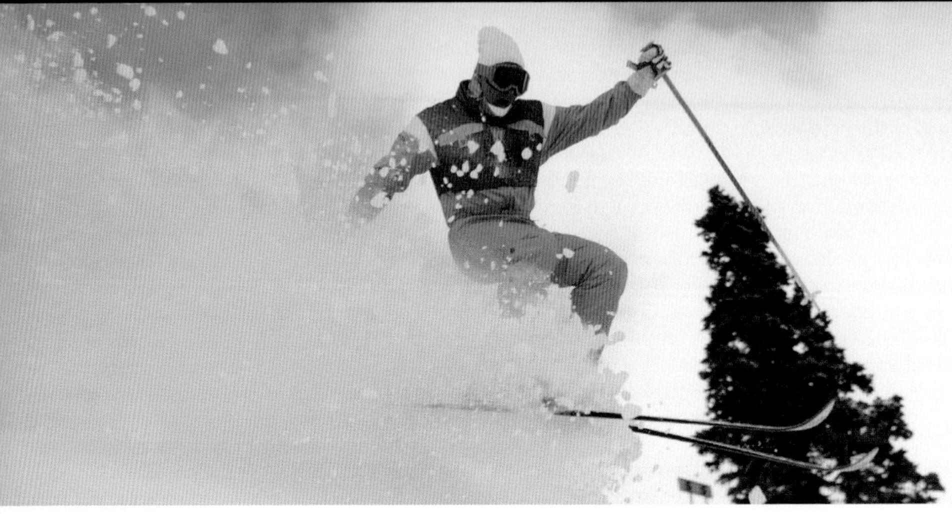

At the start of the 20th century, the artistic and literary boom of the belle époque continued, with a new generation of *arrivistes* including Pablo Picasso and Raoul Dufy. This, coupled with the high-profile celebrity status of selected resorts, highlighted the dramatic difference in the fortunes of the coast and the inland areas. As traditional rural occupations disappeared, people moved to the cities in search of work, often a fruitless journey. World War II left key cities such as Avignon and Marseille battered and bruised, with their infrastructures and industries all but wiped out. The 1950s saw road building, including the *autoroute* Esterel–Côte d'Azur, and the 1960s brought major investment, with the first plans of a TGV rail network and huge concrete industrial plants bringing jobs to the region, if compromising the aesthetics. Petrochemical plants, oil refineries and tanker terminals gave fuel to the fortunes of Marseille and the outlying area. Hydroelectric power stations and the Canal de Provence boosted the agricultural and industrial economy inland. The post-war period saw the area reinvented as a summer cultural capital. Cannes Film Festival and Avignon's theatre festival led the way to creating an international meeting place of the arts. The 1960s saw the first of the legendary jazz events in the Gould pine grove at Juan-les-Pins and brought Count Basie, Ella Fitzgerald and Dizzy Gillespie to the coast. Aix's *Art Lyrique* opera festival sees an opera house built each summer in the courtyard of the Archbishop's Palace and has been responsible for discovering some of the world's leading talents.

**Above** *Skiing is one of the sports you can try in Provence in winter*

## GO BUILD IT ON THE MOUNTAINS

The growth of air travel in the 1960s and the boom in affordable tourism led to an explosion in hotel and apartment building along the Côte d'Azur. Not all the construction projects reflected the traditional Provençal and Savoyard style of the region. Soon, concrete threatened to overshadow ochre cliffs and olive groves as the face of the coast, with controversial high-rises and schemes such as the Marina des Anges. Away from the Riviera, inland tourism promoted renovation and restoration of old village houses.
Just 90 minutes from the Promenade des Anglais, the alpine ski villages also welcomed more visitors, and in the 1970s the first new winter sports resort, Isola 2000, at 2,000m (6,560ft) above sea level, was built above the traditional old village of Isola, 17km (10.5 miles) away.

### RISE OF THE RIGHT

After nearly 3,000 years of ethnic infusion, which started when Celts, Greeks and Romans settled along the coast, immigration is still a political hot potato. In 1962, as Algeria won independence from France, thousands of *Pieds Noirs*, former colonists, returned from Africa, bringing with them the first in a wave of racist outcries that was refuelled by the rise of Jean-Marie Le Pen's far-right Front National party in the 1980s. The Front achieved its biggest political successes in the ports and urban areas of the south. Orange and Toulon were among the other key strongholds of the far right towards the end of the century.

### OCCUPATION AND RESISTANCE

From 1940 to 1944, under the German occupation, the Vichy Government of Marshal Pétain ran the southern part of France. It's a painful episode of the country's history that still divides French society. Klaus Barbie was convicted of war crimes in the 1980s. Vichy is remembered for deporting 70,000 Jews and 650,000 workers from France to Germany. But Vichy did not spring solely from Nazi occupation. Far-right politicians in 1930s France had spoken out against foreigners and pushed through the Family Code in 1939, setting down strict laws for women and sexual morality.

**Above right** *Prince Rainier and Grace Kelly, on their engagement in 1956*

**Below** *Cap Ferrat, crowned by the Villa Ephrussi de Rothschild*

### ARRIVEDERCI MERCANTOUR

The 20th century saw the final Italian retreat from Provence. The Italianate architecture of the Riviera is the enduring testament to generations of cultural occupation. However, the last corner of the region to remain part of the adjoining country has no architectural legacy. The Mercantour was Italy's 19th-century royal hunting ground, a sprawling natural landscape stretching from Piemonte to the Alpes-Maritimes and Alpes-de-Haute-Provence. The rocks, canyons, mountain peaks, alpine forests and meadows are home to eagles, kestrels, vultures, mouflons, chamois and wild boar and more than 2,000 varieties of plant life. In 1946 the area was finally split across national borders, and 68,000ha (168,000 acres) returned to France. Both nations granted the site national park status. The park has been designated a protected nature reserve since 1979.

### AMERICA-SUR-MED

If Paris was the home of 19th-century Americans in exile (Oscar Wilde said 'When good Americans die, they go to Paris'), the 20th century saw Provence stake a claim for the title. Luxury hotels and villas created a charmed combination of metropolitan society in an idyllic climate. Before World War II, author F. Scott Fitzgerald, composer Cole Porter and actor Rudolph Valentino were among the Juan-les-Pins crowd. (Juan-les-Pins formed the backdrop for the 1974 film adaptation of Fitzgerald's most famous novel, *The Great Gatsby*, starring Robert Redford and Mia Farrow.)

In the 1940s, the Cannes Film Festival introduced Errol Flynn and Clark Gable to the French Riviera. Most celebrated of all was film star Grace Kelly who, in the ultimate Hollywood love story, married Prince Rainier of Monaco and became Riviera royalty.

# THE 21ST CENTURY

The 20th century turned as the Riviera was discovering a new and unaccustomed humility. Just as the most chic resorts were launching and refurbishing ever more luxurious hotels, the area's traditional market shrank. The threat of global terrorism after 9/11 kept many wealthy overseas visitors at home, so the astronomic rents for holiday villas outside Avignon and Aix and the room charges at pampering palaces on the Med were no longer bankable guarantees. Fortunately, low-cost air travel from the UK brought new visitors to the millionaires' playgrounds, and people began exploring the backcountry in search of affordable second homes. A world away from the glitz, villages developed heritage tourism, focusing on country pursuits and traditional arts and crafts. The coast's industrial centres, Marseille and Toulon, have also seen a resurgence of a cultural kind. Marseille has been the focus of the multi-billion-euro Euroméditerranée project, a complete renovation of the former docklands. The city is gearing up to be Europe's Capital of Culture in 2013.

**Above** *Brightly coloured glassware from Biot*

### THE END OF AN ERA

The death of Prince Rainier on 6 April 2005 at the age of 81 signalled the end of the 'Hollywood glamour' era in Monaco's history. During his 56-year reign he was credited with turning an ailing principality, whose income derived almost totally from gambling, into a wealthy country and one of the world's most fashionable tax havens. He has been succeeded by his son, Prince Albert II.

### SINGLE CURRENCY, CHOICE OF EMBLEMS

On New Year's Day 2002, France said goodbye to its national currency, the franc, and adopted the euro. But Provence found itself with two local versions of the euro in its tills. Those issued in France are stamped with various images of the Republic. However, Monaco, which is not a member of the EU, was granted permission to issue its own euros, embossed with national symbols.

### RAILS 'N' WHEELS

Provence came a step closer to London in 2001 with the arrival of a Eurostar service from London to Avignon. And with slick new trains bringing the Mediterranean coast within a three-hour journey of Paris, arriving by rail is now a real possibility. New tram systems in Marseille and Nice, completed in 2007, were complemented by bike sharing schemes in 2009. There are also rent-a-bike stands in Avignon.

### THE EASYJET EFFECT

Budget airline easyJet celebrated its 15th birthday in 2010; but how people laughed when the little orange airline first arrived in Nice in 1997. Since then it's been joined by other successful low-cost operators, including Ryanair, BMIbaby and Jet2. Bringing millions of Europeans within easy striking distance of Provence had a huge effect on local house prices.

# ON THE MOVE

On the Move gives you detailed advice and information about the various options for travelling to Provence and the Côte d'Azur, before explaining the best ways to get around the region once you are there. Handy tips help you with everything from buying tickets to renting a car.

# ARRIVING

## ARRIVING BY AIR

Many visitors to Provence arrive by air, with Nice and Marseille being the main gateways to the region for visitors from Europe. Passengers from the US usually need to change planes in Paris or London, although there are daily services between New York and Nice-Côte d'Azur. The increasing number of flights from low-cost European airlines has encouraged visitors from the UK and the rest of Europe to take short breaks to Provence. The flight time from London to Provence is around two hours, from New York to Nice (direct) around eight hours and Paris to Nice around one hour 30 minutes. Regular tourists seldom visit Provence's most glamorous arrivals hall. La Môle airport, a tiny airstrip 18km (11 miles) north of St-Tropez, is used almost exclusively by VIPs, although a single scheduled summer route is laid on for wealthy bankers flying from Geneva in Switzerland.

» **Nice-Côte d'Azur** is the major airport for eastern Provence and is on the coast, 6km (4 miles) west of Nice. It is handy for reaching Monaco, Cannes and the other Riviera resorts. There are nearly 200 flights a week from Paris, as well as flights from around Europe, including low-cost airline services. Delta Air Lines currently has some services between New York and Nice. The airport's Terminal 1 serves the vast majority of international flights, with airlines including British Airways, BMIbaby and Aer Lingus. It has two restaurants, a post office, car rental offices and an information desk. Terminal 2 serves Air France, along with easyJet. Facilities include a restaurant, car rental offices and an information desk.

» **Marseille-Provence** airport, 30km (19 miles) northwest of Marseille, caters mainly for business traffic and boasts a new, albeit basic, budget-airline terminal known as MP2. The airport has two connected terminals, with shops, restaurants and a bureau de change in each. Terminal 1 has a pharmacy and first-aid station.

» **Toulon** airport is 22km (14 miles) east of Toulon and receives at least four Air France flights a day from Paris Orly, as well as seasonal European routes from Ryanair. There is one terminal, with a café/bar.

» **Avignon** airport receives several flights a week from the UK, including Flybe routes from Birmingham, Exeter, Manchester and Southampton, and a Jet2 link from Leeds. The single terminal, 10km (6 miles) southeast of Avignon, has a bar/restaurant and car rental offices.

» **Nîmes-Arles-Camargue** is a small airport 12km (7.5 miles) southeast of Nîmes and has services from easyJet and Ryanair. The small terminal has a car rental office.

» **Montpellier Mediterranée** airport is 7km (4.5 miles) southeast of Montpellier and a 40-minute drive from Nîmes, on Provence's western boundary. It has regular services

**GETTING TO THE CITY FROM THE AIRPORT**

| AIRPORT | TAXI | TRAINS |
| --- | --- | --- |
| **Nice-Côte d'Azur (NCE)** | Cost: €30 (cash only)<br>Journey time: 20 min | None |
| **Marseille-Provence, also called Marseille-Marignane (MRS)** | Cost: around €50 (day), €60 (night)<br>Journey time: 30 min | None |
| **Toulon (TLN)** | Cost: around €40<br>Journey time: 30 min | None |
| **Avignon (AVN)** | Cost: around €22<br>Journey time: 15 min | None |
| **Nîmes-Arles-Camargue (FNI)** | Cost: around €25 to Nîmes<br>Journey time: 25 min to Nîmes | None |
| **Montpellier Mediterranée (MPL)** | Cost to Montpellier: around €20<br>Journey time: 20 min | None |
| **Lyon St-Exupéry (LYS)** | Cost to central Lyon: around €38 (day), €53 (night)<br>Journey time: 45 min | TGV trains travel from the airport to destinations in Provence, including Aix-en-Provence, Arles, Avignon and Marseille.<br>Reserve ahead. |

from the UK with British Airways and Ryanair, as well as flights from Paris with Air France. *Autoroute* links with Provence are good. The airport's one terminal has a restaurant, café, car rental offices and information kiosk. There is also a hotel on site.

» **Lyon St-Exupéry** is 28km (17 miles) east of Lyon. Its TGV rail link makes the journey to Provence relatively quick, taking around one hour 30 minutes to Marseille and just over an hour to Aix-en-Provence. Its two terminals are linked by a central area containing restaurants, cafés, a pharmacy and other facilities.

## AIRPORT CONTACTS

| | | |
|---|---|---|
| Nice-Côte d'Azur | 0820 423 333 | www.nice.aeroport.fr |
| Marseille-Provence | 04 42 14 14 14 | www.mrsairport.com |
| Toulon | 0825 018 387 | www.toulon-hyeres.aeroport.fr |
| Avignon | 04 90 81 51 51 | www.avignon.aeroport.fr |
| Nîmes-Arles-Camargue | 04 66 70 49 49 | www.nimes.cci.fr |
| Montpellier | 04 67 20 85 00 | www.montpellier.aeroport.fr |
| Lyon St-Exupéry | 0826 800 826 | www.lyon.aeroport.fr |

## OTHER USEFUL CONTACTS

| | | |
|---|---|---|
| **General airport information** | | www.worldairportguide.com |
| **Information on all French airports** | | www.aeroport.fr |
| **Air France** | 0820 820 820 | www.airfrance.fr |
| **American Airlines** | 1 800 433 7300 (US number) | www.aa.com |
| **BMIbaby** | 0905 8 28 28 28 (UK number) | www.bmibaby.com |
| **British Airways** | 0870 850 9850 (UK number) | www.ba.com |
| **Delta** | 1 800 241 4141 (US number) | www.delta.com |
| **easyJet** | 0905 821 0905 (UK number) | www.easyjet.com |
| **Flybe** | 0871 700 2000 (UK number) | www.flybe.com |
| **Ryanair** | 0871 2460 000 (UK number) | www.ryanair.com |
| **Transports Alpes-Maritimes (TAM)** | 800 06 01 06 | www.cg06.fr |
| **Régie des Transports de Marseille (RTM)** | 04 91 91 92 10 | www.rtm.fr (public transportation in Marseille) |

| **BUS** | **CAR** |
|---|---|
| Bus routes 98 and 99 run to the heart of Nice every 20 min.<br>Journey time: 20 min<br>Cost: €4<br>There are also regular services to Marseille, Aix-en-Provence, Cannes and Monaco. | Take the N7 to Nice.<br>Journey time: 15–30 min |
| Buses to the Gare St-Charles train station run from 4.30am to 11.30pm every 20 min.<br>Cost: €8.50<br>Journey time: 30 min | Take the D20, D9, then A7 to Marseille.<br>Journey time: 30 min |
| A bus service runs five times a day, but does not necessarily tie in with flights.<br>Cost: €1.40. Journey time: 30 min | The A570 leads to the A57, which heads south-west to Toulon. Journey time: 30 min |
| None | Take the N7 to Avignon.<br>Journey time: 15 min |
| A bus service meets flights and takes passengers into Nîmes.<br>Cost: €5<br>Journey time: 25 min | Take the A54, northwest to Nîmes, southeast to Arles.<br>Journey time: 25 min to Nîmes |
| Bus to Montpellier and the rail station departs 7 times a day (usually on the hour) from Pont A outside the terminal.<br>Cost €5. (Local trains link Montpellier station with Marseille and Arles several times a day. The journey to Marseille takes around 1 hour 40 min and to Arles 50 min.) | Take the D21 northwest to Montpellier. Journey time: 20 min<br>(The A9, northeast, leads to Nîmes and Orange.) |
| Buses leave every 20 min. They run daily 6am–11.20pm from the airport to Lyon, and 5am–9pm from Lyon to the airport.<br>Cost: €8.40<br>Journey time: 40–50 min | Take the A432, A43 then N383 to Lyon.<br>Journey time: 45 min<br>(To head to Provence from Lyon, pick up the A7 and drive 200km/125 miles south to Orange.) |

## ARRIVING BY TRAIN

Provence has good rail links with the rest of France, into northern Europe through the hub of Paris and directly with Italy to the east. The French rail network is run by Societé Nationale des Chemins de Fer Français (SNCF), which oversees the *Grands Lignes* (long-distance services) and *Lignes Régionals* (regional services). *Grand Lignes* have the regular Corail trains and the faster *Train à Grande Vitesse* (TGV), which can reach speeds of up to 300kph (186mph). TGV services to Provence leave Paris from the Gare de Lyon.

### TICKETS

» Most trains have first and second classes, both of which are perfectly acceptable.

» Fares are split into blue (normal) and red (peak). Reduced-rate fares are generally available for normal travel on main-line routes, excluding TGV and couchette services.

» Ticket prices vary according to the level of comfort (first or second class) and departure time. First-class fares are roughly 50 per cent more expensive than second class.

» Buy tickets in the stations, at SNCF offices, online at www.voyages-sncf.com and through some travel agents. Tickets for TGV trains must be reserved. You can do this up to a few minutes before departure, although in peak season it is best to reserve well in advance. Couchettes must be reserved at least 75 minutes before the train leaves its first station.

» Stamp your ticket in the orange machines on the platforms before you start your journey. You'll risk a fine if you forget to do this.

» If you are under 26, you can get a 25 per cent discount *(Découverte 12–25)* on train travel. Seniors (over 60 years of age) also receive discounts *(Découverte Senior)*.

» When you travel second class, there are lower rates for booking more than eight days in advance *(Découverte J8)* and more than 30 days in advance *(Découverte J30)*.

» A variety of rail passes allow travel either within France only, or within France and certain other countries, or within the whole of Europe. Buy these before you enter France, either through travel agents or Rail Europe (▷ 45).

» Ticket machines, with instructions in English, accept notes, coins and credit cards. They also dispense tickets you have ordered on the internet, by telephone or Minitel.

**CATERING SERVICES**

» Catering facilities—from salads and sandwiches to hot meals—are available on most TGV and Corail services, but can be quite expensive.

» Food can be served at your seat with first-class travel on most TGV trains.

» Hot and cold drinks, sandwiches and snacks are served on most trains.

» Overnight trains have vending machines dispensing hot and cold drinks, as well as sweets (candy).

**OVERNIGHT TRAINS**

» Most overnight trains offer either reclining seats, couchette berths or a sleeper car.

» Reclining seats are available only in second class. They have adjustable head- and footrests.

» In first class, couchettes are in four-berth compartments; in second class they are in six-berth compartments.

» Sleeper car compartments are for two people in first class and three in second class.

» Overnight services include Bordeaux to Nice; Paris to Nice; Paris to Briançon.

**STATION ASSISTANCE**

» Larger stations have an information kiosk, where you can ask for advice about your journey.

» If you need assistance, look for a member of the station staff, identifiable by their red waistcoats (vests).

» You'll need a €1 deposit to use the luggage trolleys (carts).

» Porters are on hand to help with your luggage in main stations. They wear red jackets and black or navy caps.

**LEFT LUGGAGE**

» Some stations have a baggage-storage office or coin-operated lockers. Electronic locks issue a printed ticket with a code number. You'll need to keep this ticket for when you return to collect your items.

» Don't store valuables in station lockers.

» Security concerns mean that baggage-storage facilities are not always available. Ask at the information kiosk.

| FASTEST JOURNEY TIMES TO MARSEILLE (APPROXIMATE) | |
|---|---|
| **Paris** | 3 hours |
| **Lille** | 3 hours 30 min |
| **Bordeaux** | 5 hours 30 min |
| **Strasbourg** | 7 hours |
| **Lyon** | 1 hour 30 min |

**UNDERSTANDING RAILWAY TIMETABLES**

» Pick up free timetables *(horaires)* at stations.

» SNCF timetables are published twice a year—the summer one lasts from late May to late September, and the winter one from late September to late May.

» There are two styles of timetable: one for the *Grandes Lignes*, covering high-speed TGV and other main-line services, and another for the regional TER trains.

» On *Grandes Lignes* timetables, two rows of boxed numbers at the top refer to the *numéro de train* (train number) and to the *notes à consulter* (footnotes). On TER timetables, the train number is not listed.

» Footnotes explain when a train runs *(circule)*. *Tous les jours* means it runs every day; *sauf dimanche et fêtes* means it doesn't run on Sundays and holidays. *Jusqu'au*, followed by a date, indicates the service runs only up until that date.

**RAIL PASSES**

» If you are staying in France for a long time, consider buying a rail pass that is valid for a year. This entitles you to a 50 per cent discount and is available to those aged 12 to 25 *(Carte 12–25)*, those with a child under 12 *(Carte Enfant+)* and the over 60s *(Carte Senior)*.

» Foreign visitors can choose from many rail passes. To buy certain passes you must have been resident in Europe for at least six months, and have a valid passport with you.

» Rail Europe sells a variety of rail passes (www.raileurope.com for US visitors; www.raileurope.co.uk for UK visitors).

» Once you are in France it may be difficult to change reservations made abroad.

**CAR TRANSPORTER SERVICES**

» You can take your motorcycle or car on board the *Auto-Train*. The most useful services run from Paris to Marseille and Nice.

» Pick up a *Guide Auto/Train* from SNCF stations and outlets.

## TIMETABLE, FARE AND OTHER INFORMATION

›› Timetable and fare information is available from SNCF stations, ticket outlets and travel agencies, by telephone (tel 3635 in France) or the internet.

›› The website www.voyages-sncf.com is a useful source of information and has pages in English.

›› For timetable information for rail services in Provence, look for the brochures *Sud-Est* and *TGV-Méditerranée*.

## EUROSTAR

›› If you are starting from the UK, you can take the Eurostar from London to Paris (reserve ahead), then take a train to Provence.

›› Up to 16 trains per day depart from St. Pancras Station, London, to Gare du Nord, Paris. The journey time is 2 hours 40 minutes. Tel 08705 186 186 (UK); www.eurostar.com.

›› To continue to Provence, you'll need to cross Paris to the Gare de Lyon. You can do this by taking the Métro or an RER train, but if you have a lot of luggage a taxi may be simpler.

›› Eurostar offers a weekly service direct to Avignon in summer, but tickets for this should be reserved well in advance. The journey takes around 6 hours 15 minutes.

## SCENIC RAILWAYS

›› Although the majority of Provence's rail lines cut through stunning countryside, a handful are jaw-droppingly beautiful and well worth seeking out.

›› The privately run Train des Pignes (www.trainprovence.com) runs from Nice to Digne-les-Bignes in Haute-Provence through Alpine valleys.

›› The Nice to Tende route runs through the pretty towns of Breil-sur-Roya and Sospel, and eventually all the way to Turin.

›› The Riviera's coastal line from Cannes to Menton is beautiful.

## TIPS

›› If you plan to travel during peak times (mid-June to early September, holidays and rush hours), reserve your tickets well in advance. This will also grant you a much cheaper ticket.

›› You must validate *(composter)* your ticket before boarding the train. Do this by inserting it into the orange machine on the platform.

›› Bar and at-seat services on most long-distance trains are expensive.

›› If all the seats on a TGV train have been reserved, you can be placed on standby. Your ticket entitles you to board the train but does not guarantee a seat.

## RAIL JOURNEY TIMES

This chart shows the duration in hours and minutes of a train journey between various destinations in France.

### Trains from Paris

Trains usually depart hourly during the day from Paris' Gare de Lyon to Marseille. Most trains then go on to Nice. Some trains travel directly to Nice, cutting 40 minutes from the journey time.

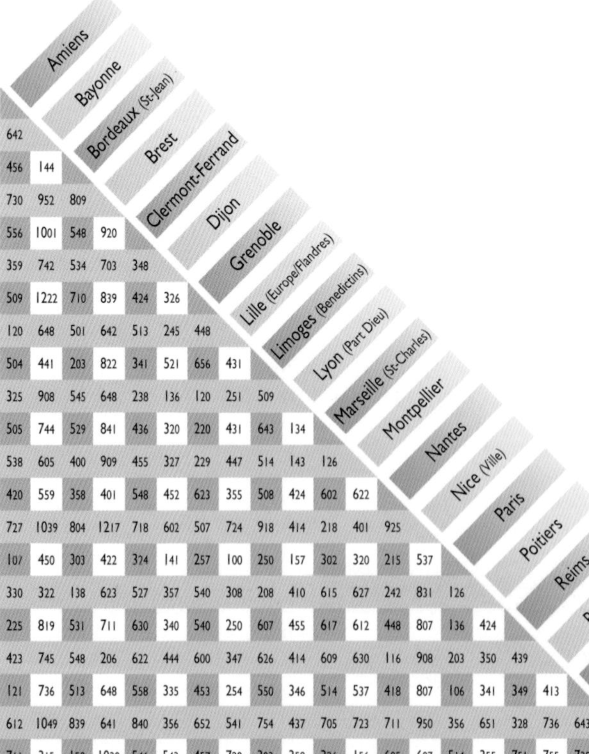

| | Amiens | Bayonne | Bordeaux (St-Jean) | Brest | Clermont-Ferrand | Dijon | Grenoble | Lille (Europe/Flandres) | Limoges (Benedictins) | Lyon (Part Dieu) | Marseille (St-Charles) | Montpellier | Nantes | Nice (Ville) | Paris | Poitiers | Reims | Rennes | Rouen (Rive Droite) | Strasbourg |
|---|---|---|---|---|---|---|---|---|---|---|---|---|---|---|---|---|---|---|---|---|
| Bayonne | 642 | | | | | | | | | | | | | | | | | | | |
| Bordeaux (St-Jean) | 456 | 144 | | | | | | | | | | | | | | | | | | |
| Brest | 730 | 952 | 809 | | | | | | | | | | | | | | | | | |
| Clermont-Ferrand | 556 | 1001 | 548 | 920 | | | | | | | | | | | | | | | | |
| Dijon | 359 | 742 | 534 | 703 | 348 | | | | | | | | | | | | | | | |
| Grenoble | 509 | 1222 | 710 | 839 | 424 | 326 | | | | | | | | | | | | | | |
| Lille (Europe/Flandres) | 120 | 648 | 501 | 642 | 513 | 245 | 448 | | | | | | | | | | | | | |
| Limoges (Benedictins) | 504 | 441 | 203 | 822 | 341 | 521 | 656 | 431 | | | | | | | | | | | | |
| Lyon (Part Dieu) | 325 | 908 | 545 | 648 | 238 | 136 | 120 | 251 | 509 | | | | | | | | | | | |
| Marseille (St-Charles) | 505 | 744 | 529 | 841 | 436 | 320 | 220 | 431 | 643 | 134 | | | | | | | | | | |
| Montpellier | 538 | 605 | 400 | 909 | 455 | 327 | 229 | 447 | 514 | 143 | 126 | | | | | | | | | |
| Nantes | 420 | 559 | 358 | 401 | 548 | 452 | 623 | 355 | 508 | 424 | 602 | 622 | | | | | | | | |
| Nice (Ville) | 727 | 1039 | 804 | 1217 | 718 | 602 | 507 | 724 | 918 | 414 | 218 | 401 | 925 | | | | | | | |
| Paris | 107 | 450 | 303 | 422 | 324 | 141 | 257 | 100 | 250 | 157 | 302 | 320 | 215 | 537 | | | | | | |
| Poitiers | 330 | 322 | 138 | 623 | 527 | 357 | 540 | 308 | 208 | 410 | 615 | 627 | 242 | 831 | 126 | | | | | |
| Reims | 225 | 819 | 531 | 711 | 630 | 340 | 540 | 250 | 607 | 455 | 617 | 612 | 448 | 807 | 136 | 424 | | | | |
| Rennes | 423 | 745 | 548 | 206 | 622 | 444 | 600 | 347 | 626 | 414 | 609 | 630 | 116 | 908 | 203 | 350 | 439 | | | |
| Rouen (Rive Droite) | 121 | 736 | 513 | 648 | 558 | 335 | 453 | 254 | 550 | 346 | 514 | 537 | 418 | 807 | 106 | 341 | 349 | 413 | | |
| Strasbourg | 612 | 1049 | 839 | 641 | 840 | 356 | 652 | 541 | 754 | 437 | 705 | 723 | 711 | 950 | 356 | 651 | 328 | 736 | 643 | |
| Toulouse (Matabiau) | 711 | 315 | 158 | 1030 | 546 | 543 | 457 | 720 | 303 | 359 | 326 | 156 | 605 | 607 | 514 | 355 | 751 | 755 | 735 | 939 |

## ARRIVING BY ROAD

Visitors from the UK and other European countries should find that driving to France is relatively easy. Plenty of car ferries, as well as Eurotunnel, link the UK with France. Once in France, a comprehensive system of *autoroutes* (motorways/expressways) fanning out from Paris enables you to cross the country with relative ease.

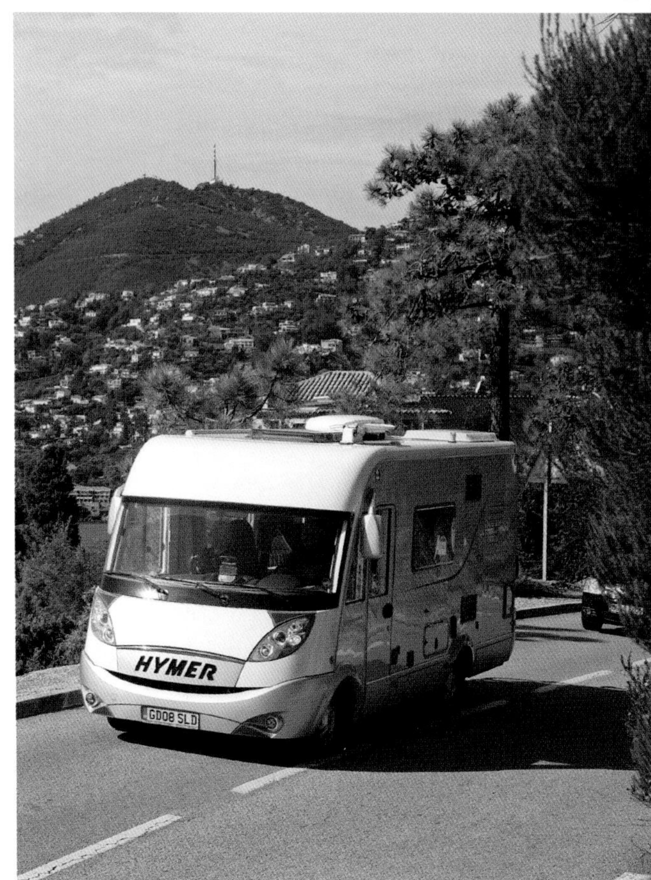


### BRINGING YOUR OWN CAR

**Legal Requirements**

» You can take private vehicles registered in another country into France for up to six months (in any 12-month period) without customs formalities.

» You must always carry the following documentation: a current passport or national ID card, a full (not provisional) valid national driver's licence (UK drivers with a photocard licence will need both the photocard and the counterpart), a certificate of insurance and the vehicle's registration document (as well as a letter of authorization from the owner if the vehicle is not registered in your name). If you are taking a UK-registered rented or leased car, ask the company to supply you with a Vehicle on Hire Certificate (VE103).

» You should always tell your insurer before you take your car abroad and buy extra cover where necessary. Third-party insurance (covering the other parties but not your own vehicle in the event of a collision) is the minimum requirement in France, but fully comprehensive insurance is strongly advised.

» Check that your insurance covers you against damage in transit, for example on the train or ferry when your car is not being driven.

» There are spot checks on cars and you may be asked to produce your documents at any time. To avoid a police fine and/or confiscation of your car, be sure that your papers are in order.

» You should display an international distinguishing sign (for example GB for Britons) at the rear of your car and on any caravan or trailer. This is not necessary if your vehicle has Euro-Plates.

» UK drivers should adjust the headlights of their vehicles for driving on the right. On older cars, use the simple black headlight beam converters that stick onto the glass. But don't use these on cars with halogen headlights—check in your owner's manual or with your dealer. If your vehicle has Xenon or High Intensity Discharge (HID) headlights, check with your dealer who may need to make the adjustment.

**Breakdowns**

» If you are taking your own car, make sure you have adequate breakdown cover. For information on AA breakdown cover, call 0800 085 2721 (UK number) or visit www.theAA.com.

### DRIVING FROM THE UK

**Eurotunnel**

» The Eurotunnel shuttle takes vehicles under the English Channel from Folkestone, in the UK, to Calais/Coquelles, in northern France. At 35 minutes, it is the shortest vehicular journey time from the UK to mainland Europe.

» For continuing travel from Calais, ▷ 48.

**Ferries from the UK**

» Numerous ferries link France with the UK (▷ 48). The cost varies widely according to the time, day and month of travel.

» Routes include Dover to Calais, Newhaven to Dieppe, Portsmouth to Caen, Portsmouth to Le Havre, Poole to Cherbourg, Portsmouth to Cherbourg, Portsmouth to St-Malo and Plymouth to Roscoff.

**Continuing Travel**

» From Calais, the fastest and easiest route to Provence is to take the A26 towards Paris/Reims. At Reims, exit onto the A26 towards Lyon and Strasbourg, thus avoiding Paris, then take the A5 and A41 towards Lyon. The A6 and A7 will lead you to Marseille, where the A8 runs along the Provence coast.

» In good conditions, you can reach Provence from the northern coast of France in around 11 hours. It is less stressful to break up your journey. You'll find numerous chain hotels near major *autoroute* exits. It's best to reserve rooms ahead, especially in summer.

» The journey to Provence from Normandy and Brittany is not as straightforward as from Calais since there are few fast roads running in a southeasterly direction across France. From Caen and Le Havre, in Normandy, the simplest and quickest route is to head south on the A13, which leads to Paris, to pick up the A6 south of the capital. From Brest and Le Mans, in western Brittany, the simplest way down to Provence is to follow the A28, A10 and A71 past Le Mans, Tours and Clermont-Ferrand. From Cherbourg, in eastern Brittany, it's slightly quicker to take the A13 to Paris, then the A6 and A7 into the heart of Provence.

» Bear in mind that *autoroutes* are toll roads and you should always have euros or a credit card readily available to pay at the toll booths. The cost of a journey from Paris to Marseille is approximately €53 (www.autoroutes.fr).

» Heavy goods vehicles are banned from French roads from Saturday evening to Sunday evening.

**CONTACT DETAILS**

**Brittany Ferries**
www.brittanyferries.com
Tel 0871 244 0744 (UK)

**Hoverspeed**
www.hoverspeed.com
Tel 0870 1642 114 (UK)

**P&O Ferries**
www.poferries.com
Tel 0871 664 5645 (UK)

**Seafrance**
www.seafrance.com
Tel 0871 423 7119 (UK)

**Eurotunnel**
www.eurotunnel.com
Tel 08705 353 535 (UK)

(To call these numbers from the US, dial 011 44, then omit the initial zero. To call from mainland Europe, dial 00 44 then omit the zero.)

## BREAKING THE JOURNEY

» France is dotted with service stations, often serving excellent freshly cooked food.

» A huge range of inexpensive motels, including Formule1 (www.hotelformule1.com) and B&B (www.hotel-bb.com) cater for long-distance drivers in France.

» You can book a budget *autoroute* hotel online for as little as €30 for a four-person room.

## GENERAL DRIVING

### The Law

» In France you drive on the right *(serrez à droite)*.

» The minimum age to drive is 18, although to rent a car you must be at least 21.

» You must wear a seatbelt.

» Children under 10 must travel in the back, with a booster seat/child safety seat, except for babies under nine months with a specially adapted rear-facing front seat (but not in cars with airbags).

» Do not overtake where there is a solid single central line on the road.

» Never drive under the influence of alcohol.

» Always stop completely at stop signs, or you may be fined.

» Remove any device to detect radar speed traps from your car.

### Road Signs

» Road signs are split into three categories. Triangular signs with a red border are warnings, circular signs are mandatory (such as speed limits or No Entry) and square signs display text information.

» Familiarize yourself with the French highway code on www.legifrance.gouv.fr.

| SPEED LIMITS | |
|---|---|
| **Urban roads** | 50kph (31mph) |
| **Outside built-up areas** | 90kph (56mph); 80kph (49mph) in wet weather |
| **Dual carriageways (divided highways), and non-toll motorways** | 110kph (68mph); 100kph (62mph) in wet weather |
| **Toll motorways *(autoroutes)*** | 130kph (80mph); 110kph (68mph) in wet weather |
| Visiting drivers who have held a licence for less than two years are not allowed to exceed the wet-weather limits, even in good weather. | |

» For more road sign information see www.permis-enligne.com.

### Roads

» The *autoroute* is the French counterpart of the British motorway or US expressway and is marked by an 'A' on maps and road signs. A few sections around key cities are free, but tolls are charged on the rest *(autoroutes à péage)*. Most foreign credit cards are accepted, although it's always prudent to have cash to hand.

» There is a comprehensive network of other roads, with generally good surfaces. A trunk road/federal highway is called a *Route Nationale* (N). Then there are *Route Départementales* (D), which can still be wide and fast. There are also quieter country roads.

### Equipment

» You must carry a red warning triangle in case you break down. Even if your car has hazard lights, a triangle is still needed as a breakdown may affect the electrical system in your car.

» Keep a spare-bulb kit (buy before you go) on hand as it is illegal to drive with faulty lights.

» Snow chains must be fitted to vehicles using snow-covered roads, in compliance with road signs. You could be fined for non-compliance. Car rental companies will supply snow chains as an option, or you can buy them from hypermarkets, especially in mountain areas.

### Fuel

» Fuel *(essence)* comes as unleaded (95 and 98 octane) and diesel *(gasoil* or *gazole)*.

» Many filling stations close on Sundays and at 6pm on other days. There are automatic 24-hour pumps at supermarkets and fuel stations; most will accept foreign credit cards.

» Prices are high at filling stations on *autoroutes*.

» Filling stations can be far apart in rural areas, so never let your tank get too low.

### Car Breakdown

» If your car breaks down on an *autoroute*, look for an emergency telephone on the roadside, which will connect you with roadside assistance.

» If you break down on an *autoroute*, you must call the police or the official breakdown service operating in that area, rather than your own roadside assistance company.

### Road Conditions

» To find out about traffic conditions visit www.bison-fute.equipement.gouv.fr (in French and English).

» For road conditions on *autoroutes* call 0892 681 077.

» For the National Road Information Service and information on national and departmental roads call 0826 022 022.

## LONG-DISTANCE BUSES

» If you're booking at the last minute, taking a long-distance bus to Provence can be much cheaper than train travel, although the journey time is significantly longer.

» Eurolines runs services to Provence from across Europe, with UK starting points at Victoria Coach Station (London), Canterbury and Dover (Kent).

### BUS CONTACTS

**Eurolines**
www.eurolines.co.uk
Tel 0871 781 8179 (UK)

**Eurolines offices in Provence**

Avignon: Gare Routière, Boulevard St-Roch
Tel 04 90 85 27 60

Marseille: 3 allée Léon Gambetta
Tel 04 91 08 95 95

Nîmes: Gare Routière
Rue Sainte-Félicité
Tel 04 66 29 50 62

## DRIVING DISTANCES AND TIMES

Use the chart below to work out the distance in km (green) and estimated duration in hours and minutes (blue) of a car journey.

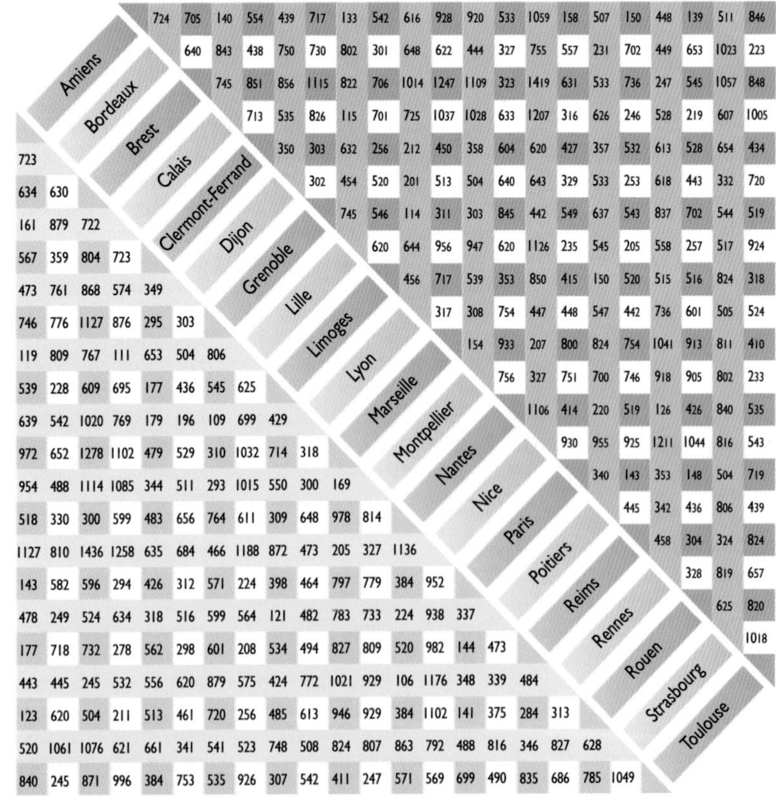

| | Amiens | Bordeaux | Brest | Calais | Clermont-Ferrand | Dijon | Grenoble | Lille | Limoges | Lyon | Marseille | Montpellier | Nantes | Nice | Paris | Poitiers | Reims | Rennes | Rouen | Strasbourg | Toulouse |
|---|---|---|---|---|---|---|---|---|---|---|---|---|---|---|---|---|---|---|---|---|---|
| Amiens | | 724 | 705 | 140 | 554 | 439 | 717 | 133 | 542 | 616 | 928 | 920 | 533 | 1059 | 158 | 507 | 150 | 448 | 139 | 511 | 846 |
| Bordeaux | 723 | | 640 | 843 | 438 | 750 | 730 | 802 | 301 | 648 | 622 | 444 | 327 | 755 | 557 | 231 | 702 | 449 | 653 | 1023 | 223 |
| Brest | 634 | 630 | | 745 | 851 | 856 | 1115 | 822 | 706 | 1014 | 1247 | 1109 | 323 | 1419 | 631 | 533 | 736 | 247 | 545 | 1057 | 848 |
| Calais | 161 | 879 | 722 | | 713 | 535 | 826 | 115 | 701 | 725 | 1037 | 1028 | 633 | 1207 | 316 | 626 | 246 | 528 | 219 | 607 | 1005 |
| Clermont-Ferrand | 567 | 359 | 804 | 723 | | 350 | 303 | 632 | 256 | 212 | 450 | 358 | 604 | 620 | 427 | 357 | 532 | 613 | 528 | 654 | 434 |
| Dijon | 473 | 761 | 868 | 574 | 349 | | 302 | 454 | 520 | 201 | 513 | 504 | 640 | 643 | 329 | 533 | 253 | 618 | 443 | 332 | 720 |
| Grenoble | 746 | 776 | 1127 | 876 | 295 | 303 | | 745 | 546 | 114 | 311 | 303 | 845 | 442 | 549 | 637 | 543 | 837 | 702 | 544 | 519 |
| Lille | 119 | 809 | 767 | 111 | 653 | 504 | 806 | | 620 | 644 | 956 | 947 | 620 | 1126 | 235 | 545 | 205 | 558 | 257 | 517 | 924 |
| Limoges | 539 | 228 | 609 | 695 | 177 | 436 | 545 | 625 | | 456 | 717 | 539 | 353 | 850 | 415 | 150 | 520 | 515 | 516 | 824 | 318 |
| Lyon | 639 | 542 | 1020 | 769 | 179 | 196 | 109 | 699 | 429 | | 317 | 308 | 754 | 447 | 448 | 547 | 442 | 736 | 601 | 505 | 524 |
| Marseille | 972 | 652 | 1278 | 1102 | 479 | 529 | 310 | 1032 | 714 | 318 | | 154 | 933 | 207 | 800 | 824 | 754 | 1041 | 913 | 811 | 410 |
| Montpellier | 954 | 488 | 1114 | 1085 | 344 | 511 | 293 | 1015 | 550 | 300 | 169 | | 756 | 327 | 751 | 700 | 746 | 918 | 905 | 802 | 233 |
| Nantes | 518 | 330 | 300 | 599 | 483 | 656 | 764 | 611 | 309 | 648 | 978 | 814 | | 1106 | 414 | 220 | 519 | 126 | 426 | 840 | 535 |
| Nice | 1127 | 810 | 1436 | 1258 | 635 | 684 | 466 | 1188 | 872 | 473 | 205 | 327 | 1136 | | 930 | 955 | 925 | 1211 | 1044 | 816 | 543 |
| Paris | 143 | 582 | 596 | 294 | 426 | 312 | 571 | 224 | 398 | 464 | 797 | 779 | 384 | 952 | | 340 | 143 | 353 | 148 | 504 | 719 |
| Poitiers | 478 | 249 | 524 | 634 | 318 | 516 | 599 | 564 | 121 | 482 | 783 | 733 | 224 | 938 | 337 | | 445 | 342 | 436 | 806 | 439 |
| Reims | 177 | 718 | 732 | 278 | 562 | 298 | 601 | 208 | 534 | 494 | 827 | 809 | 520 | 982 | 144 | 473 | | 458 | 304 | 324 | 824 |
| Rennes | 443 | 445 | 245 | 532 | 556 | 620 | 879 | 575 | 424 | 772 | 1021 | 929 | 106 | 1176 | 348 | 339 | 484 | | 328 | 819 | 657 |
| Rouen | 123 | 620 | 504 | 211 | 513 | 461 | 720 | 256 | 485 | 613 | 946 | 929 | 384 | 1102 | 141 | 375 | 284 | 313 | | 625 | 820 |
| Strasbourg | 520 | 1061 | 1076 | 621 | 661 | 341 | 541 | 523 | 748 | 508 | 824 | 807 | 863 | 792 | 488 | 816 | 346 | 827 | 628 | | 1018 |
| Toulouse | 840 | 245 | 871 | 996 | 384 | 753 | 535 | 926 | 307 | 542 | 411 | 247 | 571 | 569 | 699 | 490 | 835 | 686 | 785 | 1049 | |

## DRIVING IN PROVENCE

Driving is a good way to get around Provence's more rural areas. Roads in the region are generally in excellent condition and signposting is good.

### RENTING A CAR

» Most major car rental agencies have offices at airports, main rail stations and in the large towns and cities.

» It is often best to book your car rental in advance, either through a tour operator or online. Hiring a car in person upon your arrival will usually work out a far pricier option. SNCF, the national rail company, has inclusive train and car-rental deals from main-line stations.

» To be able to rent a car in France you must be at least 21 years old and have held a full driver's licence for at least a year. However, some companies either do not rent to, or else add a surcharge for, drivers under the age of 25. The maximum age limit varies, but the average is 70.

» You will have to show the rental company your driving licence and passport or national ID card.

» As a guide, companies should include the following in their rental agreement: unlimited mileage, comprehensive insurance cover, theft protection and 24-hour emergency roadside assistance.

» Some agencies include mileage in the cost but others may charge you extra above a certain distance, so check before you rent.

» Make sure you have adequate insurance and that you are aware of what you are covered for in the event of an accident.

» Bear in mind that low-cost operators may have an extremely high excess charge for damage to the vehicle.

» Most rental companies supply vehicles with roadside assistance, so refer to your documentation or to the information regarding breakdowns in the car, which is often kept in the glove compartment or under the sun visor.

» If your car breaks down on an *autoroute*, look for emergency telephones on the roadside. You can contact roadside assistance from here.

### PROVENCE WAYS

» Despite the many benefits of exploring Provence by car, you'll also meet several challenges. Cities such as Avignon, Nice and particularly Marseille are a confusing pattern of one-way streets linked by a grid of major boulevards. Parking is difficult and car crime is rife, so do not leave valuables in view in your car. In cities, be sure to park only in designated spaces.

» Once in the countryside, the roads become less crowded but they can be narrow and steep, especially in the mountains. Pay special attention on blind corners. If you want to admire the stunning views, pull off into a designated rest stop.

» Summer brings lots of drivers. They too may be unfamiliar with the roads so extra patience is needed. Summer also means traffic jams are a problem, particularly on the coast—it is worst on weekends, when locals also head to the beach. Traffic heading to Nice and St-Tropez is particularly heavy.

### PARKING

» Authorized parking spaces are indicated by road markings (white dotted lines). In those marked *payant*, you have to pay a fee.

» Charges usually apply from 9am to 7pm, Monday to Saturday. Sundays and holidays are generally free, but always check before parking your car.

» To pay for parking, buy a ticket from a machine at the side of the road and display it in your car.

» Some towns also have multi-level or underground parking areas.

» Many of Provence's medieval villages offer ample parking (paid) just outside the walls.

### RENTING AUTOMATIC CARS

If you are keen to rent an automatic, rather than manual, car it is best to reserve in advance, as there are fewer available in France than in countries such as the US. You may also have to pay a premium for the vehicle.

### CAR RENTAL COMPANIES

| COMPANY | TELEPHONE NUMBER | WEBSITE |
|---|---|---|
| Avis | 0820 05 05 05 | www.avis.com |
| Budget | 0825 003 564 | www.budget.com |
| Europcar | 0825 82 90 21 | www.europcar.com |
| Hertz | 0825 861 861 | www.hertz.com |
| Sixt | 0820 007 498 | www.e-sixt.com |

## TRAINS, BUSES AND TAXIS

### TRAINS

» The mountainous terrain in Provence means that not all areas are served by trains. But there are places where the regional TER trains will enhance your sightseeing, freeing you from having to find parking and avoiding traffic jams.

» Reliable services link Nice, Cannes and Fréjus with Marseille. The Rhône valley towns of Avignon, Orange, Arles and Nîmes are also connected by train. Lines from Nice run through the Roya valley and northwest into the pre-Alps.

» For local train journey planning try www.ter-sncf.com.

» You can take bicycles onto all suitable trains outside the peak hours (Mon–Fri 7am–9am and 4.30pm–6.30pm).

» Buy tickets at stations. You must validate your ticket in the orange machine on the platform before you board the train. If there is no ticket office or it is closed you can pay the conductor on board the train. Some TER platforms do not have validation machines. In this case, the conductor will validate your ticket on the train.

### BUSES

» Bus services between towns and villages in Provence range from very useful to impractical. You'll find services linking all the key towns, but the scattered villages are another matter.

» Services are severely limited on Sundays and official holidays.

» Buses usually leave from either the bus station or the central town square. You should be able to find timetable details here or at the bus company offices.

» Buses will display the route number and final destination on the front.

» You can normally buy tickets on the bus or at kiosks/*tabacs* around the town. You must validate tickets in the machine on the bus.

### TAXIS

» Taking a taxi is not the most cost-effective way of getting around, but you may consider it worthwhile for convenience, especially in the major towns and cities.

» Some taxi firms provide chauffeur-driven cars by the day if you wish to visit several locations around Provence without driving or using buses or trains.

» Taxis charge for a pick-up and a separate charge per kilometre (0.6 mile) driven. There will be an extra charge for luggage and for journeys during the evening and on Sundays. All taxis use a meter *(compteur)*. Make sure that this is reset for your journey.

» The best way to find a taxi is to head to a taxi stand (indicated by a blue *Taxi* sign). Phoning for a taxi means the meter starts from the moment it sets off to pick you up, so a journey will be more expensive.

» Some taxis accept credit cards but most will accept only cash.

## GETTING AROUND IN MAJOR TOWNS AND CITIES

All the major towns and cities have buses linking outlying districts to the central areas and it is sometimes easier to use these rather than taking your car and having to hunt for a parking space. Marseille also has an efficient Métro system, with two lines (▷ 85). Remember that on most buses in Provence you must validate your ticket by inserting it into the machine near the driver when you board the bus.

### AIX-EN-PROVENCE

**Buses**

A shuttle bus links the heart of town with the TGV station, 15km (9 miles) away. This operates from 4.25am to 8.45pm, every 15–30 minutes. Aix en Bus (tel 04 42 26 37 28; www.aixenbus.com) runs 20 lines around town and the suburbs. Buses depart from the bus station at avenue de l'Europe.

**Tickets**

Buy tickets from the bus station office or on the buses (exact change only). One ticket costs €1.10, 10 tickets cost €7.70, and a day ticket for unlimited travel within the municipality costs €3.50.

### ARLES

Arles and the Camargue are served by three bus companies—call 0810 000 816 for information on all three. Buses depart from the bus station at 24 boulevard Clemenceau, Arles. Societé des Transports d'Arles runs four lines. Ceyte Tourisme Méditerranée links the town with Tarascon, Salon, Marseille and Avignon. Cars de Carmargue runs services to Saintes-Maries-de-la-Mer.

**Tickets**

Tickets for town buses are €0.80 or €6.50 for a booklet of 10 tickets.

### AVIGNON

Transports en Commun de la Region d'Avignon (TCRA), based at avenue de Lattre de Tassigny (tel 04 32 74 18 32; www.tcra.fr), runs 31 bus lines around Avignon and to surrounding towns such as St-Rémy-de-Provence. But there are no bus services within the walls of Avignon. Buses run from 7am to 8pm. STD Gard (▷ 55, Nîmes) runs services linking Nîmes, Avignon and Tarascon.

**Tickets**

Tickets cost €1.20 and last for one hour after validation. They can be purchased on the bus or from the bus-company office. You can also buy a daily ticket for €3.60, or a book of 10 tickets for €9.40.

### CANNES

Bus Azur runs more than 20 services in Cannes and to surrounding towns.

You'll find information at the bus station at place Cournou Gentille, next to the town hall (tel 0825 825 599; www.busazur.com). Buses run from 6am to 9pm. Sillages runs services from Cannes north into the hills around Grasse (tel 04 92 42 33 80; www.sillages.eu).

**Tickets**

Single tickets cost €1, a book of 10 is €9.50 and a one-week pass is €11. Buy single tickets on the bus; others must be bought at the bus station.

**MARSEILLE**

**Métro**

The city has two fast, well-maintained Métro lines. Métro 1 runs from La Fourragére in the eastern suburbs through the northeast suburbs to La Rose. Métro 2 runs roughly north to south, from Bougainville to Sainte-Marguerite Dromel. The Métro runs Monday to Thursday from 5am to 9pm, and Friday to Sunday until 12.30am. The main office is at Espace Infos, 6–8 rue des Fabres (Mon–Fri 8.30–6, Sat 9–5.30). For a Métro map, ▷ 85.

**Buses and Trams**

Régie des Transports Marseille (www.rtm.fr) runs Métro, bus services and the two relatively new tram lines, the most convenient of which is T2 (▷ 85, Métro map). There are 81 day bus lines and 10 night lines in operation.

**Tickets**

A single trip on the bus or Métro is €1.50. A one-day pass is €5 and a carnet of ten tickets costs €12.60.

**MONACO**

Compagnie des Autobus de Monaco (www.cam.mc) runs bus services in Monaco, with six routes spanning the principality. Services run between 7am and 9pm and are less frequent on weekends. Lines 1 and 2 are most useful for visitors, linking Monaco Rock with Monte-Carlo.

**Tickets**

Single tickets cost €1, although they are slightly cheaper if you buy a pack of four or eight. A day ticket for visitors costs €3. Buy tickets on the bus. You can change buses on the same ticket if the second leg starts no more than 30 minutes after the start of the first.

**NICE**

Ligne d'Azur (tel 0810 06 10 06; www.lignedazur.com) runs more than 80 routes in the city and outlying districts. The bus station is at boulevard Jean Jaurès and the Gare Routière (long-distance bus station) is next door, although buses also depart from surrounding streets. Daytime buses run from 5.30am to 9pm. There are also five evening routes, leaving place Masséna from 9.10pm Monday to Saturday and 8.10pm on Sundays. A single tram line links the bus station with place Masséna, the train station and all points north.

**Tickets**

Buy tickets on the bus and also at electronic kiosks by each tram stop, plus various *tabacs* around the city. A single ticket costs €1 but is not valid on airport routes. You can also buy a day pass for €4.

**NÎMES**

Transports en Commun Nîmois (TCN) runs the city buses (tel 0820 22 30 30; www.tcn.fr), while a *navette* shuttle bus serves the airport (tel 04 66 29 27 29). Société des Transports Départementaux du Gard (STD Gard; tel 04 66 29 27 29; www.stdgard.com) includes routes between Nîmes, Avignon and St-Rémy-de-Provence and outlying towns. The buses start running at around 6am and continue to 7pm.

**Tickets**
Tickets cost €1 per journey within the city and can be purchased on the bus. Packs of five tickets offer savings but cannot be bought on the bus.

**ORANGE**
Transports en Commun de la Ville d'Orange (TCVO; tel 04 90 34 15 59; www.transbus.org) runs four lines within the town from 7am to 7.30pm.

**Tickets**
Tickets for buses within Orange cost €1 per journey and can be bought on the bus.

**ST-RÉMY-DE-PROVENCE**
TCRA from Avignon (▷ 53) runs bus services for St-Rémy-de-Provence. STD Gard (▷ 54, Nîmes) runs services between St-Rémy-de-Provence and Tarascon.

**Tickets**
For information on bus tickets, ▷ 53, Avignon.

**ST-TROPEZ**
There are no bus services within the town itself. Transports Var (08 10 00 61 77; www.transports.var.fr) handles bus services around the Golfe de St-Tropez from the Gare Routière at St-Tropez; these go from just outside the parking du Port. It also provides services that make the journey to markets in the area and to the SNCF rail stations at Toulon and St-Raphaël.

**Tickets**
Buy tickets (€2) on the bus.

# VISITORS WITH A DISABILITY

Getting around Provence is becoming easier for people with disabilities thanks to improvements to buses, trains and platforms. Most airports have special facilities and Eurostar and TGV trains are accessible to wheelchair-users. But you'll still find challenges when getting around the region. Before you travel it's worth checking that facilities are available at your arrival airport and your hotel, as older buildings may not have an elevator.

## ARRIVING BY AIR

» Nice airport has dedicated parking and toilets for wheelchair-users.
» Marseille airport has dedicated parking spaces and wheelchair-accessible toilets.
» Lyon airport has covered parking close to the terminals and offers a 50 per cent discount on parking charges. The set-down point is outside Terminal 1 and there is reserved parking at the airport TGV station. All toilets and phones are accessible to wheelchair-users.
» Inform your airline or travel agent when reserving or as early as possible if you require extra help while at the airport.
» If you are a wheelchair-user, inform your airline when you reserve your ticket.

## GETTING AROUND

### By Train

» France's long-distance trains are equipped for people with reduced mobility. On TGV and Corail trains, spaces for wheelchair-users are reserved in first class, although only a second-class fare is payable. Reserve at least 24 hours in advance. There are also adapted toilets.
» Most large stations have elevators or ramps to the platform. If you need assistance, it is best to request it at the time of reserving your ticket. For more information, look up SNCF's website (www.sncf.com).
» Facilities on regional trains tend to be more varied. It is always best to check before you travel. For more information, call SNCF (tel 3635 in France).

### By Bus

Bus services vary in usefulness. Bus Azur in Cannes and Ligne d'Azur in Nice have vehicles with access ramps but services in rural areas may prove more problematic. Local tourist offices will be able to give you information.

### General Information

» All new buildings must have suitable access for people with disabilities, and many of the modern museums, such as the Musée d'Art Moderne et Contemporain in Nice, have good facilities. With older buildings, you may find that access for wheelchair-users involves a member of staff unlocking a side door.
» In some towns, kerbs have been lowered at street crossings. Many large towns have traffic-free zones with reasonably flat pavements, but medieval villages often have steep cobbled lanes.
» Most parking areas have places for cars displaying the official registered-disabled sticker.

## USEFUL WEBSITES AND ORGANIZATIONS

**Tourism for All**
Tel 0845 124 9971 (from UK)
www.tourismforall.org.uk
Travel information for people with disabilities.

**Maison de la France**
www.franceguide.com
The website of the French tourist office has useful information for people with disabilities.

**Mobile en Ville**
www.mobile-en-ville.asso.fr
A website packed with information on disability access and related issues.

**Mobility International USA**
www.miusa.org
Promotes international travel and exchange schemes for people with disabilities.

**Society for Accessible Travel and Hospitality (SATH)**
Tel 212/447-7284 (from US)
www.sath.org
A US-based organization offering advice for visitors with disabilities and promoting awareness of their travel requirements.

# REGIONS

This chapter is divided into five regions of Provence, based on the area's *départements* (▷ 9), and are for the purposes of this book only. The independent principality of Monaco has been included in the Alpes-Maritimes section. Places of interest are listed alphabetically in each region.

**Provence and the Côte d'Azur's regions 58–256**

EICI-DAVANS PENJERON
LOU 14 DE DESÈMBRE 1790
JAN JÒUSÈ PÈIRE PASCALÌS
AVOUCAT-ASSESSOUR DE Z-AÌS
PROUCUROUR DÒU PAÏS DE PROUVÈNÇO
...AQUÉU GRAND PATRIOTO QUE,
DAVANS LOU PARLAMEN
E LÌS ESTAT-GENERAU DE PROUVÈNÇO,
ACAMPA PÈR LOU DARRIÉ COP,
PROUTESTÈ AUTAMEN E COURAJOUSAMEN
CONTRO L'ABOULICIOUN DÌ LIBERTA PROUVENÇAL
E MOURIGUÉ MARTIRE DE SA PROUTESTACIOUN
FREDERI MISTRAL

# BOUCHES-DU-RHÔNE

Provence's westernmost corner is delightfully varied, sweeping from flamingo-flecked marshlands to bourgeois boulevards. In contrast to more cosmopolitan enclaves between this region and the Italian border, Bouches-du-Rhône offers its visitors a mix of wide, wild nature and rich local heritage.

Ancient Provence begins here, too. Marseille may be France's second city and a thriving industrial port, but when Greek traders settled here 2,600 years ago, it was little more than a fishing village. Remains of the city's original port and ramparts are dotted between tram routes and bustling downtown commerce. The Romans, whose important trading route meandered through the nearby countryside, developed the handsome cities of Arles, Aix-en-Provence and Nîmes. Some of their buildings, whether thermal baths or glorious amphitheatres, are still in use today, and provide an irresistible year-round draw.

The violent Middle Ages saw the development and strengthening of feudal cities, such as Les Baux-de-Provence, perched on a rocky outcrop in the heart of the Alpilles. Les Baux's location—a defensive dream—offers stunning views over vineyards and olive groves to the coast beyond. Nearby, the Camargue is home to additional fortified towns, including Saintes-Maries-de-la-Mer and Aigues-Mortes.

But the Camargue's main attraction is its salty wetlands. A protected area cradled between branches of the Grand and Petit Rhônes, its southern beaches are lapped by the Mediterranean Sea. It's here that herds of sleek black bulls and indigenous white horses are interspersed with flocks of migrating birds and glowing, rosy-hued saltpans. The Camargue provides a heady outdoor foil for the region's historical sightseeing.

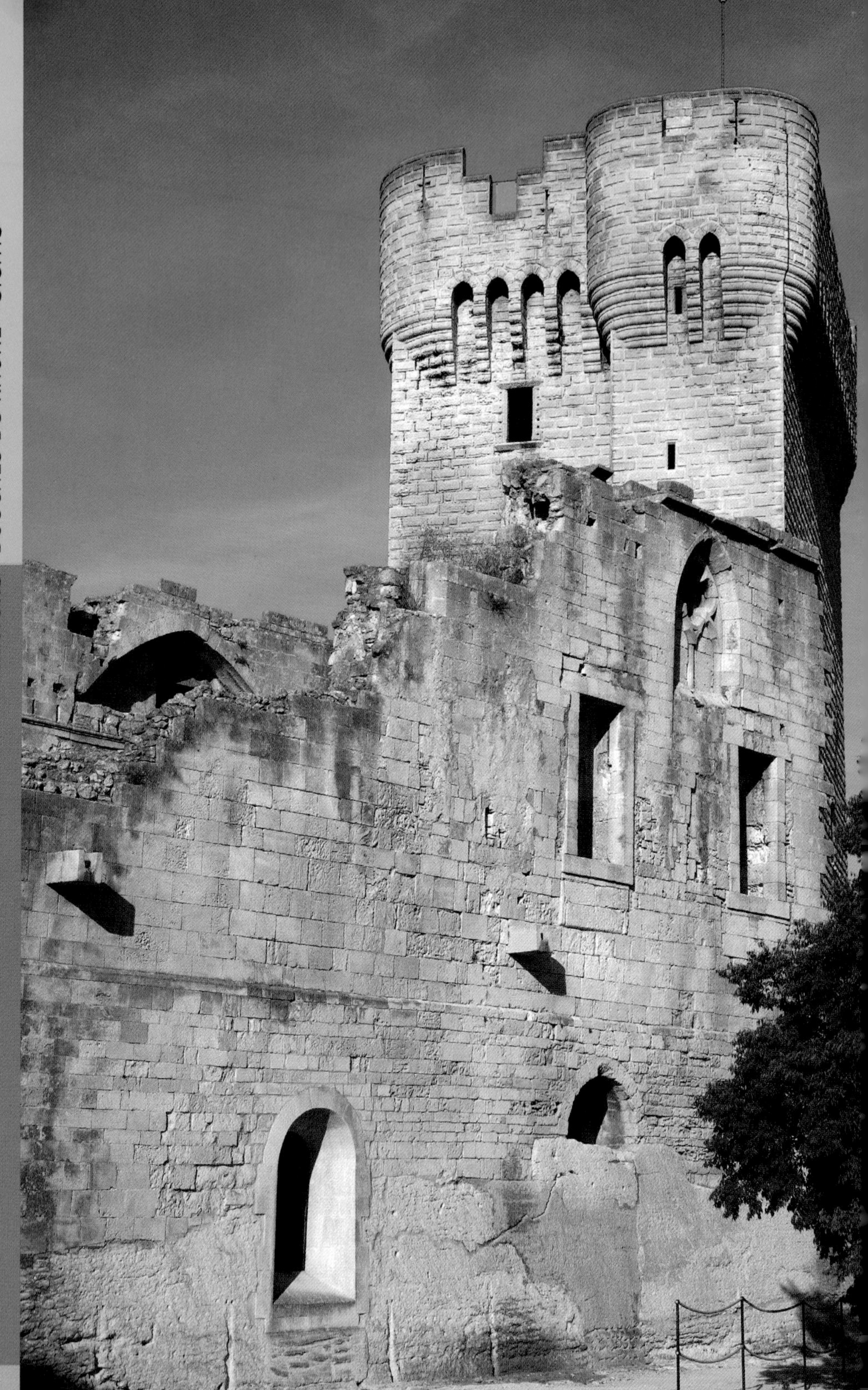

**ABBAYE DE MONTMAJOUR**

http://montmajour.monuments-nationaux.fr

These awesome, beautiful ruins of a large Romanesque fortified abbey just outside Arles include a tranquil church, beautiful cloisters and a superb view.

Montmajour was among the most powerful religious communities in medieval Provence, its wealth boosted by its landholdings and its status as an important pilgrimage site. The fortified Romanesque Benedictine monastery is on a small hill 3km (2 miles) north of Arles. Today, you can wander around the extensive ruins. The sheer scale of the buildings is striking and local people have carried out much restoration in recent years. The incomplete 12th-century Upper Church is austere but impressive. To the right of the nave is the crypt, partly built into the hillside, with fine stone carvings on the bases and capitals of the columns depicting demons and wild beasts. Note several mason's marks in the church vaulting and graffiti dating back to medieval times in the cloister. If you can face a steep climb of 124 steps, there are exceptional views of the Alpilles and Crau landscapes from the top of the 14th-century keep, 26m (85ft) high.

Montmajour's story began with the early Christian St. Trophimus, who fled here from Arles to hide in a cave, which became known as a holy place. Later a group of Christian ascetics came to reside at the site where he had lived. Their community grew and eventually the monastery was founded in the 10th century. The community was never large in numbers of monks but, thanks to its importance as a pilgrimage site, Benedictine Montmajour become one of the biggest monastic structures in Provence. Their growing wealth appears to have so corrupted the community that when, in 1639, the Benedictines sent a group to inspect and reform Montmajour, the monks in residence attempted to destroy the abbey. The community was disbanded in 1786. Restoration of the buildings began in 1907.

294 C11 Abbaye de Montmajour, route de Fontvieille, 13200 Arles 04 90 54 64 17 Apr–end Jun daily 9.30–6; Jul–end Sep daily 10–6.30; Oct–end Mar Tue–Sun 10–5 Mon–Sat 8 buses daily from Arles; Sun 2 buses only Arles, then bus Adult €7, under 18 free, EU citizens under 26 free

**ABBAYE DE SILVACANE**

This long-suffering, much-damaged masterpiece, standing close to the south bank of the Durance, could so easily be overlooked as it nestles in its deliciously peaceful waterside setting. The Abbey of Silvacane, completed in 1144, was the last of three Cistercian abbeys in Provence—known as the 'Three Cistercian Sisters of Provence'. The others are Sénanque (▷ 221) and Le Thoronet (▷ 117). Silvacane is considered the loveliest of them, and a perfect example of the simple, austere elegance promoted by the Cistercians.

The isolated setting was more wild than rural at first—the name, from *Silva Cana*, is Latin for Forest of Reeds. The monks gradually drained the soil and made it cultivable. The remoteness from the world was a deliberate attempt to encourage prayer and spirituality.

The surrounding greenery enhances this assembly of very sober buildings under Provençal red roof tiles. The abbey barely looks like an ecclesiastical building, an impression strengthened by its modest tile roof and low, damaged square tower. The church is interesting for being built on a steep slope, and having several different styles of ceiling vaults encompassing different periods. Below the church, the 13th-century cloisters with a fountain are very attractive.

Most striking is the refectory, rebuilt in 1423 in Gothic style. It has a rose window and is not as austere as other parts of the abbey, with more natural light.

295 F10 Abbaye de Silvacane, 13640 La Roque d'Anthéron 04 42 50 41 69 Late May–end Sep daily 10–6; Oct–late May Wed–Mon 10–1, 2–5 Adult €7, under 12 free

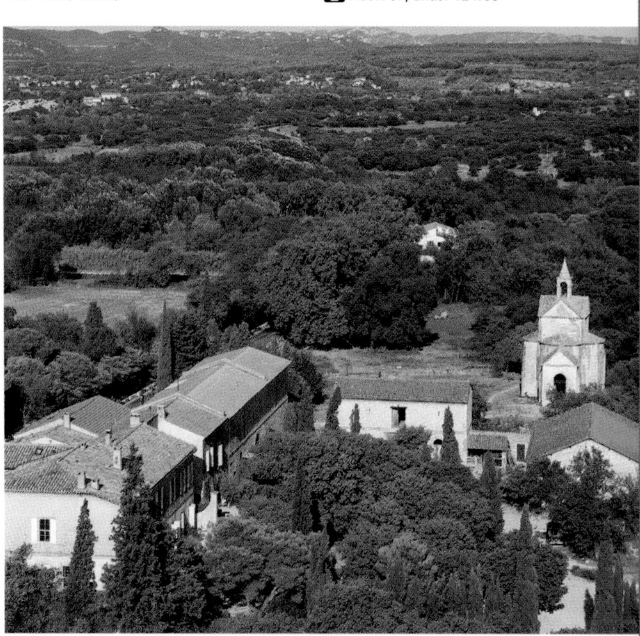

**Opposite** *The keep of the Abbaye de Montmajour*

**Right** *Climb to the top of the Abbaye de Montmajour's keep for a view over the surrounding landscape*

# AIGUES-MORTES

**INFORMATION**

www.ot-aiguesmortes.fr
294 B11 Place St-Louis, 30220 Aigues-Mortes 04 66 53 73 00 Jul, Aug daily 9–8; Sep–end Jun Mon–Fri 10–12, 1–6, Sat, Sun 10–12, 2–6 Infrequent buses from Nîmes and Montpellier Aigues-Mortes (for trains to and from Nîmes) Outside the walls, beside Porte de la Gardette Many bars and cafés in and around place St-Louis

## INTRODUCTION

The perfectly preserved, sturdily fortified walled town of Aigues-Mortes, in the sparsely populated western Camargue, is a phenomenal sight. It stands in the flat Camargue landscape like a bizarre piece of art. The medieval town is just outside Bouches-du-Rhône, across the Provence border in the Gard *département*, but is an important part of the Provence experience. Though often crowded with visitors, with many restaurant tables and souvenir shops, it remains strongly evocative of the Middle Ages. Now, though, Aigues-Mortes has less of its traditional appearance of defensive isolation, with areas of industry, vineyards and modern housing lying outside the walls.

Within its ramparts, Aigues-Mortes is a simple grid of old streets—five running east to west and five running north to south. In the heart of town is the busy main square, place St-Louis, with a statue of St. Louis in the middle.

King Louis IX (St. Louis) began building a port here in 1241. He was desperately anxious to have a French royal port on the Mediterranean so he could launch his long-dreamed-of crusades to conquer the Holy Land. By 1248, the port was ready. With 30,000 knights, Louis set off in an armada of 1,500 ships to Jerusalem. This Seventh Crusade, like the others, was a disaster, but the king survived. Unperturbed, he set off for the Eighth Crusade, this time to North Africa. He died of typhoid at Tunis in 1270—Aigues-Mortes had been his final sight of France.

Aigues-Mortes means 'dead waters', an uninviting title intended to distinguish it from the more endearingly named town of Aigues-Vives ('living waters') 20km (12.5 miles) farther north. Today, salt production is an important industry for the town. In July and August, trips by boat, horse-and-carriage or *petit train* leave from outside the town's main gate and take you into the Camargue's salt marshes.

## WHAT TO SEE

### THE RAMPARTS

Aigues-Mortes' ramparts stretch for more than 1.5km (1 mile) around the town and are in remarkably good condition. It takes about half an hour to walk the path around them. Work started on the walls in the 13th century, at the command of Philip III, and took nearly 30 years. The fortifications, including 15 towers and 10 gates, remain almost entirely intact today, partly because almost as soon as they were built Aigues-Mortes went into decline, as the seashore retreated in the mid-14th century.

### TOUR DE CONSTANCE

The impregnable Tour de Constance is by far the most impressive of Aigues-Mortes' towers. It can be reached only via the Logis du Gouverneur, starting point for the official tour of the ramparts. The tower was built as part of the town's medieval defences but became a prison early on in its life, after the town ceased to be a royal port. Philippe le Bel imprisoned 45 Templars here in 1307, but the tower's most notorious period was during the 17th century, when hundreds of Protestant women from the Cévennes were locked up here in appalling conditions. One of these women, Marie Durand, was kept in the tower for 38 years because she refused to renounce her faith. You can still see where she carved the one word *register*—'resist' in her local dialect—into the stone wall.

✉ Logis du Gouverneur, place Anatole France, 30220 Aigues-Mortes ☎ 04 66 53 61 55 ⌚ May–end Aug daily 10–7; Sep–end Apr daily 10–1, 2–5.30 ✋ Adult €7, under 18 free, EU citizens under 26 free

## MORE TO SEE

### NOTRE-DAME-DES-SABLONS

The town's main church, Our Lady of the Sands, was originally built of wood in the 12th century, then rebuilt in stone in the 13th. It has been much changed since and has modern stained glass.

✉ Place St-Louis, Aigues-Mortes ⌚ Summer daily 9–5; winter daily 9–12, 2–5 ✋ Free

### TIPS

» The Chapelle des Capucins, in the main square, is now a gallery displaying high-quality works by local artists.

» Try the Camargue delicacy *taureau à la gardiane* (slow-cooked bull's meat and olive stew) in the town's restaurants.

**Opposite** *A bustling street scene within the ramparts of Aigues-Mortes*
**Below** *A view of the town from the Tour de Constance*

# AIX-EN-PROVENCE

## INTRODUCTION

Aix is an elegant, historic university town with an impressive array of Renaissance buildings and an arty, youthful feel. It is the historic capital of Provence and has a quintessentially southern feel—joyful, busy and relaxed. For centuries a town of art and culture, it is famous as the home of Paul Cézanne (1839–1906), who was born here and did most of his work here.

Many visitors are content to get no farther than the town's tree-shaded main street, cours Mirabeau, where it is perfect just to stroll on the wide pavement or sit at an outdoor table and watch the sauntering crowds. This leisurely avenue is the epitome of all that's agreeable about a Provençal city. Yet there is a good deal to enjoy within a short walk of Mirabeau, not least the enticing, tangled lanes of Vieil Aix, the more sober Renaissance streets of the Quartier Mazarin and several good art museums.

Aix started life as a Roman spa, Aquae Sextiae. It remained an important place, especially under Good King Réné of Provence (▷ 33), a great patron of the arts, who retired here to write poetry, novels and moral treatises. It is to this day a hub for art and culture, with a distinguished annual arts festival. The university opened in 1409 and is an important presence today, with more than 40,000 students. When Provence came under the French crown, the establishment in 1501 of the Parlement de Provence—which was based here and which represented royal authority—brought a wealthy class of nobility and clerics to the town. That's when the many Renaissance mansions were built. In recent years, Aix has become one of the south's main cultural, commercial and high-tech industrial hubs.

## WHAT TO SEE

### COURS MIRABEAU

This broad central boulevard is the town's main attraction, appealing for its quiet bustle and broad, leaf-shaded walkway. Its double row of leafy plane trees shades hundreds of café tables on the north side, where the classic brasserie Les Deux Garçons (▷ 102) dates from the 1790s. Across the road

### INFORMATION

www.aixenprovencetourism.com
301 G12 2 place du Général-de-Gaulle, 13100 Aix-en-Provence 04 42 16 11 61 Apr–end Sep Mon–Sat 8.30–8, Sun 10–1, 2–6; Oct–end Mar Mon–Sat 8.30–7, Sun 10–1, 2–6 TGV Aix-en-Provence station is west of the city, in the l'Arbois district. The station in the heart of town is off rue G. Desplaces, 400m (440 yards) south of place Genéral-de-Gaulle The 'Visa for Aix and its Region' card (€2) gives reductions on the entry price to various museums, as well as discounts on bus tickets. Buy it from the tourist office or from museums

**Above** *Relaxing in place des Augustins, in Vieil Aix*
**Opposite** *A door carving at the Cathédrale St-Sauveur*

**TIPS**

» Reserve lodgings as far ahead as possible at festival time (June and July).

» Aix has nine major annual festivals, including the important *Festival d'Aix (Festival International d'Art Lyrique et de la Musique)*, an opera festival lasting for around three weeks in July (▷ 107).

» The tourist office produces a map showing locations in and around Aix where Paul Cézanne lived or worked.

there's a more sombre workaday air with banks and offices—yet these are housed in 17th- and 18th-century mansions with elaborate ironwork balconies supported by huge caryatids. Down the middle of the boulevard are four natural fountains, including the hot-water Fontaine d'Eau Thermale (▷ 67).

## QUARTIER MAZARIN

The Quartier Mazarin, off cours Mirabeau on the south side, is the neatly laid out district constructed in grid style by Archbishop Mazarin in 1646 as a grand residential area for lawyers and noblemen attending the Parlement de Provence. Among the many Renaissance houses is the remarkable former home of art collector and bibliophile Paul Arbaud, with handcrafted ceilings and fireplaces, silk wallpaper and carved wooden doorways. The house, at 2A rue 4 Septembre, is now a museum, the Musée Paul Arbaud (www.academiedaix.org; Tue–Sat 2–5), displaying his collection of faïence from Moustiers-Sainte-Marie and Marseille, works by Puget and Fragonard, sculptures and a collection of manuscripts, rare editions and books on Provence.

## VIEIL AIX

At the heart of Aix is its attractive medieval and Renaissance quarter, enclosed by a ring of avenues and squares that have replaced the town's ramparts—cours Mirabeau is the district's southern boundary. There are markets, pretty little squares with splashing fountains and narrow lanes, many for pedestrians only. Strolling in these lanes, you'll discover Renaissance and medieval buildings, and a few small museums. This is a district for fine restaurants and elegant shopping. The town's main square, place de l'Hôtel de Ville, with its Italianate town hall, is here. Rising from one corner of the building is a 16th-century belfry, the Tour de l'Horloge. On Tuesday, Thursday and Saturday the scents of a flower market fill the square. Place Richelme has a daily produce market and is a hang-out for street musicians and students. North of the Tour de l'Horloge, in rue Gaston de Saporta, is the Musée du Vieil Aix (▷ 67).

## MUSÉE GRANET

www.museegranet-aixenprovence.fr

Until the 1980s, Aix did not possess a single work by its most famous son, artist Paul Cézanne. This was remedied when the town's main art museum, Musée Granet, was given a small collection of minor early Cézanne paintings. Atypical of the artist's work, these delicate drawings and watercolours are exhibited for just a few months each year. The bulk of the museum's exhibits

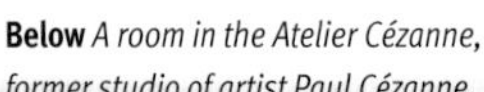

**Below** *A room in the Atelier Cézanne, former studio of artist Paul Cézanne*

are European paintings, collected by François Granet (1775–1849). There is also a 19th-century sculpture gallery and the 'De Cézanne à Giacometti' collection, plus archaeological finds dating back to Roman Aix. The most interesting exhibits are the Ligurian masks, statuary and other items discovered at nearby Entremont, which are among the oldest artworks in France.
✉ Place St-Jean-de-Malte, 13100 Aix-en-Provence ☎ 04 42 52 88 90 🕔 Jun–end Sep Tue–Sun 11–7; Oct–end May Tue–Sun 12–6 ✋ Adult €4, 18–26 €2, under 18 free; free 1st Sun of month

### ATELIER CÉZANNE

www.atelier-cezanne.com

Near the end of his life, Cézanne began to earn an income from sales of his work in Paris, Berlin and Vienna (but not in Aix). He had this handsome studio built on Les Lauves hill. From 1901 to his death in 1906, Cézanne spent most of his time here, leaving each afternoon for his landscape painting out of town. Through a series of lucky flukes, his last studio has remained perfectly preserved. The large open space was closed after the artist's death in 1906. When it was privately purchased in 1921, the buyer carefully kept all of Cézanne's personal effects. Today visitors can admire objects featured in many of the artist's drawings and paintings, including vases, chairs and mannequins, as well as photos, replica artworks and the surrounding serene gardens.
✉ 9 avenue Paul Cézanne, 13090 Aix-en-Provence ☎ 04 42 21 06 53 🕔 Jul, Aug daily 10–6; Apr–end Jun, Sep daily 10–12, 2–6; Oct, Nov, Mar daily 10–12, 2–5; Dec–end Feb Mon–Sat 10–12, 2–5 ✋ Adult €5.50, 13–25 €2, under 13 free ☞ Tour in English at 5 (Oct–end Mar at 4)

### CATHÉDRALE ST-SAUVEUR

www.cathedrale-aix.net

The cathedral is a mix of styles from Romanesque to baroque, spanning the 5th to the 17th centuries. Look for the 16th-century Flemish tapestries in the chancel, which were stolen from Canterbury Cathedral during the English Civil War. The baptistery, off the right-hand nave, contains traces of the main street of the Roman town. There are superb pieces of medieval art, notably Nicolas Froment's triptych of the *Burning Bush* in the central nave, painted for King René in 1476; the king and his queen are depicted kneeling in prayer.
✉ Rue de Laroque, Aix-en-Provence 🕔 Daily 7.30–12, 2–6 ✋ Free

## MORE TO SEE

### FONDATION VASARELY

This gallery is devoted to modern abstract artist Victor Vasarely.
✉ 1 avenue Marcel Pagnol, Jas de Bouffan, 13090 Aix-en-Provence ☎ 04 42 20 01 09 🕔 Tue–Sat 10–1, 2–6 ✋ Adult €7, child (7–18) €4, under 7 free

### FOUNTAINS

Aix has around 40 fountains. The moss-covered Fontaine d'Eau Thermale, on the cours Mirabeau, is a natural hot spring. Water pours out at 34°C (93°F).

### MUSÉE DES TAPISSERIES

The former Archbishops' Palace now shelters a tapestry museum.
✉ Ancien Palais de l'Archevêché, 28 place des Martyrs de la Résistance, 13100 Aix-en-Provence ☎ 04 42 23 09 91 🕔 Mid-Apr to mid-Oct Wed–Mon 10–6; mid-Oct to mid-Apr Wed–Mon 1.30–5 ✋ €3

### MUSÉE DU VIEIL AIX

Curiosities here include marionettes of characters from the medieval *Fête Dieu* festival.
✉ 17 rue Gaston de Saporta, 13100 Aix-en-Provence ☎ 04 42 21 43 55 🕔 Apr–end Oct Tue–Sun 2.30–6; Nov–end Mar Tue–Sun 10–12, 2–5 ✋ €4

**Above** *The 16th-century Tour de l'Horloge*

# ARLES

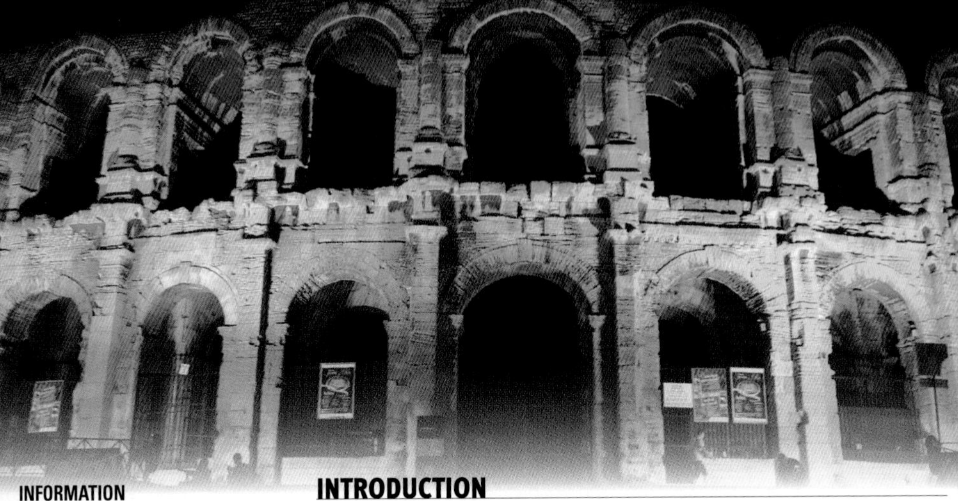

Above *Les Arènes still hosts bullfights and performances*

## INFORMATION

www.arlestourisme.com

294 C11 **Main office:** Esplanade Charles de Gaulle, boulevard des Lices 04 90 18 41 20 Apr–end Sep daily 9–6.45; Oct–end Mar Mon–Sat 9–4.45. **Gare SNCF office:** mid-Jun to mid-Sep daily 9–1, 2–6 Gare SNCF, avenue Paulin Talabot

## INTRODUCTION

Arles is a lively, arty, market town with exceptionally well-preserved Roman buildings. It is on the Rhône's left bank, at the northern edge of the Camargue. Locations in and near the town are reproduced in several paintings by Vincent Van Gogh. Extraordinarily ancient, Arles has an impressive array of historical places. Most are in the largely traffic-free old quarter, so it is convenient to stay in or near here. Especially notable are the Roman arena and, next to it, the Roman theatre, but there are considerable medieval sights too. Most of the main sights can be reached on foot. The busy main street, boulevard des Lices, runs alongside the old quarter and has many shops, bars, hotels and restaurants, as well as the tourist office. It is well served by buses.

Arles was founded by the Greeks in 600BC as a trading outpost of Massalia (Marseille). It was later taken over by the Romans, who for political reasons preferred Arles to Marseille, and built Arles up as a large port, linked to the Mediterranean by canal. It became one of the Roman Empire's most important cities (they called it Arelate). Emperor Constantine was born here. The town's fourth-century Roman baths are believed to have been the largest in Provence. In the medieval period, too, Arles remained the greatest city of Provence, until overtaken by Aix. Arles is proud of its strongly Provençal cultural identity, and it was here that 19th-century poet Frédéric Mistral based himself in his struggles to revive the Provençal language (▷ 37).

Vincent Van Gogh came to Arles in 1888, in search of a change of scene from Paris. He set up home in place Lamartine, for part of the time living with fellow artist Paul Gauguin. Van Gogh fell out with Gauguin, and, after a chaotic visit to a prostitute, famously cut off part of his ear. Despite Van Gogh's continued depression, this was a prolific, highly creative period. Surprisingly, there are no Van Gogh paintings in Arles, nor any other traces left of his two-year stay. Even his house—the little yellow house featured in his paintings—no longer exists, destroyed by wartime bombing. After cutting his ear, Van Gogh was admitted to a hospital, which has now become the Espace Van Gogh, a temporary exhibition space devoted to the study of the artist. It stands opposite the Muséon Arlaten, and still has the garden seen in his painting *Jardin de l'Hôpital à Arles*. In 1889, Van Gogh was moved at his own request to St-Paul-de-Mausole (▷ 94), a monastery and mental hospital near St-Rémy-de-Provence. A year later, his mental condition not having improved, he returned north, and in 1890 he committed suicide at Auvers-sur-Oise, near Paris.

## WHAT TO SEE

### LES ARÈNES

www.arenes-arles.com

The Roman arena stands at the quiet heart of historic Arles. Much damage has been done over the years to its sturdy structure—during the 12th century it was even turned into a walled village. The medieval towers at each end are a relic of that time, when there were 200 houses and two churches within the arena. The ancient walls were cleared out during the 1820s, and this awesome site is now used for summer bull races and performances.

✉ Place des Arènes, 13200 Arles ☎ 0891 700 370 🕐 May, Jun, Sep daily 9–7; Jul, Aug Thu–Tue 9–7, Wed 9–3; Mar, Apr, Oct daily 9–6; Nov–end Feb daily 10–5 ✋ Adult €6, under 18 free; ticket includes entrance to the Théâtre Antique

### THÉÂTRE ANTIQUE

Near the arena is the large first-century BC Théâtre Antique, or Roman theatre. Much of the stonework has been removed over the years, but although the remnants may be skeletal, the columns and tiered seating continue to create a powerful impression. The site is perhaps most famous for its large Venus sculpture, discovered here during the mid-17th century and now exhibited in the Louvre, in Paris. The theatre ruins continue to be used for concerts, drama and the July folklore festival.

✉ Rue de la Calade, 13200 Arles ☎ 04 90 49 59 05 🕐 May–end Sep daily 9–7; Mar, Apr, Oct daily 9–12, 2–6; Nov–end Feb daily 10–12, 2–5 ✋ Adult €6, under 18 free; ticket includes entrance to Les Arènes

### CATHÉDRALE ST-TROPHIME

St-Trophime Cathedral, dating from the sixth century AD, was one of the first Romanesque churches in France. However, there's little left of that original structure and the present building is mainly 12th century. Its ornate west front doorway is among the finest pieces of Provençal Romanesque stone carving. Go through the separate entrance (also on place de la République) to reach the delightful cloisters, combining Gothic and Romanesque. The upper gallery is an exhibition space.

✉ Place de la République, 13200 Arles ☎ 04 90 49 59 05 🕐 May–end Sep daily 9–7; Mar, Apr, Oct daily 9–6; Nov–end Feb daily 10–5 ✋ Cloisters: adult €3.50, under 18 free

**Below** *Intricate carvings in the Cathédrale St-Trophime*

**TIPS**

» *Passeport Avantage* allows entrance to all of Arles' museums and monuments. It costs €13.50 for adults and €12 for students. The pass is valid for one year.

» The town's huge Saturday-morning market is on boulevard Emile Combes. A second-hand market is held in place de la République on the first Wednesday of every month.

**Below** *Flowers adorn the bright yellow shutters of a house in Arles*

## MUSÉE RÉATTU

www.museereattu.arles.fr

This museum, located in a 15th-century Templar priory within the old quarter but close to the river, takes its name from its founder, local painter Jacques Réattu (1760–1833). It houses his own works, but more importantly, his remarkable collection of works by other artists. Donated to the town, it became Arles' main fine art museum, and in recent years has acquired some exceptional paintings representing all periods from the 16th century to today, especially by 19th- and 20th-century artists including Dufy, Gauguin, Léger, de Vlaminck and Rousseau. Excellent exhibits include drawings by Picasso, a regular at the Arles bullfights, as well as a collection of early 20th-century photography. The museum has been renovated extensively over the past two years.

10 rue du Grand Prieuré, 13200 Arles 04 90 49 37 58 Apr–end Sep Tue–Sun 10–7; Oct–end Mar Tue–Sun 10–12.30, 2–6.30 Adult €7, under 18 free; free to all on 1st Sun of month

## MUSÉON ARLATEN

www.museonarlaten.fr

Provençal poet Frédéric Mistral used his 1904 Nobel Prize for Literature to set up this important ethnographic museum of Provençal folk culture, and many of the displays are still exactly as he arranged them. Appropriately, the name is in Provençal dialect, meaning 'Museum of Arles', and the staff wear traditional local costume. The compendious collection includes items from all aspects of life in the region during the 17th to the 19th centuries. Household items sit alongside *santons* (figurines) and a delightful collection of pre-Revolution women's clothes. Archaeological finds are on the upper floor and there are ruins of a Roman temple in the courtyard.

29 rue de la République, 13200 Arles 04 90 93 58 11 Closed for renovations until 2013

## MUSÉE DE L'ARLES ET DE LA PROVENCE ANTIQUES

www.arles-antique.cg13.fr

Beside the Rhône, about 2km (1.2 miles) from central Arles, the Musée de l'Arles et de la Provence Antiques is a startling modern construction, a pointed triangular building with blue enamel walls. It stands at the site where a huge cache of Roman gold coins was found, next to the Roman circus, or racetrack. The N113 overpass crosses the Roman circus. On display in the museum are numerous Classical items found at Arles, including rich Roman mosaics, and the finest collection of carved marble sarcophagi outside Rome. In what appears to be a deliberate contrast, these ancient items are displayed in a bright, ultra-modern setting.

Presqu'Île du Cirque Romain, avenue de la 1ere DFL, 13635 Arles 04 90 18 88 88 Wed–Mon 10–6 Adult €7, under 18 free

## LES ALYSCAMPS

A short walk from boulevard des Lices (follow avenue des Alyscamps), the remarkable Alyscamps cemetery was once one of the most renowned burial grounds in the world. The name comes from the Latin *Elysii Campi* (the Elysian Fields). Already famous in Roman times, the cemetery continued to be used right into the Middle Ages, with tombs stacked on top of one another. It was claimed that miracles and magic occurred here. Then, in the 15th century, the grandest sarcophagi began to be stolen by clergy and officials, who coveted the fine stonework, and the cemetery was rapidly destroyed. The 20th-century construction of a railway through the grounds brought further decline, and today factory chimneys add to the ugliness. What survives is the last of the pathways between the tombs, a peaceful, melancholy and evocative tree-

lined walkway leading to a church. The graves are empty. The site was given added poignancy in the paintings of *Les Alyscamps* by Vincent Van Gogh.
✉ Avenue des Alyscamps, 13200 Arles ☎ 04 90 49 36 87 ⊙ May–end Sep daily 9–12, 2–7; Mar, Apr, Oct daily 9–12, 2–6; Nov–end Feb daily 10–12, 2–5 ✋ Adult €3.50, under 18 free

## MORE TO SEE

### CRYPTOPORTICO

Beneath the street in the old quarter is the grim Cryptoportico, two parallel galleries built by the Romans to give underground support to the Forum. The galleries were used by the Romans as a storage area for grain, wine, produce, statuary and even slaves. During World War II it was a bomb shelter.
✉ Hôtel de Ville, place de la République, 13200 Arles ☎ 04 90 49 59 05 ⊙ May–end Sep daily 9–12, 2–7; Mar, Apr, Oct daily 9–12, 2–6; Nov–end Feb daily 10–12, 2–5 ✋ Adult €3.50, under 18 free

### FONDATION VAN GOGH

www.fondationvangogh-arles.org
Facing the Roman arena, the small Fondation Van Gogh is an art museum packed with works inspired by Vincent Van Gogh. Leading modern artists including Francis Bacon, Jasper Johns and Olivier Dubré, among many others, have contributed their interpretations to the collection.
✉ Palais Luppé, 24 rond-point des Arènes, 13200 Arles ☎ 04 90 49 94 04 ⊙ Jul–end Sep daily 10–7; Apr–end Jun daily 10–6; Oct–end Mar Tue–Sun 11–7 ✋ Adult €6, child (12–18) €4, under 12 free

### THERMES DE CONSTANTIN

Arles' walled old town reaches down to the Rhône, and the last remnants of the vast spa baths of Roman Arles are spread out close to the river. What can still be seen are vestiges of the tepidarium (warm baths), caldarium (hot baths), two pools and a steam room. Part of the palace of Emperor Constantine, the Roman baths are thought to have been the largest in Provence.
✉ Rue D. Maisto, 13200 Arles ☎ 04 90 49 59 05 ⊙ May–end Sep daily 9–12, 2–7; Mar, Apr, Oct daily 9–12, 2–6; Nov–end Feb daily 10–12, 2–5 ✋ Adult €3, under 18 free

**Above** *A statue of Frédéric Mistral in place du Forum*
**Below** *Evocative Les Alyscamps*

# LES BAUX-DE-PROVENCE

**INFORMATION**

www.lesbauxdeprovence.com
294 D10 Maison du Roy, 13520 Les Baux-de-Provence 04 90 54 34 39 May–end Sep Mon–Fri 9–6, Sat, Sun 10–5.30; Oct–end Apr Mon–Fri 9.30–5, Sat, Sun 10–5.30

**Above** *The setting sun casts a golden glow over the stone houses of Les Baux-de-Provence*

## INTRODUCTION

The medieval fortress-village of Les Baux-de-Provence, with its atmospheric alleys, has an awesome location. The ruined citadel is poised on a high, stony plateau among jagged Alpilles hills on the northern limits of the Camargue. It receives up to one million visitors a year and has almost no permanent residents. In reality, Les Baux has little to offer except atmosphere and views—but these are exceptional. The citadel and place St-Vincent give sweeping vistas across Vallon de la Fontaine to the hills all around.

Les Baux came into being as a refuge for locals in the eighth century, when Saracen raiders were attacking Provence. It later became a fortress of the powerful local lords. Up to the 12th century, the Lords of Les Baux controlled a wide area of western Provence. During the 14th century, the citadel became the base of the brigand-nobleman Raymond de Turenne, who lived by kidnapping noblemen and demanding a ransom. Those whose families did not pay were thrown off the edge of the cliff. To ensure his own control over western Provence, in 1483 Louis XI ordered the destruction of the Les Baux Citadelle, but during the religious wars of the 16th century, the village was reborn as a Protestant fortress. It was defeated and largely dismantled under Richelieu in 1632. The Prince of Monaco inherited the village, as Marquis des Baux, but it remained in ruins until the 19th century, when it was taken up by well-to-do artists and romantics. It was given a boost by the opening in the 1940s of the Oustau de Baumanière, an exclusive luxury hotel-restaurant at the foot of the hill (▷ 109).

## WHAT TO SEE

### CITADELLE

www.chateau-baux-provence.com

The dominant feature of Les Baux, especially from below, is the impressive walled enclosure of the medieval citadel, whose ruins occupy most of the site. This large, windswept area is also evocatively known as the Ville Morte, or Dead City. Inside are about a dozen buildings, including a 13th-century keep, an olive museum, a chapel, a pigeon house cut out of the rock and reconstructions of medieval siege machines. A map directs you around the site. The views from this cliff-edge location take in a landscape of wild rocky terrain broken up with vineyards and woods.

Rue du Château, 13520 Les Baux-de-Provence 04 90 54 55 56 Jul–end Sep daily 9–8.30; Oct daily 9.30–6; Nov–end Mar daily 9.30–5; Apr–end Jun daily 9–6.30 Adult €7.70, child (7–17) €5.70, under 7 free Audioguide is included in entry price

### MODERN VILLAGE

Alongside the ruins of the Citadelle's Dead City is the handsome, busy, modern Les Baux, with shops, houses and a town hall. Though referred to as the 'modern' village, it dates mainly from the 16th and 17th centuries. This area occupies a narrow strip outside the original fortress. Rue du Trencat, the main street, has been carved directly from the rocky terrain. Holiday crowds saunter the streets between the ice-cream stores, souvenir shops, *crêperies*, large areas of café tables and art galleries. Sights to pause at include the 16th-century Hôtel de Manville, now the town hall, with its facade of mullioned windows, lovely Renaissance courtyard and the Musée des Santons (free) a folksy *santons* (figurines) museum.

### ART IN LES BAUX

The picturesque site has long attracted artists of renown, including Vincent Van Gogh. The medieval village has now been taken over almost entirely by seasonal artists and craftspeople, and there are many galleries and craft stalls. Several places are used for temporary exhibitions, including the town hall.

### ÉGLISE ST-VINCENT

This 12th-century church, partly hewn out of the rock, has a tower (Lanterne des Morts) and windows designed by the 20th-century stained-glass master Max Ingrand. On Christmas Eve, the popular *Fête du Pastrage* festival takes place here. In a chapel on the right-hand side of the church is the *Charette de l'Agneau* (The Lamb's Cart), which plays a key role in the festival. In a tradition dating back to the 16th century, during midnight Mass, an angel hidden behind the altar announces the Nativity to shepherds at the back of the church. The shepherds come forward, dancing and singing Christmas songs, accompanied by shepherdesses with flowers and fruits strung about them. They are followed by the chariot bearing a new-born lamb.

✉ Place St-Vincent, 13520 Les Baux-de-Provence ☎ 04 90 54 55 56 🕓 Jul, Aug daily 9–9; Mar–end Jun, Sep–end Nov daily 9–7.30; Dec–end Feb daily 9–6 ✋ Free

### CATHÉDRALE D'IMAGES AND VAL D'ENFER

www.cathedrale-images.com

There are also impressive sights at the foot of the village: Les Baux gave its name to bauxite, which was first quarried in what is now called the Val d'Enfer (the Valley of Hell), when geologists in the 1820s discovered that the red rock from the hills surrounding Les Baux could be smelted to produce aluminium. The Val d'Enfer is a spectacular gorge of wild rocks and caves to the north of the village. Its tortured-looking rock formations were supposedly the inspiration for Dante's *Inferno*. Jean Cocteau shot scenes from *Orphée* in the deserted quarries here in 1950 and one of the huge underground caverns has now been converted into the extraordinary Cathédrale d'Images, where exhibitions of bright artworks are projected onto the plain quarry walls.

✉ Route de Maillane, 13520 Les Baux-de-Provence ☎ 04 90 54 38 65 🕓 Apr–end Sep daily 10–6; Oct–end Dec, mid-Feb to end Mar daily 10–5. Closed Jan to mid-Feb ✋ Adult €7.50, child (7–17) €3.50, under 7 free

## MORE TO SEE

### MUSÉE YVES BRAYER

www.yvesbrayer.com

See vivid works by this figurative painter (1907–90), as well as pieces by other modern artists, in the 16th-century Hôtel des Porcelet. The Chapelle des Penitents Blancs, in place de l'Église, was also decorated by Brayer.

✉ Hôtel des Porcelet, place François de Hérain, 13520 Les Baux-de-Provence ☎ 04 90 54 36 99 🕓 Apr–end Sep daily 10–12.30, 2–6.30; Oct–end Dec, mid-Feb to end Mar Wed–Mon 10–12.30, 2–5.30. Closed Jan to mid-Feb ✋ Adult €4, under 18 free

### TIPS

» In summer, visit early or late to avoid the crowds.

» Cars must be parked in designated areas. When the upper parking areas are full, no cars are allowed on the access road, and you must park at the foot of the village. Occasionally the lower parking area is full too, and no further access to the village is possible except for pedestrians. A second entrance, the original Porte Eyguières, has no vehicle access.

» A combined ticket to the Citadelle, Cathédrale d'Images and Musée Yves Brayer is €15.50 (7–17 years €7.50).

» There are festivals of art and music throughout the summer.

**Below** *The entrance to the bizarre Cathédrale d'Images*

# CAMARGUE

**INFORMATION**
www.reserve-camargue.org
294 C11 Centre d'Information de la Réserve Nationale de Camargue, La Capelière, 13200 Arles 04 90 97 00 97 Apr–end Sep daily 9–1, 2–6; Oct–end Mar Wed–Mon 9–1, 2–5

## INTRODUCTION

The Camargue is a vast delta formed where the Grand Rhône and the Petit Rhône meet the sea. It is Europe's largest wetland, a place where fresh water, sea water and land meet together in a unique and haunting world of wildlife, tranquillity and wide-open spaces. Much of this curious terrain is submerged in wide, shallow *étangs*—saltwater lagoons. The most sensitive areas have been classified as protected nature reserves, including the Réserve Nationale Zoologique et Botanique de Camargue, covering 13,500ha (33,360 acres) around the Étang de Vaccarès. There are also towns here—notably Saintes-Maries-de-la-Mer (▷ 91), Aigues-Mortes (▷ 62–63) and, north of the Camargue margins, Arles (▷ 68–71). The best way to explore the Camargue is to get out of your car: walk, ride a horse, rent a bicycle or go on safari. Jeep safaris and boat tours of the canals operate from Saintes-Maries-de-la-Mer.

Monks came to the Camargue in the Middle Ages to collect salt and reclaim the swampland. They were followed in the 17th century by ranchers, who bred black, longhorn bulls and the Camargue's famous white horses. In the 1970s, much of the area was designated as the Parc Naturel Régional de Camargue. In 1993 horses, sheep and bulls had to be evacuated by helicopter and lorry after the Rhône burst its banks.

## WHAT TO SEE

### WILDLIFE

The Camargue is famous for its elegant half-wild white horses and black cattle, but many other creatures shelter in its ecosystems. The saltwater marshes attract colonies of terns and black-headed gulls, as well as species such as the oystercatcher, shelduck and redshank. In the *étangs*, pink flamingoes pick their way through the shallows in search of food, while birds of prey stand sentinel on the fence posts by the road. The silence is almost total, apart from the honking of geese as they move in fluttering ribbons across the sky. Farther inland, and closer to the Rhône, there are freshwater areas where herons, moorhens, coot, mallards and egrets thrive.

**Above** *The white horses of the Camargue*

## THE COAST

The western Camargue coast has wide sandy beaches and dunes next to Saintes-Maries-de-la-Mer. These are among the most threatened areas in the Camargue, as the natural flows of silt have been destroyed by industry. Dikes, groynes and fences have been put in place to prevent the sands disappearing. In winter, rainwater collects in the dunes and nourishes plants such as sea wormwood, sand lilies, sea rocket and sea stock. In summer, sea holly and sea spurge appear.

## ÉTANG DE VACCARÈS

From Saintes-Maries you can hike along the *digue-à-la-mer,* a sea wall that divides the lovely beaches and lagoons around the southern side of the Étang de Vaccarès. The reserve of the Étang de Vaccarès itself is open only to permit-holders, but there are many points just off the surrounding roads (especially the D37) from where you can watch bird life. The reserve's headquarters, the Centre d'Information de la Réserve Nationale de Camargue, is on the eastern side of the *étang*, and has one of the best displays on the Camargue. There are three observatories within a few minutes of here and 4.5km (3 miles) of walking trails. On the west side of the *étang* there are two more observation points.

Centre d'Information de la Réserve Nationale de Camargue, La Capelière ☎ 04 90 97 00 97 Apr–end Sep daily 9–1, 2–6; Oct–end Mar Wed–Mon 9–1, 2–5

## PONT DE GAU

www.parc-camargue.fr
www.parcornithologique.com

The Maison du Parc Naturel Régional de Camargue, 4km (2.5 miles) north of Saintes-Maries-de-la-Mer, has environmental displays and huge viewing windows. To get closer to the bird life, go to the adjacent Parc Ornithologique du Pont de Gau (Apr–end Sep daily 9–dusk; Oct–end Mar daily 10–5; adult €7, child (4–10) €4, under 4 free), which has trails around the Étang de Pont de Gau (a half-hour walk), or the more extensive Étang de Ginès sanctuary, where bulls graze in the summer. Large aviaries house predators such as buzzards, Egyptian vultures and eagle owls. The park looks after injured predators sent here from all over Europe.

Parc Naturel Régional de Camargue, Pont de Gau ☎ 04 90 97 86 32 Apr–end Sep daily 10–6; Oct–end Mar Sat–Thu 9.30–5

## TIPS

» Take precautions against mosquitoes, which breed prolifically in the marshes.
» Always take plenty of drinking water with you when you set out to explore the area.
» You can see flamingoes throughout the year, but there are larger numbers in spring and summer.
» For excursions into the Camargue, ▷ 106–107.
» For a drive in the Camargue, ▷ 98–99.
» For a bicycle ride, ▷ 100–101.

**Below left** *The grasslands look especially beautiful at sunset*
**Below right** *Elegant flamingoes in the shallows*

## BARBENTANE

www.barbentane.fr

The pretty village of Barbentane sits near the confluence of the Durance and the Rhône, south of Avignon, and is dominated by its chateau. Founded by the Marquis of Barbentane in 1674 and finished more than 100 years later, the classic grace of the great Château de Barbentane (tel 04 90 95 51 07; Jul–end Sep daily 10–12, 2–6; Easter–end Jun, Oct Thu–Tue 10–12, 2–6. Closed Nov–Easter) owes much to the great chateaux of the Île de France, around Paris. Still occupied by the Barbentane family, it has rich furnishings that reflect 400 years of acquiring the finest items—the opulent interior is often used for magazine shoots. It is adorned with 18th-century tapestries, Aubusson carpets, porcelain, statues and chandeliers.

294 D9 Le Cours, 13570 Barbentane 04 90 90 85 86 Jul, Aug Mon–Sat 9–12, 2–6.30; Sep–end Jun Mon 2–5, Tue–Fri 9–12, 2–5, Sat 9–12

## LES BAUX-DE-PROVENCE

▷ 72–73.

## CAMARGUE

▷ 74–75.

## CASSIS

www.ot-cassis.fr

Handsome cliffs rise behind this busy little modern resort and older port. The town is close to Marseille and is popular with residents of that city. It is backed by wild wooded country, as well as vineyards. This is a very old vineyard area, producing a range of local wines, especially white. Cassis has a leisurely, civilized feel to it, with memories of artists who used to meet and paint here—about a century ago it was a popular spot with painters such as Paul Signac. There's a small beach of sand and pebbles, and a pretty harbour packed with traditional wooden fishing boats. You can take a boat trip from Cassis to see the coastline's scenic *calanques* (inlets). The town is popular with walkers taking the cliff-top paths—which range from easy to arduous—leading from here westwards towards Marseille and east to La Ciotat.

301 G13 Oustau Calendal, quai des Moulins, 13260 Cassis 0892 259 892 Jun–end Sep daily 9–7; Oct–end May Mon–Fri 9.30–12.30, 2.30–6, Sat 10–12.30, 2.30–6.30, Sun 10–12.30

**Above** *Boats in the harbour at Cassis*

## CHAÎNE DES ALPILLES

This narrow range of small, pretty, rocky hills, along the northeastern edge of the Camargue plain, is an isolated extension of the Lubéron range. Among the hills are villages, vineyards, densely wooded areas of cork oak and wild Mediterranean flora. Les Baux-de-Provence (▷ 72–73), in the heart of the Alpilles, attracts many visitors, but much of the rest of the area is almost unknown to tourists. A few narrow roads penetrate the heart of the range and reach interesting places around the base of the Alpilles.

The small town of Eygalières, on the northern edge of the Alpilles, is worth a visit. You can see the ruins of the 12th-century castle keep, as well as the 17th-century Chapelle des Penitents Blancs.

For a scenic drive through the Alpilles, head south from Eygalières on the D24. The narrow, winding road is bordered by vineyards and pine forests.

Each Tuesday following Easter there is a pilgrimage from Eygalières to the nearby 12th-century Chapelle de St-Sixte, on a small hill. (The chapel is closed the rest of the year.)

At the foot of Les Alpilles, near Les Baux-de-Provence, is the wealthy village of Maussane. Its fortunes came from the surrounding olive groves. A century ago it had more than a dozen olive mills, producing high-quality olive oil. Today oil production continues, with the few remaining mills pressing olives in the traditional way.

Outside the nearby village of Le Paradou, in avenue de la Vallée des Baux-de-Provence, there's a huge indoor miniature village called La Petite Provence du Paradou (www.lapetiteprovenceduparadou.com; daily 10–6.30; Jul, Aug until 7). This features more than 400 figures of local characters—shepherds, gypsies, farmers, fishermen—integrated into a vast, wonderfully detailed tableau, called a *village des santons*, with working windmills and other features.

The attractive lane D78 snakes from Maussane around the south face of the Alpilles along an ancient route once used for the annual *transhumance* (▷ 14).

294 D10

## CHÂTEAU DE LA BARBEN

www.chateaudelabarben.fr

www.zoolabarben.com

An awesome, magnificently fortified castle on the top of a rocky hill, daunting La Barben looks almost like a film set. Originally a medieval fortress, today's castle is in reality more like a stately home, dating largely to a 17th-century reconstruction and, as of spring 2010, also housing a bed-and-breakfast.

Probably first built before the year 1000, the castle belonged to Marseille's St-Victor Abbey. In the 15th century it was acquired by King René (▷ 33), who kept it as a private residence before selling it to the de Fortins—a powerful Provençal noble family close to the French monarchy. They owned it right up until the 19th century and turned it into a luxurious home.

The highlight is a spectacular terraced garden in formal French style. This was created by André Le Nôtre, the landscape designer of Versailles, at the meeting of the Touloubre et Quatruie streams. The formality of the flower borders, statuary and basins is emphasized by the surrounding untamed woodland.

Inside the chateau are striking 16th- and 17th-century Flemish and Aubusson tapestries and elegant 18th-century painted ceilings. The entrance hall is covered with 17th-century Cordoban leather. Napoleon's sister, Pauline Borghese, once lived here, and you can visit her bedroom, which is in the Empire style. The kitchens have a bread oven made of volcanic stone brought from the Massif Central.

The chateau's lofty main terrace has a grand double staircase, which gives a dramatic view of the Étang de Berre and the town of Salon-de-Provence (▷ 95) below.

Other attractions include tours of the medieval dungeons, treasure hunts, the nearby Vivarium (reptile collection) in the castle's vaulted sheep pen, and a zoo (daily 10–6; Jul, Aug 9.30–7), with bears, lions, hippos and more.

✚ 295 F11 ✉ 13330 La Barben ☎ 04 90 55 25 41 ⌚ Apr to mid-Nov daily 2–5; Feb, Mar Sat, Sun 2–5. Closed mid-Nov to Jan ✋ Chateau only: adult €8, child (under 12) €6; Zoo and vivarium: adult €13.50, child (3–12) €8, under 3 free ? People with disabilities may find it difficult to get around the site ☞ Hourly guided tours of the chateau in French and English 🍴 🎁 ☕

### LA CIOTAT

www.tourisme-laciotat.com

La Ciotat's history as a port town stretches back to the fourth century AD. The town, southeast of Marseille, is still dominated by industrial architecture, including vast gantries and cranes that have stood idle since the dockyard closed in 1990. The port is now home to fishing boats and pleasure craft.

The town hosts a film festival in June, in memory of the Lumière brothers' first motion picture, which showed a train arriving in La Ciotat's station in 1898.

West of town, behind the dockyards, is the Parc Naturel du Mugel, a wilderness area dominated by the Bec de l'Aigle (eagle's beak) promontory, 70m (230ft) high.

✚ 301 H14 ℹ Boulevard A. France, 13600 La Ciotat ☎ 04 42 08 61 32 ⌚ Jun–end Sep daily 9–8; Oct–end May Mon–Sat 9–12, 2–6

### GÉMENOS

www.mairie-gemenos.fr

Despite being close to the *autoroute* and the spreading edges of Marseille, Gémenos is a typical Provençal village, with narrow streets and steps and old houses. It is set back from the sea at the foot of the Massif de la Sainte-Baume in 'Pagnol country', the Provence of films *Jean de Florette* and *Manon des Sources*. The author of the stories, Marcel Pagnol (1895–1974), was born in nearby Aubagne.

At the main square you can look inside the courtyard of the Granges du Marquis d'Albertas, a huge 17th- to 18th-century building that once housed agricultural workers. The beautiful 17th-century chateau of the marquis is now the town hall.

Outside the village on the D2 is the Parc de St-Pons, a protected parkland of fine deciduous trees—unusual in this region—around the ruins of the early 13th-century Cistercian ladies' abbey of St-Pons (free access). Just behind the abbey, the source of the river Frauge gushes out of a small fissure in the rockface. The abbey ruins host a series of religious music concerts in summer.

✚ 301 H13 ℹ Cours Pasteur, 13420 Gémenos ☎ 04 42 32 18 44 ⌚ Mon–Sat 9–12, 1.30–5.30

### GLANUM

▷ 94.

### GROTTES DE CALÈS

This bizarre troglodyte village has dwellings carved into caves in the steep, rocky woods outside Lamanon, 10km (6 miles) north of Salon-de-Provence (▷ 95). The caves were inhabited from Neolithic times to the 16th century and were still in use as late as the 19th century. There are more than 100 different dwellings and steps lead down into them. To reach them takes about 15 to 20 minutes: Walk out of Lamanon following signs to the Grottes de Calès.

✚ 295 E11 ✉ 13113 Lamanon ⌚ Free access; site and path closed Jul to mid-Sep, and may also be closed in dry periods if there is a risk of fire; check with Lamanon's tourist office (www.mairie-lamanon.fr) before setting out 🚌 Salon–Avignon buses stop here 🚆 Lamanon ✋ Free

**Below** *Château de la Barben*

# MARSEILLE

**INFORMATION**
www.marseille-tourisme.com
301 F13 4 La Canebière, 13001 Marseille 04 91 13 89 00
Mon–Sat 9–7, Sun 10–5
Gare St-Charles

**Above** *The elegant arches of La Vieille Charité, Marseille*

## INTRODUCTION

Ancient yet irresistibly dynamic Marseille is a Mediterranean melting pot, with an intriguing atmosphere and exhilarating *joie de vivre.* On the west coast of Provence, close to the Camargue, the city is France's premier Mediterranean sea gateway and has a distinctive mix of ethnic and cultural influences. There is plenty to see and do, including museums and art galleries, and boat trips to offshore islands. There are two Métro lines (▷ 85), plus two tram lines. The grandly beautiful Vieux Port (Old Port) and its surrounding streets form Marseille's focal point. Here are bars, art galleries, music venues and scores of little restaurants. You can walk or drive the shore road a few minutes south from Le Vieux Port to the old-fashioned little port at Anse des Auffes, where bright fishing boats are pulled up in front of a choice of fish restaurants. And the city makes a good base for some out-of-town sightseeing on the western Provence coast. While there are areas where you should be careful, on the whole the 'crime and drugs' image of the city is exaggerated.

Founded as the trading port of Massalia by the Greeks 2,600 years ago, Marseille has been the western Mediterranean's main port ever since. After the Roman conquest of Provence, the port was sacked and stripped of its fleet, although Marseille remained a busy town. A period of decline followed the Saracen raids of the seventh century, which curtailed Mediterranean trade. By the 11th century, the city had revived and continued to develop until the plague arrived in 1720, killing 50,000. By the 1760s, the city was the major port trading with the Caribbean and Latin America. The republican zeal of Marseille's oppressed workers proved a backbone of the Revolution, the city giving its name to the new national anthem, *La Marseillaise*, even though the song was composed in northeastern France (▷ 35). The city sustained extensive damage during World War II. In the second half of the 20th century, large numbers of people from Africa, particularly from Algeria and other places in North Africa, moved to the city. Today, Marseille has a total population of around one million.

## WHAT TO SEE

### LE VIEUX PORT

The focal point of the city is the large, westward-facing rectangular Old Port. Fortified, enclosed by spacious 17th-century quays, surrounded by the pale stone facades and red roofs of high, handsome old buildings, and with scores of boats jostling against one another, the port is an inspiring sight. Steep hillsides slope down to the port, overlooked on the south side by the sturdy defences of Fort St-Nicolas (no entry to visitors) and the powerfully fortified Romanesque basilica of St-Victor, which has a fifth-century crypt. Farther back is the hilltop Notre-Dame de la Garde, a 19th-century basilica topped with a huge gilded Virgin, strikingly lit at night, that locals traditionally believed gave divine protection to the city. At the foot of the hill, close to the port behind quai de Rive Neuve, is the grid of streets called the Quartier de l'Arsenal; now full of restaurants, it was once a notorious shipyard area where galley slaves were housed among the workshops. Stretching up the coast away from the Vieux Port are the dockyards, currently under renovation as part of Marseille's massive Euroméditerranée project (www.euromediterranee.fr), which aims to refresh and redevelop much of the city's urban centre. New sites include the Musée des Civilisations de l'Europe et de la Méditérranée (MuCEM), partly housed in Fort St-Jean, and director Luc Besson's multi-screen cinema in the new waterfront Euromed Centre. All projects should be completed by 2013, when Marseille is Europe's Capital of Culture (www.marseille-provence2013.fr).
82 B3 Vieux Port

### MUSÉE D'HISTOIRE DE MARSEILLE

The fascinating Musée d'Histoire de Marseille stands alongside the Jardin des Vestiges. It sets out the history of the city, with a third-century Roman ship as its focal point. The Jardin des Vestiges is an archaeological site, discovered during the late-1960s construction of the Centre Bourse shopping centre, transformed into a pretty garden. A walkway gives an overview of the ruins of the city's original Greek ramparts and parts of the dock as it was in the first century AD. Many items found in the excavations are now in the museum.
82 C2 Square Belsunce, Centre Bourse, 13001 Marseille 04 91 90 42 22
Mon–Sat 12–7 Adult €2, child (10–16) €1, under 10 free Vieux Port

### LE PANIER

Stepped alleys and run-down tenements with laundry lines strung between windows climb the Panier hill from the docks. In 1943 the occupying Nazi regime destroyed 2,000 buildings here and expelled or murdered around 25,000 residents. Among the buildings that survived is the 16th-century Maison Diamanté, so-called for a facade of stones carved into diamond-like

### TIPS

» Street parking is difficult so use the parking areas. There are five near the Vieux Port.

» The free *L'Hebdo* and *Ventilo* list hundreds of events in the city.

» The fish stew bouillabaisse is a speciality of Marseille, and at the restaurants surrounding the Vieux Port you can taste it at its most traditional.

» Beware of pickpockets in the Le Panier district and avoid the area at night. Keep a close eye on your belongings at markets, in waterfront areas and in bars.

**Below left** *Exhibits in the Musée d'Histoire de Marseille*
**Below right** *The Marché aux Poissons is a great place to buy fresh fish*

points. It houses the Musée du Vieux Marseille, with sections dedicated to Provençal furnishings, *santons* (figurines) and the esoteric playing cards called the Tarot Marseillaise (the museum is temporarily closed to the public but many of its exhibits can be seen at the Musée d'Histoire de Marseille, ▷ 79). Another survivor, in Grand Rue, is the 16th-century Hôtel de Cabre. After World War II, it was taken apart and rebuilt on a different street, which is why it says Rue de la Bonneterie on the wall. At the top of Le Panier district is the former 17th-century hospice called La Vieille Charité, a rectangle of lovely, three-floor arcaded galleries around a courtyard with a small baroque chapel. Originally a place of detention and shelter for the homeless, La Vieille Charité now hosts art exhibitions and the Musée de l'Archéologie Mediteranéenne (www.vieille-charite-marseille.org; Jun–end Sep Tue–Sun 11–6; Oct–end May Tue–Sun 10–5). Beyond is the 19th-century neo-Byzantine Cathédrale de la Major.
82 B2 Vieux Port

### PALAIS LONGCHAMP

This palace is home to the Musée d'Histoire Naturelle (Tue–Sun 10–5), which has a zoo behind it, and the Musée des Beaux-Arts (currently closed for renovations). The latter has 16th- and 17th-century French and Italian paintings, a room devoted to local architect, sculptor and painter Pierre Puget, and another room dedicated to local cartoonist Honoré Daumier.
83 F1 142 boulevard Longchamp, 13004 Marseille Palais: 04 91 14 59 50. Musée des Beaux-Arts: 04 91 14 59 30 Musée des Beaux-Arts: currently closed for renovations Cinq-Avenues-Longchamp

### CHÂTEAU D'IF

http://if.monuments-nationaux.fr
It's a 15-minute ferry ride to the island of If, with its nightmarish prison fortress, built in the 16th century and made famous by Alexandre Dumas in *The Count of Monte Cristo* (1844). The journey gives great views of the city, and a self-guided tour (leaflets in eight languages) takes you to the cells once occupied by various aristocratic prisoners.
Off map at 82 A3 04 91 59 02 30 May to mid-Sep daily 9.30–6.30; mid-Sep to end Mar Tue–Sun 9–5.30; Apr daily 9–5.30 Adult €5, under 18 free, EU citizens under 26 free From quai des Belges

**Above** *The Cathédrale de la Major*
**Opposite** *The striking statue atop the Basilique Notre-Dame de la Garde*

## MORE TO SEE

### LA CANEBIÈRE

Leading through the heart of the city in a majestic straight line from the Vieux Port's quai des Belges is the broad avenue La Canebière. Built in the 17th century, the street was for a long time rather seedy, but today is an inspiring sight. Most of the main shopping streets branch off it.
82 C2 Vieux Port

### MUSÉE CANTINI

This modern art gallery, with a good Surrealist collection and works by Matisse, Dufy, Miró, Kandinsky and Picasso, was a private home in the 17th century.
82 C3 19 rue Grignan, 13006 Marseille 04 91 54 77 75 Jun–end Sep Tue–Sun 11–6; Oct–end May Tue–Sun 10–5 Adult €2, child (10–16) €1, under 10 free Estangin-Préfecture

### MUSÉE DES DOCKS ROMAINS

At the foot of Le Panier district are several important relics and museums of the Classical period. The Museum of the Roman Docks displays a collection of first- to third-century AD Roman objects discovered during post-war rebuilding.
82 B2 28 place Vivaux, 13002 Marseille 04 91 91 24 62 Jun–end Sep Tue–Sun 11–6; Oct–end May Tue–Sun 10–5 Adult €2, child (10–16) €1, under 10 free Vieux Port

MARSEILLE
0 250 m
0 250 yds
1
2
3
4
5
A
B
C
GARE MARITIME NATIONALE
GARE DE LA JOLIETTE
Place de la Joliette
Joliette
Hôpital P Desbief
LA JOLIETTE
Place de Strasbourg
Place Marceau
ST LAZARE
Université de Provence
AV DU GÉNÉRAL
AUTOROUTE
Bourse du Travail
Arc de Triomphe
Jules Guesde
Place J Guesde
BOULEVARD CH NEDELEC
Quai Jean Charcot
Bassin de la Grande Joliette
GARE MARITIME INTERNATIONALE
QUAI DE LA JOLIETTE
AVENUE ROBERT SCHUMAN
BD DE DUNKERQUE
RUE DE FORBIN
RUE DE LA RÉPUBLIQUE
BOULEVARD DES DAMES
Rue Montolieu
Rue Duverger
Rue de la Joliette
Rue Fauchier
Rue Malaval
Rue d'Hozier
Rue Vincent Leblanc
Rue de Mazenod
Rue du Bon Pasteur
BD DE CAMILLE PELLETAN
Rue de Turenne
R Fréd Ozanam
Collège
Rue F Leca
Hôtel de la Marine
Hôtel de Région
Les Carmes
LES GRANDS CARMES
Cathédrale la Major
Cathédrale St-Lazare
Evêché
Rue de l'Evêché
La Vielle Charité
Place Sadi Carnot
Rue Ste Barbe
Cocbert Hotel de la Région
Rue Puvis de Chavannes
Rue Cocbert
COURS D'AIX
Rue du Panier
LE PANIER
Place des Moulins
Hôpital de l'Hôtel Dieu
HÔTEL DE VILLE
Quai de la Tourette
St-Cannaf
BELSUNCE
Musée d'Histoire de Marseille
Jardin des Vestiges
Rue des Precheurs
Rue H Barbusse
Rue H Fiocca
Musée des Docks Romains
Grand Rue
Rue Caisserie
Place V Gélu
Rue du Chevalier
Rue Coutellerie
Rue de la Marie
Square Protis
Théâtre Grec
Rue St-Laurent
Avenue St-Jean
Rue de Lacydon
Place J Verne
Hôtel de Ville
Rue de la Loge
Rue de Bir Hakeim
Musée de la Mode
CANEBIÈRE
Palais de la Bourse
Place du Gén De Gaulle
Fort St-Jean (MuCEM)
Chateau d'If
QUAI DU PORT
QUAI DE LA FRATERNITÉ
QUAI DES BELGES
Vieux-Port Hôtel de Ville
Vieux Port
TUNNEL ST-LAURENT
Port de Plaisance
Port de la Réserve
Rowing Club
Bas Fort St-Nicolas
Jardin du Pharo
QUARTIER DE L'ARSENAL
R Pythéas
RUE PARADIS
Opéra Municipal
Rue Molière
Rue Francis
Rue Saëns
Rue Haxo
Rue Pavillon
QUAI DE RIVE NEUVE
Pl Aux Huiles
R Fort Notre Dame
Cours Honoré d'Estienne d'Orves
Rue Fortia
Rue Sainte
Rue Lulli
Rue Grignan
RUE BRETEUIL
Musée Cantini
BOULEVARD CHARLES LIVON
Théâtre National de Marseille la Criée
Institut Pasteur
Fort d'Entrecasteaux
LE PHARO
Fort St-Nicolas
AV PASTEUR
Rue Catherine
Rue Rigaud
Rue Neuve Ste-Catherine
Rue Robert
Rue Petit Chantier
Rue de la Croix
R des Tyrans
Rue Sainte
Palais de Justice
Square Juge P Michel
Collège Anatole France
Place de la Corderie H Bergasse
Square B Albrecht
Musée du Santon
RAMPE ST-MAURICE
Rue Salute
Rue Endoume
BOULEVARD DE LA CORDERIE
Rue d Cdt d Surian
Jardin St-Nicolas
Jardin P Puget
COURS PIERRE PUGET
Préfecture
Rue Estrangin
Rue d'Arcole
Rue de Belloi
Rue R de Brignoles
Rue Edouard Delanglade
Caserne d'Aurelle
Rue Crinas
AVENUE DE LA CORSE
Rue du Rempart
Rue d'Endoume
Lycée Technologique du Rempart
Institut des Sourds Muets et Aveugles
TUNNEL PRADO CARÉNAGE
Boulevard Notre Dame
Église St-Philippe Notre-Dame de Lourdes
Rue P Codaccioni
Rue Joël
Rue Tobelem
Rue Sauveur
Rue Decazes
Rue du Coteau
Rue Recher
Rue d'Endoume
Boulevard
ST-VICTOR
Rue Bonnefoy
Rue Montévidéo
Rue Jules Moulet
VAUBAN
Rue Vendôme
Ch du Roucas Blanc
Tellène
Basilique Notre-Dame de la Garde
Place de Venise
Boulevard Vauban
LAMBERT
Bd Marius Thomas
Rue Michel Gachet
Boulevard Bompard
Avenue David
Ch du Vallon
Impasse Valon
Rue Forest
Av du Bois Sacré
Rue Lacédémone

ST-CHARLES
AVENUES
THIERS
CONCEPTION
BAILLE
NOTRE-DAME DUMONT
PREFECTURE
LODI
Lycée St-Charles
Piscine
Observatoire
Jardin Zoologique
Palais Longchamp
Cinq-Avenue-Longchamp
Place H Dunant
Musée
Petit Séminaire
Collège
GARE ST-CHARLES
St-Charles
Square de Narvick
Place des Marseillaises
Lycée V Hugo
Faculté des Sciences
Place A Labadie
Réformés-Canebière
Sq de Stalingrad
École d'Ingénieurs
Place Sébastopol
Place des Capucines
Sq Léon Blum
Universite de Droit d'Economie et des Sciences d'Art Marseille
Eglise des Réformés St-Vincent de Paul
Noailles
Théâtre du Gymnase
Marché des Capucins
Bibliothèque Collège et Lycée Thiers
Place Auguste et François Carli
St-Michel
Place Jean Jaurès
Pl du Chen Saucisse
Notre-Dame du Mont Cours Julien
Place Paul Cézanne
Place Notre-Dame du Mont
Notre-Dame du Mont
École de Méd
Hôpital de la Conception
Couvent du Refuge
Baille
Place de Rome
Préfecture des Bouches-du-Rhone
Hôpital M Levy
Eglise du T S Rosaire
Place Castellane
Castellane
Ecole de Commerce
Hôpital A Paré
Caserne Beauvau
Gare du Prado
BOULEVARD NATIONAL
BOULEVARD MONTRICHER
BOULEVARD PHILIPPON
AV DU MARÉCHAL FOCH
BOULEVARD LONGCHAMP
BOULEVARD DE LA LIBERATION
BOULEVARD JOSEPH THIERRY
BD D'ATHÈNES
BD DUGOMMIER
BD GARIBALDI
LA CANEBIÈRE
COURS LIEUTAUD
RUE DE ROME
RUE D'ITALIE
RUE PARADIS
BOULEVARD BAILLE
COURS GOUFFÉ
AVENUE DE TOULON
AVENUE DU PRADO
RUE MENPENTI
AVENUE DE CORINTHE
BOULEVARD VINCENT DELPUECH
CHEMIN DE L'ARGILE
RUE DU ROUET
A50
D
E
F

# STREET INDEX

3 F Barthélemy, Rue des D3
3 Mages, Rue des D3
3 Rois, Rue des D3

Abbé de l'Epée, Rue E2
Abeilles, Rue des D1
Académie, Rue de l' D3
Adolphe Thiers, Rue E2
Aix, Rue d' C2
A Labadié, Place D2
Alger, Rue d' E4
A Maille, Rue F5
Armeny, Rue D4
Athènes Dugommier, Boulevard d' D2
Aubagne, Rue d' C3
Auguste Blanqui, Rue E3
Auguste et François Carli, Place D3
Autoroute C1

Baille, Boulevard E5
B Albrecht, Square A4
Barbaroux, Rue E2
Belges, Quai des C3
Belsunce, Cours C2
Berceau, Rue du F4
Bergers, Rue des D4
Bernard du Bois, Rue C1
Bir Hakeim, Rue de C3
B Malon, Rue E3
Bois Sacré, Avenue du B5
Bompard, Boulevard A5
Bonnefoy, Rue C5
Bon Pasteur, Rue du C1
Bons Enfants, Rue des E3
Brandis, Rue F4
Breteuil, Rue C3
Briffaut, Rue F3
Brochier, Rue E4
Bruys, Rue de E2

Caisserie, Rue B2
Camas, Rue du F2
Camille Pelletan, Boulevard de C1
Camille, Boulevard E1
Capucines, Place des D2
Castellane, Place D5
Cdt d Surian, Rue d B4
Chape, Rue E2
Charles Livon, Boulevard A3
Chartreaux, Avenue des F1
Château Payan, Rue E3
Chauvelin, Rue E4
Chave, Boulevard E3
Chave, Boulevard F3
Chemin de l'Argile F5
Chemin du Roucas Blanc B5
Chemin du Vallon A5
Chevalier, Rue du B2
Ch Nédelec, Boulevard C1
Cocbert, Rue C2
Command Mages, Rue du E1
Consolat, Rue E2
Coq, Rue du D2
Corderie H Bergasse, Place de la C4
Corderie, Boulevard de la B4
Corinthe, Avenue de E5
Corse, Avenue de la A4
Coteau, Rue du A5
Coutellerie, Rue B2
Crinas, Rue A4
Curiol, Rue D2

Dames, Boulevard des B1
David, Avenue A5
Decazes, Rue A4
Docteur Fiolle, Rue D5
Dominicaines, Rue des C2
Dragon, Rue du C4
Dr Escat, Rue du D5
Dunkerque, Boulevard de B1
Duverger, Rue B1

Ed Dantes, Rue F2
Edmond Rostand, Rue D4
Edouard Delanglade, Rue C4
Espérandieu, Rue E1
Estrangin Pastré, Place C4
Eugène Pierre, Boulevard E2
Evêché, Rue de l' B2

F Arogo, Rue E4
Fauchier, Rue B1
Ferrari, Rue E3
Fongate, Rue D3
Forbin, Rue de B1
Fort Notre Dame, Rue B3
Fortia, Rue C3
F Pauriol, Rue E4
Francis Davso, Rue C3
Fraternite, Quai de la C3
Friedland, Rue E5
F Roosevelt, Cours E2

Garibaldi, Boulevard D2
Géneral de Gaulle, Place du C3
Général Leclerc, Avenue du C1
Gênes, Rue de E5
Goudard, Rue F3
Gouffé, Cours E5
Grand Rue B2
Grignan, Rue C4
Guy Mocquet, Rue D2

Haxon, Rue C3
H Barbusse, Rue C2
H Dunant, Place F1
Héros, Rue D1
Honnorat, Rue D1
Horace Bertin, Rue E3
Hozier, Rue d' B1
Hugueny, Rue F4

Isly, Rue d' F5
Isoard, Rue d' E1
Italie, Rue d' D4

Jardin Zoologique, Boulevard du F1
Jaubert, Rue E2
Jean Charcot, Quai A1
Jean de Bernardy, Rue E1
Jean Jaurès, Place E3
J Guesde, Place C1
J Hébert, Rue F5
Joël Recher, Rue A4
Joliette, Place de la B1
Joliette, Quai de la A2
Joliette, Rue de la B1
Joseph Thierry, Cours D2
J Roque, Rue D3
Juge P Michel, Square C4
Jules Cantini, Avenue D5
Jules Moulet, Rue C4
Julia, Rue F5
Julien, Cours D3

J Verne, Place B2

La Canebière C3
Lacédémone, Rue C5
Lacépède, Rue F1
Lacydon, Rue de B2
L Astruc, Rue F3
Lazaret, Quai du B1
L Bourgeois, Rue E1
Léon Gambetta, Allées D2
L Gozlan, Rue D1
L Grobet, Rue E1
Libération, Boulevard de la E2
Liberté, Boulevard de la D2
Lieutaud, Cours D3
Lieutaud, Cours D4
L Maurel, Rue D5
Locarn, Rue de F3
Lodi, Rue de D4
Loge, Rue de la B3
Longchamp, Boulevard E1
Longue des Capucins, Rue C1
Loubière, Rue de la E4
L Rolmer, Rue C1
Lulli, Rue C3

Malaval, Rue B1
Marceau, Place C1
Marche des Capucins D3
Maréchal Foch, Avenue du F1
Marengo, Rue D4
Marie, Rue de la B2
Marius Thomas, Boulevard A5
Marseillaises, Place des D1
Marx Dormoy, Rue F1
Mazagran, Rue D2
Mazenod, Rue de B2
M Bourdet, Boulevard C2
Melchion, Rue E4
Menpenti, Rue E5
Michel Gachet, Rue A5
Monte Cristo, Rue E2
Montévidéo, Rue C5
Montolieu, Rue B1
Montricher Flammarion, Boulevard F1
Moulins, Place des B2
Moustier, Rue D3
Musée, Rue du D3

National, Boulevard D1
Nationale, Rue C2
Neuve Ste-Catherine, Rue B4
Notre Dame, Boulevard C4
Notre-Dame du Mont, Place D3

Olivier, Rue de l' E3
Oran, Rue d' E2

Palestro, Rue D1
Palud, Rue de la D3
Panier, Rue du B2
Paradis, Rue C3
Pasteur, Avenue A4
Paul Peytrol, Boulevard C4
Pavillon, Rue C3
P Codaccioni, Rue A4
Perrin Solliers, Rue D4
Petit Chantier, Rue du B4
Petit St-Jean, Rue du C2
Philippon, Boulevard F1
Pierre Puget, Cours C4

P Laurent, Rue E4
P Maries, Rue des C2
Port, Quai du A3
Prado Carénage, Tunnel B4
Prado, Avenue du D5
Precheurs, Rue des B2
Progrès, Rue du E2
Protis, Square A2
Pythéas, Rue C3

Rampe St-Maurice A4
R de Brignoles, Rue C4
République, Rue de la B1
Rigaud, Rue B3
Rive Neuve, Quai de B3
Robert, Rue B4
Robert Schuman, Avenue B2
Roger Brun, Rue E5
Rome, Place de D4
Rome, Rue de C3
Rouet, Rue du D5
Rouet, Rue du E5

St-Anislas Torrents, Rue C4
St Bazile, Rue D2
Sainte, Rue B4
Ste Barbe, Rue C2
St-Étienne, Rue F5
Ste-Victoire, Rue D5
St-Ferréol, Rue C3
St-Jacques, Rue C4
St-Laurent, Rue A3
St-Laurent, Tunnel A3
St-Pierre, Rue E3
St-Pierre, Rue F3
Ste-Saëns, Rue C3
St-Savourin, Rue E2
St-Sébastien, Rue D5
Salute, Rue A4
Sante Cécile, Rue E4
Sauveur Tobelem, Rue A4
Sébastopol, Place F2
Sénac de Meilhan, Rue D2
Sibié, Rue D3
Stalingrad, Square de D2
Strasbourg, Place de C1
Sylvabelle, Rue C4

Telléne, Boulevard B4
Terrusse, Rue E3
Thubaneau, Rue D2
Tilsit, Rue E3
Tivoli, Rue E2
Toulon, Avenue de E5
Tourette, Quai de la A2
Turenne, Rue de C1
Tyrans, Rue des B3

Vacon, Rue C3
Vauban, Boulevard C5
Vendôme, Rue A5
Venise, Place de C5
Vertus, Rue des E4
Villeneuve, Rue D2
Vincent Delpuech, Boulevard E5
Vincent Leblanc, Rue B1
Vitalis, Rue F3
Voltaire, Boulevard D1

# MARSEILLE MÉTRO MAP

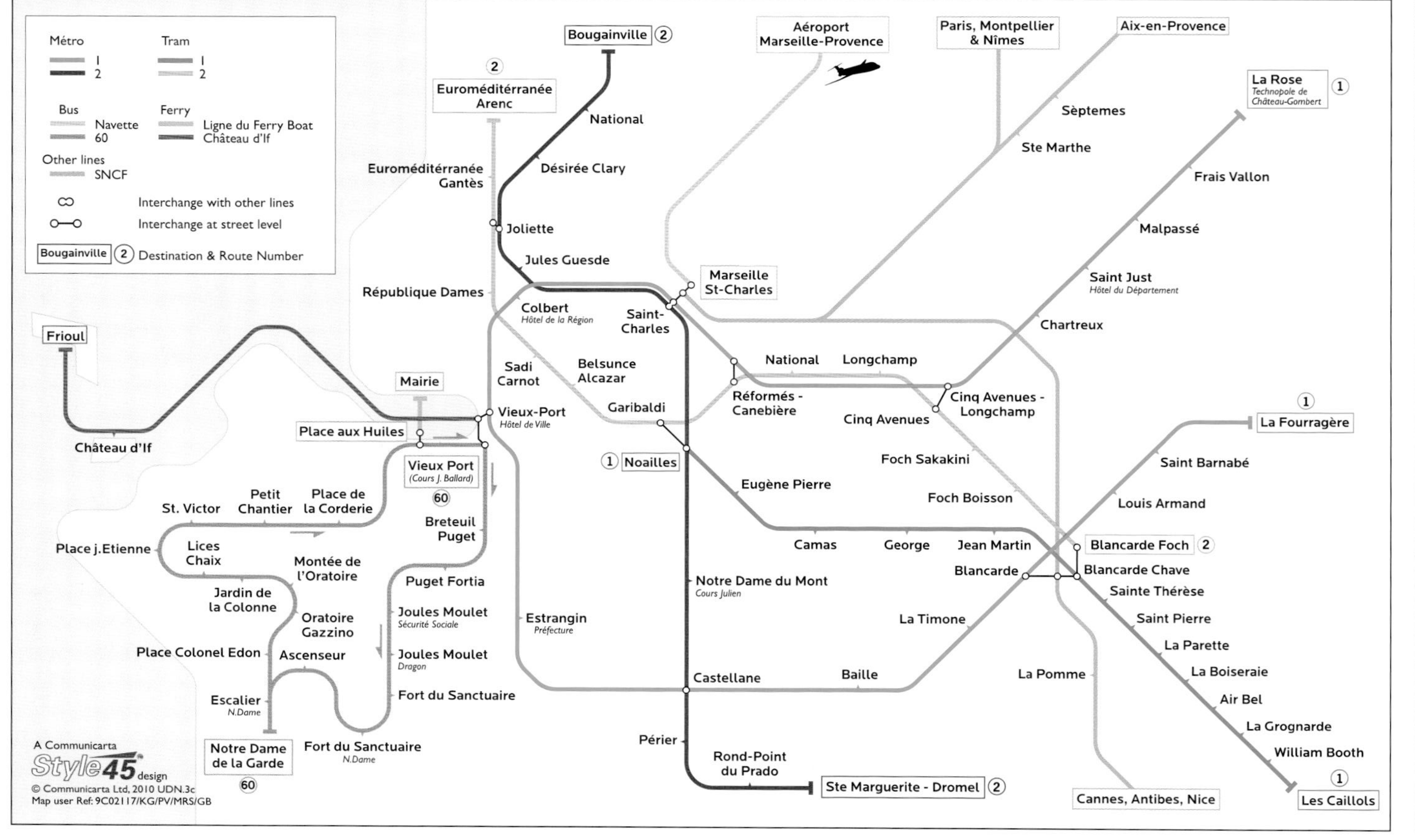

# NÎMES

**INFORMATION**

www.ot-nimes.fr

294 B10 6 rue Auguste, 30020 Nîmes 04 66 58 38 00 Jul, Aug Mon–Fri 8.30–8, Sat 9–7, Sun 10–6; Apr–end Jun, Sep Mon–Fri 8.30–7, Sat 9–7, Sun 10–6; Oct–end Mar Mon–Fri 8.30–6.30, Sat 9–6.30, Sun 10–5 Nîmes

**Above** *The Maison Carrée, beautifully floodlit at night*

## INTRODUCTION

Nîmes has wonderful Roman buildings, including one of the best-preserved amphitheatres of the ancient world. Though the town is outside the Bouches-du-Rhône *département*—it is in the Gard about 16km (10 miles) from the western edges of the Camargue—it was a vital part of Roman Provence.

The size of Nîmes is one of its key attributes. It is large enough to offer the facilities necessary for its visitors, yet small enough—especially in its old city—to generate a feeling of intimacy. The old heart of the city has been tastefully preserved and the narrow alleys are full of high-end boutiques.

Nîmes was an important settlement even before Roman times—a Celtic tribe known as the Volcae-Arecomici chose it as their capital. The Romans arrived in the first century BC. Augustus heaped privileges on the town, encircling it with a monumental wall, 8km (5 miles) long. Soon after, the amphitheatre was added, as well as the Maison Carrée and the Pont du Gard aqueduct (23km/14 miles away), which brought fresh water to the baths and fountains. In the Middle Ages, Nîmes went into decline, and suffered much bloodshed during the Religious Wars, when it sided with the Protestants. When peace returned, the city built up a thriving textile industry. One of its best-selling lines was a hard-wearing blue serge called De Nîmes. This became known as denim after Levi Strauss began, in 1848, to manufacture his famous blue jeans in California. Today, Nîmes has commissioned world-class architects to embellish the city with impressive buildings and monuments.

## WHAT TO SEE

### LES ARÈNES

www.arenes-nimes.com

Nîmes' amphitheatre is one of the best preserved from the Roman world and is the city's top attraction. From the theatre's construction during the late first century AD audiences of more than 23,000 spectators would pour inside, eager to watch gladiators battle against animals or each other at the very heart of the ancient city of Nemausus. During the sixth century, the complex was transformed into a defensive fortress and skirted by a moat. By the 12th century, the amphitheatre's purpose had shifted entirely. Hundreds of locals moved their homes within its protective walls; two churches were even built. It wasn't until the end of the 18th century that restoration commenced.

Today, visitors can explore the tiers of seating surrounding the amphitheatre. Those at the top (21m/69ft above the ground—and with no guard rail) enjoy panoramic views of Nîmes. Behind the scenes, there is a complicated arrangement of arches and passages (those beneath the arena are closed to the public), inspiring wonder at the sheer scale of the building, still much used today, not only for bullfights but for a succession of events and trade fairs. Between October and Easter, an inflatable cover keeps out the rain.

87 B2 Place des Arènes, 30000 Nîmes 04 66 21 82 56 Jul, Aug daily 9–8; Jun daily 9–7; Apr, May, Sep daily 9–6.30; Mar, Oct daily 9–6; Nov–end Feb daily 9.30–5. Closed during some events Adult €7.70, child (7–17) €5.90, under 7 free (combined ticket, Les Arènes, Maison Carrée and Tour Magne: adult €9.80, child (7–17) €7.50)

**TIPS**

» The brass studs in the pavements feature the city symbol, a crocodile and a palm tree.

» Also worth visiting are the Musée de Vieux Nîmes, in place aux Herbes, and the Musée des Beaux-Arts, in rue de la Cité-Foulc.

» Once you've taken in the history, enjoy some retail therapy at La Coupole (www.lacoupole-nimes.fr), a small shopping mall of 50 classy stores.

## MAISON CARRÉE

www.arenes-nimes.com

The Maison Carrée, in the heart of town, is a fully preserved Roman temple. The interior contains a display of panels describing its history, and some beautiful examples of Roman mosaic work. Built in the first century AD

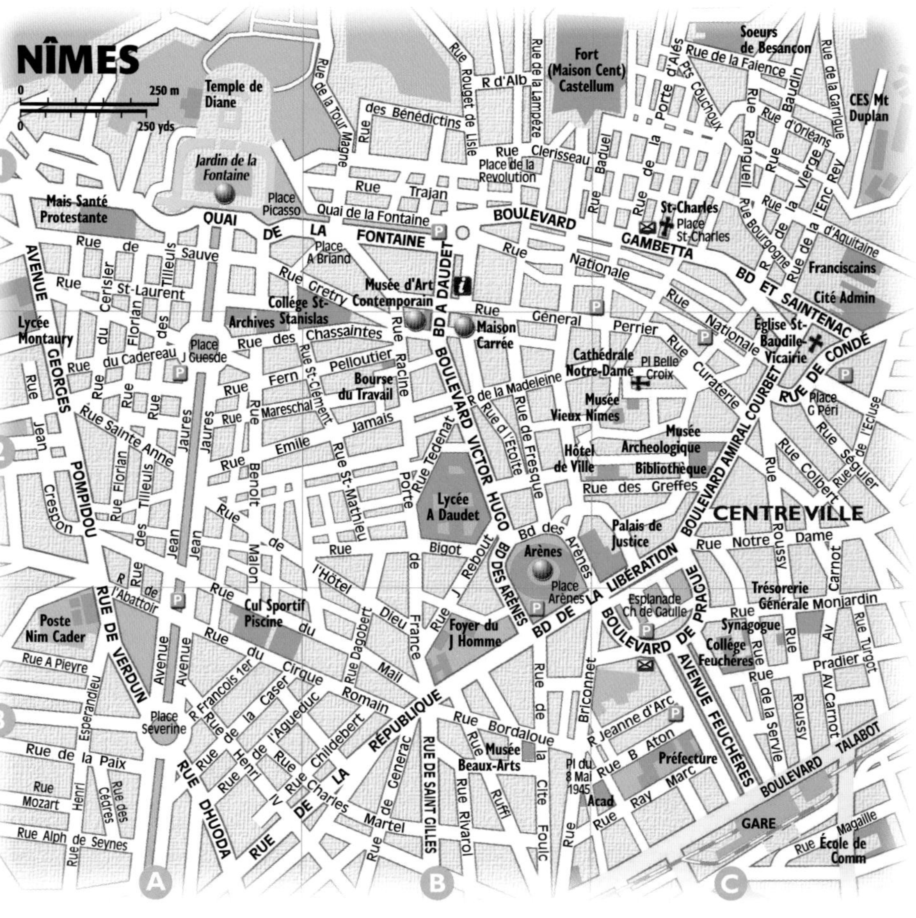

and based on the Temple of Apollo in Rome, it was dedicated to Augustus' grandsons, Caius and Lucius. Surrounded by elegant Corinthian columns, it remains almost perfectly intact, despite having been used as a stable, among other things, in the Middle Ages.

87 B2 Place de la Maison Carrée, 30031 Nîmes 04 66 21 82 56 Jul, Aug daily 10–8; Jun daily 10–7; Apr, May, Sep daily 10–6.30; Mar, Oct daily 10–6 (closed Oct daily 1–2); Nov–end Feb daily 10–1, 2–4.30 Adult €4.50, child (7–17) €3.70, under 7 free

### MUSÉE D'ART CONTEMPORAIN

Rising impressively beside the Maison Carrée, and making a striking contrast, is a gallery of contemporary art and a library designed by Sir Norman Foster. Completed in 1993, the museum has a pleasingly spacious feel and lots of natural light. The artworks date from the 1960s to today, with occasional visiting exhibitions. There's an excellent third-floor bar/restaurant, with an outside terrace overlooking the Maison Carrée.

87 B2 Carrée d'Art-Musée d'Art Contemporain, place de la Maison Carrée, 30031 Nîmes 04 66 76 35 70 Tue–Sun 10–6 Adult €5, under 25 free

### JARDIN DE LA FONTAINE

www.jardinslanguedoc.com

A short walk from the old quarter, the Jardin de la Fontaine is a beautiful park with flowing water, fountains and statues, developed in the 18th century on an ancient site that features an enigmatic temple to Diana. The area above and behind the park, on rising ground, is planted with Mediterranean evergreens, intertwined with paths up to the Tour Magne. The tower has an internal spiral staircase leading to a small viewing platform and excellent views.

87 A1 Apr to mid-Sep daily 7.30am–10pm; mid-Sep to end Mar daily 7.30–6 Free

## MORE TO SEE

### PONT DU GARD

www.pontdugard.fr

A UNESCO World Heritage Site, this aqueduct was built in the first century BC to channel huge amounts of water to the Roman settlement at Nîmes. City engineers carved out the aqueduct from a source near Uzès, 50km (30 miles) away, which necessitated spanning the Gardon river gorge at a height of 48m (156ft). Details such as the fact that no mortar was used, or that the average drop over the entire length of the aqueduct was only 24cm (10in) per km, add to the fascination of the site.

On the left bank, there is a huge parking area, information panels and a pathway leading directly to the exhibition hall, which has been carefully designed and positioned so as not to detract from the site. The exhibition shows how water was used to enrich the civilized lifestyle of the Romans—wealthy households had their own piped supply, public baths were constructed, fountains graced public areas and water powered industry.

Although people are no longer allowed onto the Pont itself, you can walk over the bridge that runs alongside it at the same level as the first tier of arches. By so doing you fully realize the size and weight of the building blocks used in the aqueduct's construction, but to appreciate it fully, you'll need to go up- or downstream for an unimpeded view from a distance.

Off map at 294 C9 Exhibition Centre, Pont du Gard, 30210 Vers-Pont-du-Gard 0820 903 330 Museum: May–end Sep Mon 2–7, Tue–Sun 9–7; Oct Mon 2–6, Tue–Sun 9–6; Nov–end Apr Mon 2–5, Tue–Sun 9–5. Site: daily 7am–1am Parking ticket (€5) gives entrance to the site. Museum: €7. Film (25 min): €4

**Left** *A statue in the Jardin de la Fontaine*
**Opposite** *One of the many fountains in the Jardin de la Fontaine*

**Above** *The Montagne Sainte-Victoire was a favourite subject of artist Paul Cézanne*

## MARTIGUES

www.martigues-tourisme.com

Once a popular spot among the Impressionists, Martigues is curiously located on a narrow strip of land with the Mediterranean on one side and the large Étang de Berre on the other. Linking the two is the Canal de Caronte, the town's main canal, while other picturesque waterways link the three separate 'villages' that make up Martigues.

Jonquières, on the southern side of the main canal, is the best village to try if you are looking for a meal or a drink. Among its tangled lanes and narrow, traffic-free streets are markets, shops and bars.

As its name suggests, the second village, L'Île (The Island), sits in the middle of the canal. Here is the lovely Église Sainte-Madeleine-de-l'Île, as well as several 17th- and 18th-century houses. Stand on the bridge at quai Brescon, next to the Église Sainte-Madeleine-de-l'Île, to admire the famous view of fishing boats moored on a curve of the canal. The scene, known as the *Miroir des Oiseaux* (the bird's mirror), was painted by Félix Ziem.

For art, head to the Musée Ziem, in Martigues' third village, Ferrières. The museum, on boulevard du 14 Juillet, has works by Ziem (1821–1911) and others (Jul, Aug Wed–Sun 10–12, 2.30–6.30; Sep–end Jun Wed–Sun 2.30–6.30).

An attractive range of low hills, the Chaîne de l'Estaque, runs along the coast between Martigues and Marseille, offering good sea views.

300 E12 Maison du Tourisme, Rond Point de l'Hôtel de Ville, 13500 Martigues 04 42 42 31 10 Easter–end May Mon–Sat 9–12.30, 1.30–5.45, Sun 10–12.30; Jun Mon–Fri 9–6, Sat 9.30–12.30, 2.30–6, Sun 9.30–12.30; Jul Mon–Fri 9–7, Sat 9.30–12.30, 2.30–6, Sun 9.30–12.30; Aug Mon–Fri 9–6.30, Sat 9.30–12.30, 2.30–6, Sun 9.30–12.30; Sep–Easter Mon–Sat 9–12, 1.45–5.30, Sun 10–12.30 Gare Martigues-Caronte

## MIRAMAS-LE-VIEUX

www.miramas.org/tourisme

Overlooking the thriving modern town of Miramas is its fortified hilltop quarter, Miramas-le-Vieux. Here the streets have been recobbled to create the kind of medieval *village perché* (perched village) you are more likely to come across in the Vaucluse. In summer you can enjoy concerts in the evocative ruins of the old chateau.

295 E11 24 avenue Falabrègues, 13140 Miramas 04 90 58 08 24 Mon–Fri 8.30–12, 1.30–6, Sat 9–12 Miramas

## MONTAGNE SAINTE-VICTOIRE

Artist Paul Cézanne loved this huge, sunlit wedge of limestone rising in the Provençal countryside east of Aix. Each afternoon he would walk from the city to capture views of the mountain, repeating this same subject endlessly, exploring the ideas of structure, form and light that it inspires. He often conveyed it as a blue-grey pyramid rising strangely above ochre soil and dark green trees.

To the ordinary eye the mountain might appear less awesome—its highest peak, Pic des Mouches, rises to only 1,010m (3,300ft)—but more satisfying as part of a rugged, dry, unchanging landscape that epitomizes Provence. The mountain is encircled by minor roads (the D10 on the north, D17 on the south) giving easy access to its viewpoints and trails. Just off the D10, the Barrage de Bimont (7km/4 miles from Aix-en-Provence) is an impressive structure damming the river Infernet to form an artificial lake, the Lac du Bimont. The area has been turned into a pleasant park.

Farther along the D10, a marked trail near Les Cabassols farm leads up the steep 3km (2-mile) path to La Croix de Provence, the peak at the western end of the mountain. Allow several hours to do this walk, as the path is difficult, but the reward is an awesome vista extending across waves of blue and purple hills.

Vauvenargues (▷ 96), on the D10, is a pretty village. The 17th-century chateau on a rock nearby was the home of artist Pablo Picasso.

At the southeastern end of the mountain is the village of Pourrières, supposedly named (from *pourri*, rotten) for the thousands of corpses of Teutons piled here after their defeat by Romans in 102BC. From here to Puyloubier, south of the mountain on the D17, is vine country producing rosé wines. For a drive, ▷ 96–97.

296 H11

## NÎMES

▷ 86–89.

# SAINTES-MARIES-DE-LA-MER

A picturesque medieval coastal town with sandy beaches, Saintes-Maries makes a perfect base for visits into the heart of the Camargue (▷ 74–75). As a medieval fortified port on the Mediterranean, with its own sandy beaches to the east, it has become the visitor capital of the Camargue region. Sports facilities include bicycle rental, horseback riding and plenty of water sports. A profusion of bird life lives in the adjacent lagoons and herds of half-wild white horses roam free in the watery terrain just outside town. The unusual name ('Holy Maries of the Sea') comes from a medieval legend that Mary Magdalene, together with St. Marie-Jacobé, sister or sister-in-law of the Virgin Mary, and St. Marie-Salomé, mother of the Apostles James and John, sailed across the Mediterranean from the Holy Land and landed here on the Camargue coast. Accompanying them on their journey were other biblical characters and their Ethiopian servant Sarah.

## MAIN SIGHTS

The town is dominated by the sturdy fortified Romanesque church (Mon–Sat 8–12.30, 2–7, Sun 8–10.30, 2–7) with its curious open bell tower. Its heavy defences date from the 12th century, and were put in place as a protection against Saracen raiders then harassing the Provençal coast. Inside the church are ancient wooden statues of Sarah. A tower standing on a corner next to the church, in rue Victor Hugo, houses the Musée Baroncelli (Apr–end Sep Wed–Mon 10–12, 2–6), which displays some interesting local historical finds. The museum tower and the church tower both give wonderful views of the town, the sea and the Camargue flatlands.

## A GYPSY CAPITAL

On landing, Mary Magdalene is said to have travelled farther into Provence, while the other two Maries and Sarah remained at Saintes-Maries, where Sarah became patron saint of gypsies. She is known among Roma people as Sarah-la-Kali, or Sarah the Black. Huge, vibrant, traditional gypsy gatherings and processions in her memory are held here annually on 24 and 25 May. Although they come from all over Europe, most of the gypsies are Spanish. Gypsy caravans are a permanent feature of the area around the town, as is Spanish entertainment such as flamenco, put on for visitors.

## INFORMATION

www.saintesmaries.com

294 B12 5 avenue Van Gogh, 13460 Saintes-Maries-de-la-Mer

04 90 97 82 55 Jul, Aug daily 9–8; Apr–end Jun, Sep daily 9–7; Mar, Oct daily 9–6; Nov–end Feb daily 9–5

## TIP

» The area beside the beach is the best place to find somewhere to park.

**Below** *The red rooftops of Saintes-Maries-de-la-Mer*

# ST-RÉMY-DE-PROVENCE

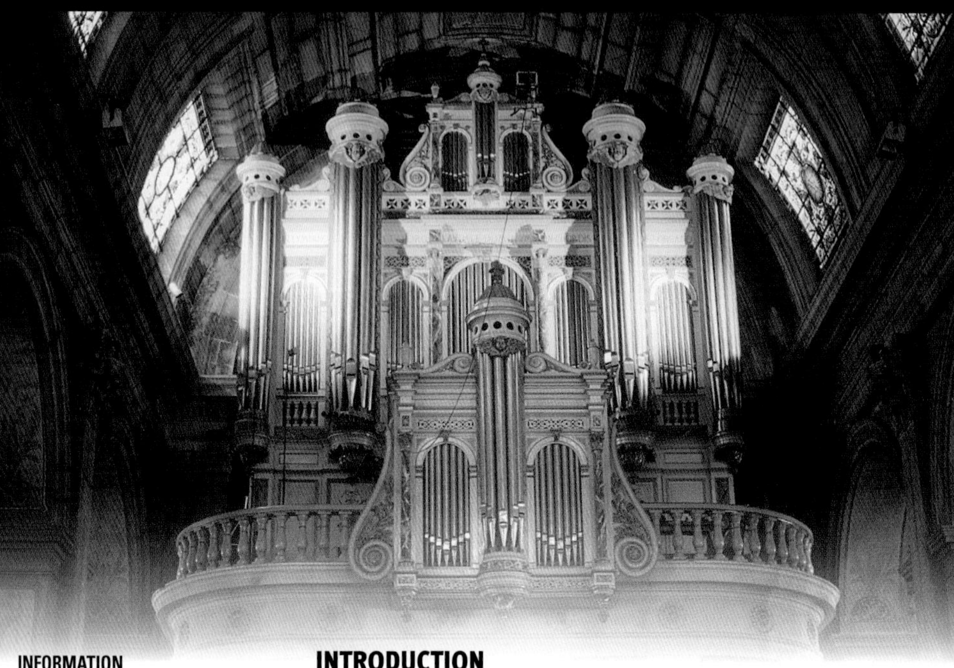

**INFORMATION**

www.saintremy-de-provence.com
294 D10 Place Jean Jaurès, 13210 St-Rémy-de-Provence 04 90 92 05 22 Easter–end Oct Mon–Sat 9–12.30, 2–7, Sun 10–12; Nov–Easter Mon–Sat 9–12, 2–6

**Above** *The vast organ at the Collegiale St-Martin*

## INTRODUCTION

St-Rémy is a bustling little town noted for its fruit, vegetables and wine, and for the ruins of Graeco-Roman Glanum, nearby. The town, which sits in countryside 5km (3 miles) north of the Alpilles hills, has many good small shops specializing in local gastronomy, antiques, pottery and traditional Provençal arts and crafts. There are few sights of importance within the town itself, but the small old quarter is pleasant, with narrow streets, plant-filled alleyways, quiet tree-shaded squares and cooling fountains. Many fine 16th- to 18th-century mansions can be seen in this quarter, and there are some small art galleries and museums. From April to October the tourist office runs a 90-minute guided tour, called 'In the steps of Van Gogh', visiting sights that the artist painted (Tue, Thu, Fri at 10am). The tour gives reduced entry fees for St-Paul-de-Mausole and the Centre d'Art Présence Van Gogh. Alternatively, there is a self-guided tour using a map from the tourist office.

St-Rémy's main attraction is about 1km (0.6 miles) south of town, where the archaeological site of the important Graeco-Roman town of Glanum (▷ 94) is located. You can take a taxi to Glanum, or reach it on foot in 10 to 15 minutes. Long before St-Rémy existed, Glanum had been built by Greek merchants from Massalia (Marseille) and had become a large, prosperous town. Taken over by the Romans, it continued to thrive until it was destroyed by Visigoths in the third/fourth centuries AD, after which the medieval town of St-Rémy grew up about 1km (0.6 miles) away. It became an important hub for the Alpilles and surrounding region.

One of St-Rémy's most illustrious sons was the astrologer Nostradamus (1503–66), whose predictions in his book *Centuries* extend even to today (▷ 34). St-Rémy also has connections to the 19th-century writer Frédéric Mistral (▷ 37), who grew up in a nearby village, and to Vincent Van Gogh. The artist came for a year (1889–90) to the nursing home at St-Paul-de-Mausole monastery (▷ 94) to seek help for depression. Cared for there by doctors and nuns, he tried to find peace of mind and to a large extent succeeded, albeit temporarily. He spent much time walking in and around the town, painting and drawing constantly. He left St-Rémy on 16 May 1890 to go to a clinic at Auvers-sur-Oise. He committed suicide a few weeks later on 29 July 1890. The Van Gogh connection has helped to make St-Rémy popular with artists and writers, such as the American novelist Gertrude Stein, who lived here in the 1920s.

## WHAT TO SEE

### OLD QUARTER

Encircled by a boulevard of plane trees, the heart of town is a warren of narrow streets and small squares with many grand houses. On the edge of the boulevard is place de la République, with an outdoor café. The Hôtel Gounod de la Ville Verte has been here for some 150 years—Charles Gounod composed the Provençal opera *Mireio* while staying here in 1864, and American author Gertrude Stein had a room here for a year in the 1920s. Facing the square is Collegiale St-Martin, with its famous modern organ, restored in 1982 and said to be one of the best contemporary organs in Europe. Recitals take place on Saturday evenings in summer. Behind St-Martin, in place Favier, are several fine Renaissance mansions—some house museums devoted to local folk culture, modern art and archaeology. Part of the house where Nostradamus was born in 1503 can be seen in rue Hoche, though it is not open to the public.

### LES ANTIQUES

Standing beside the road (D5) across from the entrance of Glanum (▷ 94), two remarkable Roman structures survive, known as Les Antiques. For many centuries, these two structures were the only visible remnants of Glanum, and it was not known that they were Roman. One of these is a two-level memorial, 18m (59ft) high and very well preserved, decorated with carvings and reliefs, dating to about 30BC and traditionally known locally as the Mausolée des Jules. It is not, however, a mausoleum and appears to have been erected by members of a Roman family in memory of their parents. Alongside is an arch, probably by Greek craftspeople (though the tiled roof was added in the 18th century), which is now thought to have marked the entrance to Glanum.

✉ Avenue Vincent Van Gogh/Routes des Baux (D5), 1km (0.6 miles) south of St-Rémy-de-Provence 💰 Free (unsupervised) access

### TIPS

» There are interesting wineries all around the town, such as Château Romanin (www.romanin.com), off the D99.

» St-Rémy makes an attractive base for visits to Les Baux-de-Provence (▷ 72–73) and Les Alpilles (▷ 76).

» To find out more about local folklore, geology and ethnology, head to the Musée des Alpilles, in place Favier.

**Below** *The arch at Les Antiques is thought to have marked the entrance to Glanum*

## ST-PAUL-DE-MAUSOLE

www.cloitresaintpaul-valetudo.com

Just outside the Glanum site is the beautiful old monastery of St-Paul-de-Mausole, where Vincent Van Gogh committed himself voluntarily for a year's rest and treatment in 1889 after mutilating his ear. It was one of the most productive periods of his life—he turned out 150 paintings and 100 drawings in 12 months, mainly set in and around the town and the sanatorium. It is still a private sanatorium for those with mental health problems. The monastery's Romanesque church and cloisters are open to the public. There is a permanent exhibition of pictures painted by the patients. These paintings are available for sale, together with Van Gogh prints—all proceeds go towards the upkeep of the hospital. The monastery's giftshop also stocks postcards, notebooks and other souvenirs printed with a range of Van Gogh's most famous paintings.

It's well worth following Van Gogh's serene trail from St-Paul-de-Mausole back into St-Rémy. The path, clearly indicated, meanders from the monastery, along quiet country roads and past 21 reproductions of Van Gogh's paintings. Each image has been positioned on the very spot from which Van Gogh created it. You can pick up maps from the St-Rémy tourist office.

✉ Avenue Vincent Van Gogh/Routes des Baux (D5), 13210 St-Rémy-de-Provence ☎ 04 90 92 77 00 ⏲ Apr–end Sep daily 9.30–7; Oct–end Dec, Feb, Mar daily 10.15–5. Closed Jan 🎟 Adult €4, under 12 free

GLANUM PLAN

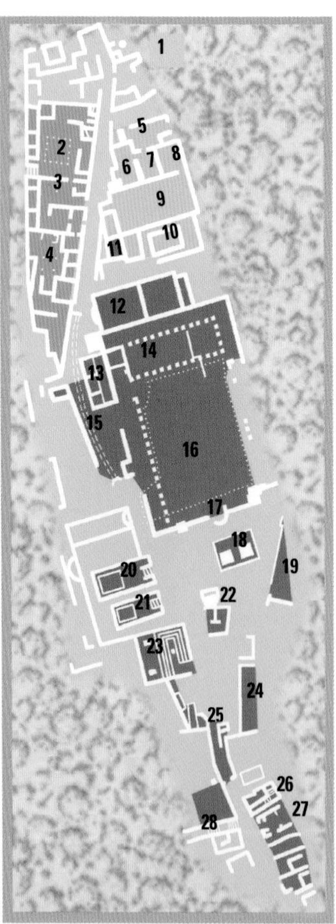


## GLANUM

http://glanum.monuments-nationaux.fr

The archaeological site of Glanum, extending over a large enclosed area of ruins next to Les Antiques and St-Paul-de-Mausole and running beside the road (D5), has been under excavation for more than 20 years. It covers three cultural periods, all of which have left extensive relics—Greek, early Roman and late Roman. Glanum is important in the study of the spread of Greek culture. It is a site rich in significance for the expert, and for the casual visitor, too, the layered excavations are fascinating. Especially interesting are the Forum (or main square) of the Roman town, the Baths and a sacred well of the Greek period. The sites of several large private houses can be made out, as well as Greek temples—one of which has been partly reconstructed using ancient tools and techniques.

✉ Glanum, avenue Vincent Van Gogh/Routes des Baux (D5), 1km (0.6 miles) south of St-Rémy-de-Provence ☎ 04 90 92 23 79 ⏲ Apr–end Sep daily 9.30–6.30 (closed Mon in Sep); Oct–end Mar Tue–Sun 10–5 🎟 Adult €7, 18–25 €4.50, under 18 free

**1** Basin of fountain

**GREEK PERISTYLE HOUSES**

**2** Maison des Antes
**3** Maison de Cybèle
**4** Maison d'Atys

**ROMAN BATHS**

**5** Heating Chamber
**6** Caldarium (hot water)
**7** Tepidarium (tepid water)
**8** Frigidarium (cold water)
**9** Palaestra (courtyard)
**10** Natatio (swimming pool)

**OTHER EXCAVATIONS**

**11** Maison de Capricorne
**12** Building with apse
**13** Basilica
**14** House of Sulla
**15** Covered water channel
**16** Forum
**17** Wall with apse
**18** Monument or altar
**19** Roman theatre
**20/21** Roman temple
**22** Well
**23** Buleuterion (council chamber)
**24** Hall with Doric columns
**25** Fortified Gate
**26** Nympheum (presumably above the sacred well of Glanum)
**27** Altars (dedicated to Hercules)
**28** Celtic shrine

### ST-CHAMAS

St-Chamas, near the Étang de Berre, was once a fishing village but has turned its attention to yachting and tourism. Its church has a striking 17th-century baroque facade. Outside the village is Pont Flavien, a first-century AD Roman bridge framed by two triumphal arches.

300 E11 Montée des Pénitents 04 90 50 90 54 Mid-Jun to mid-Sep Mon–Sat 9–12, 2–6; mid-Sep to mid-Jun Mon–Sat 9–12, 1.30–5.30

### ST-RÉMY-DE-PROVENCE

▷ 92–94.

### SALON-DE-PROVENCE

www.visitsalondeprovence.com

The large industrial town of Salon sits between the Crau plain and the hills of western Provence and at the crossroads of roads linking Arles, Avignon, Aix and Marseille. Its fortunes were founded on soap-making and olive oil. Sights include the Maison de Nostradamus, at 11 rue Nostradamus in the old quarter (Mon–Fri 9–12, 2–6, Sat, Sun 2–6). This was home to the astrologer Michel de Nostradame and is now a museum of his life. Nostradamus moved here from St-Rémy in 1547 and remained until his death in 1566. It was here he wrote the prophetic tome *Centuries*. Nearby is a 17th-century gateway, Porte de l'Horloge, with a beautiful encrusted 18th-century fountain, called the Grand Fontaine, opposite. Nostradamus' tomb is in the Église St-Laurent, in the north of the town.

Château de l'Empéri, in place des Centuries, dates back to the 10th century and houses the Musée de l'Art et d'Histoire Militaire (Wed–Mon 10–12, 2–6).

295 E11 56 cours Gimon, 13300 Salon-de-Provence 04 90 56 27 60 Jul, Aug Mon–Sat 9.30–6.30, Sun 9.45–12.15; Sep–end Jun Mon–Sat 9.30–12.30, 2–6 Salon

### TARASCON

www.tarascon.org

A former river port rising from the banks of the Rhône midway between Avignon and Arles, Tarascon is at the heart of a busy enterprise zone. It calls itself La Plus Douce des Villes Industrielles—the gentlest of industrial towns. Dominating the town is a magnificent white castle, a fairytale spectacle on the riverbank.

The town's main commercial activities revolve around food, especially preserves and canned fruit. There is also a tradition of cloth-making using vivid hues in the Provençal style, which can be explored at the beautiful Musée Souleïado, in a handsome private mansion at 39 rue Proudhon, in the old quarter (www.souleiado-lemusee.com; Tue–Sat 10–5). The town is frequently in a festive mood, with fairs, including an Orchid Festival in February, a medieval fête in September and a market in November dedicated to *santons* (traditional figurines).

Tarascon's immaculate castle (Apr–end Aug daily 9–7; Sep–end Mar Tue–Sun 10.30–5) stands on boulevard du Roi René, by the river. In the Middle Ages, the equally mighty fortresses of Tarascon and Beaucaire faced each other across the Rhône. While Beaucaire has fallen into ruin, Tarascon has been restored to near-perfect condition, complete with massive walls, turrets and towers and a bridge across the moat. Once the luxurious palace of Good King René (▷ 33), Tarascon is now one of the finest medieval chateaux in France. Built from 1400 to 1449, the defensive exterior is in sharp contrast to an elegantly styled interior. Particularly notable are the great fireplaces, mullioned windows, banquet hall and flamboyant *cour d'honneur*, where a spiral staircase makes its way to royal apartments decorated with sumptuous tapestries. From the Revolution to the 1920s, the castle was used as a prison—there is some graffiti by 18th-century English prisoners.

Tarascon is known too for its legendary or fictitious figures—the *Tarasque*, a monster banished by St. Martha (▷ 33), and the *Tartarin*, a 19th-century comic character created by Alphonse Daudet.

294 C10 16 boulevard Itam, 13150 Tarascon 04 90 91 03 52 Jul, Aug Mon–Sat 9–12, 2–7, Sun 9.30–12.30; Sep Mon–Fri 9–12, 2–6, Sat 9–12, 2–5; Oct–end Jun Mon–Fri 9–12, 2–6, Sat 9–12, 2–5 Tarascon

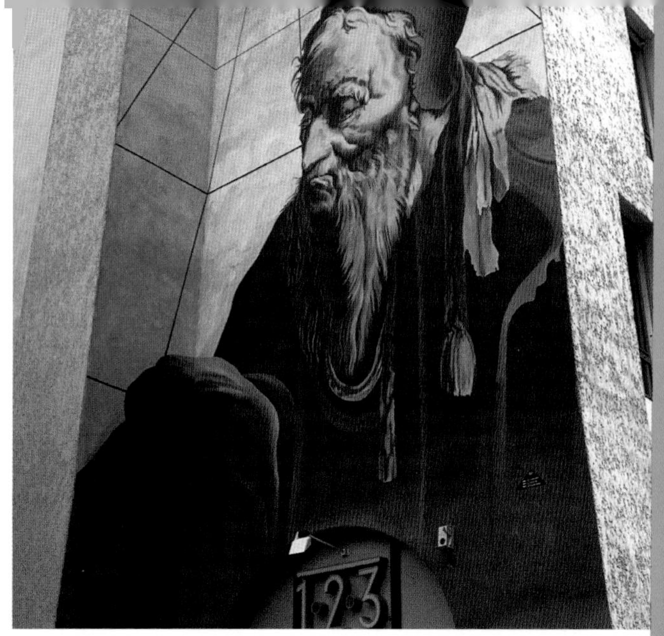


**Above** *A mural on the Maison de Nostradamus depicts the famous astrologer*

# THE HEART OF PROVENCE

**This tour starts in Aix-en-Provence and takes in the Montagne Sainte-Victoire, which inspired the painter Paul Cézanne, before turning south towards the Massif de la Sainte-Baume, where you'll have a view to Marseille. The roads are narrow in places and hilly in others, but this makes the drive interesting rather than arduous.**

**THE DRIVE**
**Distance:** 135km (84 miles)
**Time:** 1 day
**Start/end at:** Aix-en-Provence

★ The heart of Aix-en-Provence (▷ 65–67) is the cours Mirabeau, a wide boulevard planted with a double row of plane trees that provides welcome shade from the summer sun. North of here lies Vieil Aix, the oldest and most charming section of the city.

Leave Aix-en-Provence on the D10, heading towards St-Marc-Jaumegarde and Vauvenargues, to reach the Barrage de Bimont after about 7km (4 miles).

❶ The lake behind the Barrage de Bimont dam provides water for local towns. You can take a walk here if you wish.

Continue on the D10 to Vauvenargues.

❷ The pretty village of Vauvenargues is famous for its Renaissance chateau, inherited by Pablo Picasso in 1958. The artist died here in 1973 and is buried within the extensive grounds. The park and chateau are not regularly open to the public.

Rejoin the D10 by driving straight through the village (there is only one road). The D10, now signed for Jouques and Rians, runs along the northern flank of the Montagne Sainte-Victoire.

❸ The Montagne Sainte-Victoire (▷ 90) was a great inspiration to the artist Paul Cézanne.

Bear right shortly, following the D223 signed for Rians. The road narrows and climbs, but offers good views all the way. At the next major intersection, take a left turn (no sign). This is the D23 towards Rians, which ends at an intersection with the D3. Take a right turn, signed for Ollières and St-Maximin-la-Sainte-Baume. Approaching St-Maximin, turn left at the traffic lights, then right and left again as you cross St-Maximin.

❹ St-Maximin-la-Sainte-Baume has a wonderful basilica that is the best example of Gothic architecture in Provence. It was built on the site of a sixth-century church that was, according to local legend, the resting place for the remains of St. Mary Magdalene. Construction of the new basilica started in 1295 and continued until the 16th century, although no belfry was ever built and the west front was unfinished.

At a roundabout, go straight over to take the N560 signposted Nans-les-Pins. Bear right as the main road bears left. This smaller road goes under a railway bridge and is signed for Aubagne, Marseille and St-Zacharie. Continue for 100m (110 yards), then turn left at traffic lights. Go straight over at the next traffic lights on to the D64, signed Mazaugues. Follow the D64 until it reaches the D1 and turn right towards Rougiers. Turn left off the D1 into the village at the sign for Rougiers *centre*, and left again at the café/*tabac* up the rue Sainte-Anne. This goes uphill towards a ruin and a church that you'll see on top of the hill ahead. It then bears sharp left and goes through an open barrier, before continuing up the valley. Go over a crest and down to an intersection. Turn right onto the D95 (only the back of the sign is visible, so to check you are on the right road make sure the wrong side indicates Plan-d'Aups). Go past signs warning of deer, and continue to the Hôtellerie at La Sainte-Baume.

❺ The Hôtellerie is a 19th-century restoration of a Dominican friars' pilgrim hostel, dating from medieval times. It has now become an international base for spiritual studies.

Continue on the D80 through Plan-d'Aups, after which the road widens. At the next intersection, bear right onto a road signed for Auriol, which joins the D45A to make a long, twisty descent around many hairpin bends. When you reach the N560 at a roundabout, take the first exit signed St-Zacharie. When you reach the village, continue until a road on the left, the D85, is signed Trets and Col du Petit Galibier. Stay on this road, later the D12, which climbs, providing fine views, to reach Trets.

❻ Trets was originally Roman, but much of the current town dates from the Middle Ages. You can see the remains of medieval walls, as well as square 14th-century towers and a castle and church that date from the 15th century.

Approaching Trets, turn left at a roundabout, go straight over a mini-roundabout, and bear left at the next intersection to approach a roundabout with a fountain. Bear left here too onto the D908, signed Peynier.

❼ The village of Peynier has a pleasant Romanesque church.

Pass Peynier to the south and climb through wooded hills. After 4km (2.5 miles) take the D46C to the right, signed for Belcodène, and go through the village following signs for Fuveau. At a fork in the road, keep right, go over the *autoroute* and enter Fuveau. Turn left and right into the main square, then, almost immediately, take the first street on the left, which is the road to Aix-en-Provence and Gardanne. At a roundabout with a central fountain, take the exit signed for Aix and continue to the N96. Turn right and follow this road and the N7 to Aix.

## WHERE TO EAT

There is a good choice of restaurants and brasseries in St-Maximin-la-Sainte-Baume.

## INFORMATION

**HÔTELLERIE LA SAINTE-BAUME**
www.hotellerie-saintebaume.com
✉ Outside the village of Plan-d'Aups
☎ 04 42 04 54 84

**Opposite** *The Château Picasso, in Vauvenargues, where the artist died*

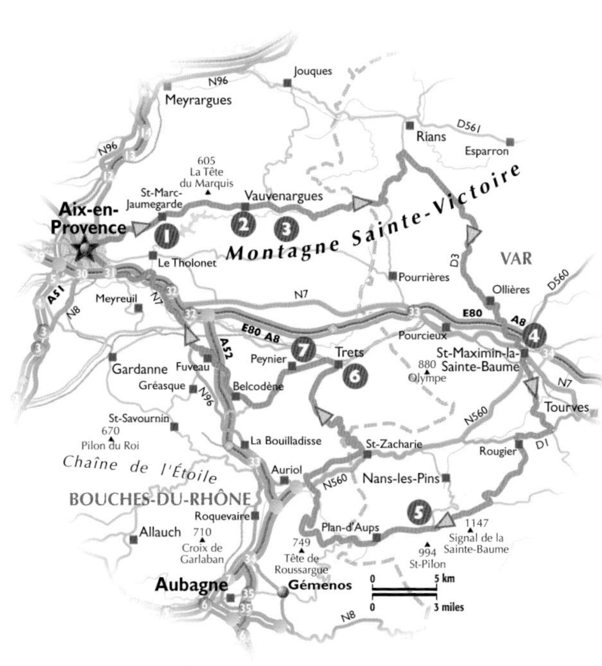

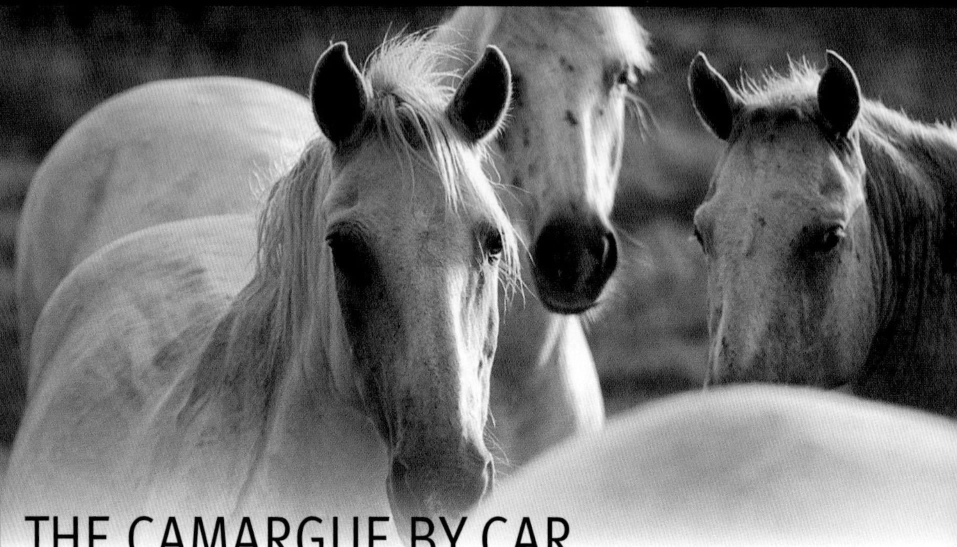

# THE CAMARGUE BY CAR

**The Camargue—the Rhône delta—is huge, and comparatively few roads penetrate its marshy secrets. To see herds of grazing Camargue bulls watched over by their cowboy *gardians*, and far more birds than can be seen from the roads, consider supplementing the drive by taking a boat trip from a town such as Saintes-Maries-de-la-Mer, or hiking or cycling (▷ 100–101) into the marshlands. As with many driving tours of the Camargue, this one begins in Arles, famous for its Roman legacies and as the haunt of artist Vincent Van Gogh.**

**THE DRIVE**
**Distance:** 95km (59 miles)
**Time:** 1 day
**Start/end at:** Arles

★ Arles (▷ 68–71), on the Rhône and north of the Camargue, has exceptionally well-preserved Roman remnants and a good art museum, Musée Réattu (▷ 70), with works by artists including Dufy and Gauguin.

Head west from Arles and cross the Grand Rhône. Take the D570 (signed for Saintes-Maries-de-la-Mer) to Albaron, once a powerful stronghold but now fighting off the sea with pumping stations rather then repelling human invaders. From here take the D37 to Méjanes.

❶ Méjanes is a small lakeside resort with a narrow-gauge railway, a bullring and ponies and horses for rent.

From here, follow the D37 as it runs past the Étang de Vaccarès, the largest of the Camargue's lagoons.

❷ The Étang de Vaccarès (▷ 75) is part of a nature reserve called the Réserve Nationale de Camargue, which has its visitor office and headquarters at La Capelière. On this stretch, stop the car at any of the laybys (pull-offs) and the distinctive smell of marsh immediately becomes apparent—a combination of salt, rotting vegetation and growing plants.

At Villeneuve, turn south towards La Capelière.

It's easy to miss the excellent visitor centre—keep a lookout for the sign and be ready to turn off the road on the left. There are marked nature trails to walk along, and the 1.5km (1-mile) path around the building has signs giving details about the area's plants and animals.

Continue south past Salin-de-Badon, noted for its birds, to Salin-de-Giraud.

❸ Salin-de-Giraud is the best known of the region's salt-producing towns. The tree-lined avenues are dominated by the Solvay refinery, where glittering piles of salt can be glimpsed through the railings.

Now take the D36 north as it slices through the marshy land to the west of the sluggish Grand Rhône. Eventually it joins the D570, which leads back to Arles.

**WILDLIFE OF THE CAMARGUE**
The Camargue is famous for its dazzling white horses and unique black bulls, but this wilderness is also home to countless birds, including ducks, waders and geese.

The wide, shallow lagoons provide excellent feeding grounds for swans, avocets and egrets, while the freshwater reed beds are used as nesting sites by bitterns, herons and warblers. Surveys have also recorded 24,000 pink flamingoes here, a truly spectacular sight. Perhaps the most remarkable of the creatures that thrive here is the brine shrimp, a crustacean just over 1.5cm (0.6in) long. It has evolved in such a way that it can live in virtually fresh or very salty water with equal ease, and so is able to survive both floods and droughts.

## INFORMATION
### RÉSERVE NATIONALE DE CAMARGUE

www.reserve-camargue.org
✉ Centre d'Information de la Réserve Nationale de Camargue, La Capelière, 13200
☎ 04 90 97 00 97

## WHERE TO EAT
### RESTAURANT DE MÉJANES

www.mejanes.camargue.fr
Generous country cooking.
✉ Domaine de Méjanes, on the D37 about 4km (2.5 miles) south of Albaron ☎ 04 90 97 10 51 ⏱ Easter to mid-Oct open for lunch daily, dinner by reservation

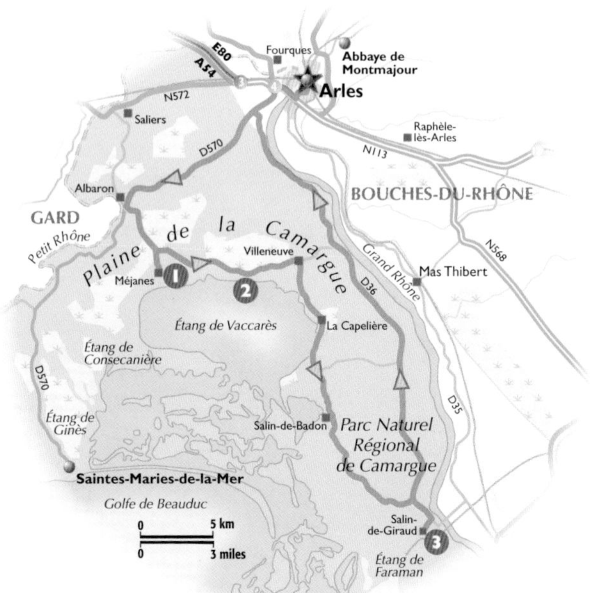


**Opposite** *The Camargue is famous for its white horses*
**Below** *The shore of the Étang de Vaccarès*

# BICYCLE TOUR

## THE CAMARGUE BY BICYCLE

**Bicycling is a good way to explore the flat, sometimes blustery, distances of the Camargue. This circular route is 20km (12.5 miles) and makes an excellent bicycle tour. It begins in Saintes-Maries-de-la-Mer, where you'll find several places that rent bicycles; the tourist office on avenue Van Gogh has a list. The route takes in the Parc Ornithologique du Pont de Gau, perfect for birdwatching.**

### THE BICYCLE TOUR

**Distance:** 20km (12.5 miles)
**Time:** 1.5 hours to 4 hours, depending on how long you spend at the bird reserve and if you do the extra 10km (6-mile) detour to the Château d'Avignon
**Start/end at:** Saintes-Maries-de-la-Mer

★ Saintes-Maries-de-la-Mer (▷ 91) is named after Mary Magdalene, Marie-Salomé (the mother of James and John the Apostles) and Marie-Jacobé (the sister or sister-in-law of the Virgin Mary), who were said to have landed here by boat from the Holy Land with Sarah, their servant. Sarah is the patron saint of gypsies and there is a large festival in her memory every May. In the crypt of the fortified Romanesque church is the black statue of Sarah, often draped in chiffon.

Leave Saintes-Maries on the D85A (also called the route de Cacharel), a minor road that runs between the Réserve Départementale des Impériaux et du Malagroy on your right and the Étang de Ginès on the left. After 4km (2.5 miles) the road bears left (there's a good view east here near the Mas de Cacharel), while an alternative route branches off right to Méjanes. After 6km (4 miles) the D85A joins the D570, the main road, at Pioch-Badet. For a longer trip, turn right and cycle 5km (3 miles) to the Château d'Avignon (closed on Tuesdays), with its collection of 19th-century furniture and contemporary art exhibitions in the gardens during the summer months. Heading south back towards Saintes-Maries will bring you past the Maison du Parc Naturel Régional de Camargue, with its environmental displays, and the Parc Ornithologique du Pont de Gau (▷ 75), with its walking trails.

❶ The Parc Ornithologique du Pont de Gau is a great place for birdwatching. The Camargue is a haven for birds, including pink flamingoes, ducks, egrets, herons, cranes, geese and swans. Large aviaries at the park show the rarer species.

To return along the Petit-Rhône after the Parc Ornithologique du Pont de Gau, turn right onto the D85 and then left onto the D38, which loops back into Saintes-Maries-de-la-Mer around the Étang des Launes with the mouth of the Petit Rhône on the left.

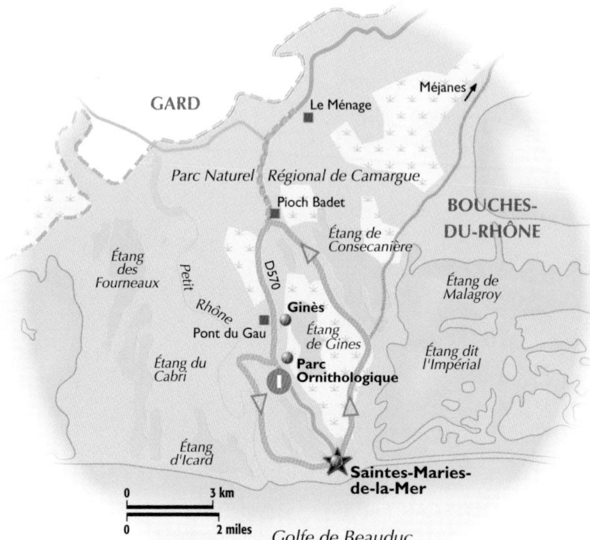


**Opposite** *Cycling through the Camargue*
**Below** *The Parc Ornithologique du Pont de Gau is ideal for birdwatching*

## WHERE TO EAT

### HOSTELLERIE DU PONT DE GAU

www.hotelpontdegau.com
This small hotel has a traditional, moderately priced restaurant.
Route d'Arles, 13460 Saintes-Maries-de-la-Mer 04 90 97 81 53 Closed Jan to mid-Feb

## INFORMATION

### TOURIST INFORMATION

www.saintesmaries.com
5 avenue Van Gogh, 13460 Saintes-Maries-de-la-Mer 04 90 97 82 55
Jul, Aug daily 9–8; Apr–end Jun, Sep daily 9–7; Mar, Oct daily 9–6; Nov–end Feb daily 9–5

## PLACES TO VISIT

### CHÂTEAU D'AVIGNON

04 90 97 58 60 Apr–end Oct Wed–Mon 9.45–5.30; Nov–end Mar Fri, last Sun of month 9.45–4.30. Closed last week in Dec Adult €3, under 16 free Apr–end Oct 3 tours daily; Nov–end Mar 2 tours daily

### PARC ORNITHOLOGIQUE DU PONT DE GAU

www.parcornithologique.com
04 90 97 82 62 Apr–end Sep daily 9–dusk; Oct–end Mar 10–dusk Adult €7, child (4–10) €4, under 4 free

## AIX-EN-PROVENCE

### BOWLING DU BRAS D'OR

www.bowlingdubrasdor.com

This ten-pin bowling venue also has a large screen showing sport.

23 boulevard Charrier, 13100 Aix-en-Provence 04 42 27 69 92 Daily 2pm–2.30am €4–€6 per game, plus €1.50 for shoe rental

### LE CÉZANNE

www.lecezanne.com

This nine-screen cinema complex focuses on Hollywood blockbusters and major hits at the French box office. Some film premieres also take place here. The films are rarely shown in their original language.

1 rue Marcel-Guillaume, 13100 Aix-en-Provence 0892 687 270 Screenings daily 10.45am–10.30pm €9.30 (evening performances)

### CHOCOLATERIE DE PUYRICARD

www.puyricard.fr

This local chocolatier is renowned internationally for the quality of its products (there is no vegetable fat; cocoa butter only). A popular chocolate is Cézanne's Nail, which reproduces the copper paving stones in Aix that indicate a circuit dedicated to the local painter.

7 rue Rifle-Rafle, 13100 Aix-en-Provence 04 42 21 13 26 Mon–Sat 9–7

### CONFISERIE ENTRECASTEAUX

This is *the* place to buy *calissons*, an Aix speciality, made from almonds. Made according to a family recipe for four generations, they come in an almond-shaped box. Other treats include glacé fruit and chocolate.

2 rue Entrecasteaux, 13100 Aix-en-Provence 04 42 27 15 02 Mon–Sat 8–12, 2–7

### LES DEUX GARÇONS

This 18th-century café has been registered as a historic monument. There's a terrace facing the city's main street, a large dining room on the ground floor and a piano bar (after 7pm) on the first floor.

53 cours Mirabeau, 13100 Aix-en-Provence 04 42 26 00 51 Daily 6am–2am

### LE DIVINO

www.divino.fr

Soothing tones dominate the interior of this temple of techno, with its talented DJs and restaurant upstairs.

4039 route de Sisteron, 13100 Aix-en-Provence 04 42 21 28 28 Thu 8pm–2am, Fri, Sat midnight–6am €15, entrance and one drink

### HAPPY DAYS

On the liveliest square in town, this bar is popular with the fashionable crowd. The funky interior has brightly coloured walls and furniture.

Place Richelme, 13100 Aix-en-Provence 04 42 21 02 35 Mon–Sat 8am–2am (food is served 12–4)

### HOT BRASS

www.hotbrassaix.com

This is the haunt of jazz-lovers and, sometimes, of great names on the music scene—the numerous pictures on the walls testify to this.

Quartier Celony, chemin d'Eguilles, 13090 Aix-en-Provence 04 42 21 05 57 Fri, Sat 11.30pm–5am €16–€20

### KEY NIGHT

Disco rhythms, foam parties and theme nights create a fun atmosphere for a young crowd.

1 route des Milles, 13100 Aix-en-Provence 04 42 27 40 90 Thu 7pm–1am, Fri–Sun midnight–6am Around €15

### MARCHÉ AUX ANTIQUAIRES

Browse this antiques market for period furniture, old books and decorative items.

Place du Verdun, 13100 Aix-en-Provence Tue, Thu, Sat 7–1

### MARCHÉ AUX HERBES

Local farmers display their cheeses, fruit and vegetables under the shade

**Opposite** *Indulge in some delicious treats from the Chocolaterie de Puyricard*

of plane trees. The produce is fresh, smells good and tastes great.
✉ Place Richelme, 13100 Aix-en-Provence
🕐 Daily 7–1

### PASINO

www.casinoaix.com
A blue glass pyramid is in the core of this 21st-century building and light plays on its facade every evening. You'll find slot machines by the hundreds and a games room, but also five restaurants and a concert hall.
✉ Avenue de l'Europe, 13626 Aix-en-Provence ☎ 04 42 59 69 00 🕐 Daily 10am–3am (until 4am Fri–Sun) 💶 Entry to the games room: €11 ❓ You must be over 18 to enter the games room

### THÉÂTRE ET CHANSONS

www.theatre-et-chansons.com
This 70-seat auditorium is entirely dedicated to songs: old-fashioned tunes, sung poetry or original performances by founder Isabelle Bloch-Delahaie. Singing workshops are also arranged.
✉ 1 rue Émile Tavan, 13100 Aix-en-Provence ☎ 04 42 27 37 39 🕐 Shows often start between 6.30pm and 8.30pm 💶 Around €12

### THERMES SEXTIUS

www.thermes-sextius.com
The spa uses naturally warm mineralized water (35°C/95°F), which has flowed from the nearby Montagne Sainte-Victoire for centuries. It opened in 1999, in an 18th-century building close to the ancient Roman pool founded by the Roman general Caius Sextius, hence the name. The hydro-therapeutic treatments focus on reducing stress and toxins.
✉ 55 avenue des Thermes, 13100 Aix-en-Provence ☎ 04 42 23 81 82 🕐 Spa Mon–Fri 8.30–7.30, Sat 9.30–7.30, Sun 10.30–4.30; general entrance Mon–Fri 8.30–8.30, Sat 9.30–7.30, Sun 10.30–5.30 💶 General entrance (pool, saunas, hammam and gym) €42, spa treatments from €89

### VINT'AGE

www.vintage-boutique.fr
Browse for high-end vintage pieces from Hermès, Chanel and Christian Dior; note that hard-to-find totes, scarves and shimmery jewels are priced accordingly.
✉ 3 rue des Epineaux, place des Trois Ormeaux, 13100 Aix-en-Provence ☎ 04 42 23 45 54 🕐 Mon 2–7, Tue–Sat 10–7

## ARLES

### BIJOUX DUMONT

This family business has been making reproductions of original Provençal jewellery since 1967. Most use 18-carat gold, silver or semi-precious stones and they incorporate emblems of the region. Choose from cicada brooches, Provençal crosses or Saintes-Maries-de-la-Mer cross pendants.
✉ 3 rue du Palais, 13200 Arles ☎ 04 90 96 05 66 🕐 Tue–Sat 9–12, 2.30–7

### LA CABANO DIS EGO

www.cabano-dis-ego.com
Horses and bulls are bred here and the owners organize horseback riding, games and traditional Camargue days, complete with themed lunches.
✉ Le Sambuc, 13200 Arles ☎ 04 90 97 20 62 🕐 Open all year

### CAMARGUE SAFARIS GALLON ORGANISATION

www.safari-4x4-gallon.camargue.fr
Get off the beaten track and discover the Camargue's wildlife on a four-wheel drive safari. See the inland waters, horses, bulls and flamingoes. Some deals also include bicycling and horseback riding.
✉ 38 avenue Edouard Herriot, 13200 Arles ☎ 04 90 93 60 31 🕐 All year long, by appointment 💶 €20 per person for 1.5 hours, €48 for 3.5 hours

### CARGO DE NUIT

www.cargodenuit.com
You'll find an eclectic mix here, from jazz fusion and salsa to reggae. The venue is a springboard for young talent every Thursday. The concert hall has a capacity of 300 and there is also a restaurant and piano bar.
✉ 7 avenue Sadi Carnot, 13200 Arles ☎ 04 90 49 55 99 🕐 Concerts and DJ club nights: Thu–Sat evening 💶 Free; €15 for the concerts

### CHRISTIAN LACROIX

www.christianlacroix.com
The celebrated haute-couture designer was born in Arles and his vibrant collections certainly capture the spirit of the south. His gilded embroideries are reminiscent of toreador costumes and use only the finest fabrics.
✉ 52 rue République, 13200 Arles ☎ 04 90 96 11 16 🕐 Mon 2.30–7, Tue–Sat 9–12, 2–7

### LE KRYSTAL

www.lekrystal.com
Enjoy theme nights at this venue, with its modern steel and pink decor and neon lights. The choice includes zouk, go-go dancers and Latin.
✉ Route de Krystal, 13280 Arles ☎ 04 90 98 32 40 🕐 Fri, Sat 11pm–6am 💶 €15, entrance and one drink; free entrance for women on Fri

### LE PATIO

www.patio.chico.fr
Here you'll be entertained by Chico, leader of the celebrated band the Gypsy Kings. At this hacienda on the banks of the Rhône, he organizes gypsy evenings with flamenco and rumba.
✉ Le Patio de Camargue, 51 chemin de Barriol, 13200 Arles ☎ 04 90 49 51 76 🕐 Sat 8pm 💶 Adult €50, child €35 ❓ Reserve ahead

### THÉÂTRE D'ARLES

www.theatre-arles.com
This theatre presents a mixture of contemporary drama and ballet from companies around France and beyond. There are also regular children's shows.
✉ Boulevard Clemenceau, 13200 Arles ☎ 04 90 52 51 55, ticket line 04 90 52 51 51 🕐 Ticket office: Sep–end Dec Mon–Fri 11–1, 3–6.30 (performance days Mon–Fri 11–1, 3 until show begins, Sat, Sun 3 until show begins); Jan–end Jul Mon–Fri 1–6 (performance days Mon–Fri 1 until show begins, Sat, Sun 3 until show begins)

## CABRIÈS

### LE FOLIE'S

This venue offers a show true to French music-hall tradition: sequins and feathers for the scantily clad dancers who sing, tap and do the cancan. Dinner is served during the show.

Zone commerciale de Plan-de-Campagne, 13480 Cabriès 04 42 02 87 20 Fri, Sat 8pm €55–€67 for show and meal (depending on which menu you choose); limited drinks are included in the price

## LA CIOTAT

### PLONGÉE 2000

www.plongee-2000.com

Scuba dives take place in areas with a high concentration of grouper; one site also has a statue of the Virgin Mary, another a Roman pool. There are also special dives for children (aged 8 years and over) and for people with disabilities.

35 quai Mitterrand, 13600 La Ciotat 04 42 71 93 02 Daily 9–12, 2–7 €35

## FONTVIEILLE

### DOMAINE OLIVIER D'AUGE

www.domaine-olivierdauge.com

Olivier d'Auge keeps alive one of the traditions of the Baux valley by producing both wine and olive oil. Among the products available are some Provençal hampers containing wine, olive oil and other local specials, including tapenade and pesto.

Auge, 13990 Fontvieille 04 90 54 62 95 Mon–Fri 8–12, 1–5, Sat, Sun by appointment only

## MALLEMORT

### GOLF DE PONT ROYAL

www.golf–pontroyal.com

Severiano Ballesteros designed this 18-hole course. The restaurant is called Esbeulavie—'life is beautiful' in Provençal.

Domaine de Pont-Royal, 13370 Mallemort 04 90 57 40 79 Jul, Aug daily 7am–8pm; May, Jun, Sep, Oct daily 8–7; Nov–end Mar daily 9–5.30 Green fee: 9 holes €39–€49, 18 holes €60–€75

## MARSEILLE

### 20,000 LIEUES

http://20000lieues.free.fr

This venue, with its beautiful wooden interior, regularly welcomes pop, rock and funk bands. It's a good place to have a drink in a convivial atmosphere, or if you fancy something to it, steaming bowls of pasta are served at all hours.

Les Goudes, 13008 Marseille 04 91 25 05 24 Daily 11am–2am; concerts Thu, Fri, Sat Free 19, 20

### ANTOINE & LILI

www.antoineetlili.com

This southern outpost of Paris brand Antoine & Lili is packed with funky women's clothes, printed pouches and quirky, animal-shaped lamps—many of the smaller items make unique gifts.

38 rue Montgrand, 13006 Marseille 04 91 52 73 70 Mon, Wed, Thu 10.30–1.30, 2.30–7.30, Tue, Fri, Sat 10–8

### LA BALEINE QUI DIT VAGUES

www.labaleinequiditvagues.org

The name of this venue means 'the whale who says waves', in reference to the traditional Native American tale in which a whale symbolizes the memory of the world. It hosts storytelling performances, many for children.

59 cours Julien, 13006 Marseille 04 91 48 95 60 Fri–Sat 8.30pm, Wed 3pm, children's performances mid-Sep–end Jun Adult €11, child (4–16) €7 Réformes

### BAR DE LA MARINE

Facing the old port, this fashionable bar has a cool atmosphere and a soundtrack of acid jazz.

15 quai de Rive Neuve, 13007 Marseille 04 91 54 95 42 Daily 7am–2am

### BAR DE LA SAMARITAINE

This 1930s bar is a local institution. Its terrace, facing the picturesque old port, becomes a piano bar from Thursday to Saturday.

2 quai du Port, 13002 Marseille 04 91 90 31 41 Daily 6am–10pm (until 11.30pm Jul, Aug)

### BIBLIOTHÈQUE DE L'ALCAZAR

www.bmvr.marseille.fr

The city's large, modern library is in a former music hall. There are film and documentary showings (often in the original language with subtitles), plus small exhibitions and conferences.

58 cours Nelsunce, 13001 Marseille 04 91 55 90 00 Tue–Sat 11–7

### BOUTIQUE OFFICIELLE DE L'OLYMPIQUE DE MARSEILLE

http://boutique.om.net

People from Marseille are passionate about their soccer team, the Olympique de Marseille or OM. This shop is entirely dedicated to it, and its TV screen broadcasts videos in praise of the team. OM's official jersey is a popular item, but you may also be tempted by a soft toy or board game.

44 boulevard de la Canebière, 13003 Marseille 04 91 33 20 01 Mon–Sat 10–7 Noailles

### LA BUTTE ROUGE

This cool tapas bar serves a range of the Spanish varieties, as well as antipasti Provençal, all washed down with French or Spanish wine by the bottle or glass.

11 rue des Trois-Mages, 13006 Marseille 04 91 47 29 66 Daily 6pm–2am Notre-Dame-du-Mont

### CENTRE DE BIEN-ÊTRE CHÂTEAU BERGER

www.chateauberger.com

A castle overlooking the Mediterranean is the classy setting for this well-being venue. It is hard not to feel relaxed in such surroundings, and the treatments also help. You can combine workouts with the benefits of seawater.

281 Corniche J.F. Kennedy, 13007 Marseille 04 91 52 61 61 Mon–Sat 9.30–6.30 Treatments from €38

### CENTRE DE LOISIRS DES GOUDES

www.goudes-plongee.com

This company will take you diving in the Bay of Marseille, around the Rioux archipelago, where caves

and old wrecks host extraordinary marine life. Some packages include meals, as well as the use of kayaks and mountain bicycles.
✉ 2 boulevard Alexandre Delabre, 13008 Marseille ☎ 04 91 25 13 16 🕐 Daily 8am–10pm ✋ €60 for first dive, €212 for a weekend 🚌 19

### LE CÉSAR

High-quality arts films and the screening of films in their original language are the attraction of this three-screen repertoire cinema. Short films and previews followed by debates with the director or the actors complete the picture.
✉ 4 place Castellane, 13006 Marseille ☎ 0892 680 597 🕐 Screenings: daily 10am–11pm ✋ Ticket around €7 Ⓜ Castellane

### LA COMPAGNIE DE PROVENCE

www.compagniedeprovence.com
Marseille soap is known all over the world. Just moments from the old port, this store offers variations on the traditional cube—it comes enriched with clay, essential oils and honey. The soap is attractively packaged with brown wrapping paper and a piece of string.
✉ 1 rue Caisserie, 13001 Marseille ☎ 04 91 56 20 94 🕐 Mon–Sat 10–7 Ⓜ Vieux-Port

### DOCK DES SUDS

www.dock-des-suds.org
These dockland warehouses are home to a 2,500-seat auditorium and an 800-seat cabaret, and also many restaurants. Cabaret, concerts and exhibitions are staged, and the annual music and art festival, *Fiesta des Suds*, is held here in October.
✉ 12 rue Urbain V, 13002 Marseille ☎ 04 91 99 00 00/0825 833 833 (information line) Ⓜ National

### ESPACE JULIEN

www.espace-julien.com
Enjoy an eclectic selection of music here, including jazz and rock. The popular venue, on a pedestrian-only street packed with bars and cafés, holds 1,000 people.
✉ 39 cours Julien, 13006 Marseille ☎ 04 91 24 34 10 🕐 Ticket office open 1 hour before performances to sell remaining tickets Ⓜ Cours Julien

### FOUR DES NAVETTES

www.fourdesnavettes.com
The city's oldest bakery, established in 1781, is the place to get *navettes*, boat-shaped biscuits scented with orange-flower water, one of Marseille's specialities. Following tradition, the bread oven, which features prominently inside the shop and dates back to 1781, is blessed on 2 February by Marseille's archbishop.
✉ 136 rue Sainte-Anne, 13007 Marseille ☎ 04 91 33 32 12 🕐 Sep–end Jul Mon–Sat 7am–8pm, Sun 9–1, 3–7.30; Aug daily 9–1, 3–7.30 🚌 55, 61, 81

### FRICHE DE LA BELLE DE MAI

www.lafriche.org
This former warehouse is home to the Système Friche theatre and the alternative Grenouille (Frog) radio station, as well as being the venue for many concerts and exhibitions; rap group IAM have regularly appeared. There is a bar on site.
✉ 41 rue Jobin, 13003 Marseille ☎ 04 95 04 95 04 🕐 Ateliers and visual arts: 9–6; concerts and club nights: times vary 🚌 49

### LA GRIFFE MESURE

www.la-griffe-mesure.fr
For the best in styling for men, this company provides bespoke tailoring and handmade suits and shirts. You can choose from a range of styles and materials and you'll then be ready to hit the exclusive restaurants and clubs along the Riviera. On the same street are numerous other designer boutiques.
✉ 8 rue de la Tour, 13001 Marseille ☎ 04 91 55 05 19 🕐 Tue–Sat 10–12.30, 1.30–6

### MADAME ZAZA OF MARSEILLE

www.zazaofmarseille.com
Zaza is the name of the local designer behind this collection, which betrays Mediterranean influences: Shirts and skirts are made of beautiful fabrics and are sometimes embroidered with gold. The store's pleasant interior has beamed ceilings and a terracotta-tiled floor typical of Provence.
✉ 73 cours Julien, 13006 Marseille ☎ 04 91 48 05 57 🕐 Tue–Sun 11–1, 2–7

### MARCHÉ DES CAPUCINS

At this market you'll find spices, fruit and vegetables from all over the world (with much from Northern Africa). Alongside these exotic offerings are some discounted household goods.
✉ Place des Capucins, 13001 Marseille 🕐 Daily 8.30–7 Ⓜ Noailles

### MARCHÉ AUX POISSONS

This vibrant market, emblematic of the city, is a must see. Fish—hauled in by small-scale, local fishermen each morning—is extremely fresh, and gutted, and is scaled on the spot.
✉ Vieux Port, 13001 Marseille 🕐 Daily 8–1 Ⓜ Vieux-Port

### MÉTAL CAFÉ

The club's decor has mixed influences: an Eastern theme for one of its mezzanines, fleur-de-lis for the second. Dance, house and disco rhythms are enjoyed by the happy few who manage to get in.
✉ 20 rue Fortia, 13001 Marseille ☎ 04 91 54 03 03 🕐 Thu–Sat 10.30pm–dawn Ⓜ Vieux Port

### O'BRADY'S IRISH PUB

www.obradys.com
Named after its owner, Jean-Luc Brady, this pub has a sports theme, with hanging flags and jerseys, and a big screen for those all-important games. You can enjoy live music on Mondays.
✉ 378 avenue de Mazargues, 13008 Marseille ☎ 04 91 71 53 71 🕐 Daily 11am–1.30am 🚌 23, 45

### L'OM CAFÉ

Named after the city's soccer team, Olympique de Marseille or OM, this café broadcasts soccer games. Sit out on the terrace facing the port.
✉ 25 quai des Belges, 13001 Marseille ☎ 04 91 33 80 33 🕐 Daily 9am–11pm Ⓜ Vieux Port

### OPÉRA DE MARSEILLE

www.marseille.fr

Built in 1787, this 1,800-seat auditorium has a profusion of frescoes and candelabras. Home to the Philharmonic Orchestra of Marseille, it also hosts operas.
2 rue Molière, 13001 Marseille 04 91 55 11 10 Closed Jul, Aug From €12 Vieux Port

### LE PELLE-MÊLE

France's greatest jazz musicians have played here. The leather and wood interior creates a warm, intimate atmosphere.
8 place aux Huiles, 13100 Marseille 04 91 54 85 26 Mon–Sat 6pm–2am From €6

### LA ROUTE DES VINS

www.laroutedesvins.com

In every one of France's wine regions, a circuit known as 'la route des vins' (the wine road) encourages the discovery of local vineyards. There is good representation of most at this shop, including those typical of Provence.
486 rue Paradis, 13008 Marseille 04 91 22 84 00 Mon–Sat 9.30–1, 3.30–8 Rond-Point du Prado

### SANTONS MARCEL CARBONEL

www.santonsmarcelcarbonel.com

A Provençal tradition, the *santons* are clay figures that represent biblical characters and craftsmen. This family business sells 700 difference figures; full Provençal crèches (Nativity scenes) are also available.
49 rue Neuve Sainte-Catherine, 13007 Marseille 04 91 13 61 36 Jan–end Nov Tue–Sat 10–12.30, 2–6.30; Dec Mon–Sat 10–12.30, 2–6.30

### STADE VÉLODROME

www.om.net

This 60,000-seat stadium is home to Olympique de Marseille, the city's soccer team. The locals are passionate about the sport and every game is a big event.
3 boulevard Michelet, 13008 Marseille Most matches begin between 7pm and 9pm From €23 Rond-Point du Prado

### THÉÂTRE NATIONAL DE MARSEILLE—LA CRIÉE

www.theatre-lacriee.com

The theatre was erected in 1981 in place of the fish market. There are two auditoriums with 782 and 260 seats. Productions range from the classics to contemporary plays, and some musicals.
30 quai de Rive Neuve, 13007 Marseille 04 91 54 70 54 Closed Aug €22 Vieux Port

### LE TROLLEYBUS

www.letrolley.com

Several distinct and spacious venues at one location means Trolleybus has something for every clubber. Whiskybar concentrates on electro and house; Terminus funk and groove; and Trolleybar rock and pop. There's also a live concert venue.
24 quai de Rive Neuve, Vieux Port, 13007 Marseille 04 91 54 30 45 Wed–Sat from 11pm

### ZÉNITH LE DÔME

www.le-dome.com

A green arch stands on top of the metal dome of this imposing concert hall, which seats 8,500 people. Productions include concerts, musicals, one-man shows and plays.
48 avenue St-Just, 13004 Marseille 04 91 12 21 21 €30–€70 St-Just

## NÎMES

### EVER'IN CAFÉ

www.ever-in.fr

Equal parts café, club and cocktail bar, Ever'in offers a myriad of garden terraces and snug indoor spots for sitting and sipping. Student, salsa and DJ nights Thursday to Saturday.
1 place Séverine, 30900 Nîmes 04 66 76 21 81 Mon–Sat 8am–2am

## ST-CANNAT

### VILLAGE DES AUTOMATES

www.parc-de-loisirs-provence.com

This is a model village with a difference; a succession of little wooden houses are home to robots that reproduce scenes from children's stories, including Jonathan Swift's *Gulliver's Travels* and La Fontaine's *Fox and Crow*. There is also a 'farm' with miniature animals, a snack bar and amusement park.
Route Nationale 7, 13760 St-Cannat 04 42 57 30 30 Jul, Aug daily 10–7; Apr, Jun, 1st 2 weeks in Sep daily 10–6; mid-Sep to end Mar Wed, Sat, Sun 10–5 Adult €10, child (3–14) €7

## SAINTES-MARIES-DE-LA-MER

### A.C.T. TIKI III

www.tiki3.fr

During this 90-minute boat excursion on the Petit Rhône river, you'll get close to the pastures and the *manade* (herds of bulls and horses), a landscape typical of Camargue.
Le Grau d'Orguon–D38, 13460 Saintes-Maries-de-la-Mer 04 90 97 81 68/04 90 97 81 22 Mid-Mar to mid-Nov €10 per person Reservations advised

### BOUTIQUE DU GARDIAN

www.legardian.com

A *gardian* is a cowboy in the Camargue, and this is where you'll find the clothes to get outfitted like one: felt hat, broad belt and *gardian* boots. You'll also find a range of outdoor brands.
9 rue Victor Hugo, 13460 Saintes-Maries-de-la-Mer 04 90 97 85 34 Summer daily 9.30–8; winter daily 9.30–12, 2–6

### MARIA MARIA

www.mariamaria.camargue.fr

There's a *feria* (festival) atmosphere at this boutique, which, in an ochre-walled and Spanish blue-tiled interior, sells clothes emblematic of the exuberance of the south: Andalusian costumes, embroidered shirts, *gardian* clothes. You'll find some big names, but the shop is also the sole authorized distributor of some local fashion designers.
7 place des Remparts, 13460 Saintes-Maries-de-la-Mer 04 90 97 71 60 Daily 10–12.30, 2–6 (9–9 in summer and during special events)

### PROMENADE DES RIÈGES

www.promenadedesrieges.com

These horseback-riding excursions let you discover the scenery of the Camargue's inland waters, beaches

and wildlife (including flamingoes). The stables have the white horses for which the Camargue is famous.
Route de Cacharel, 13460 Saintes-Maries-de-la-Mer 04 90 97 91 38 By appointment 2-hour excursion €26, full day €60

### THALACAP CAMARGUE

www.thalacap.fr
This thalassotherapy spa offers a wide range of treatments, including seaweed and mud wrap and hydromassage. It's coupled with a hotel to allow week-long treatments. Facilities include a gym, Turkish bath, sauna and two seawater pools (indoor and outdoor).
Rue Jacques Yves Cousteau, Saintes-Maries-de-la-Mer 04 90 99 22 22 Daily 9–12, 2–7. Closed mid-Nov to mid-Dec One night plus 4 treatments €200; half-day access to pool, hammam and gym €39

## ST-RÉMY-DE-PROVENCE

### CHOCOLATERIE JOËL DURAND

www.chocolat-durand.com
Chocolate-maker Joël Durand, a Breton, fell in love with Provence and has since been combining chocolate with this region's local produce. Nothing is too audacious for someone who once associated chocolate with foie gras; another creation mixes chocolate with black olives.
3 boulevard Victor Hugo, 13210 St-Rémy-de-Provence 04 90 92 38 25 Mon 9.30–12.30, 2.30–7, Tue–Sat 9.30–12.30, 2.30–7.30, Sun 10–1, 2.30–7

### LILAMAND

www.lilamand.com
Glacé fruit has been the house speciality here since 1866. For five generations, working to recipes passed from father to son, Lilamand has been preserving in sugar many of the fruits that are emblematic of Provence. Try the *Orangettes* (glazed pieces of orange meant to be dunked in chocolate), the glacé chestnuts or the glacé fruit jam.
5 avenue Albert Schweitzer, 13210 St-Rémy-de-Provence 04 90 92 11 08 Tue–Sat 10–12.30, 2.30–7

# FESTIVALS AND EVENTS

## MAY

### FÊTE DES GARDIANS

www.tourisme.ville-arles.fr
Camargue cowboys parade through Arles on horseback.
Arles 04 90 18 41 20 1 May

### FÊTE DE LA TRANSHUMANCE

www.saintremy-de-provence.com
Local people celebrate the sheep migrations (▷ 14).
St-Rémy-de-Provence 04 90 92 05 22 Whit Monday (late May or early Jun)

### THE GYPSY PILGRIMAGE

www.saintesmaries.com
Gypsy families gather for the pilgrimage to the church at the southern tip of the Carmargue, marking the traditional landing point of saints Marie-Salomé and Marie-Jacobé (▷ 91). This is France's largest gypsy gathering.
Saintes-Maries-de-la-Mer 04 90 97 82 55 24–25 May (there is a second pilgrimage on Sun closest to 22 Oct)

### FERIA DE PENTECÔTE

www.ot-nimes.fr
Five days of celebration in Nîmes include parades, lively street parties and, not to everyone's taste, bull chasing and fighting.
Nîmes 04 66 58 38 00 Late May or early Jun Free

## JUNE

### FÊTES DE LA TARASQUE

www.tarascon.org
Close to a week of festivities in Tarascon commemorate the routing of the *Tarasque* (▷ 33), including parades, concerts, boat trips, re-enactments and fireworks.
Tarascon 04 90 91 03 52 Last Sun

## JULY

### FESTIVAL D'AIX

www.festival-aix.com
This opera festival, also known as the *Festival International d'Art Lyrique et de la Musique*, lasts about three weeks.
Aix-en-Provence 04 42 17 34 00

### RENCONTRES DES SUDS

www.suds-arles.com
Dance, drama, music and opera at Arles' Théâtre Antique, plus other venues around town.
Arles 04 90 96 06 27 Mid-Jul

### TERRE È PROVENCE

www.terre-provence.com
This family business specializes in traditional pottery, including hand-painted plates and carafes. The octagonal plates decorated with flowers or olives are beautiful.
1 rue Lafayette, 13210 St-Rémy-de-Provence 04 90 92 28 52 Daily 9.30–1, 2–7. Closed Sun, Mon Jan–end Mar

## SIGNES

### PROVENCE KAYAK MER

www.provencekayakmer.fr
Take an excursion and see the spectacular *calanques* (rock formations) around La Ciotat and Cassis from the ocean. Provence Kayak Mer offers guided kayaking trips along the coast for a half day, a full day, or for a romantic sunset trip, with all equipment including lifejackets. For those with more stamina, there are two- or three-day sea safaris where you overnight in a bivouac on the seashore. Most departures are from La Ciotat.
3 rue Rompicul, 83870 Signes 06 12 95 20 12 Half day €35, sunset trip €30

## SYLVÉRÉAL

### KAYAK VERT CAMARGUE

www.kayakvert-camargue.fr
Explore the Camargue's natural reserve by canoe or kayak—picnics and overnight trips are also available, and you can rent mountain bikes.
Mas de Sylvéréal, 30600 Sylvéréal 04 66 73 57 17 From €10 per person, per hour

# EATING

**PRICES AND SYMBOLS**

The prices given are the average for a two-course lunch (L) and a three-course dinner (D) for one person, without drinks. The wine price is for the least expensive bottle.

For a key to the symbols, ▷ 2.

## AIGUES-MORTES

### EDEN RESTAURANT

www.eden-restaurant.com

Enjoy innovative seasonal cuisine in the heart of Aigues-Mortes. Opt for the foie gras teamed with prickly pear, the Camargue bull, or pork paired with sweet-and-sour green mangos. The menu changes monthly and the outdoor patio is open year round.

✉ 8 rue Denfert Rochereau, 30220 Aigues-Mortes ☎ 04 66 53 69 45 ⏰ Tue–Sat 12–3, 7.30–10, Sun 12–3. Closed mid-Jan to mid-Feb 🖐 L €19, D €29, Wine €18

## AIX-EN-PROVENCE

### L'AIXQUIS

www.aixquis.fr

The setting here, with elegantly laid tables and subtle lighting, is perfect for a romantic dinner. Fresh flowers and a tile floor give the place a Provençal feel. The food is fine Mediterranean cuisine: Warm lobster salad with coral vinaigrette is the signature dish.

✉ 22 rue Victor Leydet, 13100 Aix-en-Provence ☎ 04 42 27 76 16 ⏰ Mon 7.30–9.30, Tue–Sat 12–1.30, 7.30–9.30. Closed Aug 🖐 L €45, D €60, Wine €20

### BRASSERIE LÉOPOLD

www.hotel-saintchristophe.com

Sitting just off La Rotonde, this art deco brasserie serves traditional French dishes, plus specials with an Asian touch. Opt for grilled lamb with thyme, or salmon tartare paired with mango and ginger.

✉ 2 avenue Victor Hugo, 13100 Aix-en-Provence ☎ 04 42 26 01 24 ⏰ Daily 12–3, 7–12 🖐 L €19, D €40, Wine €18

### LES CLOS DE LA VIOLETTE

www.closdelaviolette.com

Jean-Marc and Brigitte Banzo have created an exceptional formal restaurant with the highest standards of French cuisine. The dining room has sumptuous decoration and full-length windows with views out to mature gardens. Seasonal specialities range from roasted red mullet with crispy risotto to asparagus, courgette and tapenade ravioli.

✉ 10 avenue de la Violette, 13100 Aix-en-Provence ☎ 04 42 23 30 71 ⏰ Tue–Sat 12–1.30, 7.30–9.30 🖐 L €50, D €90, Wine €25

## ARLES

### CORAZON

Corazon is in a wonderful 16th-century town house with a courtyard and fountain. The succession of small dining rooms creates a tranquil, intimate mood and the tones of white and soft brown match the exposed stone. The menu has fine regional cuisine, with some Camargue specialities such as bull served with a pepper and anchovy sauce.

✉ 1 bis rue Réattu, 13200 Arles ☎ 04 90 96 32 53 ⏰ Mon–Sat 12–2.30, 7.30–10. Closed Nov and 1–15 Jan 🖐 L €20, D €50, Wine €20

### LA GUEULE DU LOUP

The plain walls hung with pictures contrast perfectly with the exposed stone in this restaurant. Though the cuisine is true to the traditions of

**Opposite** *L'Aixquis restaurant, in Aix-en-Provence, is ideal for a romantic dinner*

the Camargue and Provence, it is also influenced by owner/chef Jean-Jacques Allard. A sample dish is eels from the Camargue served with a leek and chicory fondue in red-wine sauce.
✉ 39 rue des Arènes, 13200 Arles
☎ 04 90 96 96 69 🕓 Apr–end Sep Mon 7.30–9.30, Tue–Sat 12–1.30, 7.30–9.30; Oct–end Mar Tue–Sat 12–1.30, 7.30–9.30. Closed mid-Jan to mid-Feb ✋ L €15, D €30, Wine €18

### LOU MARQUÈS

www.hotel-julescesar.fr
A regal columned entrance welcomes you to this restaurant, in a 12th-century former convent. The refined dining room has large wood panels and drapes in shades of the south—blues subtly punctuated with touches of yellow. The inventive cuisine betrays its local influences: sea bass on pumpkin and crab ravioli, gingerbread millefeuille and caramel ice cream. The restaurant is part of a four-star hotel.
✉ 9 boulevard des Lices, 13631 Arles
☎ 04 90 52 52 52 🕓 Apr–end Oct Mon–Fri 12–1.30, 7.30–9.30, Sat 7.30–9.30, Sun 12–1.30; Nov–end Mar Mon–Fri 12–1.30, 7.30–9.30 ✋ L €21, D €40, Wine €22

### LA MAMMA

www.lamammaarles.com
There's a rustic feel to this restaurant, with a tile floor, wicker chairs, decorative agricultural items and a pizza oven. Expect Italian and regional cuisine such as sautéed beef with olives, crudités with anchovy sauce, and pizzas.
✉ 20 rue de l'Amphithéâtre, 13200 Arles
☎ 04 90 96 11 60 🕓 Tue–Sun 12–2.30, 7–10.30 ✋ L €15, D €20, Wine €15

## LES BAUX-DE-PROVENCE

### OUSTAU DE BAUMANIÈRE

www.oustaudebaumaniere.com
This restaurant, in a 16th-century Provençal country house, is part of a four-star hotel. Dine on the terrace to enjoy views of the forest of cypresses and rocky outcrops or in the elegant dining room. The exquisite dishes include truffle and leek ravioli and 'blue' lobster with a herb salad.
✉ Val d'Enfer, 13520 Les Baux-de-Provence
☎ 04 90 54 33 07 🕓 Apr–end Oct daily 12–2, 7–9; Mar, Nov–end Dec Mon–Thu 7–9, Fri–Sun 12–2, 7–9. Closed early Jan–end Feb ✋ L €90, D €150, Wine €40

### LA REINE JEANNE

www.la-reinejeanne.com
The large windows of this small restaurant are perfect for enjoying views of the valley. The regional cuisine available includes peppers marinated in olive oil, leg of lamb with garlic pickles and Provençal platter with olive tapenade. A cod and poached vegetable *aïoli* is served every Friday.
✉ Grande Rue, 13520 Les Baux-de-Provence ☎ 04 90 54 32 06 🕓 Daily 12–2, 7.30–9.30 ✋ L €16, D €25, Wine €15

## CASSIS

### RESTAURANT CHEZ GILBERT

www.restaurant-chez-gilbert.fr
Ask any local for a serious bouillabaisse recommendation, and they'll point you here. Pricey but authentic (the restaurant is a member of the elite Marseille Bouillabaisse Charter), with pretty views over the port.
✉ 19 quai des Baux, 13260 Cassis ☎ 04 42 01 71 36 🕓 Jul, Aug Thu–Tue 12–3, 7–11; Sep–end Dec, Feb–end Jun Thu–Mon 12–3, 7–11, Tue 12–3. Closed Jan ✋ L €25, D €60, Wine €22

### LE ROMARIN

www.leromarin.com
Rosemary *(romarin)* is of course used in the cuisine here, alongside many of the scents and tastes of Provence: goat's cheese salad with pine nuts, grilled lamb on skewers, plus a lot of fish. The pleasant dining room is inspired by the hues of the region.
✉ 5 rue Séverin Icard, 13260 Cassis
☎ 04 42 01 09 93 🕓 Jun–end Aug daily 7.30–11pm; Sep–end Dec, Feb–end May Wed–Sun 12–2, 7.30–10.30. Closed Jan ✋ L €20, D €35, Wine €11

## LA CIOTAT

### RIF

www.figuerolles.com
RIF stands for 'Independent Republic of Figuerolles'. Descend the 87 steps to discover the small wooden house, which looks out onto a secluded creek. The menu has a Mediterranean accent, with a hint of Russian.
✉ Calanque de Figuerolles, 13600 La Ciotat
☎ 04 42 08 41 71 🕓 Mid-Mar to end Nov daily 12–2, 7–10 ✋ L €35, D €50, Wine €15

## MARSEILLE

### LES ARCENAULX

http://arcenaulx.oxatis.com
Numerous books line the walls of Marseille's former arsenal, which has a beamed ceiling and long red banquettes. Sophisticated regional cuisine includes honey and lemon duck served with citron-scented

**Below** *Enjoy regional cuisine at La Reine Jeanne, in Les Baux-de-Provence*

courgette (zucchini) gratin. In the afternoon, Les Arcenaulx is a tea room.

25 cours Estienne d'Orves, 13001 Marseille 04 91 59 80 30 Mon–Sat 12–2, 8–11 L €30, D €50, Wine €20

**CHEZ FONFON**

www.chez-fonfon.com

The lively fishing port is the place to try bouillabaisse, Marseille's speciality dish; the crab ravioli, or squid grilled with garlic and parsley, are also exquisite. Chez Fonfon is an institution in town and has been run by the same family for more than 50 years. Its elegant interior has green wicker chairs, Provençal fabrics, and looks out over the tiny port's colourful fishing boats.

140 Vallon des Auffes, 13007 Marseille 04 91 52 14 38 May–end Oct Mon 7.30–10, Tue–Sat 12–2, 7.30–10; Nov–end Apr Tue–Sat 12–2, 7.30–10. Closed 2 weeks in Jan L €35, D €50, Wine €18

**CHEZ LOURY**

www.loury.com

This popular restaurant, close to the old port, puts the best of Mediterranean ingredients on the menu. Try herb-roasted sea urchin, home-smoked salmon or bouillabaisse.

3 rue Fortia, 13001 Marseille 04 91 33 09 73 Mon–Sat 12–2, 7.30–10.30. Closed 2 weeks in Nov L €18, D €28, Wine €15

**Above** *Marseille is a great place to try bouillabaisse*

**UN TABLE AU SUD**

www.unetableausud.com

Chef Lionel Lévy, who trained under Alain Ducasse, may have his roots in Toulouse, but his creative cooking is pan-Mediterranean. Try macaroni topped with *boutargue* (cured mullet 'caviar') from nearby Martigues; classic Marseillaise bouillabaisse is reimagined as a milkshake.

2 quai du Port, 13002 Marseille 04 91 90 63 53 Tue–Sat 12–2.30, 7.30–10. Closed Aug L €33, D €68, Wine €30

**LA VIRGULE**

http://lavirgule.marseille.free.fr

Squeezed between Marseille's Vieux Port and Le Panier district, the terrace of this petite spot makes a tasty stop mid-sightseeing. Go for the home-made foie gras, beef cheek confit or the smooth chestnut pumpkin soup topped with hazelnuts. Excellent value.

27 rue de la Loge, 13002 Marseille 04 91 90 91 11 Tue–Fri 12–2, 7.30–10, Sat 7.30–10, Sun 12–2 L €19, D €25, Wine €18

## MEYREUIL

**L'AUBERGE PROVENÇALE**

www.auberge-provencale.fr

This family-owned restaurant looks rather ordinary from the outside but the French know never to judge a book by its cover. The menu has a core of classical French staples, such as duck breast and rack of lamb, topped up by seasonal, Provençal ingredients. There's parking on site.

Impasse Le Provence—Le Canet, 13590 Meyreuil 04 42 58 68 54 Thu–Mon 12–2.30, 8–10, Tue 12–2.30. Closed first 3 weeks in Jul, 24–28 Dec L €20, D €40, Wine €15

## MOURIES

**LE VIEUX FOUR**

www.le-vieux-four.com

An imposing 18th-century oven *(four)* is the focal point of this rustic dining room, with tile floors, beamed

ceilings and wicker chairs. Dinner is served on the terrace under the shade of plane trees when the weather permits. The cuisine uses olive oil produced in Mouries. Fine regional dishes are offered and some pizzas are served in the evening.
✉ 5 cours Paul Revoil, 13890 Mouries ☎ 04 90 47 64 94 ⏲ Daily 12–2, 7–10 ✋ L €20, D €30, Wine €18

## NÎMES

### LE VINTAGE CAFÉ

This delightful little bistro is in a tiny square with a fountain, between the arena and La Maison Carrée. The daily menu is based on fresh market finds, and the dining room doubles as a gallery for local artists.
✉ 7 rue de Bernis, 30000 Nîmes ☎ 04 66 21 04 45 ⏲ Tue–Fri 11–2.30, 7–11, Sat 7–11. Closed 2 weeks Aug ✋ L €25, D €35, Wine €15

## SAINTES-MARIES-DE-LA-MER

### LE BRULEUR DE LOUPS

www.lebruleurdeloups.monsite.wanadoo.fr
Just off Sainte-Maries' seafront and boasting sea views, Le Bruleur is one of the best spots in town to try traditional Camargue cuisine—in particular, the locally sourced bull, slow roasted in a stew or grilled.
✉ 67 avenue Gilbert Leroy, 13460 Saintes-Maries-de-la-Mer ☎ 04 90 97 83 31 ⏲ Tue 12–2.30, Thu–Mon 12–2.30, 7.30–10.30. Closed mid-Nov to Christmas ✋ L €19, D €25, Wine €20

## ST-RÉMY-DE-PROVENCE

### LE BISTROT DES ALPILLES

www.lebistrotdesalpilles.com
This popular bistro has large paintings of toreadors on its walls. The food has a southern accent with fresh fish and lamb cooked traditionally over a wood fire. For dessert, don't miss the lavender, thyme and rose sorbets. There are two large dining rooms, or if the weather is good you may prefer to sit outside on the pleasant terrace.
✉ 15 boulevard Mirabeau, 13210 St-Rémy-de-Provence ☎ 04 90 92 09 17 ⏲ Daily 12–2, 7.30–10 ✋ L €20, D €35, Wine €20

### BRASSERIE LES VARIÉTÉS

A favoured local spot for lunch, a light dinner or an afternoon snack. Specials, such as an innovative spinach, mushroom and egg tart served with tomato salsa, or classic confit de canard, are scrawled on the blackboard, and wines are served by the jug.
✉ 32 boulevard Victor Hugo, 13210 St-Rémy-de-Provence ☎ 04 90 92 42 61 ⏲ Daily 11–10.30. Closed Tue in winter ✋ L €15, D €25, Wine €15

### LA SERRE

http://la.serre.free.fr
This restaurant deserves its name, 'glasshouse': It comes complete with a banana tree and other exotic plants and a little fountain. The restaurant was built in the ruins of a convent in the heart of St-Rémy. Chef Serge Gille-Nave loves to experiment with herbs, many of which he grows in the restaurant's own kitchen garden. When it comes to desserts, this grandson of Gaston Lenôtre, one of France's celebrated cake-makers, is at his best: Try the marvellous lavender-scented gingerbread and geranium sorbet. There is a vegetarian menu.
✉ 8 rue de la Commune, 13210 St-Rémy-de-Provence ☎ 04 90 92 37 21 ⏲ Tue–Sun 7.30–11 ✋ D €30, Wine €20

**Below** *Dining on the terrace at Le Bistrot des Alpilles, in St-Remy-de-Provence*

**PRICES AND SYMBOLS**

Prices are the lowest and highest for a double room for one night. Each listing states whether breakfast is included. All the hotels listed accept credit cards unless otherwise stated. Note that rates vary widely throughout the year.

For a key to the symbols, ▷ 2.

## AIX-EN-PROVENCE

### HÔTEL LE PIGONNET

www.hotelpigonnet.com

Elegant, four-star Le Pigonnet is in the heart of town, at the end of a tree-lined street. There's a wonderful view of the Montagne Sainte-Victoire. The hotel has a restaurant.

✉ 5 avenue du Pigonnet, 13090 Aix-en-Provence ☎ 04 42 59 02 90 €110–€420, excluding breakfast (€21) 49 Outdoor

## ARLES

### GRAND HÔTEL NORD-PINUS

www.nord-pinus.com

The style of this four-star hotel crosses places and times: Persian carpets, paintings, objets d'arts and antique furniture. The hotel was popular with visiting bullfighters during the mid-20th century.

✉ Place du Forum, 13200 Arles ☎ 04 90 93 44 44 €160–€295, excluding breakfast (€14) 26

### HÔTEL D'ARLATAN

www.hotel-arlatan.fr

There's quite a history to this three-star hotel: It was built on the site of Constantin Basilica and has many Roman relics, as well as a 16th-century vaulted ceiling. Take breakfast in the peaceful walled garden. There is private parking.

✉ 26 rue Sauvage, 13631 Arles ☎ 04 90 93 56 66 €85–€153, excluding breakfast 48

### LE MAS DE PEINT

www.masdepeint.com

This was the house of 17th-century Lyon draper, Antoine Peint. It became a farm in the 19th century: Rice is still grown on the estate and cattle are bred. The bedrooms are rustic yet refined. Some have beamed ceilings, others a Victorian bathroom. Enjoy farm-grown food in the evenings.

✉ Le Sambuc, 13200 Arles ☎ 04 90 97 20 62 Closed mid-Jan to mid-Mar, mid-Nov to mid-Dec €235–€295, excluding breakfast (€22) 8, plus 3 suites Outdoor

## LES BAUX-DE-PROVENCE

### HÔTEL LA BENVENGUDO

www.benvengudo.com

This ivy-covered hotel, built in 1967, has a huge garden. Inside are beamed ceilings and antique furniture; white walls give an airy feel. Some bedrooms are in adjoining buildings and some have a balcony or a terrace. There's a tennis court and boules pitch. The restaurant serves local cuisine.

✉ Vallon de l'Arcoule, 13520 Les Baux-de-Provence ☎ 04 90 54 32 54 Closed Nov–Mar €105–€370, excluding breakfast (€15) 21 rooms, 3 suites Outdoor

### LE MAS D'AIGRET

www.masdaigret.com

Nestled against a cliff, this three-star hotel has wonderful views and some surprising interiors—the breakfast room, bar, lounge and some of the guest rooms have been carved out of the rock and you can see the exposed rockface. The simple, tasteful bedrooms have floral bedspreads and white furniture, and there is a restaurant.

✉ D27A, 13520 Les Baux-de-Provence ☎ 04 90 54 20 00 Closed mid-Nov to mid-Dec €95–€190, excluding breakfast (€9) 16 Outdoor

### LE MAS DE L'OULIVIÉ

www.masdeloulivie.com

An olive grove surrounds this hotel in a Provençal cottage. The lounge has beamed ceilings and a

**Opposite** *The Grand Hôtel Nord-Pinus, Arles*

large fireplace; the bedrooms have beautiful fabrics, tile floors and subtle lighting. The pool has been attractively landscaped with rocks, a beach down to the water and a spa. Breakfast is served by the pool.
Les Arcoules, 13520 Les Baux-de-Provence 04 90 54 35 78 Closed mid-Nov to mid-Mar €110–€280, excluding breakfast (€14) 25 Outdoor

## CASSIS

### LES ROCHES BLANCHES

www.roches-blanches-cassis.com
Sitting on top of a cliff, with gardens cascading down to the sea, this four-star hotel has breathtaking views: Its pool seems to melt into the Mediterranean, which fills the horizon. Most of the bedrooms have a balcony or terrace and all have been tastefully decorated with fine fabrics and pretty shades. Enjoy dinner on the terrace or in the dining room, with its large bay windows.
Route des Calanques, 13260 Cassis 04 42 01 09 30 Closed Nov to mid-Mar €160–€260, excluding breakfast (€16) 24 Outdoor

## GÉMENOS

### LE RELAIS DE LA MAGDELEINE

www.relais-magdeleine.com
This hotel, in a pretty garden, has an attractive 18th-century facade. The interior is tastefully decorated and the bedrooms have period furniture and warm hues. The restaurant serves fine Provençal cuisine. You can eat dinner on the terrace.
Rond-point de la Fontaine, 13420 Gémenos 04 42 32 20 16 Closed mid-Nov to mid-Mar €110–€190, excluding breakfast (€15) 24 Outdoor

## MARSEILLE

### HÔTEL LE CORBUSIER

www.hotellecorbusier.com
The hotel is in a block of 300 apartments designed by Le Corbusier to re-create a city within a single building. As such, it comes complete with play areas, shops, a cinema, a bar and a library. The delightfully simple bedrooms look to the sea or the park and terrace. There is private parking.
280 boulevard Michelet, 13008 Marseille 04 91 16 78 00 €63–€120, excluding breakfast (€9) 21 Rond-point du Prado

### HÔTEL ST-LOUIS

www.hotel-st-louis.com
The Napoleonic facade of this two-star hotel, dotted with wrought-iron balconies, is listed as a historic monument. The hotel is close to the animated Canebière and Old Port. The comfortable bedrooms have been simply decorated and they all have a TV and WiFi access. The reception area has more character, with terracotta hues and a tile floor.
2 rue des Récollettes, 13001 Marseille 04 91 54 02 74 €67–€90, excluding breakfast (€8) 22 Vieux Port, Noailles

### LE PETIT NICE PASSÉDAT

www.passedat.fr
Stay here for luxury, calm and the immensity of the Mediterranean for a backdrop. The contemporary interior of this four-star hotel exudes tranquillity and the restaurant is excellent.
Anse de Maldormé, Corniche J. F. Kennedy, 13007 Marseille 04 91 59 25 92 €190–€750, excluding breakfast (€25) 13 Outdoor

## NÎMES

### HÔTEL IMPERATOR CONCORDE

www.hotel-imperator.com
This hotel fronts onto the road, but the magnificent gardens more than make up for that. Both Ernest Hemingway and Ava Gardner were lured to this wonderful place, overlooking the Jardin de la Fontaine and place Picasso. Start your evening with cocktails on the terrace overlooking the fountain and finish it in one of the spacious, well-designed rooms.
Quai de la Fontaine, 15 rue Gaston-Bossier, 30900 Nîmes 04 66 21 90 30 €180–€218, excluding breakfast (€9) 60

## ST-CANNAT

### MAS DE FAUCHON

www.mas-de-fauchon.fr
Hidden in the countryside, this small hotel offers peace and relaxation. The bedrooms have been personalized: a four-poster bed in one, flowery curtains matching the cushions in another. Each has a private terrace. The adjoining restaurant serves regional cuisine and is in a former shepherd's house with beamed ceilings and a fireplace.
1666 chemin de Berre, 13760 St-Cannat 04 42 50 61 77 €125–€285, excluding breakfast (€15) 9 Outdoor

## SAINTES-MARIES-DE-LA-MER

### AUBERGE LA LAGUNE

www.lalagune.net
In the heart of the Camargue and within walking or bicycling distance of Saintes-Maries itself, La Lagune has chalet-style cottages, each with a little terrace, set around a large swimming pool. You can follow footpaths directly from the hotel, and bicycle rental allows you to explore the region at a slower pace. There's a well-respected Provençal restaurant on site.
Route d'Arles, 13460 Saintes-Maries-de-la-Mer 04 90 97 84 34 €78–€118, excluding breakfast (€12) 20 Outdoor

## SALON-DE-PROVENCE

### ABBAYE DE SAINT-CROIX

www.hotels-provence.com
This restored 12th-century abbey sits in a prominent position surrounded by views of delightful Provençal landscapes. The original Romanesque architecture shines through in the simple yet luxurious decor of the rooms. It's a wonderful retreat after a day's sightseeing and has a gastronomic restaurant on site with a cool shaded terrace.
Route du Val-de-Cuech, 13300 Salon-de-Provence 04 90 56 24 55 Closed Nov–end Mar €182–€341, excluding breakfast (€22) 21 rooms, 4 suites Outdoor

# VAR

The Var is a fortunate land, covered with wild countryside and dotted with pretty perched villages. And thanks to its string of quiet sandy beaches and great-value accommodation, it's one of the most family-friendly places in the country. The interior is a superb place to escape. Indeed, the Abbaye du Thoronet, set in the Var's oak and cork forests, has been a scene of splendid isolation for centuries. Those with their own wheels should head farther into the Haute-Var, preferably with no fixed itinerary. The hilly towns of Aups, Cotignac and Les Arcs have enough charm—and certainly enough hearty country fare—to sustain the most demanding of visitors.

But it's the Var's splendidly serene coastline that makes it stand out. When wealthy European visitors began to head south for a dose of winter sun they settled in the resorts of Hyères, Bandol and Le Lavandou. The legacy is a row of classic seaside towns all linked by good roads, reliable bus routes and, west of Toulon, a train line. It's now the coast's white sand beaches that attract the mostly French tourists each summer, along with a trickle of visiting Brits, Germans and Italians.

The very best beaches ring the St-Tropez peninsula. This promontory is covered with vineyards and romantic hill villages like Gassin and Ramatuelle, rather than villas and traffic as some might claim. Granted, some of these sandy strips, such as Plage Pampelonne, are summer playgrounds for pop stars and models, but others, like Plage Gigaro, are windswept, quiet and linked by coastal paths. Harking for complete isolation? Then head to the Îles des Hyères, off the Var coast, where three islands lie waiting to be discovered.

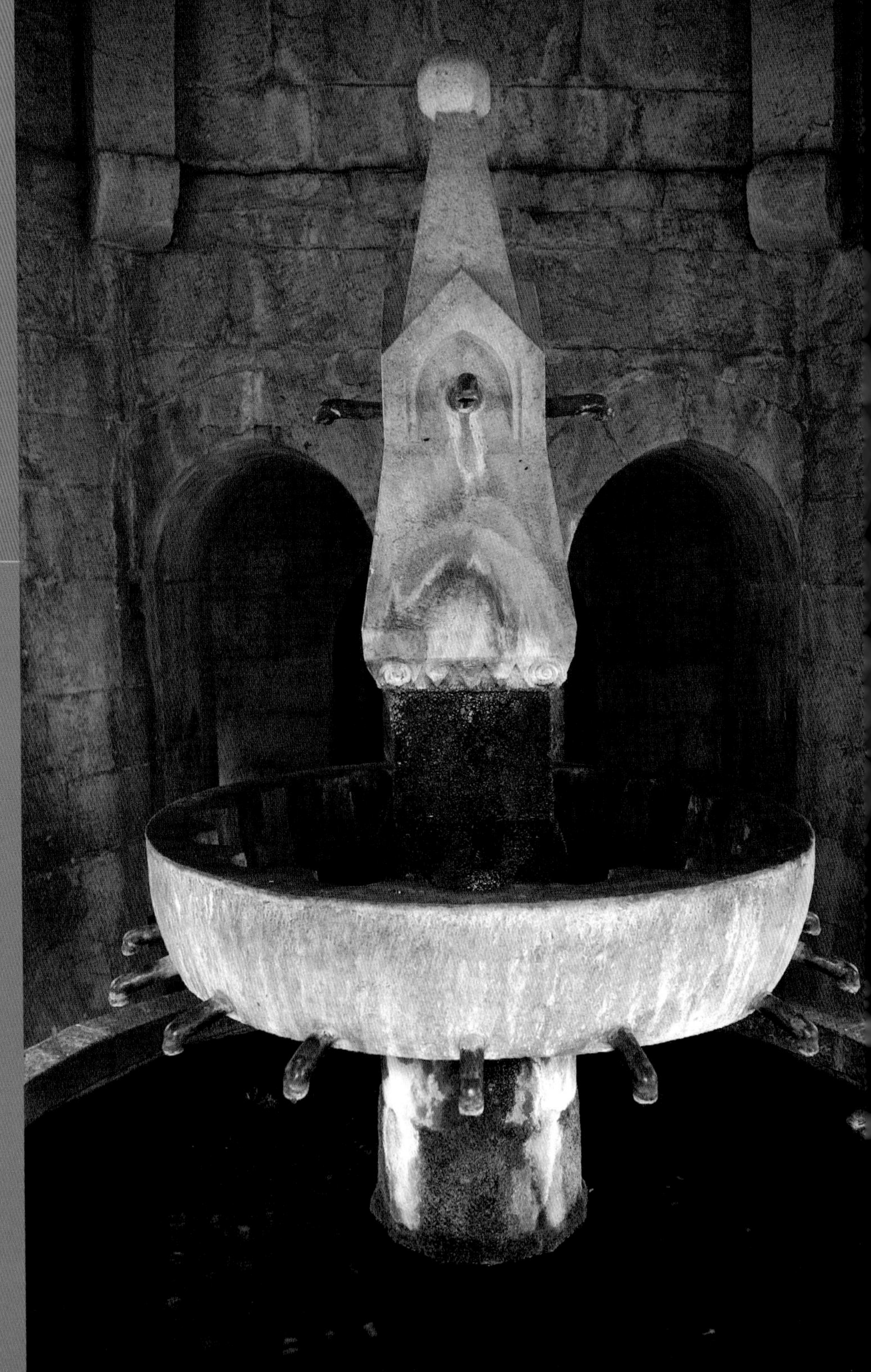

# ABBAYE DU THORONET

Hidden deep in woodland, Le Thoronet Abbey is in one of the most evocatively picturesque areas of the Provençal interior. Lying just off the D79 country road from Brignoles to Draguignan, the abbey of Le Thoronet was the first to be built of the three 12th-century Cistercian abbeys known as the 'Three Cistercian Sisters of Provence'. The buildings themselves, of great stone blocks without mortar, have survived the centuries in excellent condition, and there are beautiful, unusual cloisters. The woodland setting still conveys a sense of serenity, despite the easy accessibility of the abbey today. Several walking routes pan out from the abbey to the village of Le Thoronet, along the Argens River, and past many deserted bauxite mines.

## CISTERCIANS AT LE THORONET

The Cistercians, based at Cîteaux in Burgundy, promoted the ideal of a rigorous, harshly simple, chaste life of religious devotion and hard work. They were rebelling against the corrupt riches of the Church. As their movement grew, it founded three great abbeys in Provence—Le Thoronet, Silvacane (▷ 61) and Sénanque (▷ 221). Building started at Le Thoronet in 1146. The isolated forest setting fitted the Cistercian ideas of shunning the world. The present building, in Provençal Romanesque style, was completed in 1190, and, despite its austerity, soon became extremely wealthy through substantial donations. In the 14th century, Le Thoronet, like other abbeys, was the target of many raids, suffered poor harvests and was attacked during the Wars of Religion. It was gradually abandoned, seized by the State in the Revolution and sold, though in 1854 it was repurchased by the State and restored.

## INSIDE THE ABBEY

Going through the gatehouse, you see ahead the beautifully proportioned but rather low church, built in lovely pinkish stone, with a square bell tower and red-tile roof. The interior is very plain and undecorated. Beside the church are attractive cloisters, built on three levels because of the uneven ground. In the middle of the cloisters is a hexagonal structure containing a fountain used by the monks for hand-washing before meals. Other buildings around the cloister include the chapter house, in the early Gothic style. It has a dormitory upstairs. There's also a tithe barn, which originally stored goods given as tithes but later became an oil mill.

## INFORMATION

http://thoronet.monuments-nationaux.fr
302 K12 · Abbaye du Thoronet, 83340 Le Luc · 04 94 60 43 90 · Apr–end Sep Mon–Sat 10–6.30, Sun 10–12, 2–6.30; Oct–end Mar daily 10–1, 2–5 · Adult €7, under 18 free; free to all first Sun of month · The abbey is 11km (7 miles) from Carcès. It lies off the D79 between the D13 and D84 · Guided visits are available, depending on demand

## TIP

» Mass is sung by the Sisters of Bethlehem in the church every Sunday at noon.

**Opposite** *A fountain in the cloisters*

**Below** *Atmospheric arches in the church*

## LES ARCS-SUR-ARGENS

www.mairie-les-arcs-sur-argens.fr

In the Argens valley south of Draguignan, this attractive medieval village has an old quarter called Le Parage, which rises to the ruins of a 13th-century castle. From here, there is a wonderful view of the Massif des Maures and the surrounding vineyard country. A large Provençal-style *crèche* (Nativity) tableau inside St-Jean-Baptiste church (daily 10–2, 2–5) shows Le Parage as it once was. There is also a 15th-century polyptych by Jean de Troyes.

302 L12 Place Général-de-Gaulle, 83460 Les Arcs-sur-Argens 04 94 73 37 30 Jul, Aug daily 9.15–12.30, 2.30–8.30; Sep–end Jun Mon–Sat 9.15–12.15, 1.45–6 Draguignan-Les-Arcs

## AUPS

www.aups-tourisme.com

Dominated by the Montagne des Espiguières, the small town of Aups lies in the Haut Var woodlands. Mainly a farming town, Aups is also a popular base for exploring the Haut Var and visiting the Grand Canyon du Verdon, 23km (14 miles) to the north (▷ 204–205). As well as the remains of its medieval ramparts, several fountains and a 16th-century tower with a wrought-iron belfry, the town also has an attractive Gothic church, Église St-Pancrace, entered through a restored Renaissance doorway.

297 K11 Place F. Mistral, 83630 Aups 04 94 84 00 69 Jul, Aug Mon–Sat 9–12.30, 2–5.30, Sun 9–12.30; May, Jun, Sep Mon–Sat 8.45–12.15, 2–5.30; Oct–end Apr Mon, Tue, Thu, Fri 8.45–12.15, 1.30–5, Wed, Sat 8.45–12.15

**Below** *Bright yellow mimosa blossom*

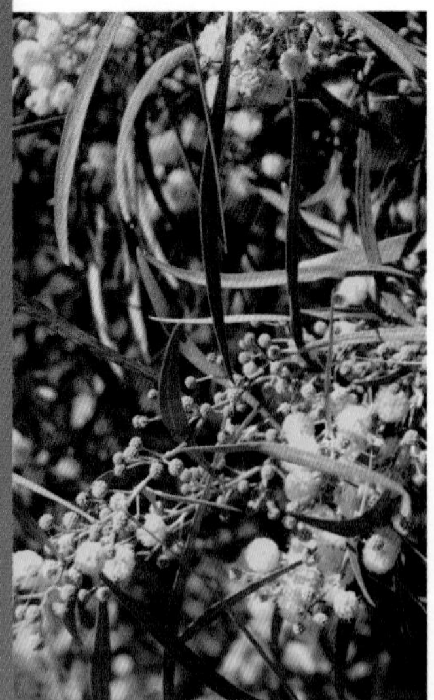

## BANDOL

www.bandol.fr

The beach resort of Bandol, between Marseille and Toulon, is popular with local families. In the past, it was a haunt of intellectuals and literati: D. H. Lawrence, Aldous Huxley and Katherine Mansfield all spent time here in the 1920s. It has a pleasant tree-lined promenade running the length of the port, and all the trappings of the Riviera—discos, nightclubs, water sports, casino—without the sky-high prices.

The hills behind the town are rather unsightly with apartments, but in town the port is picturesque and there are sandy beaches. The best of them is Anse de Renecros beach, in a sheltered position on the west of town. A frequent ferry service connects the waterfront to the Île de Bendor, where there are two hotels, a restaurant (▷ 134), diving and windsurfing facilities and a museum of wines and spirits. Bandol is famous for wine production, particularly its whites and rosés, which you can buy at several *caves* around town.

301 H14 Service du Tourisme, allée Vivien, 83150 Bandol 04 94 29 41 35 Jul, Aug daily 9.30–7; May, Jun, Sep Mon–Sat 9–12, 2–6; Oct–end Apr Mon–Sat 9–12, 2–5 Bandol

## LE BEAUSSET

www.ot-lebeausset.fr

Inland, on the main road between Toulon and Aubagne, the town of Le Beausset keeps its pleasant typically Provençal old heart. Napoleon Bonaparte stayed for a month at a house in rue Pasteur in 1793. The town square has a lovely fountain dating from 1832. On a hillside above the town is Le Beausset Vieux, site of the original Ligurian settlement, abandoned when the inhabitants moved downhill to the present location in 1506. You'll get wonderful views of Ciotat Bay from the tower on top of the Romanesque chapel, Notre-Dame du Beausset Vieux (Jul, Aug daily 3–7; Apr–end Jun, Sep daily 2–6; Oct–end Mar daily 2–5).

302 H13 Place Général-de-Gaulle, 83330 Le Beausset 04 94 90 55 10 Jun–end Aug Mon–Fri 9–12.15, 3–7, Sat 9–12.15; Sep–end May Mon–Fri 9–12, 2–6, Sat 9–12

## BORMES-LES-MIMOSAS

www.bormeslesmimosas.com

At the heart of Bormes is the steep medieval village with its pretty houses, evocative lanes, passageways and steps, and a restored fortress, the Château des Seigneurs de Fos, at the top of the hill. Perched on a Massif des Maures hilltop just inland from the beaches, Bormes is special because of its abundant bright-yellow vanilla-scented mimosa, which flower throughout the village in springtime. In summer, mimosa is replaced by bougainvillea and geraniums. There are several flower festivals, including a mimosa display in February. A *Parcours Fleuri* (flower walk), starting from near the church, leads up around the castle.

Much attention has been lavished on Bormes-les-Mimosas by the artists and second-homers who have bought property here in recent years, and there is a plethora of potteries, art galleries and craft shops. The Musée d'Art et d'Histoire, in 61 rue Carnot (Jun–end Sep Tue–Sun 10–12, 3–6.30; Oct–end May Tue–Sun 10–12, 2–5.30), traces the history of the village and holds frequent temporary art exhibitions.

302 L14 1 place Gambetta, 83230 Bormes-les-Mimosas 04 94 01 38 38 Jul, Aug Mon–Sat 9.30–1, 2.30–7, Sun 10–1, 3–7; Jun, Sep Mon–Fri 9.30–12.30, 2.30–6.30, Sun 10–1, 3–6.30; Apr, May Mon–Sat 9–12.30, 2–6, Sun 10–1, 2.30–6; Oct–end Mar 9–12.30, 1.30–5.30

## BRIGNOLES

www.la-provence-verte.net

Brignoles is a large, lively town with an extensive medieval quarter. The rather odd star attraction is the Musée du Pays Brignolais, in the 13th-century summer palace of the Counts of Provence (www.museebrignolais.com; Apr–end Sep Wed–Sat 9–12, 2.30–6, Sun 9–12, 3–6; Oct–end Mar Wed–Sat 10–12, 2.30–5, Sun 10–12, 3–5). Exhibits include a 13th-century winepress and an automated Provençal Nativity tableau.

302 J12 Carrefour d l'Europe, 83170 Brignoles 04 94 69 27 51 Jun–end Aug Mon–Sat 9–12.30, 2–7.30, Sun 9.30–12, 3–6.30; Sep–end May Mon–Sat 9–12, 2–6

## LA CADIÈRE D'AZUR

www.ot–lacadieredazur.fr

This *village perché* (perched village) may not be as scenic as nearby Le Castellet (▷ below) but it has fewer visitors and so is quieter. In summer, jazz concerts are held in the Chapelle Notre-Dame-de-la-Miséricorde, built by the Pénitents Noirs monks in 1634. The Pénitents Gris monks built the Chapelle Sainte-Madeleine at the top of the village. There is an impressive marble altarpiece in the 12th-century Église St-André.

You can buy olive oil and other local produce at the Moulin de St-Côme, on the D266 just outside the village.

301 H14 Maison des Gardes, place Général-de-Gaulle, 83740 La Cadière 04 94 90 12 56 Jul, Aug Tue–Sat 9–12, 2.30–7; Sep–end Jun Tue–Sat 10–12, 1.30–5.30

## LE CASTELLET

www.ville-lecastellet.fr

Surrounded by vineyards, the delightful, flower-filled Le Castellet was one of the first *villages perchés* (perched villages) to be taken up by artists and craftworkers, who began to move in during the 1950s. The photogenic medieval streets have several times served as film sets, most notably for Marcel Pagnol movies like *Manon des Sources.* The cinematic associations go back to the very origins of film-making, for it was here that the Lumière brothers bought a house ('Le Castel') to use as a production studio in 1895 for the making of the first-ever moving pictures.

301 H13 Hôtel de Ville, 83330 Le Castellet 04 94 32 79 13 Jul–end Sep Mon–Fri 11–5.30, Sat 1.30–6, Sun 9–1.30; Oct–end Jun Mon–Fri 9–12, 2–6, Sat 11–6

## COGOLIN

www.cogolin-provence.com

Cogolin, a short distance inland from St-Tropez and on the edge of the Massif des Maures, is known for its crafts, pipes and rugs. A handful of craftspeople in this otherwise workaday town still specialize in ironwork, pottery, corks for wine bottles, top-quality reeds for wind instruments, and cane furniture. But what many shoppers come for are the famous pipes, made at Les Pipes Ch. Courrieu, in avenue G. Clemenceau (Mon–Thu 8.30–12, 2–5.30, Fri 8.30–12, 2–5). Quirky designs include pipes with faces or with frills. Another good buy is rugs, produced in the workshops of La Manufacture de Tapis, on boulevard Louis Blanc (Mon–Thu 8.30–12, 2–5.30, Fri 8.30–12, 2–5. Closed Aug, Dec). Armenian immigrants brought the tradition of rug-making to the village in the 1920s.

303 M13 Place de la République, 83310 Cogolin 04 94 55 01 10 Jul, Aug Mon–Sat 9–1, 2–6.30; Mar–end Jun, Sep, Oct Mon–Fri 9.30–12.30, 2–6.30, Sat 9–12.30; Nov–end Feb Mon–Fri 9–12.30, 2–6, Sat 9–12.30

## COLLOBRIÈRES

www.collobrieres-tourisme.com

In the heart of the Massif des Maures coastal hills, Collobrières keeps its traditional feel, the only modern touch being a factory processing the chestnuts produced by the surrounding forests. (If you have a sweet tooth, try some *marrons glacés*—candied chestnuts). The village has modest sights,

**Above** *A view over the rooftops of Cogolin, a town on the edge of the Massif des Maures*

including a 12th-century bridge and the curiously arcaded place Rouget de l'Isle, but is mainly a rest stop on the road up to the Chartreuse de la Verne (Jul, Aug Wed–Mon 11–6; Feb–end Jun, Sep–end Dec Wed–Mon 11–5). This Carthusian nunnery stands isolated among the dense Maures forest, 12km (7 miles) from Collobrières. Founded in 1170, it has been damaged and rebuilt many times, and has recently been restored. It is a rambling complex of cloisters, chapels and cells—each with its own garden—in the rich shades of the local stone, red schist and green serpentine.

302 L13 Boulevard Charles Caminat, 83610 Collobrières 04 94 48 08 00 Mon–Sat 10–12, 3–6

## COTIGNAC

www.ot-cotignac.provenceverte.fr

Wine, olive oil and honey form the main produce of this scenic village in the Haut Var. Two ruined towers sit on top of a cliff riddled with caves. The Romanesque parish church has a facade rebuilt in the 19th century. Summer concerts are held in the nearby Théâtre de Verdure.

297 K11 2 rue Bonnaventure, 83570 Cotignac 04 94 04 61 87 Apr–end Sep Mon–Sat 9–1, 2.30–6; Oct–end Mar Mon–Fri 9–1, 3–6, Sat 9–1

## DRAGUIGNAN

www.dracenie.com

Draguignan is a busy working town in the Riviera backcountry, and former capital of the Var *département*. It has also been a military town since Roman times. The approach to the town is not particularly attractive, but persevere to the well-preserved central medieval quarter, the *vieille ville*. Of the medieval fortifications, the two gateways Porte de Portaiguières and Porte de Romaine survive. The facade of the synagogue in rue de la Juiverie dates from the same time.

The Musée Municipal (Mon–Sat 9–12, 2–6), in a former Ursuline convent on rue de la République, displays European fine art from the 17th to 19th centuries, as well as faïence and other porcelain. In nearby rue Joseph Roumanille, the Musée des Traditions Populaires (Apr–end Sep Tue–Sat 9–12, 2–6, Sun 2–6; Oct–end Mar Tue–Sat 9–12, 2–6) is an excellent ethnography museum. The market (Wed, Sat) in place du Marché is one of the region's best.

297 L11 Maison de Pôle Touristique de la Dracénie, 2 avenue Carnot, 83300 Draguignan 04 98 10 51 05 Jul, Aug Mon–Sat 9.15–12.15, 1.35–7, Sun 9.15–12.45; May, Jun, Sep Mon–Sat 9.15–12.15, 1.45–6; Oct–end Apr Mon–Fri 9.15–12.15, 1.45–6, Sat 9.15–12.45 Draguignan-Les-Arcs

## ENTRECASTEAUX

http://tourisme.entrecasteaux.fr

This pleasant inland village on the banks of the Bresque is dominated by its large chateau (open Easter–end October, closed Saturday), a rare example of the Provençal style of the 17th century, including a fine wrought-iron gateway. The building replaced an earlier fortress—you can still see the 11th-century entrance.

The chateau was restored in the 1970s by Scottish artist Ian McGarvie-Munn. Inside, the decor mixes period furnishings with modern art. Temporary art exhibitions are often held here. At the foot of the chateau is a formal garden designed in the 17th century by André Le Notre (open daily).

297 K12 21 cours Gabriel Péri, 83570 Entrecasteaux 04 94 59 95 64 Summer daily 10–12, 3.30–5.30; winter open if staff available

## EVENOS

www.evenos.com

The walls of Evenos' daunting 12th-century castle rise high above the Ollioules gorge. A twisting road reaches the castle itself (the interior is closed to the public but you can walk around the outside). Surrounding the castle and a 13th-century church is the tiny village.

302 J14 Hôtel de Ville, 83330 Evenos 04 94 98 50 86 Mon–Fri 8.30–12, 2–5.30

## FRÉJUS

▷ 121.

## LA GARDE-FREINET

www.lagardefreinet-tourisme.com

Groves of cork oaks, eucalyptus and sweet chestnut encircle this peaceful village, known as the 'capital' of the Massif des Maures (▷ 126) and perched 360m (1,180ft) above sea level. Alleys, fountains and courtyards make it a pleasant place to explore. Walk up to the Fort Freinet for lovely views of the Le Luc plain and the foothills of the Alps. La Garde-Freinet was one of the last Saracen strongholds in Provence in the 10th century and was France's main producer of cork in the 19th.

303 L13 Chapelle St-Jean, place de la Mairie, 83680 La Garde-Freinet 04 94 43 67 41 Jul, Aug Mon–Sat 9.30–1, 4–6.30, Sun 9.30–12.30; Apr–end Jun, Sep Mon–Sat 9.30–12.30, 3.30–5.30; Oct–end Mar Tue–Sun 9.30–12.30, 2–5

## GRIMAUD

www.grimaud-provence.com

The atmospheric medieval village of Grimaud stands on the eastern flanks of the Massif des Maures (▷ 126) just inland from St-Tropez. The main street, rue des Templiers, with Gothic doorways and arcades, climbs to the Romanesque church of St-Michel and the Hospice of the Knights Templar. The village was owned by the noble Grimaldi family, whose chateau ruins give broad vistas down to the Gulf of St-Tropez.

Down on the coast is Port Grimaud, an elegant marina whose canals have earned it the name 'Provençal Venice'. The resort is appealing, with its quays, waterside cafés and pastel-hued apartments. But it is enclosed by fences, has overpriced facilities, and drivers must use an expensive parking area. Boats leave from the main square for canal tours or you can rent your own electric boat for €20 per hour.

303 L13 1 boulevard des Aliziers, 83310 Grimaud 04 94 55 43 83 Jul, Aug Mon–Sat 9–12.30, 3–7; Apr–end Jun, Sep Mon–Sat 9–12.30, 2.30–6.15; Oct–end Mar Mon–Sat 9–12.30, 2.15–5.30 Annexe Port Grimaud, Chemin Communal 04 94 56 02 01 Jul, Aug Mon–Sat 9–12.30, 3–7; Jun, Sep Mon–Sat 9–12.30, 2.30–6.15

**Below** *Cork trees in La Garde-Freinet*

## FRÉJUS

This animated, long-established little beach resort makes a good base for drives along the coast and inland. On the east bank of the river Argens estuary, between the wild coastal hills of the Massif des Maures (▷ 126) and Massif d'Esterel (▷ 125), Fréjus was once a busy little Roman town and seaport. Over the centuries it moved 3km (2 miles) inland, where the medieval and Renaissance town was based. Today, it has extended back to the seashore, with the development of an appealing marina at Fréjus-Port and a narrow beachside strip called Fréjus-Plage. The town and its surroundings offer plenty of interest, including several medieval buildings, Roman ruins and modern family attractions.

### ROMAN AND MEDIEVAL REMINDERS

Although it merges into nearby St-Raphaël (▷ 124), Fréjus remains more of an inland town, St-Raphaël more of a beach resort. In the heart of Fréjus town, 17th- to 20th-century districts enclose a medieval quarter of narrow streets. At the hub of the old town is a curious *Cité Épiscopale* (Cathedral Close) with a medieval cathedral, cloisters and a fifth-century AD baptistery, possibly the oldest in France (Tue–Sun 9.30–12.30, 2–6; until 5 mid-Oct to mid-Apr). Near the cathedral close are considerable Roman ruins, including remnants of an aqueduct, a theatre, an army barracks and a fortified quay. There is also an amphitheatre called Les Arènes (Tue–Sun 9.30–12.30, 2–6; until 5 mid-Oct to mid-Apr), where concerts are still held, although it is not the most impressive amphitheatre in Provence.

### OUT OF TOWN

Out of town attractions include an extraordinary mosque in red stone, standing off the D4, built by sailors from Mali based at Fréjus in the 1920s. There's a zoo almost opposite, the Parc Zoologique de Fréjus (▷ 132). Aqualand (▷ 132) is a huge water park west of town on the N98.

### CELEBRATIONS AND MARKETS

Fréjus enjoys an extraordinary array of events, festivals and fairs, including water jousting, a *bravade* (religious festival and procession) at Easter and a grape festival in August. There are markets on Wednesday and Saturday, as well as additional summer markets.

### INFORMATION

www.frejus.fr
303 M12 · 325 rue Jean Jaurès, 83600 Fréjus · 04 94 51 83 83
Jun–end Sep daily 9–7; Apr, May Mon–Sat 9.30–6, Sun 9.30–12; Oct–end Mar Mon–Sat 9.30–12, 2–6, Sun 9.30–12
Fréjus

### TIP

›› All of the major sights in Fréjus, including the Malinese mosque, the amphitheatre, history museum and baptistery, can be visited on the same €4.60 *Fréjus Pass.*

**Above** *Brightly painted houses in Fréjus*

# HYÈRES AND THE ÎLES D'HYÈRES



**INFORMATION**
www.hyeres-tourisme.com
302 K14 (town); 302 L14–L15 (islands)
Forum du Casino, 3 avenue Ambroise Thomas, 83400 Hyères-les-Palmiers
04 94 01 84 50 Jul, Aug daily 8.30–7.30; Sep Mon–Sat 9–6; Oct–end Jun Mon–Fri 9–6, Sat 10–4 Hyères

## INTRODUCTION

A sense of remoteness and a sultry warmth greet visitors to the Côte d'Azur's most southerly resort and its unspoiled offshore islands. Exotic plants and palm trees flourish: The town is also known as Hyères-les-Palmiers, after its prolific date production.

Once an aristocratic resort, Hyères is now a budget holiday destination which is near the airport of the naval town of Toulon (▷ 127). For all that, the resort has much to recommend it, with a hotter climate and a flatter, richly cultivated fertile landscape. If you're arriving by car, it is best to park in the new town, in avenue A. Denis or avenue J. Jaurès, as parking in the old town is difficult.

You reach the Îles d'Hyères (known locally as the Îles d'Or, or Golden Islands) by public-transport ferry from two harbours: Port St-Pierre near the heart of Hyères town or the harbour on the Giens peninsula to the south. The Île de Porquerolles is the easiest island to visit as the direct ferry from La Tour Fondue harbour, 2km (1.5 miles) from Giens, takes only 20 minutes. The island has enough of interest to fill a full day. Ferries from Port St-Pierre also go to Port-Cros (taking one hour) and Le Levant (taking 90 minutes). You can take more expensive private excursions from Giens to the Île de Porquerolles and Port-Cros in high season. Ferries to Port-Cros also leave from Le Lavandou (▷ 124), farther east along the coast.

Greek traders built a port at Hyères called Olbia and the Romans renamed it Pomponiana. After the Roman withdrawal, the residents moved onto the nearby hill within fortifications built by local feudal lords. The medieval town survives today as the old quarter. In the 17th century, Hyères began to decline as Toulon grew in importance. However, by the 18th century the town had become the first holiday resort on the French Mediterranean, attracting large numbers of winter visitors. In the 19th century, many British aristocrats came for holidays—even Queen Victoria. Other 19th-century sunseekers included the writers Robert Louis Stevenson and Victor Hugo. The expression 'Côte d'Azur' was first coined (by journalist Stephen Liegeard in 1887) as a description of Hyères.

## WHAT TO SEE

### HYÈRES OLD QUARTER

The old quarter uses the backs of houses to create a defensive wall, penetrated by a Gothic gateway that leads into this atmospheric residential district of narrow streets lined with tall buildings, many with Renaissance doorways. The area climbs a slope to the ruins of a chateau in a park with wide views. The main square is the triangular place Massillon marketplace, overlooked by the Tour des Templiers, once under the command of the medieval Knights Templar. Other remnants of the Middle Ages in the town include two Romanesque–early Gothic churches, St-Paul and St-Louis. Villa de Noailles, beside the park, was a famous address in the 1920s, when the Noailles family gave exotic parties where guests included Pablo Picasso and Salvador Dalí.

### HYÈRES NEW TOWN

The area on the flat land below the old town is laid out with wide, busy boulevards edged with palm trees. In this district the Anglican church, in avenue Godillot, is evidence of the many English visitors who came in the resort's heyday. The Jardins Olbius-Riquier, covering 6.5ha (16 acres) to the southeast of the old town, are glorious tropical gardens with palm, cactus and flowering trees, a small animal enclosure and an interesting indoor area with other exotic plants and some rarer animals (May–end Sep daily 8am–9pm; Oct–end Apr daily 8–5). The gardens surround a villa in Moorish style. On the seashore, there are sandy beaches and a marina.

## GIENS

The Giens peninsula used to be one of the Îles d'Hyères, but is now connected to Hyères by a curious double sandbar, known as La Capte, 4km (2.5 miles) long. In between the two arms of the sandbar, salt pans attract numerous wading birds. The small resort village of Giens has castle ruins with an extensive view. At the eastern tip of the peninsula, La Tour Fondue is the departure point for ferries to Porquerolles.

## ÎLE DE PORQUEROLLES

At around 18sq km (7sq miles), Porquerolles is the largest of the Îles d'Hyères. Covered with Mediterranean woodland and heath, and preserved as a nature reserve, its forest paths are a haven for walkers and bicyclists. The south coast of the island has rocky cliffs, while the north coast, some 40 minutes' walk away, has a couple of sandy beaches. Ferries arrive at the enticing little quayside of Porquerolles village on the north coast, overlooked by the 19th-century Fort Sainte-Agathe (with an older corner tower), now an exhibition venue.

Daily throughout the year from Giens, departures every 30 min in Jul, Aug Adult €15.50, child (4–10) €13.50

## ÎLE DE PORT-CROS

Ferries pull in at the harbour of a small village with unpaved quays on the most southerly of the Îles d'Or. The whole island of Port-Cros, around 10sq km (4sq miles), is covered with dense Mediterranean woodland protected as a national park. There's no bicycling here, but walkers may use a network of pretty paths. The Route des Forts is a marked trail leading up to the Fort de l'Estissac and Fort du Moulin, beside the village. You can follow an underwater snorkelling trail from La Palud beach.

From Le Lavandou: Apr–end Sep daily; Oct–end Mar Thu–Tue Île de Port-Cros: adult €24.50, child (4–12) €20.30; Île du Levant and Île de Port-Cros: adult €27.50, child (4–12) €24.90

## ÎLE DU LEVANT

Tiny, rocky Île du Levant, just 8sq km (3sq miles), is the most easterly of the Îles d'Or. Around 80 per cent of the island is in the hands of the army and cannot be entered. The other 20 per cent is a nudist resort, with hundreds of permanent residents and visitors. Their small chalets rise up the wooded slopes behind the port.

From Le Lavandou: Apr–end Sep daily; Oct–end Mar Thu–Tue Île du Levant: adult €24.50, child (4–12) €20.30; Île du Levant and Île de Port-Cros: adult €27.50, child (4–12) €24.90

### TIPS

» You can't use your car on the islands; park at the ferry terminal at Giens or near Hyères port.

» The best beach on the islands is Plage de la Palud, at Port-Cros.

» Before setting off for the islands, always check the time of the last ferry back.

**Below left** *A view of the sunset from the Île de Porquerolles*
**Below right** *Looking towards the bell tower of the Ancienne Collegiale St-Paul, in Hyères*

**Above** *Sanary-sur-Mer's harbour*

## LE LAVANDOU

www.ot-lelavandou.fr

Le Lavandou stands at one end of the beautiful Corniche des Maures coast. Together with its waterfront extensions La Fossette, Aiguebelle, the nudist beach of Le Layet, and Cavalière, it has 10km (6 miles) of sandy beaches divided into 12 sandy strips—some with lifeguards, some totally wild. The town's lovely setting, yachting port and good amenities make this one of the more popular spots west of the Riviera. You can take ferries to the Île du Levant and Île de Port-Cros (▷ 123) from the port. The resort also makes a good base for exploring the Massif des Maures (▷ 126).

✚ 302 L14 ℹ Quai Gabriel-Péri, 83980 Le Lavandou ☎ 04 94 00 40 50 🕑 May–end Sep daily 9–7; Oct–end Apr Mon–Sat 9–12, 2–5.30

## LES LECQUES

www.saintcyrsurmer.com

The small waterfront resort of Les Lecques, west of Toulon, has a safe, sheltered sandy beach that attracts many local families in this built-up section of the coast. The family appeal is enhanced by a massive water park, Aqualand (mid-Jun to end Aug daily 10–7), at the nearby town of St-Cyr. St-Cyr's Musée Tauroentum, on route de la Madrague (Jun–end Sep Wed–Mon 3–7; Oct–end May Sat, Sun 2–5), displays Roman finds made locally. The town also boasts a gilded copy of the Statue of Liberty, donated by a wealthy local resident in 1913.

✚ 301 H14 ℹ Place de l'Appel du 18 Juin, Les Lecques ☎ 04 94 26 73 73 ☎ Jul, Aug Mon–Sat 9–7, Sun 10–1, 4–7; Mar–end Jun, Sep, Oct Mon–Sat 9–6; Nov–end Feb Mon–Sat 9–5

## MASSIF DE L'ESTEREL

▷ 125.

## MASSIF DES MAURES

▷ 126.

## ST-RAPHAËL

www.saint-raphael.com

Merging with Fréjus (▷ 121), the popular resort of St-Raphaël has a big sandy beach between its marinas. Once a much grander resort than today, its fine hotels and belle époque villas were destroyed by bombs in World War II. However, remnants survive of the medieval village surrounding the Romanesque church, Église St-Pierre. Beside the church, the Musée Archaeologique displays many finds discovered not just on shore but also underwater, including Roman jars and jugs, evidence of the town's busy trade during Roman times. The town hosts a New Orleans Jazz Competition every July, with performances along the promenade.

✚ 303 N12 ℹ Rue Waldeck-Rousseau, 83702 St-Raphaël ☎ 04 94 19 52 52 ☎ Jul, Aug daily 9–7; Sep–end Jun daily 9–12.30, 2–6.30 🚉 St-Raphaël

## ST-TROPEZ

▷ 128–129.

## SANARY-SUR-MER

www.sanarysurmer.com

Palm trees and pastel-hued buildings border the picturesque port at Sanary-sur-Mer. There is also a 13th-century watchtower. Look out for *pointus*—traditional boats with high, curved prows. The port dates back to Roman times. Sanary also boasts a small scuba diving museum (Jul, Aug daily 10–12.30, 4–7.30).

✚ 302 H14 ℹ Les Jardins de la Ville, 83110 Sanary-sur-Mer ☎ 04 94 74 01 04 ☎ Jul, Aug Mon–Sat 9–7, Sun 9.30–12.30; Apr–end Jun, Sep, Oct Mon–Fri 9–6, Sat 9–1, 2–5; Nov–end Mar Mon–Sat 9–12.30, 2–5.30

## TOULON

▷ 127.

## MASSIF DE L'ESTEREL

This ancient massif of volcanic rock is impenetrably wild, serene and astonishingly beautiful. The small range of the Esterel hills rises behind the coast between Fréjus and Cannes, bounded by the N7 main road and the sea. The jagged red-tinted terrain plunges into the azure sea creating exquisite bays and inlets. Until the 19th century, the Esterel was thickly covered with pine trees and Mediterranean undergrowth. However, a number of disastrous forest fires in the 1990s have savagely cut back the vegetation. The animals and birds too, including wild boar, deer, hares and partridges, have suffered from the damage to the plant cover, but are recovering. Since 1984, the massif has been a protected conservation area. Two valley zones have been designated biological reserves—the Ravin du Mal Infernet and the Ravin du Perthus—which both have cool humid conditions that have produced exceptional flora unique on the Mediterranean coast. They are both easily reached by road.

### MEMORABLE VIEWS, BY CAR OR ON FOOT

The wonderfully scenic Esterel coast road, from St-Raphaël to La Napoule, was carved into the impressive waterside cliffs a century ago. Known as the Corniche de l'Esterel or the Corniche d'Or, it is one of the most spectacular (and tortuous) drives on the Côte d'Azur. The Massif de l'Esterel is great walking country. The rocky red peaks are unforested and so offer splendid views from the top. There are several trails leading from Agay and Le Trayas train stations, as well as countryside parking spots. A popular hike leads up to the Pic de l'Ours (492m/1,600ft high).

### INFORMATION

303 N12

### TIPS

» Some paths in the massif may be closed in summer because of fire risk.

» Pick up a walking map of the massif, published by the Office National des Forêts, from tourist offices at Fréjus or St-Raphaël.

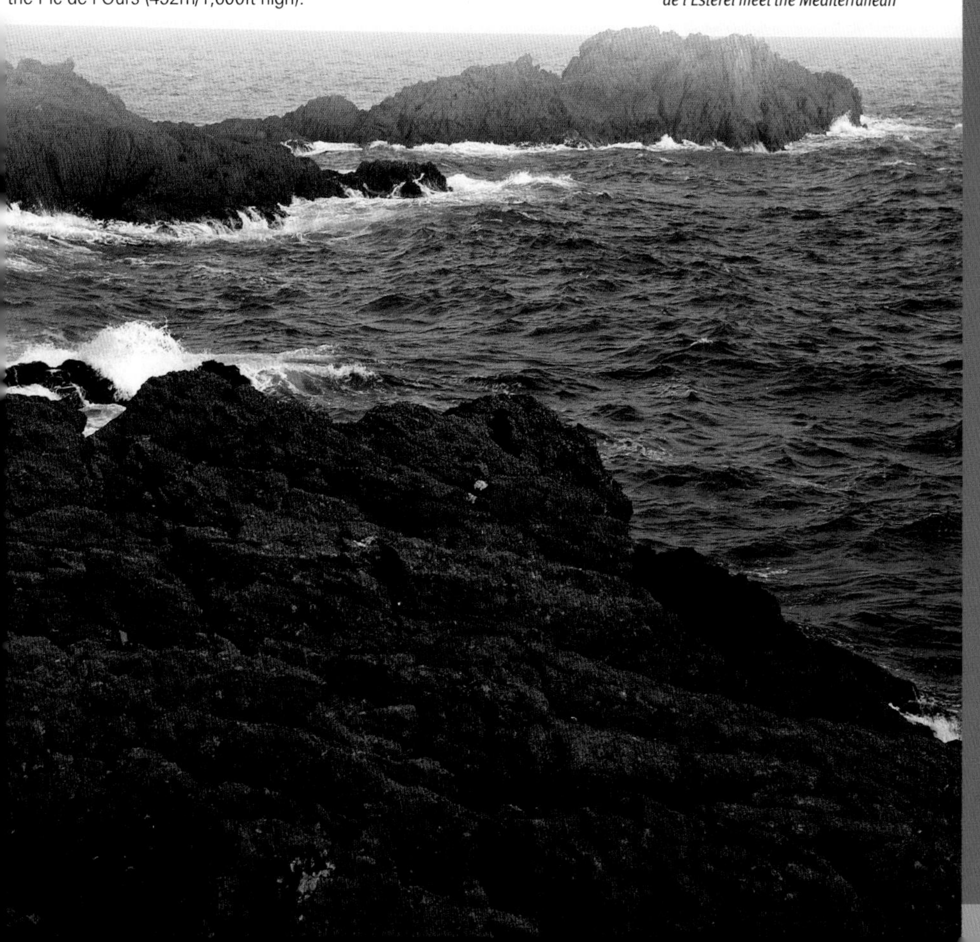

**Below** *The red-hued rocks of the Massif de l'Esterel meet the Mediterranean*

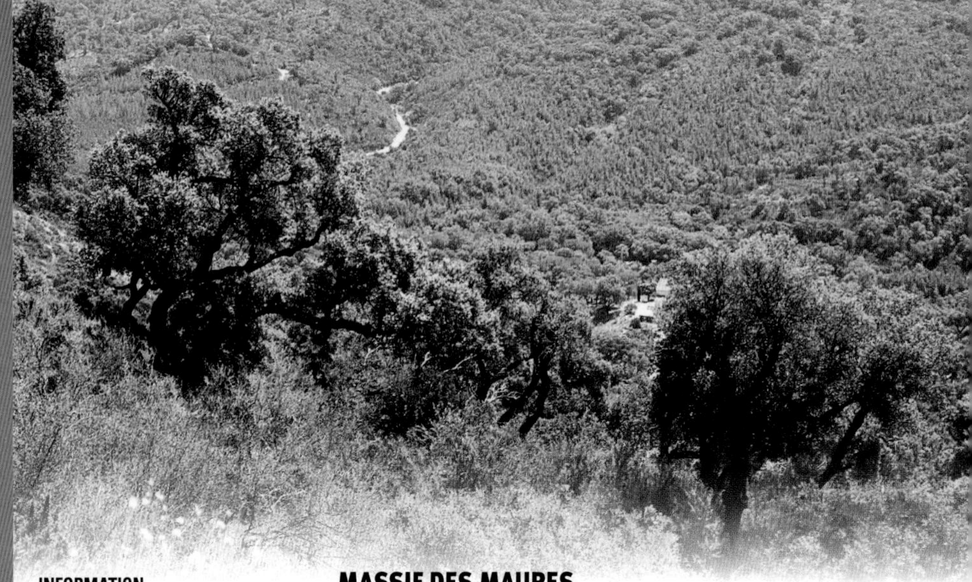

**INFORMATION**

www.st-tropez-lesmaures.com
302 K13–L13 Maison du Golfe de St-Tropez et du Pays de Maures, Carrefour de la Foux, 83580 Gassin 04 94 55 22 00 Apr–end Sep Mon–Fri 9–7, Sat 9.30–6, Sun 9.30–5.30; Oct–end Mar Mon–Fri 9–6, Sat 9.30–5.30

**Above** *Tree-covered slopes of the Massif des Maures*

# MASSIF DES MAURES

The sun-dried, half-wild Maures hills, threaded by lanes winding through the vegetation, encapsulate much that is magical about Provence. The hills, reaching heights of less than 800m (2,500ft), spread behind the coast from Hyères to Fréjus. In places they fall short of the seashore, while at other points—notably between Le Lavandou (▷ 124) and Cavalaire—they plunge directly into the sea to create a stunning coastline of dramatic views, small beaches, impressive bays and high cliffs. Detached a little from the rest of the massif stands the St-Tropez peninsula. All along the Maures shoreline, beaches are sandy and resort prices tend to be lower than farther east along the Riviera. The popular resort of Sainte-Maxime makes a good base for exploring the eastern Maures country. The massif is bordered by the D12 on the west, D7 on the east and N7 on the north.

## DIFFICULT ACCESS

Most of the hill country can be reached only on foot. Napoleon Bonaparte laid out a network of paths to enable law enforcement officers to reach areas where bandits and smugglers had their hideouts. Just one road traverses the whole length of the Massif des Maures, the N98 from St-Raphaël to Hyères, which runs along the coast as far as Port Grimaud. Three roads cut across the hills from north to south. The other zig-zagging little roads that reach into the interior reveal a hidden world of scenic landscapes thickly covered by *garrigue* (Mediterranean heath) and woods of holm oak, cork and low, aromatic pinewoods. There are also simple wine villages.

## THE INTERIOR

The village of La Garde-Freinet (▷ 120), once a remote haven of bandits and pirates in the heart of the Massif, is the little 'capital' of the Maures. North of here, on the D75, the low-key Village des Tortues (▷ 132–133) is both a delightful and entertaining outing and at the same time a serious conservation facility for tortoises, including the rare Hermann's Tortoise, a native of the Massif des Maures. Nearby is another attraction, the Hameau des Ânes (Donkey Village; Mar–end Nov daily 10–6. Last admission 5.15). Another attractive but difficult road from Grimaud winds through *garrigue*, small vineyards and cork oak forests to rustic Collobrières (▷ 119), a little village noted for its *marrons glacés* (candied chestnuts). You can try these at the farmers' market, the Marché Collobrièrois (▷ 132).

## TOULON

Toulon, at the western end of the Côte d'Azur, is France's second-largest naval port but is also a pleasant resort city. It became a naval base soon after Provence joined France in 1481. Under Louis XIV it became the strategic base for the Mediterranean fleet, a role it maintains today. France's largest aircraft carrier, the hulking great *Charles de Gaulle*, is often in port for visitors to see. Of more interest to many is Toulon's colourful fishing fleet. These boats supply the restaurants that surround the magnificent harbour, dishing up sardines, sea bass and squid for a fraction of the price charged in glitzier seaside resorts.

### SEA AND SKY

From the line of pontoons in Toulon harbour, commuters and visitors alike ride the regular Réseau Mistral boats around the bay. A €6 day pass gives unlimited travel. Popular destinations include the beach resort of Sablettes and the relaxed harbour suburb of St-Mandier. The pass also grants a return journey on the *téléphérique* (cable car) up to Mont Foron, a popular picnic, hiking and mountain-biking spot. It departs from boulevard Amiral Vence, 1km (0.6 miles) north of the train station.

### FOUNTAINS

In the heart of the city, look out for the Fontaine des Trois Dauphins, in place Puget. Made in 1782, this is one of the best of the town's 17 fountains; the three dolphins in the middle are now completely obscured by fig trees, oleander, ferns and ivy.

### CULTURE

The powerful Atlantes figures by the baroque sculptor Pierre Puget, on either side of the old town hall doorway, are based on stevedores Puget had seen unloading ships in Marseille. For those interested in maritime history, there's the Musée National de la Marine on quai de Norfolk (Jul, Aug daily 10–6; Sep–end Jun Wed–Mon 10–6). Toulon has other good museums, with themes including natural history, Asian art and photography. The excellent Hôtel des Arts (Tue–Sun 10–1, 3–7), on boulevard Maréchal Leclerc, is a freshly renovated contemporary art space. The richly decorated opera house, the grandest in Provence, stages opera, drama and ballet.

### INFORMATION

www.toulontourisme.com

302 J14 · 334 avenue de la République, 83000 Toulon · 04 94 18 53 00 · Jul, Aug Mon–Sat 9–8; Sep–end Jun Mon–Sat 9–6 · Toulon

### TIPS

» Ollioules, on the outskirts of Toulon, has pretty streets and a ruined 11th-century chateau.

» You'll find wonderful Provençal produce at the Marché de Provence, in the cours Lafayette every morning.

**Below** *Yachts moored in Toulon's harbour*

# ST-TROPEZ

**INFORMATION**

www.ot-saint-tropez.com
303 M13 Quai Jean-Jaurès, 83990 St-Tropez, 08 92 68 48 28
Jul, Aug daily 9.30–1.30, 3–8; Apr–end Jun, Sep, Oct daily 9.30–12.30, 2–7; Nov–end Mar daily 9.30–12.30, 2–6

**Above** *The harbour at night*

## INTRODUCTION

Once a Provençal seaside village, St-Tropez has become a playground of the rich and famous. Ordinary mortals come to stargaze—or to enjoy St-Tropez for what it originally was and still is, an exceptionally pretty coastal resort.

The town faces out across the large St-Tropez gulf from the north coast of the St-Tropez peninsula. It attracts celebrities from the world of pop music, movies and TV, who stay in five-star luxury. If you want to spot a celeb try the Club 55 or Tropezina beach clubs on nearby Pampelonne beach. Don't attempt to drive to St-Tropez—traffic is terrible, with waits of an hour or more to get into town and nowhere to park. Instead, use the large public parking areas at Port Grimaud or Sainte-Maxime and take the passenger ferry across the bay. If you want to relax on one of the beaches to the south of the port, the best way to get there from the town (unless you have your own speedboat) is by the bus that leaves from place des Lices in July and August. Some beaches are free but most are owned privately and you'll have to pay.

St-Tropez is named after Tropez, or Torpes, a Roman centurion martyred for his Christian faith. In the 15th century it became a fortified independent town belonging to a group of Genoese families. They started the *bravade* festival in memory of the saint. This was the first of two spectacular *bravades* held here each year. The other commemorates the involvement of the men of St-Tropez in the defeat of Spanish raiders farther along the coast in 1637. In the 19th century artist Paul Signac (1863–1935) set up house here and by the 1920s the town had become a haunt of writers and artists. In the 1950s the film star Brigitte Bardot made it her home, putting St-Tropez firmly on the media map. It remains the epitome of unconventional, carefree wealth and glitz.

## WHAT TO SEE

### PORT

St-Tropez is based around its picturesque quayside, which, despite the large numbers of visitors and huge luxury yachts, still somehow has a villagey charm. The quay curves along the edge of a beautiful blue bay. At one end of the quay are the Tour Vieille, Tour Suffren and Tour de Portalet, all remnants of the old fortifications, and the jetty called Môle Jean Réveille. Beyond it, the tiny, endearing quarter La Ponche was once a waterside fishermen's district. Another surviving fragment of the fortifications, Tour Jarlier, stands close by. At the other end of the quay is the Annonciade museum (▷ below).

### CITADELLE

East of town, on a hilltop clothed with pine and oleander, the Citadelle is an area of ruined 16th- and 17th-century defences. Inside the ruined fort is a display of relief maps and dotted around the site are cannons, drawbridges, moats and wells, along with stupendous bay views.

✉ Montée de la Citadelle, 83990 St-Tropez ☎ 04 94 97 06 53 🕐 Apr–end Sep daily 10–6.30; Oct–end Mar daily 10–12.30, 1.30–5.30 ✋ Adult and child over 8 years €2.50, under 8 free

### VIEILLE VILLE

Turning away from the quay, the old quarter or *Vieille Ville* (closed to traffic in summer) consists mainly of narrow streets of small old houses, with several chic little boutiques. Despite the large numbers of people sauntering on the nearby quayside, the streets of the old quarter are relatively uncrowded. On the edge of the quarter is the town's large main square, place des Lices (also known as place Carnot), where local men play boules under the trees. From here the town extends into more modern areas.

### MUSÉE DE L'ANNONCIADE

At the other end of the quay is the Annonciade Museum, one of Provence's finest modern art galleries, neatly housed in a 16th-century chapel. The wonderful collection takes in paintings of the pointillist, fauvist and Nabis schools by Seurat, Signac, Cross, Matisse, Vlaminck, Van Dongen, Derain, Vuillard and Bonnard, including depictions of the Riviera a century ago. You can also see personal memorabilia of Misia Godebska, friend of Bonnard, Renoir and others. Unusual drawings by Picasso show the circle of artistic friends.

✉ Place Georges-Grammont, 83993 St-Tropez ☎ 04 94 17 84 10 🕐 Jun–end Sep daily 10–1, 3–7; Oct, Dec–end May Wed–Mon 10–12, 2–6 ✋ Adult €5, 18–26 €2.50, under 18 free

### BEACHES

There are no proper beaches in town, so for a day lazing on the sand it's best to travel out onto the Cap de St-Tropez, on the peninsula. Along a sandy strip bordering the legendary Pampelonne Bay, pricey beach bars offer music, drinks and beach chairs to a cool clientele. Beaches include Tahiti-Plage, which once attracted stars such as Errol Flynn and Clark Gable, Les Bronzes, popular with celebrities, and the trendy Club 55. For water sports head for Pago Pago and for seafood try Bora Bora.

## MORE TO SEE

### ÉGLISE DE ST-TROPEZ

You'll notice this 19th-century church for its unusual yellow and pink bell tower. Inside is a golden bust of the town's patron saint.

✉ Rue de l'Église, St-Tropez 🕐 Daily 1pm–midnight

### RAMATUELLE

On a high point at the heart of the St-Tropez peninsula, Ramatuelle is a pretty village, lovingly restored by second-homers. Vineyards around it produce the local Côtes-de-Provence wines. Above Ramatuelle on the D89, three windmills give magnificent views. You can climb or drive up to the Moulin de Paillas windmill (Mar–end Oct Tue and Sat afternoons). Farther up the same road, the village of Gassin, originally a lookout guarding against Saracen invaders, has similarly fine views—and restaurant tables where you can sit and enjoy them.

✚ 303 M13

### TIPS

» Visit in mid-May or mid-June to catch one of the town's two spectacular *bravade* festivals.

» Minutes away from the crowds of St-Tropez are the beautiful villages of the St-Tropez peninsula, such as Gassin and Ramatuelle (▷ this page).

» For a walk in St-Tropez, ▷ 130–131.

**Above** *The Musée de l'Annonciade includes works by Picasso and Matisse*

# AROUND ST-TROPEZ

**This walk tempts you with chic shopping, then takes you to the marina crammed with sleek motor yachts. Equilibrium is restored with a visit to an exceptional museum of art. Then you leave the glitz behind to enter the oldest part of town, followed by an easy climb to the Citadelle, where you can enjoy views of the town and bay.**

**THE WALK**
**Distance:** 2km (1.2 miles)
**Time:** 2 hours, plus time for visits
**Start/end at:** Place des Lices

**HOW TO GET THERE**
If you are driving, you can take the D98 along the shore of the Bay of St-Tropez and follow signs for parking des Lices. However, it is probably easier to use the large public parking areas at Port Grimaud or Sainte-Maxime and take the passenger ferry across the bay.

★ Place des Lices is a large open area where markets, town gatherings and games of pétanque take place in the shade of the plane trees. The northern edge is defined by boulevard Louis Blanc; here you'll find La Tarte Tropezienne, a pastry and coffee shop whose success (there are now several in the area) has been built on a single irresistible brioche, orange blossom and cream confection, the recipe for which is protected by patent.

Descend some steps, cross the square and enter the rue Georges Clemenceau. This is lined with high-quality boutiques; at the other end is an arcade, filled with trendy boutiques, called le Grand Passage—a misnomer as it is small, unless the name refers to the size of the wallet necessary to shop here. Cross rue Allard and make a quick right then a quick left, to arrive at the quay. The Musée de l'Annonciade is 50m (54 yards) to the left.

❶ The Musée de l'Annonciade (▷ 129) is a must for enthusiasts of post-Impressionist art.

Retrace your steps along the quay, admiring the luxury boats on your left and the statue of Pierre-André de Suffen, an 18th-century admiral and founding father of St-Tropez, on the right. Pick up a town map at the tourist office next on the right, behind the resort's most famous café-terrace, Sénéquier.

❷ Sénéquier, right on the waterfront, is the place to enjoy an expresso or an ice cream while watching the well-heeled stroll by or play on their yachts just feet away.

Continue along the waterfront to reach the Môle Jean Réveille, the jetty enclosing the port, which rewards you with a wonderful view of the town on one side and views out over the Bay of St-Tropez on the other. Descend from the Môle by the Tour du Portalet and enter an alley, rue Portalet. Go left into rue St-Esprit and first right into rue du Puits. Turn left into place de l'Hôtel de Ville and then first right into rue

Commandant Guichard to reach the parish church, Notre-Dame de l'Assomption.

❸ Notre-Dame de l'Assomption's bright steeple is a town landmark, and the sound of its bells is delightful. Inside you can see the painted bust of St. Tropez (Torpes), the figurehead of processions during the town's *bravade* festivals (▷ 128).

Return to place de l'Hôtel de Ville and turn right to go through the Porte du Revelen; the small cove on the left is the original fishermen's port, known as La Ponche, where locals still take a dip from the sandy shore. Walk up rue des Remparts, bear left across place des Remparts and climb steps up to a road. Turn right down the road for 25m (27 yards), then go left between two anchors and climb more steps up to the ruined Citadelle (▷ 129).

❹ The Citadelle dates from the 16th century and its ruins now host relief maps of St-Tropez from centuries before: there's not a hotel in sight. The grounds around the Citadelle are strewn with cannons and are often used for temporary exhibitions, especially sculpture.

Retrace your path down the steps, enjoying views through oleanders and sweet-smelling eucalyptus, to the town and the bay. Cross the road and descend down rue de la Citadelle. At a tiny crossroads, 100m (110 yards) farther on, turn right into rue des Commerçants and pause for a coffee at Chez Fuchs, where a *cave à cigares* holds more than 10,000 cigars and a small spiral staircase leads to a popular Provençal restaurant. Opposite the bar is a small alley leading down to place aux Herbes.

❺ Place aux Herbes is tiny but exquisitely pretty. Here daily market stalls offer fresh fruit, vegetables and flowers. On the left, an arch leads into the shade of the morning fish market, where the night's catch is sold by the fishermen's wives.

Pass through the fish market and emerge at the other end next to the tourist office. Cross over into rue François Sibilli, walk past the olive and palm trees on place de la Garonne to place des Lices.

## WHERE TO EAT

### SÉNÉQUIER

✉ Quai Jean-Jaurès, St-Tropez ☎ 04 94 97 00 90 🕐 Summer daily 8–8; winter daily 8–7

### CHEZ FUCHS

✉ 7 rue des Commerçants, St-Tropez ☎ 04 94 97 01 25 🕐 Summer daily 8.30am–midnight; winter hours vary

## INFORMATION

### TOURIST INFORMATION OFFICE

www.ot-saint-tropez.com
✉ Quai Jean-Jaurès, St-Tropez ☎ 0892 68 48 28 🕐 Jul, Aug daily 9.30–1.30, 3–8; Apr–end Jun, Sep, Oct daily 9.30–12.30, 2–7; Nov–end Mar daily 9.30–12.30, 2–6

## WHEN TO GO

If you are driving to St-Tropez in summer, start early to avoid the heavy traffic.

**Clockwise from opposite** *Paintings on display in the harbour; cherries for sale at the market in Cours Saleya; delicious treats at La Tarte Tropezienne*

## AIGUINES

### LES GUIDES DES CALANQUES ET DU VERDON

www.les-guides.net

Explore the caves of Rampins, Néoules and Castelette or raft and rock climb above ground. Family expeditions are also available.

Le Galetas, 83630 Aiguines 04 94 84 22 55 €50–€60 for a caving expedition

## BANDOL

### LE TASTEVIN

A modern outlet dedicated to Bandol's sublime AOC wines, all of which are sourced from the surrounding vineyards. Sample wines, then buy a bottle or have a case parcelled home for you.

8 rue de la République, 83150 Bandol 04 94 05 90 64 Mon–Sun 9–12.30, 3.30–7

### THALAZUR BANDOL AND SPA

http://bandol.thalazur.fr

Water therapy, beauty treatments and massages by the beach in Bandol.

25 boulevard Louis Lumière, 83150 Bandol 04 94 29 33 00

## BORMES-LES-MIMOSAS

### PÉPINIÈRES CAVATORE

www.pepinieres-cavatore.fr

Mimosa trees are the speciality at this nursery—visit in February to see the trees in full bloom.

488 chemin de Bénat, 83230 Bormes-les-Mimosas 04 94 00 40 23 Jun–end Sep Mon–Fri 9–12; Oct–end May Mon–Fri 9–12, 1.30–5.30

## COGOLIN

### PIPES COURRIEU

www.courrieupipes.fr

Since 1802, and following methods that have been passed from father to son, the same family has been making pipes out of briar from the nearby Maures mountains. These pipes are marked with a silver cockerel, emblem of Cogolin village. A wide range of accessories for pipes and cigars is also available.

58–60 avenue Georges Clemenceau, 83310 Cogolin 04 94 54 63 82 Mon–Sat 9–12, 2–6

## COLLOBRIÈRES

### MARCHÉ COLLOBRIÈROIS

Collobrières is surrounded by chestnut groves and its vibrant farmers' market has a wide selection of chestnut products. These range from *marrons glacés* and chestnut jam to chestnut-wood wickerwork. There are also cork products and other regional specialities such as olives and honey.

Place de la Libération, 83610 Collobrières Thu, Sun 8–1

## DRAGUIGNAN

### DOMAINE RABIEGA

www.rabiega.com

This vineyard is owned by the Akesson family from Sweden, who bought the domaine from the Absolut Vodka company. It has been planted with Cabernet Sauvignon, Syrah, Cinsaut, Grenache and Carignan, which are used for rosé and red wines, and Chardonnay, Sauvignon Blanc and Viognier, for the whites.

Clos Dière, 83300 Draguignan 04 94 68 44 22 Mon–Fri 9–12, 2–5, Sat 10–12, 2–5

## FRÉJUS

### AQUALAND

www.aqualand.fr

This is the Riviera's biggest water park, covering 8ha (20 acres). Choose from a profusion of pools and water slides, including Europe's largest wave pool, the Twin-Twister (four interlaced slides) and the 'Grand Canyon' river. There are also restaurants and souvenir shops.

Quartier le Capou, RN98, 83600 Fréjus 04 94 51 82 51 Mid-Jun to 1st week in Jul daily 10–6; 2nd week in Jul–early Sep daily 10–7 Adult €25, child (3–12) €18.50, infants (under 1m/3ft tall) free

### CENTRE INTERNATIONAL DE PLONGÉE DE FRÉJUS

www.cip-frejus.com

A diving organization that arranges excursions to sites on the Bay of Cannes, including Cap Dramont. There are wreck dives in the area between Dramont and St-Tropez and night dives.

Aire de Carénage, Port Fréjus, 83606 Fréjus 04 94 52 34 99 All year long by appointment First dive: €44

### PARC ZOOLOGIQUE DE FRÉJUS

www.zoo-frejus.com

Elephants, kangaroos and hippopotamuses are among the creatures living in this safari park, covering 20ha (50 acres). Three islands are home to chimps. Don't miss the sea lion and tiger choreography.

Le Capitou, 83600 Fréjus 04 98 11 37 37 Jun–end Aug daily 10–6; Mar–end May, Sep, Oct daily 10–5; Nov–end Feb daily 10.30–4 Adult €14, child (3–9) €9.50, under 3 free

## GASSIN

### LA MAISON DES CONFITURES

You'll find every conceivable type of jam at this store, which is nestled between vineyards in a small village near St-Tropez that offers wonderful views. There are more than 500 varieties of jam, including some typically regional ones (thyme, lavender, fig and nut) and savoury jams (such as onion).

Chemin Bourrian, 83580 Gassin 04 94 43 41 58 Jul, Aug Mon–Sat 9.30–8, Sun 10–1, 5–8; Sep–end Jun Mon–Sat 9.30–7

## GONFARON

### VILLAGE DES TORTUES

www.tortues.com

A venue for the study of tortoises that is coupled with a park where you can see rare species in their natural habitat. Spring is the best time to visit, when the tortoises are more active. A tortoise clinic,

nursery and information points help you learn more about these endangered species.
✉ 83590 Gonfaron ☎ 04 94 78 26 41 🕐 Jul, Aug daily 9–7; Sep–end Jun daily 9–6 ✋ Adult €8, child (4–16) €5, under 4 free

## LORGUES

### DOMAINE DE L'ESTELLO

www.lestello.com

This 19ha (47-acre) AOC vineyard produces award-winning whites, reds and rosés. It is a very welcoming estate and the Malinge family, who own the domaine, also invite visitors to stay in their luxury gîte.
✉ Route de Garce, 83510 Lorgues
☎ 04 94 73 22 22 🕐 Mon–Fri 9–12.30, 2–6, Sat 3–6

## MONTMEYAN

### LOCATION NAUTIC

www.locationnautic.fr

This boat rental company offers you the chance to discover the Esparron de Verdon lake by kayak, pedal-boat or motorboat.
✉ Montmeyan Plage, 83670 Montmeyan
☎ 04 92 74 40 76 🕐 Apr–end Oct daily ✋ 1-hour pedal-boat rental starts at €12; electric boat rental starts at €22

## PORQUEROLLES

### PORQUEROLLES PLONGÉE

www.porquerolles-plongee.com

Porquerolles Plongée, based on one of the Îles d'Hyères, organizes dives, some onto wrecks, including cargo ships and even a submarine.
✉ Zone Artisanale 7, 83400 Porquerolles
☎ 04 98 04 62 22 🕐 Apr to mid-Nov daily dawn–dusk; rest of year by appointment
✋ €60 for the first dive

## ST-TROPEZ

### LES CAVES DU ROY

www.lescavesduroy.com

Part of luxury Hôtel Byblos, this club is the haunt of the rich and famous. Either dress to impress, or arrive earlier for a drink in the Byblos bar instead.
✉ Avenue Foch, 83990 St-Tropez
☎ 04 94 56 68 00 🕐 Mid-Apr to end Jun, Sep, Oct Fri, Sat 11.30pm–5am; Jul, Aug daily 11.30pm–5am

# FESTIVALS AND EVENTS

## FEBRUARY

### CORSO DU MIMOSA

This is a celebration of the yellow, vanilla-scented flower that gave Bormes-les-Mimosas its name.
✉ Bormes-les-Mimosas

## MAY

### BRAVADE DE ST-TORPES

St-Tropez remembers its patron saint, St. Torpes (▷ 128), in this spectacular festival.
✉ St-Tropez 🕐 16–18 May

### MARCHÉ AUX POISSONS

This fish market gives an endearing snapshot of life in St-Tropez; it's also the best place to get Mediterranean fish such as red mullet, scorpion fish and rainbow wrasse.
✉ Place aux Herbes, 83990 St-Tropez
🕐 Daily 7am–1pm

### MARCHÉ PROVENÇAL

You'll find all the typical food of Provence at this market. There's also an antiques corner, clothes and some local crafts.
✉ Place des Lices, 83990 St-Tropez
🕐 Tue, Sat 8–1

### RONDINI

www.rondini.fr

Since 1927, this family business has been making the *Tropézienne*, a Roman-style sandal worn by many celebrities, including Picasso.
✉ 16 rue Clemenceau, 83990 St-Tropez
☎ 04 94 97 19 55 🕐 Tue–Sat 9–12.30, 2.30–7

### LA TARTE TROPÉZIENNE

www.tarte-tropezienne.com

In 1955, while he was catering for the actors of the film *And God Created Woman*, confectioner Alexandre Micka created the cake filled with cream that gives this shop its name. It was a great success and Brigitte Bardot christened it *tarte Tropézienne*.
✉ 36 rue Clemenceau, 83990 St-Tropez
☎ 04 94 97 71 42 🕐 Feb–end Oct daily 8–8

### VILEBREQUIN

www.vilebrequin.com

Boys' and men's swimming trunks and shorts are sold here. The famous brand is very St-Tropez, and is worn by the A-list celebrities who frequent the peninsula's beaches.
✉ 24 rue Gametta, 83990 St-Tropez
☎ 04 94 97 62 02 🕐 Apr–end Oct Mon–Sat 10–7.30

### VIP ROOM

www.viproom.fr

The VIP Room has a classy club interior, with white wall seats, contemporary art and video projections. This is definitely the haunt of a VIP clientele. As a funky touch, the staff wear white Stetsons. There is a restaurant on site.
✉ Résidences du Nouveau Port, 83990 St-Tropez ☎ 04 94 97 14 70 🕐 Jul, Aug daily midnight–5am (restaurant open for dinner from 9)

## SALERNES

### POTERIE DU CHÂTEAU

Choose from brightly painted decorative items such as teapots, plates, cooking pots and bowls.
✉ Route de Draguignan, Quartier St-Romain, 83690 Salernes ☎ 04 94 70 63 46
🕐 Jul, Aug Mon–Sat 9–12, 3–7; Sep–end Jun Mon–Sat 9–12, 2–6

## TOULON

### BAR À THYM

www.barathym.com

There's a lot going on at Bar à Thym. A bar with a choice of 200 beers, a fusion restaurant, a gallery and a club, whatever your mood it's worth a visit. Live music ranges from rock to jazz. It gets very busy at weekends with the trendy of Toulon.
✉ 32 boulevard Cunéo, 83000 Toulon
☎ 04 94 41 90 10 🕐 Mon–Thu 6.30–midnight, Fri–Sat 6.30–3

# EATING

**PRICES AND SYMBOLS**

The prices given are the average for a two-course lunch (L) and a three-course dinner (D) for one person, without drinks. The wine price is for the least expensive bottle.

For a key to the symbols, ▷ 2.

## BANDOL

### BOUCANIER

This rustic establishment, on the restaurant strip a street back from Bandol's seaside promenade, serves excellent pizzas and grills cooked in the wood-fired oven.

✉ 13 rue Louis Marçon, 83150 Bandol ☎ 04 94 29 46 28 🕔 Feb–end Dec 12.30–3, 7–11 (closed Mon Feb–end Apr, Oct–end Dec) ✋ L €20, D €25, Wine €15

### LE CLOCHER

In the heart of Bandol you'll find this small bistro with a street-side terrace. The small number of covers makes this an intimate dining experience. The chef has received praise for the modern French menu, and the minimalist decor is in keeping with the up-to-the-minute chic.

✉ 1 rue de la Paroisse, 83150 Bandol ☎ 04 94 32 47 65 🕔 Thu–Tue 12–2, 7–9.30 ✋ L €20, D €30, Wine €14

### LE DELOS

On the Île de Bendor, this elegant but beachy restaurant has a cracking menu overseen by Provençal superchef Bruno de Lorgues. The high prices for what are admittedly superb ingredients (including truffles, foie gras and fine beef fillets) are tempered by the €29 two-course lunch menu and €55 three-course dinner menu.

✉ Île de Bendor, 83150 Bandol ☎ 04 94 05 90 90 🕔 Daily 12–2, 7–10 ✋ L €29, D €55, Wine €30 ⛴ A frequent ferry service connects Bandol's waterfront to the Île de Bendor

## LA CADIÈRE D'AZUR

### HOSTELLERIE BÉRARD

www.hotel-berard.com

At this country inn at the heart of the Bandol vineyard, chef René Bérard creates dishes that reflect his love of local produce. Dishes include *tartiflette* with crunchy pancetta and roast rabbit. Elegantly set tables, beamed ceilings and a beautiful view complete the enjoyment.

✉ 6 rue Gabriel Peri, 83740 La Cadière d'Azur ☎ 04 94 90 11 43 🕔 Wed–Sun 12.30–2.30, 7.30–9.30 ✋ L €60, D €75, Wine €20

## FRÉJUS

### L'ABRI-COTIER

There's a superb view of the port from this restaurant, with its heated terrace. Outstanding dishes such as red mullet fillets with tapenade and grilled lamb with cumin mingle happily on the menu with simple but tasty meals such as pizzas. There's a children's menu.

✉ Quai Marc Antoine, 83600 Fréjus ☎ 04 94 51 11 33 🕔 Jul, Aug Mon, Tue, Thu, Fri, Sun 12–2.30, 7–10.30, Wed, Sat 7–10.30; Easter to end Jun, Sep to mid-Oct daily 12–2.30, 7–10.30; mid-Oct to Easter Mon, Tue, Thu 12–2.30, Fri–Sun 12–2, 7–10.30 ✋ L €20, D €25, Wine €15

## HYÈRES

### LA COLOMBE

Chef Pascal Bonamy likes to innovate, mixing the finest ingredients. Creations include

**Opposite** *Place Massillon, Hyères*

swordfish fillets in risotto and red wine, and pigeon fricassée with foie gras and port. The restaurant's refined interior has a regional influence.
663 route de Toulon-La Bayorre, 83400 Hyères 04 94 35 35 16 Jul, Aug Wed–Fri, Sun 12–2, 7.30–10, Tue, Sat 7.30–10; Sep–end Jun Tue–Fri 12–2, 7.30–10, Sat 7.30–10, Sun 12–2
L €30, D €50, Wine €20

## LE LAVANDOU

### LE KRILL

This is a top option for local fare, from Provençal fish soup to *assiettes* of lightly fried squid, whitebait and prawns. Hefty portions of mains, from grilled fish to steaks, are also on the menu. Le Krill has a terrace looking out onto Le Lavandou's pretty harbour and promenade.
22 rue Patron Ravello, 83980 Le Lavandou 04 94 46 39 56 Daily 12–2.30, 6–10 L €15, D €22, Wine €14

### MATHIAS DANDINE

www.mathiasdandine.com

Sample the innovative delights of rising star Mathias Dandine at this classy seaside spot. Entrées arrive as multi-dish spreads brimming with scallops, morille mushrooms and fresh tuna. Mains are exciting takes on market-fresh fish and game. The sublime €60 set menu offers the best value.
1 avenue des Trois Dauphins, 83980 Le Lavandou 04 94 71 15 53 Daily 12.30–2, 7.30–10 L €70, D €100, Wine €40

## LORGUES

### LA FARENDOLE

www.chateauberne.com

The castle that is home to this restaurant is at the heart of a 550ha (1,358-acre) domain and its vineyard. Food comes fresh from the inn's organic garden, or from the local markets. Wonderful combinations of regional foods include scallops tartare in mustard, and roast pear with green pepper and roquefort. Eat on the terrace or in the beamed dining room. To accompany the meal, the chateau's own vintages are a must.
Château de Berne, Chemin de Berne, 83510 Lorgues 04 94 60 48 88 Mid-Mar to mid-Oct daily 12–2, 7–9.30; mid-Oct to mid-Dec Tue–Fri 7–9.30, Sat 12–2, 7–9.30, Sun 12–2. Closed mid-Dec to mid-Mar L €60, D €85, Wine €25

## ST-TROPEZ

### LE BANH-HOI

Hidden away on a lemongrass-scented backstreet, Banh-Hoi is a modern, highly acclaimed Vietnamese restaurant. Dishes are richer and meatier than traditional Southeast-Asian cuisine, with plenty of beef (satay), pork (with ginger) and tuna (tartare). There's abundant use of Thai flavours, too.
12 rue Petit St-Jean, 83990 St-Tropez 04 94 97 36 29 Apr–end Sep 7.30–11 D €60, Wine €25

### CAFÉ DES ARTS

Some think the soul of the real St-Tropez lies within these four walls. The Café des Arts is on a square in the heart of town and has one of the best terraces. Enjoy a meal while watching the bustle of the market or locals playing pétanque. It's definitely the place to be seen.
Place des Lices, 83990 St-Tropez 04 94 97 02 25 Food served daily 12–2.30, 7.30–11; café open 8am–midnight L €30, D €45, Wine €20

### LA GORILLE

La Gorille is perhaps the least expensive (and certainly the least pretentious) of St-Tropez harbour's strip of outdoor eateries. Since 1953 it has been dishing up a shortlist of well-executed staples like steak tartare and *moules et frites.*
1 quai Suffren, 83990 St-Tropez 04 94 97 03 93 May–end Sep open 24 hours; Oct–end Apr Thu–Tue 7–7 L €18, D €25, Wine €20

### SALAMA

One of St-Tropez's finest, albeit most low-key, restaurants is tucked down a dusty backstreet off place des Lices. Its North African spread is sublime: buttery couscous with lamb and prunes, plus slow-baked tagine dishes.
1 rue Tisserands, 83990 St-Tropez 04 94 97 59 62 Jun–end Aug daily 7–11; Mar–end May, Sep–end Nov Tue–Sun 7–11. Closed Dec–end Feb D €40, Wine €20

### LA TERRACE DE LA PONCHE

This classy gastronomic restaurant with a friendly twist is by St-Tropez's La Ponche town beach and ramparts. Seafood specialities rule the roost, including local sea bass and bream, plus prawns, oysters and lobster.
3 rue des Remparts, 83990 St-Tropez 04 94 97 09 29 Apr–end Sep daily 12–3, 7–11 L €50, D €70, Wine €25

## TOURTOUR

### LES CHÊNES VERT

The restaurant's name (The Green Oaks) reflects its verdant surroundings, in high oak and pine forest perched above the surrounding Provençal plains. In a renovated villa, the restaurant feels like a family home. The menu is classic French, with generous use of the grandest ingredients, such as lobster, truffles and foie gras.
Route de Villecroze, 83690 Tourtour 04 94 70 55 06 Aug–end May Thu–Mon 12–2, 7–10. Closed Jun, Jul L €30, D €50, Wine €19

**Below** *Seafood features heavily on menus on the coast*

**Above** *Provence has no shortage of elegant luxury hotels*

**PRICES AND SYMBOLS**

Prices are the lowest and highest for a double room for one night. Each listing states whether breakfast is included. All the hotels listed accept credit cards unless otherwise stated. Note that rates vary widely throughout the year.

For a key to the symbols, ▷ 2.

## BANDOL

### GOLF HOTEL

www.golfhotel.fr

Golf Hotel is simple, friendly and right on the beach. Rooms are clean, airy and uncluttered, and for a little more money you can upgrade to a terrace room, or a four-person family room. While location and price are the hotel's main selling points, amenities include free parking and an on-site ping-pong table.

✉ Plage de Rènecros, 83150 Bandol ☎ 04 94 29 45 83 €60–€85, excluding breakfast (€10) 24

### HÔTEL ILE ROUSSE

www.ile-rousse.com

This four-star hotel occupies a beautiful position with its own private beach. Rooms have a chic modern decor with some four-poster beds, and there's an elegant restaurant on site. The hotel also has a spa.

✉ 25 boulevard Louis Lumière, 83150 Bandol ☎ 04 94 29 33 00 €142–€389, excluding breakfast (€19) 54 Outdoor

## LA CELLE

### HOSTELLERIE DE L'ABBAYE DE LA CELLE

www.abbaye-celle.com

Stay in a restored 18th-century abbey at the heart of a vineyard. The takeover in 2002 by celebrated chef Alain Ducasse added a new dimension to this four-star address: It's now coupled with an excellent restaurant.

✉ Place du Général-de-Gaulle, 83170 La Celle ☎ 04 98 05 14 14 Closed Jan €250–€400, excluding breakfast (€20) 10 Outdoor

## LA CROIX-VALMER

### CHÂTEAU DE VALMER

www.chateauvalmer.com

The chateau has a private beach, tennis court and large swimming pool surrounded by palm trees. The bedrooms have Provençal furnishings and marble bathrooms. Some have a canopy bed and some suites can take up to four people. Sample Mediterranean cuisine at La Pinède Plage restaurant by the beach. Private parking is available.

✉ Route de Gigaro, 83420 La Croix-Valmer ☎ 04 94 55 15 15 Closed mid-Oct to mid-Apr €210–€540, excluding breakfast (€27) 42 Outdoor

## FRÉJUS

### L'ARÉNA

www.arena-hotel.com

This three-star hotel has a terracotta facade, palm trees in the garden, and a restaurant. In summer, enjoy breakfast by the pool.

✉ 145 rue Général de Gaulle, 83600 Fréjus ☎ 04 94 17 09 40 Closed Jan to mid-Mar €85–€140, excluding breakfast (€13) 36 Outdoor

## PAMPELONNE BAY

### CAMPING KON TIKI

www.riviera-villages.com

On the edge of Pampelonne beach, these high-class beach huts to rent by the week are extremely popular, so reserve in advance. The mobile homes come in four styles. Each has two bedrooms, a kitchenette, lounge area and bathroom. Alternatively, bring your own caravan (RV) or mobile home and hook up to water and electricity. Facilities include a grocery, restaurant, bar, tennis court and hot showers.

Route des Plages, 83350 Ramatuelle 04 94 55 96 96 Closed Nov–end Mar €50–€170 per night to rent a mobile home

### LA FERME D'AUGUSTIN

www.fermeaugustin.com

This three-star hotel combines rusticity with modern comfort—a spa bath in the bathroom, dressing rooms in the suite and a balneo pool (heated and with hydro massaging jets) in the garden. Inside there are beamed ceilings and a fireplace in the lounge. The beach is nearby.

Tahiti, 83350 Ramatuelle 04 94 55 97 00 Closed mid-Oct to mid-Mar €175–€355, excluding breakfast (€14) 46 Outdoor

### LA GARBINE

www.lagarbine.com

A ten-minute drive from St-Tropez and a 10-minute stroll to Plage Pampelonne, this country getaway offers tennis courts, a swimming pool, an exotic garden and a tranquil respite from the surrounding drama. The large, simply decorated rooms each have a terrace.

Route de Tahiti, 83350 Ramatuelle 04 94 97 11 84 Closed mid-Sep to mid-Apr €120–€200, including breakfast 25 Outdoor

## PORQUEROLLES

### L'ARCHE DE NOÉ

www.arche-de-noe.com

This is one of the few places to stay on blissful Porquerolles. It has simply furnished rooms, some with a large terrace, right on the sea. There's a cracking attached restaurant where hearty fresh breakfast is served.

Place d'Armes, 83400 Porquerolles 04 94 58 33 71 €147–€260, including breakfast 4

## SAINTE-MAXIME

### HOSTELLERIE LA CROISETTE

www.hotel-la-croisette.com

An imposing villa with a pink facade and blue shutters houses this three-star hotel. Most of the simple, sunny bedrooms give beautiful views of the bay. Lounge on the nearby beach or in the luxuriant gardens.

2 boulevard des Romarins, 83120 Sainte-Maxime 04 94 96 17 75 Closed mid-Oct to end Mar €67–€174, excluding breakfast (€11) 16

## ST-TROPEZ

### LA COLOMBIER

La Colombier boasts everything that an average St-Tropez hotel hasn't got: quiet traditional guestrooms in pastel colours, inexpensive room rates and a handful of parking spaces. Rooms look onto a quiet flower-filled courtyard where breakfast is served.

Impasse Conquêtes, 83990 St-Tropez 04 94 97 05 31 €80–€170, excluding breakfast (€8.50) 11

### PASTIS

www.pastis-st-tropez.com

In a sea-facing former mansion, and surrounding a swimming pool dotted with loungers and bathing cabins, Pastis is the epitome of unhurried charm. The unpretentious welcome is in keeping with the low-key luxury concept, while high linen counts speak of quality.

61 avenue du Général Leclerc, 83990 St-Tropez 04 98 12 56 50 Closed Nov €175–€450, excluding breakfast (€20) 9 Outdoor

### LA PONCHE

www.laponche.com

Formerly a fisherman's bar, this hotel is now a celebration of low-key elegance, where restrained finery meets French country chic. Some of the rooms in the quiet, well-placed hotel have huge terraces overlooking the rooftops of St-Tropez.

3 rue des Remparts, 83990 St-Tropez 04 94 97 02 53 €240–€310, excluding breakfast (€19) 18

## TOULON

### GRAND HOTEL DE LA GARE

www.grandhotelgare.com

This business hotel option opposite Toulon station offers complimentary WiFi, free night-time parking and comfy modern rooms. Toulon's majestic harbour is a ten-minute walk away.

14 boulevard Tesse, 83000 Toulon 04 94 22 34 82 €65–€75, excluding breakfast (€8.70) 37 rooms

**Left** *L'Arena hotel, in Fréjus, has a restaurant and a pool*

# ALPES-MARITIMES AND MONACO

The Riviera's south-facing shores makes it the sunniest place in France. Its beauty, with its backdrop of lush hills, and its warm microclimate have long attracted wealth and celebrity, beginning with visits by Queen Victoria. By the 1920s, every minor royal in Europe hopped on a train heading south come winter. A reputation for ritzy exuberance still exists, with a number of pop stars calling the Côte d'Azur their home. In high summer gossip columnists and paparazzi share the coast's great beaches with A-list celebs.

Beneath the gilded legend is a stretch of coast filled with history and culture. Nice alone has more museums than any French city outside Paris. The 2008 refurbishment of the Picasso museum in Antibes—plus the opening of the new Cocteau wing in Menton in 2010—is a tangible legacy of the region's long fixation with modern art. Step into a church in the perfume capital Grasse, or into a gallery in Vence, and you may come face to face with a canvas by Rubens or a Matisse.

Step back from the coast and the scenery becomes blissfully untamed. The perched villages of Èze and St-Paul-de-Vence, plus lesser-known settlements Peillon and Saorge, seem to cling to the craggy hills. The topography is ideal for outdoor pursuits, be it mountain biking, parascending or rafting. For bigger kicks, the wild Roya and Vésubie valleys are an hour away, as is the Gorges du Loup canyon and the ski slopes of Isola 2000. Finally, the huge Parc National du Mercantour invites serious hikers to try its 600km (370 miles) of Alpine paths.

Nestling next to Alpes-Maritimes is the tiny principality of Monaco. There's something faintly unreal about this awesome patch of rock hanging off the Provençal coast, an independent nation-state though it covers just 2sq km (less than 1sq mile). More than a millionaires' playground, it also has several worthwhile sights, including the Musée Océanographique, Monte-Carlo and the world-famous Casino.

# ANTIBES AND CAP D'ANTIBES

## INTRODUCTION

Thriving and densely packed, Antibes stands on a very attractive stretch of coast just east of Cannes and the Cap d'Antibes peninsula. This likeable, fortified Riviera town has an outstanding art museum and lovely beaches on the nearby cape. The old town was heavily fortified by Louis XIV's military engineer Vauban in the 17th century, with defences including the Grimaldi castle, now housing the Picasso Museum. Just outside the walls, Antibes' large yacht port, Port Vauban, is noted for the fine array of millionaire yachts moored alongside. Within the ramparts, the old town consists of busy squares and narrow streets lined with a lively mix of shops and restaurants. If you are driving, it is easier to find a parking space near the port rather than in the heart of town. If you are relying on buses, town bus number 2 is handy for reaching the cap.

Antibes is a town of great age. It was founded by the Greeks in 400BC and named Antipolis, meaning Opposite the City, because it faced Nice across the Baie des Anges. Subsequently, Antibes grew and became a busy Roman port. In the Middle Ages, it was harassed and almost destroyed by Saracens. It became a possession of the powerful Grimaldi dynasty, who controlled much of the Riviera coast, and it was they who first fortified the town and began to rebuild it. Antibes became part of France in 1860.

**INFORMATION**

www.antibesjuanlespins.com
299 P11 · 11 place Général-de-Gaulle · 04 97 23 11 11 · Jul, Aug daily 9–7; Sep–end Jun Mon–Sat 9–12.30, 1.30–6, Sun 10–12.30, 2.30–5 · Antibes

## WHAT TO SEE

### VIEIL ANTIBES

The attractive central historic quarter, Vieil Antibes, is bordered by Vauban's ramparts. The area is full of life, with tall 17th- and 18th-century houses lining squares and streets busy with shoppers. An open-air market in cours Masséna every morning except Monday, crowded with locals rather than visitors, gives the feel of a typical country town. Antibes is the largest horticultural hub in

**Above** *A vegetable stall in the market at cours Masséna*
**Opposite** *Yachts moored in the harbour*

the Alpes-Maritimes *département* and is well known for its flowers, with top-quality roses, tulips and carnations—all on show in the market, along with barrels of the local olives and an abundance of freshly gathered melons, figs, asparagus and other seasonal produce.

### MUSÉE D'HISTOIRE ET D'ARCHÉOLOGIE

The town's archaeology and history museum, inside a bastion south of the Château Grimaldi, contains many important archaeological finds made here. The museum draws together Etruscan, Greek, Roman and medieval items, as well as objets trouvés from shipwrecks. Next door, the old cathedral contains a 16th-century altarpiece attributed to the Niçois religious artist Louis Bréa.

✉ Bastion St-André, 06600 Antibes ☎ 04 93 34 00 39 🕑 Mid-Jun to mid-Sep daily 10–12, 2–6; mid-Sep to mid-Jun daily 10–1, 2–5 💶 Adult €3, under 18 free

### MUSÉE PICASSO–CHÂTEAU GRIMALDI

The town's major sight is the acclaimed Picasso Museum, housed in the Grimaldi's striking fortress on the cliff edge. The museum displays many ceramics, paintings and other works by Pablo Picasso (1881–1973), encompassing a range of themes and periods but with the emphasis on work created while he had a studio here in 1946. Much of the work reflects the artist's joyous post-war mood, and much explores the mythological themes that had begun to fascinate him. Photographic portraits of Picasso, by Bill Brandt and Man Ray, give further insight into the artist. Also on display are works by Nicholas de Staël, as well as pieces by Fernand Léger, Amedeo Modigliani and Joan Miró.

✉ Château Grimaldi, place Mariéjol, 06600 Antibes ☎ 04 92 90 54 20 🕑 Mid-Jun to mid-Sep Tue–Sun 10–6 (Wed, Fri until 8); mid-Sep to mid-Jun Tue–Sun 10–12, 2–6 💶 Adult €6, child (8–18) €3

### CAP D'ANTIBES

Out of town, the Cap d'Antibes, a promontory of land extending south into the sea, is a luxury haven of palatial villas, expensive hotels and sandy beaches. One of the beaches on the east side, La Salis, is a large public beach. Farther south are smaller free beaches Plage de la Garoupe and Plage Joseph, as well as private beaches that are open to the public. A footpath follows the tip of the cape for 3km (2 miles). Beneath the Garoupe plateau, Jardin Thuret (Jun–end Sep daily 8–6; Oct–end May daily 8.30–5.30) covers 4ha (10 acres) with rare and exotic plants.

## MORE TO SEE

### MARINELAND

www.marineland.fr

This big marine-life park (▷ 182) just outside Antibes has dolphins, sea lions, sharks and more. (Kids should also love the Aquasplash water park and Far West theme park just around the corner from Marineland.)

✉ On the N7, east of town ☎ 0892 300 607 🕑 Jul, Aug daily 10–10; Sep–end Jun daily 10–5.30 💶 Adult €35, child under 1.2m €27

### MUSÉE PEYNET

This museum, in place Nationale, houses the work of cartoonist Raymond Peynet. His creations featured in books and French magazines from the 1960s onwards.

✉ Place Nationale, 06600 Antibes ☎ 04 92 90 54 30 🕑 Tue–Sun 10–12, 2–6 💶 Adult €3, under 18 free

**Left** *The elegant façade of the Église de l'Immaculée Conception. Inside the church is a 16th-century altarpiece*

## LE BAR-SUR-LOUP

www.lebarsurloup.fr

Pretty Le Bar-sur-Loup sits high above the Gorges du Loup (▷ 149). The tourist office is in the dungeon of the medieval chateau that once dominated the village. The only other remains of this building are the two cylindrical towers. The Celts, Gauls, Ligurians and Romans had military encampments here. A Roman tombstone is set into the base of the clock tower of the Église St-Jacques. Inside the church is a curious 15th-century painting known as the *Danse Macabre*, thought to depict the legend of the Count of Bar, who dared to throw a party during Lent.

298 N10 Place Francis Paulet, 06620 Le Bar-sur-Loup 04 93 42 72 21 Jul, Aug daily 9–7; Sep–end Jun Tue–Fri 9.30–12.30, 2–6, Sat 9.30–12.30

## BEAULIEU-SUR-MER

http://otbeaulieu.free.fr

Beaulieu is a prosperous little waterfront hideaway between Nice and Monaco. In the lee of the Maritime Alps, and in a sheltered bay protected by Cap Ferrat and Cap d'Ail, the town has a mild winter climate and an early spring. It was popular with well-to-do English visitors in the late-19th century, and still has its Anglican church and belle époque villas, as well as a delightful palm-fringed waterfront.

The town's outstanding curiosity is the Villa Kérylos, in Impasse Gustave Eiffel (Jul, Aug daily 10–7; mid-Feb to Jun, Sep, Oct daily 10–6; Nov to mid-Feb Mon–Fri 2–6, Sat, Sun 10–6), on the tip of the northern headland. This extraordinary house, constructed in the 1900s by archaeologist Theodore Reinach and architect Emmanuel Pontremoli, has sea on three sides and is a perfect reproduction of a Greek villa of the second century BC.

Beaulieu has two beaches and both are entirely public, without a rented parasol in sight. The best, La Petite Afrique, is on the eastern edge of town past the marina. Plage du Fourmis beach is on the western side of town by the casino. Although not quite as peaceful, it forms the start of a coastal path leading all the way to St-Jean-Cap-Ferrat (▷ 153).

299 Q10 Place Georges-Clemenceau, 06310 Beaulieu-sur-Mer 04 93 01 02 21 Jul, Aug Mon–Sat 9–12.30, 2–7, Sun 9–12.30; Sep–end Jun Mon–Sat 9–12.15, 2–6 Beaulieu-sur-Mer

## BIOT

www.biot.fr

This little town, set back from the sea between Antibes and Nice, is famous for handmade glassware. Largest of the glassworks in the lower village is the Verrerie de Biot, in chemin des Combes (Jun–end Sep Mon–Sat 9.30–8, Sun 10.30–1.30, 2.30–7.30; Oct–end May Mon–Sat 9.30–6, Sun 10.30–1.30, 2.30–6.30). The earthenware tradition established here by the Romans continued until the 19th century, but then began to die out. It was the arrival in the 1950s of the innovative painter and sculptor Fernand Léger (1881–1955) that turned the town's attention back to glass and ceramics. The Musée National Fernand Léger, in chemin du Val de Pome (Wed–Mon 10–6), has a Léger mosaic on the exterior and, inside, some 400 of his works. The medieval hilltop village has 16th-century fortifications and an arcaded main square. To find out more, visit the Musée d'Histoire et de la Céramique Biotoises, in rue St-Sébastien (Jul–end Sep Wed–Sun 10–6; Oct–end Jun Wed–Sun 2–6).

298 P11 Maison du Tourisme, 46 rue St-Sébastien, 06410 Biot 04 93 65 78 00 Sep–end Jun Mon–Fri 9.30–12.30, 1.30–5, Sat, Sun 1.30–5 Biot, 3km (2 miles) from the village

## BREIL-SUR-ROYA

www.breil-sur-roya.fr

Breil, close to the Italian border, straddles the river Roya. The bell towers of the Église Sancta-Maria-in-Albis are topped with cheerful Niçois tiles. Inside the 18th-century baroque church is an altarpiece by the religious artist Louis Bréa. The town is a great base for kayaking and rafting in the lovely Roya valley.

**Above** *Biot is famous for its glassware*

299 R9 17 place Blancheri, 06540 Breil-sur-Roya 04 93 04 99 76 Jul, Aug Mon–Sat 9.30–6.30; Sep–end Jun Mon–Fri 9.30–12, 1.30–5.30, Sat 9.30–12 Breil-sur-Roya

## LA BRIGUE

www.labrigue.fr

Attractive La Brigue sits close to the Italian border. Mont Bégo, in the Mercantour mountains, can be seen to the west. Built largely of the local grey-green rock, the village is in the lovely green valley of the river Levenza. Soaring over the village is the Lombardic Romanesque tower of the 13th- to 14th-century Église Collégiale St-Martin, which has paintings by Louis Bréa.

There's more medieval art 4km (2.5 miles) up the valley to the east, in the remote Chapelle Notre-Dame des Fontaines (May–end Oct 10–12.30, 2–5.30; Nov–end Apr ask at tourist office). Here, 15th-century frescoes show the life of Christ.

299 R8 Place St-Martin, 06430 La Brigue 04 93 79 09 34 Daily 9–12, 2–5 La Brigue (Brigue-Gare)

# CANNES

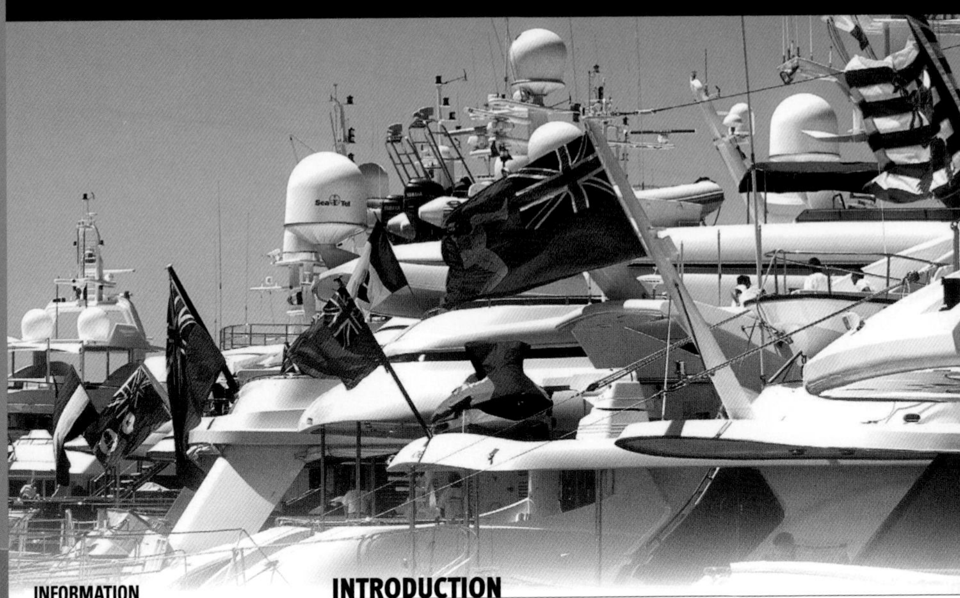

**INFORMATION**
www.cannes.fr
303 P11 **La Croisette office:** Palais des Festivals, La Croisette 04 92 99 84 22 Daily 9–7.
**Station office:** Gare SNCF, rue Jean-Jaurès 04 93 99 19 77 Daily 9–7
Cannes (in rue Jean-Jaurès)

**Above** *Luxury yachts moored at Cannes*

## INTRODUCTION

One of the world's most glamorous resorts is loaded with style and luxury—as well as having a good sandy beach, an excellent market and fine dining. The name Cannes conjures up high life and big money, an image stemming partly from the International Film Festival held here every May, with many of the world's top film stars in attendance. However, Cannes is not all about luxury. The resort, at the western end of the 'Old Riviera', has almost no 'must-see' sights, but there are many things to enjoy, including good entertainment, top-quality shopping and beach restaurants. The town's long beach is one of the few on the Riviera that is sandy, although payment is required for access to most of it. There are free sections at both ends. The hilltop old quarter, Le Suquet (▷ 145), is worth the walk for the wonderful sea view. The number 8 minibus connects Le Suquet with La Croisette.

An ancient Ligurian settlement at Cannes was taken over by the Romans, but was not a key site for them. In the 10th century, the town was a Genoese port called Canois, and in the 12th century it was given to the monks on the Îles de Lérins. It remained a fishing community until 1834, when Englishman Lord Brougham stayed here. He enjoyed his visit so much that he had a villa built—the Château Eleonore, behind avenue du Docteur Picaud—and returned each winter for the rest of his life. Lord Brougham was no ordinary English aristocrat. He was a former Lord Chancellor and inventor of the Brougham carriage and was a fantastically popular man. Numerous wealthy English visitors followed his example and built winter villas here. In the 1920s, a more artistic element began to arrive, many staying in summer. In the 1940s, the film festival took off (▷ 16), attracting top Hollywood actors, directors and producers as well as hundreds of self-promoting starlets who gave the festival, and the town, a particular air of glitz and frivolity. More than half the hotel rooms in Cannes are rated four or five stars.

## WHAT TO SEE

### BOULEVARD DE LA CROISETTE

A stroll on La Croisette is the quintessential Riviera experience. The beautiful beachside promenade, with its tamarisk and palm trees, has a glorious blue bay on one side and luxury hotels on the other. This busy waterfront road, divided by a green central strip, runs from the Palais des Festivals and old port (Vieux Port) in the west of town to Port Canto in the east. (After this, boulevard de la Croisette continues along the emptier coastal stretch to bleak Pointe de la Croisette.) The beach is divided into private sections, each with its own distinctively themed parasols. The coolest are 3.14 and Zplage. Opulent hotels across the street rank as sights in their own right: The 'top four' are the domed Carlton, the Majestic, the more recent Noga-Hilton and the white art deco masterpiece the Martinez (▷ 193). Along here, the 19th-century mansion La Malmaison houses the city's most important temporary art exhibitions. In the walkway in front of the Palais des Festivals, film stars have made handprints in the concrete. The whole of La Croisette is especially attractive at night thanks to floodlighting.

## OLD CANNES

Boulevard de la Croisette ends at the Palais des Festivals. On the other side of the Palais is the Cannes that existed before La Croisette was built. Here is the extensive old port area and its spacious waterside esplanade called La Pantiero, with large popular brasseries along one side. Behind this tree-shaded square—adorned with a statue of Lord Brougham (▷ Introduction, opposite)—run narrow shopping streets that reach the town's large covered market (Tue–Sun mornings). Steep lanes climb to the small, medieval district called Le Suquet, fortified in the 14th century by the monks of the Îles de Lérins. At the top of the hill is a 16th-century church, a terrace with lovely sea views, and the monks' watchtower, the Tour du Suquet. The Musée de la Castre (Jul, Aug daily 10–7; Apr–end Jun, Sep Tue–Sun 10–1, 2–6; Oct–end Mar Tue–Sun 10–1, 2–5), in the chateau at Le Suquet, is a large ethnographic museum with collections including musical instruments and tribal masks.

### TIPS

» Book a long way ahead for any kind of accommodation in Cannes at any time of year.

» Unless you want to star-gaze, the film festival in May is not the best time to come. Hotel prices skyrocket and the town is packed.

**Below** *The Musée de la Castre, at Le Suquet*

**FERRIES TO THE ÎLES DE LÉRINS**

**Île St-Honorat:** Planaria (tel 04 92 98 71 38) runs the only service to Île St-Honorat from Cannes. Ten services per day (€12 return) run from May–end Sep (last boat returns at 6), with eight per day from Oct–end Apr (last boat returns at 5).

**Île Sainte-Marguerite:** At least ten services per day are run year-round from Cannes to Île Sainte-Marguerite (€11.50 return) by Trans Côte d'Azur (tel 04 92 98 71 30). Services also run several times daily from Juan-les-Pins (Mar–Nov) and once daily from Nice (Jul, Aug).

**THE MAN IN THE IRON MASK**

The Man in the Iron Mask spent time at several institutions reserved for special prisoners, which hints at his importance. The writer Voltaire suggested the prisoner was the brother of then ruler Louis XIV (1638–1715), a rumour expounded by Alexandre Dumas in his *The Three Musketeers* story.

The prisoner was incarcerated, tended to only by a single high-ranking guard, and masked (allegedly with a black velvet mask, not a metal one). The fact that he wasn't simply murdered—a common enough solution in 17th-century power struggles—is probably the source of the many rumours as to his real identity. Others suggest the prisoner was either Oliver Cromwell's son, a high-ranking general or an illegitimate heir to the French throne.

### MODERN TOWN

Modern Cannes has spread far inland, embracing the formerly separate village of Le Cannet, which made an arty, less expensive alternative to Cannes for pre-World War II visitors but is now a crowded, picturesque visitor haunt with good views. To the east, Cannes encompasses the prosperous heights of Super-Cannes, where several extravagant pre-World War II villas survive. Parallel to the seashore, a couple of blocks inland, is Cannes' main shopping street, rue d'Antibes. Along here are many fashion boutiques, designer stores, perfumeries, jewellers, art specialists and chocolatiers.

## MORE TO SEE

### ÎLES DE LÉRINS

The Lérins islands, a short ferry ride from Cannes, make an enjoyable excursion. The peaceful, traffic-free islands contrast with the glitz of nearby Riviera resorts. Frequent ferries run to the larger Île Sainte-Marguerite (▷ panel), where there are paths and picnic areas under the pine trees and the shore is broken by coves and bays. By the quayside are simple fish restaurants. Close by, a Vauban fortress called Fort Royal (or Fort Vauban) houses a marine museum, the Musée de la Mer, a Huguenot Memorial Chapel and the former prison cells of the Man in the Iron Mask (Jun–end Sep daily 10–5.45; Oct–end May Tue–Sun 10.30–1.15, 2.15–4.45).

Much quieter than Île Sainte-Marguerite is Île St-Honorat. First colonized by St. Honoratus in AD410, its history has been intertwined with that of the working monastic settlement which, barring a few years during the French Revolution, has existed on the island ever since. Indeed, present-day visitors are asked to keep their voices down and their bikini tops on lest they disturb the peace. The island is ringed by footpaths and inlets, while the interior is covered with picturesque vineyards and olive groves. These are harvested by the monks and made into wine, soap and spirits, which can be brought in the monastery shop on the island's southern edge.

Note that it is not possible to sleep on either island. Ferries leaving from Cannes depart from the western tip of the Vieux Port.

303 P12

### PALAIS DES FESTIVALS ET DES CONGRÈS

This unsightly building is where the real work takes place during the film festival. Options change hands at astronomical prices at its basement screenings. Outside the building, see the handprints of film stars in the concrete of the allée des Stars.

1 La Croisette 04 93 39 01 01 Daily 9–7

**Above** *The Carlton Hotel*
**Right** *A postcard of Cannes*

## CAGNES-SUR-MER

www.cagnes-tourisme.com

Impressionist artist Renoir moved to this seaside town in 1907, hoping the warmer weather would ease his arthritis. He lived and painted here until his death in 1919. You can visit his house and gardens, the Domaine des Collettes, now known as the Musée Renoir (May–end Sep Wed–Mon 9–12, 2–6; Oct–end Apr Wed–Mon 9–12, 2–5).

The seaside section of Cagnes, known as Cros-de-Cagnes, is not as attractive as other places along the coast. Prettier is Haut-de-Cagnes, with its medieval streets and chateau built by Rainier Grimaldi in 1309. Here you'll find the Musée d'Art Méditerranéen Moderne (Jul–end Sep Wed–Mon 10–12, 2–6; Oct–end Jun Wed–Mon 10–12, 2–5) and an olive museum. The chateau hosts the *Festival Internationale de la Peinture* from July to September.

299 P10 6 boulevard Maréchal Juin, 06800 Cagnes-sur-Mer 04 93 20 61 64 Jul, Aug Mon–Fri 9–12.30, 2–6, Sat 9–12.30; Sep–end Jun Mon–Fri 9–12, 2–6, Sat 9–12

## CANNES

▷ 144–146.

## CLUES DE HAUTE-PROVENCE

www.provence-val-dazur.com

The *clues*—a southern-French word meaning openings or keys—are narrow gorges and passes in the spectacular, wild mountains in the Provençal backcountry, on the border between the Alpes-Maritimes, Haute-Provence and Var *départements*. Several provide abrupt openings in the harsh landscape between the broad valleys and plains of the Var and Alpes-Maritimes and the higher Alpine mountain country to the north. The area is popular with cross-country skiers in winter and walkers in summer.

In the sparsely populated mountains north of Grasse (▷ 151), bounded approximately by the N202 and N85 roads, the limestone hills close up and create a difficult, inhospitable and often beautiful landscape of pale rock and dense wild *garrigue* or forest. The *clues* are narrow gorges with high, steep sides, providing openings in the rocky terrain through which people, animals and rivers may pass. The focus of the region is the 1,777m (5,828ft) Montagne du Cheiron.

Many of the most dramatic sites are on the River Esteron, on the north flank of the mountain. Here is the strange fortified village of Roquestéron, with a river—formerly the border between Savoy and France—running through its heart. Before 1860, each half of the village was in a different country.

West from Roquestéron is the Clue du Riolan. Beyond is the spectacularly narrow Clue d'Aiglun, with a river gushing straight down through it as if under pressure from the mountains above. Farther west, the steep sides of the Clue de St-Auban are riddled with caves. The village of St-Auban stands at its opening.

298 N9 Maison de Pays, 06260 Puget-Théniers 04 93 05 05 05 May–end Sep daily 9–12, 2–7; Oct–end Apr Mon–Fri 9–12.30, 2–5, Sat, Sun 9–5

## COARAZE

www.ot-coaraze.com

This chic and picturesque village, perched on a cliff, calls itself *Village du Soleil* (Sun Village). Sundials have been a feature here since Jean Cocteau decorated the town hall with them. A short walk away, the Chapelle Bleue (formerly Chapelle Notre-Dame des Sept Douleurs) is named after the blue murals—pierced by green stained-glass windows—created in 1965 by Ponce de Léon.

299 Q9 Monté du Portal, 06390 Coaraze 04 93 79 37 47 Apr–end Sep Mon–Fri 8.30–12, 2–6.30, Sat, Sun 10–12, 2–6.30; Oct–end Mar Mon, Tue, Thu–Sat 8.30–12, 2–6.30

**Below** *The fortified village of Roquestéron, in the Clues de Haute-Provence*

## ÈZE

Beautiful Èze is one of the most perfect examples of a *village perché* (perched village) and is also one of the most easily accessible. Midway between Nice and Monaco, it stands on top of a 430m (1,375ft) spike of rock rising beside the Corniche Moyenne road and just a short (if steep) distance from the Riviera resorts. This fortified village is exceptionally pretty, with narrow medieval lanes and steps, and several viewpoints looking straight down onto the sea. Èze has survived with few changes since the 14th century, when the Saracens were forced out and the village reconstructed on more defensive lines to prevent further attacks.

### POPULAR

Its closeness to the coastal resorts and to the Corniche Moyenne has made Èze a chic, arty, sometimes overcrowded attraction, with a stream of visitors and tour buses arriving during the day. Yet the village has an indomitable charm and in the evenings, when visitor numbers drop, feels surprisingly unspoiled. For a better understanding of how remote and inaccessible Èze was before the invention of the car, depart from here on foot. The precipitous path that leads down to the shore is known as Sentier Friedrich-Nietzsche because Nietzsche often took this strenuous walk from the medieval village to Èze's beachy sister settlement of Èze-sur-Mer, on the coast.

### ATTRACTIONS

If you are arriving by car, park in the parking area at the foot of the village, then walk up the steep road to the large 14th-century fortified gateway into old Èze. Inside is a magical, maze-like world of pretty lanes and stairways. Head upwards to reach the ruins of a fortress, giving dazzling views out to sea. The ruins are surrounded by a brilliant, unusual cactus garden called the Jardin Exotique (daily 9–dusk), which gives unforgettable views along the Riviera coast. Below the fortress, the Chapelle des Pénitents Blancs is noted for its enamelled panelling. Within the medieval village, there are deluxe chateau-hotels, fine restaurants and little shops selling (sometimes pricey) souvenirs. On the main road below the old village there are several good shops, including branches of the Fragonard and Galimard perfumeries, a few paces up the road towards the old village.

### INFORMATION

www.eze-riviera.com

299 Q10 Place Général-de-Gaulle, 06360 Èze 04 93 41 26 00

Apr–end Oct daily 9–7; Nov–end Mar Mon–Sat 9–6.30

### TIPS

» The café terrace of the Château Eza has one of the best views in the village.

» Vehicles cannot enter the old village. There is a large parking area at the foot of the village.

**Below** *A picturesque cobbled alley*

## FONDATION MAEGHT

www.fondation-maeght.com

This art museum, in an intriguing modern building hidden in woodland outside St-Paul-de-Vence (▷ 170), has one of Europe's leading collections of 20th-century and contemporary art. The Fondation Marguerite et Aimé Maeght was opened by the Maeghts, successful art dealers, in 1964 to house their private art collection and as a memorial to their son, who died in childhood. It is still financed by their foundation. The building, designed by Catalan architect Josep-Lluis Sert, is a low simple structure with a pair of strange curved shapes resting on the roof. The interior is gloriously lit with natural light from above. The museum has several sculptures standing in the grounds, by Joan Miró, Marc Chagall, Georges Braque and others. These artists feature prominently inside the museum, together with Pierre Bonnard, Wassily Kandinsky, Alexander Calder and Fernand Léger, among others.

A tiny chapel inside the building has Braque's *White Bird on a Mauve Background* (1958–62), a striking stained-glass window created in memory of the Maeghts' son.

298 P10 Fondation Maeght, route de Pass-Prest, 06750 St-Paul-de-Vence 04 93 32 81 63 Jul–end Sep daily 10–7; Oct–end Jun daily 10–6 Adult €11, child (10–18) €9, under 10 free

## GORBIO

www.gorbio.fr

The best time to visit this attractive *village perché* (perched village) is during the *Fête Dieu* (Corpus Christi) in June, when you can see the entrancing night-time parade known as the *Procession dai Limaca*. The spectacle takes its name from the flickering lamps made from snail shells (*limaca* in Provençal) and olive oil that illuminate the village during the parade. The tradition dates back to a pagan ritual giving thanks for the winter's olive harvest.

At other times of the year, Gorbio's attractions include at least half a dozen chapels and churches in or around the village. Gorbio's residents are sometimes known as *'Les nebuleux'* ('the cloudy ones') as the village is often enveloped in clouds.

299 Q10

**Above** *The dramatic landscape of the Gorges du Loup*

## GORGES DU LOUP

The Loup river threads down through remarkable rocky ravines in the hilly country between Grasse and Vence. Many strange hollows have been carved into the rock by the rushing stream. Narrow roads alongside the ravines provide a spectacular country drive with some interesting little towns along the way. As the river approaches the small town of Pont-du-Loup, the start of the impressive gorge is marked by the curious Saut-du-Loup, a large hollow in the river bedrock, and the Demoiselles waterfall, where minerals in the water spray have 'petrified' the surrounding greenery. Farther down is the mossy Courmès waterfall, just before the river enters Pont-du-Loup.

After another 3km (2 miles) is the attractive small town of Le Bar-sur-Loup (▷ 143), among fruit groves and flowers. Its 15th-century church is noted for a vivid Danse Macabre mural. Also close to the right bank, the perched village of Gourdon (▷ below) soars above the river. On the left bank, the pretty D2210 continues to the lovely medieval village of Tourrettes-sur-Loup, standing on a rocky ridge, and known for its violets.

298 N10

## GOURDON

www.gourdon-france.com

A fascinating perched village poised on a high platform of rock in the hills behind Cannes and Nice, Gourdon justly calls itself a *nid d'aigle* (eagle's nest). With its fountains, steps, lanes and stunning views across the gorge of the river Loup, it attracts many visitors. The best view is from outside the church. The 17th-century chateau is still a private home. It also has two museums. The Musée Historique (Jun–end Sep Wed–Mon 11–1, 2–7; Oct–end May Wed–Mon 2–6) has intriguing items, including suits of armour, 16th-century furniture and a painting by Rubens. The Musée des Arts Décoratifs et de la Modernité (Jul, Aug tours daily at 12, 3, 5) displays decorative arts from the 1880s to the late 1930s. The chateau gardens were designed by landscape architect André Le Nôtre.

298 N10 Place Victoria, 06620 Gourdon 04 93 09 68 25 Daily 11–6

## GRASSE

There's more to the 'world capital of perfume' than visiting a fragrance factory, interesting though that is. Grasse also has an attractive medieval quarter and wonderful views. The large town is 15km (9 miles) inland from Cannes, on the Route Napoléon.

### THE OLD TOWN

The narrow pedestrian-only streets of the old quarter have been attractively restored. There are many fine old mansions, and a wide terrace, place du Cours, giving thrilling views towards the sea. Place aux Aires, in the heart of the old town, has a three-tiered fountain at its core. A busy flower and vegetable market takes place here every morning except Mondays. Other focal points in the old town are the 12th-century watchtower, the Tour de Guet, and the cathedral, which was originally built in the 11th century but was reconstructed in the 17th century. The cathedral, now a national monument, has a trio of Rubens paintings on the right-hand wall, as well as works by Jean Honoré Fragonard and Charles Nègre, and a triptych by Louis Bréa. It has an impressive stone double staircase, added in the 18th century, and a soaring latticework ceiling.

### PERFUMERIES

The town's major perfume makers are Molinard, Galimard and Fragonard. All three offer free guided tours in English. Fragonard has a highly enjoyable tour of its museum and shop, a short walk from the old town in boulevard Fragonard (▷ 184). Fragonard has a larger, modern site, called the Fabrique des Fleurs, 3km (2 miles) out of town on the Route de Cannes (Mar–end Oct daily 9–6; Nov–end Feb daily 10–12.30, 2–6), which is its modern perfume factory. A less poetic, more industrial approach is taken to the subject at the tours here. In the same area are Galimard, at 73 route de Cannes (Apr–end Oct daily 9–6.30; Nov–end Mar daily 9–12, 2–6), and Molinard, in boulevard Victor Hugo (Apr–end Oct daily 9–6.30; Nov–end Mar Mon–Sat 9–12, 2–6; also open lunchtimes during school holidays). If you want to learn more about the perfume business, try the Musée International de la Parfumerie, in place du Cours (Jun–end Sep daily 10–7; Oct–end May Wed–Mon 11–6). Grasse owes its perfume industry to the manufacture of scented gloves, which began in the mid-17th century. After the Revolution, gloves fell out of fashion and the town switched its attention to perfume.

### INFORMATION

www.grasse.fr

298 N11 Palais de Congrès, 22 cours Honoré Cresp ☎ 04 93 36 66 66 Jul–end Sep Mon–Sat 9–7, Sun 9–1, 2–6; Oct–end Jun Mon–Sat 9–12.30, 2–6

**Opposite** *The medieval town of Grasse*
**Below** *Perfume ingredients, sourced from local flowers*

### GUILLAUMES

www.pays-de-guillaumes.com

Guillaumes is a large village perched 800m (2,625ft) above the confluence of the Var and the Tuébi rivers, dominated by the ruins of a chateau. The chapel of Notre-Dame-du-Buyei has a painting of a fire that ravaged the village in 1682. From Guillaumes the D2202 takes you south through the dramatic Gorges de Daluis, towards Entrevaux (▷ 202).

293 N8 Mairie (town hall), 06470 Guillaumes 04 93 05 57 76 Daily 10–12, 2–6

### ISOLA 2000

www.isola2000.com

This high-quality modern ski resort is in the upper Tinée valley on the west flank of the Parc National du Mercantour, in the Provençal Alps. It offers excellent skiing, within 90 minutes' drive of the Riviera. The main part of the resort is at 2,000m (6,560ft), hence the name, while the older Isola village stands at 860m (2,800ft). Isola 2000 also makes a good summer base for exploring the peaks of the Parc National du Mercantour (▷ 168–169).

293 P7 Immeuble Le Pélevos, Isola 2000 04 93 23 15 15 Jul, Aug, Dec–end Apr daily 8.30–12, 2–7; Sep–end Nov, May, Jun Mon–Fri 8.30–12, 2–7

### JUAN-LES-PINS

www.antibes-juanlespins.com

Merging with Antibes at the head of the Cap d'Antibes peninsula (▷ 141–142), Juan-les-Pins is a popular little resort with a sandy beach, appealing to the young because of its lively nightlife. There are few traces of the large pine forest behind the coast that gave the town its name. A resort was laid out here in the 1880s by the Duke of Albany, Queen Victoria's son. It remained obscure until the 1920s, when Nice restaurateur Monsieur Baudoin went into partnership with American railway tycoon Frank Jay Gould to launch the Riviera's first summer resort, at a time when holidaying in summer was something of a novelty. Success followed, helped by the scandal of being the first beach where women wore modern-style swimsuits, and Juan developed a racy, hedonistic air.

Since 1960, the resort has hosted a Jazz Festival in July (▷ 189).

299 P11 51 boulevard Guillaumont, 06600 Juan-les-Pins 04 97 23 11 10 Jul, Aug daily 9–7; Sep–end Jun Mon–Sat 9–12, 2–6, Sun 10–12.30, 2.30–5

### LANTOSQUE

Perched on a rocky spur overlooking the Vésubie valley, Lantosque looks as if it is about to slide down the hill. Indeed, it has done so many times. Few other villages in Provence have suffered so many landslides, almost the whole village falling into the ravine on several occasions during the 15th to 17th centuries. The village had historic importance as a trading post on the Route du Sel (the salt route), along which pack animals carried salt from coastal salt pans to the mountain towns. In winter, the village is a popular little ski resort.

299 Q9 Mairie (town hall), 06450 Lantosque 04 93 03 00 02

### LEVENS

Levens dominates the plains at the mouth of the Gorges de la Vésubie. The late 18th-century friary Chapelle des Pénitents Blancs stands on the north side of the village and the Chapelle des Pénitents Noirs, with a fine baroque facade, on the east side. The Maison du Portal gateway is all that is left of the castle.

There are some scenic drives from the village: The D19 and D2565 snake around the gorges before meeting up at St-Jean-la-Rivière. A hair-raising, 6km (4-mile) detour from here leads up to the isolated sanctuary of Madone d'Utelle.There are wonderful views from the peak just past this chapel.

299 P9 3 placette Paul Olivier, 06670 Levens 04 93 79 71 00 Jul, Aug Mon–Sat 9.30–12.30, 2.30–7, Sun 10–1; Sep–end Jun Mon–Sat 9.30–12.30, 2.30–6

### MENTON

▷ 154–155.

### MONACO-VILLE

▷ 156–157.

### MONTE-CARLO

▷ 158–159.

### MOUGINS

www.mougins-coteazur.org

Mougins, a beautiful medieval perched village in the hills behind Cannes, has become a fine dining resort, with several acclaimed restaurants (▷ 191–192). Even if you're not here to eat, it's rewarding to explore Mougins' streets of carefully restored houses. There's also a Musée de la Photographie (Jul–end Sep daily 10–8; Oct, Dec–end May daily 10–6. Closed Nov) next to the Porte Sarrazine. Art exhibitions are held in the old washhouse, La Lavoir, on place de la Mairie. Southeast, on the D3, the Chapelle de Notre-Dame de Vie stands on a hilltop flanked by cypress trees. Originally 12th century, it was rebuilt in 1646. Pablo Picasso (1881–1973) owned a villa hidden among trees opposite.

298 N11 15 avenue Jean Charles Mallet, 06250 Mougins 04 93 75 87 67 Jul, Aug daily 9–7; Sep–end Jun Mon–Fri 9–5.30, Sat 9–5

### NICE

▷ 162–167.

### PARC NATIONAL DU MERCANTOUR

▷ 168–169.

### PEILLE

Reached by steep narrow roads that switchback up to a 630m (2,066ft) altitude from the Paillon valley, the peaceful perched village of Peille stands on a ridge some 20km (13 miles) inland from Monaco. Its remote, inaccessible, staunchly defended location gave the village an independent air—it even has its own dialect, called *Peilhasc*. There are several lovely old buildings in the cobbled alleys and passageways. The appearance of the village in the Middle Ages can be seen from a painting that hangs inside the Église

Sainte-Marie (ask at the Mairie for the key). The picture shows the feudal castle of the Counts of Provence, whose ruins still stand at the top of the village. Also inside the church is a fine 16th-century polyptych of the Rosary by Honoré Bertone of the Niçois school. Mountain bikes (tel 06 70 76 57 05) are available to rent in the village for those who wish to explore the region further.

✚ 299 Q10 ℹ Mairie (town hall), 06440 Peille ☎ 04 93 91 71 71

**PEILLON**

www.tourisme-peillon.com

The dramatically perched village of Peillon, soaring above the river Paillon, enjoys an 'eagle's nest' setting among rocky peaks just inland from Monaco. Although much restored, the village remains remarkably unspoiled and uncommercialized. Its 16th-century mansions line vaulted alleys and steep stairways.

Dramatic frescoes of *The Passion of Christ*, painted in 1485 by Giovanni Canavesio, decorate the interior of the Chapelle des Pénitents Blancs, at the entrance to the village. Telephone the Mairie in advance to arrange a visit (tel 04 93 79 91 04) or the tourist office.

✚ 299 Q10 ℹ 4 rue Centrale, 06440 Peillon ☎ 06 24 97 42 25

**PUGET-THÉNIERS**

Puget-Théniers is a handsome town on the border of the Alpes-Maritimes and Alpes-de-Haute-Provence, strategically located where the Var valley broadens as it leaves the higher Alps. The Redoule river, which meets the Var at this point, also flows through the town. Once a possession of the Grimaldis (the Monaco ruling family), the town is dominated by their ruined Château des Trainières, dismantled in 1691.

The old town, whose heart is the place A. Conil, was in earlier centuries a Templar stronghold. It features many fine old doorways with carved shields on the lintels. Inside the church of Notre-Dame-de-l'Assomption are two remarkable 16th-century altarpieces, the *Polyptyque de Notre-Dame-de-Secours* by Antoine Ronzen, and the carvings of the *Passion* by Mathieu d'Anvers. The town was the birthplace of Auguste Blanqui, a leader of the Paris Commune in 1870. A bronze by Aristide Maillol commemorates him.

At nearby Puget-Rostang is the excellent Ecomusée du Pays de la Roudoule (May–end Sep Tue–Sun 10–12, 2–6; Oct–end Apr Tue–Thu, Sat, Sun 10–12, 2–6), whose displays capture the identity of this region. The museum runs interesting guided tours focusing on local heritage.

✚ 298 N9 ℹ 2 rue Alexandre Barety, 06260 Puget-Théniers ☎ 04 93 05 05 05 🕒 May–end Sep daily 9–12, 2–7; Oct–end Apr Mon–Fri 9–12.30, 2–5, Sat, Sun 9–5

**ST-JEAN-CAP-FERRAT**

www.ville-saint-jean-cap-ferrat.fr

St-Jean is the small main town of the exclusive Cap Ferrat peninsula. Part ordinary village, part luxurious marina, St-Jean has an appealing quayside with a few bars and restaurants. Away from the port, the streets and houses have an Italianate appearance. St-Jean is the only part of Cap Ferrat that feels approachable to visitors who don't have a millionaire's bank balance. The rest of this rich person's hideaway consists mainly of palatial homes in vast, lush gardens half-hidden by walls, gates and hedges. Cap Ferrat's unmissable sight is the impressive Villa Ephrussi de Rothschild (▷ 172).

Paths around the Cap's 14km (9 miles) of coastline give wonderful sea views.

✚ 299 Q10 ℹ 59 avenue Denis-Semaria, 06230 St-Jean-Cap-Ferrat ☎ 04 93 76 08 90 🕒 Jun–end Sep Mon–Fri 9–5, Sat 9–4, Sun 10–2; Oct–end May Mon–Fri 9–4, Sat 10–5

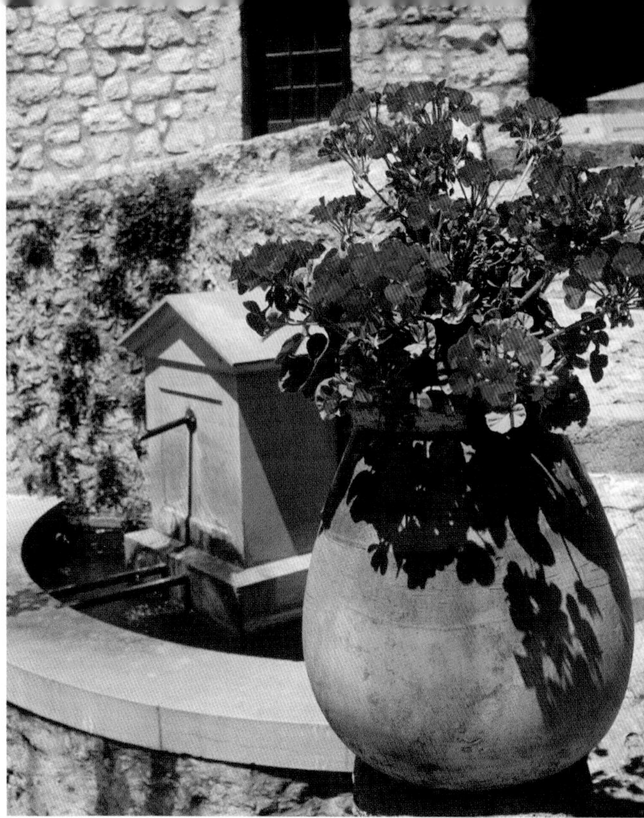

**Above** *A pot of red geraniums brightens a stone wall in the village of Peille*

# MENTON

**INFORMATION**

www.tourisme-menton.fr
299 R10 8 avenue Boyer, 06506 Menton 04 92 41 76 76 Mid-Jun to mid-Sep daily 9–7; mid-Sep to mid-Jun Mon–Sat 8.30–12.30, 2–7, Sun 9–12.30 Menton

**Above** *A view from the harbour*

## INTRODUCTION

This quiet, long-established Riviera resort with an Italian feel is famous for its gardens, lemon festival and exceptionally mild winter climate. It's close enough to the border that Italians sometimes walk here. Menton is enclosed by high mountain slopes that offer a protective barrier against wind and weather from the north. Its balmy climate—there are around 300 days of sun each year—encourages the cultivation of local gourmet varieties of lemons and oranges. There is a choice of parking areas in the town, including two underground areas at the Hôtel de Ville and St-Roch. From June to the end of September there is free parking at Rondelli. The Service du Patrimoine, based at 24 rue St-Michel (tel 04 92 10 97 10), runs guided tours of Menton and its gardens.

Menton was considered Italian until annexed by Napoleon III in 1860, although it had long belonged not to Italy but to the Grimaldis of Monaco. Even in those days it was already a winter resort popular with Russian and English aristocrats. Queen Victoria visited in 1882. A number of exotic Edwardian gardens planted behind the town are still beautifully maintained.

## WHAT TO SEE

### LA VIEILLE VILLE

The older part of town, with its alleys and covered stairways, rises steeply from the sea on the eastern side of Menton. Dating mainly from the 17th century, this Vieille Ville has an Italianate feel and gives a glimpse into the period before Menton became French. Climb along narrow rue Longue, the medieval main street, to little place de la Concepcion. With its pair of ornate ochre-painted churches, each with an Italian campanile, this square is the heart of the historic quarter.

### SALLE DES MARIAGES

Overlooking the Biovès gardens in the lower town (▷ below), Menton's attractive 17th-century Italianate town hall contains a Salle des Mariages (Wedding Room) that is decorated with wall and ceiling murals by the artist and writer Jean Cocteau (1889–1963). Marriage is the fitting theme for the paintings here.

✉ Hôtel de Ville, place Ardoïno, Menton ☎ 04 92 10 50 00 ◷ Mon–Fri 8.30–12.30, 2–5 ✋ €1.50

### MUSÉE JEAN COCTEAU

The little Bastion du Port, projecting from the shore, is the 17th-century Grimaldi fortress that Cocteau restored to house his work. It is now the remarkable Musée Jean Cocteau, displaying his mosaics and ceramics, tapestries, poems and photographs. In mid 2010 a giant new wing of the museum opened around the corner from the bastion. This collection, focusing on Cocteau artworks from 1910 until the 1950s, was donated by philanthropist and Cocteau fan Severin Wunderman.

✉ Quai Napoléon III, Menton ☎ 04 93 57 72 30 ◷ Wed–Mon 10–6 ✋ €3

### HISTORIC GARDENS

A century ago several wealthy Edwardian horticulturalists came to Menton and the adjacent Garavan district to create remarkable parks and gardens on the steep sea-facing slopes just outside town—Serre de la Madone, Jardin des Colombieres, Clos du Peyronnet and others. The nearest of these gardens, the sublime Jardin Exotique du Val Rahmeh (Apr–end Sep Wed–Mon 10–12.30, 3.30–6.30; Oct–end Mar Wed–Mon 10–12.30, 2–5), is a five-minute walk from Menton's harbour. Catching the sun during the warmest part of the winter day, these gardens enabled aristocratic experimental gardeners to cultivate an astounding variety of exotic plants from around the world. They are well worth visiting in late winter, for example in February, when spring flowers are in bloom attended by butterflies and bees.

## MORE TO SEE

### THE LOWER TOWN

The Promenade du Soleil skirts Menton's beach, close to which is the long-established—but no longer very glamorous—casino and the public gardens called the Jardin Biovès. During the town's visually stunning Lemon Festival, in February, the Biovès gardens are filled with 'sculptures' and set pieces made of oranges and lemons.

### MUSÉE MUNICIPAL DE PRÉHISTOIRE RÉGIONALE

See rock carvings from the Vallée des Merveilles, the 30,000-year-old skull of 'Menton Man' and other items from prehistoric times.

✉ Rue Lorédan Larchey, Menton ☎ 04 93 35 84 64 ◷ Wed–Mon 10–12, 2–6 ✋ Free

### PALAIS CARNOLÈS

Enjoy various works of art at this Musée des Beaux-Arts. The luxurious 18th-century palace was once a summer home for the Princes of Monaco.

✉ 3 avenue de la Madone, Menton ☎ 04 93 35 49 71 ◷ Wed–Mon 10–12, 2–6 ✋ Free

**Right** *Menton is famous for its citrus fruits and celebrates this each February with a* Fête du Citron *(Lemon Festival)*

### TIPS

» The *Fête du Citron* (Lemon Festival; ▷ 189) takes place in February.

» A chamber music festival is held in August in the Parvis St-Michel.

# MONACO-VILLE

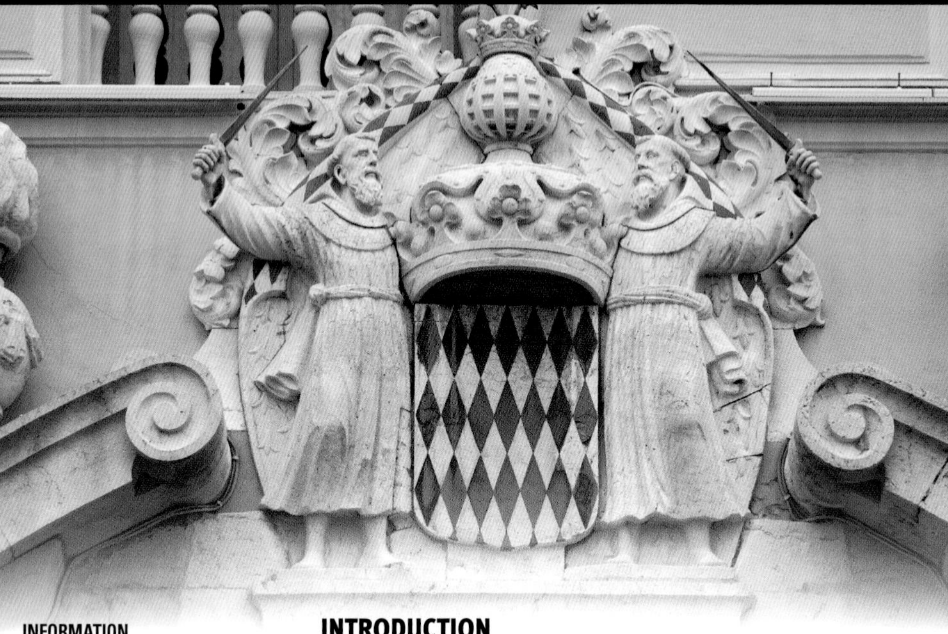

**INFORMATION**

www.visitmonaco.com
www.monaco.gouv.mc
299 Q10 2A boulevard des Moulins, Monte-Carlo, Monaco 377 92 16 61 16 Mon–Sat 9–7, Sun 11–1. In summer, additional tourist information kiosks are set up at the railway station and main sites Monaco (avenue Prince-Pierre) Frequent bus services run the length of Monaco from 7am to 9pm (€1 for a single trip). There is also a daily travel card for €3

**TIP**

» The currency in Monaco is the euro.

**Above** *The Grimaldi coat of arms*

## INTRODUCTION

The exquisite Prince's Palace makes The Rock the most extraordinary of all the Riviera's 'perched villages'.

Although so small, Monaco today is made up of several districts. However, the original town was Monaco-Ville, poised in isolation on top of its legendary rock, Le Rocher, which projects into the Mediterranean with a port on either side. It remains a tranquil, historic, relatively uncommercialized area. Unlike most other Provençal villages perched on high crests and ridges, the terrain on top of The Rock is quite flat. The Prince's Palace stands at one end and a village-like old quarter covers the rest of the area. Monaco-Ville is closed to visitors' vehicles and can be reached either on a long steep walkway from place d'Armes, or by elevator from parking des Pecheurs on the waterfront.

Monaco was originally a medieval perched fortress, its castle a possession of Barbarossa. In the 13th century, the powerful aristocratic Grimaldi family of Genoa acquired The Rock and made it their headquarters, refashioning themselves as the Princes of Monaco in the 17th century. Under Napoleon Bonaparte, most of the many such independent fiefdoms of Provence were incorporated by force into France. But the Grimaldi influence in Provence and Italy remained very powerful, and for strategic reasons Napoleon decided to make an ally of Monaco's royal family instead of seizing their land. Monaco's income had come from high taxes on its domains, but it now found a role for itself as a refuge for the aristocracy.

## WHAT TO SEE

### PALAIS PRINCIER

www.palais.mc

The sturdily fortified Prince's Palace occupies the western end of The Rock. The first Grimaldi palace here was a defensive castle built in 1215. In the 17th century it was restructured to create the present elegant building. In front is a large esplanade, place du Palais, where members of the crisply immaculate Prince's Guard are on duty. The Changing of the Guard ceremony takes place daily at 11.55am. Guided tours inside the palace reveal sumptuous rooms richly decorated and furnished, adorned with frescoes, tapestries and art. Also in the palace is a museum devoted to Napoleon Bonaparte, with an assortment of personal items, including one of his hats. The palace is open to visitors from April to October.

160 A3 Place du Palais, 98000 Monaco 377 93 25 18 31 Apr daily 10.30–5.30; May–end Sep daily 9.30–6; Oct daily 10–5 (entry is by guided tour only) Adult €8, child €3.50

## OLD QUARTER

The Palais Princier and surrounding gardens and plaza take up a large proportion of Monaco-Ville. The rest of The Rock is covered by Monaco's small historic town. Several narrow streets run parallel from place du Palais, at one end of The Rock, to place de la Visitation, at the other. They are spotlessly clean and pretty, with well-kept, pastel-shaded houses. Several of the buildings have good Renaissance doorways, especially along rue Comte Félix Gastaldi. However, there are few shops. Monaco-Ville's cathedral, in rue Colonel Bellando de Castro, has a Louis Bréa altarpiece, some fine paintings and the tombs of all Monaco's past princes.

160 A3

## MUSÉE OCÉANOGRAPHIQUE

www.oceano.mc

Carved into the flank of The Rock beside the sea is the Oceanography Museum, a world-class marine biology museum and study facility. Several floors high, it is educational and entertaining, with superb aquariums holding hundreds of thousands of creatures representing 350 species. There is a giant aquarium for sharks, a rare example of a living coral reef and sections on the human culture that has developed by the sea. The terrace offers fantastic coastal views.

160 B3 Avenue St-Martin, 98000 Monaco 377 93 15 36 00 Jul, Aug daily 9.30–7.30; Apr–end Jun, Sep daily 9.30–7; Oct–end Mar daily 10–6 Adult €13, child (6–18) €6.50, under 6 free

## OTHER DISTRICTS IN MONACO: LA CONDAMINE

160 A2

La Condamine, the old port district at the foot of The Rock and extending between Monaco-Ville and Monte-Carlo, is a busy shopping area with plenty of everyday stores. Here too is the principality's main covered market, opened in 1880. The main shopping street is rue Grimaldi. Monaco's rail station, and some of the most reasonably priced hotels, are in this part of town. The port area is packed with unpretentious restaurants—several of the best are Italian. La Condamine is the starting point for the Formula 1 Grand Prix.

## FONTVIEILLE

160 A3

Fontvieille is the area west of Monaco-Ville that has been artificially extended into the sea. This 22ha (54-acre) residential and business district stands on specially constructed platforms of rock, with a yachting port alongside. Its Roseraie Princesse Grace, in avenue des Papalins, is an exquisite rose garden dedicated to Princess Grace of Monaco. Formerly the actress Grace Kelly, the Princess died in a car accident in 1982. Other attractions include the Musée des Timbres et des Monnaies (focusing on stamps and money), the Musée Naval (model ships), the Collection des Voitures Anciennes (gleaming historic motor vehicles) and the Parc Animalier (a zoo).

## MONEGHETTI

160 A1

Climbing the steep slope between Monaco-Ville and the French border are the residential districts of Les Moneghetti and Les Révoires. At the top, just below the Moyenne Corniche road (N7), which is just outside Monaco, is the Jardin Exotique (mid-May to mid-Sep daily 9–7; mid-Sep to mid-May daily 9–6 or nightfall if earlier). This dazzling display is made up of succulents and cacti. The ticket includes a tour of the Grotte de l'Observatoire caves.

**Left** *Monaco's impressive cathedral was built between 1875 and 1903*

# MONTE-CARLO

**INFORMATION**

www.visitmonaco.com
www.monaco.gouv.mc
www.montecarloresort.com
299 Q10 2A boulevard des Moulins, Monte-Carlo, Monaco 377 92 16 61 16 Mon–Sat 9–7, Sun 11–1. In summer, additional tourist information kiosks are set up at the railway station and main sites Monaco (avenue Prince-Pierre) Frequent bus services run the length of Monaco from 7am to 8pm (€1 for a single trip)

**Above** *The Casino, floodlit at night*

## INTRODUCTION

This millionaire resort is devoted to gambling, luxury shopping and glitzy nightlife. Monte-Carlo is the large modern district along the narrow slope, close to the waterfront, in the north of the principality. It is Monaco's 'Casino quarter', with restaurants, luxurious hotels, opera and theatre, beautifully kept gardens, exclusive nightclubs and chic pricey shops, all within a short walk of the ostentatious casino. Monte-Carlo's main street, boulevard des Moulins, is lined with jewellers and boutiques selling luxurious designer clothes and expensive accessories. Avenue Princesse-Grace has exclusive sports clubs, beach clubs and nightclubs. Near the Larvotto beach area is the Jardin Japonais, a Shinto garden and a quiet, meditative refuge from the glitz that is Monte-Carlo. Unless you are into motor racing, don't come during the Grand Prix in May, when many thousands of visitors cram into the principality and many roads are closed.

Until the 19th century, Monaco consisted of Monaco-Ville (on The Rock, ▷ 156–157) and La Condamine (at the foot of The Rock, ▷ 157). In 1866, Prince Carlo III set out to develop the territory along the remainder of the Monaco shore. The result was the glamorous new district called Monte-Carlo. The architect Charles Garnier was commissioned to create a casino in similar style to his acclaimed Paris Opera House. The Casino opened in 1878 and succeeded so well in raising more funds for the royal family that all taxes were eventually abolished for Monaco citizens, and kept very low for other residents of the principality. Today, Monte-Carlo also hosts a large number of international fairs and festivals, as well as its Grand Prix motor races, which attract visitors from all over the world.

## WHAT TO SEE

### CASINO

www.casinomontecarlo.com

The wedding-cake extravagance of the Casino, along with its spacious sunlit square front-edged with café tables and the beautiful gardens, make a set-piece of gloriously ostentatious turn-of-the-19th-century style. The smart, white-gloved police officers briskly waving on the traffic complement the scene. Inside the Casino, the first halls reached are the Salons Européens and Salons Américains, which have a less-than-glamorous feel with their slot machines. You must pay to go into the more lavish Salons Privés, which is the real casino. Here is an air of riches, with high stakes and a strict dress code—and few ordinary tourists. A grand staircase leads down to an expensive nightclub featuring slick and exotic cabaret. Attached to the Casino is the equally richly decorated Monte-Carlo Opera, created by the same architect, Charles Garnier (1825–98).

161 C2 Place du Casino, Monte-Carlo, 98000 Monaco 377 98 06 21 21 Daily from 2pm, except Salons Privés, from 4pm €10, and a further €10 to enter games room Over 18s only. A passport or similar ID is required for entry. No casual dress in Salons Privés (a jacket and tie is obligatory for men after 9pm). There is an underground parking area

## MUSÉE NATIONAL

A grand villa designed by Charles Garnier north of the Casino houses this curious, eclectic collection of hundreds of dolls. Most are 19th century, with some dating back to the 18th century, but also some modern dolls. Dressed in impeccable period costume, they are amid miniature furnishings of their time. The most interesting and weird are automata—dolls that move. The mechanisms that work the dolls are fantastically delicate, and are open to view. The automata are set in motion several times a day. The museum also has a rose garden.

161 C1 17 avenue Princesse-Grace, 98000 Monaco 377 93 30 91 26 Easter–end Sep daily 10–6.30; Oct–Easter 10–12.15, 2.30–6.30. Closed the four days of the Grand Prix Adult €6, child (6–14) €3.50

## LARVOTTO

Take a break from sightseeing and lie on the beach. What Monaco does not have naturally, it creates artificially. The Larvotto area of Monte-Carlo, close to Beausoleil on the French side of the border, offers man-made beaches and swimming facilities. Next door is Le Sporting Club (including Jimmy'z nightclub), a legendary, exclusive 6ha (15-acre) waterfront area. Making a sharp contrast, near the Larvotto beach is a space for quiet reflection at the extensive, authentic Shinto garden called the Jardin Japonais (daily 9–dusk).

161 C1

## TIPS

» Monte-Carlo's open-air pool is the venue for many international swimming contests—and the view from the top diving board is excellent!

» Law enforcement is rigorous in Monaco, with 24-hour surveillance of the entire principality, including inside public buildings.

» All driving laws (and most other laws), road signs and drink-driving limits are the same in Monaco as in France.

**Below** *Take time out in the Jardin Japonais*

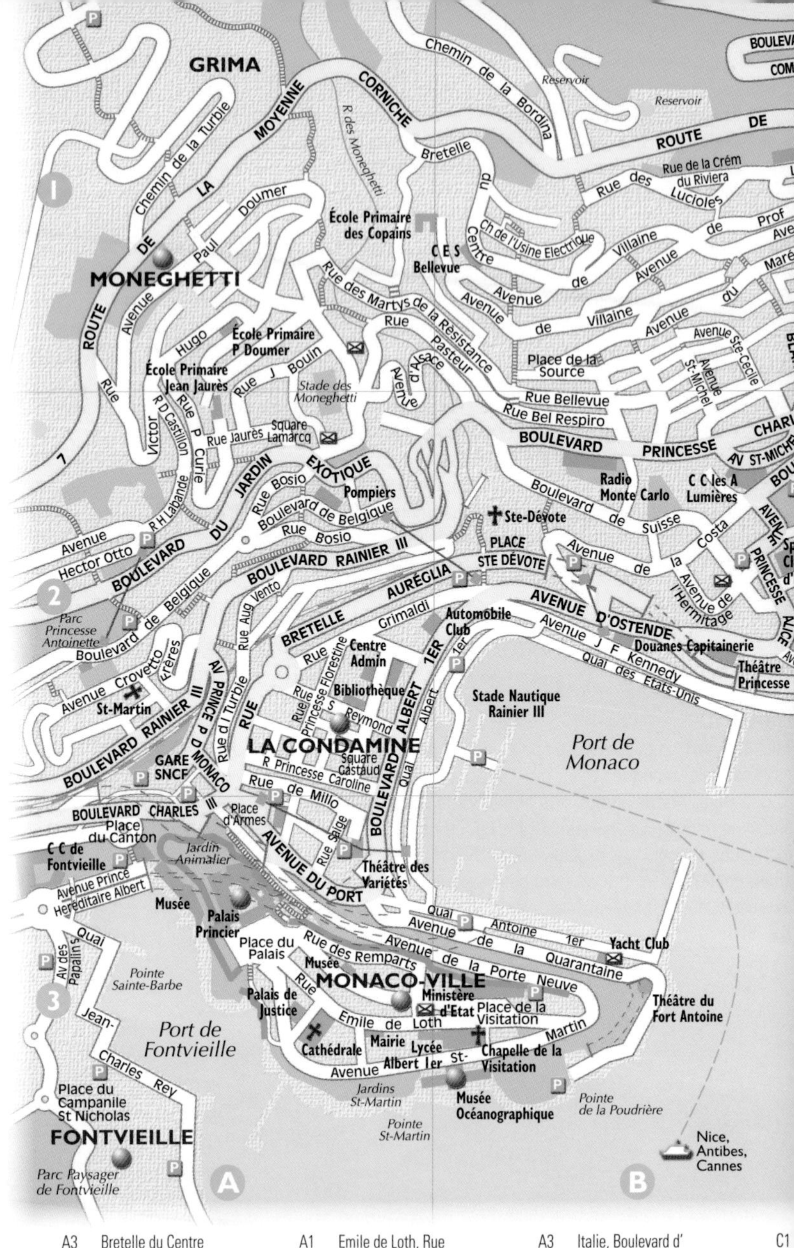
GRIMA
MONEGHETTI
LA CONDAMINE
MONACO-VILLE
FONTVIEILLE
Port de Monaco
Port de Fontvieille
Chemin de la Bordina
CORNICHE
LA MOYENNE
ROUTE DE
Chemin de la Turbie
Reservoir
R des Moneghetti
Bretelle du Centre
Rue des Lucioles
Rue de la Crém du Riviera
Ch de l'Usine Electrique
École Primaire des Copains
C E S Bellevue
Avenue de Villaine
Paul Doumer
Rue des Martys de la Résistance
Rue Pasteur
Avenue d'Alsace
Avenue Hugo
Victor Rue
École Primaire P Doumer
École Primaire Jean Jaurès
Rue J Bouin
Stade des Moneghetti
R D Castillon
Rue P Curie
Rue Jaurès
Square Lamarcq
Place de la Source
Avenue Ste-Cécile
Avenue St-Michel
Rue Bellevue
Rue Bel Respiro
BOULEVARD PRINCESSE CHARLOTTE
AV ST-MICHEL
Radio Monte Carlo
C C les A Lumières
BOULEVARD DU JARDIN EXOTIQUE
Pompiers
Rue Bosio
Boulevard de Belgique
R H Labande
Avenue Hector Otto
Boulevard de Suisse
Ste-Dévote
PLACE STE DÉVOTE
Avenue de la Costa
Avenue de l'Hermitage
BOULEVARD RAINIER III
BRETELLE AURÉGLIA
Rue Aug Vento
Parc Princesse Antoinette
Rue Grimaldi
Automobile Club
AVENUE D'OSTENDE
Avenue J F Kennedy
Quai des Etats-Unis
Douanes
Capitainerie
Théâtre Princesse
Avenue Crovetto Frères
St-Martin
AV PRINCE P D MONACO
Rue d l Turbie
Centre Admin
Rue Florestine
Bibliothèque
Rue Princesse
Rue S Reymond
BOULEVARD ALBERT 1ER
Quai Albert 1er
Stade Nautique Rainier III
R Princesse Caroline
Square Gastaud
Rue de Millo
GARE SNCF
BOULEVARD CHARLES III
Place d'Armes
Place du Canton
C C de Fontvieille
Jardin Animalier
Rue Saige
Théâtre des Variétés
AVENUE DU PORT
Avenue Prince Héréditaire Albert
Musée
Palais Princier
Quai Antoine 1er
Avenue de la Quarantaine
Yacht Club
Place du Palais
Rue des Remparts
Avenue de la Porte Neuve
Av des Papalins
Quai Jean-Charles Rey
Pointe Sainte-Barbe
Palais de Justice
Ministère d'Etat
Place de la Visitation
Rue Emile de Loth
Théâtre du Fort Antoine
Cathédrale
Mairie
Lycée
Chapelle de la Visitation
Avenue St-Martin
Avenue Albert 1er
Jardins St-Martin
Musée Océanographique
Pointe de la Poudrière
Pointe St-Martin
Place du Campanile St Nicholas
Parc Paysager de Fontvieille
Nice, Antibes, Cannes
A
B
1
2
3

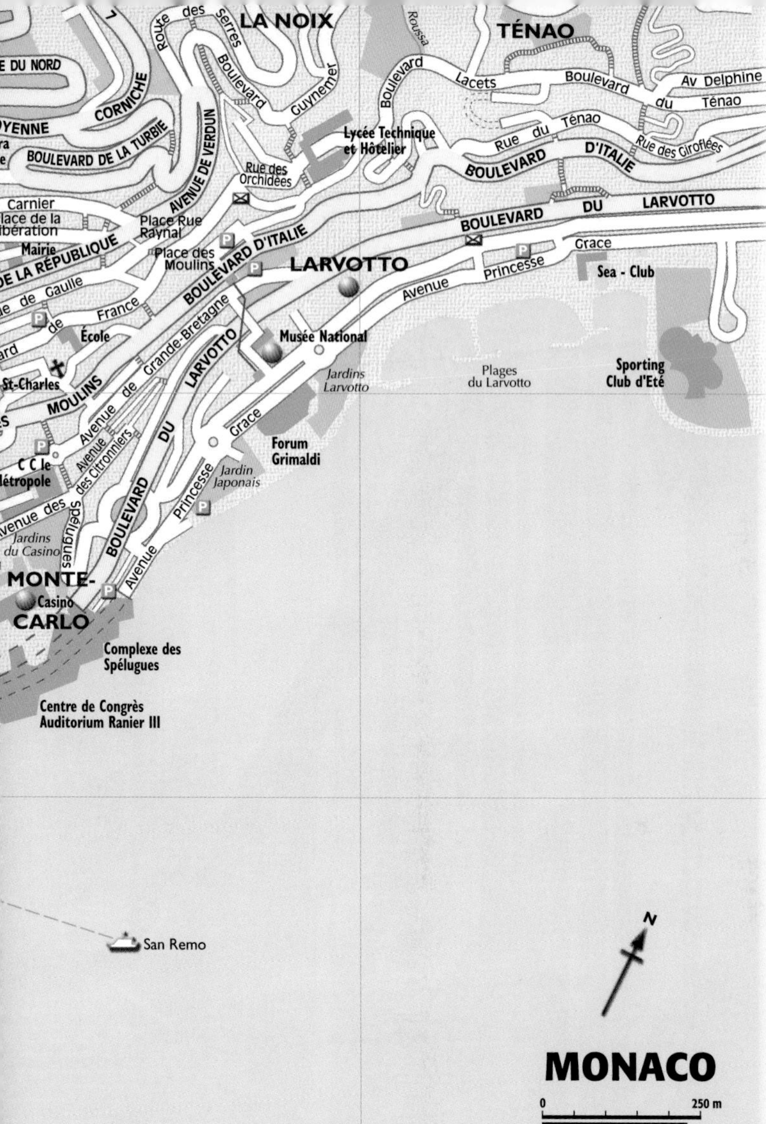
LA NOIX
TÉNAO
Route des Serres
Boulevard Guynemer
Boulevard
Lacets
Boulevard du Ténao
Av Delphine
Rue du Ténao
Rue des Giroflées
Lycée Technique et Hôtelier
BOULEVARD D'ITALIE
BOULEVARD DU LARVOTTO
CORNICHE
BOULEVARD DE LA TURBIE
AVENUE DE VERDUN
Rue des Orchidées
Carnier
Place Rue Raynal
Mairie
DE LA RÉPUBLIQUE
Place des Moulins
LARVOTTO
Avenue Princesse Grace
Sea - Club
de Gaulle
France
École
St-Charles
MOULINS
Avenue de Grande-Bretagne
Musée National
Jardins Larvotto
Plages du Larvotto
Sporting Club d'Eté
Forum Grimaldi
Jardin Japonais
Avenue des Citronniers
BOULEVARD DU LARVOTTO
Spélugues
Jardins du Casino
MONTE-CARLO
Casino
Complexe des Spélugues
Centre de Congrès Auditorium Ranier III
San Remo
N
MONACO
0
250 m
250 yds
C
D

# NICE

## INTRODUCTION

Nice is the Riviera's vivacious capital, backed by the foothills of the Provençal Alps. It is an art-lover's dream, with several major art galleries. With excellent road, rail and air connections, Nice is the busiest point of entry into Provence. The heart of town is bypassed by major roads, keeping it relatively free of through traffic. Parking is easy in the many covered parking areas, notably the useful parking area underneath place Masséna. Sights are not especially close together, but a good, inexpensive bus system, plus a tramline inaugurated in 2007, makes them all easily accessible. The 'visitor area' is mainly concentrated along the Promenade des Anglais and Le Vieux Nice. The park-like Promenade du Paillon, constructed over the concealed Paillon river, divides the old town from the new and is home to several museums. The Chagall and Matisse art museums and Cimiez hill farther back in the town deserve a special trip.

Nice has changed location several times. The original Ligurian settlement, from 1000BC, was near the waterside at the mouth of the River Paillon. The Greek town of Nikaea, from 600BC, was built on the waterfront hill now called the Château. The Roman town of Cemenelum, from 200BC, was a short distance inland on today's Cimiez hill. After the fall of Rome in the fifth century AD, the town was again based on the Château hill and the port. Medieval Nice, what is now Le Vieux Nice, belonged to the Counts of Provence and then to the Counts of Savoy. French troops occupied the area from 1792, but it was handed back in 1814. In 1860, it again became French when Napoleon III annexed the whole County of Nice, moving the Franco-Italian border to its present position. By then, Nice was already a winter resort, wealthy visitors building grand villas and extending the town westwards along the seashore. The 1920s brought a big growth in summer tourism, and many artists and writers stayed in or around Nice. Tourism continues to flourish.

### INFORMATION

www.nicetourism.com
299 Q10 **Main office:** Gare SNCF, avenue Thiers 0892 707 407 Jun–end Sep Mon–Sat 8–8, Sun 9–7; Oct–end May Mon–Sat 8–7, Sun 10–5. **Beach office:** 5 Promenade des Anglais 0892 707 407 Jun–end Sep Mon–Sat 8–8, Sun 9–6; Oct–end May Mon–Sat 9–6. **Nice-Côte d'Azur Airport:** Terminal 1 0892 707 407 Jun–end Sep daily 8am–9pm; Oct–end May Mon–Sat 8am–9pm
Nice (in avenue Thiers)
Nice is in the process of building a tram system linking downtown with the wide urban areas. This means there will be some disruption to traffic in the city until 2015

## WHAT TO SEE

### LE VIEUX NICE

Set back from the sea at the eastern end of the beach is the historic and atmospheric old quarter called Le Vieux Nice. This is a delightful tangle of picturesque narrow lanes, many lined with bars, popular restaurants and little shops selling souvenirs or traditional Provençal fabrics. There are several interesting small baroque churches too; if their doors are open, it's worth

**Above** *You can get a wonderful view from the Colline du Château*
**Opposite** *A picturesque alleyway in Le Vieux Nice*

**TIPS**

» Visit the big flower market (Tue–Sun) on cours Saleya.

» Nice's vibrant carnival takes place during the two weeks before Lent (▷ 189).

» For a different view of Nice, take a narrated tour in a land train operated by Les Trains Touristiques de Nice (adult €7, child under 9 €4). The train leaves from outside the Jardin Albert I.

» The tourist office phone line is premium rate.

looking inside to see the elaborate workmanship of the interiors. The focal point of the old quarter is cours Saleya, a long esplanade edged with restaurant tables and filled for much of the day with a big, vibrant flower market.

167 C3 There is an underground parking area at cours Saleya

## MUSÉE MASSENA

After six years of renovations, this neoclassical former palace reopened in 2008 as Nice's history museum. Over three floors it explores the modern history of the Riviera's capital by way of antique objets d'art, portraits of Nice from yesteryear and even dinner menus from the belle époque period. The carefully manicured gardens that surround the grand building are a great place to soak up the sun.

166 A3 65 rue de France, 06000 Nice 04 93 911 910 Wed–Mon 10–6 Free

## PROMENADE DES ANGLAIS

A wide waterfront road edged by mimosa and palms follows the coastal strip where Nice meets the dazzling blue curve of the Baie des Anges. Running for several kilometres beside the town's stony beach, this is the famous Promenade des Anglais. Although it's now beside a busy highway, it remains an attractive sight, and on fine days is full of people sauntering, sitting in the sun or skating. Grand facades look across from the other side of the road, including the sumptuous, traditional Hôtel Negresco and the Palais de la Mediterrannée, a state-of-the-art luxury hotel behind an art deco exterior. The Promenade des Anglais ends at the Jardin Albert I, but the promenade continues east as quai des États-Unis.

166 B3 Street parking and underground parking areas are available

## LE CHÂTEAU

The waterfront promenade ends at the Château, which is not a castle but a high headland rising up between the beach area and the port. Le Vieux Nice is just below. The medieval fortress and other buildings that stood here were demolished in 1706, leaving almost no trace. Today the hilltop is a pleasant shaded park with fantastic views of the sea and town. At the foot of the hill, the coast road turns to reach the old port, a busy area with some popular restaurants.

167 C3 Street parking is available

**Below** *The Musée Henri Matisse has many works by the artist*

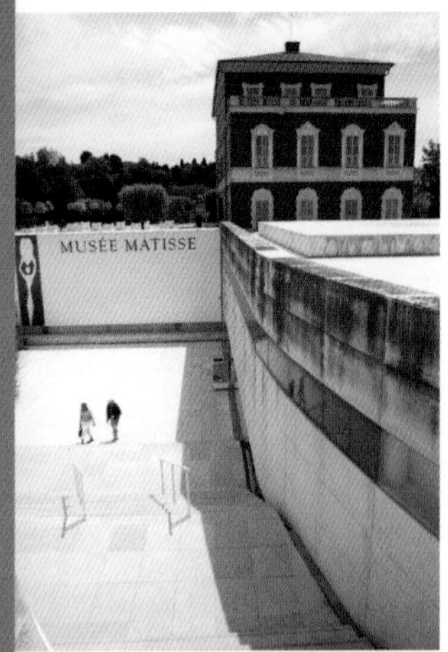


## MUSÉE HENRI MATISSE

www.musee-matisse-nice.org

Entered directly from the archaeological park, the Musée Henri Matisse houses the most important collection of Matisse's work. The museum is largely hidden from view, in a modern underground building, but above ground it also includes a 17th-century mansion. It deals with the development of Matisse's work, from exquisite line drawings to vivid gouaches to a model of his chapel at nearby Vence. There are also personal possessions and photos. Henri Matisse (1869–1954) and Raoul Dufy (1877–1953) are both buried in nearby Cimiez cemetery.

Off map at 167 C1 164 avenue des Arènes, Cimiez, 06000 Nice 04 93 81 08 08 Wed–Mon 10–6 Free 15, 17, 20, 22, 25 Guided tours (€5) Wed at 10, 2 in French; other languages by appointment

## CIMIEZ

On higher ground in the north, the Cimiez district is the site of Roman Nice. There are Roman ruins and a museum at the Parc des Antiquités, an archaeological site now laid out as a pleasant little park, known locally as Les Arènes. The oval-shaped arena, still within the ruins of its original Roman walls, now hosts open-air concerts, including jazz. Other first- to third-century AD

**CIMIEZ PLAN**

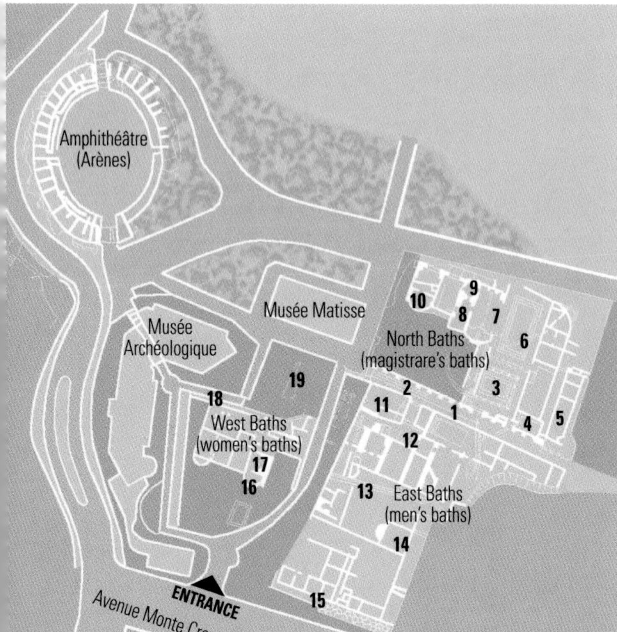


**1** Decumanus I
**2** Early boundary wall (first century AD)
**3** Natatio (swimming pool)
**4** Latrine
**5** Reservoir
**6** Courtyard
**7** Frigidarium (cold water)
**8** Tepidarium (tepid water)
**9** Laconicum (sweat bath)
**10** Caldarium (hot water)
**11** Fourth-century AD building
**12** Praefurnium (stove)
**13** Great Courtyard (Palaestra)
**14** School
**15** Decumanus II
**16** Foundations of baths (third century AD)
**17** Choir of fifth-century AD Christian basilica
**18** Baptiserium
**19** Cardo

ruins at the site include a good example of Roman baths. Beside the park, the Musée Archéologique displays objects found here and elsewhere in Nice.
166 B1 Musée Archéologique and Parc des Antiquités, 160 avenue des Arènes, Cimiez, 06000 Nice 04 93 81 59 57 Wed–Sun 10–6 Free Guided tours (€3) in French on Wed and 1st Sun in month, at 3

## MUSÉE MARC CHAGALL

www.musee-chagall.fr

Down a side road at the bottom of the Cimiez hill is the Musée Marc Chagall, with the alternative name Musée du Message Biblique. This is a phenomenal collection of Chagall's enigmatic work, including his stained glass, mosaics and art books, as well as the vast, vivid, dreamlike canvases devoted to biblical stories *(message biblique)* and Jewish subjects, including scenes from his childhood shtetl home. The museum shop has excellent books on Chagall.
166 B1 Avenue du Docteur Ménard, 06000 Nice 04 93 53 87 20 May–end Oct Wed–Mon 10–6; Nov–end Apr Wed–Mon 10–5 Adult €6.50, under 18 free; free on 1st Sun of month 15 Guided tours for pre-reserved groups only

## PLACE MASSÉNA AND CENTRAL NICE

The Paillon promenade runs into pedestrianized place Masséna and the busy heart of town. This central district is largely 18th to 20th century, with the distinctive attractive Niçois style of shallow roofs and ornate frontages with balconies and sectioned slatted shutters. Here are many stores, including Galeries Lafayette, as well as a pedestrian-only zone of narrow streets filled with specialist shops and inexpensive restaurants. The district is bisected by the city's main thoroughfare, avenue Jean Médecin, and its tram route.
166 B3 There is street parking and the underground parking area Masséna

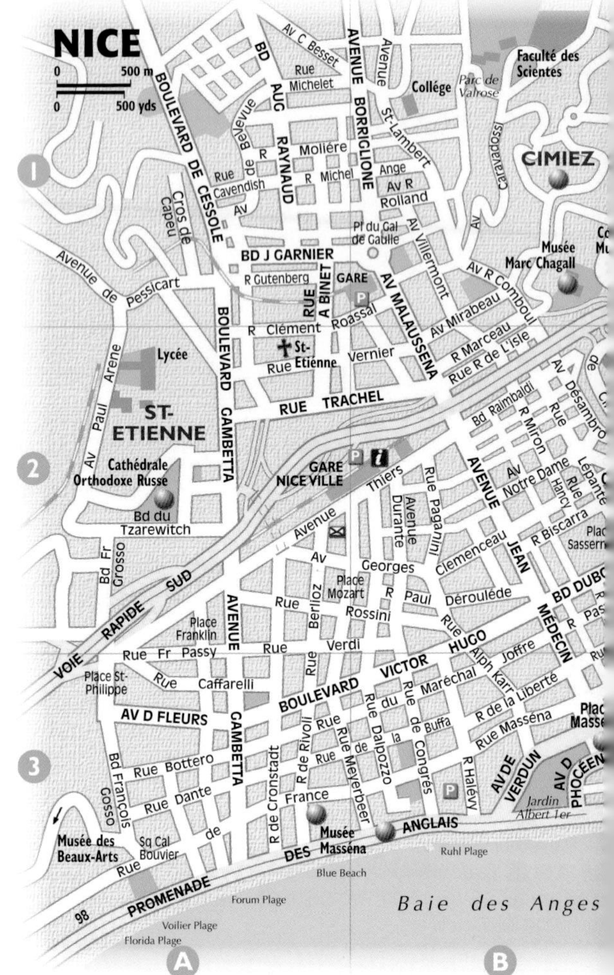


## MUSÉE DES BEAUX-ARTS

At the western end of the beach, a handsome 19th-century mansion houses the prestigious Musée des Beaux-Arts. Here you can see European fine arts of the 17th to 19th centuries, including paintings of the Riviera by Edgar Degas, Alfred Sisley and Raoul Dufy. Other exhibits include sculptures by Jean-Baptiste Carpeaux and Auguste Rodin and paintings by 17th-century Italian Old Masters. A few prize exhibits were stolen during an armed robbery in 2007.

Off map at 166 A3 · 33 avenue des Baumettes, Nice · 04 92 15 28 28 · Tue–Sun 10–6 · Free

## MUSÉE D'ART MODERNE ET D'ART CONTEMPORAIN

www.mamac-nice.org

The avant-garde Museum of Modern and Contemporary Art has the definitive collection of the 'Nice school' of 1960s artists who lived and worked in the town. See Pop Art from names such as Andy Warhol and Roy Lichtenstein. The building is unusual—four octagonal marble towers are linked by walkways.

167 C2 · Promenade des Arts, Nice · 04 97 13 42 01 · Tue–Sun 10–6 · Free

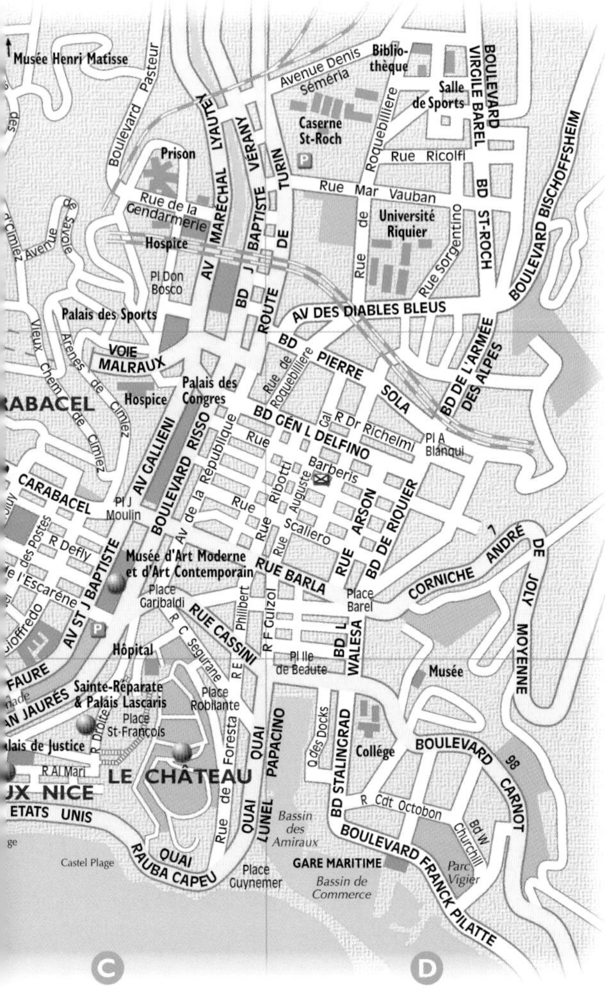

**Below** *Ornate decoration in the Cathédrale Orthodoxe Russe*

## CATHÉDRALE ORTHODOXE RUSSE

www.acor-nice.com

Tsar Nicolas II commissioned this striking cathedral in 1903, in memory of his uncle, Nicolas, who died of consumption in Nice. The glistening green cupolas are a reminder of the building's Russian origins.

166 A2 Avenue Nicolas II, Nice 04 93 96 88 02 Mon–Sat 9.15–12, 2.30–5.30, Sun 2.30–5.30 €3

# MORE TO SEE

## CATHÉDRALE DE SAINTE-RÉPARATE

This 17th-century baroque extravaganza, with a roof of bright Niçois tiles, is named after Nice's patron saint.

167 C3 Place Rossetti, Nice 04 93 62 34 40 Daily, hours vary Free

## PALAIS LASCARIS

See paintings, tapestries and furniture from the 17th and 18th centuries.

167 C3 15 rue Droite, Nice 04 93 62 05 54 Wed–Mon 10–6 Free

# PARC NATIONAL DU MERCANTOUR

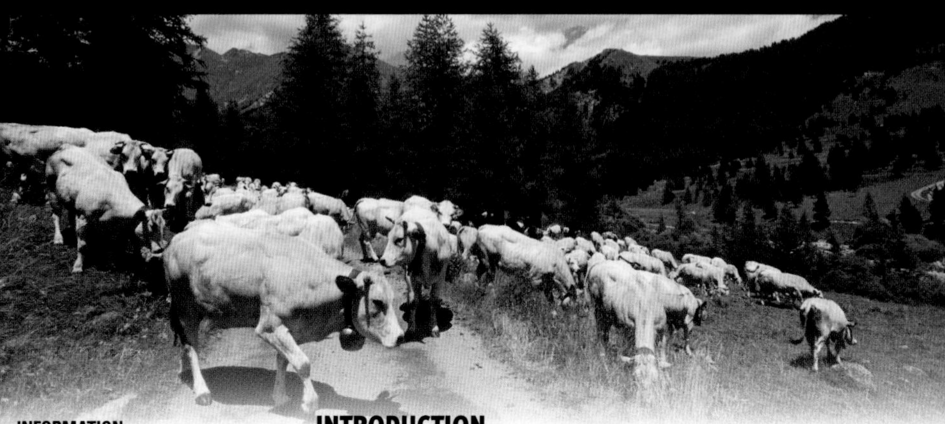

## INFORMATION

www.mercantour.eu
293 M7 Tende tourist information office: avenue du 16 Septembre 1947, 06430 Tende-Val-des-Merveilles
04 93 04 73 71 Mon–Sat 9–12, 2–5, Sun 9–12

Above *Cattle graze in the park*

## INTRODUCTION

An awesomely beautiful mountain region with superb wildlife, the Mercantour combines the warmth of the Mediterranean with the harsher world of the Alps. The National Park lies along the Franco-Italian border in the Provençal Alps, and can be reached relatively easily from the Riviera coast on roads climbing the Tinée, Vésubie and Roya valleys. The main entry point is the small town of Tende (▷ 171), on the Roya river. The landscapes are extremely varied, ranging from gentle green pasture and alpine forests to glacial lakes, canyons and soaring peaks in the inaccessible protected zone. Popular with walkers and climbers, this is a genuine adventure land, but carefully managed, with guides, park rangers and facilities. *Refuges* or chalets on well-marked mountain trails offer shelter or overnight lodgings, but these must be reserved well in advance. There are 600km (370 miles) of paths in the park and several nature trails, such as those at Lac d'Allos (▷ 199) and Col de la Bonette. Two long-distance hiking trails, GR5 and GR52, also cross the area.

The Mercantour was a hunting reserve for the Italian royal family in the second half of the 19th century. It remained in Italian hands until after World War II, when it was split between Italy and France. The two halves were symbolically joined in 1980 to form the Argentera National Park.

## WHAT TO SEE

### VALLÉE DES MERVEILLES

The most popular and remarkable excursion into the Parc is the trek to the Vallée des Merveilles (▷ 176–177). This is a valley on a high tributary of the Roya, just below Mont Bégo (2,872m/9,420ft), where thousands of odd, repetitive drawings are inscribed on the rocks. Many more can be seen in the nearby Vallée de Fontanalbe. In a simple style resembling stick men, and actually rather hard to discern, these images are thought to have been made in the Bronze Age (1800–1500BC) and depict hands, weapons, tools and horns. No one knows what purpose the pictures served, if any, but an explanation popular with the guides and others is that the Bronze Age inhabitants of the site here worshipped Mont Bégo as a sacred place of the Bull-God and Earth-Goddess religion. There is, however, no convincing evidence for this. The most striking of the drawings have been given names, such as *The Sorcerer*. The walk to the Vallée takes you through a dramatically wild scene of forests, flower meadows, lakes and mountains.

The Park's website lists the websites and telephone numbers of several practised mountain guides On the D91 at Lac des Mesches there is a parking area at the start of the path to the Refuge des Merveilles (a 3-hour walk away)

## FLORA AND FAUNA

For walkers and climbers venturing deep into the national park, there is a great wealth of animal and plant life to be seen. Pines and larches on the lower slopes give way to Alpine meadows at higher altitudes. There is permanent snow above 3,000m (9,840ft). Hovering overhead are birds such as eagles, kestrels and falcons, and the rare lammergeyer vulture. Smaller birds include the ptarmigan, great spotted woodpecker, hoopoe, citril finches, ortolan and rock buntings. Mouflons (wild sheep) were reintroduced in the 1950s, while red deer, chamois, blue hare, ibex and boar are increasing in numbers. There are numerous other animals, and 200 rare plant species, including 35 endemic to this region.

## THE SEASONS

In spring, mountain meadows are dotted with bellflowers and blue gentians. You may sometimes see saxifrage, the symbol of the park. In summer you can wander through glades of pines, spruce, larches and silvery wild olives without the need for all-weather clothing. Autumn, like spring, is a quieter time to visit and the park is arguably at its most beautiful. In winter the entire region is frequently dusted with snow.

## TIPS

» The following are not allowed in the park: pets, fires, camping, waste disposal or removing any plant or natural object.

» The park's main office (23 rue d'Italie, 06006 Nice, tel 04 93 16 78 88) is not open to the public.

» Col de la Cayolle refuge (tel 04 93 05 54 90) is open from mid-June to mid-September.

» Most of the park's higher reaches are covered in snow from mid-October to mid-June, limiting accessibility for all but the most experienced climbers.

**Left** *Cycling through the Vallée des Merveilles*
**Below** *Flowers brightening the slopes*

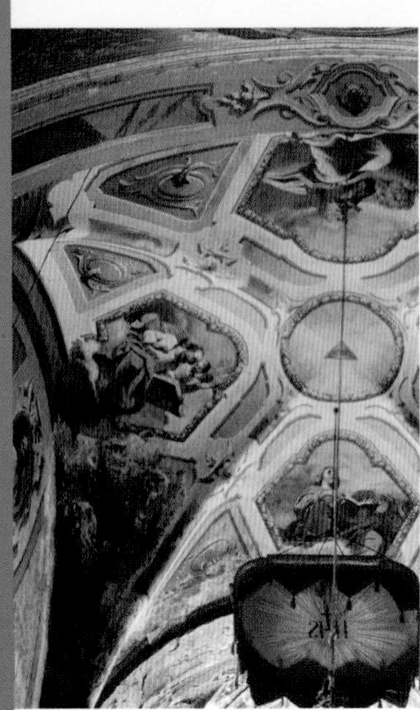

**Above** *Frescoes in Église St-Sauveur, Saorge*

## ST-MARTIN-VÉSUBIE

www.saintmartinvesubie.fr

The upper Vésubie valley and surrounding peaks form a spectacularly scenic landscape on the edge of the high-altitude Parc National du Mercantour (⊳ 168–169). The main town of the region, St-Martin-Vésubie, is a popular little resort among the green hills on the twin streams of Le Boréon and La Madone de Fenestre, which pour down from the Mercantour heights and meet in the town to form the river Vésubie. Water even flows down the heart of the cobbled main street, rue Dr. Cagnoli, overhung with chalet-style houses. The effect is delightful—but was not always so, since this stream once served as the town's main sewer. Rue Dr. Cagnoli runs from the main square, place Félix-Faure, down to the Gothic Maison des Contes de Gubernatis, passing the bulbous tower of the Chapelle des Pénitents-Blancs.

Inside the parish church is an altarpiece from the Bréa school and, for part of the year, the polychrome wooden statue of the Madone de Fenestre, brought to the town by 12th-century Templars. In July the statue is carried in procession to its summer quarters, the Sanctuaire de la Madone de Fenestre, 12km (7.5 miles) northeast. It returns in September. The chapel gets its curious name ('Madonna of the Window') from a natural opening in the rocks above it, through which you can see the sky.

✚ 299 P8 ℹ Place Félix-Faure, 06450 St-Martin-Vésubie ☎ 04 93 03 21 28 ⌚ Jul, Aug daily 9–12, 2–7; Sep–end Jun Mon–Sat 9–12, 2–6, Sun 9–12

## ST-PAUL-DE-VENCE

www.saint-pauldevence.com

Visually stunning, the hilltop village of St-Paul is well defended within its ring of ramparts. The busy, commercialized streets lead to picturesque sights like the old washhouse, while the church has fine medieval art. The village is in a constant battle to preserve something of its authentic atmosphere, while thousands of visitors come each day from Riviera resorts just 30 minutes' drive away. Packed with workshops, art galleries, antiques stores and gift shops, its narrow streets are crowded in summer.

The village appealed to the Riviera's artists of a century ago, such as Pablo Picasso and Marc Chagall. They used to meet at a tavern called the Auberge de la Colombe d'Or and pay for meals by donating art every now and then. Some of these still hang on the walls of the *auberge*, now one of the region's most prestigious restaurants. The Musée d'Histoire (Apr–end Sep daily 10–12, 3–6; Oct, Dec–end Mar daily 2–5), in a 12th-century keep next to the town hall, has photos of some of the celebrities who have visited or lived in the village.

✚ 298 P10 ℹ 2 rue Grande, 06570 St-Paul-de-Vence ☎ 04 93 32 86 95 ⌚ Jun–end Sep daily 10–7; Oct–end May daily 10–6

## SAORGE

Seen from below, this perched village in the Roya valley in the Provençal Alps is a jumble of dark fortifications, towers and tall houses, with glazed roof tiles catching the light. The precipitous drive up to the village is worth it to see how this peculiar place has been built, with houses piled one on top of the other and connected by stairways and alleyways where daylight hardly penetrates. The village stands guard over the entrance to the awesome Roya Gorge and the approaches to the Col de Tende. It was a key defensive post in the Middle Ages, but the fort was destroyed by Napoleon Bonaparte in 1794. The church at the heart of the village has some intriguing trompe l'oeil frescoes. The fine carved organ was built in Genoa and brought up here by pack mules. At the end of the main street, a path leads to a 17th-century Franciscan monastery with an 11th-century chapel, La Madone del Poggio.

✚ 299 R8 ℹ Mairie (town hall) ☎ 04 93 04 51 23 🚉 Saorge-Fortan station 1km (0.6 miles) from the village

## SOSPEL

www.sospel-tourisme.com

The charmingly Italianate town of Sospel sits among terraces and groves on the banks of the river Bévéra, in the hills that separate Provence from Italy. Located on an important medieval trade route, the town grew up around its distinctive fortified toll bridge. The 11th-century bridge—still with its tollgate halfway across—remains an evocative sight.

In the western half of the town, narrow streets open up into place St-Michel, which is lined with baroque facades. The 17th-century Église St-Michel has a Romanesque bell tower, inherited from the 12th-century church it replaced. Inside the church are magnificent altarpieces by Louis Bréa.

Out of town on the D2204 is Fort St-Roch, a Maginot Line fortress built in 1932. It now houses a museum of the Alpine resistance (Jun–end Sep Tue–Sun 2–6; Oct–end May Sat, Sun 2–6).

✚ 299 Q9 ℹ Avenue Jean Médecin, 06380 Sospel ☎ 04 93 04 15 80 ⌚ Mon–Sat 10–4, Sun 10–12.30 🚉 Sospel

## TENDE

www.tendemerveilles.com

Tende is the last town in France on the mountain road from Provence into Italy's Piedmont—and until 1947, Tende itself was in Italy. It remained in Italy when the rest of the County of Nice became French in 1860 because Victor Emmanuel II begged Napoleon III to let him keep these high hills, where he loved to hunt chamois. As a gesture of goodwill, Napoleon III agreed to the request. Tende joined France after World War II.

The town is a curious steep collection of high balconied houses under dark stone roofs rising one above the other, a warren of little streets running between, all dominated by a rather bizarre bulbous church spire. Many of the houses, stone built and roofed with stone slabs, date from the 15th century. Ruins of a castle stand above the town. The unusual church, St-Marie des Bois, has a handsome Renaissance doorway and 17th-century organ.

The town has become the main base for excursions into the Mercantour (▷ 168–169), especially walkers heading to the Vallée des Merveilles (▷ 176–177). The Musée des Merveilles, in avenue du 16 Septembre 1947 (May to mid-Oct Wed–Mon 10–6.30; mid-Oct to end Apr Wed–Mon 10–5) has displays explaining the history, archaeology and mythology of the valley and the rock drawings, as well as giving insight into the local culture. The museum is also an information venue for walks to the Vallée des Merveilles.

✚ 299 R8 ℹ Avenue du 16 Septembre 1947, 06430 Tende-Val-des-Merveilles ☎ 04 93 04 73 71 ⏲ Mon–Sat 9–12, 2–5, Sun 9–12 🚉 Tende

## LA TURBIE

www.ville-la-turbie.fr

La Turbie sits on a lofty ridge in beautiful sunlit hills above Monaco. The small town dates back to early Roman times, when it was the highest point on the Via Julia highway (480m/1,575ft above sea level). Here in the first century BC, the massive Trophée des Alpes was erected as a triumphal monument to commemorate Augustus' conquest of the Alpine tribes. A small part is still standing, on cours Albert 1er, and its chunky silhouette is a memorable landmark overlooking the town. The Trophée (mid-May to mid-Sep daily 9.30–1, 2.30–6.30; mid-Sep to mid-May daily 10–1.30, 2.30–5) was originally 50m (165ft) high and 38m (125ft) wide, with a statue of Augustus on top. In the Middle Ages it was used as a fortress, and later much vandalized, eventually being largely dismantled on the orders of Louis XIV in 1705. It was further destroyed in the 19th century when the stonework was quarried to build the nearby church. Despite all this damage, enough of the vast monument survived to make partial restoration feasible (financed by an American, Edward Tuck). The present structure has a height of 35m (115ft). A long inscription on its base lists all 44 local tribes conquered by Augustus. The gardens surrounding the trophy offer panoramic views of the Riviera.

✚ 299 Q10 ℹ 2 place Detras, 06320 La Turbie ☎ 04 93 41 21 14 ⏲ Jul, Aug Mon–Sat 9–1, 2.30–6.30, Sun 9–1; Sep–end Jun Mon–Fri 9.30–1, 2.30–5.30, Sat 9.30–1

## VENCE

www.vence.fr

Vence is best known for its artistic connections, especially Henri Matisse's chapel. The town is an easy drive inland from Cannes or Antibes and is in an attractive part of the Riviera backcountry. It has an enjoyable old town, with surviving sections of the ramparts including five gateways. At the heart of town are place du Frêne, dominated by an ancient ash tree, and place du Peyra, with a fountain of drinkable mineral-rich water. Next to the square, Château de Villeneuve has a 13th-century watchtower; today the chateau is used for exhibitions of 20th-century art. Head down rue du Marché, which is crammed with excellent little patisseries, charcuteries, cheese specialists and fishmongers with sacks of mussels and mounds of freshly cooked prawns.

Rue du Marché leads to place Clemenceau, at the heart of the old quarter, where Roman tombstones are incorporated into the walls of the 10th-century cathedral—the site was formerly a Roman temple. In the baptistery at the back there's a mosaic by Marc Chagall (1887–1985).

Vence is noted for artistic and literary connections. André Gide, Paul Valéry and D. H. Lawrence are among the writers who have lived in the town. Vence's main attraction is in the modern suburbs in the north: the exquisite little Chapelle du Rosaire, designed by Henri Matisse (1869–1954). Stained glass throws patterns of yellow, green and blue onto walls of white tiles on which line drawings depict biblical scenes. A rule of silence inside the chapel greatly enhances the effect. Matisse built the chapel as a thank you to Dominican nuns who cared for him when he was gravely ill. After five years of work, he declared that this was his masterpiece.

✚ 299 P10 ℹ 8 place du Grand Jardin, 06140 Vence ☎ 04 93 58 06 38 ⏲ Jul, Aug Mon–Sat 9–7, Sun 10–6; Sep, Oct, Mar–end Jun Mon–Sat 9–6; Nov–end Feb Mon–Sat 9–5

**Below** *The Trophée des Alpes, in La Turbie*

**INFORMATION**

www.villa-ephrussi.com
299 Q10 Fondation Béatrice Ephrussi de Rothschild, chemin du Musée, 06230 St-Jean-Cap-Ferrat 04 93 01 33 09 Jul, Aug daily 10–7; Feb–end Jun, Sep, Oct daily 10–6; Nov–end Jan Mon–Fri 2–6, Sat, Sun, school hols 10–6 Guided tours of the villa take place at 11.30, 2.30, 3.30 and 4.30 (€3) Adult €10, child (7–17) €7.50 Elegant tea room Buses from Nice every half hour to Beaulieu, which is around 2km (1.2 miles) from the Villa Beaulieu, around 2km (1.2 miles) from the Villa

**Above** *Elegant arches in the patio*

## VILLA EPHRUSSI DE ROTHSCHILD

This luxurious Italianate villa contains around 5,000 works of art. Béatrice de Rothschild, wife of wealthy banker Baron Ephrussi, created the spacious villa and gardens here in 1912, wanting a place for banquets and entertaining. She also needed somewhere to house her huge collection of important items gathered from around France and the rest of the world. She chose a delightful setting, on the quiet and exclusive Cap Ferrat peninsula (▷ 153) close to Beaulieu, with sea views on both sides. Construction took seven years, with a succession of around 40 architects—some didn't last more than a few hours, thanks to the baroness' capriciousness. The baroness died in 1934, leaving the villa to France's Académie des Beaux-Arts. Now, visitors can wander around the beautiful gardens and the ground floor of the villa, although to see the collections on the first floor you have to take a guided tour.

### THE ART

The art collection is diverse, with some 5,000 works, ranging from French period furniture and tapestries to Renaissance religious art, fine 18th-century porcelain and bas-reliefs. The Far Eastern art is also remarkable, with a wonderful display of pink jade and some rare Chinese chests. The Salon des Singes (Monkey Room) on the first floor reflects the Baroness' love of monkeys and other animals.

### OUTSIDE

The grounds are divided into a series of separate areas encapsulating different garden styles from around the world. Along the length of the central garden are musical fountains (you can have *Happy Birthday* played for you as the waters dance for your delight), surrounded by the seven other gardens in such styles as Spanish, Florentine and Japanese.

### TEA AND SHOPPING

The villa has an elegant tea room with wonderful views of the Bay of Villefranche from its large windows. The site's shop has an interesting range of jewellery, porcelain and good-quality rugs and wallhangings.

## VILLEFRANCHE-SUR-MER

With fishing boats in the port and pastel-painted houses climbing steep narrow lanes, Villefranche-sur-Mer is thought by many to be one of the loveliest places on the Riviera. The pretty, unpretentious small port town is very close to Nice. Historically a military base as well as a fishing village, Villefranche now hosts summertime cruise ships in its deep, sheltered port. The rue Obscure, a vaulted 13th-century street running beneath the houses close to the port, was used as a community bomb shelter in World War II. After the war, Villefranche's bay was frequently used as a harbour by the US Navy's 6th Fleet. Although it's difficult to imagine today, this lovely village had a very seedy side throughout the 1950s. Present-day visitors may recognize the area as the setting for two high-grossing movies, conman comedy *Dirty Rotten Scoundrels* (1988) starring Steve Martin and Michael Caine, and action film *Ronin* (1998) featuring Robert de Niro.

### FAMOUS RESIDENT

Artist, writer and film director Jean Cocteau lived here from 1924 to 1926; he decorated the Chapelle St-Pierre (Apr–end Sep daily 10–12, 3–7; Oct, mid-Dec to end Mar daily 10–12, 2–6. Closed Nov to mid-Dec). His dazzling frescoes show the life of St. Peter as if among the people of the town.

### SIGHTS

Above the port, the massive walls of the 16th-century Citadelle enclose the Mairie (town hall), an open-air theatre and two museums. Fondation-Musée Volti (Jul, Aug Mon, Wed–Sat 10–12, 2.30–7, Sun 2–7; Jun, Sep Mon, Wed–Sat 9–12, 2.30–6, Sun 2.30–6; Oct, Dec–end May Mon, Wed–Sat 10–12, 2–5, Sun 2–5. Closed Nov) is dedicated to sculptures of voluptuous female figures by local artist Volti. The Musée Goetz-Boumeester (Jul, Aug Mon, Wed–Sat 10–12, 2.30–7, Sun 2–7; Jun, Sep Mon, Wed–Sat 9–12, 2.30–6, Sun 2.30–6; Oct, Dec–end May Mon, Wed–Sat 10–12, 2–5, Sun 2–5. Closed Nov) contains works by modern artists Christine Boumeester and Henri Goetz, two works by Pablo Picasso and one by Joan Miró, as well as displays of ceramics. At the citadel entrance you can see finds from the wreck of a Genoese trading ship that sank in Villefranche port in 1516.

### INFORMATION

www.villefranche-sur-mer.com

299 Q10 Jardin François-Binon, 06230 Villefranche-sur-Mer

04 93 01 73 68 Jul, Aug daily 9–7; Jun, Sep Mon–Sat 9–12, 2–6.30; Oct–end May Mon–Sat 9–12, 2–6

Villefranche-sur-Mer

**Below** *A view across the bay*

# NICE OLD TOWN

**Most of the Italian-style buildings in Nice's Old Town are around 300 years old, and date from the House of Savoy era, 150 years before Nice became part of France. This walk takes in its history-packed side streets and three majestic main squares.**

**THE WALK**
**Distance:** 2km (1.3 miles)
**Time:** 1.5 hours
**Start/end at:** place du Palais, Nice Old Town

★ From the fountain in the place du Palais (or Palace Square) several *palais* are clearly visible. The grey colonnaded building is the imposing Palais de Justice, the region's law court. In 1976, the famous French bank robber Albert Spaggiari jumped out of a courtroom window into a waiting car, never to be seen again. Opposite is the orange Palais Rusca, a town hall building, once a training school for the French military.

Walk south under the arch marked by a palm tree, which leads to the seafront. Stop before the road. On the way, pass Nice's colourful flower market, the Marché aux Fleurs (▷ 187), on your left, and catch a glimpse of Nice's grand opera house on your right.

❶ This seafront area is dotted with open-air sculptures. Walk 50m (55 yards) to the left to the Galerie des Ponchettes, at 77 quai des États-Unis, a free gallery where artist Henri Matisse had one of his first exhibitions.

Carry on past Galerie de Ponchettes for 100m (110 yards), with the buildings, which are actually former fishermen's houses, on your left. Turn left after the Sun, Sea, Beach Café into the cours Saleya square.

❷ In cours Saleya, straight ahead is the huge Mairie, the office of the mayor of Nice and formerly the Palais de Rois Sardes: the palace of the Sardinian kings who ruled the city. Ahead on the right is a baroque masterpiece, the Chapelle de la Miséricorde. Running left and right all along the cours Saleya are colourful fruit and vegetable stalls (Tue–Sun 7–12.30) or al fresco dining tables and cafés (daily 12.30–11).

Turn right and head to the large yellow mansion at the cours Saleya's end. Matisse once lived, and painted, in the building's third and fourth floors. Turning left, walk up rue Jules Gilly, which becomes rue Droite, one of the Old Town's most atmospheric streets. Pass the eye-poppingly ornate Église de Gésu on your left, walk over rue Rossetti, and stop at the Palais Lascaris (15 rue Droite).

❸ The Palais Lascaris (▷ 167) is yet another former palace, but one which welcomes visitors inside. Head up the stone stairs for several floors of fabulous frescoes, coats of armour and ritzy 17th-century furniture.

Carry on down rue Droite, pausing to peek at the cannonball lodged in the wall above the junction of rue de la Loge. This dates from the Turkish navy's assault on Nice in 1543. At no. 11 rue Droite is the gallery of

C. Gall, one of the street's most innovative artists. Carry on to the fish market at place St-François.

❹ You can smell Nice's fish market (Tue–Sun 8–12.30) before you can see it. Notice the water pouring from the four carved dolphin heads in the fountain. The day's catch is still washed here.

Carry on in the same direction along Rue Pairolière. Traditionally, the old city was split up into guilds, and this is most certainly still the butchers' area. Notice hanging game and the odd stuffed pig. Turn left onto place de la Tour.

❺ Attractive place de la Tour contains Nice's ancient clock tower, several pavement cafés, and the excellent Cave de la Tour, a wine shop and old-fashioned bar.

Turn right from place de la Tour and follow the tram down boulevard Jean Jaurès. Pass Café de Turin (⊳ 192), the best seafood restaurant in Nice, as you walk into the wide expanse of place Garibaldi.

❻ Place Garibaldi is home to heaps of great restaurants, regular markets and a statue of Italian reunification hero Giuseppe Garibaldi (he was born around the corner). It's one of Nice's most vibrant squares.

Stop for refreshments or retrace your steps along the wide pavements of boulevard Jean Jaurès all the way to rue du Marché, 300m (330 yards) on your left. This leads down into place du Palais.

### WHEN TO GO
This short route can be walked at any time of year. Beware the lunchtime dining rush as you wander along the cours Saleya.

### WHERE TO EAT
Around 20 cafés dot this walk, including several on cours Saleya, two on place St-François and several more on place Garibaldi.

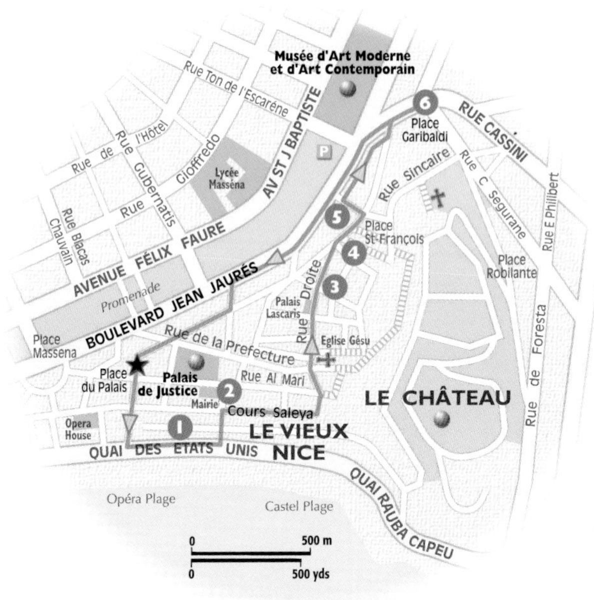


### PLACES TO VISIT
### GALERIE DES PONCHETTES
✉ 77 quai des États-Unis ☎ 04 93 62 31 24 🕐 Tue–Sun 10–6 Free

### FISH MARKET
✉ Place St-François 🕐 Tue–Sun 8–12.30

**Opposite** *Vibrant blooms at the flower market in cours Saleya*
**Below** *The Chapelle de la Miséricorde*

# VALLÉE DES MERVEILLES

**The Valley of Marvels is in the Parc National du Mercantour (▷ 168–169), a vast scenic area of peaks, valleys and lakes spanning the Alpes-Maritimes and Alpes-de-Haute-Provence *départements* and joined to the Parco Naturale dell'Argentera in Italy. The park shelters Alpine and Mediterranean flora and fauna. At least 25 of its plant species are not found anywhere else in the world and at least half of all France's flower species are represented. Protected animals include ibex, wild sheep and wolves. This hike takes you past glacial boulders with images of figures and tools carved by ancient Ligurians.**

**BE PREPARED**

The only way to reach the Vallée des Merveilles is on foot—not only are there no real roads, but private vehicles are generally banned from this section of the park because it is a protected zone. (Some four-wheel-drive visitor vehicles are allowed on the first section to the Refuge des Merveilles.) You need to allow at least a day for this hike and start early in the morning. If you want to stay in the area overnight, options include the *refuges* (Refuge des Merveilles at Lac Long or Refuge de Valmasque at Lac Vert) or one of the hotels at the winter ski resort of Castérino, although not all are open year round. Camping is not allowed. Sudden storms are frequent and violent; plan your hike with the park office in Tende and take their map with you, wear suitable hiking boots and take food and drinks. The final part of this walk involves a taxi ride, so have cash available.

**THE WALK**

**Distance:** 30km (18.5 miles)
**Time:** 1 to 2 days
**Start/end at:** parking area, Lac des Mesches

**HOW TO GET THERE**

St-Dalmas-de-Tende is in the far southeast of France near the Italian border, off the E74 south of Tende.

★ St-Dalmas-de-Tende, a small village, is the gateway to the Vallée des Merveilles. To reach the start of the walk, drive up the D91 towards Lac des Mesches, passing through peaceful woods with the rocky heights of Cime de la Nauque to the left. At the lake there is a spacious parking area.

Follow the footpath towards Lac Long, which will take several hours. At first the walking is pleasant and easy, winding through wooded slopes, but then the path begins to rise steeply.

❶ Lac Long's chilly shores are surrounded by pines and in spring the area is a wonderful sight as wild flowers bloom. All around is the stony mass of mountains, with Mont Bégo looming to the north.

This is the southern end of the Vallée des Merveilles and here is the ❷ Refuge des Merveilles. The valley can be sinister in dull light, with the rocks a threatening dark shade.

At this point you join the GR52 *Grandes Randonnées* trail. Climb until you reach Mont des Merveilles, where you can start to look for the carvings. As there are few obvious landmarks to describe where they are, refer to the maps from the park offices.

❸ These ancient carvings number more than 100,000. Yet it is easy to miss them, especially in winter when many are covered in snow. It is thought that the oldest date from about 1800BC, with others added in Roman times. No one knows why these intriguing images were carved, although one theory is that Mont Bégo (sometimes called the Magic Mountain) was a sacred site, and the images were etched into the rocks as votive offerings by prehistoric pilgrims. The drawings were not properly studied until the 1890s, when naturalist Clarence Bicknell excavated and catalogued them. He showed how the diagrams of hunting weapons, daggers, animals and mysterious symbols provide a unique insight into the Ligurian culture.

The trail continues past a string of lakes through the valley towards Lac du Basto. Although difficult to find, engravings are littered along the path, some of them close and others towards the slopes of the mountains. Before Lac du Basto, GR52 heads off to the left, while your path continues towards Valmasque.

❹ There is a *refuge* at Valmasque, near Lac Vert, a lovely place where Mont Sainte-Marie looks down from a height of 2,738m (8,981ft).

Here the path turns northeast for the home stretch. After Mont Peracouerte farther on, turn right and head south to Castérino.

❺ The tiny resort of Castérino is in an attractive setting on the D91.

Take a taxi from Castérino for the final 3km (2 miles) to the parking area at Lac des Mesches, where your walk began.

## WHEN TO GO

Spring is the best time to come for the wild flowers. Always reserve in advance if you are planning to stay or eat in one of the *refuges*. Bear in mind that they are not always open.

## WHERE TO EAT

You can have meals at the *refuges* if you reserve ahead. There are seasonal cafés and *auberges* at Castérino; some have terraces with good views.

## REFUGE DES MERVEILLES

www.cafnice.org
☎ 04 93 04 64 64 or 04 93 04 88 90
🕔 Mid-Jun to late Sep; late Sep to mid-Jun by appointment

## REFUGE DE VALMASQUE

☎ No phone; write to Refuge de Valmasque, 06430 Tende 🕔 Jun–end Sep

## INFORMATION

## MAISON DU PARC NATIONAL

www.mercantour.eu
✉ Casterino, 06430 Tende ☎ 04 93 04 89 79 🕔 Mon–Sat 9–12, 2–5, Sun 9–12

**Opposite and below** *There's no shortage of stunning scenery in the Vallée des Merveilles*

# CÔTE D'AZUR AND THE PARC NATIONAL DU MERCANTOUR

**There could hardly be a greater contrast than that between the Côte d'Azur coast and the Parc National du Mercantour. One is glitter and bustle, the other peace and unspoiled beauty. This driving tour combines the two, starting in Menton, one of the most pleasant of the Côte d'Azur towns, and then heading north into the hills. Be aware that the roads to the north of the Côte d'Azur tend to be winding and slow.**

**THE DRIVE**
**Distance:** 150km (93 miles)
**Time:** 1 day
**Start/end at:** Menton

★ Menton (▷ 154–155) describes itself as the warmest town on the Côte d'Azur, and the citrus orchards seem to reinforce this claim. It is a picturesque Italian town that finds itself on the French side of the border.

From the middle of town, take the road signed *Autoroute (Nice, Italia)* and *Sospel*. Follow signs for Sospel on the D2566, going under the A8 and passing through Castillon-Neuf, until you reach Sospel.

❶ The village of Sospel (▷ 170) has an 11th-century bridge, rebuilt in 1947 after it was damaged during World War II.

At Sospel, go over the rail crossing and then turn left, following signs for Moulinet and Col de Turini. Bear left at a bend onto the D2204 and climb up to Col St-Jean, where there are superb views down to Sospel. Go over Col de Braus (1,002m/ 3,287ft) and descend around hairpin bends almost into l'Escarène. Just after a rail bridge take a right turn, signed for Lucéram and Peïra-Cava. Drive through the village of Lucéram.

❷ Lucéram is a haphazard collection of medieval alleys.

At the next junction, isolated and on a steep hill, bear left, following signs for Turini. The road climbs around 16 hairpin turns and passes through Peïra-Cava.

❸ Peïra-Cava is one of the best viewpoints on the route, with a superb panorama across to the Parc National du Mercantour (▷ 168–169).

Continue to the Col de Turini.

❹ The Col de Turini, at an altitude of 1,607m (5,271ft), has fine views and is often included as one of the toughest climbs in the Tour de France. There is a hotel, café and restaurant.

Turn left onto the D70, signed for La Bollène-Vésubie and Nice, carefully descending the long, winding road from the pass. After about 10km (6 miles), look for a chapel on the left (on a bend) just after the Chapelle-St-Honorat tunnel.

❺ There is a parking place at this chapel and superb views over La Bollène-Vésubie.

Continue through La Bollène. At an intersection turn left onto the D2565, signed for Nice and St-Martin-Vésubie, to reach a valley bottom. There, follow signs for Lantosque and Nice, going straight on at first, then turning left along the main road. After 1km (0.6 miles) you can either go right and drive through Lantosque village, or take the bypass. The road through the village rejoins the main road; if you go that way turn right (signed for Nice).

Continue through St-Jean-de-la-Rivière. About 1km (0.6 miles) beyond St-Jean, take the left fork, the D19, signed *Nice par Levens*—be sure to follow this sign since both directions are signed for Nice. The road narrows and climbs up the side of the Vésubie valley. After you leave the tunnel just before Duranus, there is a viewpoint to the right, the Saut des Français, above sheer cliffs. Continue along the road into Levens.

❻ Levens (▷ 152) has a main square with shady gardens and some good views.

Leave Levens on the D19, signed for Nice. Continue for about 16km (10 miles), passing Tourrette-Levens. Just after St-André you'll go under the A8. Take a left turn at the traffic lights here, signed for Sospel, cross a river and go straight over at the next set of traffic lights to go back under the A8. Take the next right turn, signed for Route de Turin, crossing the river and a level crossing (rail crossing). Take a left turn at the traffic lights, signed for La Trinité and Drap, and at a roundabout (traffic circle) take the road signed for La Turbie and Laghet. Follow the D2204A up a winding valley to the sanctuary at Laghet. There, a hairpin turn takes the road sharply to the right. Pass under the A8 again, and turn left at the next intersection (an *autoroute* access road, signed for Menton). Turn left again at the next intersection onto a road signed for La Turbie and Monaco. Continue to La Turbie.

❼ La Turbie (▷ 171) is an ancient village on the Via Julia, a road built by Julius Caesar to link Genoa with Cimiez, on the northern outskirts of Nice. Its triumphal arch, the Trophée des Alpes, was erected in the first century BC.

Drive through La Turbie and bear left past a hotel, following signs for Roquebrune and Menton, and then go downhill. At the bottom, take a right turn at the traffic lights, signed for Nice and Beausoleil. Take a left turn at the next set of traffic lights, signed for Cap Martin. As it leaves the heart of the village, the road veers sharply left. Go straight ahead here, on the road signed for Cap Martin. This road soon reaches the sea. Park here for the start of the walk on page 180.

Follow the coast road back to Menton.

**WHERE TO EAT**
**LES TROIS VALLÉES HOTEL-RESTAURANT**
✉ Col de Turini ☎ 04 93 04 23 23

There are several bars and restaurants in Sospel.

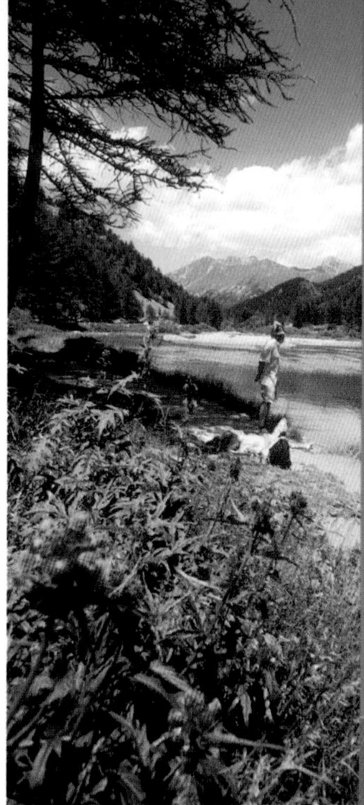

**Above** *Taking in the scenery in the Parc National du Mercantour*
**Opposite** *Sospel's 11th-century bridge*

# CAP MARTIN COAST

**This coastal walk visits what many consider to be the most attractive section of the Côte d'Azur. A long linear walk (you return by train), it is best done in the afternoon, after the heat of the day has passed and the sun is at the best angle for the views. The walk takes you past rhododendrons, cascades of honeysuckle and huge cactus plants to the right, with the turquoise sea to the left and coastal towns ahead. You can extend the walk by continuing into Monaco.**

**THE WALK**
**Distance:** 6km (4 miles)
**Time:** 2 hours (longer if you continue to Monte-Carlo)
**Start at:** Cap Martin
**End at:** Roquebrune train station or Monte-Carlo
? The journey back to the start point involves a train ride

**HOW TO GET THERE**

Cap Martin is east of Monaco, close to the Italian border.

★ Cap Martin's thrusting headland has long been a lookout point—the ruined tower at its heart was once a fortified medieval watchtower. At the base of the tower are the remains of an 11th-century priory. Legend has it that the prior had an agreement with the local folk that if the tower's bell rang, they would all hurry to the site to defend the monks. One night, just to test the system, the prior rang the bell and was very pleased with the speedy response. The local people were less pleased and a few nights later, when the bell rang again, they did not bother to turn out. But this time it was no trial run, and the priory was sacked by pirates and all the monks killed. Today Cap Martin is a rich suburb of Menton (▷ 154–155), its mansions set among sweet-smelling mimosa and olive trees.

Start from the parking area at the seaward end of avenue Winston Churchill, so-called as the British wartime leader used to paint on this very spot. Go back in the direction in which you drove, then pass to the left of the hotel entrance, along a wide path at the edge of the sea. The path is marked at its start by a sign for Ville de Roquebrune–Cap Martin, and a list of times for walks. Follow the path as it skirts the edge of private gardens and smart hotels. The path heads west along the edge of Cap Martin. There is a superb view of Monaco ahead and the sea to the left.

❶ The path is named Promenade Le Corbusier after the highly influential architect of the 1920s, who is connected with this stretch of coast through his association with artist and designer Eileen Gray. Her imaginative house above the shore was designated a historic monument in 1998. The house, which the thoroughly modern Gray anointed as E.1027, is hidden from view, lying below the path. It was being renovated at the time of writing and may be open to the public in the future. Here the path is very close to the rail line.

In several places, steps lead up to the Cap, but the best route continues to Roquebrune rail station, from where trains run back into Carnolès. From Carnolès station, head seaward and follow the coastal path back to the parking area.

Alternatively, to extend the walk, continue from Roquebrune along the path into Monte-Carlo, another 4km (2.5 miles) in length.

❷ Monte-Carlo (▷ 158–159) is part of the principality of Monaco.

Trains from Monaco also serve Carnolès. This longer walk has the advantage of a glorious entrance to Monaco.

**WHERE TO EAT**

There are expensive, high-quality restaurants in Cap Martin and less expensive places near Roquebrune rail station.

**WHEN TO GO**

Before you set off, check there is a suitably timed train from Roquebrune or Monaco to take you back to Carnolès.

**Opposite** *A view over the rooftops at Roquebrune*
**Right** *Rhododendrons in bloom*
**Below** *If you extend the walk to Monte-Carlo you can visit the famous Casino*

# WHAT TO DO

**Above** *A market stall in Nice*

## ANTIBES

### ANTIBES BATEAUX SERVICES

www.antibes-bateaux.com

This boat-hire specialist offers speedboats for rent from under a parasol in Antibes harbour. You can rent six-horsepower boats without a licence, or more powerful options if you are an experienced skipper.

✉ Port du Plaisance, 06160 Antibes ☎ 06 15 75 44 36 🕐 May–end Sep daily 8.30–6.30 ✋ €140 per day for 6hp boat

### CAFÉ PIMMS

Antibes' most unhurried café lies at the entrance to town, making it a people-watching paradise. Try the signature, and inexpensive, Pimms cooler.

✉ 3 rue de la République, 06600 Antibes ☎ 04 93 34 04 88 🕐 Daily 12–8

### HEIDI'S ENGLISH-LANGUAGE BOOKS

Heidi's is the pick of Antibes' bookshops, with new titles upstairs and thousands upon thousands of second-hand classics downstairs.

✉ 24 rue Aubernon, 06600 Antibes ☎ 04 93 34 74 11 🕐 Tue–Sun 10–7

### MARINELAND

www.marineland.fr

Watch sharks from the safety of a glass tunnel, or choreography involving seals, killer whales and dolphins. Marineland is part of a complex that also includes a farm, Butterfly Jungle, Aqua-Splash (summer only) and Adventure Golf.

✉ On the N7, east of town ☎ 0892 300 607 🕐 Jul, Aug daily 10–10; Sep–end Jun daily 10–5.30 ✋ Adult €35, child (under 1.2m) €27

### LA SIESTA

www.lasiesta.fr

This trendy club, which is packed all summer, has several dance floors, a swimming pool, restaurant, casino and access to the beach.

✉ Route du Bord de Mer, 06600 Antibes–Juan-les-Pins ☎ 04 93 33 31 31 🕐 Mid-Jun to mid-Sep daily 8pm–5am; mid-Sep to mid-Jun Fri, Sat 8pm–5am ✋ €15–€20

## BEAULIEU-SUR-MER

### GRAND CASINO DE BEAULIEU

www.casinobeaulieu.com

One of the belle époque wonders of the Riviera coast, the casino at Beaulieu-sur-Mer takes you back to the heyday of this refined resort. You can enjoy an elegant meal here too.

✉ 4 avenue Fernand Dunan, 06310 Beaulieu-sur-Mer ☎ 04 93 76 48 00 🕐 Mon–Fri 11am–4am, Sat–Sun 11am–5am (gaming tables open 9pm)

## BIOT

### VERRERIE DE BIOT

www.verreriebiot.com

Biot is known as the glassblowers' capital. On this site, you'll find a gallery and museum dedicated to glass, and a showroom. You can buy beautiful hand-blown dishes and glasses and visit the workshop.

✉ 5 chemin des Combes, 06410 Biot ☎ 04 93 65 03 00 🕐 Jun–end Aug Mon–Sat 9–8, Sun 10–1, 2.30–7.30; Sep–end May Mon–Sat 9.30–6, Sun 10.30–1, 2–6.30

## CAGNES-SUR-MER

### CASINO DE CAGNES-SUR-MER

www.groupetranchant.com

There is a relaxed atmosphere at this modern casino, with nearly 200 slot machines, a games room with poker and blackjack and a restaurant.

✉ 116 boulevard de la Plage, 06800 Cagnes-sur-Mer ☎ 04 92 27 14 40 🕐 Daily 10am–4am ✋ Entry to games room €10

## CANNES

### ALEXANDRE III

This old cinema-turned-theatre stages plays, ranging from the classics to more modern works.
✉ 19 boulevard Alexandre, 06400 Cannes
☎ 04 93 94 33 44 ⓘ Open all year

### BATHROOM GRAFFITI

You'll find vintage airline bags, funky shorts, colourful beachwear and off-the-wall souvenirs at this store, on Cannes' most fabulous shopping boulevard.
✉ 52 rue d'Antibes, 06460 Cannes
☎ 04 93 39 02 32 ⓘ Mon–Sat 10.30–7

### CANNES ENGLISH BOOKS

www.cannesenglishbookshop.com
The large collection of books in English at this store should meet all literary tastes: novels, bestsellers, cookbooks, travel guides. A friendly bilingual welcome and a prime location (right behind the Palais des Festivals) also explain why it is popular with the English-speaking community.
✉ 11 rue Bivouac-Napoléon, 06400 Cannes
☎ 04 93 99 40 08 ⓘ Mon–Sat 10–6.45

### LE FESTIVAL

Between two luxury hotels and facing the sea, this bar's terrace is a popular place for people-watching and admiring the beautiful expanse of blue to the horizon.
✉ 52 La Croisette, 06400 Cannes
☎ 04 93 38 04 81 ⓘ Daily 9am–midnight

### JACQUES LOUP

www.jacques-loup.com
In addition to its own collection, this shoe shop carries the hottest designs from international shoemakers such as Bottega Veneta, Rossi, Church's and Tod's. It also stocks clothes from Prada, Marni and Miu Miu. It's an institution for every fashionista in Cannes.
✉ 21 rue d'Antibes, 06400 Cannes
☎ 04 93 39 28 35 ⓘ Mon–Sat 9.30–8

### MARCHÉ DE FORVILLE

Even if you're not planning to buy anything (but it's going to be hard to resist), Cannes' biggest market is worth seeing for its bright displays of fruit, vegetables, flowers and cheeses. The venue is partially covered.
✉ Rue du Marché de Forville, 06400 Cannes ⓘ Tue–Sun 7am–1pm (there is an antiques market on Mon)

### MORRISON'S IRISH PUB

www.morrisonspub.com
This pub, with its convivial wooden interior, boasts a big screen, beloved of sports fans. In addition, there is live music every Wednesday and Thursday evening. Guinness and Kilkenny are on tap, served by friendly Irish staff.
✉ 10 rue du Teisseire, 06400 Cannes
☎ 04 92 98 16 17 ⓘ Mon–Thu 5pm–2am, Fri–Sun 1pm–2am

### PALAIS DES FESTIVALS ET DES CONGRÈS

www.cannes.fr
The Cannes Film Festival takes place in this venue, built in 1982. At other times, the *palais* welcomes international exhibitions, as well as staging performances in its 2,300-seat Lumière auditorium and plays, ballets and concerts in the 1,000-seat Théâtre Debussy. Check out the handprints of the stars in the 'walk of fame' just outside.
✉ 1 boulevard de la Croisette, 06400 Cannes ☎ 04 93 39 01 01

### ZANZIBAR

www.lezanzibar.com
Popular with the gay community, this club has a prime location near the Palais des Festivals, pleasant decor with a marine theme and good techno rhythms.
✉ 85 rue Félix-Faure, 06400 Cannes
☎ 04 93 39 30 75 ⓘ Daily 6pm–4am

### Z PLAGE

www.hotel-martinez.com
The private beach of the luxury Hôtel Martinez (▷ 193) isn't exclusively reserved for its clients. Munch on organic bites, take a dip in the sea or lie back and enjoy the sun next to

**Above** *Try your luck at a casino*

Cannes' A-list, as this is the coolest beach club in town.
✉ Hotel Martinez, 73 boulevard de la Croisette, 06400 Cannes ☎ 04 92 98 74 22 ⏲ May–end Sep daily 10–7 ✋ Lounge chair rental in high season around €40 per day

## CANNES LA BOCCA

### AIR ODYSSEY

www.air-odyssey.com
Hop on a light aircraft for an hour-long tour over St-Tropez or the Gorges du Verdon.
✉ Mandelieu Airport, 06150 Cannes La Bocca ☎ 04 93 48 39 26 ⏲ By reservation

### CANNES BOWLING

www.rivieraloisirsbowling.com
There are 16 bowling lanes and 21 pool tables here. A DJ spices up the atmosphere on weekends and there's a restaurant on site with Formula 1-themed decor.
✉ 189 avenue Francis-Tonner, 06150 Cannes La Bocca ☎ 04 93 47 02 25 ⏲ Daily 3pm–4am ✋ €6 per game; €2 for shoe rental

## LE CANNET ROCHEVILLE

### MARCHÉ BIOLOGIQUE

Buy regional products that are certified organic at this small market. It's the true taste of Provence.
✉ Quartier l'Aubarède, 06110 Le Cannet Rocheville ⏲ Wed 7am–1pm

**Below** *Perfume makes a good souvenir*

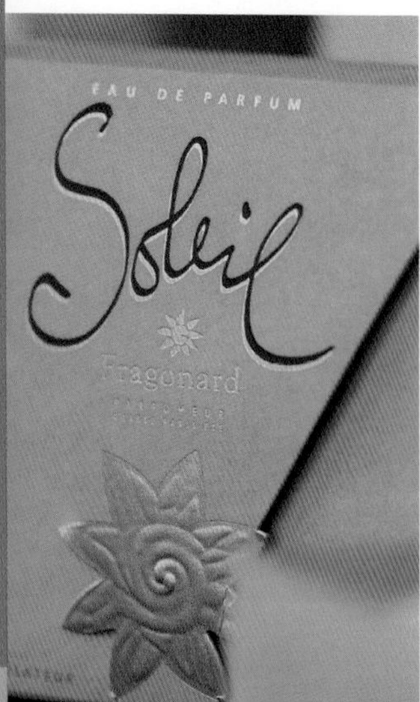


## ÈZE

### ASTRORAMA

www.astrorama.net
This astronomy group invites the public to come and star-watch. Powerful telescopes bring the planets closer than you've ever seen them before.
✉ Route de la Revère, 06360 Èze ☎ 04 93 85 85 58 ⏲ Jul, Aug Tue–Sat 7–11; Mar–end Jun, Sep, Oct Fri, Sat 7–11 ✋ Adult €9, child (6–18) €7

### L'ÉCHOPPE PROVENÇALE

This pretty boutique has a comprehensive range of Provençal arts and crafts, including printed fabrics, pottery, olive-wood articles and edibles.
✉ 55 avenue de Verdun, 06360 Èze ☎ 04 93 41 00 23 ⏲ Jun–end Aug daily 9–7; Sep–end May Mon–Sat 9–12.30, 3–7, Sun 10–4

### LA PROVENCE PAR MARC FERRERO

www.ferrerogallery.com
Marc Ferrero is a native of Provence and his art captures the essence of the Mediterranean landscapes and lifestyle in strong colours with a 'Van Gogh-esque' feel.
✉ 6 rue de la Paix, 06360 Èze ☎ 04 92 10 82 92 ⏲ Daily 10–7

## GRASSE

### FRAGONARD

www.fragonard.com
World-renowned as a perfume capital, Grasse is home to many perfumeries. Fragonard (▷ 151), dating back to the 18th century, is one of the oldest and the most prestigious. Visit the perfume museum, then shop for fragrances.
✉ 20 boulevard Fragonard, 06130 Grasse ☎ 04 93 36 44 65 ⏲ Shop: Mar–end Oct daily 10–7; Nov–end Feb daily 10–12.30, 2–7. Factory (3km/2 miles out of town on the Route de Cannes): Mar–end Oct daily 10–6; Nov–end Feb daily 10–12.30, 2–6.

## ISOLA

### ISOLA 2000

www.isola2000.com
At an altitude of 2,000m (6,500ft), this ski resort offers 50 tracks and one snow park with heli-skiing, snow scooters and an ice rink. In summer, the outdoor activities continue with hiking and horseback riding.
✉ Tourist office: Immeuble le Pélevos, Isola 2000 ☎ 04 93 23 15 15 ✋ Ski pass: adult €28.80

## JUAN-LES-PINS

### PAM PAM

www.pampam.fr
Open from early afternoon until after sunrise during the summer, Pam Pam offers drinks and ice cream in the afternoon and aperitifs and snacks as evening arrives. But it really takes off later in the evening when the rhythms of Brazil drift across the south of France with colourful and energetic Latin and tribal stage shows. The drink of choice here is rum, for sipping or in a cocktail.
✉ 137 boulevard Wilson, 06160 Juan-les-Pins ☎ 04 93 61 11 05 ⏲ Late Mar to mid-Nov and Christmas–early Jan 2pm–4am

### ULM MOROSINI

www.hydro-ulm.com
Touring the Rade du Golfe on a hybrid of a super-light plane and a boat gives you a wonderful bird's-eye view of islands and lighthouses.
✉ 7 bis avenue Doctor Hochet, 06160 Juan-les-Pins ☎ 04 93 67 05 11 ⏲ Daily by appointment. Closed Jan ✋ €60 for a 25-min flight

### LE VILLAGE

Drinkers from Juan's strip of alfresco bars heap in here at midnight for house, disco and pop tunes.
✉ Boulevard de la Pinede, 06160 Juan-les-Pins ☎ 04 92 93 90 00 ⏲ Jun–end Aug daily 11pm–5am; Apr, May, Sep Fri, Sat 11pm–5am

## MENTON

### CASINO DE MENTON

www.lucienbarriere.com
Behind a Moorish-style facade are slot machines, gaming rooms, two bars, a restaurant and club Le Brummell. Tea dances and theatre also take place here. Formal dress is required.

**Right** *The harbour at Monaco*

✉ 2 avenue Félix Faure, 06500 Menton ☎ 04 92 10 16 16 🕑 Daily 10am–3am (until 4am Fri, Sat); table game room opens at 8pm

### LES IMAGES DE PROVENCE

This company designs and prints its own beautiful Provençal fabrics, which it sells by the metre or transformed into finished items, such as soft furnishings.

✉ 21 rue St-Michel, 06500 Menton ☎ 04 93 57 09 98 🕑 Mon–Sat 9–12, 3–7

## MONACO

### BOUTIQUE FORMULE 1

A whole shop full of Formula 1 paraphernalia, including T-shirts, caps and posters. Go from one-of-a-kind items to kitsch, mass-produced stuff.

✉ 15 rue Grimaldi, 98000 Monaco ☎ 377 93 15 92 44 🕑 Mon–Sat 10–12.30, 2–7

### CASINO DE MONTE-CARLO

www.montecarlocasino.com

The rich and famous flock to this grand belle époque gambling temple, decorated with frescoes and paintings and featured in several movies, including James Bond films. The dress code is smart and you must be over 18.

✉ Place du Casino, 98000 Monaco ☎ 377 98 06 21 21 🕑 Daily from 2pm, except Salons Privés, from 4pm 🎫 Entry €10 and a further €10 to enter games room

### CENTRE COMMERCIAL LE MÉTROPOLE

www.ccmetropole.com

Near the Casino, this shopping complex has majestic belle époque decor. There are three levels, with 80 boutiques selling top-notch fashion, beauty products, household goods and leisure equipment.

✉ 17 avenue des Spélugues, 98000 Monaco 🕑 Mon–Sat 10–7.30

### COUNTRY CLUB DE MONTE-CARLO

www.mccc.mc

This club has 21 clay tennis courts, which all look out to the sea. A squash court, fitness club and pool come as a bonus. It is home every year to the prestigious ATP Masters Series (▷ 189).

✉ 155 avenue Princesse Grace, 06190 Roquebrune (just outside Monaco) ☎ 04 93 41 30 15 🕑 Jun–end Aug daily 8am–9pm; Sep–end May daily 8–8 🎫 €41 for a day pass

### JIMMY'Z

You'll face highly selective entry here and extraordinary prices once you get in—entering the haunt of the jet set has its toll. The reward is partying with faces seen in magazines, in a luxurious interior with a Cuban smoking room and Japanese garden.

✉ Sporting d'Été, avenue Princesse Grace, 98000 Monaco ☎ 377 98 06 70 68 🕑 May–end Oct daily 11pm–5am; Nov–end Apr Wed–Sun 11pm–5am 🎫 Free

### LULL

www.lull.mc

Monaco's hippest clothing atelier has cool jackets, demin dresses and sunglasses. It's completely non-designer, and well worth seeking out.

✉ 29 rue de Millo, 98000 Monaco ☎ 377 97 77 54 54 🕑 Mon–Sat 10–8, Sun 2–8

### MUSÉE OCÉANOGRAPHIQUE

www.oceano.mc

Hundreds of tropical fish are protected from sharks by coral reef at this fascinating giant aquarium (▷ 157). Another attraction is the micro-aquarium: A magnifying glass is used with a camera to film microscopic aquatic animals. In the basement, discover the skeletons of sea animals, including a blue whale.

✉ Avenue St-Martin, 98000 Monaco ☎ 377 93 15 36 00 🕑 Jul, Aug daily 9.30–7.30; Apr–end Jun, Sep daily 9.30–7; Oct–end Mar daily 10–6 🎫 Adult €13, child (6–18) €6.50, under 6 free

### OPÉRA DE MONTE-CARLO

www.opera.mc

Since its inauguration by actress Sarah Bernhardt in 1879, this impressive belle époque opera house has welcomed the world's greatest voices. The architect, Charles Garnier, also designed the Opéra Garnier in Paris.

✉ Place du Casino, 98000 Monaco ☎ 377 98 06 28 00 🎫 From €15

### PLAGE DU LARVOTTO

Lifeguards are on site during the high season at this sandy beach, making it a good place to swim. Changing rooms and showers are available and there are bars and restaurants nearby.

✉ Avenue Princesse Grace, 98000 Monaco

### LE SPORTING

www.cinemasporting.com

Most films are shown in their original language at this three-screen cinema. It also hosts an open-air cinema from June to August.

✉ Galerie du Sporting d'Hiver, place du Casino, 98000 Monaco ☎ 0892 682 072 🕑 Daily 2–9 🎫 €9.50

### LE SPORTING D'ÉTÉ

www.sportingmontecarlo.com

With a sunroof and large windows facing the sea, this concert hall has a majestic setting. It welcomes the biggest international stars. There is also a casino and club on site.

Avenue Princesse Grace, 98000 Monaco 377 92 16 36 36 Late Jun–early Sep show daily 10.30pm

### THERMES MARINS DE MONTE-CARLO

www.montecarlospa.com

The pools, solariums and gym here have large windows that look onto the sea. There are beautiful hammams (Turkish baths) whose decor obeys the Moresque tradition, with blue-and-white tiled mosaics and little fountains. Treatments include Eastern massages and the latest innovations in marine therapy.

2 avenue Monte-Carlo, 98000 Monaco 377 92 16 40 40 Daily 8–8 €143 for 4 thalassotherapy treatments; €75 for a day pass to the pool and hammam; 'Lift 6' facial treatment €50 for 30 min

## MOUGINS

### BUGGY CROSS

Next to the Automobile Museum, you can experience the thrill of speed on one of three tracks in a quad bike, kart or mini-motorcycle. There are also vehicles for children aged four and over.

909 chemin Font-de-Currault, 06250 Mougins 04 93 69 02 74 Wed, Sat, Sun and all school holidays 11am–dusk Quad 50cc €9 for 10 min, 125cc €13 for 10 min

### SPA SHISEIDO AU MAS CANDILLE

www.lemascandille.com

East meets West at this spa, which offers massages combining body sculpting with the ancient Japanese arts of shiatsu and chi. These come complete with aromatherapy products, aimed at both the skin and the mind. Regular massages, manicures and pedicures are also offered.

Boulevard Clément-Rebuffel, 06250 Mougins 04 92 28 43 43 Daily 10–7 Express facial €65; pedicure €30

## NICE

### AKATHOR

www.akathor.com

This Scandinavian pub is very popular with students and is one of the liveliest venues in town. The concert hall upstairs is used for live bands, as well as for English-language stand-up comedy.

32 cours Saleya, 06300 Nice 04 93 62 49 90 Daily 5.30pm–2am

### BAR DES OISEAUX

www.bardesoiseaux.com

A gem of a jazz club with a near nightly calendar of live music. Great pre-spectacle dining and drinking, plus occasional comedy and theatre.

5 rue St-Vincent, 06300 Nice 04 93 80 27 33 Tue–Sat 12.30–3, 7–1 Admission price for shows from €10

### LE BEFORE

This rather chic venue is known in French as a *bar-apéro,* where everyone meets for a pre-dinner drink, though it's open until late and offers dance music and live acts. There's a great terrace for those sultry summer nights.

18 rue du Congrès, 06000 Nice 04 93 87 85 59 Mon–Sat 6pm–12.30am

### LA BODÉGUITA DEL HAVANA

Hopping Cuban joint with authentic drinks and music, plus wild dancing. View the dance floor from the balcony, then join in.

14 rue Chauvain, 06000 Nice 04 93 92 67 24 Wed–Sat 8pm–3am

### THE CAT'S WHISKERS

Browse through books in English, including detective novels, bestsellers, children's stories and classics. Some are second-hand.

30 rue Lamartine, 06000 Nice 04 93 80 02 66 Mon–Sat 10–12.30, 3–7

### LE CENTRE

www.accueil-beaute.com

On the ninth floor of the luxury Meridien hotel, this beauty venue will pamper you from top to toe. Facilities include a sauna, hammam (Turkish bath), Jacuzzi, fitness equipment and tanning beds.

1 promenade des Anglais, 06000 Nice 04 93 87 82 14 Mon–Sat 9–8 Regenerating facial €70; Dead Sea mud wrap €40

### LA CHAPELLERIE

www.chapellerie.com

Find hats for every occasion: from the panama to the beanie, and wedding hats. A custom-made service is available. This shop, along with its sister branches at 12 rue de France and 56 rue Giofreddo, often provides accessories to the entertainment industry.

36 cours Saleya, 06300 Nice 04 93 62 52 54 Mon–Sat 9.30–12.30, 2–7

### LE CHAT PERCHÉ

This vibrant venue regularly organizes exhibitions and has a DJ every Friday night. Otherwise sporting events are shown on a big screen; table football and a dartboard are also available.

4 place Garibaldi, 06000 Nice 04 93 89 20 80 Daily 8am–12am

**Below** *La Chapellerie, Nice, is the ideal place to buy a summer hat*

**CHEZ WAYNE'S**
www.waynes.fr
Food, drink and nightly live music are available at this English-American bar and restaurant. There is a sunny terrace and an interior that pays tribute to rock music, with guitars and concert posters on the walls.
✉ 15 rue de la Préfecture, 06000 Nice ☎ 04 93 13 46 99 🕐 Daily noon–1am

**CINEMA MERCURY**
Vintage three-screen cinema where every film is shown in its original language. An average of three arty flicks are shown each night.
✉ 16 Place Garibaldi, 06300 Nice ☎ 04 93 55 37 81 🕐 Daily 2pm–10pm 🖐 €5–€8

**CINÉMATHÈQUE**
www.cinematheque-nice.com
Henri Langlois created this impressive film archive more than 20 years ago. Every month, theme-based retrospectives and festivals put the great classics on the bill.
✉ Acropolis 3, esplanade Kennedy, 06300 Nice ☎ 04 92 04 06 66 🕐 Tue–Sat 2–8 (start of film), Sun 11–3 🖐 €2

**CONFISERIE FLORIAN**
www.confiserieflorian.com
The Florian family perfected the art of preserving Provence's luscious fruits in sugar at this beautiful establishment in Nice port in 1974. The result: adult sweeties, paired with grown-up jams, *marrons glacés* and liqueurs made from rich French fruit. Complimentary guided visits in five languages are available.
✉ 14 quai Papacino, 06300 Nice ☎ 04 93 55 43 50 🕐 Daily 9–12, 2–6.30

**L'F**
On the liveliest street in town, this café-bistro has one of Nice's best terraces, heated during colder spells. Inside is a 1930s and 1940s interior, with a black-and-white chequered floor.
✉ 6 place Charles-Félix, 06300 Nice ☎ 04 93 85 74 10 🕐 Daily 12pm–2am

**GHOST HOUSE**
This fashionable bar has comfortable sofas, gleaming mirrors and great cocktails. To curtail neighbourhood noise, 'Le Ghost' operates a 'closed door' policy: Ring the bell to gain entrance. The resident DJ plays techno, hip hop or soul.
✉ 3 rue Barillerie, 06300 Nice ☎ 04 93 92 93 37 🕐 Daily 7pm–2.30am

**GLACIER FENOCCHIO**
Quite simply Nice's best ice-cream maker. The key to its success? Big servings and truly original tastes: Alongside the traditional peach melba and *café liegeois*, you may want to try the tomato or chewing-gum sorbet. The pretty location, facing Sainte-Réparate Cathedral, comes as a bonus.
✉ 2 place Rossetti, 06300 Nice ☎ 04 93 80 72 52 🕐 Mar–end Nov daily 9am–11.30pm

**GRAND CAFÉ DE LYON**
www.cafedelyon.fr
This art nouveau-style bistro, established in 1900, is an institution in Nice. It's a brasserie at lunchtime, a tea room in the afternoon and, later, a good place for a glass of rosé.
✉ 33 avenue Jean Médecin, 06000 Nice ☎ 04 93 88 13 17 🕐 Daily 7am–11pm

**JEAN-LOUIS MARTINETTI**
www.martinetti.fr
Jean-Louis Martinetti's photography is an ode to Nice. He uses simple compositions (for example, a palm tree framed by the sea) in bold tones. On occasion, the friendly photographer can even be seen manning the till.
✉ 17 rue de la Préfecture, 06300 Nice ☎ 04 93 85 61 30 🕐 Tue–Sat 10–12.15, 3–7

**LOCAVENTURE**
www.locaventure.com
Snowboarding, scuba diving, rock climbing, caving, inline skating and much more: This shop rents out all the equipment you'll need for an outdoor adventure. Its staff also offer advice on activities.
✉ 13 rue Fontaine-de-la-Ville, 06300 Nice ☎ 04 93 56 14 67 🕐 Mon–Sat 8–12, 3–7, Sun 8–12, 6–8

**MARCHÉ À LA BROCANTE**
This antiques market mostly welcomes professionals, and the items on display are often highly collectable. Among the possibilities are genuine Gallé glasswork, old postcards, jewellery and ethnic artwork.
✉ Cours Saleya, 06300 Nice 🕐 Mon 8–5

**MARCHÉ AUX FLEURS**
This flower market is in the animated cours Saleya, with its many shops and cafés. Exotic plants and trees on sale include orange and lemon trees and cacti. In February, mimosa is in full blossom.
✉ Cours Saleya, 06300 Nice 🕐 Tue–Sat 6.30–5.30, Sun 6.30–1.30

**MARCHÉ SALEYA**
This fruit and vegetable market keeps the spirit of Provence alive. You'll find lots of locally grown produce, including olives, artichokes, asparagus and mushrooms.
✉ Cours Saleya, 06300 Nice 🕐 Tue–Sun 7am–1pm

**MARCHÉ SALEYA D'ARTISANAT D'ART**
Take a stroll through Nice's evening arts and crafts market. You'll find Provençal handicrafts, plus crafts from other regions of the world.
✉ Cours Saleya, 06300 Nice 🕐 Jun–end Sep daily 6pm–midnight

**MARTIN FLEURS**
www.martin-fleurs.com
This florist offers an impressive range of bouquets—some could even qualify as floral sculpture. Exotic flowers are widely used.
✉ 28 rue Hôtel-des-Postes, 06000 Nice ☎ 04 93 62 08 00 🕐 Mon–Sat 8.30–7.30

**MASTER HOME**
www.master-home.com
Choose between scores of beers and cocktails at this upmarket French 'pub'. Tables spill outside most evenings, as nightly DJs rev up indoors.
✉ 11 rue de la Préfecture, 06300 Nice ☎ 04 93 80 33 82 🕐 Mon– Fri 10am–2.30am, Sat, Sun 2pm–2.30am

**MOULIN À HUILE ALZIARI**
www.alziari.com.fr
The olive oil on sale in this shop comes from a mill in Nice's northwest corner, which you can visit by appointment. The olive soaps and colourful cans of oil make wonderful souvenirs.
4 rue St-François-de-Paule, 06300 Nice 04 93 85 76 92 Tue–Sat 8.30–12.30, 2.15–7

**OLIVIERA**
www.oliviera.com
Try-before-you-buy oil tastings are available at Oliviera. Products cover most of France's AOC oil regions, including the limited-production run from a network of local producers.
8 bis rue du Collet, 06300 Nice 04 93 13 06 45 Tue–Sat 12–10, Sun 12–3

**OPÉRA DE NICE**
www.opera-nice.org
Frescoes and a massive chandelier decorate this Italianate theatre, inaugurated in 1885, which stages opera, classical music and ballet.
4–6 rue St-François-de-Paule, 06300 Nice 04 92 17 40 00 Tue–Sat, shows at 4pm and 8pm €10–€85

**PATHÉ MASSÉNA**
www.pathe.fr
The 12 screens at this cinema show Hollywood blockbusters and the latest French releases.
31 avenue Jean-Médecin, 06000 Nice 0892 69 66 96 Daily 10–10 €8

**STADE MUNICIPAL DU RAY (LÉO LAGRANGE)**
www.ogcnice.com
This 17,000-seat stadium is home to the OGC Nice soccer club, better known as *Les Aiglons* (The Eaglets).
35 avenue du Ray, 06100 Nice 0892 702 106 Matches usually start around 8pm €8–€35

**THÉÂTRE NATIONAL DE NICE**
Both classic and contemporary plays are on the bill at this theatre.
Promenade des Arts, 06300 Nice 04 93 13 90 90 Ticket office: Tue–Sat 2–7 €10–€30

**THÉÂTRE DE LA TRAVERSE**
www.la-traverse.com
Adjoining La Traverse publishing house and its bookstore, this 45-seat theatre likes to experiment. The plays vary from one-person shows and comedy to drama and historical works.
2 rue François-Guisol, 06300 Nice 04 93 35 67 46 Oct–end Jun: shows on Fri and Sat at 8.30pm and Sun at 4pm €15

**VÉLO BLEU**
www.velobleu.org
Nice's rent-a-bike scheme lets you insert a credit card deposit into the electronic bicycle stands around town, then borrow a bicycle.
Nice 04 93 72 06 06
Rental free for first 30 min, €1 for 30 min thereafter

**Below** *Catch a performance at the Théâtre National de Nice*

## OPIO

**GOLF D'OPIO VALBONNE**
www.opengolfclub.com
English architect Donald Harradine designed this 18-hole golf course, in a 220ha (545-acre) park.
Route de Roquefort, 06650 Opio 04 93 12 00 08 Daily 8–5.30 Green fee from €38

## ST-ÉTIENNE DE TINÉE

**AURON ST-ÉTIENNE DE TINÉE**
www.auron.com
This ski resort, at an altitude of between 1,600m (5,250ft) and 2,400m (7,900ft), has 39 runs and 27 ski lifts. You can ski, snowboard or choose from hang-gliding, sleigh tours, ice-skating and snow scooters.
Grange Cossa, 06660 Auron 04 93 23 02 66 Ski resort open Dec–end Apr, depending on snowfall Ski pass €28–€80 per day

## ST-JEAN-CAP-FERRAT

**ZOO DU CAP-FERRAT**
www.zoocapferrat.com
Attempting to reproduce the natural habitat of more than 300 animals, including crocodiles, monkeys and tigers, this zoo has numerous pools and grottos. You can get really close to the tigers, protected by a Plexiglas wall. There is a snack bar and playground on site.
117 boulevard Général-de-Gaulle, 06230 St-Jean-Cap-Ferrat 04 93 76 07 60 Apr–end Oct daily 9.30–7; Nov–end Mar daily 9.30–5.30 Adult €14, child (3–10) €10, under 3 free

## LA TURBIE

**GOLF CLUB DE MONTE-CARLO**
At an altitude of 900m (3,000ft), this 18-hole golf course has great views of the French and Italian mountains and the sandy coastline.
Route du Mont Agel, 06320 La Turbie 04 92 41 50 70 Mon 8–5, Tue–Sun 8–6 Green fee €120

# FESTIVALS AND EVENTS

## JANUARY

### FESTIVAL INTERNATIONAL DU CIRQUE

www.montecarlofestivals.com

This circus festival in Monaco, established in 1974, involves animal tamers, clowns and magicians. Trophies are awarded to the best acts, which are performed for a second time during the closing night's gala.

✉ Espace Fontvieille, avenue des Ligures, 98000 Monaco ☎ 377 92 05 23 45 (ticket office) 🕐 End Jan ✋ Adult €25–€100, child (under 13) €10 (or adult price for good seats)

### MONTE-CARLO RALLY

www.acm.mc

This four-day trial tests the driving skills of participants as they follow a route through the snow- and ice-covered minor roads in the Alps behind Monaco.

✉ Automobile Club de Monaco, 23 boulevard Albert Ier, 98000 Monaco ☎ 377 93 15 26 00 🕐 Last week in Jan

## FEBRUARY

### FÊTE DU CITRON

www.feteducitron.com

This festival celebrates the main crop of the area—lemons. The highlight is a parade of eye-catching floats decorated with thousands of lemons.

✉ Jardin Biovès, Menton ✋ Entry to static displays €8; seat for start of parade €21; seat for finish of parade €23 (parade prices include entry to static displays)

### NICE CARNIVAL

www.nicecarnaval.com

The Riviera celebrates Mardi Gras with two weeks of parades. Huge papier-mâché floats proceed through Nice to be set alight at sea on the final night. You can pay to sit in the stands or look out of your hotel window for free.

✉ Nice ☎ 0892 707 407 (tourist office)

## APRIL

### ATP MASTERS TENNIS CHAMPIONSHIP

www.mccc.mc

Top names in tennis gather for this championship.

✉ Country Club de Monte-Carlo, 155 avenue Princesse Grace, 06190 Roquebrune ☎ 377 97 98 70 00

### NICE HALF MARATHON

www.nicesemimarathon.com

The summer sporting calendar starts with this run along the Promenade des Anglais. It attracts an international field.

✉ Nice ☎ 0892 707 407 (tourist office)

## MAY

### CANNES FILM FESTIVAL

www.festival-cannes.fr

May means Hollywood comes to the Riviera as stars are photographed along the Croisette and the steps of the Palais des Festivals. All the biggest screenings and parties are invitation only, but there are some public screenings.

✉ Palais des Festivals, Cannes ☎ 01 53 59 61 00

### FÊTE DU ROSE

www.ville-grasse.fr

A mid-May event, where tens of thousands of roses cover Grasse's Cathedral and town centre.

✉ Grasse ☎ 04 97 05 57 90 ✋ €7.50

### MONTE-CARLO GRAND PRIX

www.acm.mc

Monte-Carlo's annual weekend in the spotlight, when the city becomes a race track.

✉ Automobile Club de Monaco, 23 boulevard Albert Ier, 98000 Monaco ☎ 377 93 15 26 00 ✋ €70–€450

## JUNE

### FESTIVAL DE MUSIQUE SACRÉE

Nice's Festival of Sacred Music celebrated its 35th anniversary in 2009. Religious music is played in the chapels and churches of Vieux Nice nightly over a two-week period.

✉ 8 rue St-François-de-Paule, 06364 Nice ☎ 04 97 13 23 95/04 97 13 36 89 ✋ Free–€25

### FÊTE DE LA MUSIQUE

www.fetedelamusique.culture.fr

This annual event marks the longest day of the year with music on literally every street corner. You'll find jazz bands, classical outfits and sound systems along the beach and in the old town.

✉ Nice 🕐 21 Jun

## JULY

### JAZZ À JUAN

www.jazzajuan.fr

Juan-les-Pins' jazz festival is one of Europe's best. Expect some of the greatest names, such as Maceo Parker and Marcus Miller. The festival celebrated its 50th anniversary in 2010.

✉ Pinède Gould, 06600 Antibes ☎ Tourist office: 04 92 90 53 00 🕐 One week around mid-Jul

### NICE JAZZ FESTIVAL

www.nicejazzfestival.fr

Les Arènes de Cimiez is the venue for this lively event.

✉ Arènes de Cimiez ☎ 0892 70 75 07 ✋ Day tickets €29–€49

## AUGUST

### OPERA LES AZURIALES

www.azuriales-opera.com

The Villa Ephrussi de Rothschild (▷ 172) plays host to this ten-day open-air opera festival. It's a classy event, with champagne bars and beautifully decorated stages, all against a Mediterranean backdrop.

✉ Cap Ferrat ☎ 04 93 56 51 41

### MONTE-CARLO FIREWORKS COMPETITION

www.visitmonaco.com

Sit at the harbour and watch a spectacular fireworks show for free.

✉ Monaco 🕐 Various dates in August

# EATING

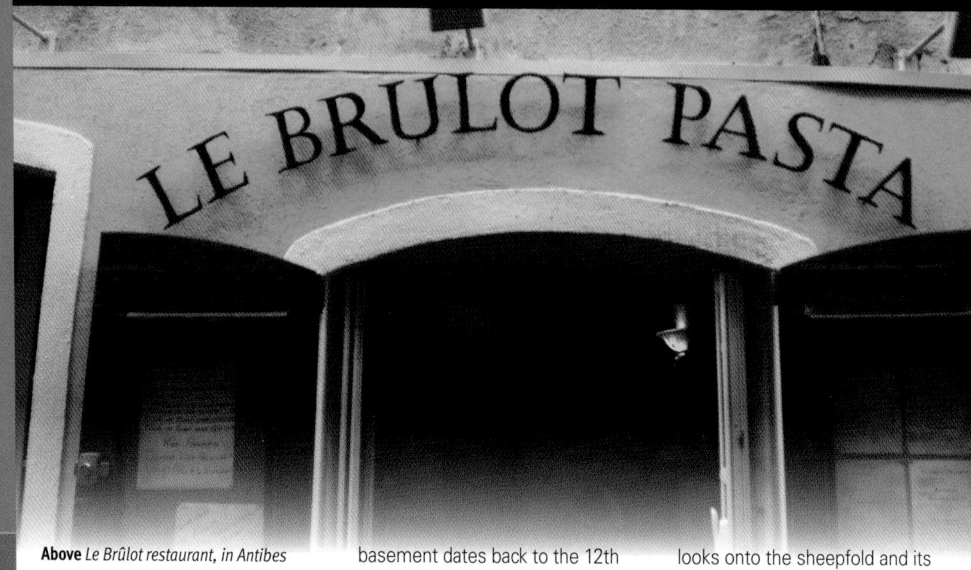


**Above** *Le Brûlot restaurant, in Antibes*

**PRICES AND SYMBOLS**

The prices given are the average for a two-course lunch (L) and a three-course dinner (D) for one person, without drinks. The wine price is for the least expensive bottle.

For a key to the symbols, ▷ 2.

## ANTIBES

### BACON

www.restaurantdebacon.com

A restaurant that boasts six decades of award-winning seafood and lies on a street named in honour of its own existence doesn't come cheap. But the house speciality bouillabaise and crustacean range are worthy treats. The €49 lunch menu and varying prices on the all-encompassing wine list can make a pricey visit more palatable.

✉ Boulevard de Bacon, Cap d'Antibes, 06160 Antibes ☎ 04 93 61 65 19 🕐 Mar–end Oct Wed–Sun 12–2.30, 7–10, Tue 7–10 ✋ L €50, D €100, Wine €26

### LE BRÛLOT

www.brulot.com

Authenticity is key at this restaurant, with its exposed stone, beamed ceilings and antique baker's oven. A second room in the vaulted basement dates back to the 12th century. The cuisine makes good use of the wood oven: grilled steak with Provençal herbs and grilled scampi flambéed with pastis (a local aniseed spirit). Specials include couscous on Thursdays and ham on the bone on Fridays.

✉ 3 rue Frédéric Isnard, 06600 Antibes ☎ 04 93 34 17 76 🕐 Mon–Wed 7.30–10, Thu–Sat 12–2.30, 7.30–10 ✋ L €25, D €35, Wine €14

### LA TAVERNE DU SAFRANIER

This flamboyant and funky restaurant makes the most of its location on place Safranier, Antibes' answer to London's Notting Hill. Chalkboards casually tacked up the piazza's walls offer simple yet well-executed seafood dishes, like baked sea bass with Provençal sauce.

✉ Place Safranier, 06600 Antibes ☎ 04 93 34 80 50 🕐 Mid-Feb to mid-Nov daily 12–2.30, 7–10.30 ✋ L €25, D €35, Wine €28

## AURIBEAU-SUR-SIAGNE

### LA VIGNETTE HAUTE

www.vignettehaute.com

This inn, off the beaten track, has a dining room lit by oil lamps. There are beamed ceilings, exposed brick vaults and arches, and the restaurant looks onto the sheepfold and its flock. The upscale cuisine includes monkfish and chorizo skewers, and truffle *risotti* with roasted scallops. Ask to visit the private museum, Le Curiosa, displaying a collection entitled Love and Humour.

✉ 370 route du Village, 06810 Auribeau-sur-Siagne ☎ 04 93 42 20 01 🕐 Wed–Fri 7–10.30, Sat, Sun 10–3, 7–10.30 ✋ L €50, D €95 (wine is included)

## CANNES

### CHEZ ASTOUX

www.astouxbrun.com

Seafood is the speciality at this popular bistro. The large shellfish platters are a tasty option but you can also enjoy fish soup and poached or grilled fish, including saffron cod. There is a covered terrace and take-out service is available.

✉ 27 rue Félix Faure, 06400 Cannes ☎ 04 93 39 21 87 🕐 Café: daily 8am–midnight. Kitchen: daily 12–2, 7–11 ✋ L €25, D €40, Wine €15

### CHEZ VINCENT ET NICOLAS

A flamboyantly original establishment at the foot of Le Suquet, Cannes' old town. The restaurant tumbles out onto the tiny piazza in front, where the tables are

packed with a young crowd digging into foie gras hamburgers and French dishes with an Asian twist.
✉ 92 rue Meynadier, 06400 Cannes ☎ 04 93 68 35 39 ⌚ Tue–Sun 6pm–midnight ✋ L €25, D €40, Wine €18

### CIRO

www.cirocannes.com

Arguably the best, and perhaps one of the least expensive, Italian restaurants in Cannes. Try pizzas fresh from the wood-fired oven, or the signature *linguine fruits de mer* in papery crust.
✉ 28 rue du Suquet, 06400 Cannes ☎ 04 93 29 21 24 ⌚ Daily 12–3, 7–12 ✋ L €20, D €30, Wine €16

### CLARIDGE

Come here for a drink, ice cream or traditional brasserie fare until late into the night. There's a pub atmosphere, with sports shown on a large screen, although the decor sticks to the brasserie theme, with marble tables.
✉ 2 place du Général de Gaulle, 06400 Cannes ☎ 04 93 39 05 86 ⌚ Daily 7am–2.30am ✋ L €14, D €20, Wine €15

### ESCALE DE CHINE

The ornate decoration in this Chinese restaurant includes a profusion of exotic wood, mirrors, columns and gilded panels, yet it manages to avoid kitsch. The refined cuisine includes dishes such as Chinese fondue and Peking duck.
✉ 58 rue Jean Jaurès, 06400 Cannes ☎ 04 93 99 15 99 ⌚ Wed–Sun 12–2.30, 7–11, Mon, Tue 7–11 ✋ L €12, D €20, Wine €12

### LA POTINIÈRE DU PALAIS

www.lapotiniere.fr

The *palais* (palace) refers to the Palais des Festivals, where major events in Cannes take place. But there's more to this restaurant than a choice location. The cooking is exceptionally good and the menu has a lot of fish and classics such as sole *meunière* and lobster ravioli.
✉ 13 square Mérimée, 06400 Cannes ☎ 04 93 39 02 82 ⌚ Mon–Sat 12–2.30, 7.30–10 ✋ L €30, D €40, Wine €20

## ÈZE

### LE CHÈVRE D'OR

www.chevredor.com

The luxury Château de la Chèvre d'Or hotel is home to this restaurant with fantastic views along the coast. The establishment boasts two Michelin stars thanks to the stewardship of head chef Philippe Labbé. The menu has an excellent selection of luxury ingredients, including truffles, cèpes and lobster, balanced by an excellent wine list. This is a favourite with the Riviera glitterati.
✉ Moyenne Corniche, rue du Barri, 06360 Èze ☎ 04 92 10 66 66 ⌚ Mid-Mar to end Sep daily 12–3, 7–9.30; Oct Wed–Sun 12–3, 7–9.30 ✋ L €120, D €200, Wine €40

## GILETTE

### LA CAPELINE

This small, rustic *auberge* is one of the last of its kind. Delicious and uncomplicated food using the season's freshest ingredients is complemented by local wines. The country setting is splendid. For an inexpensive but very French experience, spend a couple of hours enjoying lunch out on the shady terrace.
✉ 06830 Gilette ☎ 04 93 08 58 06 ⌚ Mar–end Oct Thu–Tue 12–2.30; Nov–end Feb Sat, Sun 12–2.30 ✋ L €25, Wine €12

## GRASSE

### LA BASTIDE ST-ANTOINE–JACQUES CHIBOIS

www.jacques-chibois.com

An olive grove surrounds this 18th-century Provençal town house. The elegant dining room has period furniture and fine tableware and makes discreet use of materials from the area: tile floor and fine fabric for the curtains. The Mediterranean cuisine includes the finest ingredients: John Dory with fennel and asparagus, and butterflied langoustines with orange pulp. Reservations are essential.
✉ 48 avenue Henri-Dunant, 06130 Grasse ☎ 04 93 70 94 94 ⌚ Daily 12–1.30, 8–9.30 ✋ L €80, D €130, Wine €40

## MONACO

### AMICI MIEI

Amici Miei is a traditional Italian restaurant much frequented by Monaco's huge Italian community. The location in modern Fontvieille may be incongruous, but you can expect classics such as *spaghetti alla vongole* and grilled fish. There's a huge outdoor dining terrace.
✉ 16 quai Jean-Charles Rey, 98000 Monaco ☎ 377 92 05 92 14 ⌚ Daily 12–3.30, 7–11 ✋ L €25, D €30, Wine €15

### LE LOUIS XV

www.alain-ducasse.com

The height of luxury, this restaurant is within the majestic Hôtel de Paris, built in 1864. The Mediterranean-inspired menu changes with the seasons and is thematic. Topics include the kitchen garden, hunting, the farm, the sea and rivers. The sumptuous Louis XV-style interior provides a fitting backdrop for a feast fit for a king.
✉ Hôtel de Paris, place du Casino, 98000 Monaco ☎ 377 98 06 88 64 ⌚ Jan, Mar–end Nov Thu–Mon 12.15–1.45, 8–9.45. Closed Feb, Dec ✋ L €120, D €200, Wine €90

### STARS 'N' BARS

www.starsnbars.com

This ever-popular American-style bar-restaurant, with a predominantly Tex-Mex menu, is the perfect place for families tired of more formal French restaurants. The bar has lots of games to keep kids occupied. In the evenings there's disco or live music.
✉ 6 quai Antoine I, La Condamine, 98000 Monaco ☎ 377 97 97 95 95 ⌚ Food is served Tue–Sun 11.30am–midnight; the bar is open until 2am ✋ L €20, D €25, Wine €15

## MOUGINS

### LE MOULIN DE MOUGINS

www.moulindemougins.com

Surrounded by greenery and decorated with contemporary works of art, this 16th-century former olive mill provides a gastronomic treat. The cuisine is a sophisticated combination of Mediterranean

tastes reinvented by the day. The excellent wine cellar has more than 5,000 vintages. You can also take cooking classes here.
✉ Quartier Notre-Dame-de-Vie, 06250 Mougins ☎ 04 93 75 78 24 ⏲ May–end Oct daily 12–2, 7.30–10; Nov–end Apr Tue–Sun 10–12, 7.30–10. Closed last 2 weeks in Jan 🖐 L €49, D €100, Wine €25

## NICE

### L'ÂNE ROUGE

www.anerougenice.com
Chef Michel Devillers likes to cook fish, and his creations are tantalizing: succulent scallops roasted with chorizo, fresh and dried tomatoes and thyme flower. There's a fireplace in the elegant interior and the flower-filled terrace has a view of the port.
✉ 7 quai des Deux-Emmanuel, 06300 Nice ☎ 04 93 89 49 63 ⏲ Fri–Tue 12–2.30, 7.30–9.30, Thu 7.30–9.30 🖐 L €40, D €55, Wine €18

### CAFÉ DE TURIN

Thanks to a century of experience, Café de Turin serves up platters of oysters, snails, sea urchins, crab pincers and snails with aplomb, all washed down with the establishment's own inexpensive white wine.
✉ 5 place Garibaldi, 06300 Nice ☎ 04 93 62 29 52 ⏲ Daily 8am–10pm 🖐 L €20, D €30, Wine €14

### LA MAISON DE MARIE

www.lamaisondemarie.com
This restaurant is ideal for a romantic meal, with candlelit tables in the evening. In fair weather, a couple of tables are set out on the terrace. The Mediterranean cuisine includes sardines stuffed with pine nuts and lamb with a herb crust.
✉ 5 rue Masséna, 06000 Nice ☎ 04 93 82 15 93 ⏲ Tue–Sat 12–2, 7–11 🖐 L €25, D €35, Wine €15

### RESTAURANT BOCCACCIO

www.boccaccio-nice.com
There are no less than six dining rooms here, all of which have a marine theme. One has a large aquarium, another with a vaulted wooden ceiling is reminiscent of the interior of a caravel (a historic small ship), and model boats carry on the theme. The menu has Mediterranean seafood dishes such as bass in a salty crust, bouillabaisse and seafood platters.
✉ 7 rue Masséna, 06000 Nice ☎ 04 93 87 71 76 ⏲ Daily 12–2.30, 7–11 🖐 L €40, D €50, Wine €25

### ROSSETTISSERIE RESTAURANT

Pluck a revolving half-chicken or joint of lamb or beef from the oven straight onto your plate at this rotisserie specialist. Proprietor-cum-chef Jean-Michel can also make you a picnic box (€2 less than the menu price) of meat and vegetables for the beach. Wine by the *pichet* (pitcher) makes this an excellent-value bet.
✉ 8 rue Mascoinet, 06300 Nice ☎ 04 93 76 18 80 ⏲ Tue–Sat 12–2.30, 7–11 🖐 L €15, D €20, Wine €13

### LE SAFARI

This restaurant is on a lively street and its terrace bulges with people in good weather. The interior is bistro-style, complete with a little blackboard displaying the menu. On offer are Nice specialities (salad of chopped fresh artichokes with olive oil and lemon, crudités with warm anchovy sauce) and a great choice of freshly baked pizza.
✉ 1 cours Saleya, 06300 Nice ☎ 04 93 80 18 44 ⏲ Tue–Sun 12–2.30, 7–11 🖐 L €25, D €40, Wine €14

### L'UNIVERS DE CHRISTIAN PLUMAIL

www.christian-plumail.com
One of the most chic addresses in Nice, chef Christian Plumail is climbing the ladder of gastronomic success with this restaurant on place Masséna, which now boasts a Michelin star. The clean lines of the dining room with its modern sculpture and art make a perfect canvas for the beautifully presented dishes. There are also seasonal menus featuring local produce.
✉ 53 boulevard Jean Jaurès, 06300 Nice ☎ 04 93 62 32 22 ⏲ Tue–Fri 12.30–2.30, 7.30–9.30, Sat, Sun 7.30–9.30 🖐 L €30, D €50, Wine €20

## RAYOL-CANADEL

### MAURIN DES MAURES

www.maurin-des-maures.com
This brasserie is named after a legendary character who spent his life hunting in the Maures mountains. In the dining room, a painting depicts part of his story. The brasserie fare has a southern accent, with dishes including courgette (zucchini) and goat's cheese tart, and the house fried fish. Wok-friendly Asian vegetables and marinated meats are additional specialities, best eaten while looking out to sea from the panoramic terrace.
✉ Avenue Mistral, 83820 Rayol-Canadel ☎ 04 94 05 60 11 ⏲ Daily 12–2, 7–10 🖐 L €25, D €35, Wine €15.50

## VILLEFRANCHE-SUR-MER

### LE COSMO

A people-watcher's paradise hogging most of Villefranche's prettiest old town square. Wine can be brought by the *pichet* (pitcher), and guests are welcome anytime for a beer and the house speciality: *anchoïade* and crudités dip. Seared tuna, giant salads and meats on the grill complete the mix.
✉ Place Amelie Pollonais, 06230 Villefranche ☎ 04 93 01 84 05 ⏲ Daily 8am–11pm 🖐 L €25, D €35, Wine €18

**Below** *In summer, dining out on a restaurant terrace is ideal*

**Above** *Hotel Martinez, Cannes*

**PRICES AND SYMBOLS**

Prices are the lowest and highest for a double room for one night. Each listing states whether breakfast is included. All the hotels listed accept credit cards unless otherwise stated. Note that rates vary widely throughout the year.

For a key to the symbols, ▷ 2.

## ANTIBES

### RELAIS DU POSTILLON

www.relaisdupostillon.com

As near as you can get to Antibes' historic centre, the Postillon is an inexpensive treat with heaps of period charm, wood and subtle shades. Rooms blend modern beds and linen with antique chairs and mirrors, some with a balcony or terrace to boot. Breakfast is served in the cosy café or outdoors on the square.

✉ 8 rue Championnet, 06600 Antibes ☎ 04 93 34 20 77 € €68–€96, excluding breakfast (€8) 16

## CANNES

### CHALET DE L'ISÈRE

Breakfast is served in a tiled garden at this two-star hotel. Bedrooms have been simply decorated, yet each has its own touch. There is a restaurant with a large outdoor terrace. The Palais des Festivals is a 10-minute walk away.

✉ 42 avenue de Grasse, 06400 Cannes ☎ 04 93 38 50 80 € €81, excluding breakfast (€8) 8

### HOTEL MARTINEZ

www.hotel-martinez.com

This mythical palace, popular with celebrities during the Film Festival, faces the Bay of Cannes. The luxurious decor shows art deco influence: Dark woods and marble or deep carpets set the tone. Services include a bar, restaurants, business facilities and private beach.

✉ 73 boulevard de la Croisette, 06400 Cannes ☎ 04 92 98 73 00 € €300–€900, excluding breakfast (€27 continental, €34 buffet) 386 rooms, 27 suites Outdoor

### HÔTEL DE PARIS

www.hotel-de-paris.com

This three-star hotel has a pink 19th-century facade, which contrasts beautifully with the blue of the outdoor pool. Inside, there is antique furniture and even some medieval armour. Facilities include a private beach, swimming pool, Jacuzzi and hammam (Turkish bath). Bedrooms have satellite TV, a safe and connection point for laptops.

✉ 34 boulevard d'Alsace, 06400 Cannes ☎ 04 97 06 98 88 € €75–€150, excluding breakfast (€13) 50 Outdoor

## MENTON

### CLARIDGE'S

www.claridges-menton.com

This two-star hotel is just a couple of kilometres from chic Monaco and close to beaches. The simply decorated bedrooms are quite small but they are comfortable and have satellite TV. There's a bar and lounge, and a terrace looks out onto the street.

✉ 39 avenue de Verdun, 06500 Menton ☎ 04 93 35 72 53 € €62–€79, excluding breakfast (€6) 39 (In 24 rooms)

### HÔTEL AIGLON

www.hotelaiglon.net

Close to the sea, this prestigious three-star hotel is in a 20th-century town house. Cross its luxurious garden, climb its marble stairs and you'll discover an elegant interior, with fine furniture. The bedrooms have satellite TV, a safe and minibar. Other facilities include a kids'

playground, table tennis and parking. The pool is heated and there's a solarium. Le Riaumont restaurant serves fine Provençal cuisine. You can enjoy breakfast on the poolside terrace.
✉ 7 avenue de la Madone, 06500 Menton ☎ 04 93 57 55 55
€90–€172, including breakfast
29 Outdoor

## MONACO

### HOTEL DE FRANCE

www.monte-carlo.mc
This quiet, simple hotel, a ten-minute walk from the train station, is a real find in wallet-crunching Monaco. Modern rooms feature satellite TV and en-suite bathrooms, plus there's a little café and bar on site. Public parking is available nearby (charge).
✉ 6 rue de la Turbie, 98000 Monaco
☎ 377 93 30 24 64 €85–€112, excluding breakfast (€9)
10 rooms

### HÔTEL HERMITAGE

www.hotelhermitagemontecarlo.com
This belle époque luxury hotel faces the Mediterranean. It has a panoramic restaurant, Le Vistamar, and you can have breakfast under a glass ceiling designed by Gustave Eiffel. The services are those you would expect of a luxury hotel, including a helicopter shuttle service between Monaco and Nice airports. There is direct access to Les Thermes Marins de Monaco Spa and Health Resort.
✉ Square Beaumarchais, 98000 Monaco
☎ 377 98 06 40 00 €380–€975, excluding breakfast (€32) 280 rooms, 45 suites and 8 apartments
Indoor

## MOUGINS

### LE MANOIR DE L'ETANG

www.manoir-de-letang.com
In a park dotted with ponds, this three-star hotel is housed in an elegant, ivy-clad 19th-century residence. The interior is decorated with antique furniture. The restaurant serves fine local cuisine, either by the pool or in the dining room.
✉ 66 allée du Manoir, 06250 Mougins ☎ 04 92 28 36 00 Closed Nov–end Mar €200–€275, excluding breakfast (€17) 21
Outdoor

**Above** *Les Muscadins, in Mougins, has a restaurant serving fine local cuisine*

### LES MUSCADINS

www.hotel-mougins-muscadins.com
Pablo Picasso once stayed at this former guest house, which is now a four-star hotel. The ochre facade and tile floor are inspired by the region, and antiques add to the elegance. Each room has a personal touch, such as a wrought-iron four-poster bed or patterned tile floors. Tasty local cuisine is served in the restaurant; lobster is one of the specials.
✉ 18 boulevard Courteline, 06250 Mougins
☎ 04 92 28 43 43 €185–€295, excluding breakfast (€15) 10

## NICE

### AUBERGE DE JEUNESSE DE NICE

www.fuaj.org
This youth hostel is located in the wooded hills of Mont Boron. There are beautiful views down to Nice. Dormitories have six to eight beds and there is a communal room with a TV. Facilities also include a kitchen, laundry service and internet access. The hostel is 4km (2.5 miles) from the city and the beach. Credit cards are not accepted.
✉ Route Forestière du Mont-Alban, 06300 Nice ☎ 04 93 89 23 64 Closed Oct–end May €18.20, including breakfast 56

### HÔTEL ARMENONVILLE

www.hotel-armenonville.com
This two-star hotel is in a 20th-century mansion surrounded by a flower garden. Some of the rooms have a terrace and look onto this greenery. All are bright and have been tastefully decorated with antique furniture and beautiful tiled bathrooms. Breakfast can be served in the garden.
✉ 20 avenue des Fleurs, 06000 Nice
☎ 04 93 96 86 00 €49–€99, excluding breakfast (€9) 12

### HÔTEL NEGRESCO

www.hotel-negresco-nice.com
Built in 1912, this palace and its signature dome have been given landmark status. The interior is an ode to fine art, from the Renaissance to the modern: In the Salon Royal, Niki de Saint-Phalle's *Nana*, an oversize sculpture of a woman, sits happily next to classical portraits. This venerable hotel, rated as Nice's finest, has two

equally established restaurants, Le Chantecler and La Rotonde.
✉ 37 promenade des Anglais, 06000 Nice ☎ 04 93 16 64 00 €250–€650, including breakfast 121 rooms, 24 suites

### HÔTEL WINDSOR

www.hotelwindsornice.com

This is no ordinary hotel, rather a sanctuary for the soul. A protector Buddha sits enthroned in the reception area. Massages are available. Contemporary artists have personalized each of the rooms. The tranquil tropical garden, complete with bamboo, a swimming pool, a palm tree and even a parrot, is sublime

✉ 11 rue Dalpozzo, 06300 Nice ☎ 04 93 88 59 35 €78–€175, excluding breakfast (€12) 57 Outdoor

## ROQUEBRUNE-CAP-MARTIN

### LES DEUX FRÈRES

www.lesdeuxfreres.com

Most of the rooms at this hotel have wonderful views of the Mediterranean and Monaco. The rooms are refined and original: The Moroccan room has a leopard skin, the Marine room has blue-and-white striped bed linen and the Medieval room has a wrought-iron bench. Gourmet cuisine is served in the restaurant, on the terrace, or by the fireplace in winter.

✉ Le Village, 06190 Roquebrune-Cap-Martin ☎ 04 93 28 99 00 €75–€110, excluding breakfast 10

## ST-JEAN-CAP-FERRAT

### HÔTEL BRISE MARINE

www.hotel-brisemarine.com

This three-star hotel is in an Italian-style villa, built in 1878. The ochre facade has blue shutters and faces the sea. There are excellent views from the garden, the patio and terraces, and from some of the simple, elegant bedrooms. Each room has a TV, safe and minibar. There is no restaurant on site. Parking is available.

✉ 58 avenue Jean Mermoz, 06230 St-Jean-Cap-Ferrat ☎ 04 93 76 04 36 Closed Nov–end Jan €150–€178, excluding breakfast (€14) 16

## ST-PAUL-DE-VENCE

### HÔTEL LE HAMEAU

www.le-hameau.com

Overlooking the village of St-Paul-de-Vence and its valley, this three-star hotel is in an 18th-century farm complex with whitewashed walls and arched entrances. Some bedrooms have a private terrace. The garden has fragrant jasmine, citrus trees and honeysuckle.

✉ 528 route de la Colle, 06570 St-Paul-de-Vence ☎ 04 93 32 80 24 Closed Jan €105–€170, excluding breakfast (€15) 14 Outdoor

### LE MAS DE PIERRE

www.lemasdepierre.com

Spread across a hillside near St-Paul-de-Vence, this beautifully renovated *mas* (stone farmhouse) has spacious, stylish accommodation set around a gorgeous pool and in 2ha (5 acres) of lush gardens. The chic colonial-style furnishings contrast beautifully with the Provençal architecture. The rooms each have a private balcony or garden and there's a luxury spa on site.

✉ Route des Serres, 06570 St-Paul-de-Vence ☎ 04 93 59 00 10 Closed Jan, Feb €230–€570, excluding breakfast (€30) 48

## VILLEFRANCHE-SUR-MER

### HÔTEL WELCOME

www.welcomehotel.com

Hôtel Welcome is in a modern building overlooking the bay. The bright bedrooms have balconies—their views seduced writer and film director Jean Cocteau, a former guest. The interior has a contemporary elegance. There is no restaurant.

✉ 1 quai Courbet, 06230 Villefranche-sur-Mer ☎ 04 93 76 27 62 Closed mid-Nov to Christmas €98–€228, excluding breakfast (€11) 36

**Below** *The reception area of the Hôtel Negresco, Nice*

# ALPES-DE-HAUTE-PROVENCE AND HAUTES-ALPES

With a landscape of soaring mountains and lofty plateaux, this is Provence at its most wild. It's also one of the greenest areas of the country, with Alpine snowmelt watering scores of valleys and sustaining forests, meadows and even the odd vineyard. Best of all, its natural beauty is readily accessible thanks to a superb network of roads and buses, plus the single-gauge Train des Pignes that runs down to Nice. To help you explore the countryside, each tourist office has invaluable local walking and bicycling guides.

The regional centres of Gap, Sisteron and Digne-les-Bains have all been around since Roman times and are alive with culture. The modern museums in each town contrast with surrounding old ramparts and glorious churches. Several nearby fortified villages, including Entrevaux, Castellane and Briançon, cling to the cliffs like fairy-tale castles.

It's not the Sisteron lamb or wealth of outdoor activities that divert most visitors to the Alpes-de-Hautes-Provence, even though these are fine attributes in themselves. The Gorges du Verdon—the world's second-largest canyon—occupies a good part of the region and is one of Europe's most awe-inspiring spectacles. Put on the map only in 1905, it's now a haven for birdwatchers and climbers, while the adjoining Lac de Sainte-Croix is perfect for rowboats and canoes. Of the several tempting local bases, Moustiers-Sainte-Marie's status as a centre of the faïence industry and a den of fine dining makes it a good bet.

Come December, the ski slopes around Val d'Allos open up in earnest. In summer they host similarly adventurous types in search of skydiving, hiking and canyoning. And if taking a mountain bike up in a cable car, then descending 1,000m (half a mile) downhill is your thing, this is the place to do it.

## ALLOS AND VAL D'ALLOS

www.valdallos.com

The Allos valley is a large, modern mountain resort area just south of the Col d'Allos pass, on the edge of the beautiful Parc National du Mercantour. In winter it's the largest skiable area in the southern Alps; in summer it's a good starting point for walks and drives.

On the northern side is the Alpine-style resort called Val d'Allos 1800 (or La Foux). To the south is the sports-based Val d'Allos 1500 (or Le Seignus). It is next to Val d'Allos 1400 (or Allos), the valley's original village. The greener lower slopes, formerly sheep pastures, are now dotted with ski chalets and summer holiday homes.

The most important outing is to the spectacularly beautiful Lac d'Allos, in the peaks to the east of Allos village. Located at 2,220m (7,300ft), and covering some 60ha (150 acres), it's the largest lake in the High Alps. To reach the lake involves a 15km (9-mile) drive zig-zagging upwards on the D266 (open mid-Jun to mid-Oct only), then a walk of some 40 minutes to the amphitheatre of slopes looking across the lake itself. Its still water, reflecting the surrounding mountain peaks like a giant mirror, is so cold that, reputedly, nothing can grow in it.

✚ 293 M7 ℹ Place du Presbytère, 04260 Val d'Allos ☎ 04 92 83 02 81 ⊕ Mid-Dec to late Mar, Jun–end Aug daily 8.30–12, 2–6.30; late Mar–end May, Sep to mid-Dec Mon–Sat 9–12, 2–5

## BARCELONNETTE

www.barcelonnette.net

Far up in the Alpine northern limits of Provence, close to ski resorts, this tranquil and rather remote old town is surrounded by high peaks, tiny farms and mountain meadows. The town, in the valley of Ubaye, is worth seeing for its curious Mexican cultural connection.

The Mexican link arose by chance in the 19th century, when many local young men went to Mexico to seek their fortunes. The first were the two Arnaud brothers, Jacques and Marc-Antoine, whose huge financial success tempted others to follow in their footsteps. In Mexico itself, the men of Barcelonnette and its nearby villages assisted each other and many had a degree of success—a few even became millionaires. After some years, a number of them returned to the Provençal Alps, building houses in a strange mix of styles reflecting their New World culture and prosperity. Wander along avenue de la Libération to see some of the grander Mexican houses.

Barcelonnette is especially popular in summer as a starting point for walks and drives into the Mercantour National Park (▷ 168–169). The Maison du Parc, near the heart of town, is an information point for the park. Downstream from the town, organizations offer kayaking, canoeing and rafting.

Barcelonnette was built by the Counts of Barcelona (hence its name) and vestiges survive of their 13th-century fortifications. It is a picturesque and atmospheric town, with cobbled lanes and small squares. Place Manuel, the main square, is especially attractive, surrounded by old buildings. There are fine old houses in several streets, as well as villas in a bizarre mix of styles influenced by the town's Latin American links. The Musée de la Vallée de l'Ubaye, in avenue de la Libération (Jul, Aug daily 10–12, 2.30–7; Sep to mid-Nov, mid-Dec to end Jun Wed–Sat 2.30–6. Closed mid-Nov to mid-Dec), itself in one of the Mexican villas, tells the town's story.

✚ 293 M6 ℹ Place Frédéric Mistral, 04400 Barcelonnette ☎ 04 92 81 04 71 ⊕ Daily 9–12.30, 1.30–7.30

## BRIANÇON

www.ot-briancon.fr

Briançon is the highest town in Europe, at 1,320m (4,330ft), and is surrounded by scenic mountain peaks. Two national parks, the Parc National des Écrins and the Parc National Régional du Queyras, are in the surrounding area.

The town is on the Col de Montgenèvre, one of the major Alpine passes linking France and Italy, and has been settled since pre-Roman times. It now promotes itself as a ski station of the Serre Chevalier ski area, with more than 250km (155 miles) of ski runs between four villages.

At the end of the 17th century Louis XIV's military planner, Vauban, turned Briançon's old medieval town into an impenetrable walled city. Now known as Cité Vauban, this area is traffic free and the focus of visitor interest. Go through Porte de Pignerol into Grande Rue, with its impressive houses.

Other highlights include the Maison des Templier (which houses the tourist information office), the 14th-century Église des Cordeliers and the Fort du Château, where 19th-century defences replaced the last vestiges of the original chateau, built in the 11th century. The 18th-century Collégiale (Notre-Dame de St-Nicolas) was built to Vauban's design.

✚ 289 M3 ℹ 1 place du Temple, 05100 Briançon ☎ 04 92 21 08 50 ⊕ Mon–Sat 9–12, 2–6, Sun 10.15–12.15, 2.30–5 🚉 Briançon

**Opposite** *A snow-covered Briançon*
**Below** *The mountain peaks of the Val d'Allos*

## CASTELLANE

www.castellane.org

In some ways a typical attractive old Provençal hill town, Castellane becomes exceptional because of its dramatic location. It stands on the Route Napoléon (the Emperor rested here on 3 March 1815) and is the key starting and finishing point for a trip along the Grand Canyon du Verdon (▷ 204–205).

Alongside the town, and rising above it, soars a remarkable narrow ridge of rock, 184m (603ft) high, with the chapel of Notre-Dame du Roc perched on the top. Though a steep climb, it's accessible on a trail that winds up to the summit. The walk takes about 30 minutes.

The old town of Castellane has remnants of its 14th-century walls. The town is also a centre for adventure tourism, with plenty of places to rent bicycles or kayaks, or embark on a white-water rafting or hiking trip. It is incongruously surrounded by campsites and is terribly crowded in summer.

297 L10 · 34 rue Nationale, 04120 Castellane · 04 92 83 61 14 · Jul, Aug Mon–Fri 9–7, Sat, Sun 9–6; Sep–end Jun Mon–Sat 9–12, 2–5

## COLMARS

Colmars is a lovely old fortified town nestled amid woodland and mountain peaks just down the Haut Verdon Valley from Allos (▷ 199). It is dominated by two forts, the Fort de France to the south and the Fort de Savoie to the north, built at the end of the 17th century, when the border town faced constant attacks by the Savoyards.

293 M8 · Place Joseph Girieud, 04370 Colmars · 04 92 83 41 92 · Tue–Sat 9–12.15, 2–5.45, Sun 9–12.15 during holiday periods

## DIGNE-LES-BAINS

▷ 201.

## ENTREVAUX

▷ 202.

## FORCALQUIER

▷ 203.

## GAP

www.gap-tourisme.fr

At an altitude of 750m (2,500ft), Gap is the highest *département* capital in France. The town, capital of the Hautes-Alpes, enjoys excellent skiing conditions in winter and Provençal warmth in summer.

The Romans established Gap in the first century AD, and 18 centuries later Napoleon Bonaparte spent a night here on his route back to Paris from Elba. For reminders of the town's history, head to rue Jean Eymar, now one of the main shopping streets, which has houses built along the ramparts, the town's oldest window, a small sundial and a washhouse.

Just outside town is the 220ha (500-acre) Charance Botanical Garden (mid-Apr to end May, Sep, Oct Wed–Mon 2–5; Jun–end Aug Wed–Mon 10–12, 2–6.30). It grows more than 3,000 species of mountain flowers and houses the world's largest collection of old roses. Its terraced gardens are listed as a historic monument.

Northeast of Gap is the Parc National des Écrins, one of France's largest but lesser-known parks.

292 J5 · 2a cours Frédéric Mistral, 05000 Gap · 04 92 52 56 56 · Jul, Aug Mon–Sat 9–7, Sun 10–1; Sep–end Jun Mon–Sat 9–12, 2–6 · Gap

## GRAND CANYON DU VERDON

▷ 204–205.

## GRÉOUX-LES-BAINS

www.greoux-les-bains.com

Around 3 million litres (660,000 gallons) a day emerge from the Gréoux springs, at an average temperature of 36°C (97°F). The Romans built spa baths here in the second century AD. They were reopened in the 17th century, were fashionable in the 19th and were rebuilt in 1962.

Gréoux is dominated by its ruined 12th-century castle of the Knights Templar. The village's pleasant streets have many art galleries. See vivid stained glass and mosaics at the Atelier Musée du Vitrail et de la Mosaïque, in Grande Rue. The town makes a tranquil base for excursions to the water-sports centre Lac de Sainte-Croix. The village of Esparron, with a smaller lake packed with boats, is a few kilometres east.

296 J10 · 5 avenue des Marronniers, 04800 Gréoux-les-Bains · 04 92 78 01 08 · Jul, Aug Mon–Sat 9–7, Sun 9–12.30, 2.30–7; Apr–end Jun, Sep, Oct Mon–Sat 9–12.30, 2–6.30, Sun 9–1; Mar, Nov Mon–Sat 9–12, 2–8; Jan, Feb, Dec Mon–Sat 9–12, 2–5

**Below** *Castellane's dramatically located Chapelle Notre-Dame du Roc*

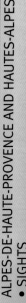

## DIGNE-LES-BAINS

This bright, airy prosperous spa resort is the largest town in the mountainous backcountry of Provence. It makes an excellent base for touring the hills by foot, by car or on the old narrow-gauge Chemin de Fer de Provence railway, known as the Train des Pignes (▷ 212), that connects the town to Nice. A spa during Roman times, Digne flourished into the Middle Ages, as can be seen from the beautiful 12th-century Romanesque church, Notre-Dame du Bourg, in the main boulevard. The old town, which also has some modern buildings, encloses a crumbling 15th-century hilltop Gothic cathedral, St-Jerome.

### SPA

At Digne's ultra-modern spa, Thermes de Digne-les-Bains, 3km (2 miles) south of town, you can enjoy anti-stress remedies and other treatments (tel 04 92 32 58 46; closed Sat afternoon and Sunday). The mineral waters emerge from eight hot springs and one cold spring. In town, a 150-year-old 'Great Fountain' in boulevard Gassendi is cloaked with deposits from the calcium-rich water.

### MUSEUMS

The Musée de la Seconde Guerre Mondiale (Museum of World War II), in place Paradis, is in a former bomb shelter carved into the mountain (Jul, Aug Mon–Thu 2–6, Fri 2–5.30; mid-Apr to end Jun, Sep to mid-Nov Wed 2–5). Here you can learn about Digne's curious fate during the war, when it was occupied by the Italians. The Musée Gassendi (Apr–end Sep Wed–Mon 11–7; Oct–end Mar Wed–Mon 1.30–5.30), close to the 'Great Fountain', focuses on fine art. Out of town, at 27 avenue Maréchal Juin, is a Tibetan museum, the Fondation Alexandra David-Neel (tours at 10, 2 and 3.30 all year round).

### OUTDOOR

A popular local activity is *Via Ferrata*—travelling by ropes, iron stairways and zip lines across the craggy countryside. Visitors can now hire equipment from the Tourist Office and attempt the Rocher de Neuf Heures trail (▷ 212).

### INFORMATION

www.ot-dignelesbains.fr

292 K8 Rond Point 11 Novembre, 04001 Digne-les-Bains ☎ 04 92 36 62 62 Jul, Aug daily 9–12, 2–6; Sep–end Jun Mon–Sat 9–12, 2–6 Digne

### TIPS

» Digne is the lavender capital of Provence and you can buy wonderful lavender products at the market on Wednesdays and Saturdays, in place du Général-de-Gaulle.

» The town hosts a lavender festival, the *Corso de la Lavande*, for five days in early August.

» The Tourist Office has a list of local hikes into the hills around Digne.

**Above** *The church of Notre-Dame du Bourg dates from the 12th century*

## INFORMATION

www.entrevaux.info

298 N9 Porte Royale du Pont Levis, 04320 Entrevaux 04 93 05 46 73 Jul, Aug daily 9–6.30; mid-Jan to end Jun, Sep, Oct Mon–Fri 9–12, 2–5.30. Closed Nov to mid-Jan Entrevaux (on the Chemins de Fer de Provence line from Digne to Nice)

## TIP

›› The village hosts concerts and festivals in summer.

# ENTREVAUX

Entrevaux, above a narrow gorge in the mountains between Nice and Digne, is an impressive sight. The spectacular fortified medieval village and its castle stand guard over a dramatic mountain scene. Originally a Ligurian settlement, then a Roman garrison, the compact village has a fortified drawbridge and an awesome 17th-century citadel. Approaching Entrevaux from either direction along the Var valley, it is easy to see why it was such an important town in the 17th century, when this was the French border with Savoy. The gorges here narrow to just a few hundred metres across—plug this and you block a major route between the two states. On the west bank of the Var, a jagged curtain of rock makes the hillside impassable. On the east bank, this natural barrier is reflected in the grand fortifications, built by Vauban, Louis XIV's military architect, which zig-zag up to La Citadelle, perched 135m (440ft) above the town.

## CITÉ VAUBAN

The main access to the town is via a fortified single-arch river bridge, built by Vauban, which enters through the Porte Nationale or Porte Royale. A remarkable ramp, strikingly punctuated by a score of bastions, goes from the town up a sheer rock face to reach Vauban's ruined Citadelle, crowning a steep crest of rock. There is little to see at the fortress, but the view is exceptional. Vauban's work started in 1692 and was completed in 1706. When Napoleon Bonaparte annexed the County of Nice to France, Vauban's defences became redundant and the village returned to its previous obscurity, but with its remarkable legacy of military architecture. During most of the 19th and 20th centuries, Entrevaux was unknown, and few visitors found their way here. In recent years, the dramatic setting and Vauban's work have been rediscovered, and Entrevaux has been revitalized.

## THE OLD TOWN

Within the town walls, the narrow streets keep their historic appearance, especially around the fortified cathedral, the walls of which form part of the city's defences. The town's other gateway, Porte d'Italie, opens onto a pleasant riverside walk. There's plenty to see around the village, including a restored oil mill and flour mill, a communal bread oven and even a collection of historic motorcycles.

**Below** *Entrevaux's Citadelle, perched high on a rock*

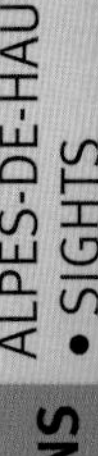

## FORCALQUIER

This historic, attractive market town in the beautiful Provençal hills has a peaceful, hard-working atmosphere. Originally a small Roman town, it became the seat of a powerful independent county controlling a wide area in the 12th century and was capital of Haute-Provence from the end of the 11th century to the beginning of the 13th century. Its old buildings are reminders of these times. Today, the surrounding countryside attracts bicyclists and walkers, who set off on the many marked trails.

### EXPLORING THE TOWN

The former citadel is raised up on a hill, but everything has now vanished except the ruins of just one tower. In town, in place du Bourguet, the large Romanesque and Gothic Cathédrale Notre-Dame du Marché, dating partly from the 12th century, survives. South of the cathedral is the old quarter, including what was once an enclosed Jewish ghetto. The convent in place du Bourguet now houses a cinema and the Musée Municipal (check with tourist office for opening times), with displays of local costumes, furnishings and other examples of folk culture. Outside the town gate (the Porte des Cordeliers) is the Couvent des Cordeliers, in boulevard des Martyres, a 12th-century monastery much changed in modern times, though with fine cloisters that are open to the public. It is one of the oldest Franciscan monasteries in France. (The tourist office organizes guided tours of the whole convent in July and August. Places must be pre-reserved.)

### STAR-GAZING

The Observatoire de Haute-Provence sits on a plateau southwest of Forcalquier, near the village of St-Michel-l'Observatoire. Its 14 domes house various telescopes pointed at the stars. Tours are available. See the website for details of bi-monthly public openings (www.centre-astro.fr; tel 04 92 76 69 69). The observatory was built here in 1936, after experts spent much effort hunting for the place in Provence with the clearest atmosphere.

### INFORMATION

www.forcalquier.com
296 H9 L'Office de Tourisme Intercommunal du Pays de Forcalquier et Montagne de Lure, 13 place du Bourguet, 04310 Forcalquier 04 92 75 10 02 Mid-Jun to mid-Sep Mon–Sat 9–12.30, 2–7, Sun 10–1; mid-Sep to mid-Jun Mon–Sat 9–12, 2–6

### TIPS

» Breathe deeply—Forcalquier is said to have the cleanest air in France.
» There's a big market on Mondays.
» Forcalquier hosts a renowned classical music festival each July.
» The citadel gives sweeping views across the surrounding countryside.

**Above** *Looking out over the rooftops of Forcalquier to the hills beyond*

# GRAND CANYON DU VERDON

**INFORMATION**

www.moustiers.eu
www.castellane.org
297 K10 Place de l'Église, 04360 Moustiers-Sainte-Marie (western edge of canyon) 04 92 74 67 84 Jul, Aug Mon–Fri 9.30–7, Sat 9.30–12.30, 2–7; Apr–end Jun, Sep daily 10–12.30, 2–6; Mar, Oct, Nov daily 10–12.30, 2–5.30; Dec–end Feb 10–12, 2–5

**Above** *An adventurous way to get a great view of the canyon*

## INTRODUCTION

The plunging ravine of the river Verdon, 21km (13 miles) long and edged on each side by narrow clifftop roads, is one of the most dramatic natural sights in Europe. It is promoted by tourist offices as the 'Grand Canyon' of the Verdon. Rising just above La Foux d'Allos in the Mont des Trois Evêchés, the Verdon river flows south before looping west above Castellane to carve its way through the limestone plateau of Haute-Provence on its way to the river Durance. Between Castellane and Moustiers-Sainte-Marie the river has hewn the spectacular Grand Canyon into the plateau. From sheer cliffs some 700m (2,300ft) above the flowing river there are panoramic views down the length of this rocky corridor. The town of Moustiers-Sainte-Marie (▷ 207) is at the western end of the gorge and Castellane (▷ 200) is near the eastern end. From both these towns, winding, precipitous roads run along the top of each side of the ravine, sometimes close to the edge. These reach a succession of breathtaking viewpoints giving fantastic vistas along the ravine and across the rocky terrain. Try to avoid July and August, when there is nose-to-tail traffic.

A fantastic way to see the canyon is on foot—a path runs the full length, although be ready for narrow ledges and dark tunnels. Always take a torch (flashlight), sweater, water and food, and beware of sudden changes in water levels due to upstream power stations. Wear suitable footwear and use bridges to cross the river. The paths are not suitable for children or for dogs. Before you set out, ask for the walking routes from the tourist offices at Moustiers-Sainte-Marie or Castellane. Kayaking and canoeing are other adventurous options, and are best tried on the Lac de Sainte-Croix, the calm emerald-green lake that the floodwaters of the Gorge flow into.

The first inhabitants of the gorges were the Ligurians, followed centuries later by shepherds fleeing the Saracens. 'Wild men' were said to live in the caves in the Middle Ages. The eminent speleologist E. A. Martel carried out the first scientific expedition to the gorges in 1905—it took him more than three days to travel the length, armed with a canoe, climbing rope and cameras. The first paths and viewpoints were constructed shortly after, and in 1947 the Corniche Sublime road was built on the south side. In 1997 the Gorges du Verdon became a Parc Naturel Régional, but the theoretical protection this gives is sometimes hard to appreciate amid the heavy traffic that crawls along the road in summer.

## WHAT TO SEE

### SOUTH BANK

The south side of the Grand Canyon, called the Corniche Sublime, has the grander scenery and a string of better viewpoints. Along the winding road at the top of the canyon, several of these pull-offs and *points sublimes* allow you to linger over the view. One reason why this is more rewarding on the south side of the river is that the road is closer to the cliff edge for more of the distance. The best stretch here is the Balcons de la Mescla, at the east end of the Corniche Sublime.

### NORTH BANK

The north side is also extremely impressive, but the road is more hair-raising and there are fewer viewpoints, although the north bank's *point sublime* is perhaps the very best location on either side. What you see is rock face dropping sometimes more or less vertically several hundred metres down to the slender river at the bottom.

**Right** *Taking to the water*
**Below** *The Route des Crêtes offers stunning views*

### TIPS

» Even a short drive along the Corniche Sublime is enough to be very impressive.

» For a drive alongside the canyon, ▷ 210–211.

» On the canyon's south side, Balcons de la Mescla on the Corniche Sublime gives the best view.

» On the north bank, the Route des Crêtes drive and the *point sublime* are highlights.

## LURS

Lurs, high above the west bank of the Durance, owes its survival to a group of graphic designers and printers. In the Middle Ages the village was the summer home to the Bishops of Sisteron, but by the 20th century its fortunes had plummeted and local people had abandoned it because of its lack of electricity and water. It was saved from oblivion by the designers and printers, led by typographer Maximilian Vox, who moved in after World War II. The village, with its neatly kept streets and attractive houses, is now classified as a historic site.

In the last week of August, Lurs hosts the *Rencontre Internationale de Lure*, aimed at graphic designers, photographers and printers.

296 J9 Place de la Fontaine, 04700 Lurs 04 92 79 10 20 (Apr, Jun–end Sep); 04 92 79 95 24 (rest of year)

## MANE

This medieval village, on a hill 4km (2.5 miles) south of Forcalquier, is dominated by its 12th- to 15th-century fortress. There's also a 16th-century church and a well-preserved old quarter, but the highlight is the Romanesque Prieuré de Salagon, a remarkable medieval priory outside the village on the N100. It has a lovely medicinal herb garden and also houses the Musée Jardins de Salagon (Jun–end Aug daily 10–7.30; May, Sep daily 10–12.30, 2–6.30; Oct, Feb–end Apr daily 2–5; Nov–end Dec Sun 2–5. Closed Jan), dedicated to the preservation of local tradition. Farther along the same road, the palatial Château de Sauvan, built in 1720 in Classical style, has lavish interiors and extensive gardens. Visits are by guided tour (Jul, Aug Sun–Fri 3.30; Apr–end Jun, Sep to mid-Nov Thu, Sat, Sun 3.30; Feb, Mar Sun 3.30. Closed mid-Nov to end Jan).

296 H9

## MANOSQUE

www.manosque-tourisme.com

Penetrate the industrial periphery of this large town, on the banks of the Durance, to reach the appealing old quarter at its heart, entered via the 14th-century Porte Saunerie. The pedestrian-only rue Grande is the main street, lined with shops. It hosts a market on Monday, Wednesday, Friday and Saturday mornings. The Église Notre-Dame de Romigier has a sixth-century black wood Virgin (▷ 31) and a Renaissance carved doorway.

At the L'Occitane factory shop, fabulous Provençal beauty products are sold for a fraction of the retail price. Contact the Manosque tourist office to book a one-hour free tour of the factory.

296 H10 Place du Docteur Joubert, 04100 Manosque 04 92 72 16 00 Jul, Aug daily 9–1, 2–7; Sep–end Jun Mon–Fri 9–12.15, 1.30–6, Sat 9–12.15 Manosque

**Below** *The honey-coloured houses of Mane rise up a small hill*

## MOUSTIERS-SAINTE-MARIE

▷ 207.

## RIEZ-LA-ROMAINE

www.ville-riez.fr

Riez, on the road from Gréoux to Moustiers (D952) as it crosses the high Valensole plateau, was a Roman trading town. Four Corinthian marble columns of a temple to Apollo, standing incongruously in a field on the edge of town, are the sole visible remnant of that era. In the fifth century AD, the Roman baths were used as the foundation for a baptistery (ask at the tourist office if you would like to visit), one of a handful of Merovingian structures surviving in France. Inside is a small museum.

There are Renaissance houses in Grand Rue, while the side streets have workshops making *santons* (figurines) and pottery. The village hosts a truffle market on Wednesdays in winter.

297 K10 4 allée Louis Gardiol, 04500 Riez 04 92 77 99 09 Jul, Aug Mon–Sat 9.30–12.30, 3–7, Sun 9.30–12.30; Sep–end Jun Mon–Fri 8.30–12, 1.30–5, Sat 8.30–12

## SIMIANE-LA-ROTONDE

www.simiane-la-rotonde.fr

Simiane-la-Rotonde takes its name from a curious, truncated, 12th-century chateau with a rotunda at the top of the village (May–end Aug daily 10.30–1, 1.30–7; Mar, Apr, Sep to mid-Nov Wed–Mon 1.30–6. Closed mid-Nov to end Feb). It is one of the few pieces of non-religious Romanesque architecture left in Provence.

The village winds around a little hill and is surrounded by farmland and scenic lavender fields.

296 G9 Mairie (town hall), 04150 Simiane-la-Rotonde 04 92 75 91 40

## MOUSTIERS-SAINTE-MARIE

An exceptional village in a striking location, Moustiers clings to a river gorge in wild rocky hills. It is one of the main access points for driving along the Grand Canyon du Verdon (▷ 204–205) and stands at the edge of a large lake, Lac de Sainte-Croix, an attractive and popular holiday area with trails, bicycle rental, horseback riding and water sports. But this sun-basking village makes a phenomenal sight in its own right. It is located beside a gorge, watched over by a chapel on a rocky ledge. A chain across the gorge suspends a gilded star high above the village.

### FAÏENCE

The village has long been famous for its high-quality glazed ceramics, known as faïences. The faïence industry dates from 1668, when, according to legend, a local potter learned the secrets of glazed ceramics from an Italian monk. Faïence manufacturing died out at the Revolution, but was revived in the 1920s. To see precious 17th- and 18th-century Moustiers work, as well as modern faïence, visit the Musée de la Faïence, in the town hall (Jul, Aug daily 10–12.30, 1.30–7; Apr–end Jun, Sep, Oct Wed–Mon 10–12.30, 1.30–6; Nov, Dec, Feb, Mar Sat, Sun 2–5. Closed January). The village also has many shops selling pottery and workshops where you can buy straight from the producer.

### CHAPEL AND STAR

The village came into being after monks from the Îles de Lérins (▷ 146) settled here in the fifth century AD. The monastic site was replaced in the 12th century by a chapel, Notre-Dame de Beauvoir, subsequently altered. The present building, a pleasant 20-minute walk from the heart of the village, dates mainly from the 12th and 16th centuries and has a Renaissance doorway and Romanesque and Gothic interior. There are two annual pilgrimages to the chapel. The famous star was originally an offering by a 12th-century seigneur of the Blacas family to Notre-Dame de Beauvoir in thanks for his freedom from captivity. The star (and its chain) have been replaced several times and the tradition of keeping it there is now sacrosanct.

### THE VILLAGE

Red-tiled old houses huddle along a tangle of vaulted alleys, narrow lanes and stairways arranged up the ravine's steep slopes. There's an attractive church with a landmark Italianate bell tower. Originally 12th century, reworked in the 14th and 16th centuries, the church has a Romanesque porch, Romanesque nave and Gothic choir.

### INFORMATION

www.moustiers.eu

297 K10 Place de l'Église, 04360 Moustiers-Sainte-Marie 04 92 74 67 84 Jul, Aug Mon–Fri 9.30–7, Sat 9.30–12.30, 2–7; Apr–end Jun, Sep daily 10–12.30, 2–6; Mar, Oct, Nov daily 10–12.30, 2–5.30; Dec–end Feb daily 10–12, 2–5

### TIPS

» Highlight of the year is the week-long Diana festival in September, ending with the *Fête de la Nativité* procession to the chapel on 8 September.

» It's worth walking up to the chapel, if only to see the fantastic view.

**Above** *The old town of Moustiers appears to be clinging to the rockface*

**INFORMATION**

www.sisteron.com

292 J8 Place de la République, 04200 Sisteron 04 92 61 36 50

Jul, Aug Mon–Sat 9–7, Sun 10–6; Easter–end Jun, Sep–end Nov Mon–Sat 9–12, 2–6; Dec–Easter Mon–Sat 9–12, 2–5

## SISTERON

Here is an intriguing old town, a remarkable setting and an impressive hilltop citadel with a wonderful view. Sisteron, on the Route Napoléon (N85), stands at the frontier of Haute-Provençe in stupendous surroundings. The Alpine-Italianate town straddles the river Bévéra, in a narrow valley edged by cliffs, known as a *clue*. The cliffs are high, almost vertical and dramatically scored with various geological strata. The *clue* once marked the border between Provence and Dauphiné. An 11th-century bridge connects the two sides of the town and was once a tollgate. From the road bridge farther down the river there is a lovely view of the tollgate bridge and the mountains behind it.

### THE OLD TOWN

The fortified *vieille ville*, or old town, with five towers surviving from what was once a complete ring of defences, occupies a vantage point overlooking the rocky ravine. Inside the old quarter is a tangle of stepped alleys, narrow streets and covered passageways, known locally as *andrones*. There's an attractive and interesting Romanesque church—the 12th-century Notre-Dame des Pommiers—a strong, simple building with later additions.

### THE CITADEL

Sisteron's gaunt citadel (Jun–end Sep daily 9–7; Apr, May Oct daily 9–6; late Mar, early Nov daily 9–5) stands on a high ridge overlooking the town, its walls narrowing as they follow the rocky ledge. What remains—gates, towers, bastions—is very impressive, and it's well worth the climb. Napoleon Bonaparte stopped here on his march back to Paris in 1815. The citadel survived until World War II, when the Nazis used it as a garrison, strategic base and prison. Destroyed by Allied bombers on 15 August 1944, all that remains are the outer walls and the fantastic view.

### HIKING AND BIKING

The area around Sisteron takes in some of the most beautiful countryside in Provence. It's a hot spot for hikers, not least because the GR6 walking trail passes through town. This *grande randonnée* route threads its way from the Atlantic, past the Pont du Gard (▷ 88), Tarascon (▷ 95) and Forcalquier (▷ 203) to St-Paul-sur-Ubaye on the edge of the Mercantour National Park. Sisteron's tourist office has a wealth of different walking guides for sale, including one listing 17 local routes and another detailing the Gorge de la Méouge, an area of natural rock swimming pools spanned by a Roman bridge, 9km (5.5 miles) northeast of town. The Alpes-de-Haute-Provence region now boasts 1,500km (930 miles) of mountain-bike tracks. Again, the tourist office has details of several local routes and can point visitors in the right direction for bicycle hire.

**Opposite** *Sisteron's Citadel stands guard over the town*

**Below** *The church of Notre-Dame des Pommiers dates from the 12th century*

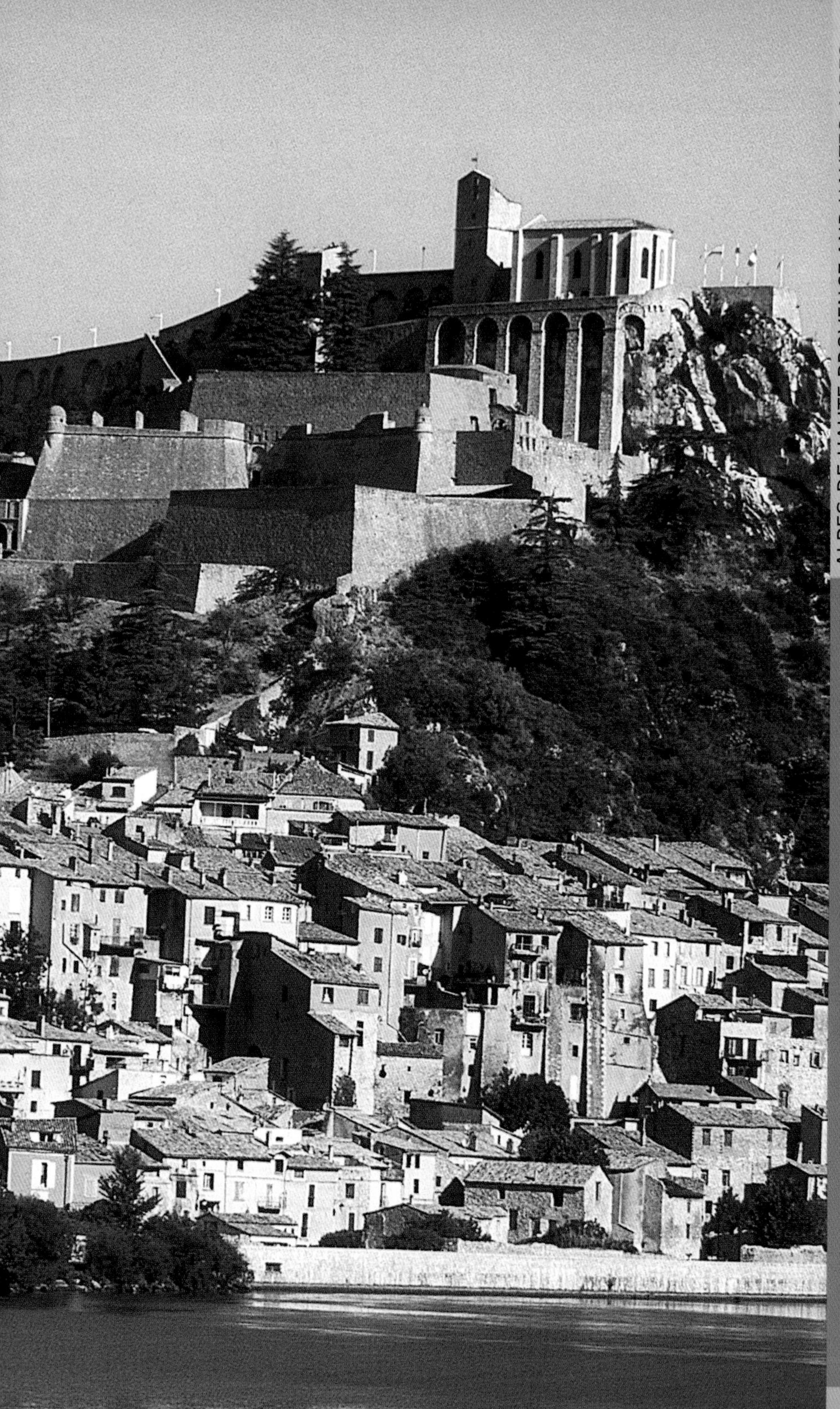

# DRIVE

# GRAND CANYON DU VERDON

**This drive offers dramatic views of the Grand Canyon du Verdon, as you follow the river west from Castellane to the vast Lac de Sainte-Croix. After refreshment in the village of Moustiers-Sainte-Marie, you return by following the Verdon's south bank—a slightly easier drive, with equally superb views.**

**THE DRIVE**
**Distance:** 137km (85 miles)
**Time:** 1 day (excluding walks)
**Start/end at:** Castellane

**BE PREPARED**
If you intend to leave your car and do any walking, ask for the walking routes from the tourist office at Castellane or Moustiers-Sainte-Marie before you set out. Always check weather conditions and take a torch (flashlight), water and food (▷ 204).

★ The hill town of Castellane (▷ 200) is a popular base for walkers and climbers, sitting at an altitude of 730m (2,372ft). The Chapelle Notre-Dame du Roc watches over the town from a rock 184m (603ft) farther up, but Castellane's main attraction is as the starting point for one of Europe's most exciting drives, along the Gorges du Verdon.

Leave Castellane from the roundabout by the Grand Hôtel du Levant, where the D952 is signed for Moustiers-Sainte-Marie. Soon you'll see the striking rock formation—the Crête des Traversières—reach for the sky above the picturesque village of Chasteuil. The road splits at the Pont de Soleils; this is the bridge you'll reach on the return route to Castellane. Bear right to stay on the D952 signed Moustiers; soon you'll enter a short tunnel. Immediately at the tunnel exit a sign on the left indicates the D23B to the Belvédère du Couloir Samson. A short, dead-end road takes you to this viewpoint, at the bottom of the Verdon valley.

❶ The Belvédère du Couloir Samson has parking spaces. From here you can follow part of a seven-hour walk to a summit called La Maline at 1,460m (4,745ft). Noticeboards emphasize the need for careful preparation, professional equipment and watchful attention to the rapidly changing water level of the river.

Back in your car, return to the D952 and turn left. Bear left in the village of Rougon, and about 1km (0.6 miles) before reaching the small village of La Palud-sur-Verdon, a sign left indicates the Route des Crêtes.

❷ The Route des Crêtes offers unforgettable views of the canyon. It climbs to the highest points of the north bank of the river, with numerous *belvédères* where you can stop and enjoy the view.

A sign indicates whether the Route des Crêtes is *ouvert* (open) or closed because of snow. If it is closed, skip to point 3. Otherwise, turn off onto the dramatic road. When you reach the Pas de la Baou, at an altitude of 1,285m (4,176ft), the river is 715m (2,313ft) below. From these heights, the road starts to descend and there are expansive views to the west, with frequent sightings of the route on the south bank that you will follow later. But don't take your eyes from the road: There are few safety barriers or walls around these hairpinned descents. You are likely to encounter walkers along this stretch until the road returns you to La Palud-sur-Verdon, where you can pause for coffee.

❸ La Palud-sur-Verdon is a good place to visit if you enjoy outdoor activities. You can rent mountain bicycles or find a guided walk or climb. The town hall, in a small chateau, has an exhibition on the geology, flora and fauna of the area.

Turn left on the D952, signed for Moustiers. As the road reaches the end of the Grand Canyon, there are tremendous views to the Lac de Sainte-Croix, which on a sunny day glows an almost luminous blue. At a roundabout, bear right to Moustiers-Sainte-Marie—an ideal place to eat lunch.

❹ Moustiers-Sainte-Marie (▷ 207) is known for its faïence (fine glazed ceramics) and for a gilded star suspended on a chain between two rock faces. The star is replaced whenever the chain breaks—about twice every century. The current star measures nearly 1.15m (4ft) across.

Leave Moustiers by retracing your route back to the roundabout, going straight over on the D957 and following the sign for Aiguines. The road crosses a bridge where the Verdon river flows into the lake. You can rent kayaks and electric boats here and take them for a short distance beneath the steep canyon walls. Shortly, take a left turn onto the D19 to Aiguines.

❺ Aiguines has a privately owned chateau with tiled turrets, which is a picturesque sight as you approach the village from below. Park in the road in the heart of the village and go by foot down steps on the right to a small arcade of artisanal shops. One of these specializes in the production of beautiful handmade *santons* (small figurines).

Continue along the D19 as it climbs out of Aiguines and stop at the orientation table about 1km (0.6 miles) farther on. The river and views are now mainly on your left, with numerous stopping places and well-signed viewing points. Care should be taken on these sometimes narrow corners, and especially at a short series of mini-tunnels cut into the rock face—the Tunnel de Fayet. The last of the viewing opportunities is at the Balcons de la Mescla.

❻ The Balcons de la Mescla has a bar-restaurant where you can stop for refreshments and enjoy more superb views.

After several kilometres, watch for signs to Trigance and a Maison de l'Information. Turn left onto the recently surfaced stretch of road and descend to the village.

❼ Trigance has small shops, a well, an art gallery and the last working water-powered flour mill in Provence, all dominated by a sombre chateau recently converted into a family-run luxury hotel.

The tourist office is a farther 5km (3 miles) out of the heart of the village. Follow the road as it skirts Trigance to the south. At an intersection with the D955, turn right; the tourist office is on the right after 500m (545 yards).

❽ The tourist office has excellent displays about local geology and you can also buy local produce there, including wonderful Provençal soap.

Head back along the D955 until you reach the Pont de Soleils; turn right on the D952 to return to Castellane.

**WHEN TO GO**

July and August are best avoided, as the roads will be jam-packed.

**INFORMATION**

**CASTELLANE TOURIST INFORMATION**

▷ 200.

**MOUSTIERS TOURIST INFORMATION**

▷ 207.

**WHERE TO EAT**

**LA TREILLE MUSCATE**

✉ Place de l'Église, Moustiers-Sainte-Marie ☎ 04 92 74 64 31 🕐 Fri–Wed 12–2, 7.30–10. Closed mid-Nov to end Jan

**Opposite** *The scenic Routes des Crêtes*

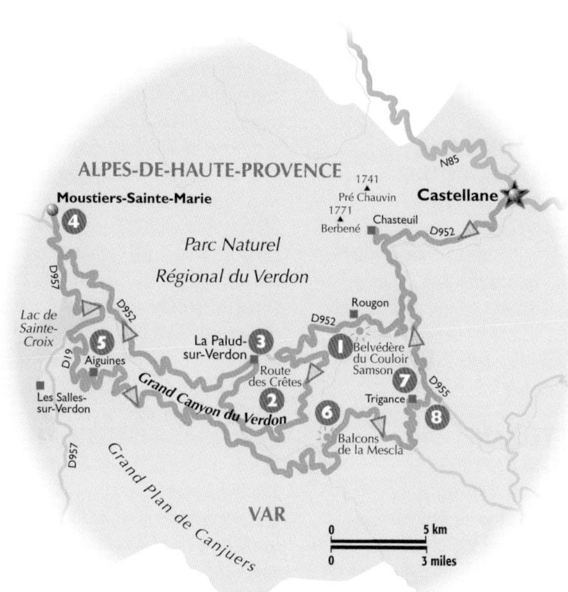

# WHAT TO DO

## BARCELONNETTE

### CINÉ UBAYE

This two-screen cinema shows general releases in a jam-packed calendar, mostly in their original language.
Rue Mercier, 04400 Barcelonnette 04 92 81 37 26 Tue–Sun 3–9pm €8

### ÉCOLE DE PARAPENTE DE LA VALLÉE DE L'UBAYE

www.ubaye-parapente.com
Discover the beautiful Ubaye valley from the sky on a paraglide, accompanied by an instructor. In winter, you can wear your skis!
Le Pont Long, 04400 Barcelonnette 04 92 81 34 93 All year long by appointment From €45

### RANDO PASSION

www.rando-passion.com
Try a wide range of activities with Rando Passion. In winter there's cross-country skiing, snowshoeing and the possibility of spending the night in an igloo. In summer, you can hike and mountain bicycle.
31 rue Jules Béraud (start points vary), 04400 Barcelonnette 04 92 81 43 34 Cross-country skiing 2.5-hour class: €19; one-day mountain bicycle rental: €25; luge descent €39

## BREIL-SUR-ROYA

### LOISIRS MERCANTOUR

www.loisirs-mercantour.com
The central reservation point for a host of outdoor activities in the Roya Valley, from sled riding in Casterino to white-water rafting near Sospel.
394 route St-Pierre, 06540 Breil-sur-Roya 04 93 04 92 05 Mountain snowshoe tour €25

## CASTELLANE

### ABOARD RAFTING

www.aboard-rafting.com
Experience the thrill of white-water rafting through the gorges of Verdon or see waterfalls and natural pools by canoe. You can avoid getting wet by renting a mountain bicycle and seeing the area on two wheels.
8 place de l'Église, 04120 Castellane 04 92 83 76 11 Apr to mid-Oct daily 9–7 Day rafting €50

## DIGNE-LES-BAINS

### DECATHLON

www.decathlon.fr
Camping, hiking and mountain-biking equipment for exploring Digne's wild environs.
5 route de Marseille, 04000 Digne-les-Bains 04 92 36 67 50 Mon–Sat 9–7.30

### GOLF DE DIGNE LES BAINS

www.golfdignelalavande.com
You'll get wonderful views from this 18-hole course, nestled between mountains. A restaurant, two-star hotel, swimming pool and tennis court are also on site.
57 route du Chaffaut, 04000 Digne-les-Bains 04 92 30 58 00 Daily 9–6 (mid-Jul to end Aug 8–8) Green fee €36.70–€53

### RÉSERVE NATURELLE GÉOLOGIQUE DE HAUTE PROVENCE

www.resgeol04.org
Explore this nature reserve following one of the many trails, then learn more at the three museums: 'Earth and Time' in Sisteron, 'Fossils' in Castellane and the 'Walking Museum' in Digne-les-Bains.
Parc St-Benoît, 04005 Digne-les-Bains 04 92 36 70 70 Earth and Time museum: Jun–end Sep Tue–Sat 9–12, 2–6. Closed Oct–end May. Fossils museum: May–end Sep Wed–Mon 10–1, 3–6.30. Closed Oct–end Apr. Walking Museum: Jul, Aug Mon–Fri 9–1, 2–7, Sat, Sun 10.30–12.30, 2–7; Apr–end Jun, Sep, Oct Sat–Thu 9–12, 2–5.30, Fri 9–12, 2–4.30; Nov–end Mar Mon–Fri 9–12, 2–5.30. Park: Apr–end Oct daily 8–7; Nov–end Mar Mon–Fri 8–7 Earth and Time museum: adult €2.50; Fossils museum: adult €4; Walking museum: adult €4.60; reduced prices for children; under 4 free

### ROCHER DE NEUF HEURES

www.ot-dignelesbains.fr
Traverse the zip lines and metal stairs across the Alps, on this 500m-long beginners trail, which opened in 2009, a short walk from Digne. Equipment is available on site, or from Digne's tourist office.
Rocher de Neuf Heures, 04000 Digne-les-Bains 04 92 36 62 62 Apr–Oct daily Adult €12, child €10

### SAVEURS ET COULEURS

The tastes *(saveurs)* and colours are those of Provence: fine oils, vinegars, prepared dishes, alcohol, perfumes, Marseille soap, plaids and tablecloths made from Provençal fabrics and other decorative items made of olive wood and terracotta. The store also stocks products from Hédiard, a famous Parisian *épicerie*.
7 boulevard Gassendi, 04000 Digne-les-Bains 04 92 36 04 06 Tue–Sat 8.30–12.30, 2.30–7

### TRAIN DES PIGNES

www.trainprovence.com
Since 1891, a single steam-powered carriage has chugged along a track linking the Alps to Provence. The train is a stylish way to see Provence's mountain scenery.
Espace Pierre Ferrié, 04000 Digne-les-Bains 04 92 31 01 58 May–end Oct daily from 7am From €13 (€35.30 to Nice and back)

## ENTREVAUX

### PAIN D'EPICERIE

This shop is laden with regional foodstuffs, including honey, which is poured from a huge vat. Jams, cheese and liqueurs are also sold.
Rue de Marché, 04320 Entrevaux 04 93 05 49 89 Thu–Tue 9–12, 3–5.30

## ESPARRON

### CLUB NAUTIQUE D'ESPARRON DE VERDON

http://cnev.online.fr
Learn the basics of sailing in three to five half-day lessons. Authorized

Fédération Française de Voile (French Sailing Federation) techniques are taught on the Lac d'Esparron; classes are suitable for ages seven and up.
✉ Le port, 04800 Esparron de Verdont ☎ 04 92 77 15 25 ✋ €86–€135

## FORCALQUIER

### DISTILLERIES ET DOMAINES DE PROVENCE

www.distilleries-provence.com
Since 1898, this distillery has been producing the 'Pastis Henri Bardouin', a local speciality. Other Provençal liqueurs are also available.
✉ Z.A. Les Chalus, 04300 Forcalquier ☎ 04 92 75 15 41 ⌚ Jul, Aug Mon–Sat 9–7, Sun 9–12; Apr–end Jun, Sep–end Dec Mon, Wed–Sat 9–12, 2–8. Closed Jan–end Mar

## GRÉOUX-LES-BAINS

### ETABLISSEMENT THERMAL DE GRÉOUX-LES-BAINS

www.chainethermale.fr
Thermal cures have been practised at Gréoux for more than two millennia. These baths, surrounded by luxuriant parkland, specialize in both health and relaxation, using hot pools, hydrotherapy, massage and water gymnastics.
✉ Quai des Hautes Plaines, 04800 Gréoux-les-Bains ☎ 0826 468 185 ⌚ Mid-Mar to mid-Dec Mon–Sat ✋ €49 for discovery package (4 treatments)

### GRAND CASINO DE GRÉOUX-LES-BAINS

www.casinogreoux.com
Alongside the casino and its games room, you'll find a bar and restaurant. There is a tea dance every Wednesday 4–7pm. The interior follows a Venetian theme, with masks and candelabras.
✉ Avenue des Thermes, 04800 Gréoux-les-Bains ☎ 04 92 78 00 00 ⌚ Daily 10am–4am

## MANOSQUE

### MOULIN DE L'OLIVETTE

www.moulinolivette.fr
Buy produce from the region's olive groves from this agricultural cooperative. Pressing and bottling takes place on site and you can visit the mill in November and December, when it is in operation just after the harvest. The oil produced here bears the 'AOC' label and won the prestigious Concours Général Agricole de Paris in 2007.
✉ Place de l'Olivette, 04000 Manosque ☎ 04 92 72 00 99 ⌚ Jul, Aug daily 8–12, 2.30–6.30; Sep–end Jun daily 8–12, 2–6.30

### LA REMISE DU PAYSAN

You'll find a great selection of local produce at this grocery, including fruit and vegetables, vintages of olive oil, fine vinegar and fruit juices.
✉ Avenue Georges Pompidou, 04100 Manosque ☎ 04 92 87 33 37 ⌚ Mon–Sat 8–12.30, 3–7.30, Sun 7–1

## MOUSTIERS-SAINTE-MARIE

### ATELIER SOLEIL

www.soleil-deux.fr
In a former oil mill, this studio produces faïence. You can browse the beautiful collection of vases, plates and pitchers.
✉ Chemin Marcel Provence, 04360 Moustiers-Sainte-Marie ☎ 04 92 74 63 05 ⌚ Mar–end Nov daily 9–6.30; Dec–end Feb Mon–Fri 9–5

### NOËL VOYER

www.verdon-vtt.fr
You can rent mountain bicycles for all the family here, including helmets and baby seats. The company can also provide guiding services for groups/families of 5–12.
✉ Chateau Ségriès, 04360 Moustiers-Sainte-Marie ☎ 04 92 74 68 83 ✋ Bicycle rental €13 for a morning, €19 per day

## LA PALUD

### LE PERROQUET VERT

www.leperroquetvert.com
This is the first stop for climbers and outdoor enthusiasts hoping to tackle the nearby Gorges du Verdon. It also rents inexpensive double rooms.
✉ Rue Grande, 04120 La-Palud-sur-Verdon ☎ 04 92 77 33 39 ⌚ May–end Aug daily 9–7; Mar, Apr, Sep, Oct Tue–Sun 10–6

## PRA-LOUP

### STATION DE PRA-LOUP

www.praloup.com
In winter, 53 ski lifts take you up the slopes, at an altitude of up to 2,500m (8,200ft). In summer, activities include paragliding, rafting, canyoning and mountain bicycling.
✉ Tourist office: Maison de Pra-Loup, 04400 Pra-Loup ☎ 04 92 84 10 04 ✋ Ski pass: adult €29 per day, child (6–12) and over 64 €24, under 6 and over 75 free

## ST-JACQUES

### FERME AUBERGE DU DOMAINE D'AIGUINES

This farm specializes in ducks. Products for sale include foie gras, pâté, gizzard, breast and rillettes. The farm is coupled with an inn offering duck dishes.
✉ Le Village, 04330 St-Jacques ☎ 04 92 34 25 72 ⌚ Opening hours vary; call before you visit

# FESTIVALS AND EVENTS

## JULY

### BARCELONNETTE FÊTE DU JAZZ

www.barcelonnette.com
International jazz festival.
✉ Barcelonnette ⌚ Two weeks, mid-Jul

## AUGUST

### CORSO DE LA LAVANDE

A celebration of lavender.
✉ Digne-les-Bains ⌚ Five days around the 1st weekend in Aug

## SEPTEMBER/OCTOBER

### TERRES D'ÉTOILE

Every year, the ceramicists of Moustiers-Sainte-Marie celebrate the lighting of the kiln fires for a new season. Over a period of one week the new styles are fired and put on display in venues around the town.
✉ Moustiers-Sainte-Marie ☎ 04 92 74 67 84 (tourist office) ⌚ End Sep–early Oct

# EATING

**Above** *Café de la Poste, Manosque*

**PRICES AND SYMBOLS**

The prices given are the average for a two-course lunch (L) and a three-course dinner (D) for one person, without drinks. The wine price is for the least expensive bottle.

For a key to the symbols, ▷ 2.

## BRIANÇON

### RESTAURANT LES ÉCRINS

Just outside Briançon, this wooden-beamed restaurant focuses on hearty local mountain cuisine, including *raclette*, grilled local trout and pork in cider sauce.

✉ 11 place du Champ de Mars, 05100 Briançon ☎ 04 92 20 35 16 🕐 Thu–Mon 12–2, 7–10.30, Tue 12–2 L €20, D €25, Wine €15

## CASTELLANE

### AUBERGE DU TEILLON

www.auberge-teillon.com

This former coaching inn, in a small hamlet outside Castellane, offers good-quality dishes at a reasonable price. It's ideal if you are touring the Gorges du Verdon region.

✉ Route Napoléon, La Garde, 04120 Castellane ☎ 04 92 83 60 88 🕐 Jul, Aug Wed–Mon 12–2.30, 7–10, Tue 7–10; mid-Mar to end Jun, Sep to mid-Nov Tue–Sat 12–2.30, 7–10, Sun 12–2.30 L €25, D €35, Wine €14

## CHÂTEAU-ARNOUX

### L'OUSTAOU DE LA FOUN

A house built of Durance stone, with an internal courtyard and fountain, is home to this restaurant. One dining room has exposed stone; the other is vaulted. The finest ingredients are used. The langoustines, Sisteron lamb and truffle dishes (in season) are excellent.

✉ RN 85, 04160 Château-Arnoux ☎ 04 92 62 65 30 🕐 Apr–end Dec Tue–Sat 12–2, 7.15–9.30, Sun 12–2 L €30, D €45, Wine €16

## DABISSE

### LE VIEUX COLOMBIER

This 19th-century coaching inn on the banks of the Durance has a rustic dining room and tree-lined terrace. It serves classic French dishes.

✉ D4, 04190 La Bastide Dabisse ☎ 04 92 34 32 32 🕐 Mon–Sat 12–2, 7.30–11. Closed first two weeks Jan L €30, D €45, Wine €15

## DIGNE-LES-BAINS

### L'OLIVIER

www.resto-lolivier.fr

Enjoy beautifully presented refined cuisine. Starters include snail kebabs with lardons and foie gras with lavender honey. The ten meaty mains include shoulder of lamb with olive confit.

✉ 1 rue des Monges, 04000 Digne-les-Bains ☎ 04 92 31 47 41 🕐 Tue–Sat 12–1.30, 7.15–9.30 L €20, D €30, Wine €15

## ENTREVAUX

### LE VAUBAN

www.hotel-le-vauban.com

Order the local speciality, *secca d'Entrevaux* (cured beef) or opt for one of Chef Fabrice's hearty dishes, such as tasty Daube Provençale (slow-cooked beef stew). In summer, dine on the shady terrace, against the picturesque backdrop of Entrevaux village.

✉ Hôtel Le Vauban, place Moreau, 04320 Entrevaux ☎ 04 93 05 42 40 🕐 Daily 12–2.30, 7.30–9.30 L €12, D €17, Wine €15

## FORCALQUIER

### TERRASSES DE LA BASTIDE

Chef Joël Juglaret presides over the Provençal and Savoyard dishes at this country inn, 2km (1.3 miles) from Forcalquier centre. A host of inexpensive set menus accompany the à la carte selection, which includes scallops and bean tagine, and pigeon with lavender honey.

✉ Restanque de Beaudines, 04300 Forcalquier ☎ 04 92 73 32 35 🕐 Mid-Jun to mid-Sep daily 12–2, 7–10; mid-Sep to mid-Jun Wed–Sat 12–2, 7–10, Tue 7–10, Sun 12–2 L €18, D €25, Wine €15

## FOUX D'ALLOS

### LE VERDON

www.restaurant-leverdon.com

This restaurant is in an imposing chalet in the Foux d'Allos ski resort. The rustic interior has wood and exposed bricks, while outside, the sunny terrace gives wonderful views of the mountain. The place is famous for pizza, but you can also enjoy cheese fondue, *confit de canard*, grilled fish and many other dishes.

✉ Galerie Commerciale, 04260 Foux d'Allos ☎ 04 92 83 83 77 🕑 Jun to mid-Sep, Dec–end Apr daily 12–2, 7–9.30 L €20, D €28, Wine €10

## GAP

### PATALAIN

This grand bourgeois dining room is in a fine late 19th-century mansion. As befits the setting, the menu is classical French (dishes include veal cutlets and foie gras terrine) and the service professional yet discreet. There's also a beautiful garden terrace for alfresco lunches and dinners. Enjoy the setting and the excellent food.

✉ 2 place Ladoucette, 05000 Gap ☎ 04 92 52 30 83 🕑 Mon–Sat 12–2, 7.30–9.30. Closed 26 Dec to mid-Jan L €30, D €40, Wine €20

## MANOSQUE

### CAFÉ DE LA POSTE

www.cafedelaposte.com

This café and its terrace look onto the city's oldest public garden. Inside there is contemporary decor. Enjoy salad and cold platters, or more elaborate dishes such as foie gras with fig marmalade, Calabrian spaghetti and steak tartare. There are some excellent vegetarian options.

✉ Rue Reine-Jeanne, 04100 Manosque ☎ 04 92 72 69 02 🕑 Mon–Sat 7am–1am L €18, D €25, Wine €12

### LE SOUBEYRAN

Despite the kooky 1970s-style interior, this restaurant is an excellent choice for inexpensive, classic French cuisine. Cassoulet and *steak au poivre* feature alongside a few culinary blasts from the past, prawns marie-rose included.

✉ 3 boulevard Tilleuls, 04100 Manosque ☎ 04 92 72 54 82 🕑 Tue–Sun 12–12.30, 7–10 L €20, D €30, Wine €15

### LE TABLE DE PRÉ SAINT MICHEL

Enjoy expert takes on hearty, country cuisine, dished up by wonderfully friendly staff. Reserve a table for inventive starters (foie gras terrine with fig chutney) and hearty mains (sea bass fillet with onion compote). A three-course set menu (€25) is also available.

✉ Route de Dauphin, 04100 Manosque ☎ 04 92 72 512 79 🕑 Mon–Fri 12–2, 7–10, Sat 7–11 L €20, D €30, Wine €16

### LES VOÛTES DU MONT D'OR

In a 17th-century cotton mill, this elegant restaurant has attractive vaults, along with Parisian-style street lamps and a tile floor. Chef Rémy Tchekemian uses the finest local ingredients and impeccable presentation to excite the taste buds.

✉ La Filature, 43 boulevard des Tilleuls, 04100 Manosque ☎ 04 92 72 32 28 🕑 Tue–Sat 12–2, 7.30–9.30, Sun 12–2 L €20, D €35, Wine €14

## MOUSTIERS-SAINTE-MARIE

### LA BASTIDE DE MOUSTIERS

www.bastide-moustiers.com

This gorgeous 17th-century Provençal *bastide* (country house) is owned by renowned master chef Alain Ducasse, who took personal charge of the renovations. The restaurant is managed with great aplomb by his personally chosen team. The menu changes daily, taking into account what is in season in the vast *bastide* gardens or at local markets, but every dish displays its haute-cuisine pedigree. The price remains reasonable for the quality. The restaurant is part of a four-star inn (▷ 217).

✉ Chemin de Quinson, 04360 Moustiers-Sainte-Marie ☎ 04 92 70 47 47 🕑 Mar–end Dec Thu–Mon 12.30–2, 7.30–9.30. Closed Jan, Feb L €40, D €60, Wine €40

### FERME SAINTE-CÉCILE

www.ferme-ste-cecile.com

The restaurant is in a former 18th-century hillside farm. The interior has beamed ceilings, white wooden chairs and cheerful blue-and-yellow tablecloths. The menu makes the most of local ingredients, including scallops in chanterelle sauce and veal cannelloni. In fine weather, opt for the terrace and enjoy views of the surrounding mountains.

✉ Route des Gorges du Verdon, 04360 Moustiers-Sainte-Marie ☎ 04 92 74 64 18 🕑 Tue–Sun, holiday Mons 12–2, 7–9. Closed Jan, Feb L €30, D €45, Wine €20

## SISTERON

### LES BECS FINS

http://becsfins.free.fr

Chef and owner Raphaël Videau masters rustic local specialities: lamb terrine with thyme and mint and home-made foie gras. A pleasant shaded terrace looks onto a pedestrian-only street.

✉ 16 rue Saunerie, 04200 Sisteron ☎ 04 92 61 12 04 🕑 Mon, Tue, Thu–Sat 12–1.30, 7–9.30, Sun 12–1.30 (daily Jul, Aug) L €17, D €30, Wine €12

### LA CITADELLE

This is a great place to try local dishes, including stuffed mutton tripe, Sisteron lamb and frozen nougat. Dishes include sea bass with garlic mayonnaise and, in season, there's a game menu.

✉ 126 rue Saunerie, 04200 Sisteron ☎ 04 92 61 13 52 🕑 Daily 12–2.30, 7.30–10 L €20, D €30, Wine €10

### LE RATELIER

www.la-bouisse.com

You'll find traditional cuisine at this unpretentious, friendly eatery. Sisteron is famous for its lamb, and the house speciality has it grilled and served with a garlic sauce. For a real local experience, try the *pied paquets* (stuffed mutton tripe). There is an as-much-as-you-can-eat hors d'oeuvre buffet.

✉ 55 place Paul Arène, 04200 Sisteron ☎ 04 92 61 01 83 🕑 Feb–end Dec Mon–Sat 12–2, 7.30–9.30. Closed Jan L €14, D €25, Wine €15

# STAYING

**Above** *La Bastide de Moustiers, in Moustiers-Sainte-Marie*

### PRICES AND SYMBOLS

Prices are the lowest and highest for a double room for one night. Each listing states whether breakfast is included. All the hotels listed accept credit cards unless otherwise stated. Note that rates vary widely throughout the year.

For a key to the symbols, ▷ 2.

## BARCELONNETTE

### CHEZ ARLETTE SIGNORET

www.domainedelara.com

With only five bedrooms, there's an intimate atmosphere in this cottage, a couple of kilometres from Pra-Loup and Sauze ski resorts. Inside, there are beamed ceilings and antique furniture. You can dine with your hostess. Credit cards are not accepted.

✉ Domaine de Lara, St-Pons, 04000 Barcelonnette ☎ 04 92 81 52 81 €75–€84 5

## CHÂTEAU-ARNOUX

### LA BONNE ETAPE

www.bonneetape.com

Rooms in this ancient ivy-covered *bastide* (country house) are a picture of period luxury. Original art, wooden bedsteads and high linen counts can be found in each room, and the lounge is filled with club chairs and antiques. There's a luxurious swimming pool and parking too.

✉ Chemin du Lac, 04160 Château-Arnoux, ☎ 04 92 64 00 09 Closed Jan €98–€116, excluding breakfast (€12) 18 Outdoor

## DIGNE-LES-BAINS

### HOTEL CENTRAL

www.lhotel-central.com

This great-value family-run hotel in downtown Digne has heaps of information about hiking and biking in the surrounding countryside. Rooms are simple, but come with sturdy beds, TV, WiFi and a view over the quiet streets below.

✉ 28 boulevard Gassendi, 04000 Digne-les-Bains ☎ 04 92 31 31 91 €41–€55, excluding breakfast (€6) 8

## ENTREVAUX

### HOTEL LE VAUBAN

www.hotel-le-vauban.com

Overlooking the fortified village of Entrevaux, this is a relaxed family-run hotel with a country restaurant attached. The rooms are resolutely simple but are clean and quiet. Parking is available, as is a full-board tariff.

✉ Place Moreau, 04320 Entrevaux ☎ 04 93 05 42 40 €50–€65, excluding breakfast (€7) 8 rooms

## FORCALQUIER

### AUBERGE CHAREMBEAU

www.charembeau.com

This two-star country inn, close to the picturesque village of Niozelles, is in an 18th-century farmhouse. Some rooms can take up to four people and have a kitchenette. There's a tennis court outside.

✉ Route de Niozelles, 04300 Forcalquier ☎ 04 92 70 91 70 Closed mid-Oct to end Feb €58–€100, excluding breakfast (€9) 23 Outdoor

## GAP

### HOTEL LE CLOS

www.leclos.fr

A landscaped garden surrounds this comfortable two-star hotel. There is a large restaurant on site and the terrace is popular with diners in summer. Rooms are simple and comfortable.

✉ 20ter, avenue Cdt Dumont, 05000 Gap ☎ 04 92 51 37 04 Closed late Oct–end Nov €48–€61, excluding breakfast (€8) 29

## GORGES DU VERDON

### AUBERGE DU POINT SUBLIME

This family-owned *auberge* (inn) sits in the stunning wild landscapes of the Gorges du Verdon region. Rooms are clean and simple and there's a restaurant on site offering a good country-style menu. For those who are keen on walking, there are numerous walking and hiking trails in the region. The *auberge* makes a good budget stopover.

✉ D952, 04120 Rougon
☎ 04 92 83 60 35
🕒 Closed mid-Oct to mid-Apr ✋ €61, excluding breakfast (€8) 🛈 13

## MONETIER-LES-BAINS

### AUBERGE DU CHOUCAS

www.aubergeduchoucas.com

In the heart of the Serre-Chevalier ski area, this 17th-century farmhouse offers an elegant base for both summer and winter stays. The restaurant serves regional cuisine and the ski lifts are within walking distance.

✉ Rue de la Fruitier, 05220 Monetier-les-Bains ☎ 04 92 24 42 73 ✋ €80–€200, excluding breakfast (€17) 🛈 12

## MOUSTIERS-SAINTE-MARIE

### LA BASTIDE DE MOUSTIERS

www.bastide-moustiers.com

This 17th-century cottage turned four-star inn houses one of chef Alain Ducasse's restaurants (▷ 215). The 12 sumptuous bedrooms are named after local ingredients and each is decorated according to its name.

✉ Chemin de Quinson, 04360 Moustiers-Sainte-Marie ☎ 04 92 70 47 47
✋ €190–€370, excluding breakfast (€20)
🛈 12 ❄ 🏊 Outdoor

### LA FERME ROSE

www.lafermerose.com

The pink *(rose)* facade gave this two-star inn its name. Inside there are beamed ceilings, a tile floor and, in the restaurant, bistro furniture and some 1950s-style pieces such as a jukebox. Enjoy breakfast in the garden in summer.

✉ 04360 Moustiers-Sainte-Marie ☎ 04 92 75 75 75 🕒 Closed mid-Jan to mid-Mar, Nov–Christmas ✋ €78–€148, excluding breakfast (€9.50) 🛈 11

## SISTERON

### HOTEL DU COURS

www.hotel-lecours.com

Guest rooms are a cut above the area's average here, with elegant decor, a minibar and air conditioning. Some have views over Sisteron and its ancient city walls. As well as a central location, Hotel du Cours has a great restaurant that serves dishes on a leafy terrace in summer, or under a beamed ceiling in spring and autumn.

✉ Place de l'Église, 04200 Sisteron
☎ 04 92 61 04 51 🕒 Closed Dec–end Feb ✋ €75–€90, excluding breakfast (€10)
🛈 45 ❄

**Below** *Beautiful flowers mark the entrance of an* auberge *in Barcelonette*

# VAUCLUSE

Vaucluse is the true heart of Provence. Pale-stone villages clutch perilously to hilltops, backed by sheer blue skies. Below them, verdant vineyards roll along, alternating with fields of dazzling purple lavender. Old ochre quarries surround the russet-hued town houses of Roussillon, glowing a deep fiery red at sunset. This fragrant wilderness, stretching loosely from Vaison-la-Romaine in the north to Ansouis in the south, is prettier than any picture.

Outdoor enthusiasts will no doubt be drawn to the craggy, snow-capped summit of Mont Ventoux, its ascent a legendary stage in the Tour de France. The prominent landmark is visible from pretty much anywhere in the region. Nearby, the Parc Naturel du Lubéron provides more gentle activities, including trekking, climbing, cross-country cycling and bird-spotting.

The region is also home to jaw-dropping Roman ruins, including Orange's Théâtre Antique, with its perfectly preserved stage wall, and Pont Julien, dating from the third century AD, just north of Bonnieux. But it was really one thousand years later, when papal headquarters were temporarily shifted to Avignon during the 14th century, that attention focused here.

Today, vibrant Avignon still dominates the region culturally, economically and spiritually. Tourists pour through the preserved walls of the city to visit the vast Palais des Papes (Pope's Palace), clamber along Pont St-Bénézet over the river Rhône or attend its biggest annual event, the *Festival d'Avignon*. Wine-lovers should take time out for a trip to nearby Châteauneuf-du-Pape, where the popes spent their summers, cultivating what have become exceptionally fine wines.

## ABBAYE DE SÉNANQUE

One of the 'Three Sisters' of the Cistercians in Provence, the Abbaye de Sénanque has a pure and simple beauty. It stands in the quiet, attractively wooded little valley of the Senancole, 4km (2.5 miles) upstream from Gordes (▷ 231), at the foot of the Plateau of Vaucluse. Lavender is cultivated beside it, beautiful with bright purple blooms in early summer. The honeyed stone abbey was built in the 12th century by the Cistercian Order, as the third—and last—of their monasteries in Provence. The three monasteries were known as the 'Three Cistercian Sisters of Provence'. The other two were Silvacane (▷ 61) and Le Thoronet (▷ 117). The sturdy, unadorned Romanesque main building is a perfect example of the Cistercian style.

### AN ENDURING COMMUNITY

The community dedicated itself to austerity and hard work, received many gifts, and prospered for a period. It went into decline after being attacked by the local sect known as the Vaudois in 1544. However, the damaged buildings were repaired at the beginning of the 18th century, and the monastery survived. It has remained in continuous occupation throughout its history, except for 60 years following the anti-religious violence of the French Revolution and also in the years 1969–88.

### MONASTIC LIFE

The abbey buildings at Sénanque today are still partly occupied by a Cistercian monastery, with a pious atmosphere and a rule of silence—which visitors, too, are requested to respect. Notices advise that Sénanque abbey is not a tourist site but a place of monastic life. At present, all visitors must join a guided tour (in French only, although multilingual explanations are handed out at the start of each tour). Off the central courtyard extends a long, cool stone dormitory block under a barrel vault: Here 30 monks would sleep—fully clothed—on straw mattresses on the floor. This leads into the abbey church, its extremely plain appearance slightly softened by the rounded lines of the Romanesque pillars and arches. There is some modern stained glass, in a suitably simple style, added in 1994. The church is almost unique in facing north instead of east. Outside, the cloisters are at the heart of the abbey. The cloister pillars are decorated with carved capitals with simplified motifs of flowers and foliage. There is also a 'calefactory', which was the only heated room in the monastery and was where the monks worked.

### INFORMATION

www.senanque.fr

295 F9 Abbaye Notre-Dame de Sénanque, 84220 Gordes 04 90 72 05 72 Guided tours: Jul, Aug Mon–Sat 9.50, 10.10, 10.30, 2.30, 2.50, 3.10, 3.30, 3.45, 4, 4.15, 4.30, Sun afternoon tours only; Jun, Sep Mon–Sat 10.10, 10.30, 2.30, 3.10, 3.30, 4.10, 4.30, Sun afternoon tours only; Apr, May Mon–Sat 10.10, 10.30, 2.30, 3.30, 4.30, Sun afternoon tours only; Feb, Mar, Oct–early Nov Mon–Sat 10.30, 2.30, 3.30, 4.30, Sun afternoon tours only; mid-Nov to end Jan daily 2.50, 4.20 Adult €7, child (6–18) €3, under 6 free All visitors must join a guided tour (in French)

### TIPS

» After your visit, buy lavender oils and soaps, handmade by the monks.
» Closure is very prompt.
» Dress modestly.

**Opposite** *A path of lavender leads to the Abbaye de Sénanque*
**Below** *The abbey dates from the 12th century*

**INFORMATION**

www.tourisme-ansouis.com
295 G10 Place du Château, 84240 Ansouis 04 90 09 86 98 Tue–Fri 10–12, 2–6, Sat 10–12

**TIP**

» The Musée de la Vigne et du Vin (Wine Museum), on route de Pertuis (Sep–end Jun Mon, Tue, Thu–Sat 9.30–12, 2.30–6; Jul, Aug Mon–Sat 9.30–1, 2.30–7) is just outside Ansouis, in the Château Turcan. The chateau is still a working vineyard and visitors are encouraged to sample and purchase wines directly from the owners.

# ANSOUIS

Pretty Ansouis is well off the beaten track, 5km (3 miles) from the D973 midway between the small towns of Cadenet and Pertuis. The village is on the south-facing side of a rocky crest on the summit of which stands a palatial chateau (accessible by guided tour only, Wed–Mon 2.30, 3.45; contact the tourist office for details). Originally a 12th-century fortress, it was modernized and made more elegant during the Renaissance. More of a large country house than a castle, it has impressive halls and rooms, a large kitchen and superb formal gardens arranged on terraces (closed to visitors). Although the chateau was the private home of the Sabran-Pontevès family for several centuries, it was sold to new owners in 2008. The building underwent extensive renovations, before reopening to the public in 2010.

## DUAL-IDENTITY CHATEAU

Viewing the chateau from the north, you're faced with an impenetrable fortress, part of the original building. As you move around the exterior, the scene changes to an 18th-century mansion, with gardens and terraces. The interior, too, reflects this dual identity. There are reminders of the chateau's fortress days on the ground floor, with weapons and armour. Upstairs, there are Flemish tapestries and elegant Italian-Renaissance furniture. The Provençal kitchen dates from the 18th century. Visitors are not allowed access to the exquisite garden, but you can get a lovely view of it from the upstairs gallery.

## A CELIBATE COUPLE

St-Martin's church, next to the chateau, contains busts of two 13th-century saints, St. Delphine and St. Elzéar. Delphine, the daughter of an aristocratic family, took a vow of chastity as a young woman and not even marriage pursuaded her to break it. She accepted a politically arranged marriage with Elzéar, son of the Sabran family, in a deal intended to unite support for Charles II of Naples, but she kept her chastity pledge. Elzéar also made a pledge, and the pious pair lived together in celibacy, although Elzéar soon died. Delphine lived another 37 years, patiently enduring poverty and carrying out good works.

## EXTRAORDINARY MUSEUM

Created by artist and scuba expert Georges Mazoyer, the quirky Musée Extraordinaire, in rue du Vieux Moulin (Sep–end Jun daily 2–6; Jul, Aug daily 2–7) has fossils, coral, artworks and installations created from items collected during more than four decades of deep-sea diving.

**Below** *The hills surrounding Ansouis*

## APT

www.ot-apt.fr

Apt is a busy, lightly industrial country town, with tree-shaded squares, fountains and a vibrant street market every Saturday. It's the main town for the Lubéron area and has Roman origins. Its prosperity is partly thanks to agriculture, although ochre-processing is also important—the ochre quarries are nearby.

The heart of Apt has the typical appearance of a busy Provençal inland town, with stone houses, red-tile roofs, narrow old streets and pretty squares. The main square is place de la Bouquerie.

Apt's main sight is the former cathedral church of Sainte-Anne, whose two crypts date from the 4th and 11th centuries. Two 14th-century stained-glass windows at the end of the apse depict St. Anne. Next door to the church is the 16th-century Tour de l'Horloge, straddling the rue des Marchands.

Apt is especially known for its crystallized fruit and fruit preserves. It was once noted for faïence with a distinctive marbled design, and examples of this fine workmanship can be seen in the modest Musée de l'Aventure Industrielle, in place du Pestel (Jun–end Sep Mon, Wed–Sat 10–12, 3–6.30, Sun 3–7; Oct–end May Mon, Wed–Sat 10–12, 2–5.30).

Place Jean Jaurès is home to the Maison du Parc du Lubéron (www.parcduluberon.fr), an information point for the Lubéron Regional Park.

295 G9 20 avenue Philippe de Girard, 84400 Apt 04 90 74 03 18 Jul, Aug Mon–Sat 9–7, Sun 9.30–12.30; Sep–end Jun Mon–Sat 9.30–12.30, 2.30–6.30, Sun 9.30–12.30

## AVIGNON

▷ 224–227.

## BARRY

In wild and rocky hills 5km (3 miles) from Bollène (▷ this page), the extraordinary troglodyte village of Barry is one of the best preserved in Provence. Known locally as Le Village Troglodyte, the site was inhabited continuously for thousands of years—possibly from as long ago as the early Neolithic era (around 4000BC). The *bories* (drystone huts) were abandoned as recently as 1925 after some fatal rockslides.

From the parking area a track leads past a series of 'houses' consisting only of handsome stone facades placed across caves. The caves have been carved into rooms, and some have a surprising level of home comfort. A map of walks in the area can be downloaded from the Bollène tourist office website.

290 D7

## BEAUMES-DE-VENISE

www.ot-beaumesdevenise.com

A noted wine village on the steep, rocky southern flank of the Dentelles de Montmirail in northern Vaucluse, Beaumes-de-Venise has for many centuries been known for its rich muscat dessert wine. The village produces other good wines too, and is also known for its high-quality olive oil and fruits, including melons, apricots and cherries. The Avignon popes owned a vineyard here in the 14th century, while Anne of Austria visited in 1660 to present a set of liturgical vestments in recognition of the village's winemaking skills.

Venise refers to the papal territory, the Comtat Venaissin, while *Beaumes* comes from *Baume*, Provençal for 'grotto'. The rocky terrain above the village is dotted with caves where the area's original inhabitants lived. Above them are the ruins of a 12th-century chateau.

290 E8 Maison des Dentelles, place du Marché, 84190 Beaumes-de-Venise 04 90 62 94 39 May–end Sep Mon–Sat 9–1, 2–6.30; Oct–end Apr Mon–Sat 9–12.30, 2–6

## BOLLÈNE

www.bollenetourisme.com

The highly industrialized Canal de Donzère-Mondragon runs parallel to the Rhône river between Montélimar and Orange, at the foot of pretty hills on the northwestern edge of Vaucluse. Standing beside the canal, the commercial and market town of Bollène has become

**Above** *A statue on the church of Sainte-Anne, Apt*

the main economic hub of the industrial zone. It is dominated by a vast nuclear plant just north of the town.

Traces of the historic Bollène survive, and there are some fine old houses with beautifully decorated doors in the old town around the church. Louis Pasteur was staying here in 1882 when he discovered an inoculation against swine fever.

From the upper town, the view looks out onto the Cévennes hills.

290 D7 Place Reynaud de la Gardette, 84500 Bollène 04 90 40 51 45 Apr, May, Oct Mon–Sat 8.30–12, 2–5.30; Jun–end Sep Mon–Sat 9–12.30, 2.30–6; Nov–end Mar Mon–Fri 8.30–12, 2–5.30, Sat 9–12 Bollène

## BONNIEUX

www.bonnieux.com

This lofty village on the north side of the Lubéron hills has a church at the top and a church at the bottom. Steep lanes and cobbled steps lead up to the 12th-century church, now disused but offering lovely views from its terrace. A 17th-century building in rue de la République houses the Musée de la Boulangerie, a museum about bread-making. The lower church, built in 1870, displays four 15th-century painted wooden panels.

295 F10 7 place Carnot, Bonnieux 04 90 75 91 90 Easter–end Sep Mon–Sat 9.30–12.30, 2–6, Sun 10–12.30; Oct–Easter Mon–Fri 9.30–12.30, 2–6, Sat 2–5

# AVIGNON

**INFORMATION**

www.ot-avignon.fr
294 D9 41 cours Jean-Jaurès 84004 Avignon 04 32 74 32 74 Easter–end Oct Mon–Sat 9–6 (until 7 during the Festival), Sun 9.45–5; Nov–Easter Mon–Fri 9–6, Sat 9–5, Sun 10–12 Main station in boulevard St-Roch; TGV station 5km (3 miles) from the middle of the city

**Above** *Villeneuve-lès-Avignon*

## INTRODUCTION

Romantic, riverside Avignon, with its massive stone fortifications, nursery-rhyme bridge and towering fortress of the medieval popes, has a long tradition of vivacity, art, culture and *joie de vivre*. It is easily accessible, with excellent road and rail connections. Impressive ramparts enclose the whole of the old city, creating a clearly defined area of manageable, walkable size—visitors don't have to grapple with the rest of this industrial city at all, but can generally spend their entire stay in the historic central area. The main entrance to the walled town is Porte de la République, opposite the rail station. A central shopping avenue (cours Jean-Jaurès and rue de la République) makes its way from the city gate to the main square, place de l'Hôtel de Ville, with its hundreds of outdoor tables. Most of the narrow backstreets either side have been attractively restored, and there is good shopping. At festival time in July, hundreds of thousands of visitors arrive from across Europe. Avignon has a long history as a hub of entertainment. Its cultural influence was confirmed in 1947, when the annual Theatre Festival was launched.

Prehistoric Avignon sat on the Rocher des Doms, which, in about 500BC, was developed by Greek settlers into the town of Avenio. The Romans enlarged Avenio and laid out a Forum on what is now the place de l'Hôtel de Ville, although the town was eclipsed by Arles and Nîmes. In 1309 the papal court moved to Avignon from Rome (▷ 32) and the city grew in size and importance. The area remained in papal hands (initially in Avignon, later governed from Rome) for centuries, only becoming part of France again in 1791. During its time under papal control, the city attracted a large wealthy clerical class, but also political refugees and outcasts on the run, who were given refuge. Something of that dichotomy survives today—there are many luxury shops and well-to-do inhabitants but also poorer enclaves ringing the old city.

## WHAT TO SEE

### PALAIS DES PAPES

www.palais-des-papes.com

The 14th-century fortress of the popes of Avignon is a vast, forbidding building soaring above the rest of central Avignon. It stands on one side of a huge piazza, and was the home of the popes from 1309 to 1403. Inside is a maze of passageways, galleries, rooms and chapels. You may visit independently or join a guided tour in English. The main things to see are the Large Audience Hall and the Papal Bedroom, its walls decorated with birds and golden vines on a blue background. The Grand Tinel banquet hall, 45m (150ft) long, has Gobelin tapestries and beautifully restored panelling in the shape of a ship's keel on the ceiling. There's a good view from the Terrasses des Grands Dignitaires.

226 B1 Place du Palais, 84008 Avignon 04 90 27 50 00 Mar–end Jun, mid-Sep to end Oct daily 9–7; Jul and 1st 2 weeks in Sep daily 9–8; Aug daily 9–9; Nov–end Feb daily 9.30–5.45. Last tickets sold one hour before closing Mar to mid-Nov adult €10.50, child (8–17) €8.50, under 8 free, joint ticket including Pont St-Bénézet adult €13, child (8–17) €10, under 8 free; mid-Nov to end Feb adult €8.50, child (8–17) €7, joint ticket including Pont St-Bénézet adult €11, child (8–17) €8.50, under 8 free Guided tours several times a day; audioguides (included in entry price) are available in 9 languages There is parking under place du Palais

### PETIT PALAIS

The Petit Palais is an art museum with a remarkable collection of medieval works. It is noted for Italian Primitives, but there are also works of the Sienese, Venetian, Florentine and Avignon schools, Romanesque and Gothic sculpture and frescoes, as well as its star exhibit, Sandro Botticelli's *Madonna and Child.* The palace dates from the 14th century. In the 16th century it was the luxurious palace of Cardinal Rovere, the future Pope Julius II. It is his acclaimed personal art collection that forms the nucleus of the art museum.

226 B1 Palais des Archevêques, place du Palais, 84000 Avignon 04 90 86 44 58 Wed–Mon 10–1, 2–6 Adult €6, child €3.50 There is parking under place du Palais

### PONT ST-BÉNÉZET

www.palais-des-papes.com

A ramparts walkway gives access to what survives of the narrow, cobbled bridge of St-Bénézet. This is the *pont d'Avignon* on which *on y danse* in the nursery rhyme *Sur le Pont d'Avignon.* Built in 1177 under the inspiration of a shepherd boy called Bénézet, the bridge originally went all the way across the

## PALAIS DES PAPES FLOORPLAN

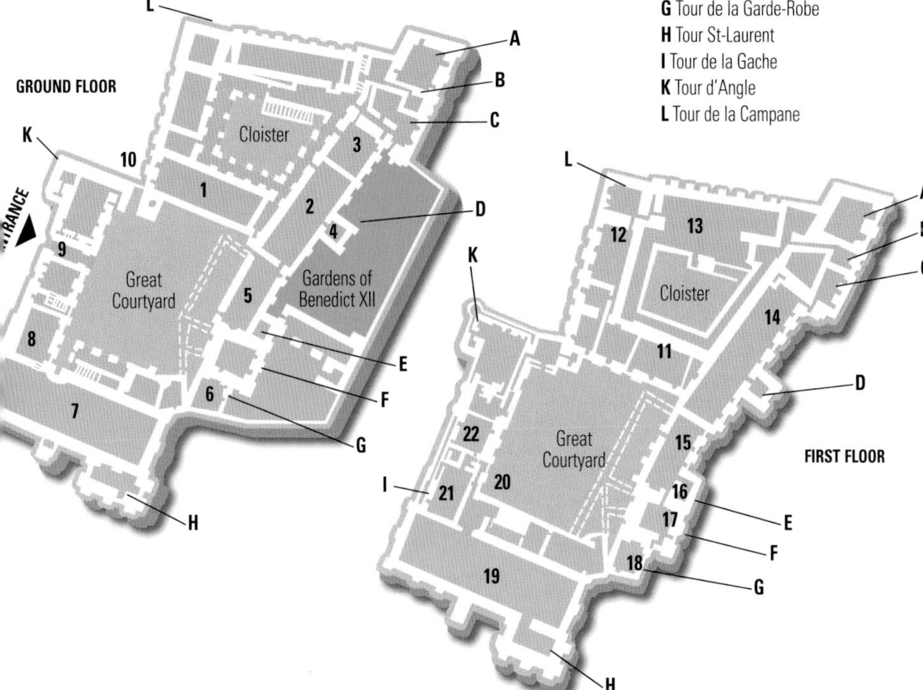


### PALAIS DES PAPES FLOORPLAN

**1** Conclave Wing
**2** Consistory Hall
**3** Wine store, bakery
**4** St. John's Chapel
**5** Treasury
**6** Wardrobe, bathroom
**7** Large Audience Hall
**8** Small Audience Hall
**9** Porte des Champeaux
**10** Porte de Notre-Dame
**11** Guest room
**12** Confidants' Wing
**13** Chapel of St. Benedict
**14** Grand Tinel (banquet hall)
**15** Ante-room
**16** Study
**17** Papal bedroom
**18** Room of the Stag (above St-Michael's Chapel)
**19** Great Chapel
**20** Window of Indulgence
**21** Servants' quarters
**22** Wing of the Dignitaries
**A** Tour de Trouillas
**B** Tour de la Glacière
**C** Tour des Cuisines
**D** Tour St-Jean
**E** Tour de l'Étude
**F** Tour des Anges
**G** Tour de la Garde-Robe
**H** Tour St-Laurent
**I** Tour de la Gache
**K** Tour d'Angle
**L** Tour de la Campane

**TIPS**

» The *Avignon Passion* gives reductions on entry tickets to the main sights. You can buy it at the tourist office or at the participating sights.

» Two little sightseeing land trains set off frequently throughout the day from place du Palais (mid-Mar to mid-Oct).

» The *Festival d'Avignon* (Avignon International Festival of Theatre), for three weeks in July, offers top-name entertainment, plus many fringe shows (www.festival-avignon.com).

» For a walk in Avignon, ▷ 246–247.

Rhône to Villeneuve-lès-Avignon. In 1668 the Rhône flooded and washed away a large part of the bridge, leaving only what can be seen today. The surviving arches reach about halfway to Île de la Barthelasse, the island in midstream. The endearing little chapel of St-Nicolas, standing on the bridge, has two levels—simple Romanesque down below and Gothic on top.

Off map at 226 B1 Rue Ferruce, 84000 Avignon 04 90 27 51 16 Mar–end Jun, mid-Sep to end Oct daily 9–7; Jul and 1st 2 weeks in Sep daily 9–8; Aug daily 9–9; Nov–end Feb daily 9.30–5.45. Last tickets sold 30 min before closing time Mar to mid-Nov adult €4.50, child (8–17) €3.50, joint ticket including Palais des Papes €13, child (8–17) €10, under 8 free; mid-Nov to end Feb adult €4, child (8–17) €3, joint ticket including Palais des Papes €11, child (8–17) €8.50, under 8 free Guided tours are available; audioguides (included in entry price) are available in 9 languages There is parking under place du Palais

## FONDATION ANGLADON

www.angladon.com

This modern art museum, founded in 1995, has become one of Avignon's most important sights. It displays the remarkable personal collection of artists Jean and Paulette Angladon-Dubrujeaud and is housed in their backstreet mansion. It focuses on 19th- and 20th-century art, with works by Paul Cézanne, Picasso and leading Impressionists. There is also Vincent Van Gogh's *Railroad Cars*.

226 B2 Hôtel de Massilian, 5 rue Laboureur, 84000 Avignon 04 90 82 29 03 Apr–end Nov Tue–Sun 1–6; Dec, Jan Wed–Sun 1–6; Feb, Mar Tue 2–5, Wed–Sun 1–6 Adult €6, child (7–12) €1.50, under 7 free Guided visit with art historians by appointment; language and price depends on demand There is street parking nearby

## MORE TO SEE

### MUSEE CALVET

Inside one of the town's many grand 18th-century mansions, the Calvet Museum displays important collections of 15th- to 20th-century paintings and sculptures, period furniture, faïence and fine gold and silver work. Among the modern painters on display are Chaim Soutine, Édouard Manet and Alfred Sisley.

226 B2 | 2 Hôtel Villeneuve Martignan, 65 rue Joseph Vernet, 84000 Avignon | 04 90 86 33 84 | Wed–Mon 10–1, 2–6 | Adult €6, child (12–18) €3, under 12 free

### ROCHER DES DOMS

Leading off the place du Palais next to the papal palace, a steep path climbs up onto the peaceful Rocher des Doms garden, which covers a rocky outcrop. There are dramatic views of the Rhône, Pont St-Bénézet and the countryside of western Provence.

226 B1

### VILLENEUVE-LÈS-AVIGNON

One of the best vantage points to gain a sense of Avignon's medieval grandeur is the 13th-century Fort St-André at Villeneuve-lès-Avignon, on the other side of the river. The view is especially stirring at sunset, as the golden southern light bathes the town. When the popes moved to Avignon, the cardinals made their base at Villeneuve. It is very popular for an evening out.

Off map at 226 A1

**Below** *A statue in a niche on a street corner*

**CARPENTRAS**

www.carpentras-ventoux.com

Intriguing reminders of times past can be seen in this country town, on the fertile plain northeast of Avignon. Originally a Roman settlement, it became an important religious town under papal rule. The historic old quarter is a tangled mass of lanes and narrow streets, once ringed with 14th-century ramparts but now enclosed by a circle of boulevards. Its Porte d'Orange gateway survives, and a first-century AD Roman Triumphal Arch stands behind the town's main sight, the 15th-century Ancienne Cathédral, in place du Général-de-Gaulle (daily 7.30–12, 2–6.30). The cathedral has a superb Gothic doorway, called Porte Juive (Jewish Door), supposedly because Jewish converts to Christianity came in through this door. There was a big Jewish community here from Roman times onwards, and the 14th-century synagogue, in place Maurice-Charretier (Mon–Thu 10–12, 3–5, Fri 10–12, 3–4), is said to be the oldest in France that is still in use. However, having been extensively modernized in the 20th century, it does not give much indication of its age.

If you're in Carpentras on a Friday, visit the market in the old town.

290 E8 Maison de Pays, 97 place du 25 Août 1944, 84200 Carpentras 04 90 63 00 78 Jul, Aug Mon–Sat 9–1, 2–7, Sun 9.30–1; Sep–end Jun Mon, Wed–Sat 9.30–12.30, 2–6, Tue 9.30–12.30, 3–6 (also Sun 9.30–1 Easter–end Jun)

**CAVAILLON**

www.cavaillon-luberon.com

Known as the 'Melon Capital of France', this prosperous town, irrigated by the Durance and Coulon rivers, grows a vast quantity of prime fruit and vegetables. Surrounded by lush market gardens, Cavaillon is one of the most productive agricultural hubs in France. Its high-quality produce has been praised since Roman times.

The only relic of the Roman era is a small, first-century AD triumphal arch, moved from next to the Cathédrale St-Véran to its present position in 1880. The Cathédrale St-Véran is an elegant 12th-century Romanesque structure with charming cloisters. Nearby, on rue Hebraïque, is the old synagogue, sole remnant of a once populous Jewish district. The ornate interior is impressive. The bakery under the main prayer hall is now a museum of the Jewish life of the Comtat Venaissin.

295 E10 Place François-Tourel, 84305 Cavaillon 04 90 71 32 01 Jul, Aug Mon–Sat 9–12.30, 2–6.30, Sun 10–12; mid-Mar to end Jun, Sep to mid-Oct Mon–Sat 9–12.30, 2–6.30; mid-Oct to mid-Mar Mon–Fri 9–12, 2–6, Sat 9–12 Cavaillon

**CHÂTEAUNEUF-DU-PAPE**

▷ 229.

**CRESTET**

Quiet, charming and completely uncommercialized, this village is south of Vaison-la-Romaine on a crest of the Dentelles de Montmirail (▷ below). Cobbled alleyways climb through the village. The tiny main square has a bubbling fountain and a 12th-century church. A pathway makes its way up to the former chateau (closed to the public).

290 E7

**DENTELLES DE MONTMIRAIL**

www.ot-beaumesdevenise.com

The Dentelles are an intriguing small range of jagged hills with limestone pinnacles rising from an important little wine area in northern Vaucluse. They get their name from *dentelle*, which means lace, as the jagged limestone peaks imitate the points around the edges of handmade lace.

The higher part of the slopes is wild wooded country, but the lower slopes are covered with vines producing Côte du Rhône red wines. A number of wine villages lie on the slopes: Séguret (▷ 238) and Gigondas are among the prettiest. Others include Vacqueyras and Beaumes-de-Venise (▷ 223). There is wine tasting at all the villages.

At the foot of the Dentelles' north slope is Vaison-la-Romaine (▷ 240–241), with some intriguing Roman ruins and the Romanesque cathedral of Notre-Dame-de-Nazareth.

290 E8 Maison des Dentelles, place du Marché, 84190 Beaumes-de-Venise 04 90 62 94 39 May–end Sep Mon–Sat 9–12, 2–6.30; Oct–end Apr Mon–Sat 9–12, 2–6

**Below** *Viewed beyond a mass of yellow broom, the peaks of Les Dentelles de Montmirail*

## CHÂTEAUNEUF-DU-PAPE

Châteauneuf is a picture-book medieval fortified village by a little river, not far from the Rhône. Old stone houses and lanes have been perfectly restored. The village is surrounded by its famous vineyards, all neatly tended. It is a popular visitor destination, with people coming not just to see the village but, more importantly, to taste the wines.

### MUSÉE DU VIN PÈRE ANSELME

This free museum, with cellars (www.brotte.com; Apr–end Sep daily 9–1, 2–7; Oct–end Mar daily 9–12, 2–6), in avenue Pierre de Luxembourg, makes a good starting point for gathering basic knowledge about local wines, historical methods of winemaking and the Châteauneuf denomination. Explore the museum exhibits—which include a 600-year-old chestnut wine barrel—or simply sip, savour and purchase a few fine samples.

### WINE TASTING

Châteauneuf's tourist office can help to arrange visits to vineyards and wineries. Among the best-known vineyards in the town are Château Rayas, Château Le Nerthe, Château de Beaucastel, Château de la Gardine and the Château des Fines Roches.

### WINEMAKING

Winegrowers here choose from 13 types of grapes. The vineyard soil is covered with pebbles, to magnify the sun's heat during the day and seal it in at night. This, and the wide spacing between vines, results in a wine with a high alcohol content (12.5 per cent or higher). Most of the 14 million bottles of wine made here are a full-bodied red, although it's worth trying one of the 850,000 bottles of white. An authentic bottle of Châteauneuf-du-Pape has the crossed keys of the chateau embossed on the bottle.

### POPES' SUMMER GETAWAY

The village, whose name means 'Pope's new castle', was a summer hideaway of the 14th-century Avignon popes. They ordered the first vineyards to be laid out. Little survives of the papal fortress at the top of the village, blown up by the Germans in 1944. The ruins give good views of the Rhône valley.

### INFORMATION

www.ccpro.fr

290 D8 Place du Portail, Châteauneuf-du-Pape 04 90 83 71 08 Jun–end Sep Mon–Sat 9.30–6; Oct–end May Mon, Tue, Thu–Sat 9.30–12.30, 2–6

### TIPS

» Pop into the tourist office to pick up one of seven hiking or five cycling guides to the region.

» The *Fête de la Véraison* (▷ 251), in early August, is a good time to come and try the wine.

**Above** *Châteauneuf-du-Pape, surrounded by vineyards*

**INFORMATION**

www.oti-delasorgue.fr

295 E9 Résidence Jean Garcin, 84800 Fontaine-de-Vaucluse 04 90 20 32 22 May–end Sep daily 10–1, 2–6; Oct–end Apr Mon–Sat 9.30–12.30, 1.30–5.30, Sun 1.30–5.30 For a drive in the area, ▷ 242–243

# FONTAINE-DE-VAUCLUSE

From this village, a pleasant riverside path leads to one of the world's most powerful natural springs. This spring, which gives the village its name, has long fascinated both visitors and locals because the actual source has never been located. Water gushes from beneath a sheer cliff into a still and very deep pool, surrounded by rocks and vegetation and often by a dense spray. At its height, the Fontaine de Vaucluse is among the world's most powerful natural flows of fresh water: 630 million cubic metres (22,260 million cubic feet) of water emerge from it each year, flowing down the narrow valley to become the river Sorgue. For maximum effect, come in March or April.

## CHEMIN DE LA FONTAINE

To reach the spring, you have to walk for some 15 minutes along the traffic-free Chemin de la Fontaine beside the Sorgue. In this enclosed valley, now so full of visitors, the 14th-century poet Francesco Petrarch lived as a hermit for 16 years in the total isolation described in *De Vita Solitaria*. In the village, in quai du Château Vieux, there is the Musée Bibliothèque Pétrarque (closed Tue, and Nov–end Mar), in what is said to be his own house. Along the *chemin* are several other interesting attractions focusing on local history. The Musée d'Histoire 1939–45 (Apr–Oct closed Tue; Nov, Dec, Mar closed Mon–Fri; Jan, Feb closed) reflects daily life under the Nazi occupation and the Resistance, but also deals with the art and literature of the 'spirit of liberation'. A little farther on, the Ecomusée du Gouffre (open daily; closed mid-Nov to end Jan) deals vividly with efforts to discover the source of the Fontaine. A few paces farther along the *chemin*, Moulin à Papier Vallis Clausa (open daily) is a fascinating traditional water-powered paper mill.

## THE CHATEAU

Southeast of Fontaine-de-Vaucluse's town centre, the remains of an 11th-century castle are perched on a hill above both the village and the river Sorgue. Originally built on the site of a former monastery, the chateau was destroyed during the 17th century. Like much of the surrounding wilderness, the site makes for a pleasant afternoon's exploration.

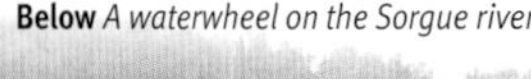

**Below** *A waterwheel on the Sorgue river*

## GORDES

An exceptionally pretty and unusual village, medieval Gordes is a chic, arty hideaway noted for its curious *bories*. The village, in the southern part of the Vaucluse plateau, was abandoned during the early 20th century, but was quickly rediscovered and restored by artists and well-to-do visitors. Now a rather chic place to have a second home, it is popular with media people. As a result, it is well served with shops and restaurants at the expensive end of the scale. The houses appear to be built one on top of the other as they climb the steep hill on which this picturesque old village stands. Narrow stairways and covered passages wind steeply around the hill, which is topped by a Renaissance chateau fancifully restored by modern artist Victor Vasarely. It now contains a gallery of the work of another modern artist, Pol Mara (daily 10–12, 2–6). The tourist office is on the first floor of the chateau. The Grande Salle, which is part of the Mairie, has a Renaissance fireplace wonderfully ornamented with shells and flowers. Follow Gordes' winding streets downhill, duck into the ornate church of St-Firmin, then continue on to admire the panoramic views from the town's *terrasses*.

### *BORIES*

Around the village are numerous *bories*—windowless dome-shaped drystone dwellings, many of them centuries old. They were used as shepherds' huts, storage sheds, animal shelters and seasonal or even permanent homes; some were inhabited until the 19th century. Provence has up to 6,000 *bories*, some dating back to prehistoric times and others built only a few hundred years ago. Vaucluse has a particularly high concentration of them. Their ingenious construction does not involve mortar—instead, each layer of flat stone slightly overlaps the next. To see a restored museum-village of these structures, follow the signs to the Village des Bories, off the D2, 4km (2.5 miles) from Gordes (daily 9am–dusk). The *bories* here are between 200 and 500 years old.

### INFORMATION

www.gordes-village.com
295 F9 Le Château, 84220 Gordes
04 90 72 02 75 Mon–Sat 9–12, 2–6, Sun 10–12, 2–6

### TIP

» The village has a lively two-week music festival in August.

**Above** *The hillside village of Gordes*

## L'ISLE-SUR-LA-SORGUE

www.oti-delasorgue.fr

This curious old town stands on a large island in the river Sorgue and is enclosed by water channels, with several large, mossy waterwheels. The town's rich architecture is a legacy of once-thriving silk and leather industries. Today it has art galleries and antiques shops, and is the main town for buying and selling Provençal antiques, with a Sunday antiques market. At the town's heart is a 17th-century church, Notre-Dame-des-Anges (Tue–Sun 10–12, 3–5) with a highly decorated baroque interior. There is also an 18th-century Hôtel-Dieu, in rue J. Théophile, preserving its original pharmacy (30-min guided tours—contact tourist office for times; reserve ahead).

295 E9 Place de la Liberté, 84800 L'Isle-sur-la-Sorgue 04 90 38 04 78 Jul, Aug Mon–Sat 9–12.30, 2.30–6, Sun 9.30–1; Sep–end Jun Mon–Sat 9–12.30, 2.30–6, Sun 9–12.30

## LACOSTE

Little lanes stepping up towards a huge ruined chateau, and glorious rural views, have made this Lubéron hilltop village popular with second-homers. Remnants of the ramparts survive, with two gateways. The chateau (▷ 15) dominating the village was the family home of the notorious Marquis de Sade (1740–1814), who in fact spent very little time here. Built in the 11th century, it used to be one of the grandest in the region. In 2001, Pierre Cardin bought it, and every summer the *Festival d'Art Lyrique et de Théâtre de Lacoste* (www.festivaldelacoste.com) is held here.

295 F10

## LUBÉRON

www.parcduluberon.fr

The exceptionally picturesque and varied landscapes of the Lubéron hills are the epitome of the Provence heartland. Extending roughly from Cavaillon (Vaucluse) to Villeneuve (Alpes-de-Haute-Provence), the hills reach their highest point at Mourre Nègre (1,125m/ 3,690ft). Typical of the region are gaunt medieval hilltop villages with terraced fields and drystone *bories* (▷ 231), interspersed with expanses of dense wild heath. Many of the village houses have been restored as holiday homes or arty getaways. The village of Ménerbes is the setting for British writer Peter Mayle's bestseller *A Year in Provence* (1989), while Lourmarin was the home of writer Albert Camus (1913–60), who is buried in the cemetery.

Much of the region is protected as a Parc Naturel Régional, ensuring its character and culture are preserved. The hills are rich in flora and fauna, with numerous species of wild flowers and colonies of rare birds such as Bonelli's Eagle, Egyptian Vulture and the Eagle Owl.

295 F10–G10 Maison du Parc Naturel du Lubéron, 60 place Jean Jaurès, 84404 Apt 04 90 04 42 00 Mon–Fri 8.30–12, 1.30–6

## MALAUCÈNE

This small town has become a popular base for hiking, horseback riding and bicycling on nearby Mont Ventoux (▷ 233) and Dentelles de Montmirail (▷ 228). Four fortified gates mark the entrances into the evocative medieval quarter. Next to Porte Soubeyran is a fortified church noted for its wood carving and 18th-century organ loft. Rue St-Étienne and rue du Château climb past the crumbling old clock tower (a lookout during the Wars of Religion), reaching a high belvedere created from the ruins of the old chateau.

290 E8 Place de la Marie, 84340 Malaucène 04 90 65 22 59 Jul, Aug Mon–Sat 9.30–12, 2.30–6; Sep–end Jun Mon–Thu 9.30–12, 2.30–6, Fri 9–12

## MAZAN

www.mazantourisme.com

Little Mazan lies beside the minor road that follows the Auzon river into the countryside east of Carpentras. Solid gateways lead into the mainly 16th- and 17th-century central part of town, which is rich with statues in niches, fountains and

**Above** *A waterwheel, L'Isle-sur-la-Sorgue*

ancient doorways. The Chapelle des Pénitents Blancs, opposite the church, now houses the Musée de Mazan (Jun–end Sep Wed–Mon 3.30–6.30). Its most remarkable exhibit is the skeleton of a young fourth-century woman, who was supposedly killed by a stone from a catapult, which has left a gaping hole in the front of her skull.

290 E8 83 place du 8 Mai, 84380 Mazan 04 90 69 74 27 Jul, Aug Mon–Fri 9–12, 2–6, Sat 9–12, 2–5, Sun 9–12; Apr–end Jun, Sep Mon–Fri 9–12, 2–6, Sat 9–12; Oct–end Mar Mon–Fri 9–12, 2–6

## MONT VENTOUX

▷ 233.

## OPPÈDE-LE-VIEUX

Oppède-le-Vieux was once a bustling village with its own castle, but now is partly in ruins. The castle was ransacked during the Revolution and the village fell into decline when the Comtat Venaissin became part of France in 1791. But its fortunes began to look up in the 1940s, when a colony of artists moved in. You have to leave your car at the bottom but can then walk up to the summit of the village, passing an old church, but take care as there are many unprotected drops.

295 F10

## MONT VENTOUX

Rising high above the rest of the region, the neatly conical summit of Ventoux is one of the most distinctive sights in western Provence. The awesome peak rises to 1,909m (6,261ft) and the mountain has been declared a World Biosphere Reserve. A paved road makes Ventoux accessible for fine-weather walks and drives. Even in winter, there are plenty of visitors, who come to Ventoux's own ski resort, Mont Serein. The snow lasts well into spring. In summer, the peak is often shrouded in cloud while the rest of Provence basks in sunshine. The 14th-century poet Francesco Petrarch was the first person to write about his ascent of the mountain—it took him two days. Today, some walks and excursions, including night visits, are organized from Bedoin tourist office (tel 04 90 65 63 95) and Malaucène tourist office (tel 04 90 65 22 59).

### TO THE SUMMIT

Around the foot of the mountain is wooded hill country with a few simple villages. The road to the top climbs steeply, with sharp hairpins, its surface painted with graffiti and advertising most of the way. Provence seems to end as you continue the climb to the summit in summer, and another land is entered—bleak, cold, stony, unearthly, with howling winds. Yet there is plenty of low, tenacious vegetation, and in April or May there can be blankets of flowers even at the very top. Surprisingly, the road actually goes all the way to the summit of the mountain, where high-tech observation and communications equipment is installed. From here you look across another world, of distant crests and peaks and mountain ranges: It has been described as one of the best views in Europe. The vista takes in the Alps, the Rhône valley, the Vaucluse plateau, the Cévennes and the Mediterranean.

### WINDY MOUNTAIN

The winds near the summit are rarely light, and reach more than 160kph (100mph) when the *mistral* is blowing. Legend has it that the mountain owes its name to these winds—*ventour* is Provençal for windy. From November to the end of May sudden heavy snowfalls are possible at any time.

### INFORMATION

291 F8 Chalet d'Accueil du Mont Ventoux ☎ 04 90 63 42 02

### TIPS

» Check the weather forecast, and do not ascend Mont Ventoux in windy weather or when storms or snow are expected.

» Be prepared for low temperatures at the summit, averaging 11°C colder than at the foot of the mountain.

» *Epeautre*, the wild barley that grows on the mountain, has become something of a local speciality—look for it on restaurant menus.

**Below** *An unusual landscape*

# ORANGE

## INFORMATION

http://uk.otorange.fr
290 D8 Cours Aristide Briand, 84100 Orange 04 90 34 70 88
Jul, Aug Mon–Sat 9.30–7.30, Sun 10–1, 2–7; Apr–end Jun, Sep Mon–Sat 9.30–6.30, Sun 10–1, 2–6.30; Oct–end Mar Mon–Sat 10–1, 2–5 Orange

**Above** *The belfry*

## INTRODUCTION

A vibrant, attractive and ancient town at the gateway to Provence, Orange is noted for some remarkable reminders of Roman times. Well placed for visitors coming down the Rhône valley highways, the attractive provincial town makes an enjoyable pause. It has impressive Roman structures, with two World Heritage Sites, one of which is the Roman theatre, whose huge backdrop wall was famously described by Louis XIV as 'the finest wall in my kingdom.' The central district of the town dates from medieval times and is lively and bustling, with picturesque lanes and squares. It is small and easily explored on foot and the tourist office organizes guided tours. Orange is also the place to take stock of alternative routes and destinations: Here the roads diverge for access to Nîmes and western Provence; Avignon and the heart of Provence; or Carpentras, Mont Ventoux and the wine towns of Vaucluse. If you are driving into Orange, be aware that navigating your way around the outer boulevards can be tricky.

Originally a Celtic settlement called Arausio, Orange was conquered, with difficulty, by the Romans in 102BC. The town stood on the Via Agrippa highway and became a prosperous city. The Romans were driven out by Visigoths in the fifth century AD. Orange was an independent principality in medieval times. In 1622 the Dutch Prince of Nassau, later to become Prince of Orange, took possession of the city and it became a refuge for dissenters from Catholicism. To protect its small territory in southern France, the Dutch royal house enclosed Orange with ramparts, largely constructed with masonry from Roman buildings. Orange did not become part of France until the 1713 Treaty of Utrecht. In the 19th and 20th centuries, the town's position beside the Rhône and at the gateway to the south encouraged commercial and industrial development.

## WHAT TO SEE

### THÉÂTRE ANTIQUE

www.theatre-antique.com
The remarkable Roman theatre at the heart of Orange is one of the most important Roman structures surviving anywhere. The semi-circular auditorium, built into the slope of St-Eutrope hill, could hold 10,000 spectators and staged

anything from circus acts to Greek tragedies. Its stage still hosts many performances, including the annual *Chorégies* choral music festival. But the main focus is the stage wall. Standing 36m (119ft) high and measuring 103m (338ft) from end to end, the grandeur of the wall, decorated with columns, marbles, statues and mosaics, testifies to the important role the theatre played in the life of the Roman town. Actors moved about unseen through hidden passageways within the wall. The statue of Augustus above the central royal door dates from the first century AD and was pieced together from fragments.
✉ Rue Madeleine Roch, 84100 Orange ☎ 04 90 51 17 60 🕑 Jun–end Aug daily 9–7; Apr, May, Sep daily 9–6; Mar, Oct daily 9.30–5.30; Jan, Feb, Nov, Dec daily 9.30–4.30 ✋ Adult €7.90, child (7–17) €5.90, under 7 free. Ticket includes entry to the Musée Municipal ☛ Audioguide included in entry price

### MUSÉE MUNICIPAL

The light and airy rooms of the first-rate municipal museum trace the history of the town and display some of the town's more important Roman and medieval relics, notably the Romans' remarkable Land Survey of Orange carved on marble. Old engravings and prints show the neglected state of the Roman theatre before it was restored.
✉ Rue Madeleine Roch, 84100 Orange ☎ 04 90 51 17 60 🕑 Jun–end Aug daily 9–7; Apr, May, Sep daily 9–6; Mar, Oct daily 9.30–5.30; Nov–end Feb daily 9.30–4.30 ✋ Adult €7.90, child (7–17) €5.90, under 7 free. Ticket includes entry to the Théâtre Antique

### ARC DE TRIOMPHE

The Arc de Triomphe is the grandiose three-arched monument erected to mark the defeat of the local tribes. Roman forces were defeated here by the local tribes in 105BC and it became an urgent priority for the Romans to conquer the area decisively. The triumphal arch was erected in 20BC to celebrate their eventual victory. It survives in astonishingly good condition, and is one of the oldest in existence. Rich carvings tell the story of other victories, including naval battles. The Arc is on a roundabout surrounded by traffic from the N7.
✉ Avenue de l'Arc de Triomphe, 84100 Orange

## MORE TO SEE

### COLLINE ST-EUTROPE

The hill rising behind the theatre is called Colline St-Eutrope, and here many of the Roman items were found. There are great views from in front of the ruined foundations of a fortress here.

### TIPS

» There is parking alongside cours A. Briand and in cours Pourtoules near the Théâtre Antique.

» *Chorégies* (the International Festival of Music and Theatre) is held in July and early August at the Théâtre Antique and other venues—see www.choregies.asso.fr for information on the coming programme in English.

**Below left** *A Roman statue in the old town*
**Below right** *Roman columns at the Théâtre Antique*

# PERNES-LES-FONTAINES

It is delightful to stroll in the narrow streets and squares of this aptly named little town, discovering the many fountains. Medieval Pernes, in the papal territory of the Comtat Venaissin, was enclosed by its ramparts in the 14th century, and a great deal survives from those days. Pernes (*les Fontaines* was added to the name only in 1936) is a historic town, with impressive fortifications, towers, lovely old squares, Renaissance houses and a cluster of old chapels. Its particular charm, though, derives from harnessing the waters of the otherwise unremarkable Nesque river into numerous fountains. Just south of Carpentras, and 25km (16 miles) east of Avignon, it can easily be visited on a tour of the Vaucluse area.

## THE FOUNTAINS

From the 15th century onwards, the Nesque was channelled into fountains in the village. More have been added over time, even in recent years, bringing the total to 36, along with 4 *lavoirs* (public washing areas). They range from the oldest, La Fontaine Reboul, more than 400 years old, to the modern, La Fontaine Villeneuve, added in 1952 and reputedly so awful that no one wishes to remove the moss that now obscures it. Among the most beautiful is La Fontaine de Cormoran, added in 1761.

## BUT NOT JUST FOUNTAINS

The Tour Ferrande, in rue Barbes, shelters a remarkable series of 13th-century frescoes depicting religious and historical scenes in cartoon-strip style. The lovely 16th-century Porte Notre-Dame has a small chapel—Notre-Dame-des-Graces—built onto one of the piles of the river bridge. The 13th-century Tour de l'Horloge, or clock tower, is a last remnant of the chateau of the Counts of Toulouse. Rainy-day museums in the town include the Musée du Costume Comtadin (Jun–end Sep Mon 3–6.30, Tue–Sat 10–12, 3–6.30), devoted to 19th-century local costume and housed in the Magasin Drapier, a fascinating preserved former drapers' shop in rue de la République. The Musée des Traditions Provençales (Jun–end Sep Mon 3–6.30, Tue–Sat 10–12, 3–6.30), focusing on Provençal tradition and culture, is in the 17th-century Maison Fléchier, in place Fléchier. The walkway beside the Nesque gives an exquisite view of the bridge, the chapel, the keep and the town's clock tower.

### INFORMATION

www.ville-pernes-les-fontaines.fr
295 E9 Place Gabriel Moutte, 84210 Pernes-les-Fontaines 04 90 61 31 04 Jul, Aug Mon–Fri 9–12, 2–6.30; Apr–end Jun, Sep Mon–Fri 9–12, 2–6, Sat 9–12, 2–5; Oct Mon–Fri 9–12, 2–6, Sat 9–12; Nov–end Mar Mon–Fri 9–12, 2–5, Sat 9–12

### TIPS

» Visit in mid-September for the *Fête du Patrimoine.*

» Contact the tourist office to arrange a visit to the Tour Ferrande.

**Above** *The 16th-century Porte Notre-Dame*

## ROUSSILLON

The vast ochre quarries next to this pastel-tinted village are an astonishing sight. You'll often see artists sketching or painting in this village high in the Lubéron hills. Roussillon is a curiosity, and a very attractive one. For centuries housing a community of ochre miners, the streets are edged by pretty homes tinted with 17 different shades of ochre across a warm spectrum from golden yellow to blood red. This beauty happened entirely by chance, as ochre miners over the centuries built cottages from the most conveniently available material, ochre rocks.

### VISIT THE QUARRIES

The extensive area of former ochre quarries, extending like a bizarre dazzling wilderness next to the village, makes an unforgettable outing. The underground galleries are now closed but you can visit the disused quarries following the Ochre Path, or *Sentier des Ocres,* (Mar to mid-Nov daily 9–5.30; mid-Nov to end Feb Sat, Sun 1–5). To enjoy it fully, you'll need to be able to walk well in difficult terrain.

### LOCAL INDUSTRY

Ochre mining was an important industry here for hundreds of years. Indeed, Provençal ochre is thought to have been in use since prehistoric times. The Romans first developed the quarries into a major enterprise. After a decline in the medieval period, the ochre industry was restarted on a large scale in the 18th century, when ochre powders were shipped from Marseille to countries all over the world. At the beginning of the 20th century, nearly every adult in Roussillon was employed by the mine owners. Ochre was mined either in tall, underground galleries or in the open air. A new decline began in the 1920s, when synthetic dyes were first manufactured, and within a decade the mining of natural ochre was no longer viable. But artists and visitors continue to give life to this exceptional place.

### RED ROOTS

The scientific explanation for the striking red hue of Roussillon's ochre is the combination of oxides. But legend blames it on the bloody death of a medieval lady called Seremonde, wife to Raymond of Avignon, who threw herself from the cliffs after her affair with a troubadour was discovered.

### INFORMATION

www.roussillon-provence.com
295 F9 Place de la Poste, 84220 Roussillon 04 90 05 60 25
Jul, Aug Mon–Sat 9–12, 2–6, Sun 2–6; Apr–end Jun, Sep, Oct Mon–Sat 9–12, 2–6; Nov–end Mar Mon–Sat 2–5
€2.40 to enter the quarries

### TIPS

» The simplest place to leave your car is in one of the parking areas close to the entrance to the quarries.

» For a walk in the quarries, wear something that you don't mind having stained with ochre.

» The rough terrain of the quarries could be difficult for young children. Even for others, there are some areas where it is necessary to take extra care.

**Below** *Roussillon's houses, glowing red in the sunlight*

### SAIGNON

www.saignon.fr

In a quiet area of the eastern Lubéron, the ancient hilltop fortress village of Saignon rises high above the Calavon valley. It is stretched along a ledge with its medieval castle at one end and the 12th-century Romanesque church of Notre-Dame-de-Pitié at the other. Approaching Saignon from Apt, it becomes clear why the village has been a natural fortress since Celto-Ligurian times—the towering rocks on which it stands would be enough to deter any attacker. At the same time, Saignon is open, bright and approachable, a typical Provençal village of picturesque streets, fountains, fine doorways on grand old houses and a clock tower and tree-shaded square.

Walkers can climb to the top of the high Saignon rock for an immense panorama with views reaching Mont Ventoux (▷ 233) and the Montagne de Lure.

295 G10 Mairie (town hall): place de l'Église, 84400 Saignon 04 90 74 16 30

### ST-DIDIER

www.provence-ventoux-village.com

Between Pernes-les-Fontaines (▷ 236) and Venasque (▷ 239), this peaceful village, 6km (4 miles) from Carpentras (▷ 228), is known for its waters and enjoys an impressive setting in the Vaucluse upland. The tree-lined main street leads to a medieval gateway and church, behind which stands the Château de Thézan (closed to the public). This 15th-century building was converted in 1863 into a hydrotherapy venue still in use for the treatment of nervous disorders. Peek into the courtyard to see its Renaissance doorways and windows.

295 E9 Mairie (town hall): place de la Mairie, 84210 St-Didier 04 90 66 01 39

### ST-SATURNIN-LES-APT

www.saintsaturninlesapt.fr

The extensive fortified village of St-Saturnin looks towards the Lubéron from the southern slopes of the Vaucluse plateau. It is a richly productive agricultural village, surrounded by vineyards and cherry orchards, olives and lavender. It is known too for asparagus, honey and truffles. There are many holiday villas around the village.

Despite St-Saturnin's peaceful setting, a more turbulent past is recalled by the village's ruined defences: the gateways Portail Ayguier, Porte de Rome and Porte de Roque, the Tour du Portalet tower and vestiges of an 11th-century chateau. Remnants of a small Romanesque chapel at the top provide views far across the region.

295 G9 Avenue Jean Geoffroy, 84490 St-Saturnin-les-Apt 04 90 05 85 10 Mon–Sat 9.30–12, 3.30–6, Sun 9.30–12

### SAULT

www.saultenprovence.com

The airy little town of Sault is on a rock spur on the edge of the Vaucluse plateau, close to the towering presence of Mont Ventoux (▷ 233). The vivid upland landscape is decorated in early summer with fields of wheat and bright lavender; the countryside around Sault produces almost half the region's lavender essential oil. The main attraction is as a base for excursions into the mountains.

Little remains of the town's chateau, but the old quarter has several medieval and Renaissance houses. The church is remarkable for its barrel-vaulted nave supported by slender columns. The Musée de Sault (Jul, Aug Mon–Sat 3–6) displays prehistoric and Gallo-Roman finds, as well as an incongruous Egyptian mummy. Opened in 1859, the museum also houses ancient coin collections, armoury and an extensive library. The Centre de Découverte de la Nature et du Patrimoine Cynégetique (Jul, Aug Mon–Fri 10–12, 3–7; Sep–end Jun Mon–Fri 10–12, 2–6) looks at the area's wildlife and the role of hunting in local culture.

291 G8 Avenue de la Promenade, 84390 Sault 04 90 64 01 21 Jul, Aug daily 9–1, 2–7; May, Jun Mon–Sat 9–12, 2–6, Sun 9.30–12.30; Sep, Oct, Jan–end Apr Mon–Sat 9–12, 2–6; Nov, Dec Mon–Sat 9–12, 2–5

### SÉGURET

www.seguret.fr

This delightful village high on the slopes of the Dentelles de Montmirail (▷ 228) had fallen largely into ruins by the mid-20th century, when it was saved by the enthusiastic *Amis de Séguret* (Friends of Séguret), who restored its houses and monuments and instigated customs like the *Pegouado* torchlight procession at Christmas and the Provençal Folklore Fair in August. The village has a 15th-century fountain and a 12th-century church and is a local hub for crafts and culture.

Don't miss the view from the village's main square, of vineyards below and rocky summits above.

290 E8 Mairie (town hall): rue des Poternes, 84110 Séguret 04 90 46 91 06

### SÉRIGNAN-DU-COMTAT

www.serignanducomtat.com

Jean-Henri Fabre put this village on the map. Born in 1823, Fabre rose to become a leading scientist. Acclaimed for his work in many fields outside of his specialism—the study of insects—Fabre became known too as an author of school textbooks. In March 1879, he purchased the house and land outside Sérignan that was to become his *harmas*, from a Provençal word meaning a secure enclosure. He cultivated this site as a haven for insect life. After Fabre's death in 1915, the Paris-based Musée National d'Histoire Naturelle purchased the *harmas*. Between 2000 and 2006, a total of more than one million euros was invested in the restoration of the property.

290 D8 L'Harmas de Fabre, route d'Orange, 84830 Sérignan-du-Comtat 04 90 30 57 62 Jul, Aug Mon, Tue, Thu, Fri 10–12.30, 3.30–7, Sun 3.30–7; Apr–Jun, Sep, Oct Mon, Tue, Thu, Fri 10–12.30, 2.30–6, Sun 2.30–6. Closed Nov–end Mar

**Left** *The baptistery at Venasque*

## LE THOR

www.oti-delasorgue.fr

One of the most impressive churches in the Vaucluse is Notre-Dame-du-Lac (consult tourist office for times), on the banks of the Sorgue river at the market town of Le Thor. Completed at the end of the 12th century, it marks the first transitional steps from Romanesque to Gothic. The Gothic vaulting in the nave is one of the earliest examples in Provence. The finely decorated west portal shelters a wooden statue of the Virgin.

See stalactites and small pools in the beautiful caves called Grotte de Thouzon, 3km (2 miles) north of Le Thor (www.grottes-thouzon.com; Jul, Aug daily 10–6; Apr–end Jun, Sep, Oct daily 10–12, 2–6, last visit 5.30; Mar Sun 2–6, last visit 5.30).

295 E9 Place du 11 Novembre, 84250 Le Thor 04 90 33 92 31 Mon 2–6, Tue–Fri 9.30–12.15, 2–6, Sat 9.30–12.15

## VAISON-LA-ROMAINE

▷ 240–241.

## VALRÉAS

www.ot-valreas.info

Valréas is a pleasant town whose economy is based on the cardboard industry, winemaking and lavender products. Administratively it is a curiosity: Officially in the Vaucluse *département*, it is surrounded by the Drôme *département*. This arrangement dates back to the 14th century, when the popes in Avignon wished to expand their territory by purchasing land on the French side of the border. When King Charles VII heard that the popes had acquired Valréas, he ordered no more land to be sold to them—leaving Valréas and the surrounding villages isolated. When the *départements* of France were created in the 18th century, Valréas opted to remain part of the Vaucluse (and hence part of Provence). This is why Valréas likes to add *L'Enclave des Papes* to its name.

The historic heart of town has many fine old houses, the Romanesque church of Notre-Dame-de-Nazareth and the imposing 18th-century Château de Simiane, now housing the town hall and hosting temporary art exhibitions in summer. The town's cardboard manufacturing has flourished here since the 19th century, giving rise to an unexpectedly fascinating museum, the Musée du Cartonnage et de l'Imprimerie, in avenue Maréchal Foch (Apr–end Oct Mon, Wed–Sat 10–12, 3–6, Sun 3–6; Nov–end Mar Mon, Wed–Sat 10–12, 2–5, Sun 2–5).

Travel to the nearby village of Richerenches, 7km (4.5 miles) southeast, to see the famous truffle market every Saturday from December to the end of March.

290 E7 Avenue Maréchal Leclerc, 84601 Valréas 04 90 35 04 71 Nov–end Feb Mon–Sat 9.15–12.15, 2–5; Mar–end Jun, Sep, Oct Mon–Sat 9.15–12.15, 2–6; 1st 2 weeks in Jul, last 2 weeks in Aug Mon–Sat 9–12.30, 2.30–6.30; mid-Jul to mid-Aug Mon–Sat 9–12.30, 2.30–6.30, Sun 9–12.30 The town celebrates *La Nuit du Petit-St-Jean* on 23 Jun with a spectacular torchlight procession

## VENASQUE

www.tourisme-venasque.com

Venasque's cherry orchards look magnificent in spring, with their snow-like blossom. The town is on a high point in the Vaucluse hills, with a commanding view of the Carpentras plain. Its wild and lonely position has been of strategic importance for millennia, since the Ligurian settlement of Vindasca was founded here. Dominating the route from Carpentras to Apt, Venasque became a refuge for the bishops of Carpentras after the Roman withdrawal in the third to fifth centuries AD.

The town's baptistery (mid-Apr to mid-Oct daily 9–12, 1–6.30; mid-Oct to mid-Apr daily 9.15–12, 1–5; closed mid-Dec to early Jan), beside the church, dates from the sixth century AD and is said to stand on the remains of a Roman temple. It is one of the oldest surviving religious buildings in France. Inside are fragments of a fifth-century sarcophagus and there is an octagonal font set in the floor.

At the other end of Venasque is the medieval rampart wall with three turrets, which once blocked the approach to this fortress village. Venasque was so important in the Middle Ages that it gave its name to the papal territories, the Comtat Venaissin.

295 E9 Grand 'Rue, 84210 Venasque 04 90 66 11 66 Jul, Aug Sun, Mon 3–7, Tue–Sat 10–12.30, 3–7; Apr–end Jun, Sep, Oct Sun, Mon 2–6, Tue–Sat 10–12, 2–6. Closed Nov–end Mar

# VAISON-LA-ROMAINE

### INFORMATION

www.vaison-la-romaine.com
290 E7 Place du Chanoine-Sautel, 84110 Vaison-la-Romaine 04 90 36 02 11 Jul, Aug daily 9–12.30, 2–6.45; mid-Oct to end Mar Mon–Sat 9–12, 2–5.45; Apr–end Jun, Sep to mid-Oct Mon–Sat 9–12, 2–5.45, Sun 9–12

**Above** *An intricate Roman mosaic*

## INTRODUCTION

The largest archaeological site in France is also a pleasing little market town set among Provençal hills. Vaison rises from the narrow gorge of the Ouvèze river in an attractive setting on the north side of the Dentelles de Montmirail (▷ 228), near where the hills meet the plain. The town's great attraction is its two connected archaeological sites, totalling 15ha (37 acres), where exceptional ruins of the Roman period have been uncovered. On the other side of the Ouvèze, reached by crossing a Roman bridge that is still in daily use, the town's medieval quarter, or Haute Ville (upper town), stands high on a hill. Apart from its impressive historical sights, Vaison is a thriving and appealing little market town. The Roman sites, archaeological museum and other sights may be visited on a single ticket, *Billet Tous Monuments*, available from the ticket office next to the Roman sites.

Vaison started out as a Gaulish settlement called Vasio. Colonized by the Romans in the second century BC, it became a prosperous town named Vasio Vocontiorum, linked to the other side of the Ouvèze by the Pont Romain, still in use today. After invasion by Visigoths and the fall of the Roman Empire, the town was re-established on the better protected hillside on the other side of the Ouvèze. In the 18th century the town spread back across the river, and was built largely on top of the Roman ruins. In the 20th century excavations saved what was left of the ruins of the Roman town. The popularity of the Roman site with visitors led Vaison to develop other attractions, including hotels, restaurants and a summer festival of drama, music and dance.

## WHAT TO SEE

### QUARTIER DU PUYMIN

The Puymin quarter is the higher and larger of the two Roman sites. It has a visible street layout, some surviving walls and even some patches of frescoes and mosaic floors. The highlight is the Roman theatre, the Théâtre Antique

(▷ 241). Other points of interest include the extensive House of Apollon Lauré, named for a white marble head of Apollo; the even larger Tonnelle House; the public space known as the Sanctuary, decorated with statuary and probably with some religious connection; and an area of smaller houses and workshops.
✉ Avenue Général-de-Gaulle, 84110 Vaison-la-Romaine ☎ 04 90 36 50 48 🕐 Jun–end Sep daily 9–6.30; Nov, Dec, Feb daily 10–12, 2–5; Mar, Oct daily 10–12, 2–5.30; Apr, May daily 9.30–6. Closed Jan ✋ *Billet Tous Monuments:* Adult €8, child (12–18) €3.50, under 12 free

### THÉÂTRE ANTIQUE
Cut into the Puymin hill is first-century AD Roman Vaison's fine theatre, which was restored in the 20th century and is now the venue for a range of events. Its tiered rows of seating, joined by stairs and topped with a portico, could accommodate 6,000 spectators.
✉ Within the Quartier du Puymin, same ticket and opening hours

### QUARTIER DE LA VILLASSE
A modern road separates the Villasse and Puymin sites. The lower site, called Quartier de la Villasse, is smaller but has a remarkable street of small shops, workshops and villas with mosaic floors. One notable structure is the ruins of the House of the Silver Bust, the largest house excavated in Vaison. The street's large paving stones are still in place, and there are sewers and other plumbing works beneath. On one side it is clear that the walkway was arcaded as the supporting columns survive. On the east side of the site are baths. The Théo Desplans Musée Archéologique (Theo Desplans Archaeology Museum, included in entry ticket for Villasse) on the site displays a collection of sculpture unearthed there.
✉ Avenue Général-de-Gaulle, 84110 Vaison-la-Romaine ☎ 04 90 36 50 48 🕐 Apr–end Sep daily 10–12, 2.30–6.30; Nov, Dec, Feb daily 10–12, 2–5; Mar, Oct daily 10–12.30, 2–5.30. Closed Jan ✋ *Billet Tous Monuments:* Adult €8, child (12–18) €3.50, under 12 free

### HAUTE VILLE
The medieval quarter (Haute Ville) stands apart from modern Vaison, rising on a hill on the other side of the river. A short walk leads up to this attractive district of lanes and alleys. At the top stand the ruins of the castle built in the 12th century by the Counts of Toulouse, and partly reconstructed in the 15th century. From here you can enjoy views down to the town and across to Mont Ventoux (▷ 233).

### PONT ROMAIN
Vaison's main street, Grande Rue, runs down between old houses to the Roman bridge, which crosses the Ouvèze river. A single arch with a single-track cobbled roadway on top, it has not been widened or hardly even repaired in 2,000 years, although the parapet on top is modern. The present parapet was put in place in 1993, replacing the 17th-century parapet that was swept away in the catastrophic floods of 22 September 1992.

## MORE TO SEE

### NOTRE-DAME DE NAZARETH
About 10 minutes' walk from the Quartier de la Villasse site, the Romanesque cathedral, Notre-Dame de Nazareth, has lovely 12th-century cloisters.
✉ Avenue Général-de-Gaulle, 84110 Vaison-la-Romaine 🕐 Jul–end Sep daily 10–12.30, 2–6.30; Apr–end Jun daily 3–6; Oct daily 10–12, 2–5; last 3 weeks in Feb, 1st week in Mar daily 3–5; doors close 15 min earlier. Closed Nov to 1st week in Feb, last 3 weeks in Mar ✋ *Billet Tous Monuments:* Adult €8, child (12–18) €3, under 12 free

**Right** *A statue of a Roman warrior*

### TIPS
» There's a large, lively street market every Tuesday morning.

» There are large parking areas next to the two Roman sites.

» A summer festival of drama, music and dance is held at the Roman theatre from early July to mid-August. Every three years, there is also a Festival of Choral Music (www.choralies.fr).

# FONTAINE-DE-VAUCLUSE

**The Fontaine de Vaucluse is one of the most powerful resurgent springs in the world, and visitors flock to the village that bears its name to see the water flow. An early admirer was Petrarch, who lived here in the 14th century. This tour begins in the village, before heading out to explore the surrounding area. It takes in L'Isle-sur-la-Sorgue, with its canals and waterfalls, L'Abbaye de Sénanque, famous for its lavender, and the hill village of Gordes.**

**THE DRIVE**
**Distance:** 65km (40 miles)
**Time:** 1 day
**Start/end at:** Fontaine-de-Vaucluse

★ The Fontaine de Vaucluse (▷ 230) is at its most powerful in March and April, when water levels are boosted by the melting snow and up to 200 cubic metres (7,000 cubic feet) of water per second thunder out. It is here that the river Sorgue begins. The spring is around 2km (1.2 miles) from the heart of the village. There are several attractions on the way, including a history museum and a traditional water-powered paper mill.

Park in the village and walk to place de la Colonne, with its statue of Petrarch. Follow the woodland path to the spring.

Walk back to your car and start the drive by heading for L'Isle-sur-la-Sorgue on the D25.

❶ L'Isle-sur-la-Sorgue (▷ 232), as its name suggests, is on an island in the river Sorgue. Stroll past the soothing canals and watermills or visit the magnificent baroque Notre-Dame-des-Anges. The town is also the antiques capital of Provence.

Take the D938 north to Pernes-les-Fontaines, 11km (7 miles) away.

❷ Pernes-les-Fontaines (▷ 236) has 36 fountains, many dating from the 18th century. Visit the Tour Ferrande (tours through the tourist office) to see some of the oldest frescoes in France, dating from the 13th century. Notre-Dame-des-Graces and the 16th-century Porte Notre-Dame are also worth seeing.

Leave Pernes-les-Fontaines and follow signs for St-Didier (D28), and then Le Beaucet (D39).

❸ At Le Beaucet you'll find a ruined castle, cave dwellings and a pilgrimage site dedicated to rainmaker St. Gens. A monument to French Resistance fighters was added to the parking area in 1995.

Take the D247 to Venasque, a beautiful clifftop village that was once the seat of bishops.

❹ Venasque (▷ 239) was once a formidable stronghold and gave shelter to the bishops of Carpentras during the barbarian invasions. The

**Opposite** *Pretty Fontaine-de-Vaucluse*

baptistery, founded in the sixth century AD, is one of the oldest religious buildings in France.

The D4 winds its way through a sea of vines until it meets the D177. Take the D177, which runs through the Forêt du Murs and then plunges through a steep and mysterious gorge, with towering limestone walls on either side. The Abbaye de Sénanque waits at the other end.

❺ The Abbaye de Sénanque (▷ 221) is a Cistercian monastery dating from the mid-12th century. At dusk, listen for the clank of bells as sheep are rounded up for the night.

After Sénanque, you reach the picturesque hill village of Gordes, whose houses seem to cling precariously to the terraces.

❻ Gordes (▷ 231) is dominated by a Renaissance chateau restored by Hungarian artist Victor Vasarely. An art gallery displays pop art works by Pol Mara. The Grande Salle, on the first floor, has a wonderful Renaissance fireplace.

Leave Gordes on the D2 and follow signs to the Village des Bories, 4km (2.5 miles) away.

❼ The Village des Bories (▷ 231) is intriguing. The stone huts *(bories)* have been used for shelter, storerooms, ovens and agricultural huts. This style of dwellings was first used in megalithic times.

The D2 ends with signs to Fontaine-de-Vaucluse pointing in opposite directions. Take the tourist route (D100A), which is more scenic, to return to the village.

## WHEN TO GO

The Fontaine de Vaucluse is in full flow in spring. During late summer, it can be less impressive.

**Right** *A house in L'Isle-sur-la-Sorgue*

## WHERE TO EAT

All the towns and villages on the route have restaurants and cafés.

### AU FIL DE TEMPS

✉ Place Giraud, 84210 Pernes-les-Fontaines ☎ 04 90 30 09 48 🕑 Tue–Sat 12–2.30, 7.30–10. Closed late Dec to mid-Jan

## INFORMATION

### TOURIST INFORMATION

www.oti-delasorgue.fr ✉ Chemin du Gouffre, 84800 Fontaine-de-Vaucluse ☎ 04 90 20 32 22 🕑 May–end Sep daily 10–1, 2–6; Oct–end Apr Mon–Sat 9.30–12.30, 1.30–5.30, Sun 1.30–5.30

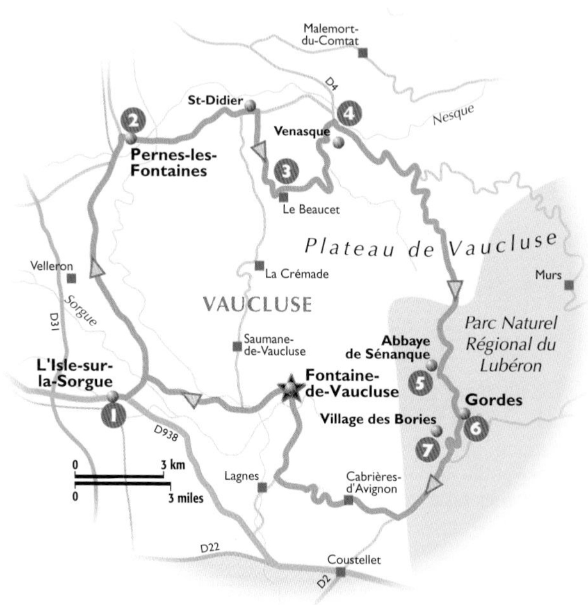

# VAISON-LA-ROMAINE

**The legacy of the Romans lives on in Vaison-la-Romaine, where you can see ruins dating back around 2,000 years. This walk takes you past the town's Roman bridge, medieval gateway and 12th-century cathedral.**

**THE WALK**
**Distance:** 3.5km (2.2 miles)
**Time:** 1.5 hours
**Start/end at:** Vaison-la-Romaine's main parking area, avenue Général-de-Gaulle
**?** The walk has some steep climbs.

**HOW TO GET THERE**
Vaison-la-Romaine is 30km (19 miles) northeast of Orange.

★ Vaison-la-Romaine (▷ 240–241) straddles the river Ouvèze and over the centuries its inhabitants have moved back and forth from one bank to the other. The Celts were the first to build a settlement on the hill here. The Romans arrived in the second century BC, choosing to set up *Vasio Vocontiorum* on the other side of the river. Today, you can see excavated Roman ruins in the lower half of town, while the upper part has reminders of its late-medieval heyday.

Start from the main parking area, next to the Roman sites on avenue Général-de-Gaulle. Walk through the busy and appealing heart of town down to the ancient Pont Romain.

❶ The Pont Romain is a Roman bridge, 17m (56ft) long. Note the level of the Ouvèze river below the bridge: Usually a trickle at the bottom of the deep valley, in the disastrous floods of September 1992 the river flowed over the top of the Pont Romain.

Take the road opposite the bridge, which leads up to the Haute Ville. Go through the arched gateway, a remnant of the medieval ramparts.

❷ Upper Vaison is an almost complete medieval town, with attractive alleys of houses dating from the 13th and 14th centuries. The fortifications were constructed in part with stones from the ruins of the Roman town.

Turn sharply left, backtracking a little, up the narrow rue de l'Horloge. Continue climbing, looking towards the clock tower that gives the road its name. Follow the road around to the right, and turn left at an intersection onto rue de l'Église, following signs for the chateau. There is a viewpoint to the left, near the church. Pass the church and continue uphill to Plan Pascal and on again, up some steps, to the rue de la Charité. This road narrows into a rough track. At the end of the stone wall on the left, turn left and climb to the ruins of the chateau.

❸ The chateau gives you wonderful views of the Roman ruins and the lower town. A Celtic fortress once stood here. The current chateau was built by Count Raymond of Toulouse in the 12th century. It now stands in ruins and is closed to the public.

Return to the stone wall. Turn right and left under an arch and down the steps. These lead to a beautiful square with a fountain and the Hôtel de Prévôt.

Leave the square to the left and go down rue des Fours, one of the prettiest streets in old Vaison. When a road leads off to the right, keep straight ahead. Turn right at the next junction to reach an intersection. Turn left, then take the next turn on the right, which opens up to a view of the lower town. Descend the steps on the left and then more steps to the right, to reach rue du Château. Turn left and follow the road to a main road junction. Bear right and cross the river Ouvèze by the Pont Neuf. Take the first right into avenue Jules Ferry and then go left to reach the cathedral.

❹ The Romanesque Cathédrale Notre-Dame de Nazareth was built in the 12th century, on the site of a 6th-century Merovingian church. The old bishop's throne sits behind the altar and there are lovely 12th-century cloisters.

Return to avenue Jules Ferry and walk the 500m (545 yards) or so along it to avenue Général-de-Gaulle and the entrance to the Quartier du Puymin.

❺ The Quartier du Puymin has some fascinating Roman ruins, including several villas and a theatre that held around 6,000 people. You can also see intricate mosaic floors.

After visiting this extensive Roman site, cross the road to enter the town's other major area, the Quartier de la Villasse, where you'll find the Roman baths. The parking area is nearby.

## WHEN TO GO

You can do this walk at any time of year. On cool, clear days there are good views of Mont Ventoux (▷ 233) from the chateau ruins.

## INFORMATION

### TOURIST INFORMATION

✉ Place du Chanoine-Sautel, 84110 Vaison-la-Romaine ☎ 04 90 36 02 11 🕐 Jul, Aug daily 9–12.30, 2–6.45; mid-Oct to end Mar Mon–Sat 9–12, 2–5.45; Apr–end Jun, Sep to mid-Oct Mon–Sat 9–12, 2–5.45, Sun 9–12

## WHERE TO EAT

There are plenty of restaurants on and around the Grande Rue and place Chanoine-Sautel.

**Opposite** *Intricately carved columns at the cathedral*
**Below** *The ancient Pont Romain*

# AVIGNON

**Avignon offers a winning combination: culture, history, cafés and shops. This walk includes some of the city's most well-known sights, including the famous bridge and the mighty Palais des Papes, but also leads you down quieter cobbled streets and to small shady squares.**

**THE WALK**
**Distance:** 3km (2 miles)
**Time:** half a day
**Start/end at:** place du Palais, Avignon

**HOW TO GET THERE**
Avignon is just off the A7 *autoroute*.

★ The formidable Palais des Papes was created for the popes in the 14th century (▷ 224–225). Inside, vivid frescoes help you imagine the sumptuous conditions that once existed here. Several other interesting buildings sit around the place du Palais, including the 17th-century Hôtel des Monnaies, the 14th-century Petit Palais at the far end and the 12th-century cathedral, Notre-Dames-des-Doms, right beside the palace.

Start from the place du Palais. Take the ramp rising from the square beside the cathedral, to the park and gardens of the Rocher des Doms.

❶ The Rocher des Doms is a high point overlooking the Rhône river. From one side it offers a fine view of Pont St-Bénézet, the legendary medieval Pont d'Avignon.

Follow the signs back down narrow streets and worn steps to the river. This is the Quartier de la Balance, a renowned gypsy area in the 19th century. Visit the Pont St-Bénézet and its chapel.

❷ Pont St-Bénézet owes its fame to the children's rhyme *Sur le Pont d'Avignon* and was built in the 12th century, legend has it, by a shepherd called Bénézet, who was acting on the orders of an angel. A terrible flood in the 17th century caused it to lose all but four of its 22 arches.

Leave the bridge through the small shop and walk back alongside the remains of the papal fortifications to the Porte du Rhône. Pass through and turn immediately right to walk in their shadow until you come to place Crillon, with its shady trees and pretty paved square. Pass the Hôtel d'Europe, then turn right and walk for some 400m (430 yards) along rue Joseph Vernet to the Musée Calvet.

❸ The Musée Calvet houses a beautiful collection of French, Italian, Flemish and Dutch paintings, sculptures, porcelain and furniture from the last five centuries. Nearby is the Musée Requien, with a small natural history collection (free).

At the end of rue Joseph Vernet, turn left into rue de la République, Avignon's main thoroughfare. Almost immediately, on the right side of the road, is the Musée Lapidaire.

❹ The Lapidaire museum is an annex of the Musée Calvet, housing local architectural finds. It is in a 17th-century Jesuit college.

Turn left out of the museum and left again down rue F. Mistral. Turn left into rue Laboureur. Number five is the Fondation Angladon.

❺ Fondation Angladon is a wonderful art museum that opened in the mid-1990s in the Hôtel de Massilian. It features mainly 19th- and 20th-century art, and highlights include paintings by Cézanne, Picasso and Degas. There are also personal works by the two founders.

Continue along rue Laboureur to place St-Didier.

❻ Place St-Didier is home to the lovely Provençal-style church of St-Didier and the striking tower of the Livrée de Ceccano.

Make your way back to the hectic rue de la République along the small rue du Prevôt, then turn right and continue until you reach place de l'Horloge.

❼ Place de l'Horloge is a large, shady square boasting a medieval clock tower and plenty of cafés. Enjoy a drink and watch the antics of the street musicians, jugglers and painters.

Take the pedestrian-only rue des Marchands to reach the Église St-Pierre, with its Renaissance carvings, then cross place St-Pierre and follow signs to the Palais des Papes. The route weaves through narrow alleys to reach a rear entrance to the shop in the Palais. Keep left to follow the lane back to the place du Palais.

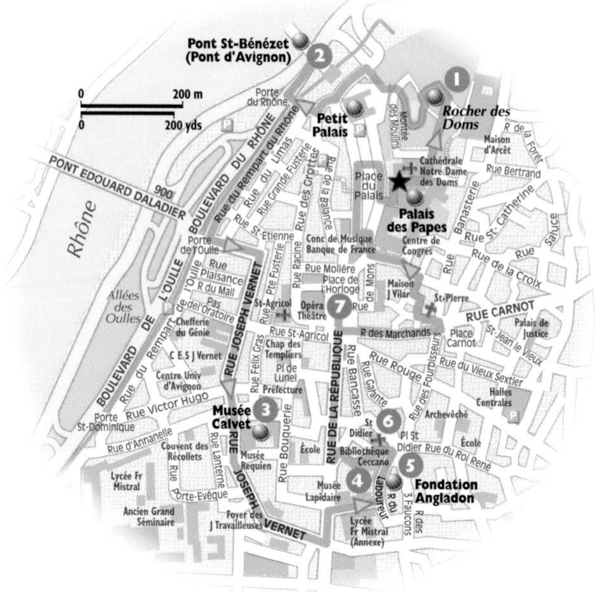


## WHEN TO GO

You can enjoy this walk any time of year. The shrubs in the gardens of Rocher des Doms are at their best in April, and the views early in the morning are stunning.

## INFORMATION

### TOURIST INFORMATION

www.ot-avignon.fr
✉ 41 cours Jean-Jaurès, 84004 Avignon
☎ 04 32 74 32 74 ⌚ Easter–end Oct Mon–Sat 9–6 (until 7 during the Festival), Sun 9.45–5; Nov–Easter Mon–Fri 9–6, Sat 9–5, Sun 10–12

## WHERE TO EAT

There are many restaurants and cafés on the route, especially in place de l'Horloge.

**Opposite** *Pont St-Bénézet by day*
**Below** *...and at dusk*

# WHAT TO DO

**Above** *Stocking up on fresh fruit and vegetables at Avignon's Marché des Halles*

## APT

### APT UNION

www.lesfleurons-apt.com

This confectioner is a world leader when it comes to the glacé cherry. Beautiful wooden boxes contain the fruits. To visit the factory, reserve ahead.

✉ Quartier Salignan, BP 137, 84405 Apt ☎ 04 90 76 31 31 🕐 Jul, Aug Mon–Sat 8.30–7; Dec daily 8.30–7; Sep–end Nov, Jan–end Jun Mon–Sat 9–12, 2–6

## AVIGNON

### BAR DE L'HÔTEL D'EUROPE

www.heurope.com

This elegant bar is part of a four-star hotel in a 16th-century building. Sit out in the pleasant shady courtyard in fair weather.

✉ 12 place Crillon, 84000 Avignon ☎ 04 90 14 76 76 🕐 Daily 12pm–1am

### LA BOUTEILLERIE DU PALAIS DES PAPES

www.palais-des-papes.com

In the Palace's former Artillery Room, La Bouteillerie sells more than 40 types of local Côtes du Rhône wines by the bottle or case. Thirsty visitors can try before buying; prices start at €2 a glass.

✉ Palais des Papes, entrance through place du Palais des Papes or place de l'Amirande, 84000 Avignon ☎ 04 90 27 50 85 🕐 Open during Palais hours (▷ 225)

### BOWLING

www.bowlingavignon.com

Test your skills on one of the 16 computerized bowling alleys here.

✉ Avenue Paul-Claudel, 84000 Avignon ☎ 04 90 88 50 11 🕐 Mon, Tue, Thu, Fri 3pm–2am, Wed, Sat, Sun 2pm–2am 💶 €3.90–€6.50 per game

### CADILLAC CAFÉ

http://cadillac-cafe.fr

Go back to 1950s Americana at this venue, with its frescoes of Marilyn and Elvis, pool tables and video games. There are plenty of theme nights and barbecues in summer.

✉ 11 bis route de Lyon, 84000 Avignon ☎ 04 90 86 99 57 🕐 Daily 2pm–1am

### CHAPELIER MOURET

www.chapelier.com

The same family has been making hats here since 1860, following methods passed from father to son. There's a great collection of panamas and *capelines* (wide-brimmed hats typical of the region).

✉ 20 rue des Marchands, 84000 Avignon ☎ 04 90 85 39 38 🕐 Tue–Sat 10–12.30, 2–7

### LE CID

www.lecidcafe.com

Seventies pop decor (updated annually) and house and lounge rhythms are the key elements of this bar, popular with the gay and lesbian community. On the first Friday of the month, Le Cid serves up sushi plates (€4) with evening aperitifs (7–11pm).

✉ 11 place de l'Horloge, 84000 Avignon ☎ 04 90 82 30 38 🕐 Daily 6.30pm–1am

### LE CUBANITO CAFÉ

Che Guevara posters adorn the walls at this Cuban den where you can enjoy a rum cocktail. Try a free salsa class any evening at 9pm.

✉ 51 rue Carnot, 84000 Avignon ☎ 04 90 86 98 04 🕐 Tue–Sun 10am–1am

### MARCHÉ FORAIN

Avignon's biggest market takes you to the other side of the Mediterranean, with North African spices, vegetables and fruit, plus clothes, housewares and bric-a-brac.

✉ Jardins de la Préfecture, 84000 Avignon 🕐 Sat, Sun 6am–1pm

### MARCHÉ DES HALLES

www.avignon-leshalles.com

Sample or purchase a wide range of local produce at this market.

✉ Place Pie, 84000 Avignon 🕐 Tue–Sun 6am–1.30pm

### MARCHÉ AUX PUCES

Antiques dealers mix with locals at this large bazaar. Arrive early to have the best chance of finding a bargain. After browsing, you can enjoy a drink in one of the nearby cafés.
✉ Place des Carmes, 84000 Avignon
🕒 Sun 7–1

### OPÉRA CAFÉ

This contemporary chic bar-restaurant, on Avignon's busiest square, is a hit with the trendy crowd. There is a DJ most evenings.
✉ 24 place de l'Horloge, 84000 Avignon
☎ 04 90 86 17 43 🕒 Daily 9am–1am (until 3am in Jul)

### OPÉRA-THÉÂTRE D'AVIGNON ET DES PAYS DE VAUCLUSE

www.operatheatredavignon.fr
There is lavish decor at this Italian-style theatre, with gilded panels, painted ceilings and statues of playwrights Molière and Racine.
✉ 1 rue Racine, 84000 Avignon ☎ 04 90 82 42 42 🕒 Tue–Sat 8.30pm, Sun 2.30pm

### PATINOIRE D'AVIGNON

www.patinoire-avignon.com
This ice rink is home to the Castors (the Beavers) ice-hockey team.
✉ 2483 chemin de l'Amandier, 84000 Avignon ☎ 04 90 88 54 32 🕒 Mon–Thu 9.30–12, 2.30–5, Fri 9.30–12, 2.30–5, 9–11.30, Sat 2.30–5, 9–11.30, Sun 2.30–5
✋ Adult €9.50, child (under 13) €6.50

### RED ZONE BAR

www.redzonebar.com
Here you'll find salsa on Tuesday night, club night on Wednesday, student night on Thursday, dancing on Friday and Saturday, and electro/house on Sunday.
✉ 25 rue Carnot, 84000 Avignon ☎ 04 90 27 02 44 🕒 Tue–Sat 9pm–3am, Sun–Mon 10pm–3am

### LE ROUGE GORGE

On Fridays and Saturdays this place hosts cabaret-style dinner theatre. The rest of the week sees jazz, rock, samba and flamenco.
✉ 10 rue de la Peyrollerie, 84000 Avignon
☎ 04 90 14 02 54 🕒 Sep–end Jul Fri, Sat (and other show nights) 8pm–3am

### SHAKESPEARE LIBRAIRIE

There are many second-hand books in English at this store, which also has a tea room. No visit is complete without some tea and cake.
✉ 155 rue de la Carreterie, 84000 Avignon
☎ 04 90 27 38 50 🕒 Tue–Sat 9.30–12, 2–6

### SOULEIADO

www.souleiado.com
Browse beautiful Provençal cotton and silk, linens and printed clothes, at Souleiado's newest boutique.
✉ 9 rue Joseph Vernet, 84000 Avignon
☎ 04 90 86 32 05 🕒 Mon–Sat 10–7

### TAPALOCAS

www.tapalocas.com
Always bustling, this former warehouse turned bodega, with long wooden tables and a mosaic-adorned bar, offers a large choice of tapas. There are concerts on Thursdays from 8.30pm, plus free WiFi.
✉ 15 rue Galante, 84000 Avignon ☎ 04 90 82 56 84 🕒 Daily 11.45am–1.30am (until 3am in Jul)

**Below** *Hats for sale in Avignon*

### THÉÂTRE DU CHIEN QUI FUME

www.chienquifume.com

Enjoy theatre, songs and dance here. Popular since its opening in 1982, the Chien's performances range from choreographed fairy tales to quirky monologues, in French.

75 rue des Teinturiers, 84000 Avignon 04 90 85 25 87 €12–€22

## CARPENTRAS

### CONFISERIE BONO

www.confiseriebono.fr

Glacé fruits have been prepared at this store since 1925. The traditional methods that made its reputation are still used.

280 allée Jean Jaurès, 84200 Carpentras 04 90 63 04 99 Mon–Fri 9–12, 2–6, Sat 10–12

### JOELLE

www.lesolivades.fr

Les Olivades (the brand sold in this shop) has been making printed fabrics since 1818, first seeking its inspiration in the *indiennes* (fabrics imported from India during the 17th century), then establishing the product as a tradition of Provence. The beautiful collection includes tableware and clothing.

102 rue Moricelly, 84200 Carpentras 04 90 63 33 50 Mon–Sat 9.30–12, 2–6

### MARCHÉ DE LA TRUFFE

Black truffle is cultivated in the Vaucluse and collected during winter with the help of dogs. This market displays this regional speciality.

Place Aristide Briand, 84200 Carpentras Mid-Nov to mid-Mar Fri 8am–11am

## CAVAILLON

### LE GRENIER À SONS

www.grenier-a-sons.org

This 350-seat concert hall stages jazz, rock, blues, reggae and more.

157 avenue du Général-de-Gaulle, 84301 Cavaillon 04 90 06 44 20 €10–€15

## COUSTELLET

### LA GARE COUSTELLET

www.aveclagare.org

Formerly a railway station, this is now a 280-seat venue hosting anything from jazz to rock. There are also art and photography exhibitions, and multimedia spaces.

105 quai Entreprises, 84660 Coustellet 04 90 76 84 38 Multimedia centre: Tue, Thu–Sat 4–6.30, Wed 10–12, 4–6.30; performances: Fri, Sat 9pm–2am Concerts €5–€15

## GORDES

### HERVÉ THIBAULT

http://hervethibault.free.fr

Artist Hervé Thibault exhibits worldwide but keeps a permanent gallery at his home in a tiny hamlet close to Gordes.

Grand'Rue, Les Baumettes, 842220 Gordes 04 90 72 27 53 Call for opening hours

### HOT AIR BALLOON PROVENCE

www.montgolfiere-provence-ballooning.com

These hot-air balloons fly over the picturesque villages of the Lubéron, including Gordes, Roussillon and Lacoste. The tour lasts between 40 and 80 minutes. Enjoy a picnic and champagne after landing.

Joucas, 84220 Gordes 04 90 05 76 77 By appointment €175–€245

## L'ISLE-SUR-LA-SORGUE

### BOUTIQUE RETOUR DE VOYAGE

Browse through an exotic medley of furniture, cookbooks and crafts, collected from all over the world by next door's B&B owners Frédéric and Marie Claude.

6 rue Rose Goudard, 84800 L'Isle-sur-la-Sorgue 04 90 20 74 86 Tue–Sun 10.30–6

### MARCHÉ ANTIQUITÉS AND BROCANTE

L'Isle-sur-la-Sorgue's winding streets overflow with stands selling clothes, jewellery, local foods but primarily antiques. Surrounding antique shops remain open during the market, too.

84800 L'Isle-sur-la-Sorgue Sun 9–6

## LAURIS

### CAP RANDO

www.cap-rando.com

This equestrian venue organizes various routes for discovering Provence on horseback. These include exploring the Parc Naturel Régional du Lubéron, following the lavender route (from the Lubéron to Verdon and then Nice) and crossing the Provençal Alps. Some carriage tours are also available.

Chemin de Recaute, 84360 Lauris 04 90 08 41 44 All year long by appointment From €50 (half day) to €790 (one week, including room and board)

## LOURMARIN

### LA BOUTIQUE DU MOULIN

This petite space is packed with elegant homewares, such as traditional textiles and hand-painted ceramic bowls.

Rue du Temple, 84160 Lourmarin 04 90 68 82 97 Tue–Sat 10–6.30

### LE SPA DE CLARICE

www.lespadeclarice.com

Within the spa's pared down, Provençal ambiance, expert Karine Isnard offers massages (from €38), manicures (€8) and other luxurious treatments. Reserve in advance.

Clos de la Treille, 84160 Lourmarin 04 90 68 61 31

### LE THÉ DANS L'ENCRIER

On Lourmarin's backstreets, this pretty little shop stocks English and French books. There's also a café on site, as well as free WiFi.

Rue de la Juiverie, 84160 Lourmarin 04 90 68 88 41 Tue–Sat 10.30–6.30

## LUBÉRON

### VÉLO LOISIR EN LUBÉRON

www.veloloisirluberon.com

This bicycling club organizes tours in the Parc Naturel Régional du Lubéron. It provides excellent free maps, as well as information on renting a bicycle, finding a bed for the night and transporting luggage.

203 rue Oscar Roulet, 84440 Robion 04 90 76 48 05 Mon–Fri 9–12.30, 2–6

## MONIEUX

### LES ANES DES ABEILLES

www.ane-at-rando.com

Spend a day travelling at donkey pace through the countryside around Mont Ventoux. The animals don't

carry you, but they do carry your bags—a perfect pace for children.
✉ Le Col de Abeilles, Les Isnards, 84390 Monieux ☎ 04 90 64 01 52 🕐 Daily by appointment Feb–end Dec. Closed Jan 💶 €45 per day

## MORIÈRES-LÈS-AVIGNON

### GOLF DE CHÂTEAUBLANC

www.golfchateaublanc.com
There are two courses here: one 9-hole and one 18-hole. After your game, have a bite to eat at the restaurant.
✉ Les Plans, 84310 Morières-lès-Avignon ☎ 04 90 33 39 08 🕐 Daily 8–7 💶 18 holes: Mon–Fri €42, Sat, Sun €53; 9 holes: Mon–Fri €30, Sat, Sun €35

## ORANGE

### SAFRAN D'ORANGE

www.safran-orange.com
Valérie Marcoup Ricard produces her own unique saffron, harvesting and drying the precious crocus threads in October and November. Weighing in as the world's most expensive spice, her prettily packaged saffron makes an exquisite present.
✉ Chemin des Ramas, Quartier Chaponnet, 84100 Orange ☎ 06 20 52 80 23 🕐 Visits by appointment only 💶 From €16 for 0.5g

## PIERRELATTE

### LA FERME AUX CROCODILES

www.lafermeauxcrocodiles.com
La Ferme aux Crocodiles lets children see crocodiles, alligators and other reptiles. The farm is under cover, with a huge dome ceiling. There's a playground and snack bar.
✉ Les Blanchettes, 26700 Pierrelatte ☎ 04 75 04 33 73 🕐 Mar–end Sep daily 9.30–7; Oct–end Feb daily 9.30–5 💶 Adult €11.50, child (3–12) €7, under 3 free

## RUSTREL

### COLORADO AVENTURES

www.colorado-aventures.com
Take a journey through the forest canopy on a series of rope bridges and walkways while securely fastened to a series of safety ropes. It's part assault course, part nature trail. There are four routes; allow between 2–4 hours.
✉ Le Château, 84400 Rustrel ☎ 06 78 26 68 91 🕐 Jul, Aug daily 9.30–5.40 (reservations advised); Mar–end Jun, Sep to mid-Nov Sat, Sun 10–4.30 (reservations obligatory) 💶 Adult €18, child (from age 6, with a height of 1.5m/5ft with hands raised) €14

## LE THOR

### AUDITORIUM DE VAUCLUSE

www.auditoriumlethor.com
This venue welcomes French and international high-quality shows.
✉ 971 chemin des Estourans, 84250 Le Thor ☎ 04 90 33 97 32 🕐 Ticket office: Mon–Sat 10–12.30, 2–6

# FESTIVALS AND EVENTS

## JULY

### AVIGNON FESTIVAL

www.festival-avignon.com
The biggest names in theatre, dance and music flock to Avignon for a season of spectacular performances against a stunning backdrop. There's also plenty of free street entertainment and fringe events (www.avignonleoff.com).
✉ Avignon ☎ 04 90 27 66 50 🕐 Three weeks in Jul

### CHORÉGIES

www.choregies.asso.fr
Orange's world-famous opera and classical music festival.
✉ Orange ☎ 04 90 34 24 24 🕐 Mid-Jul to early Aug

## AUGUST

### FÊTE DE LA LAVANDE

Sweet-smelling festivities in Sault, a town surrounded by lavender.
✉ Jardin des Lavandes, Sault ☎ 04 90 64 01 21 🕐 Mid-Aug

### FÊTE DE LA VÉRAISON

Medieval pageantry celebrates the maturing of the grapes in Châteauneuf-du-Pape. Wine producers set up stalls in the village, where you can taste their produce.
✉ Châteauneuf-du-Pape 🕐 Early Aug

**Below** *Residents of the Lubéron take part in a colourful procession, dressed in traditional Provençal costume*

## VAISON-LA-ROMAINE

### CAVE LA ROMAINE

www.cave-la-romaine.com
The first wine cooperative in the Vaison and Haut-Comtat regions, Cave La Romaine has been gathering and selling top-notch wines since 1924. The communal cellars stock quality Côtes du Rhône and Côtes du Ventoux, among other varieties, from more than 350 regional vineyards.
✉ Quartier le Colombier, 84110 Vaison-la-Romaine ☎ 04 90 36 55 90 🕐 Daily 8–12, 2–6.30; tastings by appointment

# EATING

**Above** *L'Entrée des Artistes, Avignon*

**PRICES AND SYMBOLS**

The prices given are the average for a two-course lunch (L) and a three-course dinner (D) for one person, without drinks. The wine price is for the least expensive bottle.

For a key to the symbols, ▷ 2.

## AVIGNON

### CHRISTIAN ÉTIENNE

www.christian-etienne.fr

This elegant restaurant is in a 14th-century palace and its dining room has beautiful painted ceilings and frescoes. The terrace looks onto the Palais des Papes. Christian Étienne, former sous-chef at Paris' Ritz Hotel, creates exquisite regional dishes, with truffles and tomatoes his preferred ingredients—black truffle omelette is a house special. In summer, try the tomato sorbet from the *Menu Tomate*.

✉ 10 rue de Mons, 84000 Avignon ☎ 04 90 86 16 50 🕐 Tue–Sat 12–1.15, 7.30–9.15 L €30, D €65, Wine €20

### LA COMPAGNIE DES COMPTOIRS

www.lacompagniedescomptoirs.com

Dine in elegant surroundings at this top-quality restaurant, launched by Olivier Château and the Pourcel brothers. The delicious cuisine has a Provençal accent.

✉ 83 rue Joseph Vernet, 84000 Avignon ☎ 04 90 85 99 04 🕐 Tue–Sat 12–2.30, 7–11 L €15, D €35, Wine €20

### LA CUISINE D'OLIVIER

www.hotelgolfgrandavignon.com

This light and modern dining room welcomes golfers and tourists throughout the day, so you aren't tied to standard French lunch and dinner times. There is a range of menus, from brasserie style to formal gourmet dishes, and the quality is good.

✉ Les Chênes Verts, 84270 Vedène, Avignon ☎ 04 90 31 96 11 🕐 Daily 8am–11pm L €18, D €35, Wine €14

### L'ENTRÉE DES ARTISTES

There's a retro bistro-style interior behind the red facade of this restaurant. Pictures of famous actresses and old opera posters hang on the walls. The pleasant terrace looks onto a lively square. The chef accommodates market finds and the menu changes frequently. You may be lucky enough to sample the home-smoked salmon, the daube of duck (the meat is slowly cooked in wine) or the crêpes Suzette (pancakes flambéed with bitter orange liqueur).

✉ 1 place des Carmes, 84000 Avignon ☎ 04 90 82 46 90 🕐 Mon–Fri 12–1.30, 7.30–10.30, Sat 7.30–10.30. Closed 2 weeks in Aug, last week in Dec L €19, D €30, Wine €12

### LA FOURCHETTE

Wood panels, wicker chairs and a multitude of forks *(fourchettes)* hanging on the wall give this restaurant a simple yet original feel. The menu offers innovative regional cuisine. Smoked haddock ravioli, sardines marinated in coriander and thyme custard showcase the interesting use of local food. The menu varies depending on what's available at the market each day.

✉ 17 rue Racine, 84000 Avignon ☎ 04 90 85 20 93 🕐 Mon–Fri 12–2, 7.30–9.30. Closed first 3 weeks of Aug L €26, D €31, Wine €18

### GRAND CAFÉ

www.legrandcafe-avignon.com

The Grand Café, next to Cinéma Utopia, is perfect for a drink or some regional cuisine before or after a film. The interior is impressive—the former warehouse has kept

its red-brick vaulted ceiling and also has four huge mirrors.
✉ 4 rue des Escaliers Sainte-Anne, 84000 Avignon ☎ 04 90 86 86 77 ⏲ Tue–Sat 12–12. Closed Jan 🖑 L €19, D €30, Wine €15

### LE PRIEURÉ

www.leprieure.fr
Across the Rhône from Avignon and so technically just outside the Provence border is this luxury hotel in a renovated old convent. There's a majestic dining room with stone arches and vaults, or eat out in the shady courtyard. The menu changes with the season but a speciality is Catalan lamb.
✉ 7 place du Chapitre, 30400 Villeneuve-lès-Avignon ☎ 04 90 15 90 15 ⏲ Apr–end Oct Tue 7.30–9.30, Wed–Sat 12–2, 7.30–9.30 (also Sun 12–2 Jun–end Sep). Closed Nov–end Mar 🖑 L €35, D €65, Wine €25

### LE SIMPLE SIMON

This is a little piece of old England in the heart of Avignon. Inside there are beamed ceilings, plates hanging on the walls, a collection of teapots and a large round table in the middle of the room where the cakes and other desserts are displayed. During the afternoon it's a great place to enjoy a cup of tea and a cake. At lunchtime, the dish of the day is often of British influence.
✉ 26 rue Petite-Fusterie, 84000 Avignon ☎ 04 90 86 62 70 ⏲ Tue–Sat 12–7. Closed Aug 🖑 L €17 (lunch only)

### WOOLOOMOOLOO

www.woolloo.com
A collection of African masks and other works of art, trinkets and low tables with cushions as seats create an unusual atmosphere. Order *maffe* (beef cooked slowly in a peanut butter sauce) or other tastes from around the world. The terrace looks onto one of Avignon's most picturesque streets.
✉ 16 rue des Teinturiers, 84000 Avignon ☎ 04 90 85 28 44 ⏲ Restaurant: daily 11.45–2, 7.30–12. Tea room: winter only, Sat, Sun 2–6 🖑 L €15, D €26, Wine €15

## BONNIEUX

### LA BASTIDE DE CAPELONGUE

www.capelongue.com
This exquisite, elegant restaurant is in a country-house hotel perched on a hill. The refined decor makes good use of local materials. Local specialities are served and there is a large choice of salads, fresh from the organic garden, for lunch. From June to September, chef Edouard Loubet opens his *table d'été* (12–5), which serves up light meals, aperitifs and stunning views.
✉ Les Claparèdes, Chemin des Cabanes, 84480 Bonnieux ☎ 04 90 75 89 78 ⏲ Mid-Mar to mid-Nov Thu–Mon 12–1.30, 7–9 🖑 L €70, D €130, Wine €30

### LE PONT JULIEN

www.lepontjulien.com
At the heart of Lubéron's regional park, Le Pont Julien is in a traditional Provençal house. The unpretentious interior includes lamps and paintings. There are two dining rooms and a terrace, and the menu offers a tour of the Mediterranean region with meats, fish and cheeses typical of Haute-Provence.
✉ Le Pont Julien, D90, 84480 Bonnieux ☎ 04 90 74 48 44 ⏲ Mon 12–1.45, Wed–Sun 12–1.45, 7.45–8.45 🖑 L €18, D €25, Wine €12.50

## CAIRANNE

### AUBERGE CASTEL MIREÏO

www.castelmireio.fr
There are fine views from the terrace of this welcoming restaurant, which is part of a hotel. The menu includes local dishes: rabbit terrine marinated in wine from Cairanne served with an onion marmalade, poultry from the Drôme region, truffles (in season). Plus there is a good selection of local wines.
✉ Route d'Orange, 84290 Cairanne ☎ 04 90 30 82 20 ⏲ Sun, Mon, Wed 12–2.30, Tue, Thu–Sat 12–2.30, 7.30–9.30. Closed Jan 🖑 L €19, D €26, Wine €15

## CHEVAL-BLANC

### L'AUBERGE DE CHEVAL BLANC

www.auberge-de-chevalblanc.com
Chef Hervé Perrasse prepares the great classics of Provençal cuisine with obvious pleasure. The *escabèche millefeuille* (anchovies in puff pastry) or melt-in-your-mouth Provençal flan made with fresh, local herbs and white wine are excellent choices. Many dishes are organic and there's a pleasant shaded terrace, which looks onto a garden. The dining room has beamed ceilings, wicker chairs and displays of works by local artists.
✉ 481 avenue de la Canebière, 84460 Cheval-Blanc ☎ 04 32 50 18 55 ⏲ Jul, Aug daily 7.30–10, also Sun 12–2; Sep–end Jun Tue–Fri 12–2, 7.30–10, Sat 7.30–10, Sun 12–2 🖑 L €23, D €38, Wine €19

## LE CRESTET

### LE MAS D'HÉLÈNE

www.lemasdhelene.com
There's a lovely setting in a country house in a park planted with oak trees for this restaurant. Eat on the terrace or in the elegant dining room, decorated in Provençal style with a romantic twist. Blue, yellow and white set the tone, with mirrors and subdued lighting. Dishes to try include terrine of foie gras, chicken with a mushroom sauce and zabaglione for dessert.
✉ Quartier Chante Coucou, 84110 Le Crestet ☎ 04 90 36 39 91 ⏲ May–end Sep Thu–Tue 7.30–9 🖑 D €30, Wine €12

## GIGONDAS

### L'OUSTALET

www.restaurant-oustalet.fr
This restaurant, under new young chef Cyril Glémot, is at the heart of a small medieval town surrounded by olive groves and vineyards. Enjoy dinner on the terrace, under the shade of plane trees, or in the rustic dining room, with beamed ceilings and exposed brick. Dishes include aubergine with *brousse* (sheep's cheese), or roasted pigeon served alongside chantarelle-stuffed *nems* (Vietnamese spring rolls). There's a vegetarian menu, and the local Gigondas wine is worth sampling.
✉ Place du Village, 84190 Gigondas ☎ 04 90 65 85 30 ⏲ Apr–end Sep daily 12–2, 7.30–9.30; Oct–end Mar Sun–Thu 12–2, Fri, Sat 12–2, 7.30–9.30 🖑 L €21, D €35, Wine €20

## GORDES

### HOSTELLERIE LE PHEBUS

www.lephebus.com

Le Phebus is a restaurant and a four-star hotel. Chef Xavier Mathieu's sophisticated regional cuisine includes fillet of sole pan-fried in salt butter with tangy jasmine and vanilla and farmhouse duck foie gras. Patrons can opt to dine in the more relaxed environs of Mathieu's new Café de la Fontaine.

Route de Murs, 84220 Joucas-Gordes 04 90 05 78 83 Apr to mid-Oct Mon, Fri, Sat 12–1.30, 7–9.30, Tue–Thu, Sun 7–9.30. Closed mid-Oct to end Mar L €60, D €89, Wine €30

### LE MAS HERBES BLANCHES

www.herbesblanches.com

This restaurant, between Gordes and Roussillon, offers upscale French cuisine with gorgeous views. Chef Akhara Chay has created a menu of ornately crafted, seasonal specials: red mullet with olive carpaccio, or crab with beetroot, capers and watercress.

Lieu dit Toron, 84220 Joucas, Gordes 04 90 05 79 79 Daily 12–1.30, 7–10 L €39, D €55, Wine €25

## LOURMARIN

### LE COMPTOIR

www.moulindelourmarin.com

An 18th-century oil mill is home to this restaurant. Under beautiful vaults, tables have been dressed with blue and yellow, and are lit by candles. Chef Edouard Loubet uses vegetables fresh from the restaurant's garden, and herbs and spices typical of the Lubéron region.

Le Moulin de Lourmarin, rue du Temple, 84160 Lourmarin 04 90 75 98 76 Mon–Fri 7–10, Sat, Sun 12–2.30, 7–10. Closed mid-Jan to mid-Feb and last 2 weeks of Nov L €40, D €60, Wine €25

## MANE

### LE CLOÎTRE

www.couventdesminimes-hotelspa.com

Le Cloître is in a restored 17th-century convent, now a luxury hotel. Philippe Guérin's creations are seasonal: pea soup with mint, aubergine (eggplant) and goat's cheese or John Dory with lemon confit, spring onions and dried fruits.

Le Couvent des Minimes, chemin des Jeux de Maï, Mane 04 92 74 77 77 Daily 12–2, 7.30–10 L €35, D €60, Wine €25

## ORANGE

### LA TABLE DU VERGER

www.masdesaigras.com

Run by chef Alain Davi and his charming wife Sylvie, La Table du Verger serves up almost exclusively organic, seasonal cuisine. Opt for scallops and sweet potato purée, or foie gras topped with the lightest truffle mousse. In summer, there are tables in the sun-dappled garden.

Le Mas des Aigras, chemin des Aigras, Russamp Est, 84830 Orange 04 90 34 81 01 Daily 12–2, 7.30–10. Closed 2 weeks in Feb, 1 week in Oct, 1 week in Dec L €20, D €30, Wine €18

## LE PONTET-AVIGNON

### AUBERGE DE CASSAGNE

www.aubergedecassagne.com

In a fine Provençal mansion dating from around the middle of the 1800s, this excellent kitchen is overseen by chef Philippe Boucher. The restaurant has a professional sommelier in André Trestour, who will provide expert advice to accompany your chosen dish. There is an excellent selection of local wines to choose from.

450 allée de Cassagne, 84130 Le Pontet-Avignon 04 90 31 04 18 Daily 12–1.30, 7.30–9.30. Closed second week in Jan to early Feb L €33, D €60, Wine €25

## ROCHEGUDE

### CHÂTEAU DE ROCHEGUDE

www.chateauderochegude.com

In a hamlet 10km (6 miles) north of Orange, this amazing 12th-century fortress, once the summer residence of the local Marquis, is now a beautifully presented hotel and restaurant. The menu is seasonal, using the best Provençal ingredients, including the famed truffle. In winter, meals are served in the medieval armoury, in summer on the chateau terrace.

26790 Rochegude 04 75 97 21 10 Apr–end Oct Mon–Sat 12–2, 7.30–9.30, Sun 12–3, 7.30–9.30; Dec–end Mar Tue 7.30–9.30; Wed–Sat 12–2.30, 7.30–9.30; Sun 12–3. Closed Nov L €26, D €40, Wine €22

## VAISON-LA-ROMAINE

### HOSTELLERIE LE BEFFROI

www.le-beffroi.com

This hotel-restaurant, in a 16th- and 17th-century building in the old town, has an ornate dining room. The menu concentrates on traditional Provençal dishes and the wine cellar stocks predominantly local Côte du Rhône and Ventoux labels that complement the food.

Rue de l'Evêché, Cité Médiévale, 84110 Vaison-la-Romaine 04 90 36 04 71 Easter–end Oct Mon, Wed–Fri 7.30–9.30, Sat, Sun 12–2, 7.30–9.30 (also open Tue 7.30–9.30 in Jul) L €25, D €35, Wine €18

**Below** *A table set for dinner at the Hostellerie Le Phebus, Gordes*

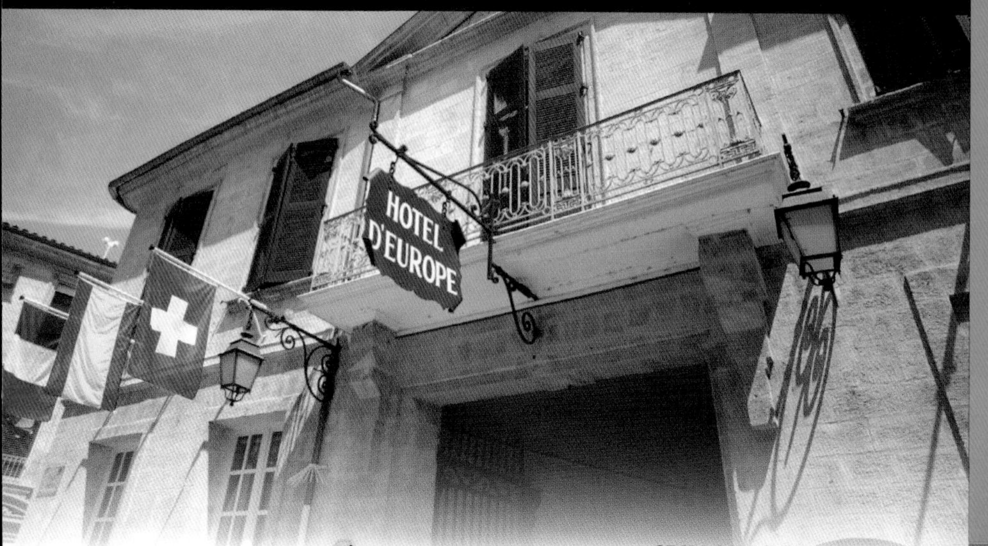


**Above** *Avignon's Hôtel d'Europe*

**PRICES AND SYMBOLS**

Prices are the lowest and highest for a double room for one night. Each listing states whether breakfast is included. All the hotels listed accept credit cards unless otherwise stated. Note that rates vary widely throughout the year.

For a key to the symbols, ▷ 2.

## AVIGNON

### CAMPING DE BAGATELLE

www.campingbagatelle.com

This camping ground, with room for 230 tents or caravans (RVs), is on the Île de la Barthelasse, an island on the Rhône connected to Avignon by a bridge and surrounded by greenery. Bring your own tent or caravan. Facilities include bars, a grocery store, a restaurant, children's playgrounds, a laundrette and parking. And if you don't want to sleep under canvas, there's also a youth hostel and a small hotel.

25 allées Antoine Pinay, Île de la Barthelasse, 84000 Avignon 04 90 86 30 39 €5.06–€7.16 for one person plus tent, additional person €5.06–€7.16; €10.26–€18.46 for one person plus caravan or mobile home; additional person €3.06–€4.46 Outdoor

### HÔTEL D'EUROPE

www.heurope.com

Follow in the steps of Napoleon Bonaparte, Pablo Picasso and Salvador Dalí, who stayed at the Marquis of Graveson's former house, built in 1580 and turned into a hotel in 1799. The luxury furnishings include antiques, candelabra, paintings and ornate carpets. The suites have a terrace with wonderful views over Avignon. There's a gastro restaurant and parking.

12 place Crillon, 84000 Avignon 04 90 14 76 76 €195–€480, excluding breakfast (€17) 41 rooms, 3 suites

## CABRIÈRES-D'AVIGNON

### LA BASTIDE DE VOULONNE

www.bastide-voulonne.com

Behind the ochre facade and blue shutters of this 18th-century former farmhouse is a tastefully decorated interior, where wrought iron, wood and shades of terracotta dominate. Most of the rooms have king-size beds; there is a garden and a bread oven in the dining room.

D148, 84220 Cabrières-d'Avignon, Gordes 04 90 76 77 55 Closed Dec–end Feb €90–€150, excluding breakfast (€12) 13 rooms, 3 suites Outdoor

## CRILLON LE BRAVE

### HOSTELLERIE DE CRILLON LE BRAVE

www.crillonlebrave.com

An exceptional property, the *hostellerie* is a small hamlet of stone buildings linked by cobbled lanes and renovated in a stylish but indomitably Provençal way. Chef Philippe Monti presides over Le Restaurant, with its southern French menu. The hotel has received accolades from a host of international publications.

Place de l'Église, 84410 Crillon le Brave 04 90 65 61 61 Closed Nov–end Mar €240–€490, excluding breakfast (€12) 32 rooms and suites Outdoor

## FONTAINE-DE-VAUCLUSE

### HÔTEL DU POÈTE

www.hoteldupoete.com

In a former mill, the Hôtel du Poète has a swimming pool, Jacuzzi and cool leafy garden, edged by the bubbling waters of La Sorgue. The serene rooms are decorated in natural materials and neutral tones; the two on the fourth floor have views over the town's rooftops.

Le Village, 84800 Fontaine-de-Vaucluse 04 90 20 34 05 €70–€40, excluding breakfast (€17) 21 rooms and suites Outdoor

## GORDES

### LES BORIES

www.hotellesbories.com

This four-star hotel is named after the drystone buildings once used by local shepherds. The dining room is actually in a former *borie*. The bedrooms have large bay windows that open onto private terraces and have wonderful views. The hotel has its own spa, including a sauna and Turkish baths.

Route de l'Abbaye de Sénanque, 84220 Gordes 04 90 72 00 51 €200–€430, excluding breakfast (€23) Indoor and outdoor

## LAGNES

### LE MAS DES GRÈS

www.masdesgres.com

You'll be welcomed like a family friend at this restored country house. The tastefully decorated bedrooms are simple but comfortable. Breakfast and dinner are served outside, in the shade of a 200-year-old plane tree. The parking area is fully enclosed.

Route d'Apt, 84800 Lagnes 04 90 20 32 85 Closed mid-Oct to mid-Mar €80–€230, excluding breakfast (€12) 14 Outdoor

## LOURMARIN

### LE MAS DE GUILLES

www.guilles.com

Check in and switch off: These rooms (some with private patios), suites and a peaceful pool are in three hectares (seven acres) of aromatic gardens. Every Wednesday, chef Patrick Lherm offers a special set menu at the restaurant. The hotel is located between Lourmarin and Vaugines, where parts of the 1986 film *Jean de Florette*, starring Gérard Depardieu, were shot.

Route des Vaugines, 84160 Lourmarin 04 90 68 30 55 Closed Dec–end Feb €76–€148, excluding breakfast (€15) 26 rooms, 2 suites Some rooms

## ORANGE

### HÔTEL ARÈNE

www.hotel-arene.fr

In a tree-lined square in the historic heart of Orange, the Arène offers good-value quiet rooms with a safe, air conditioning and mini-bar and a private garage (a separate fee is charged for parking). The small breakfast room serves regional specials and there is a separate restaurant on site.

Place des Langes, 84100 Orange 04 90 11 40 40 €78–€145, excluding breakfast (€8) 35

## PERNES-LES-FONTAINES

### MAS LA BONOTY

www.bonoty.com

This 17th-century farm has been beautifully restored with tiled floors and regional furniture in the bedrooms and exposed brick walls in the living room. The surrounding park has been landscaped with lavender, olive trees and fruit trees. Fine regional cuisine is on the restaurant menu and your dinner and breakfast can be served by the swimming pool, weather permitting.

Chemin de la Bonoty, 84210 Pernes-les-Fontaines 04 90 61 61 09 Closed Jan €75–€90, including breakfast 8 Outdoor

## ROUSSILLON

### HÔTEL LES SABLES D'OCRE

www.roussillon-hotel.com

A 15-minute walk from the hilltop town of Roussillon, Les Sables d'Ocre offers simple guest rooms, most with balcony or terrace, arranged around a pretty pool and gardens. Half-board options are available.

Les Sablières, Roussillon 04 90 05 55 55 €69–€82, excluding breakfast (€10) 22 Outdoor

### MAS DE GARRIGON

www.masdegarrigon-provence.com

Each of the stunning, individually decorated rooms at this renovated *mas* (stone farmhouse) is named after a famous artist. Styles include vivid red or blue walls or soft pale colours, but each room is simple and elegant and has a balcony or garden area. The communal areas have comfortable sofas for relaxing and there's a pretty pastel dining room.

Route de St-Saturnon d'Apt, 84220 Roussillon 04 90 05 63 22 €105–€135, excluding breakfast (€16) 7 Outdoor

## SAULT

### HOSTELLERIE DU VAL DE SAULT

www.valdesault.com

Among pine trees and facing Mont Ventoux, this quiet three-star hotel has wonderful views. The rustic building has wooden floors and beamed ceilings. Bedrooms are simple yet the artful use of fabrics is warming. All have a private terrace. High-quality regional cuisine is served in the adjoining restaurant.

Route de St-Trinit, 84390 Sault 04 90 64 01 41 Closed Nov–end Mar €87–€135, excluding breakfast (full-board options are available) 11 Outdoor

## VACQUEYRAS

### DOMAINE DE LA PONCHE

www.hotel-laponche.com

This 17th-century cottage is in a park dotted with cypress and olive trees. Beamed ceilings and a tiled floor set the tone inside. Each spacious, comfortable bedroom has a personalized detail, such as a canopy bed or a fireplace. The restaurant serves excellent regional cuisine.

84190 Vacqueyras 04 90 65 85 21 Closed mid-Nov to mid-Mar €120–€130, excluding breakfast (€15) 3 rooms, 2 suites Outdoor

## VAISON-LA-ROMAINE

### HOSTELLERIE LE BEFFROI

www.le-beffroi.com

Housed in a 16th-century mansion and an adjoining building that dates from the 17th century, this three-star hotel certainly doesn't lack character. You'll have panoramic views of the medieval town of Vaison-la-Romaine from some of the bedrooms, and from the terraced garden, where breakfast is served in good weather. Facilities include a restaurant (▷ 254) and a garage.

Rue de l'Evêché, Cité Médiévale, 84110 Vaison-la-Romaine 04 90 36 04 71 Closed Feb–end Mar €90–€144, excluding breakfast (€12) 22 Outdoor

# PRACTICALITIES

Practicalities gives you all the important practical information you will need during your visit, from money matters to emergency phone numbers.

# ESSENTIAL INFORMATION

## WEATHER

### CLIMATE

» Long hot summers are the signature of Provence but winters can be bitter, especially in the mountains. Winds also play an important role: The strongest is the *mistral*, blowing south down the Rhône valley.

» There are sheltered micro-climates, such as the coastal corniches near the Italian border.

» Mountain meltwater in spring and heavy rains in autumn mean there is a risk of flash floods, especially in the Rhône valley.

### WHEN TO GO

» **Spring:** The days get longer and warmer and everything seems to be in bloom, including the flower fields that provide the raw materials for the perfume industry of Grasse. It is warm enough to take your lunchtime drinks on the terrace in April.

» **Summer:** Temperatures can rise to the mid 30s°C (93°F). School holidays in late July and August see families heading south from northern France, so make reservations for all types of accommodation. Roads are busy, particularly on the coast. Fire risk in the forest is at its peak and some areas may be off-limits. On the plus side, all the facilities, from water sports to campsites, are open and festivals are in full swing. To escape the heat, head to the Alpes-de Haute-Provence.

» **Autumn:** High season ends when the children go back to school and Paris opens up again at the end of August. The heat tempers in September and early October but it is still warm. You can get a seat at the most popular restaurants and prices for hotel rooms drop a little. From mid-September, water sports stop and some artisans take a few weeks off, but it is *vendange* (picking time) in the vineyards.

» **Winter:** Cool weather sets in during November, with snow arriving on high ground in early December (although the area around Nice rarely suffers snow). Inland, many restaurants and hotels close until spring and some coastal resorts empty. To avoid the dreaded *mistral*, which blows down the Rhône valley, head farther east to the Côte d'Azur.

### TIME ZONES

| CITY | TIME DIFFERENCE | TIME AT 12 NOON IN FRANCE |
|---|---|---|
| Amsterdam | 0 | 12 noon |
| Berlin | 0 | 12 noon |
| Brussels | 0 | 12 noon |
| Chicago | -7 | 5am |
| Dublin | -1 | 11am |
| Johannesburg | +1* | 1pm |
| London | -1 | 11am |
| Madrid | 0 | 12 noon |
| Montréal | -6 | 6am |
| New York | -6 | 6am |
| Perth, Australia | +7* | 7pm |
| Rome | 0 | 12 noon |
| San Francisco | -9 | 3am |
| Sydney | +9* | 9pm |
| Tokyo | +8* | 8pm |

Clocks in France go forward one hour on the last Sunday in March, until the last Sunday in October.

* One hour less during French Summer Time.

## AVIGNON

### TEMPERATURE

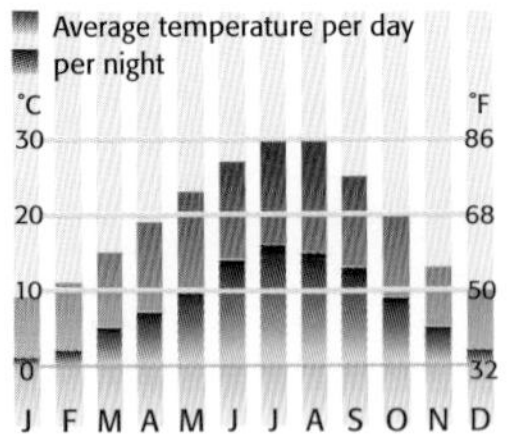


### RAINFALL

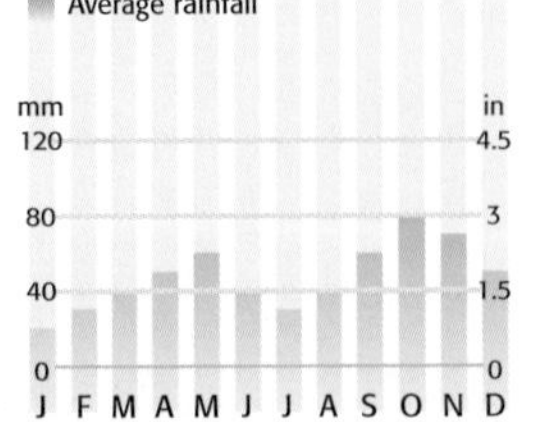


## MARSEILLE

### TEMPERATURE

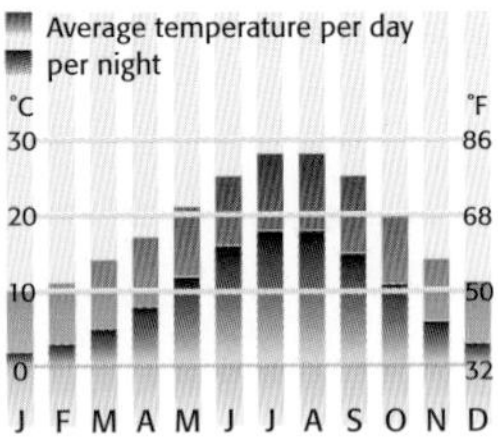


### RAINFALL

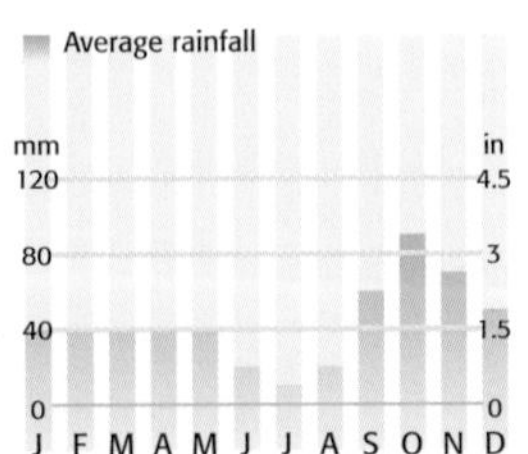


## NICE

### TEMPERATURE

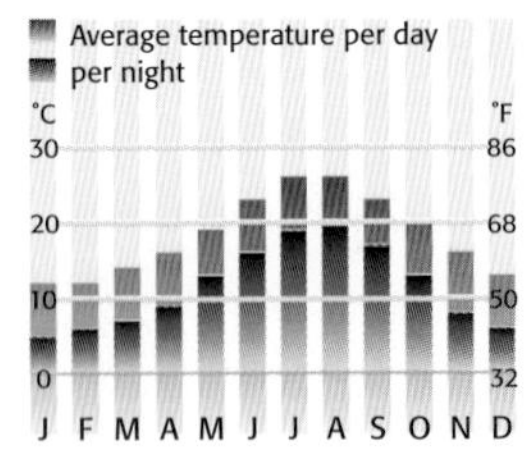


### RAINFALL

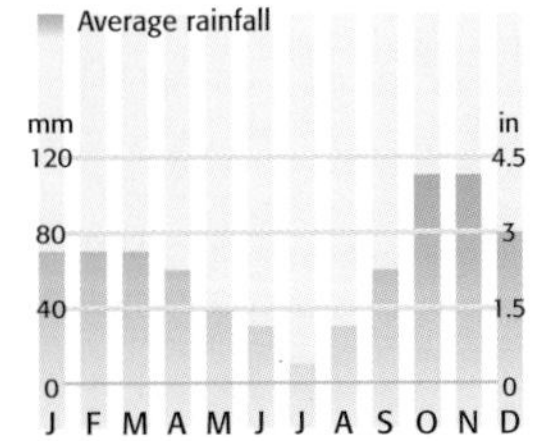

## WHAT TO TAKE

» The key things to remember are passports, tickets, travel and health insurance documents, money, credit cards and any medication you'll need. If you plan to drive, take your driver's licence and, if using your own car, the vehicle registration and insurance certificates (▷ 47).

» If you go skiing, and in the sunnier months, you'll need sunscreen and sunglasses.

» You may like to take more formal clothes for going out in the evening.

» A small backpack or shoulder bag is useful for sightseeing. Bear in mind that these are attractive to pickpockets, so keep your money tucked away and an eye on your bag when you're in restaurants and other crowded places, especially in cities.

» Take the addresses and phone numbers of emergency contacts, including the numbers to call if your credit cards are stolen. Make photocopies of your passport, insurance documents and tickets, in case of loss. Keep a separate note of your credit card numbers in case you need to report a theft to the police.

» Visitors from the UK and US will need adaptors for electrical equipment (▷ 263).

» There is a language guide on pages 281–285 of this book, but if you wish to communicate in French you may find a separate phrase book helpful.

» A first-aid kit is useful.

» If you wear glasses, take a spare pair and your prescription.

» Don't forget your camera! Digital peripherals are widely available, along with photo printing booths.

### PASSPORTS AND VISAS

» Entry requirements differ depending on your nationality and are also subject to change. Always check prior to a visit and follow news events that may affect your situation.

» UK, US and Canadian visitors need a passport, but not a visa, for stays of up to three months. You should have at least six months' validity remaining on your passport.

» For more information about visa and passport requirements, look up the French tourist office website (www.franceguide.com) or the French Embassy website (www.ambafrance-uk.org, or www.ambafrance-us.org for the US).

» Photocopy the relevant pages of your passport to carry with you, so you can leave your actual passport in your hotel safe.

### LONGER STAYS

» UK citizens who want to stay longer than three months may need to apply for a *Carte de Séjour* from the Préfecture de Police. US and Canadian visitors need a *Carte de Séjour* and a visa. For information call the Immigration Department of the French Consulate.

### TRAVEL INSURANCE

» Make sure you have full health and travel insurance.

» EU nationals receive reduced-cost health treatment in France (but not Monaco) with the relevant documentation (the EHIC for British visitors; see www.ehic.org.uk), but health and travel insurance is still advisable. For other visitors, full health insurance is a must.

### CUSTOMS

**From another EU country**

Below are the guidelines for the quantity of goods you can bring to France from another EU country, for personal use:

| | |
|---|---|
| • 800 cigarettes | • 110 litres of beer |
| • 400 cigarillos | • 10 litres of spirits |
| • 200 cigars | • 90 litres of wine (of which only 60 litres can be sparkling wine) |
| • 1kg of smoking tobacco | • 20 litres of fortified wine (such as port or sherry) |

**From a country outside the EU**

You are entitled to the allowances shown below only if you travel with the goods and do not plan to sell them.

| | |
|---|---|
| • 200 cigarettes or | • 250cc/ml of eau de toilette |
| 100 cigarillos or | • 2 litres of still table wine |
| 50 cigars or | • 1 litre of spirits or strong liqueurs over 22% volume; |
| 250g of tobacco | or 2 litres of fortified wine, sparkling wine or other liqueurs |
| • 60cc/ml of perfume | • Up to €175 of all other goods (or €90 for under 15s) |

### FRENCH EMBASSIES AND CONSULATES ABROAD

| COUNTRY | ADDRESS | WEBSITE |
|---|---|---|
| **Australia** | Level 26, St. Martins Tower, 31 Market Street, Sydney tel (02) 9268 2400 | www.ambafrance-au.org |
| **Canada** | 501 McGill College, Bureau 1000, Montréal H3A 3M8 tel 514 878-4385 | www.consulfrance-montreal.org |
| **Ireland** | 36 Ailesbury Road, Ballsbridge, Dublin 4 tel (01) 277 5000 | www.ambafrance.ie |
| **New Zealand** | 34–42 Manners Street, Wellington, 12th floor, PO Box 11-343 tel 644 384 25 55 | www.ambafrance-nz.org |
| **UK** | 21 Cromwell Road, London, SW7 2EN, tel 020 7073 1200 | www.ambafrance-uk.org |
| **US (Los Angeles)** | 10990 Wilshire Boulevard, Suite 300, Los Angeles, CA 90024 tel 310/235 3200 | www.consulfrance-losangeles.org |
| **US (New York)** | 934 Fifth Avenue, New York, NY 10021, tel 212/606 3600 | www.consulfrance-newyork.org |

## MONEY

### THE EURO

» France is one of 16 European countries that have adopted the euro as their official currency. Euro notes and coins were introduced in January 2002, replacing the former currency, the French franc.

### BEFORE YOU GO

» It is advisable to use a combination of cash and credit cards rather than relying on only one means of payment during your trip.
» Check with your credit or debit card company that your card can be used to withdraw cash from Automatic Teller Machines (ATMs) in France. It is also worth checking what fee will be charged for this and what number you should call if your card is stolen.
» Surprisingly, it is becoming increasingly difficult to change cash in France, with many banks posting a 'No Change' notice in their windows each summer. Purchase euros before you arrive, or plan to take out money using your credit or debit card.

### TRAVELLER'S CHEQUES

» Traveller's cheques are increasingly hard to change in France, and have, by and large, been replaced by credit cards.

### ATMS

» ATMs are common in France, often with on-screen instructions in a choice of languages. Among the cards accepted are Visa, MasterCard and Diners Club. You'll need a four-digit PIN.
» Your card issuer may charge you for withdrawing cash.

### BANKS

» Hours vary, but usual opening hours are Monday to Friday 8.30 or 9–12 and 2–5, although banks in cities may not close for lunch.
» In smaller towns and villages banks often close on Mondays but open on Saturday mornings instead.
» Banks close at noon on the day before a national holiday, as well as on the holiday itself. Only banks with *change* signs change traveller's cheques or foreign currency and you'll need your passport to do this.

### BUREAUX DE CHANGE

» Bureaux de Change have longer opening hours than banks, but the exchange rates may not be so good. You'll find them in all the major cities across Provence.
» Avoid changing large amounts of traveller's cheques at hotels, as the rates may not be competitive.

### CONCESSIONS

» If you are a student or teacher, apply to the International Student Travel Confederation (www.isic.org) in your own country for an International Student Identity Card (ISIC). This entitles you to various discounts during your visit.
» Seniors often get reduced-rate tickets on public transportation and on admission to museums and sights by showing a valid identity card or passport.
» Younger children often have free entry to sights.

### CREDIT CARDS

» Most restaurants, shops and hotels accept credit cards, although some have a minimum spending limit.

### POST OFFICES

» Most post offices have ATMs.
» Cards accepted are listed on each ATM, and instructions are available in English.
» Money can be wired, through Western Union, via most post offices.
» International Money Orders can be sent from all post offices (a charge is applied).

### TAXES

» Non-EU residents can claim a sales-tax refund (*détaxe*) of 12 per cent on certain purchases, although you must have spent more than €175 in one shop, at one time.
» Ask the store for the relevant forms, which the store should complete and stamp. Give these forms to customs when you leave the country, along with the receipts, and they will be stamped. Send the forms back to the shop and they will either refund your credit card account or send you a cheque.
» You may have to show the goods to Customs when you leave France, so keep them within easy reach.
» Exempt products include food and drink, medicine, tobacco, unset gems, works of art and antiques.
» The company Global Refund offers a reimbursement service (01 41 61 51 51; www.globalrefund.com).

### WIRING MONEY

» In an emergency, you can have money wired to you from your home country, but this can be expensive (as agents charge a fee for the service) and time-consuming.
» You can send and receive money via agents such as Western Union (www.westernunion.com) and Travelex (www.travelex.fr).

| PRICES OF EVERYDAY ITEMS | | |
|---|---|---|
| Takeout sandwich | | €3.50 |
| Bottle of mineral water | (from a shop, 0.5 litres) | €1 |
| Cup of coffee | (from a café, espresso) | €1–€2 |
| | (*Crème*, larger cup with milk) | €3–€4 |
| Beer | (*Un demi*, half a litre) | €3–€4 |
| Glass of house wine | | €3 |
| French national newspaper | | €1–€1.20 |
| International newspaper | | €3 |
| Litre of petrol | (98 unleaded) | €1.35 |
| | (diesel) | €1.05 |
| AA-sized batteries | | €6 |
| 20 cigarettes | (on average) | €7 |

» Money can be wired from bank to bank, taking up to two working days, or through Travelex and Western Union, which is normally faster.

### TIPS

» Try to avoid using higher denomination notes when paying taxi drivers and when buying low-cost items in smaller shops.

» Never carry money or credit cards in back pockets, or other places that are easy targets for thieves.

» Keep spare money in your hotel safe *(coffre-fort)* until you need it.

» Check the exchange rates for traveller's cheques and cash offered in post offices as well as in banks, as banks do not always offer the best rate.

» In France, MasterCard is sometimes known as Eurocard and Visa is known as Carte Bleue.

» Some smaller hotels and inns don't accept credit cards, so find out before you check in.

| TIPPING GUIDE | |
|---|---|
| Restaurants (service included) | Change * |
| Hotels (service included) | Change * |
| Cafés (service included) | Change * |
| Taxis | 10 per cent |
| Tour guides | €2 |
| Porters | €2 |
| Hairdressers | €2 |
| Cloakroom attendants | €1 |
| Toilets | Change |

* Or more if you are impressed with the level of service

## HEALTH

### BEFORE YOU GO

» EU citizens receive reduced-cost healthcare in France (but not Monaco) with the relevant documentation. For UK citizens, this is the European Health Insurance Card (EHIC). For details on how to obtain a card consult www.ehic.org.uk, tel 0845 605 0707 or pick up a form at your local post office. Full health insurance is still strongly advised. For all other countries full insurance is a must.

» Make sure you are up to date with anti-tetanus boosters. Bring any medication you need with you and pack a first-aid kit. In summer, bring sunscreen.

### IF YOU NEED TREATMENT

» The French national health system is complex. Any salaried French citizen who receives treatment by a doctor or public hospital can be reimbursed by up to 70 per cent. The same is true if you are an EU citizen and have a valid EHIC.

» If you are relying only on the EHIC, rather than travel insurance, make sure the doctor you see is part of the French national health service (a *conventionné*), rather than the private system, otherwise you may face extra charges. In any case, you will have to pay up front for the consultation and treatment. To reclaim part of these costs, send the *feuille de soins* (a statement from the doctor) and your EHIC details to the Caisse Primaire d'Assurance-Maladie (state health insurance office) before you leave the country. Call 0820 904 175 to find the nearest office. Remember that you should also attach labels of any medicine you have to buy.

» If you have to stay overnight in a public hospital, you will have to pay 25 per cent of the treatment costs, as well as a daily charge *(forfait journalier)*. These are not refundable. It is far better to have full health insurance than to rely solely on the EHIC.

» Citizens of non-EU countries must have full health insurance.

» If you are hospitalized and have insurance, ask to see the *assistante sociale* to arrange the reimbursement of the costs through your insurers.

» In an emergency, dial 15 for the *Service d'Aide Médicale d'Urgence* (SAMU) unit (ambulance). They work closely with hospital emergency units and are accompanied by trained medical personnel.

» If you are able to get yourself to a hospital, make sure it has an emergency department *(urgences)*.

### FINDING A DOCTOR

» You can find a doctor *(médecin)* by asking at your hotel, a pharmacy or the town hall. Appointments are usually made in advance, but few doctors will refuse to see an emergency case.

» Emergency house calls (24 hours) can be arranged in the Marseille area by calling SOS Médecins (tel 36 24). Otherwise call 15 for emergencies or SOS Help (tel 01 46 21 46 46) for practical help in English.

### FINDING A HOSPITAL

» Hospitals are listed in the phone book under *hôpitaux* and around-the-clock emergency services are called *urgences*.

» Private hospitals are a lot more expensive than public ones and treatment is not necessarily better. If you choose a private hospital, check that you are covered for the costs before receiving treatment.

### DENTAL TREATMENT

» EU citizens can receive reduced-cost emergency dental treatment with the EHIC, although insurance is still advised. The procedure for reclaiming money is the same as for general medical treatment.

» Other visitors should check their insurance covers dental treatment.

### PHARMACIES

» A pharmacy *(pharmacie)* will have an illuminated green cross outside. Most are open Mon–Sat 9–7 or 8, but they usually post on the door details of another pharmacy that is open later (called the *pharmacie de garde*).

» Pharmacists are highly qualified and provide first aid, as well as supplying medication (some drugs are by prescription, or *ordonnance*, only). But they cannot dispense prescriptions written by doctors outside the French health system, so bring sufficient supplies of any prescribed drugs you need.

» Pharmacists also sell a range of health-related items, although it is less expensive to go to the supermarket for items such as soap, toothbrushes and razors.

›› Some commonly used medicines sold in supermarkets at home (such as cold remedies) can only be bought in pharmacies in France.

**TAP WATER**

›› Tap water is safe to drink and restaurants will often bring a carafe of water to the table, although most French people opt for bottled water.

›› In public places look for the sign *eau potable* (drinking water). Don't drink from anything marked *eau non potable*.

**LOCAL HAZARDS**

›› The sun can be strong so use a high-factor sun block. You may like to take insect repellent, although insect bites in France are more likely to be irritating than dangerous.

›› If you are planning on any high-altitude walks, take plenty of water, warm clothing and check weather reports before you go.

›› Recent hot dry summers have led to forest fires. The nearest tourist office should be able to tell you whether the area you intend to visit is at risk. At times of high risk some roads and trails may be closed.

›› Don't pick and eat wild mushrooms as some varieties are poisonous.

**ALTERNATIVE MEDICINE**

›› Alternative medicine, such as homeopathy, is available from most pharmacies.

›› Alternative treatment is on the increase, although chiropractic and reflexology are not widespread.

Useful websites include www.chiropratique.org (the Association Française de Chiropratique), www.aea-org.com (Association Europe Acupuncture) and www.naturosante.com (a site about alternative medical treatments).

**HEALTHY FLYING**

›› Visitors to France from as far as the US, Australia or New Zealand may be concerned about the effect of long-haul flights on their health. The most widely publicized concern is Deep Vein Thrombosis, or DVT. Misleadingly called 'economy class syndrome', DVT is the forming of a blood clot in the body's deep veins, particularly in the legs. The clot can move around the bloodstream and could be fatal.

›› Those most at risk include the elderly, pregnant women, those using the contraceptive pill, smokers and the overweight. If you are at increased risk of DVT see your doctor before departing. Flying increases the likelihood of DVT because passengers are often seated in a cramped position for long periods of time and may become dehydrated.

**To minimize risk:**

Drink water (not alcohol)

Don't stay immobile for hours at a time. Stretch and exercise your legs periodically

Do wear elastic flight socks, which support veins and reduce the chances of a clot forming

**Exercises**

**Ankle rotations**

Lift feet off the floor. Draw a circle with the toes, moving one foot clockwise and the other counterclockwise.

**Calf stretches**

Start with heel on the floor and point foot upward as high as you can. Then lift heels high, keeping balls of feet on the floor.

**Knee lifts**

Lift leg with knee bent while contracting your thigh muscle. Then straighten leg, pressing foot flat to the floor.

Other health hazards for flyers are airborne diseases and bugs spread by the plane's air-conditioning system. These are largely unavoidable, but if you have a serious medical condition seek advice from a doctor before flying.

**PUBLIC HOSPITALS**

| NAME | ADDRESS | TELEPHONE |
|---|---|---|
| Centre Hospitalier Général | 305 rue Raoul Follereau, 84000 Avignon | 04 32 75 33 33 |
| Centre Hospitalier du Pays d'Aix | Avenue Tamaris, 13100 Aix-en-Provence | 04 42 33 50 00 |
| Hôpital Les Broussailles | 13 avenue Broussailles, 06400 Cannes | 04 93 69 70 00 |
| Hôpital Général Joseph Imbert | Quartier Haute de Fourchon, 13200 Arles | 04 90 49 29 22 |
| Hôpital St-Roch | 5 rue Pierre Dévoluy, 06006 Nice | 04 92 03 33 33 |
| Hôpital de la Timone | 264 rue St-Pierre, 13005 Marseille | 04 91 38 60 00 |

**OPTICIANS**

It's always a good idea to pack a spare pair of glasses or contact lenses and your prescription, in case you lose or break your main pair.

| NAME | WEBSITE |
|---|---|
| Alain Afflelou | www.alainafflelou.com |
| Lissac Opticien | www.lissac.com |
| Optic 2000 | www.optic2000.fr |
| Optical Center | www.optical-center.com |
| Opticiens Krys | www.krys.com |

**USEFUL NUMBERS**

| | |
|---|---|
| **Emergency medical aid/ambulance** | 15 |
| **General emergencies** | 112 |
| **Police** | 17 |
| **Fire (Pompiers)** | 18 |
| **SOS Help (English crisis information hotline; daily 3pm–11pm)** | 01 46 21 46 46 |

## BASICS

### CAR RENTAL

›› See page 51 for details of car rental companies.
›› See pages 47–51 for information on driving in France.

### CHILDREN

›› The French *autoroute* system has service stations at intervals of approximately 40km (25 miles), which sell food and have recreation areas. At intervals of about 10km (6 miles), there are *aires*, rest stops with toilets and recreation areas but no food or fuel, good for restless children to run around.
›› Most restaurants welcome children, although not many have high chairs, and children's menus are not common outside family-friendly resorts, so it's probably best to aim for family-style bistros where facilities are better and staff are more helpful.
›› If you need special facilities in your hotel, such as a cot, or a child seat in your rented car, reserve them in advance.
›› For baby-changing facilities while out and about, try the rest rooms in department stores and the larger museums.
›› Supermarkets and pharmacies sell nappies (diapers) and baby food, although they are often closed on Sunday so make sure you stock up.
›› Entrance to museums is often free to young children.
›› Don't underestimate the power of the Provençal sun. Make sure children wear a hat and sunscreen. Carry clothing to cover shoulders, arms and legs.

### ELECTRICITY

›› Voltage in France is 220 volts. Sockets take plugs with two round pins.
›› UK electrical equipment will need an adaptor plug, which you can buy at airport terminals.
›› American appliances using 110–120 volts will need an adaptor and a transformer. Equipment that is dual voltage should need only an adaptor.

### LAUNDRY

›› There are two options if you need a laundry service—a *laverie automatique* (laundrette) and a *pressing/nettoyage à sec* (dry-cleaners). Dry-cleaners are easier to find, but are more expensive. Some have an economy service, but this is not recommended for your best silk jacket.

### LOCAL WAYS

›› Greetings are often quite formal in France. Offer to shake hands when you are introduced to someone, and use *vous* rather than *tu*. It is polite to use *Monsieur, Madame* or *Mademoiselle* when speaking to people you don't know. For very young women and teenage girls use *Mademoiselle*; otherwise use *Madame*.
›› The continental kiss is a common form of greeting between friends, and the number of times friends kiss each other on the cheek varies from region to region.
›› Address waiters and waitresses as *Monsieur, Madame* or *Mademoiselle* when you are trying to attract their attention. Never use *garçon*.

| CONVERSION CHART | | |
|---|---|---|
| FROM | TO | MULTIPLY BY |
| Inches | Centimetres | 2.54 |
| Centimetres | Inches | 0.3937 |
| Feet | Metres | 0.3048 |
| Metres | Feet | 3.2810 |
| Yards | Metres | 0.9144 |
| Metres | Yards | 1.0940 |
| Miles | Kilometres | 1.6090 |
| Kilometres | Miles | 0.6214 |
| Acres | Hectares | 0.4047 |
| Hectares | Acres | 2.4710 |
| Gallons | Litres | 4.5460 |
| Litres | Gallons | 0.2200 |
| Ounces | Grams | 28.35 |
| Grams | Ounces | 0.0353 |
| Pounds | Grams | 453.6 |
| Grams | Pounds | 0.0022 |
| Pounds | Kilograms | 0.4536 |
| Kilograms | Pounds | 2.205 |
| Tons | Tonnes | 1.0160 |
| Tonnes | Tons | 0.9842 |

›› Communicating in French is always the best option, even if you can manage only *bonjour, s'il vous plaît* and *merci*. The French are protective of their language and your efforts to speak it will be appreciated. If your knowledge of French is limited, ask the fail-safe *Parlez-vous anglais?* and hope the answer is *oui*.
›› Remember that it is traditional to say hello as you enter a shop, bar or café, particularly in small towns and villages, and that you are greeting your fellow customers as well as the proprietor. For a mixed audience, a *bonjour Messieurs Dames* is the appropriate phrase. When it is your turn to be served, greet the server with *Bonjour Madame* or *Bonjour Monsieur*, then don't forget to say *merci* and *au revoir* or *bonne-journée* as you leave.
›› The hill villages of Provence still carry on the tradition of the siesta between lunchtime and 3pm.

### MEASUREMENTS

›› France uses the metric system. Road distances are measured in kilometres, fuel is sold by the litre and food is weighed in grams and kilograms.

## PLACES OF WORSHIP

›› Some of the most magnificent buildings in Provence are the great cathedrals found in the major cities and the tiny parish churches in towns and villages. They have become so popular as visitor attractions that it's easy to forget that they are still active places of worship. As such, it's important to respect these churches and the people who worship in them by dressing appropriately. Men should wear long trousers rather than shorts and should avoid sleeveless shirts. Women should keep their knees and shoulders covered and men should remove hats on entering the building.

›› Take photos only if it is permitted and don't forget to turn off your mobile phone.

›› Every town and village in France has its Roman Catholic church, usually at the physical heart of the community as well as the spiritual heart.

›› There are Anglican churches around Nice and Monte-Carlo.

›› Avignon, Carpentras, Cavaillon, Nice and Marseille are among the places with synagogues.

›› There are mosques along the coast and in larger cities, including Marseille.

## SMOKING AREAS

›› Smoking is banned in all public areas, including train stations, restaurants, buses and cafés.

## TICKETS

›› Tourist information offices in French cities often sell a pass that gives entry to the main sights at a reduced rate. It's worth investing in one of these if you plan on spending a few days in one city.

›› Since 2008 many of the state-owned museums in France have been free. Nice has taken this edict very seriously, and the majority of its museums are now free.

›› For information on bus and rail tickets ▷ 52–55.

›› Students with an International Student Identity Card (ISIC) and seniors get reduced-price entry at some museums.

›› For information on show and concert tickets, ▷ 273.

## TOILETS

›› France's modern unisex public toilets are a vast improvement on previous facilities. Coin-operated and self-cleaning, you can find them in most large cities.

›› In smaller towns and villages, free public toilets can normally be found by the market square or near tourist offices, although cleanliness varies.

›› The two most reliable options are to take advantage of facilities in museums or other visitor attractions or in restaurants and cafés, though you should be a customer to use the facilities, so be sure to buy a drink.

›› Ask for *les toilettes*.

## VISITORS WITH DISABILITIES

›› France has made great headway in recent years in providing access and facilities for visitors with disabilities. All new buildings in France must take the needs of people with special requirements into account, and, where possible, existing buildings such as town halls, airports and train stations must be adapted with ramps and automatic doors.

›› However, bear in mind that some tourist offices, museums and restaurants that are in historic, protected buildings are still not fully accessible. A telephone call before going to a restaurant is a good idea to arrange for an easily accessible table.

›› The Association des Paralysés de France (17 boulevard Auguste Blanqui, 75013, Paris; 0800 800 766; www.apf.asso.fr) provides some useful information on wheelchair access.

›› For other organizations that give advice to people with disabilities, ▷ 56.

## FINDING HELP

Most visits to Provence are trouble-free, but make sure you have adequate insurance to cover any health emergencies, thefts or legal costs that may arise. If you do become a victim of crime, it is most likely to be at the hands of a pickpocket, so keep your money and mobile phone safely tucked away. Petty crime is high in Provence compared with most of the rest of France, especially in the resorts.

### PERSONAL SECURITY

» Make a note of your traveller's cheques numbers and keep it separate from the cheques themselves, as you will need it to make a claim in case of loss.

» Most areas of Provence are relatively safe, but in larger cities, it's wise to avoid poorly lit streets at night, particularly around the train station. Walk in a pair or a group, and explore unknown neighbourhoods only by day.

» Don't keep wallets, purses or mobile phones in the back pockets of trousers, or anywhere else that is easily accessible to thieves. Money belts and bags worn around the waist are targets, as thieves know you are likely to have valuables in them. Keep an eye on your bags in restaurants and bars and on trains. Carry shoulder bags across your chest to foil thieves on scooters who grab bags as they pass by.

» Thieves and pickpockets are especially fond of crowded trains, airports, rail stations, markets and beaches. Beware if someone bumps into you—it may be a ploy to distract you while someone else snatches your money.

» If you are the victim of theft, you must report it at the local police station *(commissariat)* if you want to make a claim on your insurance. Keep the statement the police give you. Contact your credit card company as soon as possible to cancel any stolen cards.

» Keep valuable items in your hotel safe *(coffre-fort)*.

» Theft of cars and theft from cars are significant problems in some parts of Provence. When you park your car, don't leave anything of value inside. It's even risky to leave anything in view that could attract the attention of a thief. Carry your belongings with you or leave them in your hotel.

### LOSS OF PASSPORT

» Always keep a separate record of your passport number and a photocopy of the page that carries your details, in case of loss or theft. You can also scan the relevant pages of your passport and then email them to yourself at a secure email account that you can access anywhere.

» If you do lose your passport or it is stolen, report it to the police and then contact your nearest embassy or consulate.

### POLICE

» There are various types of police officer in France. The two main forces are the *Police Nationale*, under the control of the local mayor, and the *Gendarmerie Nationale*, who you often see at airports.

» You are likely to encounter the armed CRS riot police only at a demonstration.

» The police have wide powers of stop and search. It is wise to carry a photocopy of your passport in case a police officer requests your ID.

### FIRE

» The French fire service deals with anything from stranded cats to road accidents and gas leaks. Officers are trained to give first aid.

### HEALTH EMERGENCIES

See pages 261–262.

**MAIN POLICE STATIONS IN PROVENCE**

| PLACE | ADDRESS | TELEPHONE |
|---|---|---|
| Aix-en-Provence | 28 avenue Henri Malacrida, 13100 | 04 42 26 31 96 |
| Arles | 1 boulevard des Lices, 13200 | 04 90 18 45 00 |
| Avignon | Boulevard St-Roch, 84000 | 04 90 16 81 00 |
| Cannes | 1 avenue de Grasse, 06400 | 04 93 06 22 22 |
| Marseille | Angle Canabière/Garibaldi, 13001 | 04 88 77 58 00 |
| Nice | 1 avenue Maréchal Foch, 06000 | 04 92 17 22 22 |
| Nîmes | Avenue Pierre Gemal, 30000 | 04 66 28 30 00 |
| St-Tropez | Avenue 8 Mai, 83990 | 04 94 54 86 65 |
| Toulon | La Colombe, 1 rue Henri Poincaré | 04 98 03 24 00 |

**CONSULATES IN PROVENCE**

| COUNTRY | ADDRESS | TELEPHONE |
|---|---|---|
| Canada | Rue Lamartine, 06000 Nice | 04 93 92 93 22 |
| Germany | La Minotaure, 34 avenue Henry Matisse, 06200 Nice | 04 93 83 55 25 |
| | 338 avenue du Prado, Marseille | 04 91 16 75 20 |
| Ireland | No office in operation; phone for appointment | 06 77 69 12 36 |
| Italy | Boulevard Gambetta, 06000 Nice | 04 92 14 40 90 |
| Spain | 20 boulevard des Moulins, Monaco | 377 93 30 24 98 |
| UK | 24 avenue du Prado, Marseille | 04 91 15 72 10 |
| | 26 avenue Notre-Dame, 06000 Nice (consulate in Nice by appointment through the Marseille consulate) | |
| US | 7 avenue Gustave V, 06000 Nice | 04 93 88 89 55 |
| | 12 boulevard Paul Peytral, 13006 Marseille | 04 91 54 92 00 |

**EMERGENCY NUMBERS**

| | |
|---|---|
| **112** | General emergency number |
| **15** | Ambulance |
| **17** | Police |
| **18** | Fire |

## COMMUNICATION

### TELEPHONING

**French numbers** Numbers have 10 digits. France is divided into five regional zones, indicated by the first two digits of the phone number. You must dial these two digits even if you are calling from within the zone. Numbers in Provence begin with 04. Monaco numbers have the prefix 377.

**International calls** To call France from the UK dial 00 33, then drop the first zero from the 10-digit number. To call the UK from France, dial 00 44, then drop the first zero from the area code. To call France from the US, dial 011 33, then drop the first zero from the number. To call the US from France, dial 00 1, followed by the number.

**Call charges** For calls within France, peak period is from 8am to 7pm, Monday to Friday. You'll save money if you call outside this time. Numbers beginning with 08 have special rates. 0800 or 0805 numbers are free. 0810 and 0811 numbers are local rate. Other 08 numbers cost more than national calls—sometimes considerably more. The prefixes 0893, 0898 and 0899 are particularly expensive.

**Directory** For national directory assistance dial 09 69 36 39 00; for international assistance, dial 3212.

### PAYPHONES

›› Most public payphones in France use a phone card *(télécarte)* rather than coins. Buy these at post offices, *tabacs*, newsstands and France Telecom shops. Some phones accept credit cards, although this may make the calls more expensive. You do not need to pay to call the emergency services.

›› The phone gives instructions in various languages—press the flag button to select your choice. If the phone has a blue bell sign, you can receive incoming calls.

›› Public phones in cafés and restaurants use cards or coins or need to be switched on by staff and you pay after the call. They tend to be more expensive than public payphones. Check the rates for hotel phones, as they can be much higher than from a public payphone.

### MOBILE PHONES

›› Before you leave, contact your Customer Service department to find out if you have restrictions on making calls from France.

›› Make sure the numbers pre-programmed in your phone are in the international format.

›› Check the call charges, which can rise steeply when you are abroad.

›› Mobile phone numbers in France begin with 06.

›› If you're travelling through France for a longer period, you could buy a French SIM card. Orange (www.orange.fr) and SFr (www.sfr.fr) are France's most popular operators; cards cost around €5, and you'll need to show a valid form of ID.

### SENDING A LETTER

›› You can buy stamps *(timbres)* for a letter *(lettre)* or a postcard *(carte postale)* at post offices and *tabacs*. Write *par avion* (by air) on the envelope if sending overseas.

›› For registered mail, ask at the post office for the letter to be sent *recommandé*. For a parcel *(colis)*, choose *prioritaire* (priority) or the less expensive but slower *économique*.

›› Mailboxes are yellow and often have two sections, one for local addresses and one for farther afield *(autres destinations)*.

### POST OFFICES

›› Post offices *(bureaux de poste)* are well signposted. The postal service is known as La Poste.

›› Opening hours are generally Monday to Friday 8–5 or 6, Saturday 8–12. Some branches close for lunch. Queues are worst at lunchtime and late afternoon.

›› Facilities usually include phone booths, photocopiers, fax *(télécopieur)* and, sometimes, internet access. *Poste Restante* services are available for a fee.

### INTERNET ACCESS

›› You'll find internet cafés in the major towns. Many hotels and libraries have internet terminals, as do many post offices.

### LAPTOPS

›› Most hotels of two stars and above provide WiFi access, as do many cafés and public places.

| COUNTRY CODES FROM FRANCE | |
|---|---|
| Australia | 00 61 |
| Belgium | 00 32 |
| Canada | 00 1 |
| Germany | 00 49 |
| Ireland | 00 353 |
| Italy | 00 39 |
| Monaco | 00 377 |
| Netherlands | 00 31 |
| New Zealand | 00 64 |
| Spain | 00 34 |
| Sweden | 00 46 |
| UK | 00 44 |
| US | 00 1 |

| POSTAGE RATES FOR LETTERS UP TO 20g | |
|---|---|
| Within France | €0.54 |
| To Western Europe | €0.60 |
| To Eastern Europe (outside EU) | €0.85 |
| To America | €0.85 |
| To Africa | €0.85 |
| To Asia | €0.85 |
| To Australia | €0.85 |

**GUIDE PRICES**

| TYPE OF CALL | CONNECTION FEE | FEE PER MINUTE |
|---|---|---|
| Local, peak | €0.10 | €0.028 |
| Local, off-peak | €0.10 | €0.014 |
| National, peak | €0.10 | €0.078 |
| National, off-peak | €0.10 | €0.053 |
| Calling the UK, off-peak | €0.12 | €0.12 |
| Calling the US, off-peak | €0.12 | €0.12 |

## OPENING TIMES

» Banks open Monday to Friday 8.30 or 9–12, 2–5, but this can vary. They close at noon on the day before a national holiday, as well as on the holiday itself.

» Shops tend to close on Sundays, even chain stores. Family-owned shops may close also on Mondays, but are often open on Sunday until 12.30 or 1. Smaller shops often close 12–2. Bakers *(boulangeries)* open on Sunday mornings and supermarkets and hypermarkets are open Monday to Saturday and have long business hours, opening at about 9am and staying open until 9 or 10pm. Some also remain closed on Monday mornings. Shops in rural areas often close from 12–3.

» Museums are generally closed on Mondays if they are municipal museums, or Tuesdays if they are national museums. Some close at lunchtime (12–2), except in August. Entrance to some museums is free on the first Sunday of the month, although this can lead to crowds. If you plan to travel a long distance to see a museum, call in advance as opening hours can be idiosyncratic (some museums open on public holidays and some do not, and the renovation craze has not helped).

» Post offices open Monday to Friday 8–5 or 6 on weekdays and 8–12 on Saturday. Small branches may close for lunch.

» Pharmacies are generally open Monday to Saturday 9–7 or 8. They all display a list of local pharmacies that open later and on a Sunday.

» Restaurants usually serve lunch 12–2 or 2.30 and dinner 7.30–10 or 11. Restaurants away from resorts and major towns close earlier, often at around 9.30, and may close on Sunday evenings and one other day, often Monday. Brasseries tend to serve food all day. Some restaurants on the coast close from November to Easter.

» Cafés tend to open 8–8, while bars are lively until around midnight. Nightclubs usually open from 10 or 11pm until 2am or later, although Provence's nightlife can be limited during the winter.

### NATIONAL HOLIDAYS

France has 11 national holidays *(jours fériés)*, when train and bus services are reduced and banks and many museums and shops close. The most steadfastly respected are 1 January, 1 May, 1 November, 11 November and 25 December. If you're in France during a national holiday, it's a good idea to call ahead to see if the sight you want to visit is open.

| | |
|---|---|
| 1 January | New Year's Day |
| March/April | Easter Monday |
| 1 May | Labour Day |
| 8 May | VE Day |
| A Thursday in May | Ascension Day |
| May/June | Whit Monday |
| 14 July | Bastille Day |
| 15 August | Assumption Day |
| 1 November | All Saints' Day |
| 11 November | Remembrance Day |
| 25 December | Christmas Day |

## TOURIST OFFICES

### FRENCH TOURIST OFFICES

**Australia**
Level 20, 25 Bligh Street, Sydney NSW 2000
Tel 02 9231 5244;
email: info.au@franceguide.com

**Canada**
1800 avenue McGill College, Suite 1010, Montreal, H3A 3J6
Tel 514 288 2026;
email: canada@franceguide.com

**Germany**
Zeppelinallee 37, D-60325 Frankfurt am Main
Tel 0900 1 57 00 25 (€0.49 per min);
email: info.de@franceguide.com

**Ireland**
30 Merrion Street Upper, Dublin
Tel 15 60 235 235;
email: info.ie@franceguide.com

**Italy**
Via Tiziano 32, 20145, Milan
Tel 899 199 072 (€0.52 per min);
email: info.it@franceguide.com

**Spain**
Plaza de España 18, Torre de Madrid 8a Pl. Of. 5, 28008, Madrid
Tel 0807 117 181 (€0.31 per min);
email: info.es@franceguide.com

**UK**
Lincoln House, 300 High Holborn, WC1V 7JH, London; tel 09068 244123 (60p per min);
email: info.uk@franceguide.com

**US (New York)**
825 Third Avenue, 29th floor (entrance on 50th Street), New York, 10022
Tel 514/288 1904;
email: info.us@franceguide.com

**US (Los Angeles)**
9454 Wilshire Boulevard, Suite 715, 90212, Beverly Hills, California
Tel 514/288 1904;
email: info.us@franceguide.com

## USEFUL WEBSITES

**www.aeroport.fr**
Information on all of France's airports. (French)

**www.angloinfo.com**
A forum for English life on the Côte d'Azur, with English services and chat rooms.

**www.decouverte-paca.fr**
The website of the regional tourist organization for the French Riviera. You can order a range of brochures here or find links to other sites.

**www.fodors.com**
A comprehensive travel planning site that lets you research prices, reserve air tickets and put questions to fellow visitors. (English)

**www.franceguide.com**
Practical advice from the French Tourist Office on everything from arriving in France to buying a property. The site also has features on holidays and attractions. (French, English, German, Spanish, Italian, Dutch, Portuguese)

**www.guideriviera.com**
The Tourist Office website for the region has information on a range of attractions.

**www.lemonde.fr**
Catch up on current events on the site of *Le Monde* newspaper. (French)

**www.meteofrance.com**
Weather forecasts for France. (French)

**www.monum.fr**
Information on France's most historic monuments. (French and English)

**www.pagesjaunes.fr**
France's telephone directory, online. (French and English)

**www.provencebeyond.com**
Information about Provence beyond the French Riviera. (English)

**www.provenceweb.fr**
Packed with information, including links to online shopping for Provençal goods. (English and French)

**www.radio-france.fr**
News, music and sport. (French)

**www.skifrance.fr**
Search for a resort, find out the latest snow conditions and see the slopes in real time via webcam. (English and French)

**www.theAA.com**
The AA website contains a route planner, helpful if you are driving in France. You can also order maps of the country. (English)

**www.tourist-office.org**
Details of every tourist office in France. (French)

Other websites are listed alongside the relevant sights and towns in the Sights section, and in the On the Move section.

### KEY SIGHTS QUICK WEBSITE FINDER

| SIGHT/TOWN | WEBSITE | PAGE |
|---|---|---|
| Aigues-Mortes | www.ot-aiguesmortes.fr | 62–63 |
| Aix-en-Provence | www.aixenprovencetourism.com | 65–67 |
| Antibes | www.antibesjuanlespins.com | 141–142 |
| Arles | www.arlestourisme.com | 68–71 |
| Avignon | www.ot-avignon.fr | 224–227 |
| Les Baux-de-Provence | www.lesbauxdeprovence.com | 72–73 |
| Camargue | www.reserve-camargue.org | 74–75 |
| Cannes | www.cannes.fr | 144–146 |
| Hyères | www.hyeres-tourisme.com | 122–123 |
| Marseille | www.marseille-tourisme.com | 78–85 |
| Monaco | www.visitmonaco.com | 156–161 |
| Nice | www.nicetourism.com | 163–167 |
| Nîmes | www.ot-nimes.fr | 86–89 |
| Orange | http://uk.otorange.fr | 234–235 |
| Parc National du Mercantour | www.mercantour.eu | 168–169 |
| St-Rémy-de-Provence | www.saintremy-de-provence.com | 92–94 |
| St-Tropez | www.ot-saint-tropez.com | 128–129 |
| Vaison-la-Romaine | www.vaison-la-romaine.com | 240–241 |

# MEDIA, BOOKS AND FILMS

## TELEVISION

» France has five non-cable television stations: the nationally owned and operated channels 2 and 3, the privately owned 1 and 6, and the Franco-German ARTE (channel 5). Almost all the shows are in French. There are commercials on all these channels except ARTE.

» **TF1** has news, recent American and French films, soaps and shows.

» **France 2** has news, recent French and foreign films, soaps, shows and documentaries.

» **France 3**, a regional and national channel, has regional and national news, regional shows, documentaries, mostly French films and, once a week, a film in its original language.

» **ARTE** is a Franco-German channel with shows in French and German. International films are shown in their original language and there are also cultural documentaries.

» **M6** shows a lot of pop music videos, low-budget films and past American sitcoms and soaps. There are also some interesting documentaries.

» Digital television has now taken off in France. More than 100 channels are available.

» If the TV listings mention *VO (version originale)*, the film will be in the language in which it was made, with French subtitles (Channel 3 usually screens a good film in *VO* every Sunday around midnight).

| NEWSPAPERS | |
|---|---|
| French daily newspapers have clear political leanings. | |
| **Le Monde** | A stately paper, left-of-centre. |
| **Libération** | This lively youth-focused paper is more clearly leftist. |
| **L'Humanité** | Left wing. |
| **Le Figaro** | Mainstream conservative daily. |
| **Le Parisien** | This tabloid paper is written at a level of French that makes it fairly easy for non-native readers to understand. |
| **Journal du Dimanche** | Sunday newspaper. |

| CABLE TV | |
|---|---|
| BBC Prime | With a mix of BBC shows, old and new |
| Canal+ | Shows recent films (some in their original language) |
| MTV | Contemporary music channel |
| MCM | The French version of MTV |
| Eurosport or Infosport | For major sporting events |
| Planète | Nature and science documentaries |
| RAI Uno | Italian |
| TVE 1 | Spanish |
| Euronews | A European all-news channel |
| LCI | All news in French |
| Canal Jimmy | Screens some British and American shows like *Friends* and *NYPD Blue* in English or multilingual versions |
| Paris Première | A cultural channel with some films in English |
| Canal J | With children's shows until 8pm |
| Téva | A women's channel that runs some English-language shows such as *Sex and the City* |

» Note that French television channels do not always keep exactly to schedule.

» Most hotels have at least a basic cable service, which is likely to include BBC World and CNN. Cable channels now offer multilingual versions of some shows. Ask at your hotel how to use this option as the mechanics vary. ARTE usually offers a choice between French and German for its cultural shows.

## RADIO

» French radio stations are available mainly on FM wavelengths, with a few international stations on Long Wave. Stations (with their Marseille frequencies) include:

» **Chérie FM:** 100.1 FM; French mainstream pop, news, reports.

» **France Infos:** 105.3 FM; news bulletins every 15 minutes.

» **France Musique:** 94.7 FM; classical and jazz music, concerts, operas, news.

» **NRJ:** 106.4 FM; French and International pop, techno, rap, R'n'B.

» **Radio Classique:** 100.9 FM; classical music.

» **Skyrock:** 90 FM; rap, hip-hop, R'n'B.

» **BBC Radio 4:** 198 kHz MW; news, current affairs, drama.

» **BBC Five Live:** 909 kHz MW; news and sport.

» **BBC World Service:** morning and early afternoon 15485 kHz LW, evening 6195 kHz and night 198 kHz.

» **Riviera Radio:** an English-speaking station operating from Monaco. Frequencies are 106.5 FM in the Alpes-Maritimes and 106.3 FM in Monaco.

## NEWSPAPERS

» In resorts and the major cities, you can buy the main British dailies, usually a day old, at a premium.

» *The Economist, USA Today* and *The Wall Street Journal* can be found at newsstands in cities, along with the *International Herald Tribune*, which reports international news from a US standpoint.

» You may be disappointed to find an international edition of your preferred paper rather than the one you would get at home.

» Local press plays an important part in the political sphere in France and there are several influential local newspapers published in Provence. City newspapers *La Marseillaise* and *Nice-Matin* are widely read beyond urban boundaries and reflect a southern perspective on national matters. *Département*-wide *Vaucluse* and *Var-Matin* include coverage of local issues, as does the cross-region *La Provence*.

» Local papers will normally have listings for the coming few days, with movie, concert and exhibition information and contact details. Magazines with events listings include *Hello Nice* (in English) and *Proximité* (in French and English), both published monthly and available at tourist offices, and Avignon-based *Le Rendezvous*, produced monthly in English. You can pick up free listings magazines at tourist offices, music stores or cafés.

» Weekly news magazines include *Le Nouvel Observateur, Le Point* and *L'Express*.

» For women's fashions, options include *Elle, Vogue* or *Marie Claire*.

» When you want celebrity gossip and lots of pictures, buy *Paris Match, Voici* or *Gala*.

## FILMS

» Watching a French film is a good way to get the feel of the place before you visit.

» For a classic, try *Les Enfants du Paradis* (1945) directed by Marcel Carné. For *nouvelle vague* (new wave) cinema—often filmed with a hand-held camera—try *Jules et Jim* (1962) directed by François Truffaut and starring Jeanne Moreau, or *À Bout de Souffle* (1959), directed by Jean-Luc Godard. The surreal *Belle de Jour* (1967), starring Cathérine Deneuve, caused a scandal at the time due to its erotic subject matter. The 1987 weepie *Au Revoir les Enfants* tells the story of a Jewish boy in occupied France in World War II.

» No reference to French movies would be complete without mentioning Gérard Départdieu, the actor who conquered France and then Hollywood. His best-known works include *Cyrano de Bergerac* (1990) and *Jean de Florette* (1986). The sequel to this, *Manon des Sources* (1986), stars Emmanuelle Béart, one of France's leading actresses.

» Jean-Pierre Jeunet's *Delicatessen* (1991) turns the controversial subject of cannibalism into a black comedy.

» The vibrant underbelly of Provence's urban centres is shown in full colour in these movies: Marseille in *The French Connection* (1975) and *Taxi* (1998), and Nice in *Ronin* (1998) and *The Good Thief* (2002).

» For something lighter try *French Kiss* (1995), which romps around Provence and the Riviera, or *Mr Bean's Holiday* (2007) for scenes in Avignon, Cannes and the countryside in between.

» Cannes hosts Europe's most prestigious film festival in May. It attracts top international actors, directors and producers, as well as starlets and self-promoting wannabes whose antics contribute much to the atmosphere. Millions of euros of business is conducted during the 12-day festival. For more details, look up www.festival-cannes.fr.

» Studios de la Victoirine made Nice a player in the French and international cinema scene from 1920 until the 1960s.

» Watch out for some great Riviera mountain scenery in *Herbie Goes to Monte-Carlo* (1977), when the famed 'Love Bug' cruises the boulevards and races along the country lanes.

» *And God Created Woman* (1956) by Roger Vadim launched Brigitte Bardot onto the world stage and kick-started the enduring reputation of St-Tropez.

» *To Catch a Thief* (1955) brought the pride of Hollywood to the Côte d'Azur in the form of Grace Kelly, Cary Grant and director Alfred Hitchcock. The film offers some great views of Monaco and the Riviera.

» One of the successes of 2006, *A Good Year* starring Russell Crowe, immerses the viewer in the archetypal landscapes of southern France.

## BOOKS

» For those who prefer to find their atmosphere on the page, there is no shortage of choices.

» Books about Provence written from a foreigner's perspective have dominated the bestseller list over the last couple of decades. Peter Mayle's *A Year in Provence* (1989), charting the author's first months living in the area, kick-started the process, followed by the sequel, *Toujours Provence* (1991). English actress Carol Drinkwater recounts her Provençal experiences in *The Olive Farm* (2001), *The Olive Season* (2003) and *The Olive Harvest* (2005).

» Classic literature set in Provence includes some fine 20th-century works. Ernest Hemingway wrote much of *The Garden of Eden* (unfinished when he died and published in 1986) during a sojourn here. F. Scott Fitzgerald captures the essence of expat life on the Riviera in *Tender is the Night* (1934), which was partly inspired by his own life and social circle.

» The modern French classic *Bonjour Tristesse* (1954), a story of the flowering of a young Frenchwoman, by Françoise Sagan, is set on the Esterel Coast.

» For something more modern try cop-drama *Total Chaos* (2005), by Jean-Clause Isso, and *Jacquot and the Waterman* (2005), by Martin O'Brien. Both are set around Marseille.

» Factual historical accounts of life in Provence can be found in *High Season in Nice* (2001), by Robert Kanigel, and *Chasing Matisse* (2005), by James Morgan.

# WHAT TO DO

## SHOPPING

Provence is a seductive shopping destination, whether you're after local produce at the lively markets or chic Riviera fashion at a Cannes boutique. Herbs, soaps, perfumes, pottery, olive oil and wine are among the best buys of the region.

### FOOD

Dried wild herbs, virgin olive oil and strings of garlic are the musts for any market shopping trip. The west coast of France may be more famous for its truffles, but the vast majority selected by top chefs come from Provence. For sensational jam, try the Les Merveilles range, and for other sugary treats sample candied fruits in Apt, *calissons* (candied-fruit paté) in Aix-en-Provence, *berlingots* (fruit humbugs) in Carpentras, nougat in Vence and *marrons glacés* (glazed chestnuts) in Collobrières.

Food is taken very seriously in France, with quality and freshness high on every shopper's list of priorities. Most food stores, except supermarkets, specialize and usually sell only one type of product. The ones you are most likely to see are the *boulangerie* (bakery), *pâtisserie* (pastry/cake shop), *fromagerie* (cheese shop), *boucherie* (butcher's shop), *charcuterie* (delicatessen) and *poissonnerie* (fishmonger's).

### WINES AND SPIRITS

*Hypermarchés* sell an excellent range of French wines, and British visitors in particular will find prices less expensive than back home. It is also fun to buy from the vineyards *(domaines)* themselves. The Rhône and Lubéron have specialist wine routes, as do many smaller AOC areas, such as Bandol and Cassis.

### REGIONAL SPECIAL BUYS

The air in the south is heavy with the scent of flowers, particularly around Grasse, famous for its perfumes. *Savon* (soap) *de Marseille* is known for its quality, and is often made with a base of olive oil. Nothing of the olive tree is wasted: The wood is carved into items, ranging from salad bowls to coasters.

Terracotta pottery is also widespread and you'll find bright ceramics in any market square. Ceramics in the shape of crickets and special garlic-scraper saucers make unusual gifts, and are widely available throughout the region. For faïences (fine glazed ceramics) head to Moustiers-Sainte-Marie and for glassware try Biot.

### INDIVIDUAL BOUTIQUES

Chain stores are finding their way into larger Provence towns, but there are many more individual boutiques selling fashion, shoes, and items such as kitchenware. In cities, the department store *(grand magasin)* brings these specialists under one roof.

### MARKETS

The *marché* (market) is a French institution. Large cities hold at least one daily market and smaller towns have a weekly one. They usually start around 7am and finish at noon. Discover the freshest seasonal produce, including fruit, vegetables and cheeses, and other products, from basketware to pottery. Buy *herbes de Provence* at Arles' Saturday market and flowers in old Nice. Other types of market advertise in the local paper or on posters. *Foires artisanales* bring together potters, sculptors and other artists, and are held during the holiday season. A summer treat is the *marché nocturne*, a craft market that gets going after sunset, away from the sweltering afternoon sunshine. One of the best is at Aix's cours Mirabeau. At Christmas there are wonderful Yuletide markets selling the famous *santons* (figurines), often based on local and well-known characters.

*Marchés aux puces* (flea markets) can be found in many cities. They are a bargain hunter's delight, with a mix of genuine antiques and flea-market goods—anything from furniture to china. Look out for genuine art nouveau glassware and top-quality hand-embroidered bed linens.

### MODERN STORES

Supermarkets and hypermarkets *(hypermarchés or grandes-surfaces)* have sprung up on the outskirts of every big town or city. The main names include Carrefour, Auchan, Champion and E. Leclerc. Here you will find the *boulangerie, boucherie* and *charcuterie* under one roof. Often the *hypermarchés* are surrounded by other stores, such as DIY stores, in a *centre commercial* (shopping mall). The larger malls have restaurants.

### CLOTHES

You'll find designer labels in the chic Riviera resorts and a good range of fashion stores in all the main towns. You can buy traditional Provençal cotton prints, known as *indiennes*, either by the length or ready-made into scarves, tops and skirts. Souléiado and Les Olivades stores are good places to look.

### PRACTICALITIES

Some shops close from noon until mid-afternoon. Hypermarkets usually remain open over lunch.

Non-EU visitors can reclaim VAT on certain purchases (▷ 260).

## ENTERTAINMENT AND NIGHTLIFE

Quality performances combine with amazing venues on the Provence arts scene. Enjoy epic opera in Orange's Roman theatre, jazz in Nice's Cimiez gardens or major theatrical performances at the Avignon festival. For more intimate productions, try a fringe show in a café-theatre or chamber music in the cloisters of a church. Magazines in hotel foyers and tourist information offices are a good source of information.

Don't expect great nightlife in the heart of the Provençal countryside—the serious clubbing takes place in town or along the coast. University towns are best, so party animals should consider checking out the bars of Marseille for flyers announcing the next big event. During winter, clubs in the Côte d'Azur resorts appear deceptively sleepy. But from carnival time in spring right up to New Year, the chic club scene comes alive, with minor royals and major celebs regularly on the guest list.

### THEATRE

France has a rich cultural heritage in the performing arts, ranging from acknowledged classics to the most avant-garde productions. Every major city in Provence has a theatre. Seasons usually run from October until late spring. The fringe scene, with café-theatres and alternative productions, is usually more lively and has a year-round schedule.

In Avignon in July the famous festival (▷ 251) attracts troupes from around the world and you can often see Shakespeare in any of five or six languages. During the festival, Avignon stages many French premieres featuring top stars. Expect to see plays by Molière, Henrik Ibsen and Anton Chekhov in venues ranging from the Papal Palace to side-street cafés. Fringe theatres in Marseille and the Théâtre des Ateliers in Aix-en-Provence (www.theatre-des-ateliers-aix.com) specialize in works by local playwrights. Huge auditoriums in exhibition venues on the outskirts of major towns host touring productions of French rock musicals such as Starmania and *The Hunchback of Notre-Dame.*

### DANCE

Contemporary dance festivals in Aix and Marseille draw crowds in summer, and Avignon's festival attracts international companies. The Centre Choréographique National is based at the Pavillion Noir in Aix, where the Ballet Preljocaj (www.preljocaj.org) hosts performances throughout the year. For information on the Ballet National de Marseille, check www.ballet-de-marseille.com.

### OPERA

In summer, Provence hosts many operatic productions, usually in historic settings. Most famous is the *Chorégies* (▷ 235) in Orange, when the Roman theatre hosts a couple of large-scale pageant productions of popular pieces such as *Carmen* and *La Traviata.* In Aix-en-Provence the *Festival d'Art Lyrique* (▷ 107) sees a temporary opera house erected in the courtyard of the Archbishop's Palace. This festival, with an emphasis on the works of Mozart and Benjamin Britten, is famous for discovering the international opera stars of tomorrow.

### CLASSICAL MUSIC

Aix and Orange's summer music festivals have orchestral concerts alongside the more famous opera. In Nice, you can enjoy sacred music in churches and summer concerts at the Cimiez monastery. Chamber music is celebrated through July and August, and features international performers in Menton (www.festivalmusiquementon.com).

### JAZZ

The Riviera is a beacon to the world's leading jazz musicians. Its two main events overlap, giving you the chance to overindulge in the most potent music. The pine groves of Juan-les-Pins have hosted the legends of jazz and swing for decades, with stars from both sides of the Atlantic (▷ 189). Rival

performers line up in Nice's Cimiez gardens for the Nice Jazz Festival (▷ 189).

### RESERVING TICKETS

Most box offices will accept telephone reservations with payment by credit card. FNAC stores (www.fnac.com) and Virgin Megastores (www.virgin mega.fr) have ticket agencies selling seats for high-profile events, and tourist offices often sell tickets for smaller festivals. Matinées are often less expensive than evening shows.

### ETIQUETTE

Events in concert halls and opera houses require smart but not necessarily formal clothing—although you can dress up if you wish without feeling overdressed. Festivals have no dress code, although turning up in beachwear or shirtless may cause offence. As in all indoor facilities in France, smoking is banned in auditoriums.

### THE CAFÉ-BAR

The inextricably linked café-bar is the lifeblood of French nightlife. Even the most humble village will have at least one place for a few drinks. In country areas French bars have multiple personalities—they are a place for teenagers to hang out over a game of pool, and somewhere for farmers to meet to discuss the latest subsidy controversy. In the cities, and especially in the resorts, bars are more sophisticated—diners drop in for an aperitif before dinner or a coffee and digestif afterwards.

Every bar worth its salt will have tables outside in summer, and the most popular are those where the clientele can watch the world go by as evening turns to night.

A PMU bar is a branch of the French tote system where you can bet on horse races and often watch races live on TV. In cities, bars open as early as 7am to serve breakfast and stay open until the early hours of the morning. Out of season and out of the cities, bars may close as early as 7pm.

Unaccompanied children under 18 are not allowed into bars and the legal age for drinking is 18.

### CLUBS

Major cities and resorts have a lively club scene. Find flyers at tourist offices, music stores or trendy cafés. Clubs may open from 10pm but don't get started until midnight. Smart dress is usually the rule. There is an admission charge on weekends and some week nights, but this usually includes your first drink.

### CASINOS

Not necessarily just for James Bond types, a night at a casino is part entertainment, part spectator sport and, provided you don't go totally over the top and lose your shirt, a great place to mix with European high rollers. Dress well to avoid doormen's sneers. Tables open around 10pm and close around 4am. The doyenne has to be Monte-Carlo's Casino (▷ 158–159, 185). Money from the gaming tables is Monaco's principal income. Only foreigners are allowed to play, so you'll need your passport. Locals, even the royals, are barred from gambling. There is also a casino in Cagnes-sur-Mer (▷ 182).

### GAY AND LESBIAN

Nice and St-Tropez have a lively gay bar and club scene (www.gay-provence.org). Inland, Aix-en-Provence and Avignon have a choice of venues. Marseille's gay community is student-led and tends to be more political, with a Gay Pride march in late June or early July.

# SPORTS AND ACTIVITIES

Provence has plenty to offer when it comes to outdoor activities—whether it's skiing in the Hautes-Alpes, windsurfing near Hyères or horseback riding through the Camargue. The French have great enthusiasm for sports. If you can climb it, jump from it, ski down it, sail on it, swim under it, ride on it or slither through it, the French do it—and there will be an association to organize and publicize the activity. There are also plenty of spectator sports to enjoy, attracting sportsmen and women from across the world.

## AIR SPORTS

Local aerodromes host clubs specializing in flying *(vol)*, gliding *(vol à voile)* or launching themselves out of planes *(parachutisme)*. These are privately run members' clubs that generally welcome foreign members (although the price, at around €200, may be prohibitive). They also offer introductions *(baptêmes)* to the sport, with prices of around €75 for a flight, €400 for parachute training and €230 for a tandem parachute jump.

Fédération Française de Vol Libre: www.ffvl.fr

Fédération Française de Vol à Voile: www.ffvv.org

## BICYCLING

Bicycling *(cyclisme)*, either off or on road, is a popular pastime, as well as a serious sport. It is easy to rent bicycles in towns and around most railway stations. Many tourist offices can offer itineraries for riders with mountain bicycles (*vélo tous terrains*—VTT), while Vélo Loisir, in Lubéron, (www.veloloisirluberon.com) is a good, bilingual website, with maps and practical information for cycling through the Lubéron countryside.

Fédération Française de Cyclisme: www.ffc.fr

The Tour de France is arguably the most important sporting event in France (www.letour.fr). The three-week event crosses the country in July, with its own carnival-style roadshow following along. It often includes a stretch in Provence. You don't need a ticket, just find a suitable spot along the route on any stage. You'll need to arrive early as the roads are closed at least a couple of hours before the race is due to pass by.

## CLIMBING

The Lubéron area attracts climbers from all over the world, and the Dentelles de Montmirail have been popular year round since the 1940s. The Club Alpin de Français (www.ffcam.fr) has information about climbing lessons or equipment rental for experienced climbers. Local tourist offices can put you in touch with caving groups.

## FISHING

While fish farming is now one of the region's biggest growth industries, thousands of kilometres of waterways in Provence offer

more tranquil angling and fly-fishing. Vaucluse alone has almost 3,000km (1,800 miles) of river banks. On rivers and lakes, some of which are private, you will need a licence (available from fishing shops) to cast your line.

**GOLF**

Golfers have plenty of courses to choose from in Provence, especially on the coast. In some resorts, such as those along the coast or near Avignon, the golf course is seen as an extension of the four-star luxury experience.

Tourist offices have details of special offers on green fees for visitors, including passes allowing holidaymakers to visit a selection of courses, and can organize combined golfing and dining breaks. Choose from various 18-hole courses, such as the Golf Club d'Aix-Marseille (www.golfaixmarseille.com) or the Riviera's Golf d'Opio Valbonne (www.opengolfclub.com). For more information, look up the website of the Fédération Française de Golf (www.ffg.org).

**HORSE RACING**

Horse racing is a popular sport in France and there are hippodromes—racecourses—in some of Provence's coastal towns and resorts. The Riviera's main venue is at Cagnes-sur-Mer (www. hippodrome-cotedazur.com) and Marseille has a choice of tracks (www.hippodrome-borely.com).

**HORSEBACK RIDING**

The flat marshes of the Camargue offer some of the most spectacular yet undemanding routes for horseback riding *(équitation/randonée équestre)*. You'll also find riding clubs close to major towns and cities, including Les Milles, near Aix.
Fédération Française d'Équitation: www.ffe.com

**KAYAKING**

Many of Provence's rivers are excellent for kayaking and canoeing, including the Sorgue and the Durance. The most spectacular settings are the Grand Canyon du Verdon (go with a trained guide) and the Ubbaye valley in the Alpes-de-Haute-Provence. You can rent equipment on site by the hour, the day or longer, or you can take an escorted kayak trip. The fast-flowing waters in the region are linked to hydroelectric power stations, so currents alter suddenly as barrages are raised or lowered. Do get up-to-the-minute local advice before venturing out.
Fédération Française de Canöe-Kayak: www.ffck.org

**MOTOR SPORTS**

There is only one destination for Formula 1 fans: The most glamorous race on the circuit is at Monte-Carlo, where the cars twist and turn through the narrow streets rather than a specially built racetrack. Seeing legends of racing speeding past famous buildings and the magnificent views is breathtaking stuff. The presence of the jet set turns Monaco into much more than a Grand Prix, but if you simply want to watch the racing, prices for hillside viewing start at €70, with stand seats costing from €270–€450 (www.formula1monaco.com). Racing under far more hazardous conditions, the Trophée Andros is the classic alpine ice-driving championship, one of the main events of Provence's winter resorts (www.tropheeandros.com).

**PARAPENTE**

The *parapente* is a little like a parachute but is more controllable, and you don't need to take a plane ride—a running jump from any high point launches you into the air. Pioneered in France, it is a popular sport.
Fédération Française de Vol Libre: www.ffvl.fr

**RUGBY**

There is a strong rugby following in France and the season (running from September to the end of May) culminates in the international Six Nations Tournament (www.rbs6nations.com), when France takes on England, Scotland, Wales, Ireland and Italy in a bid to be the best in Europe. RC Toulonnais is currently the only Provençal team to play in the professional Top 14 leading league—most of the big money, big teams and big crowds are in southwest France—but Pays d'Aix RC play in Rugby Pro D2, rugby's second division in France.

**SAILING**

Most of Provence's 125 ports and marinas have sailing schools and boats for rent (www.voilecotedazur.com). For a change from Mediterranean scenery, head to the mountain lakes of the Alpes-de-Haute-Provence, such as Lac de Quinson and Lac du Castillon, where sailing is also popular.

**SKIING/SNOWBOARDING**

These are the principal sports of the winter season, and the Alpine resorts, including Isola 2000 (www.isola2000.com) and Val d'Allos (www.valdallos.com), have a wide range of activities and training packages. Equipment rental and ski-school classes can vary in price according to the time of year. It is worth checking dates of the French school holidays, since outside these periods excellent bargains may be had, with discounts on hotels as well. Contact the École du Ski Français: www.esf.net or Club Alpin Français: www.ffcam.com and www.skifrance.com.

**SOCCER**

Soccer is one of the premier sports in France. Olympique de Marseille are among the south's sporting heroes. A.S. Monaco are also in contention in Ligue 1. The season runs from August to the end of May and tickets for matches are like gold. A.S. Monaco plays at Stade Louis II (tel 377 92 05 40 00; www.asm-fc.com); Olympique de Marseille at Stade Velodrome 3, boulevard Michelet (www.om.net).

### TENNIS

The mild winter climate means the tennis stars come out in Provence as early as February. Both Monaco (Apr) and Nice (May) feature early on the ATP Masters tour (www.atpworldtour.com).

### WALKING AND HIKING

Provence is criss-crossed by trails, with a series of *Sentiers de Grandes Randonnées* (long-distance trails) and *Petites Randonnées* (shorter walking routes) that are included on maps published by Institut Géographique National (www.ign.fr). Topographical guides are sold at tourist offices and park bookstores.

To supplement this network, every *département* and even local *communes* have shorter walks, including marked trails around lakes, along river banks or linking historical monuments. Most tourist offices have information about trails and walks in their area, and town halls usually have free maps of local walks. Alternative options are *RandOxygène* (www.randoxygene.org), detailed booklets that comprehensively cover Provençal walks for all abilities (in French), or the *Randonnée avec Âne*, where hikers travel with donkeys who carry baggage and picnics in their panniers (www.bourricot.com).

### WINDSURFING

The happiest side effect of Provence's notorious *mistral* wind is that it produces champion windsurfers. When the weather is less stormy, gentler but effective winds are harnessed by experts at Saintes-Maries-de-la-Mer and at l'Almanarre, near Hyères. There are windsurfing schools all along the coast.

### GENERAL INFORMATION

Each district has some form of sporting facility, be it a boules pitch, sports hall, swimming pool *(piscine)*, tennis court or golf course. Information about these facilities appears in tourist publications under *loisirs* (leisure). Most tourist offices publish separate booklets focusing on their leisure facilities. The French Government Tourist Office (FGTO) produces some excellent brochures on leisure and sporting activities.

## HEALTH AND BEAUTY

What the rest of the world has discovered in the last few decades, the French have known for centuries—that a little pampering is good for everyone.

### SPAS AND THALASSOTHERAPY

France discovered the therapeutic value of its natural water sources soon after it began to enjoy the taste of the waters themselves. One of the oldest is at Aix-en-Provence, where, long before the Romans built their spa resorts, Celtic women used to take to the 35°C (95°F) waters for their alleged fertility benefits. Today's Thermes Sextius Hydrotherapy Complex (⊳ 103) uses those same hot waters and adds mud treatments and gym toning to the recipe. The most luxurious hotels on the Riviera now boast health spas and pampering suites. The French invented thalassotherapy—the use of sea water in a variety of therapies—and thalassotherapy venues are dotted along the Mediterranean coast.

## FOR CHILDREN

There is plenty to entertain children in Provence, whether they prefer splashing in the warm waters of the Mediterranean, visiting an adventure park or waving at a parade during one of the many festivals. Museums are usually child-friendly and often have activity packs or treasure hunts for younger visitors. The region's Roman ruins have their own attraction for youngsters, bringing to life school history lessons.

### BEACHES

There are excellent beaches along the Mediterranean coast, although some of the more exclusive addresses tend to frown on children being children. The best option is to find a less fashionable stretch of beach, close to a water park, and sacrifice parental calm in preference for family harmony. Good family beaches include Le Lavandou, Bandol, La Ciotat, La Couronne (near Martigues) and Sausset-les-Pins.

### FESTIVALS AND FAIRS

These are held throughout the year and are perfect for children. There are marching bands, merry-go-rounds, costumed minstrels, clowns and face painting. The Carnival parades often have child-friendly themes. Menton's *Fête du Citron* (⊳ 189), in late February, regularly turns to fairy tales and exotic themes, and floats in recent years have evoked Asterix, Alice in Wonderland and mythical Indian gods.

### FOOD

Food tasting is always popular, with many a baker ready to share a slice of chocolate bread or sweetmaker some home-made candies. There are lots of olives and cheeses to sample on a trip to the weekly market.

### ADVENTURE PARKS

More than 30 adventure parks and water parks provide a useful bribe to guarantee good behaviour on longer drives. Zoos and animal parks are also popular.

### SPORTS

France has a comprehensive range of sports (⊳ 274–this page). The level of training and supervision is usually very high, so children can try a new sport or simply enjoy one in which they are already proficient—from horseback riding to bicycling, or windsurfing to snowboarding. Ski resorts have kids' clubs where youngsters can enjoy supervised training and entertainment while the adults play at their own pace.

# FESTIVALS AND EVENTS

You are unlikely to go hungry or thirsty at one of Provence's 500 or so festivals. Whatever the theme, glasses and plates are filled and refilled. In addition to the food and free-flowing wine, festivals often involve a lively procession with participants dressed in traditional costume. The events give you a glimpse into the history and character of the town or village, and of Provence itself.

**RELIGIOUS**

Provence is famous for its Nativity scenes: Artisans make *santons* (figurines) for Nativity displays and shepherds lead their flocks to church on Christmas Eve. Saintes-Maries-de-la-Mer brings together Christian and folk traditions with its gypsy pilgrimage (▷ 107). Saints' days are celebrated with gusto: St. Eloi festivities (25 Jun) see fabulous processions, with garlanded horses pulling wagons piled with wheat.

**ARTS**

The Cannes Film Festival (www.festival-cannes.com) in May has the highest profile, but summer nights are filled with the sound of sopranos in open-air operas across Provence. Avignon has a lively fringe (www.avignonleoff.com) where you can enjoy the off-beat on a budget. Jazz is France's adopted art form, with top artists appearing along the Côte d'Azur in the summer. The nationwide *Fête de la Musique* on 21 June (fetedelamusique.culture.fr) sees every town corner crowded with free performances of every type of music and dancing revellers.

**FOOD AND DRINK**

In October, France has a week of food festivals, street fairs and cookery contests (*La Semaine du Goût*, www.legout.com). This pleasure is prolonged in Provence with an extra week of gastronomy in Vaison-la-Romaine (*Les Journées Gourmandes*, www.journees-gourmandes.com), but the eating continues year round. Provence's wine country produces some excellent festivals, with chestnuts, roasted, puréed and baked, served with local wines along the Rhône, and olives complementing the wines of the Lubéron.

**TRADITIONAL**

May Day is the *Fête des Gardians*, when the cowboys of the Camargue display their rodeo skills and race in the Roman theatre at Arles. St-Tropez's noisy and ebullient *bravades* are nominally a celebration of the town's patron saint, but it's also a commemoration of the rout of a Spanish armada.

# EATING OUT IN PROVENCE AND THE CÔTE D'AZUR

Provençal cuisine is as much a reflection of the region as the landscape and architecture. The sultry climate encourages wonderful fresh produce, bursting with aromatic, sun-drenched tastes. The staples of dishes *à la provençale* include virgin olive oil, garlic, tomatoes and wild herbs. Fish is in plentiful supply, fresh from the Mediterranean ports.

### BRASSERIES AND BISTROS

Brasseries and bistros are good places to enjoy local dishes, such as bouillabaisse, in a friendly, informal setting. Brasseries open longer hours than restaurants and bistros. Bistros are often small, independent or family-run restaurants serving traditional cooking, with a modest wine list.

### RESTAURANTS

Celebrity chefs are the standard-bearers of haute cuisine, and their dining rooms in Provence are regarded as the equal of any Parisian establishment. Alain Ducasse and Joël Robuchon are among those who dictate the food fads of tomorrow. Every town has its respected restaurants, where you'll find starched linen, polished glass and silverware and a sense of hushed reverence for the gastronomic offerings to come. Remember to dress well and reserve in advance. The dining rooms of Logis de France hotels offer quality regional food.

The *menu dégustation*, found in only the finest restaurants, is a *prix-fixe* menu with a sample of the top dishes and a choice of appropriate wines. The best value are the weekday set lunchtime menus, bringing a meal at even the most stellar establishments down to a realistic price.

### CAFÉS AND BARS

Cafés and bars serve coffee, soft drinks, alcohol, snacks and often herbal and traditional teas too. They open from breakfast until late in the evening and you can expect to pay a little more for your drink if you sit at a table or on the outdoor terrace. You'll notice the locals tend to stand at the bar. Bars often have newspapers and you can linger over your cup of coffee.

### CUTTING COSTS

If you are on a budget, have your main meal at lunchtime, when most restaurants serve a *menu du jour* of two or three courses with a glass of wine for around 50 per cent of the evening cost. Many restaurants also have *prix-fixe* meals in the evening too, with three, four or more courses, the best of which is the *menu gastronomique*.

### OPENING TIMES

Most restaurants and bistros keep strict serving times. Restaurants open at 12, close at 2.30, then reopen at 7.30. Except in the bustling heart of a lively city, restaurants stop taking orders between 10pm and 11pm, although in summer people tend to dine later. Many restaurants are closed for lunch on Saturday and Monday and for dinner on Sunday evenings. Some on the coast close completely between November and Easter.

### ETIQUETTE

Only the very top restaurants have a dress code, but it is usual to dress up when dining in a more formal venue. Most restaurants include the tip in the price of dishes, indicated by *service compris* or *s.c.*

You may want to leave an extra tip if you are especially impressed with the service. Smoking has long been banned in all French cafés and restaurants. Address staff as *Monsieur, Madame* or *Mademoiselle*.

### VEGETARIAN AND WORLD CUISINE

In recent years, a move to lighter dishes and simpler techniques has, belatedly, acknowledged vegetarian tastes, although France's concept of vegetarianism is a little hazy, sometimes involving beef stock, chicken and bacon. Larger towns have North African, Lebanese and Vietnamese restaurants and Italian restaurants are also popular.

# PROVENÇAL CUISINE

**STYLES**
**... provençale:** with olive oil, garlic, tomatoes, onion and herbs.
**... niçoise:** with olive oil, garlic, tomatoes, onion, herbs, olives, capers, anchovies and tarragon.

**MEAT**
**Agneau de Sisteron:** this lamb has grazed on mountain pastures and is lean and tasty.
**Boeuf gardiane:** the Camargue's version of beef braised in red wine.
**Daube:** meat stewed in wine.
**Lapin:** rabbit often comes simmered in wine and herbs, as does hare *(lièvre)*.

**SALADS AND OTHER DISHES**
**Aïoli:** a delicious garlic mayonnaise, often served with raw vegetables as a hors d'oeuvre.
**Cargolade:** stew of snails in wine.
**Pissaladière:** a tasty flan containing olives, onions and anchovies.
**Pistou:** sauce made of ground garlic, basil and cheese bound with olive oil.
**Ratatouille:** tomatoes, onions, courgettes (zucchini) and aubergines (eggplant) slow-cooked in garlic and olive oil.
**Rouille:** a spicy mayonnaise made with garlic and chilli.
**Salade niçoise:** the traditional Nice salad includes tomatoes, French beans, anchovies, olives, peppers and boiled egg.
**Socca:** this tasty pancake, made from chick-pea flour, is a Nice speciality and is sure to satisfy hunger pangs.

**FISH**
**Bouillabaisse:** fish stew served with *aïoli* or *rouille*.
**Bourride:** fish soup-cum-stew.
**Brandade de morue:** paste of salt cod mixed with milk, garlic and olive oil.
**Crabe:** crab.
**Gambas:** giant prawns.
**Homard:** lobster.
**Loup de mer:** sea bass—this tastes best grilled with vine shoots or fennel.
**Merlan:** hake.
**Moules:** mussels.
**Oursins:** sea urchins.
**Palourdes:** clams.
**Rouget:** red mullet.
**Soupe de poisson:** this is a classic, inexpensive soup of puréed mixed fish.
**Truite:** trout, often fresh from mountain streams.
**... à la meunière:** a method of serving fish, fried in butter then presented with lemon juice, butter and parsley.

**CHEESE**
Be sure to try some local cheeses made from the milk of goats *(chèvres)* or ewes *(brebis)*.
**Banon:** creamy sheep's cheese.
**Petits chèvres:** these small roundels of goat's cheese have often been rolled in herbs.
**Poivre d'âne:** there's a peppery taste to this goat's cheese.

**FRENCH SAUCES**
**Béarnaise:** egg yolk, vinegar, butter, white wine, shallots and tarragon.
**Béchamel:** a classic sauce of flour, butter and milk. Often a base of other sauces such as Mornay, with cheese.
**Chasseur:** hunter-style, with wine, mushrooms, shallots and herbs.
**Demi-glace:** brown sauce of stock with sherry or Madeira wine.
**Sauce au poivre:** spicy green-pepper sauce used all over Provence.

**HOW TO ORDER STEAK**
The French like their meat lightly cooked. Lamb will come rare unless you demand otherwise. If you order steak, you will be asked how you would like it cooked. The options are:
**Bleu:** blue, the rarest steak, warm on the outside but uncooked and cool in the middle.
**Saignant:** bloody, or rare, the steak is cooked until it starts to bleed and is warm in the middle.
**À point:** literally 'at the point'. The meat is cooked until it just stops bleeding. Many restaurants serve steak *à point* with some blood in the middle. If you want a warm pink middle but no visible blood, ask for steak *plus à point*. It's not an official French term, but good restaurants should oblige.
**Bien cuit:** 'well cooked', with only a narrow pink middle. If you want no pink to remain, ask for it *bien bien cuit*, although your waiter may not be impressed.

For more French food terms, ▷ 284.

# STAYING IN PROVENCE AND THE CÔTE D'AZUR

Simplicity or luxury is the key choice for a stay in Provence, with the grand hotels of the Riviera contrasting with old stone buildings inland and homey chalets in the mountains. A new generation of boutique hotels combines the two, with minimalistic decor and high-tech luxuries.

## GENERAL INFORMATION

Hotels are inspected regularly and classified into six categories: no star, one-star, two-star, three-star, four-star and five-star. They must display their rates (including tax) both outside the hotel and in the rooms, and charge per room and not per person. You generally have to pay extra for breakfast and for any additional beds you may want in your room.

## LUXURY

Traditional haunts of the rich and famous include the fabulous belle époque hotels on the Riviera, which offer the full luxury treatment. These have been joined by new designer hotels such as the Hotel Windsor (⊳ 195) in Nice, which offers guest rooms designed by artists and a Turkish bath upstairs. Smaller, but no less expensive, are the boutique hotels, with a couple of dozen rooms styled by fashion gurus. For true luxury, find a top-of-the-range *mas* (country house) with a swimming pool or a first-class restaurant with rooms. Many restored country houses also offer pampering, and a chance to get back to basics by learning old country recipes from their chefs. In most of the luxury hotels on the coast, health and beauty treatments are provided in state-of-the-art spas.

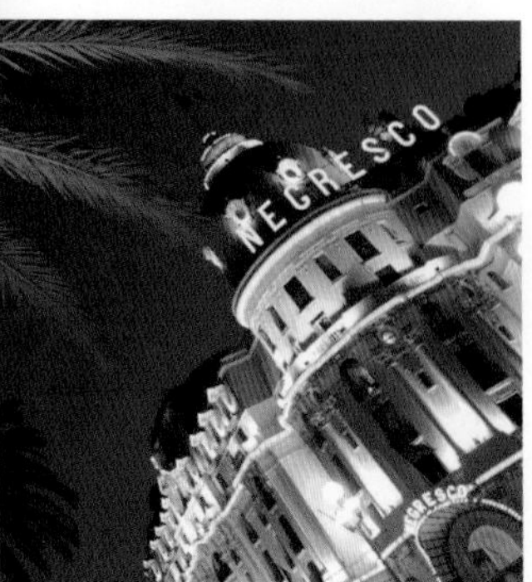


## ON A BUDGET

Independent city hotels are often surprisingly chic, although occasionally horribly dated and draughty. International chain hotels and motels are the easy option, and while the like of www.hotelformule1.com and www.etaphotel.com may be useful overnight stops on long *autoroute* journeys south, there are far more interesting options available at similar prices. Best of all are the Logis de France—small, family-run inns and hotels offering good standards, from basic and comfortable to charming. Most have restaurants, serving traditional local dishes. All are regularly inspected and listed on the website www.logis-de-france.fr. Some offer themed packages which promote winter sports, fishing or hiking.

Budget beds are also offered at the region's many youth hostels *(Auberges de Jeunesse)*. You will get a discount if you are a member of the International Youth Hostelling Federation or of the Youth Hostelling Federation of your home country. Look up the website www.fuaj.org for a list of youth hostels.

## BED-AND-BREAKFAST

The *chambre d'hôte* is France's answer to the traditional bed-and-breakfast, and tourist offices have lists of families who offer rooms to visitors. However, the best *chambres d'hôte* are affiliated with the Gîtes de France organization (⊳ below). Often in converted farm buildings or restored watermills, they give you the opportunity to experience French life. Breakfast usually includes home-made treats, from fresh croissants to jams. Since many are run by farmers' wives and vineyard owners, it is worth taking the *table d'hôte* option and dining with the host family at least once.

## SELF-CATERING

*Gîtes* are self-contained cottages, houses and apartments, often with swimming pools, in small towns and country areas, and may be classified by the organization Gîtes de France (www.gites-de-france.fr). The accommodation is usually simple and decent (bring your own linen or rent on site), but with a certain rustic charm. Other self-catering options range from isolated farmhouses to grand villas or beach apartments on the Riviera.

## CAMPING

Provence has around 900 campsites, the majority of which are in the Var *département*. Campsites, officially graded from no stars to four stars, are regularly inspected. Most have excellent facilities, with mobile homes and pre-pitched tents. Some have swimming pools, supermarkets and restaurants. Visitors with their own caravans (RVs) and tents can find inexpensive sites offering electricity, showers and bathrooms. In July and August it is important to reserve ahead.
National Federation of Campsites: www.campingfrance.com.

# WORDS AND PHRASES

Even if you're far from fluent, it is always a good idea to try to speak a few words of French while in France. The words and phrases on the following pages should help you with the basics, from ordering a meal and buying goods in a shop to posting a letter and dealing with emergencies.

**CONVERSATION**

**I don't speak French.**
Je ne parle pas français.

**Do you speak English?**
Parlez-vous anglais?

**I don't understand.**
Je ne comprends pas.

**Please speak more slowly.**
Pouvez-vous parler plus lentement?

**Please repeat that.**
Pouvez-vous répéter?

**My name is ...**
Je m'appelle ...

**Hello, pleased to meet you.**
Bonjour, enchanté(e).

**I'm on holiday.**
Je suis en vacances.

**I live in ...**
J'habite à ...

**Good morning.**
Bonjour.

**Good evening.**
Bonsoir.

**Goodnight.**
Bonne nuit.

**Goodbye.**
Au revoir.

**See you later.**
A plus tard.

**May I/Can I?**
Est-ce que je peux?

**How are you?**
Comment allez-vous?

**I'm sorry.**
Je suis désolé(e).

**Excuse me.**
Excusez-moi.

**NUMBERS**

| | |
|---|---|
| **1** | un |
| **2** | deux |
| **3** | trois |
| **4** | quatre |
| **5** | cinq |
| **6** | six |
| **7** | sept |
| **8** | huit |
| **9** | neuf |
| **10** | dix |
| **11** | onze |
| **12** | douze |
| **13** | treize |
| **14** | quatorze |
| **15** | quinze |
| **16** | seize |
| **17** | dix-sept |
| **18** | dix-huit |
| **19** | dix-neuf |
| **20** | vingt |
| **21** | vingt et un |
| **30** | trente |
| **40** | quarante |
| **50** | cinquante |
| **60** | soixante |
| **70** | soixante-dix |
| **80** | quatre-vingts |
| **90** | quatre-vingt-dix |
| **100** | cent |
| **1,000** | mille |

**SHOPPING**

**How much is this?**
C'est combien?

**I'm looking for ...**
Je cherche ...

**I'm just looking, thank you.**
Je regarde, merci.

**Could you help me, please?**
(Est-ce que) vous pouvez m'aider, s'il vous plaît?

**When does the shop close?**
A quelle heure ferme le magasin?

**Do you accept credit cards?**
(Est-ce que) vous acceptez les cartes de crédit?

**This is the right size.**
C'est la bonne taille.

**Do you have anything less expensive/smaller/larger?**
(Est-ce que) vous avez quelque chose de moins cher/plus petit/plus grand?

**I'll take this.**
Je prends ça.

**Do you have a bag for this?**
(Est-ce que) je peux avoir un sac, s'il vous plaît?

**I'd like ... grams.**
Je voudrais ... grammes.

**I'd like a kilo of ...**
Je voudrais un kilo de ...

**What does this contain?**
Quels sont les ingrédients?

**I'd like ... slices of that.**
J'en voudrais ... tranches.

**Bakery**
Boulangerie

**Bookshop**
Librairie

**Chemist**
Pharmacie

**Market**
Marché

**Sale**
Soldes

**DAYS**

| | |
|---|---|
| **Monday** | lundi |
| **Tuesday** | mardi |
| **Wednesday** | mercredi |
| **Thursday** | jeudi |
| **Friday** | vendredi |
| **Saturday** | samedi |
| **Sunday** | dimanche |
| | |
| **today** | aujourd'hui |
| **yesterday** | hier |
| **tomorrow** | demain |
| | |
| **morning** | matin |
| **afternoon** | après-midi |
| **evening** | soir |
| **night** | nuit |

**MONTHS**

| | |
|---|---|
| **January** | janvier |
| **February** | février |
| **March** | mars |
| **April** | avril |
| **May** | mai |
| **June** | juin |
| **July** | juillet |
| **August** | août |
| **September** | septembre |
| **October** | octobre |
| **November** | novembre |
| **December** | décembre |
| | |
| **month** | le mois |
| **year** | l'année |

**SEASONS**

| | |
|---|---|
| **spring** | printemps |
| **summer** | été |
| **autumn** | automne |
| **winter** | hiver |
| | |
| **holiday** | vacances |
| | |
| **Easter** | Pâques |
| **Christmas** | Noël |

**HOTELS**

**Do you have a room?**
(Est-ce que) vous avez une chambre?

**I have a reservation for ... nights.**
J'ai réservé pour ... nuits.

**Double room.**
Une chambre pour deux personnes/double.

**Twin room.**
Une chambre à deux lits/avec lits jumeaux.

**Single room.**
Une chambre à un lit/pour une personne.

**With bath/shower/lavatory.**
Avec salle de bain/douche/WC.

**Is the room air conditioned?**
(Est-ce que) la chambre est climatisée?

**Is there a lift?**
(Est-ce qu') il y a un ascenseur?

**How much each night?**
C'est combien par nuit?

**Is breakfast/lunch/dinner included in the cost?**
(Est-ce que) le petit déjeuner/le déjeuner/le dîner est compris dans le prix?

**Is room service available?**
Il y a le service en chambre?

**When do you serve breakfast?**
À quelle heure servez-vous le petit déjeuner?

**May I have breakfast in my room?**
(Est-ce que) je peux prendre le petit déjeuner dans ma chambre?

**Do you serve evening meals?**
(Est-ce que) vous servez le repas du soir/le dîner?

**The room is too hot/cold.**
Il fait trop chaud/froid dans la chambre.

**Will you look after my luggage until I leave?**
Pouvez-vous garder mes bagages jusqu'à mon départ?

**Is there parking?**
(Est-ce qu') il y a un parking?

**Do you have babysitters?**
(Est-ce que) vous avez un service de babysitting?

**Could I have another room?**
(Est-ce que) je pourrais avoir une autre chambre?

**Can I pay my bill?**
(Est-ce que) je peux régler ma note, s'il vous plaît?

**May I see the room?**
(Est-ce que) je peux voir la chambre?

**Swimming pool.**
Piscine.

**Sea view.**
Vue sur la mer.

**USEFUL WORDS**

| | |
|---|---|
| **Yes** | Oui |
| **No** | Non |
| **There** | Là-bas |
| **Here** | Ici |
| **Where** | Où |
| **Who** | Qui |
| **When** | Quand |
| **Why** | Pourquoi |
| **How** | Comment |
| **Later** | Plus tard |
| **Now** | Maintenant |
| **Open** | Ouvert |
| **Closed** | Fermé |
| **Please** | S'il vous plaît |
| **Thank you** | Merci |

**GETTING AROUND**

**Where is the information desk?**
Où est le bureau des renseignements?

**Where is the timetable?**
Où sont les horaires?

**Does this train/bus go to ...?**
Ce train/bus va à ...?

**Do you have a Métro/bus map?**
Avez-vous un plan du Métro/des lignes de bus?

**Train/bus/Métro station.**
La gare SNCF/routière/la station de Métro.

**Where can I buy a ticket?**
Où est-ce que je peux acheter un billet/ticket?

**Where can I reserve a seat?**
Où est-ce que je peux réserver une place?

**Please can I have a single ticket to ...?**
Je voudrais un aller simple pour ..., s'il vous plaît.

**Please can I have a return ticket to ...?**
Je voudrais un aller-retour pour ..., s'il vous plaît.

**Is this seat free?**
(Est-ce que) cette place est libre?

**Do I need to get off here?**
(Est-ce qu') il faut que je descende ici?

**Where can I find a taxi?**
Où est-ce que je peux trouver un taxi?

**How much is the journey?**
Combien coûte le trajet?

**I'd like to rent a car.**
Je voudrais louer une voiture.

**No parking.**
Interdiction de stationner.

**I'm lost.**
Je me suis perdu(e).

**Is this the way to ...?**
C'est bien par ici pour aller à ...?

**Go straight on.**
Allez tout droit.

**Turn left/right.**
Tournez à gauche/à droite.

**Cross over.**
Traversez.

**Traffic lights.**
Les feux.

**Intersection.**
Carrefour.

**Corner.**
Coin.

**MONEY**

**Is there a bank/currency exchange office nearby?**
(Est-ce qu') il y a une banque/un bureau de change près d'ici?

**Can I cash this here?**
(Est-ce que) je peux encaisser ça ici?

**I'd like to change sterling/dollars into euros.**
Je voudrais changer des livres sterling/dollars en euros.

**Can I use my credit card to withdraw cash?**
(Est-ce que) je peux utiliser ma carte de crédit pour retirer de l'argent?

**What is the exchange rate today?**
Quel est le taux de change aujourd'hui?

**COLOURS**

| | |
|---|---|
| **brown** | marron/brun |
| **black** | noir(e) |
| **red** | rouge |
| **blue** | bleu(e) |
| **green** | vert(e) |
| **yellow** | jaune |
| **orange** | orange |
| **pink** | rose |

**POST AND TELEPHONES**

**Where is the nearest post office/mail box?**
Où se trouve la poste/la boîte aux lettres la plus proche?

**How much is the postage to ...?**
A combien faut-il affranchir pour ...?

**I'd like to send this by air mail/registered mail.**
Je voudrais envoyer ceci par avion/en recommandé.

**Where can I buy a phone card?**
Où est-ce que je peux acheter une télécarte?

**Please put me through to ...**
Pouvez-vous me passer ..., s'il vous plaît?

**What is the charge per minute?**
Quel est le tarif à la minute?

**Hello, this is ...**
Allô, c'est ... (à l'appareil).

**Who is speaking please?**
Qui est à l'appareil, s'il vous plaît?

**I would like to speak to ...**
Je voudrais parler à ...

**RESTAURANTS**

**I'd like to reserve a table for ... people at ...**
Je voudrais réserver une table pour ... personnes à ... heures, s'il vous plaît.

**A table for ..., please.**
Une table pour ..., s'il vous plaît.

**Could we sit there?**
(Est-ce que) nous pouvons nous asseoir ici?

**Is this table taken?**
(Est-ce que) cette table est libre?

**Are there tables outside?**
(Est-ce qu') il y a des tables dehors/à la terrasse?

**Could we see the menu/wine list please?**
(Est-ce que) nous pouvons voir le menu/la carte des vins, s'il vous plaît?

**Do you have nappy-changing facilities?**
(Est-ce qu') il y a une pièce pour changer les bébés?

**Where are the toilets?**
Où sont les toilettes?

**We'd like something to drink.**
Nous voudrions quelque chose à boire.

**Could I have bottled still/sparkling water please?**
(Est-ce que) je peux avoir une bouteille d'eau minérale/gazeuse, s'il vous plaît?

**What do you recommend?**
Qu'est-ce que vous nous conseillez?

**Is there a dish of the day?**
(Est-ce qu') il y a un plat du jour?

**I can't eat wheat/sugar/salt/pork/beef/dairy.**
Je ne peux pas manger de blé/sucre/sel/porc/bœuf/produits laitiers.

**I am a vegetarian.**
Je suis végétarien(ne).

**I'd like ...**
Je voudrais ...

**How much is this dish?**
Combien coûte ce plat?

**Is service included?**
(Est-ce que) le service est compris?

**Can I have the bill, please?**
(Est-ce que) je peux avoir l'addition, s'il vous plaît?

**The bill is not right.**
Il y a une erreur sur l'addition.

**The food was excellent.**
Le repas était excellente.

**FOOD AND DRINK**

**Breakfast**
Petit déjeuner

**Lunch**
Déjeuner

**Dinner**
Dîner

**Coffee**
Café

**Tea**
Thé

**Orange juice**
Jus d'orange

**Apple juice**
Jus de pomme

**Milk**
Lait

**Beer**
Bière

**Red wine**
Vin rouge

**White wine**
Vin blanc

**Bread roll**
Petit pain

**Bread**
Pain

**Sugar**
Sucre

**Wine list**
Carte/liste des vins

**Main course**
Le plat principal

**Dessert**
Dessert

**Salt**
Sel

**Pepper**
Poivre

**Cheese**
Fromage

**Knife**
Couteau

**Fork**
Fourchette

**Spoon**
Cuillère

**Soups**
Soupes/potages

**Chicken soup**
Soupe au poulet

**Vegetable soup**
Soupe de légumes

**Lentil soup**
Soupe aux lentilles

**Mushroom soup**
Soupe aux champignons

**Sandwiches**
Sandwichs

**Ham sandwich**
Sandwich au jambon

**Dish of the day**
Plat du jour

**Fish dishes**
Les poissons

**Prawns**
Crevettes roses/bouquet

**Oysters**
Huîtres

**Salmon**
Saumon

**Haddock**
Églefin

**Squid**
Calmar

**Meat dishes**
Viandes

**Roast chicken**
Poulet rôti

**Casserole**
Plat en cocotte

**Roast lamb**
Gigot

**Potatoes**
Pommes de terre

**Green beans**
Haricots verts

**Peas**
Petits pois

**Carrots**
Carottes

**Spinach**
Épinards

**Onions**
Oignons

**Tomatoes**
Tomates

**Fruit**
Les fruits

**Apples**
Pommes

**Strawberries**
Fraises

**Peaches**
Pêches

**Pears**
Poires

**Pastry**
Pâtisserie

**Chocolate cake**
Gâteau au chocolat

**Cream**
Crème

**Ice cream**
Glace

**ILLNESS AND EMERGENCIES**

**I don't feel well.**
Je ne me sens pas bien.

**I need to see a doctor/dentist.**
Il faut que je voie un médecin/docteur/dentiste.

**Is there a doctor/pharmacist on duty?**
(Est-ce que) il y a un médecin/un docteur/une pharmacie de garde?

**I have left my medicine at home.**
J'ai laissé mes médicaments chez moi.

**Could you call a doctor?**
(Est-ce que) vous pouvez appeler un médecin/un docteur?

**Please tell me how to get to the hospital.**
(Est-ce que) vous pouvez m'indiquer le chemin pour aller à l'hôpital, s'il vous plaît?

**I have a headache.**
J'ai mal à la tête.

**I've been stung by a wasp/bee/jellyfish.**
J'ai été piqué(e) par une guêpe/abeille/méduse.

**I have a heart condition.**
J'ai un problème cardiaque.

**I am diabetic.**
Je suis diabétique.

**I'm asthmatic.**
Je suis asmathique.

**I'm on a special diet.**
Je suis un régime spécial.

**I am on medication.**
Je prends des médicaments.

**I have bad toothache.**
J'ai mal aux dents.

**I don't want an injection.**
Je ne veux pas de piqûre.

**Help!**
Au secours!

**I need to make an emergency appointment.**
Je dois prendre rendez-vous d'urgence.

**I have lost my passport/wallet/purse/handbag.**
J'ai perdu mon passeport/portefeuille/porte-monnaie/sac à main.

**I have had an accident.**
J'ai eu un accident.

**My car has been stolen.**
On m'a volé ma voiture.

**I have been robbed.**
J'ai été volé(e).

**TOURIST INFORMATION**

**Where is the tourist information office, please?**
Où se trouve l'office du tourisme, s'il vous plaît?

**Do you have a city map?**
Avez-vous un plan de la ville?

**We are staying here for a day.**
Nous sommes ici pour une journée.

**Where is the museum?**
Où est le musée?

**Can you give me some information about ...?**
Pouvez-vous me donner des renseignements sur ...?

**What are the main places of interest here?**
Quels sont les principaux sites touristiques ici?

**Please could you point them out on the map?**
Pouvez-vous me les indiquer sur la carte, s'il vous plaît?

**What sights/hotels/restaurants can you recommend?**
Quels sites/hôtels/restaurants nous recommandez-vous?

**I am interested in ...**
Je suis intéressé(e) par ...

**Does the guide speak English?**
Est-ce qu'il y a un guide qui parle anglais?

**Do you have any suggested walks?**
Avez-vous des suggestions de promenades?

**Are there guided tours?**
Est-ce qu'il y a des visites guidées?

**Are there organized excursions?**
Est-ce qu'il y a des excursions organisées?

**What is the admission price?**
Quel est le prix d'entrée?

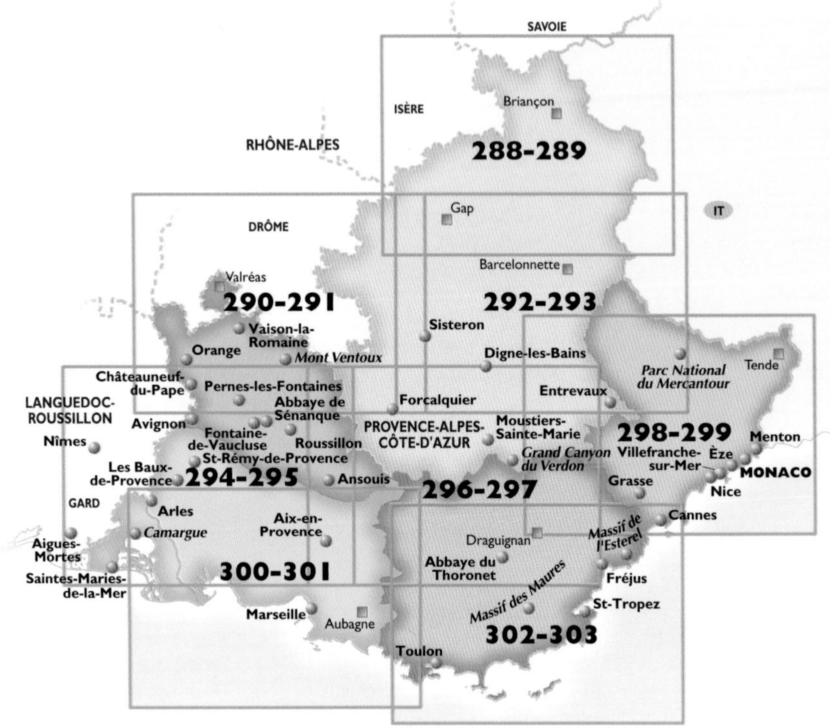

SAVOIE
ISÈRE
Briançon
RHÔNE-ALPES
288-289
Gap
IT
DRÔME
Barcelonnette
Valréas
290-291
292-293
Vaison-la-Romaine
Sisteron
Orange
Mont Ventoux
Digne-les-Bains
Parc National du Mercantour
Tende
Châteauneuf-du-Pape
Pernes-les-Fontaines
Entrevaux
LANGUEDOC-ROUSSILLON
Abbaye de Sénanque
Forcalquier
Avignon
PROVENCE-ALPES-CÔTE-D'AZUR
Moustiers-Sainte-Marie
298-299
Menton
Nîmes
Fontaine-de-Vaucluse
Roussillon
Grand Canyon du Verdon
Villefranche-sur-Mer
Èze
MONACO
Les Baux-de-Provence
St-Rémy-de-Provence
294-295
Ansouis
296-297
Grasse
Nice
GARD
Arles
Cannes
Aix-en-Provence
Camargue
Draguignan
Massif de l'Esterel
Aigues-Mortes
Abbaye du Thoronet
300-301
Fréjus
Saintes-Maries-de-la-Mer
Massif des Maures
Marseille
Aubagne
St-Tropez
302-303
Toulon

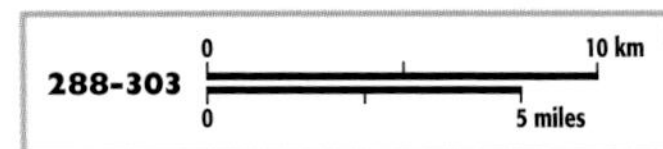


Toll motorway
Motorway
Motorway junction with and without number
National road
Regional road
Local road
Railway
International boundary
Administrative region boundary
Département boundary
Featured place of interest
Town / Village
Built-up area
National park
Airport
Aerial cableway
621 Height in metres
Ferry route
Mountain pass
Viewpoint

# MAPS

Map references for the sights refer to the atlas pages within this section or to the individual town plans within the regions. For example, Toulon has the reference 302 J14, indicating the page on which the map is found (302) and the grid square in which Toulon sits (J14).

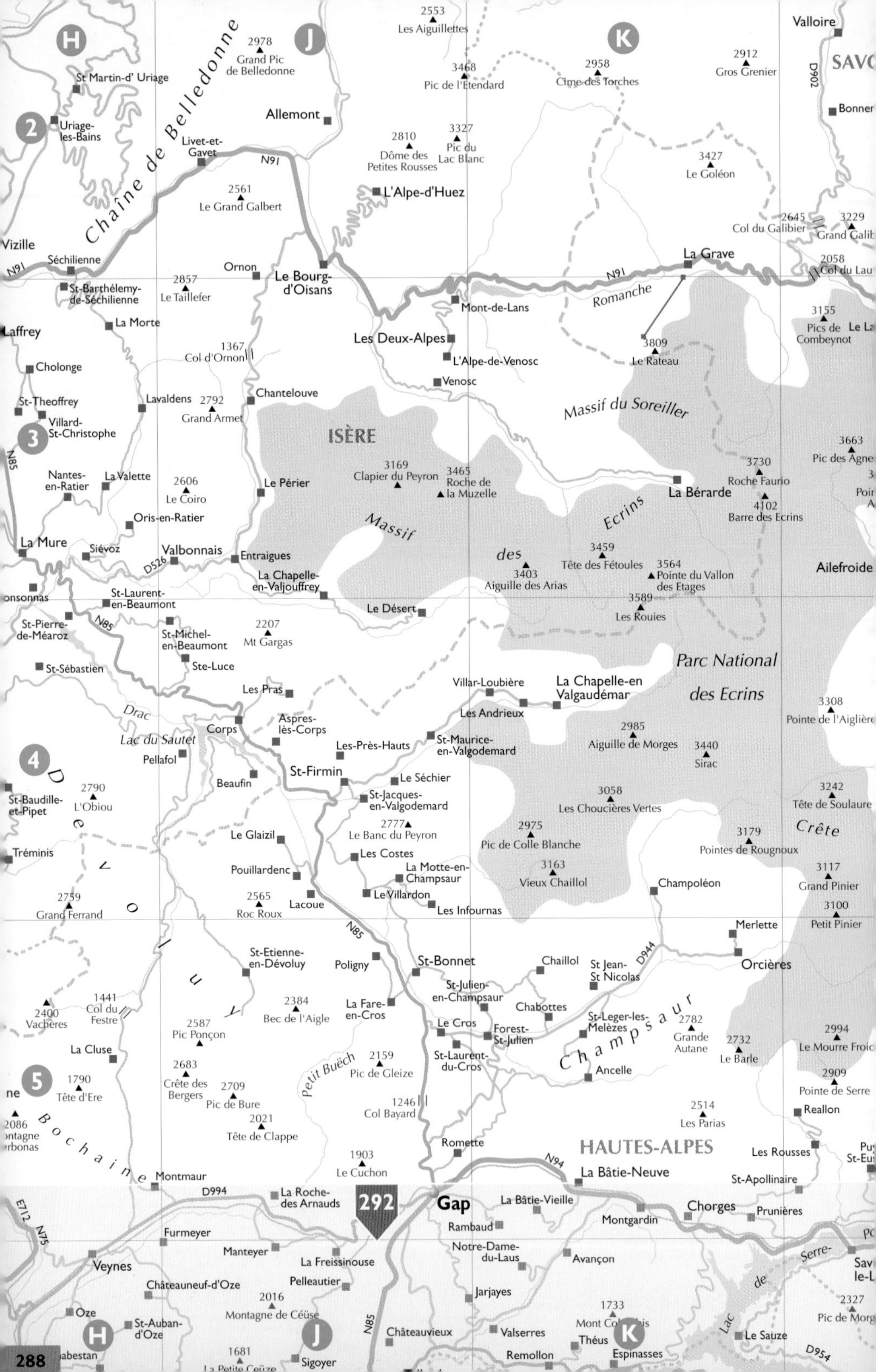

Chaîne de Belledonne
2978 Grand Pic de Belledonne
St Martin-d' Uriage
Uriage-les-Bains
Livet-et-Gavet
Allemont
2553 Les Aiguillettes
3468 Pic de l'Etendard
2958 Cime des Torches
2912 Gros Grenier
Valloire
2810 Dôme des Petites Rousses
3327 Pic du Lac Blanc
3427 Le Goléon
L'Alpe-d'Huez
2561 Le Grand Galbert
2645 Col du Galibier
3229 Grand Galib
Vizille
Séchilienne
Ornon
Le Bourg-d'Oisans
La Grave
2058 Col du Lau
St-Barthélemy-de-Séchilienne
2857 Le Taillefer
Romanche
Mont-de-Lans
3155 Pics de Combeynot
La Morte
Laffrey
Les Deux-Alpes
1367 Col d'Ornon
3809 Le Rateau
L'Alpe-de-Venosc
Cholonge
Venosc
Chantelouve
Massif du Soreiller
Lavaldens
2792 Grand Armet
St-Theoffrey
Villard-St-Christophe
ISÈRE
3663 Pic des Agne
3169 Clapier du Peyron
3465 Roche de la Muzelle
3730 Roche Faurio
Nantes-en-Ratier
La Valette
2606 Le Coiro
Le Périer
La Bérarde
4102 Barre des Ecrins
Oris-en-Ratier
Massif des Ecrins
La Mure
Siévoz
Valbonnais
Entraigues
3403 Aiguille des Arias
3459 Tête des Fétoules
3564 Pointe du Vallon des Etages
Ailefroide
La Chapelle-en-Valjouffrey
St-Laurent-en-Beaumont
Le Désert
3589 Les Rouies
St-Pierre-de-Méaroz
St-Michel-en-Beaumont
2207 Mt Gargas
Ste-Luce
St-Sébastien
Parc National des Ecrins
Les Pras
Villar-Loubière
La Chapelle-en Valgaudémar
Drac
Corps
Aspres-lès-Corps
Les Andrieux
3308 Pointe de l'Aiglière
Lac du Sautet
Pellafol
Les-Près-Hauts
St-Maurice-en-Valgodemard
2985 Aiguille de Morges
3440 Sirac
Dévoluy
St-Firmin
Le Séchier
Beaufin
St-Baudille-et-Pipet
2790 L'Obiou
St-Jacques-en-Valgodemard
3058 Les Choucières Vertes
3242 Tête de Soulaure
2777 Le Banc du Peyron
2975 Pic de Colle Blanche
Crête
Le Glaizil
Tréminis
3179 Pointes de Rougnoux
Les Costes
La Motte-en-Champsaur
Pouillardenc
3163 Vieux Chaillol
Champoléon
3117 Grand Pinier
Le Villardon
Lacoue
2565 Roc Roux
Les Infournas
2759 Grand Ferrand
3100 Petit Pinier
Merlette
St-Etienne-en-Dévoluy
Poligny
St-Bonnet
Chaillol
St Jean-St Nicolas
D944
Orcières
St-Julien-en-Champsaur
1441 Col du Festre
2400 Vachères
2384 Bec de l'Aigle
La Fare-en-Cros
Chabottes
2587 Pic Ponçon
Le Cros
Forest-St-Julien
St-Leger-les-Melèzes
2782 Grande Autane
2994 Le Mourre Froid
La Cluse
St-Laurent-du-Cros
Champsaur
2732 Le Barle
2683 Crête des Bergers
2159 Pic de Gleize
Petit Buëch
Ancelle
1790 Tête d'Ere
2709 Pic de Bure
2909 Pointe de Serre
Bochaine
2086 ontagne rbonas
1246 Col Bayard
2514 Les Parias
Reallon
2021 Tête de Clappe
HAUTES-ALPES
Romette
Les Rousses
1903 Le Cuchon
N94
La Bâtie-Neuve
Montmaur
St-Apollinaire
D994
La Roche-des-Arnauds
292
Gap
La Bâtie-Vieille
Chorges
Prunières
Montgardin
E712
N75
Furmeyer
Rambaud
Notre-Dame-du-Laus
Manteyer
Veynes
La Freissinouse
Avançon
Lac de Serre-
Pelleautier
Châteauneuf-d'Oze
Jarjayes
2016 Montagne de Céüse
1733 Mont Colombis
2327 Pic de Morg
Oze
St-Auban-d'Oze
N85
Châteauvieux
Valserres
Théus
Le Sauze
D954
Remollon
Espinasses
1681 La Petite Ceüze
Sigoyer
N91
N85
D526
D902

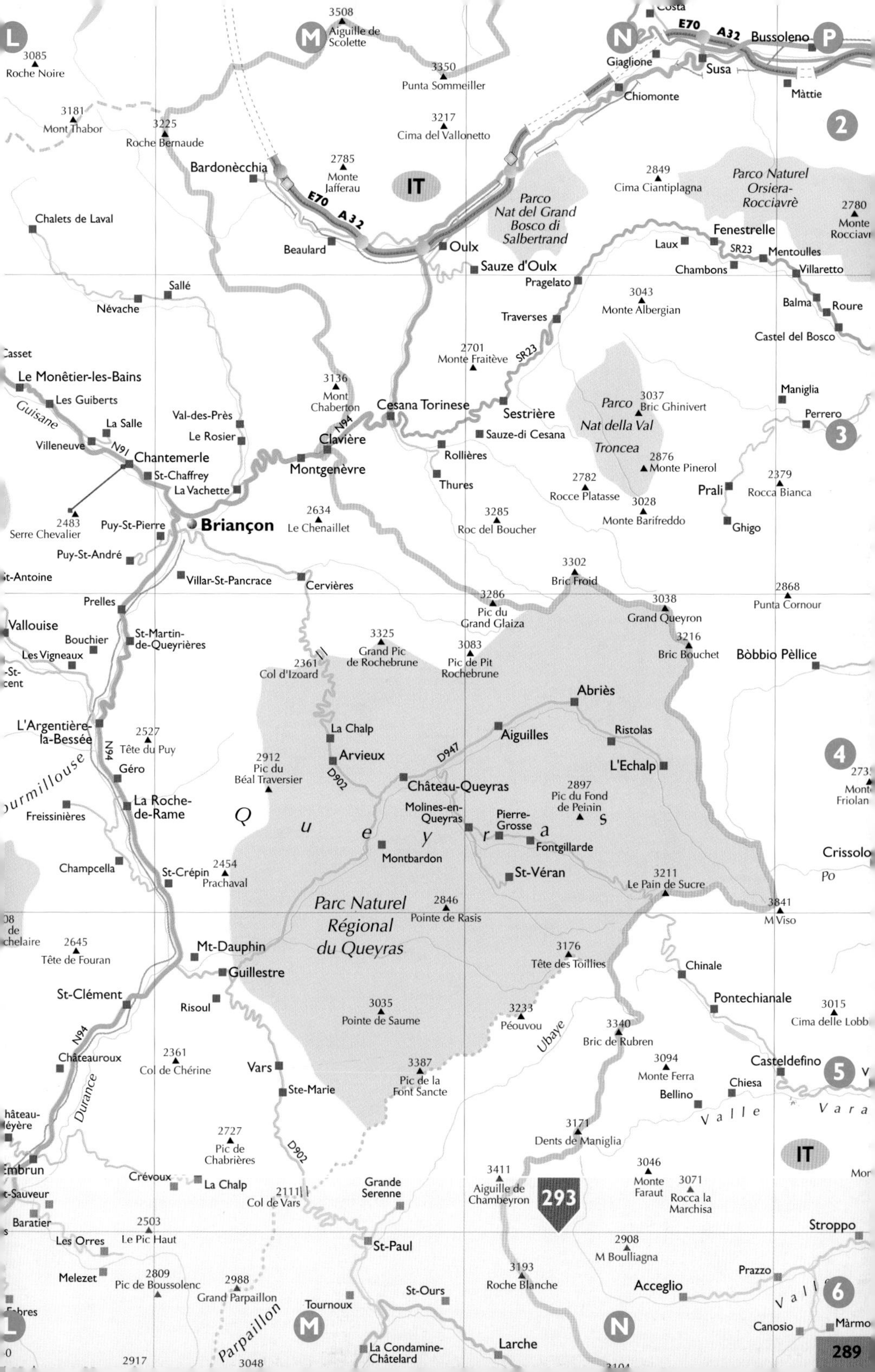
L
3085
Roche Noire
3508
Aiguille de Scolette
M
Costa
E70
A32
Bussoleno
N
P
Giaglione
Susa
3350
Punta Sommeiller
Chiomonte
Màttie
3181
Mont Thabor
3225
Roche Bernaude
3217
Cima del Vallonetto
2
2785
Monte Jafferau
Bardonècchia
IT
2849
Cima Ciantiplagna
Parco Naturel Orsiera-Rocciavrè
2780
Monte Rocciavr
Chalets de Laval
E70
A32
Parco Nat del Grand Bosco di Salbertrand
Beaulard
Oulx
Laux
Fenestrelle
SR23
Mentoulles
Sauze d'Oulx
Chambons
Villaretto
Sallé
Pragelato
3043
Monte Albergian
Névache
Balma
Roure
Traverses
Castel del Bosco
Casset
2701
Monte Fraitève
SR23
Le Monêtier-les-Bains
3136
Mont Chaberton
Maniglia
Les Guiberts
Guisane
Cesana Torinese
Parco
3037
Bric Ghinivert
Sestrière
Perrero
La Salle
Val-des-Prés
N94
Nat della Val
Le Rosier
Clavière
Sauze-di Cesana
3
Villeneuve
N91
Troncea
Chantemerle
Rollières
2876
Monte Pinerol
St-Chaffrey
Montgenèvre
2782
2379
La Vachette
Thures
Rocce Platasse
Prali
Rocca Bianca
2483
Serre Chevalier
Puy-St-Pierre
Briançon
2634
Le Chenaillet
3285
Roc del Boucher
3028
Monte Barifreddo
Ghigo
Puy-St-André
3302
Bric Froid
St-Antoine
Villar-St-Pancrace
Cervières
2868
Punta Cornour
Prelles
3286
Pic du Grand Glaiza
3038
Grand Queyron
Vallouise
Bouchier
St-Martin-de-Queyrières
3325
Grand Pic de Rochebrune
3216
Bric Bouchet
Bòbbio Pèllice
Les Vigneaux
3083
Pic de Pit Rochebrune
2361
Col d'Izoard
Abriès
L'Argentière-la-Bessée
La Chalp
Ristolas
2527
Tête du Puy
Aiguilles
N94
D947
Arvieux
4
2912
Pic du Béal Traversier
L'Echalp
Géro
D902
Château-Queyras
2897
Pic du Fond de Peinin
Monte Friolan
La Roche-de-Rame
Molines-en-Queyras
Pierre-Grosse
Freissinières
Q u e y r a s
Fontgillarde
Montbardon
Crissolo
Champcella
St-Crépin
2454
Prachaval
St-Véran
Po
3211
Le Pain de Sucre
Parc Naturel Régional du Queyras
2846
Pointe de Rasis
3841
M Viso
2645
Tête de Fouran
Mt-Dauphin
3176
Tête des Toillies
Chinale
Guillestre
St-Clément
Pontechianale
Risoul
3035
Pointe de Saume
3233
Péouvou
3015
Cima delle Lobb
N94
Ubaye
3340
Bric de Rubren
Châteauroux
2361
Col de Chérine
Vars
3387
Pic de la Font Sancte
3094
Monte Ferra
Casteldefino
5
Durance
Ste-Marie
Chiesa
Bellino
Valle Vara
2727
Pic de Chabrières
D902
3171
Dents de Maniglia
IT
Embrun
Crévoux
La Chalp
3411
Aiguille de Chambeyron
293
3046
Monte Faraut
3071
Rocca la Marchisa
2111
Col de Vars
Grande Serenne
Baratier
2503
Le Pic Haut
Stroppo
Les Orres
St-Paul
2908
M Boulliagna
Melezet
2809
Pic de Boussolenc
3193
Roche Blanche
Prazzo
2988
Grand Parpaillon
St-Ours
Acceglio
6
Tournoux
Parpaillon
M
N
Canosio
Màrmo
Larche
2917
3048
La Condamine-Châtelard

St-Lager-Bressac
Les Reys-de-Saulce
St-Sauveur-en-Diois
Espenel
C
D
E
Berzème
Cruas
les Tourrettes
St-Martin-sur-Lavezon
St-Vincent-de-Barrès
La Coucourde
Saou
1513
Roche Courbe
Plateau du Coiron
5
St-Martin-l'Inférieur
Derbières
Puy-St-Martin
Soyans
Francillon-sur-Roubion
Mornans
1544
Meysse
N86
Savasse
La Laupie
D6
Cleon-d'Andran
Le Poët-Célard
Bézaudun-sur-Bine
1516
Montagne de Couspeau
St-Pons
Rochemaure
Sauzet
Bonlieu-sur-Roubion
Manas
Pont-de-Barret
Bourdeaux
Aubignas
St-Marcel-lès-Sauzet
Charois
Ancône
St-Gervais-sur-Roubion
Rochebaudin
D538
Montboucher-sur-Jabron
Eyzahut
971
Serre Gros
Alba
Le Teil
La Bâtie-Rolland
Mélas
Montélimar
Puygiron
La Bégude-de-Mazenc
Le Poët-Laval
Dieulefit
D107
E15 A7
Espeluche
Bouvières
N7
La Touche
D9
898
Mont Rachas
Allan
Montjoux
Valvignères
Malataverne
18
Roche-St-Secret-Béconne
Viviers
Châteauneuf
Montjoyer
1259
La Lance
6
Salles-sous-Bois
Larnas
Donzère
Réauville
Montbrison
St-Montan
N86
Roussas
Tauligan
Le Pègue
Valaurie
1214
Cougoir
Rhône
Grignan
Les Granges-Gontardes
Chantemerle-lès Grignan
St-Pantaléon-les-Vignes
Condorcet
Chamaret
Grillon
D941
Venterol
La Garde-Adhémar
Valréas
Aubres
Pierrelatte
D538
Bourg-St-Andéol
Montségur-sur-Lauzon
VAUCLUSE
Nyons
B
St-Paul-Trois-Châteaux
Richerenches
Montaulieu
D94
Solérieux
St-Marcel-d'Ardèche
N7
La Baume-de-Transit
Vinsobres
Cité de l'Usine
Eygues
Mirabel-aux-Baronnies
Visan
St-Maurice-sur-Eygues
Lapalud
Barry
7
Just
Bouchet
Suze-la-Rousse
19
Villedieu
Bollène
Buisson
Puyméras
St-Julien-de-Peyrolas
D94
St-Roman-de-Malegarde
Faucon
N86
Pont-St-Esprit
E15 A7
Rochegude
Roaix
Vaison-la-Romaine
Pierrelongue
St-Paulet-de-Caisson
Ste-Cécile-les-Vignes
Rasteau
Mondragon
Cairanne
Mollans-sur-Ouvèze
Carsan
St-Alexandre
Lagarde-Paréol
Crestet
Entrechaux
La Galle
Séguret
D938
Mornas
Sérignan-du-Comtat
D976
D8
Sablet
Beaumont-du-Ventoux
Vénéjan
Dentelles de Montmirail
St-Etienne-des-Sorts
Travaillan
Malaucène
Cèze
N7
Suzette
Bagnols-sur-Cèze
Camaret
20
Ouvèze
Lafare
8
Chusclan
Mon
Orange
La Roque-Alric
Le Barroux
N580
Vacqueyras
Orsan
Codolet
21
Bédoin
N86
Jonquières
Beaumes-de-Venise
St-Pons-la-Calm
Laudun
Caromb
Tresques
Caderousse
A7
22
Modène
St-Pierre-de-Vassols
Connaux
Courthézon
St-Paul-les-Fonts
Sarrians
Mormoiron
Gaujac
D950
St-Genies-de-Comolas
Châteauneuf-du-Pape
Mazan
D942
St-Victor-la-Coste
Carpentras
St-Laurent-des-Arbres
D942
Roquemaure
Blau
N7
Malemort-du-Comtat
Pouzilhac
294
Lirac
Bédarrides
Monteux
295
Sauveterre
22
D49
9
Tavel
St-Didier
Valliguières
Sorgues
Entraigues
Venasque
Pujaut
Nesque
D942
Althen-des-Paluds
Pernes-les-Fontaines
St-Hilaire-d'Ozilhan
Rochefort-du-Gard
23
Vedène
Les Valayans
A9
Villeneuve-
290

F
G
H
J
DRÔME
Barnave
Serre Chauvière
Menglon
Recoubeau-Jansac
D93
Montlaur-en-Diois
Luc-en-Diois
Boulc
D539
1916
Toussière
Lus-la-Croix-Haute
2400
Vachères
Col du Festre
La Cluse
Pic
2683
Crête des Bergers
2709
St-Julien-en-Beauchêne
1790
Tête d'Ere
2086
Montagne Durbonas
Bochaine
5
288
Tête
Pradèlle
Poyols
1613
La Servelle
Lesches-en-Diois
1430
Pierre Blanche
Val-Maravel
Creyers
Montbrand
Montmaur
D994
Jonchères
La Haute Beaume
La Beaume
D993
E712
N75
Volvent
Furmeyer
1412
Serre la Chaud
1180
Col de Cabre
Bellegarde-en-Diois
Les Prés
Aspres-sur-Buëch
Veynes
Châteauneuf-d'Oze
St-Dizier-en-Diois
Chalancon
Valdrôme
Oze
St-Auban-d'Oze
Establet
1389
Serre Embouc
Montagne de l'Aup
Aspremont
La Motte
Rottier
La Piarre
Chabestan
Le Saix
1681
La Petite
Bruis
1757
Le Duffre
D994
Sigottier
Esparron
Ste-Marie
La Bâtie-Montsaléon
Cornillon-sur-l'Oule
Montmorin
Serre de la Bouisse
Cornillac
1645
6
Villeperdrix
1473
Montagne de Raton
Serres
La Flamence
le Bersac
Savournon
St-May
L'Epine
D994
Rémuzat
Montagne de St-Genis
Rosans
Mereuil
D994
Verclause
1545
Rocher de Beaumont
Montrond
Pelonne
St-André-de-Rosans
Vaucluse
1214
1313
Ventavon
A51
Montjay
Chanousse
Lazer
Bellecombe
Eyguians
Ste-Jalle
1213
Crête de Rascuègne
292
St-Sauveur-Gouvernet
1324
Le Suillet
E712
N75
Laragne-Montéglin
N85
Bésignan
Laux-Montaux
Chauvac
Villebois-les-Pins
Etoile-St-Cyrice
Orpierre
1359
Montagne de la Claveliére
Ste-Euphémie-sur-Ouvèze
Le-Poët
Laborel
Les Bégues
Montagne de Chabre
D942
St-Auban-sur-l'Ouvèze
Montguers
7
La Roche-sur-le-Buis
La Rochette-du-Buis
Barret-le-Bas
Ouvèze
Antonaves
Ballons
St-Pierre-Avez
Eygaliers
Gresse
Eygalayes
Salérans
Ribiers
Mévouillon
Lachau
D542
Eourres
1615
Crête de l'Ane
Sèderon
1427
Chante Duc
Barret-de-Lioure
Brantes
Montbrun-les-Bains
Noyers-sur-Jabron
Savoillan
Les Omergues
Montfroc
1909
St-Vincent-sur-Jabron
Ventoux
Reilhanette
1393
Montagne d'Albion
1370
Le Grand Terme
Crête de la Faye
1535
Valbelle
1214
Le Tréboux
Montagne de Lure
Ferrassières
1826
Signal de Lure
de la Canaud
Aurel
Le Contadour
8
Château
Saumane
Sault
Revest-du-Bion
D950
Monieux
Lardiers
Cruis
Mallefoug
Montlaux
Gorges de la Nesque
St-Jean
St-Étienne-les-Orgues
Peyru
St-Christol
Banon
Ongles
Montsalier
296
Fontienne
Vaucluse
919
St Pierre
Sigonce
9
Calavon
UCLUSE
D943
Lagarde-d'Apt
Simiane-la-Rotonde
Largue
Lurs
1054
Le Cluyer
1256
St Pie
1120
Le Buisseron
Carniol
Revest-des Brousses
Forcalquier
D12
Pierrerue

2384
Bec de l'Aigle
La Fare-en-Cros
Chabottes
Le Cros
Forest-St-Julien
St-Laurent-du-Cros
St-Léger-les-Mélèzes
Champsaur
2782
Grande Autane
2732
Le Barle
2994
Le Mourre Froid
2909
Pointe de Serre
Reallon
Ancelle
2587
Pic Ponçon
2683
Crête des Bergers
2709
Pic de Bure
2021
Tête de Clappe
Petit Buëch
2159
Pic de Gleize
1246
Col Bayard
2514
Les Parias
Romette
288
HAUTES-ALPES
Les Rousses
Puy-St-Eusèbe
Le Château Caléyère
1903
Le Cuchon
N94
La Bâtie-Neuve
Montmaur
D994
La Roche-des Arnauds
Gap
La Bâtie-Vieille
St-Apollinaire
Chorges
Prunières
Montgardin
Rambaud
Furmeyer
Manteyer
La Freissinouse
Notre-Dame-du-Laus
Avançon
Veynes
Pelleautier
Jarjayes
Lac de Serre-Ponçon
Savines-le-Lac
Crots
Châteauneuf-d'Oze
2016
Montagne de Céüse
2327
Pic de Morgon
St-Auban-d'Oze
N85
Châteauvieux
Valserres
1733
Mont Colombis
Théus
Le Sauze
D954
1681
La Petite Ceüze
Sigoyer
Remollon
Espinasses
Le Saix
Tallard
D900
La Bréole
2440
Le Petit Ferrand
Esparron
Piégut
Rochebrune
St-Vincent-les-Forts
Le Lauzet-Ubaye
Lardier-et-Valença
Bréziers
Saulce
Curbans
Gigors
Bellaffaire
Faucon-du-Caire
Turriers
La Chapelle
Montclar
Monêtier-Allemont
1561
Malaup
Crête des Mélèzes
Montagne de la Blanche
A51
de St-Genis
1313
Ventavon
1425
Les Croix
Le Caire
Astoin
2430
Pic de Bernardez
Chardavon-Bas
Seyne
Lazer
Melve
La Motte-du-Caire
Bayons
291
2032
Tête Grosse
Clamensane
1962
Clot de Bouc
1346
Col de Maure
2739
Roche Close
N75
Laragne-Montéglin
Thèze
2071
l'Oratoire
1930
Le Marzenc
Le-Poët
Le Vernet
Nibles
1886
Montagne de Jouere
2115
Les Monges
Verdaches
Châteaufort
Barles
Le Haut Vernet
Clues de Verbaches
1770
Set de la Croix
Valernes
Montagne de Gache
Bès
2189
Blayeul Sommet
1240
Col du Labouret
St-Geniez
Authon
1909
Sommet de Nibles
1365
Crête de Géruen
Prads-Haute-Bléone
Ribiers
1880
1667
Sommet de Chappe
1551
Sisteron
Vilhosc
Le Castellard
La Robine
Crête de Liman
Blégiers
La Javie
1435
Sommet de Vaumuse
1313
Le Brusquet
Salignac
Valbelle
Thoard
Sourribes
Montagne du Cheval Blanc
2305
Draix
Peipin
Durance
Marcoux
Aubignosc
D900
2223
Volonne
1298
Sommet du Ruth
Lure
1140
Pic d'Oise
Champtercier
Château-Arnoux
Châteauneuf-Val-St-Donat
Digne-les-Bains
Les Sieyes
Tartonne
E712 A51
l'Escale
ALPES-DE-HAUTE-PROVENCE
Mirabeau
Cruis
Mallefougasse
Montfort
Mallemoisson
Lambruisse
Montlaux
N85
Malijai
Peyruis
D4
Le Chaffaut-St-Jurson
Clumanc
St-Étienne-les-Orgues
Les Mées
Bléone
Châteauredon
Chabrières
Asse
296
Mézel
297
Sigonce
N96
Chaudon-Norante
St-Lions
Lurs
Puimichel
Plateau
D907
N202
Barrême
Entrevennes
St-Jeannet

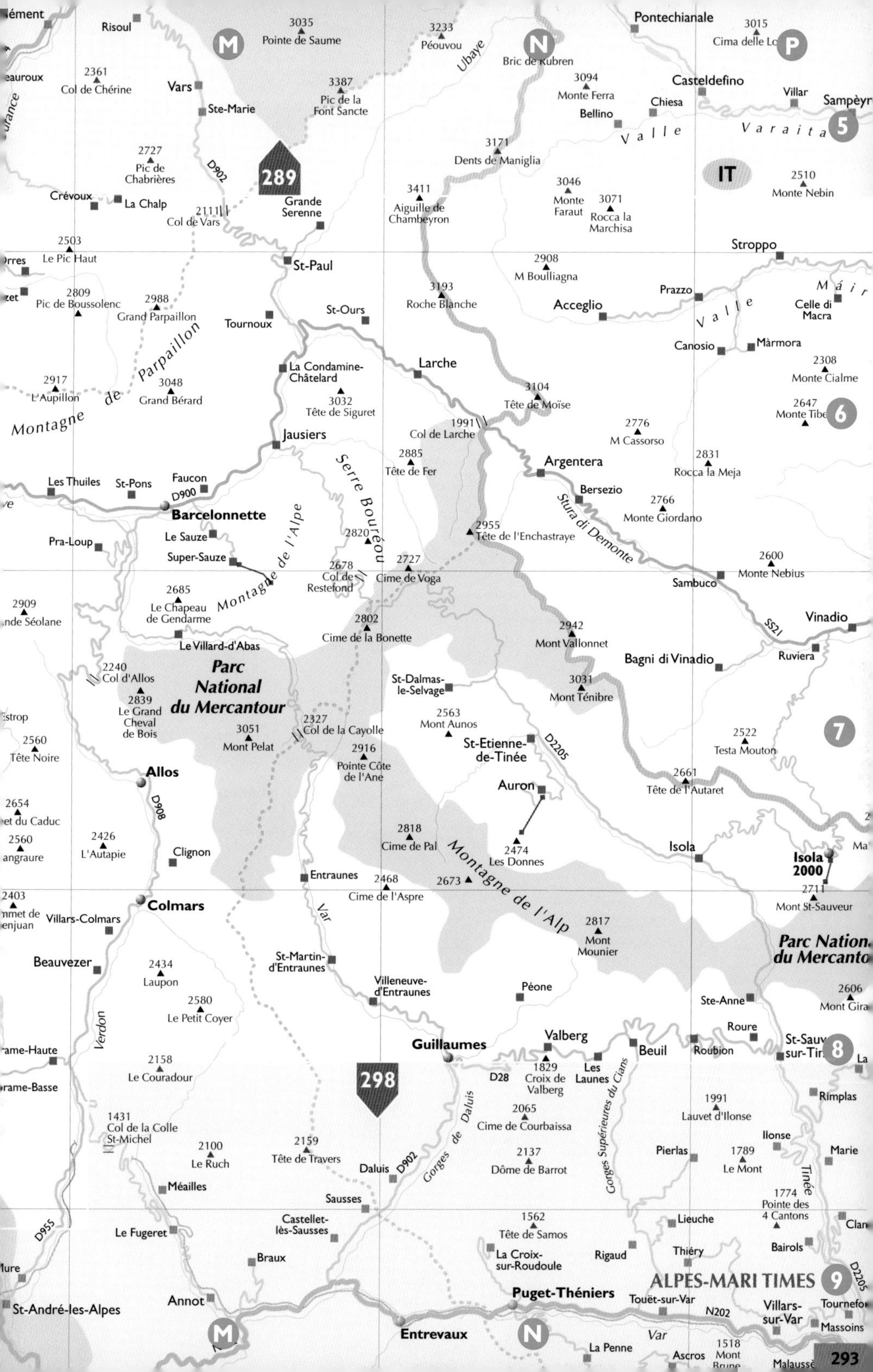

Risoul
3035
Pointe de Saume
3233
Péouvou
Ubaye
Pontechianale
3015
Cima delle Lo
M
N
P
2361
Col de Chérine
Vars
Ste-Marie
3387
Pic de la
Font Sancte
Bric de Rubren
3094
Monte Ferra
Casteldefino
Chiesa
Bellino
Villar
Sampèyr
Valle
Varaita
5
2727
Pic de
Chabrières
D902
289
3171
Dents de Maniglia
IT
2510
Monte Nebin
Crévoux
La Chalp
2111
Col de Vars
Grande
Serenne
3411
Aiguille de
Chambeyron
3046
Monte
Faraut
3071
Rocca la
Marchisa
2503
Le Pic Haut
St-Paul
Stroppo
2908
M Boulliagna
2809
Pic de Boussolenc
2988
Grand Parpaillon
3193
Roche Blanche
Prazzo
Acceglio
Valle
Máir
Celle di
Macra
Tournoux
St-Ours
Canosio
Màrmora
La Condamine-
Châtelard
Larche
2308
Monte Cialme
2917
L'Aupillon
3048
Grand Bérard
3032
Tête de Siguret
3104
Tête de Moïse
Montagne de Parpaillon
2647
Monte Tibe
6
1991
Col de Larche
2776
M Cassorso
Jausiers
Serre Bouréou
2885
Tête de Fer
Argentera
2831
Rocca la Meja
Les Thuiles
St-Pons
Faucon
D900
Bersezio
Barcelonnette
Stura di Demonte
2766
Monte Giordano
Le Sauze
Montagne de l'Alpe
2955
Tête de l'Enchastraye
Pra-Loup
2820
Super-Sauze
2678
Col de
Restefond
2727
Cime de Voga
2600
Monte Nebius
Sambuco
2685
Le Chapeau
de Gendarme
2909
2802
Cime de la Bonette
2942
Mont Vallonnet
Vinadio
SS21
Le Villard-d'Abas
Ruviera
Bagni di Vinadio
Parc
National
du Mercantour
2240
Col d'Allos
St-Dalmas-
le-Selvage
3031
Mont Ténibre
2839
Le Grand
Cheval
de Bois
2327
Col de la Cayolle
2563
Mont Aunos
3051
Mont Pelat
St-Etienne-
de-Tinée
D2205
2522
Testa Mouton
7
2560
Tête Noire
2916
Pointe Côte
de l'Ane
Allos
D908
Auron
2661
Tête de l'Autaret
2654
2560
2426
L'Autapie
2818
Cime de Pal
Montagne de l'Alp
2474
Les Donnes
Isola
Isola
2000
Clignon
Entraunes
2468
Cime de l'Aspre
2673
2711
Mont St-Sauveur
2403
Colmars
Villars-Colmars
Var
2817
Mont
Mounier
Parc Nation
du Mercanto
Beauvezer
2434
Laupon
St-Martin-
d'Entraunes
Villeneuve-
d'Entraunes
Péone
2606
Mont Gira
2580
Le Petit Coyer
Ste-Anne
Verdon
Guillaumes
Valberg
Beuil
Roubion
Roure
St-Sauv
sur-Tin
8
2158
Le Couradour
298
D28
1829
Croix de
Valberg
Les
Launes
Gorges Supérieures du Cians
1991
Lauvet d'Ilonse
Rimplas
1431
Col de la Colle
St-Michel
2065
Cime de Courbaissa
Ilonse
2100
Le Ruch
2159
Tête de Travers
Daluis
D902
Gorges de Daluis
2137
Dôme de Barrot
Pierlas
1789
Le Mont
Marie
Tinée
Méailles
Sausses
1774
Pointe des
4 Cantons
D955
Le Fugeret
Castellet-
lès-Sausses
1562
Tête de Samos
Lieuche
Bairols
Braux
La Croix-
sur-Roudoule
Rigaud
Thiéry
ALPES-MARI TIMES
9
D2205
Annot
Puget-Théniers
Touët-sur-Var
N202
Villars-
sur-Var
Tournefo
St-André-les-Alpes
M
Entrevaux
N
Massoins
Var
La Penne
1518
Mont
Ascros
293

GARD
Seynes
La Bruguière
St-Laurent-la-Vernède
Fontarèches
Belvézet
Euzet
Le Pin
Masmolène
La Capelle-et-Masmolène
St-Pons-la-Calm
Tresques
Laudun
Connaux
St-Paul-les-Fonts
Gaujac
St-Victor-la-Coste
St-Genies-de-Comolas
Caderousse
Courthézo
Châteauneuf-du-Pape
Roquemaure
St-Laurent-des-Arbres
Lirac
Sauveterre
Tavel
Pujaut
Sorgues
St-Jean-de-Ceyrargues
Baron
Foissac
Montaren-et-St-Médiers
Serviers-et-Labaume
D981
St-Hippolyte-de-Montaigu
Pouzilhac
Valliguières
Uzès
St-Maximin
Garrigues
Arpaillargues-et-Aureillac
Brignon
Moussac
Bourdic
Sauzet
St-Geniès-de-Malgoires
La Calmette
Collias
Vers-Pont-du-Gard
St-Hilaire-d'Ozilhan
Rochefort-du-Gard
Villeneuve-lès-Avignon
Pont du Gard
Remoulins
E15 A9
N100
Saze
Estézargues
Domazan
Avignon
Gorges du Gardon
Sernhac
Fournès
Théziers
Barbentane
Rognonas
204
Pic de Guerre
Gajan
Aramon
Meynes
Montfrin
D2
Châteaurenard
N106
Les Fontilles
Boulbon
La Montagnette
N570
Graveson
D571
N86
Marguerittes
Vallabrègues
Comps
Eyragu
Maillane
NÎMES
D999
Redessan
Jonquières-St-Vincent
Clarensac
Caveirac
Vistre
Rodilhan
Manduel
Tarascon
Beaucaire
Langlade
Caissargues
Bouillargues
D99
St-Rémy-de-Provence
Nages-et-Solorgues
Milhaud
N113
D38
St-Etienne-du-Grès
Chaîne des Alpil
Bernis
Garons
Aubord
Uchaud
Bellegarde
Vestric-et-Candiac
Vergèze
E80 A54
Rhône
Fontvieille
Les Baux-de-Prove
Générac
Codognan
Paradou
Maussane-les-Alpilles
Beauvoisin
Fourques
Abbaye de Montmajour
D17
Aimargues
Vauvert
GARD
St-Gilles
Arles
Mouriès
N572
Le Cailar
Saliers
Raphèle-lès-Arles
St-Martin-de-Crau
Étang de Grey
Étang de Scamandre
Rhône à Sète
Étang du Charnier
Plaine d
Petit Rhône
Aigues-Mortes
D58
Camargue
Mas Thibert
N568
Étang du Lairan
Parc Naturel Régional de Camargue
Étang de la Ville
Étang de Vaccarès
300
Étang des Caïtives
Étang des Fourneaux
Étang de Consecanière
D570
Étang du Roi
Étang du Cabri
Étang de Gines
D35
Parc Naturel Régional de Camargue
Étang d'Icard
Saintes-Maries-de-la-Mer
N268
Golfe de Beauduc
Salin-de-Giraud

Carpentras
VAUCLUSE
Plateau de Vaucluse
Cavaillon
Apt
Parc Naturel Régional du Lubéron
Montagne du Lubéron
Salon-de-Provence
Aix-en-Provence
BOUCHES-DU-RHÔNE
Étang de Berre
Martigues
Chaîne de la Trévaresse
Chaîne de Vitrolles
291
296
301

Sault
Revest-du-Bion
Saumane
Lure
Châteauneuf-Val-St-Donat
Lardiers
Cruis
Mallefougasse
Montfort
Montlaux
St-Christol
Banon
291
Ongles
St-Étienne-les-Orgues
Peyruis
Les Mées
Montsalier
Fontienne
Sigonce
Simiane-la-Rotonde
Calavon
919
St Pierre
Lagarde-d'Apt
1054
Le Cluyer
1256
St Pierre
Carniol
Largue
Lurs
Puimichel
1120
Le Buisseron
Revest-des Brousses
Forcalquier
D12
Pierrerue
St-Saturnin-les-Apt
Mane
Entrevennes
Le Castellet
Rustrel
Oppedette
Niozelles
La Brillanne
St-Michel-l'Observatoire
St-Maime
Oraison
Viens
Ste-Croix à-Lauze
Villeneuve
Caseneuve
Lincel
Dauphin
Reillanne
Apt
Volx
St-Martin-de-Castillon
N100
N96
Saignon
Céreste
Valensole
Parc Naturel Régional du Lubéron
Manosque
Parc Naturel Régional du Verdon
Auribeau
Pierrevert
1125
Mourre Nègre
Vitrolles
E712
A51
Lubéron
Cabrières d'Aigues
Peypin-d'Aigues
Ste-Tulle
St-Martin-de-Brômes
D952
Gréoux-les-Bains
La Bastide-des-Jourdans
Vaugines
Cucuron
La Motte-d'Aigues
Corbières
295
St-Martin de-la-Brasque
Grambois
Ansouis
Cadenet
Beaumont-de-Pertuis
Durance
Verdon
Esparron-de-Verdon
Vinon-sur-Verdon
La Tour d'Aigues
Mirabeau
Villelaure
D973
St-Pierre
Pertuis
La Bastidonne
St-Julien
Les Rouvières
St-Paul-lès-Durance
Ginasservis
691
Grand Blé
Peyrolles-en-Provence
Jouques
N96
Meyrargues
La Verdière
Venelles
Rians
D561
Varages
Artigues
Esparron
St-Martin
Tavernes
Puyricard
Barjols
605
La Tête du Marquis
Vauvenargues
Montagne Sainte-Victoire
606
Séouve Sommet
Aix-en-Provence
Brue-Auriac
Le Tholonet
Puyloubier
D560
Beaurecueil
301
Pourrières
Seillons-Source-d'Argens
Milles
Châteauneuf-le-Rouge
Meyreuil
N7
Ollières
N8
Rousset
E80 A8
Bras
Pourcieux
Gardanne
Fuveau
A52
Mont Aurélien
Bouc-Bel-Air
Peynier
880
Olympe
Trets
St-Maximin-la-Sainte-Baume
Gréasque
Cité Biver
Belcodène
Simiane-Collongue
Mimet
St-Savournin
Tourves
Les Peyrets
Cadolive
La Bouilladisse
N560
Rougier
Chaîne
590
296

Digne-les-Bains
ALPES-DE-HAUTE-PROVENCE
Les Sieyes
Tartonne
La Bâtie
Lambruisse
Le Chaffaut-St-Jurson
292
Clumanc
1789 Montagne de l'Allier
1431 Col de la Coll
St-Michel
2100 Le Ruch
Méailles
Châteauredon
Chabrières
Asse
N85
Mézel
Chaudon-Norante
St-Lions
La Mure
D955
Le Fugeret
Braux
Annot
Moriez
St-André-les-Alpes
N202
Barrême
D907
St-Jeannet
Estoublon
Gorges de Trévans
1620 La Barre
1621 Crête de Montmuye
Senez
1725 Sommet du Castellard
St-Julien-du-Verdon
Barrage de Castillon
Vergons
1124 Col de Toutes Aures
Rouainette
1941 Sommet de la Bernarde
St-Julien-d'Asse
St-Jurs
Blieux
1146 Col des Leque
1741 Pré Chauvin
Castellane
Soleilhas
St-Auban
Moustiers-Sainte-Marie
1771 Berbené
D953
Riez
Roumoules
Parc Naturel Régional du Verdon
Peyroules
Le Mousteiret
Rougon
La Palud-sur-Verdon
D952
Le Bourguet
Châteauvieux
La Marte
Aiguines
Les Salles-sur-Verdon
Grand Canyon du Verdon
Trigance
Brenon
298
Ste-Croix-de-Verdon
Lac de Ste Croix
Montpezat
Bauduen
Bargeme
La Bastide
La Roque-Esclapon
St-Laurent-du-Verdon
Baudinard-sur-Verdon
D957
Grand Plan de Canjuers
Comps-sur-Artuby
Artignosc-sur-Verdon
Montagne de Barjaude
Vérignon
1173
D955
Moissac-Bellevue
Régusse
Montmeyan
Seillans
Aups
Montferrat
Bargemon
Ampus
St-Pierre-de-Tourtour
Châteaudouble
Claviers
D562
Callas
Fox-Amphoux
Villecroze
Tourtour
Rebouillon
D560
Sillans-la-Cascade
Salernes
Figanières
Draguignan
Bagnols-en-Forêt
813
Cotignac
Flayosc
Entrecasteaux
VAR
St-Antonin-du-Var
Lorgues
La Motte
302
Correns
D562
Le Muy
E80 A8
Carces
Abbaye du Thoronet
Les Arcs
N7
Argens
Montfort-sur-Argens
Taradeau
Puget-sur-Argens
Le Thoronet
Vins-sur-Carami
Le Val
Cabasse
Vidauban
A8
Brignoles
E80 A8
N7
N7
Le Luc
St-Ayg
D25
Camps-la-Source
Aille
K
L
M
8
9
10
11
12

Set de la Croix
Allos
de l'Ane
Auron
Tête de l'Autaret
2654
Sommet du Caduc
2560
Sangraure
2426
L'Autapie
Clignon
D908
2818
Cime de Pal
2474
Les Donnes
Isola
Montagne de l'Alp
Entraunes
2468
Cime de l'Aspre
2673
2403
Sommet de Denjuan
Villars-Colmars
Colmars
Blégiers
Var
2817
Mont Mounier
Beauvezer
2434
Laupon
St-Martin-d'Entraunes
Montagne du Cheval Blanc
2305
Villeneuve-d'Entraunes
Péone
2580
Le Petit Coyer
Ste-An
Verdon
293
Guillaumes
Valberg
Beuil
Roubion
Thorame-Haute
2158
Le Couradour
1829
Croix de Valberg
Les Launes
D28
Château-Garnier
Thorame-Basse
La Bâtie
1991
Lauvet d'Il
1431
Col de la Colle St-Michel
2065
Cime de Courbaissa
PROVENCE
2100
Le Ruch
2159
Tête de Travers
Gorges de Daluis
Gorges Supérieures du Cians
Pierlas
Daluis
D902
2137
Dôme de Barrot
Méailles
Sausses
1789
Montagne de l'Allier
Castellet-lès-Sausses
1562
Tête de Samos
Lieuche
D955
Le Fugeret
La Croix-sur-Roudoule
Rigaud
Thiéry
La Mure
Braux
St-Lions
Moriez
St-André-les-Alpes
Annot
Puget-Théniers
Touët-sur-Var
ALPES-MA
202
N202
Entrevaux
Var
La Penne
Ascros
Rouainette
St-Pierre
Vergons
1124
Col de Toutes Aures
St-Antonin
1725
Sommet du Castellard
St-Julien-du-Verdon
1941
Sommet de la Bernarde
Collongues
N85
Barrage de Castillon
Les Mujouls
Sallagriffon
Roquesteron
1146
Col des Leque
Briançonnet
Gars
Clues de Haute-Provence
Esteron
1741
Pré Chauvin
Soleilhas
St-Auban
1471
Le Mas
Conségudes
Castellane
1474
1541
Montagne du Ch
Gréolières-les-Neiges
771
1777
Cime du Cheiron
Peyroules
Parc Naturel Régional du Verdon
297
Thorenc
Coursegoules
Le Mousteiret
Valderoure
Gréolières
Cipières
Caille
Châteauvieux
Le Bourguet
Séranon
Andon
La Marte
Brenon
N85
Montagne de l'Audibergue
1642
Gorges du Loup
Col de
Trigance
Caussols
Touret-sur-L
Bargeme
La Bastide
Gourdon
La Roque-Esclapon
Le Bar-sur-Loup
Comps-sur-Artuby
St-Vallier-de-Thiey
N85
Magagnosc
Roquefort-les-Pins
Mons
N2085
Grasse
Cabris
Spéracèdes
Plascassier
D955
St-Cézaire-sur-Siagne
Le Tignet
Peymeinade
Valbonne
Seillans
Mouans-Sartoux
Callian
Fayence
Montauroux
Siagne
N85
Montferrat
Bargemon
Auribeau
Mougins
Tanneron
Pégomas
St-Jean
Châteaudouble
Claviers
D562
Callas
Lac de St-Cassien
Cann
Massif du Tanneron
Figanières
303
Draguignan
Bagnols-en-Forêt
Mandelieu-la-Napoule
Golfe de Napoule
Les Adrets-de-l'Esterel
La Napoule
N7

P
Q
R
7
8
9
10
11
3088
Monte Matto
2687
Cima del Lausetto
2451
Monte Bussáia
Terme di Valdieri
Limone
Piemonte
2938
Mt
Malinvern
Isola
2000
2711
3297
Cima d'Argentera
2306
Monte Garbella
2650
Pointe Marguareis
Parco Regionale
Alta Valle Pésio
e Tánaro
Viozer
Parco Regionale
delle Alpi Marittime
1871
Col de Tende
2241
Cime de l'Evêque
1896
Cima di Piar
Cavallo
3143
Cime du Gélas
Le Boréon
2606
Mont Giraud
2250
Baus de la Frema
2786
Mont Neillier
E74 N204
Tende
Mónesi
1500
Col St-Martin
St-Martin-Vésubie
2496
Cime de
la Valette
2873
Mont Bégo
La Brigue
2200
Monte
Saccarello
La Bolline
Rimplas
St-Dalmas
Venanson
D2565
2685
Cime du Diable
2414
Pointe de la
Corne de Bouc
2136
Cime de Marte
Marie
Roquebillière-
Vieux
Belvédère
2085
Mont Tournairet
Roquebillière
1677
Cima de Coss
Roya
Fontan
Triora
Tinée
1889
L'Authion
La Bollène-
Vésubie
Ft de Cayrons
Saorge
2038
Mont Peyrevieille
1971
Mont Torrage
Clans
Lantosque
1607
Col de Turini
1610
L'Arpette
1587
Tête d'Alpe
D2205
La Tour
1606
Brec d'Utelle
D2565
Moulinet
Breil-
sur-Roya
Pigna
1063
Monte Mera
1627
Monte
Ceppo
Tournefort
Massoins
1481
Pierre Plate
Peïra-Cava
879
Col de Brouis
Castel Vittório
St-Jean-la-Rivière
Baiardo
1504
Cime de
Rocca Seira
Utelle
D2566
Piene
Rocchetta
Nervina
1026
Mont Colombin
Apricale
1299
Monte Bignone
1549
Mont Vial
Duranus
Gorges de la Vésubie
Lucéram
1002
Col de Braus
Sospel
Isolabona
Olivetta
San Michele
Perinaldo
Tourette-
du-Château
Bonson
1413
Mont Férion
Coaraze
Collabassa
SS20
Dolceacqua
Levens
D2566
1281
Mt Razet
1378
Mont Grammont
Seborga
Gilette
N202
Bendejun
Berre-
des-Alpes
Castillon
San Biagio
d Cima
San
Remo
L'Escarène
Camporosso
A10
E80
Bouyon
St-Martin-
du-Var
St-Antoine
La Garde
1264
Pic de Baudon
Ste-Agnès
Coldiro
Ospedaletti
St-Blaise
Contes
Peille
Le Broc
Castagniers
Châteauneuf-
de-Contes
Gorbio
Ventimiglia
SS1
Bézaudun
Mortola
1085
Mouton d'Anou
Carros
Tourrette-
Levens
Peillon
Garavan
Bordighera
Aspremont
D2204
Menton
Roquebrune
San
Remo
Gattières
Colomars
Drap
Laghet
La Turbie
Cap Martin
Riviera di Ponente
St-Jeannet
Falicon
E80 A8
Monte-Carlo
Monaco-Ville
MONACO
La Gaude
Èze
Cap d'Ail
Fondation
Maeght
Villefranche-sur-Mer
Beaulieu-sur-Mer
Villa Ephrussi de Rothschild
St-Paul-
de-Vence
N7
N202
St-Jean-Cap Ferrat
NICE
Cagnes-
sur-Mer
St-Laurent-
du-Var
Plage de la Ville
Cap Ferrat
Nice
(Cotê d'Azur)
Biot
La Brague
Bastia
l'Ile Rousse
Calvi
Ajaccio
Antibes
Golfe
Juan
Juan-les-Pins
Cap d'Antibes

les-Alpilles
Aureille
Eyguières
de Calès
Lamanon
C
D
E
Fourques
Abbaye de Montmajour
Arles
D17
Mouriès
N572
Salon-de-Provence
N538
Vernègues
11
Raphèle-lès-Arles
St-Martin-de-Crau
N113
E80 A54
La B
Grans
Plaine de la Crau
Entressen
Le Pont-du-Raud
Lançon-Provence
Miramas
Miramas-le-Vieux
Camargue
294
Mas Thibert
N568
Cornillon-Confoux
295
St-Chamas
Étang de Vaccarès
BOUCHES-DU-RHÔNE
N1569
Istres
Rassuen
D35
D5
Étang de Berre
Berre-l'Étang
12
Parc Naturel Régional de Camargue
St-Mitre-les-Remparts
-la-Mer
N268
Fos-sur-Mer
N568
Martigues
Salin-de-Giraud
Port-de-Bouc
Port-St-Louis-du-Rhône
Château-les-Mart
Étang de Faraman
Grand Rhône
Golfe de Fos
Chaîn
Plage de Piemancon
Carro
Ste-Croix
Sausset-les-Pins
Cap Couronne
13
14
C
D
E

Pertuis
La Bastidonne
St-Estève-Janson
St-Paul-lès-Durance
Ginasservis
Rognes
Chaîne de la Trévaresse
Peyrolles-en-Provence
Jouques
Meyrargues
St-Cannat
Venelles
Rians
Artigues
Esparron
Puyricard
Eguilles
Coudoux
605
La Tête du Marquis
Vauvenargues
296
Montagne Sainte-Victoire
606
Aix-en-Provence
Ventabren
Le Tholonet
Puyloubier
Velaux
Les Milles
Beaurecueil
Pourrières
Chaîne de Vitrolles
Meyreuil
Châteauneuf-le-Rouge
Ollières
Le Petit Arbois
Rousset
Pourcieux
Calas
Vitrolles
Gardanne
Fuveau
Peynier
Trets
880
Olympe
Mont Aurélien
Bouc-Bel-Air
Cabries
Cité Biver
Gréasque
Belcodène
Simiane-Collongue
Mimet
St-Savournin
Les Pennes-Mirabeau
St-Victoret
670
Pilon du Roi
Les Peyrets
Cadolive
La Bouilladisse
Chaîne de l'Étoile
590
Grande Etoile
Nans-les-Pins
l'Estaque
Le Rove
Château-Gombert
Roquevaire
Huveaune
Plan-de-Cuques
Le Logis-Neuf
Allauch
710
Croix de Garlaban
749
Tête de Roussargue
Plan-d'Aups
994
St-Pilon
1147
Signal de la Ste-Baume
Massif de la Sainte Baume
Rade de Marseille
MARSEILLE
La Valentine
Aubagne
Gémenos
302
Île Ratonneau
Île Pomègues
Carnoux-en-Provence
Roquefort-la-Bédoule
Massif de Marseilleveyre
432
Cap Croisette
Île Tiboulen
Les Goudes
Île Maire
Cassis
Ceyreste
Le Brulat
Le Castellet
Le Beausset
La Cadière-d'Azur
St-Cyr-sur-Mer
Cap Morgiou
Cap Canaille
Les Calanques
Île de Jarre
Île Calseraigne
Congloué
Île de Riou
La Ciotat
Les Lecques
Île Verte
Bandol
Sanary-sur-Mer
Île de Bendor
Ajaccio
Propriano
Porto-Vecchio
Bastia
l'Ile-Rousse
Six-Fours-les-Plages
Le Brusc
Île des Embiez
F
G
H
11
12
13
14

La Verdière
H
J
K
Ampus
St-Pierre-de-Tourtour
Rians
D561
Varages
11
Artigues
Esparron
St-Martin
Tavernes
Fox-Amphoux
Villecroze
Tourtour
Reboull
D560
Salernes
Sillans-la-Cascade
Barjols
Pontevès
toire
606
Séouve Sommet
Brue-Auriac
813
Gros Bessillon
Cotignac
Flayosc
296
Entrecasteaux
297
urrières
Seillons-Source-d'Argens
VAR
St-Antonin-du-Var
Châteauvert
Lorgues
Correns
D562
Ollières
Carces
Abbaye du Thoronet
Bras
Argens
Montfort-sur-Argens
Pourcieux
Le Thoronet
12
Mont Aurélien
St-Maximin-la-Sainte-Baume
Vins-sur-Carami
Olympe
E80
A8
Le Val
Cabasse
Vida
N7
Tourves
Brignoles
E80 A8
N7
N7
Le Luc
N560
Rougier
Camps-la-Source
Flassans-sur-Issole
D558
les-Pins
830
Montagne de la Loube
Sainte Baume
La Roquebrussanne
Besse-sur-Issole
Mazaugues
Forcalqueiret
Ste-Anastasie-sur-Issole
994
St-Pilon
1147
Signal de la Ste-Baume
D5
Gonfaron
915
Le Mourré d'Agnis
Garéoult
N97
la
Néoules
Rocbaron
Carnoules
Pignans
Les Mayon
301
Signes
Méounes-lès-Montrieux
705
Pilon St-Clément
Puget-Ville
A57
779
La Sauvette
13
D554
N97
826
Jas de Laure Serra
Belgentier
Cuers
440
Le Peyrol
Collobrières
Capeau
Pierrefeu-du-Var
340
Baisse du Castellas
Le Brulat
605
Rocher de l'Aigle
Massif
Le Castellet
Sollès-Toucas
Le Beausset
Solliès-Pont
D12
801
Mont Caume
Le Revest-les-Eaux
Solliès-Ville
zur
N8
Evenos
La Farlède
Bormes-les-Mimosas
Le Lavanc
507
Mont Faron
La Crau
A50
Ollioules
A570
La Londe-les-Maures
N98
D559
dol
Sanary-sur-Mer
A57
N98
La Garde
Hyères
Baie du
Plage de la F
Port-de Miramare
14
TOULON
Le Pradet
Berriau-Plage
D559
La Seyne-sur-Mer
Carqueiranne
Six-Fours-les-Plages
Hyères-Plage
Rade d'Hyères
Cap Blanc
Les Sablettes
St-Mandrier-sur-Mer
Le Brusc
La Capte
Île des Embiez
Golfe de Giens
Étang des Pesquiers
Cap Cépet
Cap Sicié
Giens
Île de Bagaud
Port-Cros
Ajaccio
Bastia
Porquerolles
Parc National de Port-Cros
Île de Porquerolles
Cap d'Arme
Îles d'H
15
J
K

Bargemon
Montauroux
Auribeau
Mougins
Tanneron
Pégomas
St-Jean
Golfe-Juan
Châteaudouble
Claviers
D562
Callas
Lac de St-Cassien
298
Cannes
Massif du Tanneron
Figanières
Bagnols-en-Forêt
Draguignan
Mandelieu-la-Napoule
Golfe de Napoule
Île Ste-Marguerite
Les Adrets-de-l'Esterel
La Napoule
N7
Théoule-sur-Mer
Île St-Honorat
618
Mont Vinaigre
Îles de Lérins
Miramar
Le Trayas
496
Pic de l'Ours
La Motte
Massif de l'Esterel
Le Muy
E80 A8
452
Pic du Cap Roux
Arcs
Valescure
Puget-sur-Argens
Agay
Argens
Fréjus
St-Raphaël
Anthéor
N98
Le Dramont
Cap du Dramont
Golfe de Fréjus
St-Aygulf
D25
Corniche de l'Esterel
Les Issambres
Maures
Plan-de-la-Tour
Val d'Esquières
Ste-Maxime
La Garde-Freinet
636
Golfe de St-Tropez
Beauvallon
Pointe de Rabiou
Port-Grimaud
Cap de St-Tropez
Grimaud
St-Tropez
N98A
Plage des Salins
Cogolin
Plage de Tahiti
Gassin
Ramatuelle
Plage de Pampelonne
La Croix-Valmer
Cap Camarat
528
Les Pradels
D559
Plage de l'Escalet
Baie de Cavalaire
Le Rayol-
Cavalaire-sur-Mer
Cap Cartaya
Plage de la Briande
Cap Ladier
Corniche des Maures
Cap Nègre
Côte d'Azur
Île du Levant
Pointe Maupertuis
M
N
P
11
12
13
14
15

## C



## D



## E

## F



## G



## H



## I

## PICTURES

The Automobile Association would like to thank the following photographers and companies for their assistance in the preparation of this book.
Abbreviations for the picture credits are as follows –
(t) top;
(b) bottom;
(c) centre;
(l) left;
(r) right;
(AA) AA World Travel Library

**2** AA/C Sawyer
**3t** AA/C Sawyer
**3tc** AA/C Sawyer
**3bc** AA/A Baker
**3b** AA/C Sawyer
**4** AA/Y Levy
**5** AA/Y Levy
**6** AA/C Sawyer
**7** AA/Y Levy
**8** AA/T Oliver
**10** AA/Y Levy
**11l** AA/A Baker
**11r** AA/J Tims
**12** AA/Y Levy
**13** AA/C Sawyer
**14** Photolibrary
**15t** © Owen Franken/CORBIS
**15b** AA/C Sawyer
**16** AA/C Sawyer
**17l** © Bettmann/CORBIS
**17r** Photo by Eamonn McCormack/ Getty Images
**18** AA/C Sawyer
**19t** AA/C Sawyer
**19bl** AA/C Sawyer
**19br** AA/C Sawyer
**20** AA/Y Levy
**21l** AA/J Tims
**21r** AA/Y Levy
**22** AA/Y Levy
**23t** AA/C Sawyer
**23b** AA/R Strange
**24** ©Tim De Waele/Corbis
**25t** AA/C Sawyer
**25b** AA/C Sawyer
**26** HI hotel eco spa & beach/ Patrick Gries
**27** AA/C Sawyer
**28** AA/R Strange
**29t** AA/R Moore
**29b** AA/Y Levy
**30** AA/R Strange
**31l** AA/Y Levy
**31r** AA/R Strange
**32** AA/R Strange
**33l** © Patrick Ward/Alamy
**33r** AA
**34** AA/R Strange
**35t** Song sheet for the Marseillaise, mid-19th century (coloured engraving) (detail) by French School, (19th century) Private Collection/ Archives Charmet/ The Bridgeman Art Library Nationality/copyright status: French/out of copyright
**35b** © Bettmann/CORBIS
**36** AA/R Strange
**37l** 'Winter in Nice', poster advertising P.L.M trains (colour litho) by Alesi, Hugo d' (1849-1906) Bibliotheque-Musée Forney, Paris, France/ Archives Charmet/ The Bridgeman Art Library Nationality/copyright status: French/out of copyright
**37r** Photo by Hulton Archive/ Getty Images
**38** Photodisc
**39t** SNAP/Rex Features
**39b** AA/R Strange
**40** AA/Y Levy
**41** AA/K Blackwell
**43** Digitalvision
**44** AA/K Blackwell
**45** AA/C Sawyer
**47** AA/Y Levy
**48** AA/Y Levy
**49** AA/C Sawyer
**51** AA/C Sawyer
**52** AA/J Tims
**53** AA/J Tims
**54** AA/J Tims
**55** AA/Y Levy
**56** AA/C Sawyer
**57** AA/R Strange
**58** AA/Y Levy
**60** AA/Y Levy
**61** AA/Y Levy
**62** AA/Y Levy
**63** AA/Y Levy
**64** AA/C Sawyer
**65** AA/Y Levy
**66** AA/Y Levy
**67** AA/Y Levy
**68** AA/Y Levy
**69** AA/C Sawyer
**70** AA/C Sawyer
**71t** AA/Y Levy
**71b** AA/Y Levy
**72** AA/R Strange
**73** AA/Y Levy
**74** © Arco Images GmbH/Alamy
**75l** © WoodyStock/Alamy
**75r** AA/C Sawyer
**76** AA/C Sawyer
**77** AA/C Sawyer
**78** AA/C Sawyer
**79l** AA/Y Levy
**79r** AA/A Baker
**80** AA
**81** AA/C Sawyer
**86** Photolibrary
**88** AA/A Baker
**89** AA/C Sawyer
**90** AA/Y Levy
**91** AA/R Moore
**92** AA/C Sawyer
**93** AA/Y Levy
**95** AA/A Baker
**96** AA/C Sawyer
**98** AA/C Sawyer
**99** AA/Y Levy
**100** AA/C Sawyer
**101** AA/Y Levy
**102** AA/Y Levy
**108** AA/C Sawyer
**109** AA/C Sawyer
**110** AA/Y Levy
**111** AA/C Sawyer
**112** AA/C Sawyer
**114** AA/Y Levy
**116** AA/Y Levy
**117** AA/Y Levy
**118** AA/ A Mockford & N Bonetti
**119** AA/Y Levy
**120** AA/Y Levy
**121** AA/C Sawyer

**123l** © Hemis/Alamy
**123r** AA/A Baker
**124** Photolibrary
**125** AA/Y Levy
**126** AA/C Sawyer
**127** Photolibrary
**128** AA/Y Levy
**129** AA/C Sawyer
**130** AA/C Sawyer
**131l** AA/C Sawyer
**131r** AA/J Tims
**134** AA/Y Levy
**135** AA/J Tims
**136** AA/C Sawyer
**137** AA/C Sawyer
**138** Photolibrary
**140** AA/Y Levy
**141** AA/Y Levy
**142** AA/C Sawyer
**143** AA/Y Levy
**144** AA/C Sawyer
**145** AA/C Sawyer
**146l** AA/R Strange
**146r** AA
**147** AA/C Sawyer
**148** AA/C Sawyer
**149** AA/C Sawyer
**150** Photolibrary
**151** AA/C Sawyer
**153** AA/A Baker
**154** AA/C Sawyer
**155** © niceartphoto/Alamy
**156** AA/Y Levy
**157** AA/R Strange
**158** AA/C Sawyer
**159** AA/Y Levy
**162** AA/C Sawyer
**163** AA/C Sawyer
**164** AA/J Tims
**167** AA/J Tims
**168** AA/C Sawyer
**169l** AA/C Sawyer
**169r** AA/C Sawyer
**170** AA/R Moore
**171** AA/C Sawyer
**172** The Covered patio©Culturespaces/C. Recoura
**173** AA/R Moore
**174** AA/J Tims
**175** AA/J Tims
**176** AA/C Sawyer
**177** AA/C Sawyer
**178** AA/R Moore
**179** AA/C Sawyer
**180** Photolibrary
**181t** AA/J Smith
**181b** AA/R Strange
**182** AA/C Sawyer
**183** AA/ J Wyand
**184** AA/C Sawyer
**185** AA/C Sawyer
**186** AA/C Sawyer
**188** AA/C Sawyer
**190** AA/C Sawyer
**192** AA/C Sawyer
**193** AA/C Sawyer
**194** AA/C Sawyer
**195** AA/J Tims
**196** AA/C Sawyer
**198** John Miller/Robert Harding
**199** AA/R Moore
**200** AA/R Moore
**201** AA/R Strange
**202** AA/C Sawyer
**203** Photolibrary
**204** AA/C Sawyer
**205l** AA/C Sawyer
**205r** AA/C Sawyer
**206** AA/R Strange
**207** AA/A Baker
**208** AA/C Sawyer
**209** AA/C Sawyer
**210** AA/C Sawyer
**214** AA/C Sawyer
**216** AA/C Sawyer
**217** AA/C Sawyer
**218** Roy Rainford/Robert Harding
**220** © Brian Jannsen/Alamy
**221** AA/A Baker
**222** AA/Y Levy
**223** AA/C Sawyer
**224** AA/Y Levy
**227** AA/Y Levy
**228** AA/R Strange
**229** AA/Y Levy
**230** AA/Y Levy
**231** AA/Y Levy
**232** AA/Y Levy
**233** AA/C Sawyer
**234** Photolibrary
**235l** David Hughes/Robert Harding
**235r** AA/Y Levy
**236** AA/C Sawyer
**237** Photolibrary
**239** AA/R Strange
**240** AA/C Sawyer
**241** AA/A Baker
**242** AA/Y Levy
**243** AA/Y Levy
**244** AA/C Sawyer
**245** AA/C Sawyer
**246** AA/C Sawyer
**247** Photolibrary
**248** AA/C Sawyer
**249** AA/C Sawyer
**251** AA/A Baker
**252** AA/C Sawyer
**254** AA/C Sawyer
**255** AA/C Sawyer
**257** AA/Y Levy
**263** AA/J Tims
**264** AA/C Sawyer
**267** AA/C Sawyer
**268** AA/A Mockford & N Bonetti
**270** AA/K Blackwell
**272** Photolibrary
**273l** AA/J Wyand
**273r** AA/C Sawyer
**274** AA/C Sawyer
**277** © niceartphoto/Alamy
**278** AA/J Tims
**279** AA/P Kenward
**280** AA/C Sawyer
**287** AA/C Sawyer

Every effort has been made to trace the copyright holders, and we apologise in advance for any accidental errors. We would be happy to apply any corrections in the following edition of this publication.

# CREDITS

**Managing editor**
Sheila Hawkins

**Project editor**
Kathryn Glendenning

**Design**
Tracey Butler

**Picture research**
Elisabeth Stacey

**Image retouching and repro**
Sarah Montgomery

**Mapping**
Maps produced by the Mapping Services Department of AA Publishing

**Main contributors**
Lindsay Bennett, Colin Follett, David Halford, Nick Hanna, Josephine Perry, Laurence Phillips, Rutherford Tomasetti Partners, Andrew Sanger, The Content Works

**Updater**
Rutherford Tomasetti Partners

**Indexer**
Marie Lorimer

**Production**
Lorraine Taylor

Published by AA Publishing, a trading name of AA Media Limited, whose registered office is Fanum House, Basing View, Basingstoke, RG21 4EA. Registered number 06112600.
A CIP catalogue record for this book is available from the British Library.

**ISBN 978-0-7495-6759-0**



KeyGuide is a registered trademark in Australia and is used under license.
Colour separation by AA Digital Department
Printed and bound by Leo Paper Products, China

We believe the contents of this book are correct at the time of printing. However, some details, particularly prices, opening times and telephone numbers, do change. We do not accept responsibility for any consequences arising from the use of this book.
This does not affect your statutory rights. We would be grateful if readers would advise us of any inaccuracies they may encounter, or any suggestions they might like to make to improve the book. There is a form provided at the back of the book for this purpose, or you can email us at travelguides@theaa.com

A04201
Maps in this title produced from mapping © MAIRDUMONT/Falk Verlag 2011
and with reference to mapping ISTITUTO GEOGRAFICO DE AGOSTINI, Novara
Weather Chart statistics supplied by Weatherbase © Copyright 2004 Canty and Associates, LLC
Communicarta assistance with distance/time charts gratefully acknowledged.
Transport map © Communicarta Ltd, UK

Find out more about AA Publishing and the wide range of travel publications and services the AA provides by visiting our website at **theAA.com/shop**

# READER RESPONSE

Thank you for buying this KeyGuide. Your comments and opinions are very important to us, so please help us to improve our travel guides by taking a few minutes to complete this questionnaire.

You do not need a stamp (unless posted outside the UK). If you do not want to cut this page from your guide, then photocopy it or write your answers on a plain sheet of paper.

Send to: **KeyGuide Editor, AA World Travel Guides**
**FREEPOST SCE 4598, Basingstoke RG21 4GY**

Find out more about AA Publishing and the wide range of travel publications the AA provides by visiting our website at www.theAA.com/bookshop

## ABOUT THIS GUIDE

Which KeyGuide did you buy? ..........................................................................................................................

Where did you buy it? ..........................................................................................................................

When? .............month ............... year

Why did you choose this AA KeyGuide?
☐ Price ☐ AA Publication
☐ Used this series before
title
☐ Cover ☐ Other (please state)

Please let us know how helpful the following features of the guide were to you by circling the appropriate category: very helpful (VH), helpful (H) or little help (LH)

| | | | |
|---|---|---|---|
| Size | VH | H | LH |
| Layout | VH | H | LH |
| Photos | VH | H | LH |
| Excursions | VH | H | LH |
| Entertainment | VH | H | LH |
| Hotels | VH | H | LH |
| Maps | VH | H | LH |
| Practical info | VH | H | LH |
| Restaurants | VH | H | LH |
| Shopping | VH | H | LH |
| Walks | VH | H | LH |
| Sights | VH | H | LH |
| Transport info | VH | H | LH |

What was your favourite sight, attraction or feature listed in the guide?

Page................. Please give your reason ..........................................................................................................................

..........................................................................................................................

Which features in the guide could be changed or improved? Or are there any other comments you would like to make?

..........................................................................................................................

## ABOUT YOU

Name (Mr/Mrs/Ms).......................................................................................................................................................

Address .....................................................................................................................................................................
.....................................................................................................................................................................................
.....................................................................................................................................................................................
.....................................................................................................................................................................................
Postcode.................................................... Daytime tel nos..............................................................................................

Email.........................................................................................................................................................................
Please only give us your mobile phone number/email if you wish to hear from us about other products and services from the AA and partners by text or mms.

Which age group are you in?
Under 25 ☐ 25–34 ☐ 35–44 ☐ 45–54 ☐ 55+ ☐

How many trips do you make a year?
Less than 1 ☐ 1 ☐ 2 ☐ 3 or more ☐

## ABOUT YOUR TRIP

Are you an AA member? Yes ☐ No ☐

When did you book?............. month................. year

When did you travel?............. month................ year

Reason for your trip? Business ☐ Leisure ☐

How many nights did you stay? ...........................

How did you travel? Individual ☐ Couple ☐ Family ☐ Group ☐

Did you buy any other travel guides for your trip? .........................................................................................

If yes, which ones?....................................................................................................................................................

Thank you for taking the time to complete this questionnaire. Please send it to us as soon as possible, and remember, you do not need a stamp (unless posted outside the UK).

**Titles in the KeyGuide series:**
Australia, Barcelona, Berlin, Britain, Brittany, Canada, China, Costa Rica, Croatia, Florence and Tuscany, France, Germany, Ireland, Italy, London, Mallorca, Mexico, New York, New Zealand, Normandy, Paris, Portugal, Prague, Provence and the Côte d'Azur, Rome, Scotland, South Africa, Spain, Thailand, Venice, Vietnam, Western European Cities.